Lecture Notes in Computer Science 14130

Founding Editors

Gerhard Goos
Juris Hartmanis

Editorial Board Members

The series Lecture Notes in Computer Science (LNCS), including its subseries Lecture Notes in Artificial Intelligence (LNAI) and Lecture Notes in Bioinformatics (LNBI), has established itself as a medium for the publication of new developments in computer science and information technology research, teaching, and education.

LNCS enjoys close cooperation with the computer science R & D community, the series counts many renowned academics among its volume editors and paper authors, and collaborates with prestigious societies. Its mission is to serve this international community by providing an invaluable service, mainly focused on the publication of conference and workshop proceedings and postproceedings. LNCS commenced publication in 1973.

Ida Lindgren · Csaba Csáki ·
Evangelos Kalampokis · Marijn Janssen ·
Gabriela Viale Pereira · Shefali Virkar ·
Efthimios Tambouris · Anneke Zuiderwijk
Editors

Electronic Government

22nd IFIP WG 8.5 International Conference, EGOV 2023
Budapest, Hungary, September 5–7, 2023
Proceedings

 Springer

Editors
Ida Lindgren 🆔
Linköping University
Linköping, Sweden

Csaba Csáki 🆔
Corvinus University of Budapest
Budapest, Hungary

Evangelos Kalampokis 🆔
University of Macedonia
Thessaloniki, Greece

Marijn Janssen 🆔
Delft University of Technology
Delft, The Netherlands

Gabriela Viale Pereira 🆔
University for Continuing Education Krems
Krems an der Donau, Austria

Shefali Virkar 🆔
Vienna University of Economics
and Business
Vienna, Austria

Efthimios Tambouris 🆔
University of Macedonia
Thessaloniki, Greece

Anneke Zuiderwijk 🆔
Delft University of Technology
Delft, The Netherlands

ISSN 0302-9743   ISSN 1611-3349 (electronic)
Lecture Notes in Computer Science
ISBN 978-3-031-41137-3   ISBN 978-3-031-41138-0 (eBook)
https://doi.org/10.1007/978-3-031-41138-0

This Springer imprint is published by the registered company Springer Nature Switzerland AG
The registered company address is: Gewerbestrasse 11, 6330 Cham, Switzerland

Preface

The EGOV-CeDEM-ePart 2023 conference, or for short EGOV 2023, is the sixth conference in the series after the successful merger of three formerly independent conferences, e.g., the IFIP WG 8.5 Electronic Government (EGOV), the Conference for E-Democracy and Open Government Conference (CeDEM), and the IFIP WG 8.5 IFIP Electronic Participation (ePart). This larger, united conference is dedicated to the broad area of digital or electronic government, open government, smart governance, artificial intelligence, e-democracy, policy informatics, and electronic participation. Scholars from around the world have found this conference to be a premier academic forum with a long tradition along its various branches, which has given the EGOV-CeDEM-ePart conference its reputation as the leading conference worldwide in the research domains of digital/electronic, open, and smart government as well as electronic participation.

The call for papers attracted completed research papers, work-in-progress papers on ongoing research (including doctoral papers), project and case descriptions, as well as workshop and panel proposals – in total 106 papers. This volume contains only completed research papers. All submissions were assessed through a double-blind peer-review process, with at least three reviewers per submission, and the acceptance rate for completed research papers was 36%. The review time took 44 days this year, thanks to the contribution of the many PC members.

The review process was focused on ensuring a double-blind reviewing process and avoiding any conflicts of interest. Authors of papers submitted their papers to a track. The track chairs handled the papers within their own track by assigning reviewers and proposing acceptance decisions. The lead track chair became part of the editorial team of the proceedings, in addition to the general chairs. Track chairs were not allowed to submit to their own track, nor were persons from the same university or close collaborators of a track chair allowed to submit, to avoid any conflict of interest. Track chairs could either submit to another track or to the 'track chairs' track. The latter was handled by the general chairs. The general chairs checked after the submission deadline whether there was any conflict of interest among the papers submitted to tracks; if so, then papers were moved to another track. The track chairs checked that all papers were submitted anonymously. If not, the authors were asked to resubmit within days. Track chairs assigned the reviewers and selected the program committee members in such a way that there were no conflicts of interest. After at least three reviews were received, the track chairs made a proposal for a decision per paper. The decisions were discussed in a meeting with the general chairs and track chairs to ensure that the decisions were made in a consistent manner across the tracks.

Electronic Government is an evolving field of research and practice. The conference tracks of the 2023 edition reflect the development and progress in this field:

- General E-Government and E-Governance
- General E-Democracy and e-Participation
- ICT and Sustainable Development Goals

- AI, Data Analytics, and Automated Decision Making
- Digital and Social Media
- Digital Society
- Emerging Issues and Innovations
- Legal Informatics
- Open Data: Social and Technical Aspects
- Smart Cities (Government, Districts, Communities, and Regions)

Among the full research paper submissions, 28 papers (empirical and conceptual) were accepted for this year's Springer LNCS EGOV proceedings (vol. 14130) from the General E-Government and E-Governance; AI, Data Analytics, and Automated Decision Making; Emerging Issues and Innovations; Open Data; and Smart and Digital Cities tracks. The LNCS ePart proceedings (LNCS vol. 14153) contain the completed research papers from the General E-Democracy and e-Participation, ICT & Sustainability, Digital and Social Media, Legal Informatics and Digital Society tracks.

The papers included in this volume (vol. 14130) have been clustered under the following headings:

- Digital Government
- Artificial Intelligence, Algorithms, and Automation
- Open Government and Open Data
- Smart Cities, Regions, and Societies
- Innovation and Transformation in Government

As in the previous years and per the recommendation of the Paper Awards Committee, under the leadership of Noella Edelmann (Danube University Krems, Austria), Evangelos Kalampokis (University of Macedonia, Greece), and Manuel Pedro Rodríguez Bolívar (University of Granada, Spain), the IFIP EGOV-CeDEM-ePart 2023 Conference Organizing Committee granted outstanding paper awards in three distinct categories:

- The most interdisciplinary and innovative research contribution
- The most compelling critical research reflection
- The most promising practical concept

The winners in each category were announced during the obligatory awards ceremony at the conference.

The EGOV 2023 conference was hosted by Corvinus University of Budapest. Corvinus University is the leading educational institution in Hungary in the fields of economic, management, and social sciences. The institution offers state-of-the-art knowledge, a professional network, and a secure future for its 10k+ students. The university has 120+ years of history and 10,000+ students, including 1,500 international students from 80+ nationalities. The institution is ranked in the Top 300 in the QS World rankings for 2021 in the fields of Business and Management, Economics, and Social Sciences. The institution has over 250 partner universities worldwide. It is an AMBA-accredited Business institution and the only member of CEMS in Hungary. Corvinus essentially educates the social and economic elite of the region. It strives to produce scientific results that are relevant for Hungary, Europe, and the world. The founders of the university believed that only talent and ambition should count – social or financial status should not prevent anyone from studying. We were very happy to be hosted here and enjoyed the beautiful city of Budapest and the many in-depth discussions advancing the EGOV field.

Many people behind the scenes make large events like this conference happen. We would like to thank the members of the Program Committee, the reviewers, and the track chairs for their great efforts in reviewing the submitted papers. We would also like to express our deep gratitude to Csaba Csáki and his local team at Corvinus University of Budapest for hosting the conference.

We hope that the papers included in this volume will help to advance your research and that you will enjoy reading them,

September 2023

Ida Lindgren
Csaba Csáki
Evangelos Kalampokis
Marijn Janssen
Gabriela Viale Pereira
Shefali Virkar
Efthimios Tambouris
Anneke Zuiderwijk

Organization

Conference Chairs

Csaba Csáki	Corvinus University of Budapest, Hungary
Lieselot Danneels	Ghent University, Belgium
Noella Edelmann	Danube University Krems, Austria
Marijn Janssen	Delft University of Technology, The Netherlands
Evangelos Kalampokis	University of Macedonia, Greece
Ida Lindgren	Linköping University, Sweden
Anna-Sophie Novak	Danube University Krems, Austria
Panos Panagiotopoulos	Queen Mary University of London, UK
Peter Parycek	Fraunhofer FOKUS, Germany/Danube-University Krems, Austria
Gabriela Viale Pereira	Danube University Krems, Austria
Gerhard Schwabe	University of Zurich, Switzerland
Iryna Susha	Utrecht University, The Netherlands
Jolien Ubacht	Delft University of Technology, The Netherlands
Efthimios Tambouris	University of Macedonia, Greece

Program Committee Chairs

Török Bernát	Ludovika – University of Public Service, Hungary
Joep Crompvoets	KU Leuven, Belgium
Csaba Csáki	Corvinus University - Corvinus Business School, Hungary
Lieselot Danneels	Ghent University / Vlerick Business School, Belgium
Noella Edelmann	Danube University Krems, Austria
J. Ramon Gil-Garcia	University at Albany, SUNY, USA
Sara Hofmann	University of Agder, Norway
Marijn Janssen	Delft University of Technology, The Netherlands
Marius Rohde Johannessen	University of South-Eastern Norway, Norway
Evangelos Kalampokis	University of Macedonia, Greece
Hun-Yeong Kwon	Korea University, South Korea
Thomas Lampoltshammer	University for Continuing Education Krems, Austria
Habin Lee	Brunel University London, UK

Katarina Lindblad-Gidlund	Mid Sweden University, Sweden
Ida Lindgren	Linköping University, Sweden
Euripidis Loukis	University of the Aegean, Greece
Gianluca Misuraca	Universidad Politécnica de Madrid, Spain
Francesco Mureddu	Lisbon Council, Belgium
Anastasija Nikiforova	Tartu University, Estonia
Anna-Sophie Novak	Danube University Krems, Austria
Panos Panagiotopoulos	Queen Mary University of London, UK
Peter Parycek	Danube-University Krems, Austria
Manuel Pedro Rodríguez Bolívar	University of Granada, Spain
Gerhard Schwabe	University of Zurich, Switzerland
Anthony Simonofskim	Université de Namur, Belgium
Iryna Susha	Utrecht University, The Netherlands
Efthimios Tambouris	University of Macedonia, Greece
Jolien Ubacht	Delft University of Technology, The Netherlands
Gabriela Viale Pereira	Danube University Krems, Austria
Shefali Virkar	Vienna University of Economics and Business, Austria
Anneke Zuiderwijk	Delft University of Technology, The Netherlands

Chair of Outstanding Papers Awards

Noella Edelmann	Danube University Krems, Austria
Evangelos Kalampokis	University of Macedonia, Greece
Manuel Pedro Rodríguez Bolívar	University of Granada, Spain

PhD Colloquium Chairs

Gabriela Viale Pereira	Danube University Krems, Austria
Ida Lindgren	Linköping University, Sweden
J. Ramon Gil-Garcia	University at Albany, SUNY, USA

Web Master

| Gilang Ramadhan | Delft University of Technology, The Netherlands |

Program Committee

Karin Ahlin	Mid Sweden University, Sweden
Suha Alawadhi	Kuwait University, Kuwait
Valerie Albrecht	Danube University Krems, Austria
Laura Alcaide-Muñoz	University of Granada, Spain
Cristina Alcaide-Muñoz	University of Malaga, Spain
Joao Alvaro Carvalho	University of Minho, Portugal
Renata Araujo	Mackenzie Presbyterian University, Brazil
Wagner Araujo	UNU EGOV, Portugal
Frank Bannister	Trinity College Dublin, Ireland
Ana Alice Baptista	University of Minho, Portugal
Peter Bellström	Karlstad University, Sweden
Flavia Bernardini	Universidade Federal Fluminense, Brazil
Török Bernát	Ludovika – University of Public Service, Hungary
Radomir Bolgov	Saint Petersburg State University, Russia
Alessio Maria Braccini	University of Tuscia, Italy
Paul Brous	Delft University of Technology, The Netherlands
Iván Cantador	Autonomous University of Madrid, Spain
Wichian Chutimaskul	King Mongkut's University of Technology Thonburi, Thailand
Vincenzo Ciancia	Istituto di Scienza e Tecnologie dell'Informazione, Italy
Antoine Clarinval	Université de Namur, Belgium
María Elicia Cortés-Cediel	University Complutense of Madrid, Spain
Joep Crompvoets	KU Leuven, Belgium
Peter Cruickshank	Edinburgh Napier University, UK
Jonathan Crusoe	Gothenburg University and University of Borås, Sweden
Csaba Csáki	Corvinus University of Budapest, Hungary
Frank Danielsen	University of Agder, Norway
Lieselot Danneels	Ghent University, Vlerick Business School, Belgium
Gabriele De Luca	University for Continuing Education Krems, Austria
Bettina Distel	Universität Münster, Germany
Dirk Draheim	Software Competence Center Hagenberg, Austria
Noella Edelmann	Danube University Krems, Austria
Montathar Faraon	Kristianstad University, Sweden
Shahid Farooq	Freelance Governance & Institutional Development Specialist, Pakistan
Cesar Casiano Flores	University of Twente, The Netherlands

Gerhard Schwabe	University of Zurich, Switzerland
Walter Seböck	University for Continuing Education Krems, Austria
Andreiwid Sheffer Corrêa	Federal Institute of Sao Paulo, Brazil
Tobias Siebenlist	Rhine-Waal University of Applied Sciences, Germany
Kerley Silva	University of Porto, Portugal
Anthony Simonofski	Université de Namur, Belgium
Leif Sundberg	Mid Sweden University, Sweden
Iryna Susha	Utrecht University, The Netherlands
Øystein Sæbø	University of Agder, Norway
Efthimios Tambouris	University of Macedonia, Greece
Luca Tangi	Joint Research Centre - European Commission, Italy
Lörinc Thurnay	Danube University Krems, Austria
Daniel Toll	Linköping University, Sweden
Jolien Ubacht	Delft University of Technology, The Netherlands
Marco Velicogna	IRSIG-CNR, Italy
Gabriela Viale Pereira	Danube University Krems, Austria
Shefali Virkar	Vienna University of Economics and Business, Austria
Gianluigi Viscusi	Linköping University, Sweden
Jörn von Lucke	Zeppelin Universität Friedrichshafen, Germany
Bianca Wentzel	Fraunhofer FOKUS, Germany
Guilherme Wiedenhöft	Federal University of Rio Grande, Brazil
Elin Wihlborg	Linköping University, Sweden
Mete Yildiz	Hacettepe Üniversitesi İİBF, Türkiye
Maija Ylinen	Tampere University of Technology, Finland
Sang Pil Yoon	Korea University, South Korea
Chien-Chih Yu	National Chengchi University, Taiwan
Thomas Zefferer	Graz University of Technology, Austria
Dimitris Zeginis	University of Macedonia, Greece
Anneke Zuiderwijk	Delft University of Technology, The Netherlands

Additional Reviewers

Jörg Becker	University of Münster, ERCIS, Germany
Bettina Distel	University of Münster, ERCIS, Germany
Corinna Funke	public GmbH, Germany
Amirhossein Gharaie	Linköping University, Sweden
Junchul Kim	Brunel University London, UK

Ini Kong   Delft University of Technology, The Netherlands
Yannik Landeck   Fortiss, Germany
Changwon Park   Brunel University London, UK
Elham Shafiei Gol   Brunel University London, UK
Yao Hua Tan   Delft University of Technology, The Netherlands

Contents

Open Government and Open Data

Smart Cities, Regions, and Societies

Innovation and Transformation in Government

Digital Government

Construct Hunting in GovTech Research: An Exploratory Data Analysis

Mattias Svahn[1] ⓘ, Aron Larsson[2,3](✉) ⓘ, Eloísa Macedo[4,5] ⓘ,
and Jorge Bandeira[4,5] ⓘ

[1] Swedish Defence Research Agency, 164 90 Stockholm, Sweden
mattias.svahn@foi.se
[2] Department of Computer and Systems Sciences, Stockholm University, 16440 Kista, Sweden
aron@dsv.su.se
[3] Department of Communication, Quality Management and Information Systems, Mid Sweden University, 851 70 Sundsvall, Sweden
[4] TEMA Centre for Mechanical Technology, University of Aveiro, 3810-193 Aveiro, Portugal
{macedo,jorgebandeira}@ua.pt
[5] LASI - Intelligent Systems Associate Laboratory, Guimarães, Portugal

Abstract. The concept of "GovTech" has emerged as a business-oriented model and practice for enabling the public sector to take advantage of digital solutions as service towards the citizen, while the private for-profit sector is responsible for innovation, development, and profitable maintenance of the GovTech services, hence making the whole area of solutions seemingly desirable to invest in.

However, the current literature on stakeholder views of the GovTech market remains rather generic, less connected to concrete examples of GovTech solutions as these are perceived within a given and delimited GovTech domain. The objective of this paper is to apply exploratory quantitative data analysis for phenomena detection and evaluation. We explore to what extent the constructs of the area actually are disparate and ill-suited to use for quantitative GovTech research, and find five factors showing a degree of mistrust between the public and private sector and prescribe further research into developing constructs that can cut across the research area, enabling for a build-up of a stronger theoretical base for tech business in the public-private markets.

Keywords: GovTech · quantitative method · constructs · exploratory data analysis · mobility-as-a-service · MaaS

1 Introduction

During the latter decade the concept of "GovTech" has emerged as a form of business-oriented model and practise for enabling the public sector to take advantage of digital solutions as a service towards the citizen, while the private for-profit sector is responsible for innovation, development, and profitable maintenance of the GovTech services, hence

---

The original version of this chapter was revised: The name of the author Eloísa Macedo has been corrected. The correction to this chapter is available at
https://doi.org/10.1007/978-3-031-41138-0_29

I. Lindgren et al. (Eds.): EGOV 2023, LNCS 14130, pp. 3–17, 2023.
https://doi.org/10.1007/978-3-031-41138-0_1

making the whole area of solutions seemingly desirable to invest in. Perhaps not surprisingly, both the public sector and the private tech sector have put a lot of hope on the GovTech concept. Global bodies such as the World Bank promote the GovTech model as a means for a "whole-of-government approach to public sector modernization that promotes simple, efficient, and transparent government with the citizens at the centre of reforms" [10]. Thus, the narrative of GovTech is in line with that of digitalisation in general, serving as the means for a quicker, more innovative, and more inclusive market setup for economic growth and sustainability spanning all levels from the international to regional, cf. [25].

However, the GovTech setup has been problematised in recent literature from various standpoints, as it entails that public services stand within the constraints of public-private partnerships. The complexity of forming business solutions that can pinpoint public utility and democratic value, as well as building business value from e-government solutions has been an issue for a long time even before the rise of GovTech as a concept, see, e.g., [3, 6, 30].

Other concerns raised is that the public sector will be less able to maintain its own technological skill set and thus be more open to exploitation, as well as that the rise of GovTech becomes a path on which the public sector becomes less aware of, and less responsible for, the public values it exists to protect, cf., e.g., [8]. Furthermore, although it is often claimed by the private sector that the GovTech market is extremely large in size estimated to exceed 430 872 Million USD in 2021 [11], there are concerns that when the application domain of a GovTech solution as desired by governments becomes more concrete and less of a vision then serious for-profit businesses are not able or willing to commit due to reasons of legislation or low profitability leading to a missing market case [7]. In turn, facilitating the "unleash" of the GovTech potential is most often considered to be a matter for the public organisations who shall open up public infrastructure for private business experimentation, offer lucrative marketplaces for SMEs, create market incentives and increase what the private sector calls the public sectors' competence and flexibility in public procurement, or even develop market-shaping and market stimulating policies [21, 22, 26]. However, even if such a role for the public sector does not per se contradict with its core values, it is less in line with the traditions of administration and the common rationales for its existence like providing safe and equal services and support to citizens and businesses while ensuring that they abide by laws and regulations and take corrective actions otherwise [28].

1.1 The State of the GovTech Research Area

This mentioned state with conflicting forces, wishes, and traditions, is a state that necessitates more research. Of great interest would be research that has a tripartite stakeholder focus, taking into account; i) the governance of GovTech, together with ii) the markets of GovTech, and iii) taking into perspective the differing traditions of the public sector in different countries. However, the current literature on stakeholder views of the GovTech market remains highly generic, less connected to concrete examples of GovTech solutions as perceived within a given and delimited GovTech domain. And given that we accept that there is a market, albeit complex in nature, little research has been done to address GovTech endeavours from the mentioned tripartite perspective. Furthermore, and perhaps due to the complex nature of public-private partnerships within the tech domain as well as due to differing administrative traditions across the EU, it has been claimed in e-government studies that there is lack of "clarity and rigour" about methodologies and data collection and that quantitative studies are underrepresented [5, 16, 30, 32]. Thus, broader scaled quantitative evaluations where a degree of certainty underpins the concepts, notions, thoughts, wishes, where these can be measured and evaluated across countries to bring more clarity to the research area of GovTech is desirable. However, it is less clear just how to set up such a mainstream quantitative research design enabling for this, and from contemporary theory derive what constructs that actually are meaningful.

Given the above, an interesting question to pose is how to develop viable research constructs for the quantitative research on the GovTech uptake, its barriers, and its prerequisites and do it in a European context? One point of departure for such a question is to have a concrete GovTech domain with respondents that are active, viz. Have a stake or mission to improve a public sector service level by the means of 'tech' and pursue an exploratory data analysis to initialise the basis for quantitative work [19].

Based upon an understanding that quantitative research demands stability in the investigated constructs, we aim to conduct an analysis of a quantitative evaluation where the research constructs are provided according to a prima facie understanding of the relationships between actors in a GovTech domain. Due to a perceived lack of clarity in the research area we anticipate that such prima facie constructs for the quantitative research on GovTech are disparate. We therefore firstly aim to explore to what extent such constructs are disparate and ill-suited to use for quantitative GovTech research and what needs to be addressed in order to pursue quantitative GovTech research on a pan-European level. Secondly, we draw some conclusions from the data analysis with respect to the relationships between GovTech actors.

2 Research Approach and Method

In the social sciences, emphasis is placed on the importance of causal analysis, whether qualitative, quantitative, or multi-method. Out of such analysis we aim to understand and predict events in the world. Thus, good theories are crucial, and such derive from observations and understanding of phenomena. The starting point of theory can therefore be to at all identify phenomena to explain [19]. In that approach we also take a cue from Ref. [27] and agree that "social science exploration is a broad-ranging, purposive, systematic prearranged undertaking designed to maximise the discovery of generalisations leading to description and understanding". However, we disagree with Stebbins notion that exploratory research should not use traditional structures like, e.g., hypotheses, instead we follow the notion of Ref. [9] that exploratory research should not be limited to only qualitative approaches, as argued in [19].

The objective of this paper is therefore to apply exploratory quantitative data analysis for phenomena detection and evaluation. This to lay a groundwork for coming deductive research into GovTech market and development analysis. We apply exploratory quantitative data analysis as it is characterised by a flexibility in identifying and investigating a range of statistical and hopefully also substantive phenomena, in a way that is necessary when hunting for constructs for GovTech.

Our approach can be called "interpretive research" as the authors are invested in philosophical and methodological ways of understanding social reality, along the lines of "Verstehen" as first discussed by Max Weber, cf. [14]. While interpretative approaches are usually associated with qualitative social science, we, in the way of Ref. [2] put forth that interpretative research philosophies are equally applicable to the analysis of quantitative data. We exploit variance based quantitative methods to shed light on the unobservable latent data that underlie the observed data, in line with exploratory quantitative data analysis, where the aim to find indications of constructs that can lie as the basis for confirmatory quantitative data analysis, as exploratory and confirmatory data analysis necessitates each other, cf. [19].

2.1 Constructs in Quantitative Data Analysis

Constructs are abstractions of thought that researchers use to express ideas, and or concepts that are interesting for research. Constructs are a way of bringing theory down to a hands-on level, helping to explain the different components of theories, as well as build road maps towards operationalizing the components of theory into graspable elements. Well conducted quantitative research can bring together theory and variables and clarify how a concept and its relation to other concepts is to be estimated, and part of that is to have clear constructs. Broadly speaking, constructs are the building blocks of operationalizable theories, helping to explain how and why certain phenomena behave the way that they do, whether in GovTech or in governance in general. Constructs are often referred to as mental abstractions because seldom are constructs directly observable. For instance, we cannot directly observe "depression", but we may associate depression with measurable signs such as a person that often engages in self-harm, is withdrawn, has mood swings and so on. We cannot really measure "brand equity" even though large parts of the consumer economy are based on it. Constructs vary significantly in their complexity. Some constructs may seem to be very easy to understand and measure, e.g., age, sex (but not gender), height, but others are more difficult and abstract, e.g., "sexism", "self-esteem", "brand equity", and "family". A discussion about modern lifestyles can become confused if the concept of "family" is different among participants to the discussion. The question that then arises are what are the nuts and bolts that make up such abstractions? And in our case, what nuts and bolts can be said to make up "GovTech"?

2.2 MaaS as the Testbed for Developing GovTech Constructs

As the testbed for the exploration of GovTech constructs we choose the area of MaaS - Mobility-as-a-Service. MaaS is a form of organising personal mobility. It can be done through combining various forms of personal "non-private-car" transport into one single, combined, and on-demand personal mobility service. MaaS strives to offer users the added value of accessing personal mobility through one single source and one single payment channel, instead of multiple ticketing and payment methods. This can be public transport, bike, car sharing services etc. MaaS is to be not only a convenient, but also sustainable alternative to using the private car and so reduce congestion and constraints in transport capacity. The development of MaaS challenges business and operation models for public transport and mobility service, municipal planning prerogatives, and the larger macro-organisation of society [23]. MaaS is a suitable test domain for this study, as building a society that can bring down private individual use of the personally owned car, is one of the key public governance issues for a sustainable future. It is also one of the most difficult, as MaaS cuts across consumer identities, business models, local and higher levels of public governance, societal traditions, and urban-versus-rural planning. It is also an area where public-private partnerships may be both necessary due to the wide spectrum of mobility services that a successful MaaS implementation requires, and difficult, as traditions of public governance are old, entrenched, strong and vary between regions and countries [1]. In the area of Maas, Ref. [8] find that MaaS supply side barriers are lack of public-private cooperation, support from established businesses and from the political side, and that the demand side barriers are lack of appeal to older generations, public transport users, and private vehicle users. Ref. [20] finds that lack of appropriate business models, cultures of collaboration, and unclear roles and responsibilities are significant factors holding up the development of MaaS. Both those problematizations indicate a need for clearer constructs among the forces working to develop MaaS.

Hence, we view MaaS as an area with a complexity of forming combined business models and public governance models that can pinpoint both public value for citizens and business value for companies that belong to the area of GovTech. It is therefore to be expected that the shared common ideas that underlie a construct in quantitative research are both extra necessary and extra hard to find in the area of MaaS as an example of a GovTech domain.

Screening for Face Validity. To execute the analysis, a secondary Likert scale data set on commercial and public sector stakeholders' attitudes to MaaS development was used. The data set was gathered through an online survey launched between 2020 and 2021 within the scope of the INTERREG EUROPE project "PriMaaS"[1]. It contains 20 Likert scale survey items, and the initial sample consists of 107 respondents from Sweden, Italy, Portugal and Germany. The respondents were researchers, senior executives in private and public transportation settings, and policymakers in the public sector in the four countries. The structure of the survey was inspired by a previous work in [20] who performed a qualitative study on several multiscale factors with a claimed impact on the development and implementation of MaaS.

At first, the data set was screened for face validity in order to have it represent a prima facie set of survey items for investigating MaaS stakeholders' attitudes to the necessary private-public partnerships deemed necessary for MaaS and by extension GovTech development. The face validity of an item is how well it, based on the researchers' or experts' experience and training, intuitively appears to measure the concept it is intended to measure, cf. [18]. Face validity is essential because it affects a measurement's perceived credibility and acceptability [13]. Even though the data set used could be considered to be face valid at the outset as it has been subject to a construct development and face validity judgement to devise measurements for the MaaS area when originally designed as the primary data set in [24], three items were excluded from the analysis herein.

The item *"It is not clear if MaaS actually provides a business opportunity with acceptable margins of profitability"* was excluded as it is a measure of perceived uncertainty with respect to future consumers and business making it speculation prone. Furthermore,

---

[1] https://projects2014-2020.interregeurope.eu/primaas/ (Retrieved 2023–03-28).

the item *"There is a high level of uncertainty about travellers' actual willingness and intention to adopt MaaS"* was excluded as it is an item as it was deemed speculative and a question about the opinions of others, while most of the items are about the respondents' own opinions. Finally, the item *"National legislation hinders innovation and renewal in the transport sector"* was also excluded as it is not clear whether the respondents associated the national legislation issue with MaaS and that the terms 'innovation' and 'renewal' are problematic to use in a survey item when not being explicitly defined and at the same time having a 'buzzword connotation' making the item too much into a leading question. The item still expresses a central concept for MaaS, GovTech and governance studies. Hence it can be seen as an expression of the ambiguity of constructs in the Gov-Tech research area. This face validity analysis left seventeen items to be included in the exploratory data analysis. Given that the dataset was designed for exploring strengths and obstacles for rolling out MaaS, a sub-area within GovTech, then a construct situation that relates to GovTech should also, if existing, be visible in an observation of MaaS data.

3   Results

3.1   Exploratory Factor Analysis

The seventeen variable dataset was first put to an analysis for Skewness and Kurtosis with SPSS 29. This showed the variables had Skewness values ranging from -0.983 to 0.053 indicating a general tendency towards left skewness, i.e., careful low-end answers. The variables also showed kurtosis values ranging from -1.133 to 0.323 indicating an overall tendency towards negative platykurtic kurtosis i.e., with thinner tails than a normal distribution resulting in fewer extreme positive or negative answers, than in the case of full statistical normality. These values still fall within the acceptable normality range for an exploratory factor analysis [31].

To explore the factorial structure of constructs in the dataset, all remaining 17 items of the dataset were subjected to an exploratory factor analysis (EFA)/PCA with Varimax rotation, to reduce the dimensions. We see that Principal Component Analysis (PCA) and Factor Analysis (FA) are not the same, although they do share similarities and are often used for similar purposes in data analysis. For instance, Ref. [12] discusses the use of exploratory factor analysis in psychological research, highlighting its applications in identifying latent constructs and assessing construct validity, or Ref. [29] who compares PCA and factor analysis.

The minimum factor loading criteria was set to 0.45. The Kaiser-Meyer-Olkin measure verified the sampling adequacy for the analysis KMO = 0.631. Bartlett's test of sphericity was 347.514 with $p < 0.001$, indicating that the correlation structure of the remaining data set is adequate for exploratory factor analyses. The Kaiser's criterion of eigenvalues was greater than 1. This in the end yielded a 5-factor solution as the best fit for the data, accounting for 57% of the variance. The results of this factor analysis are presented in Table 1.

Table 1 above shows us the rotated component matrix from an exploratory factor analysis. Such a table is the end output of an exploratory factor analysis. The numbers

Table 1. Results from exploratory factor analysis as a rotated component matrix. Extraction method: Principal Component Analysis, Rotation Method, Varimax with Kaiser Normalization. Rotation converged in 7 interactions.

For collaborative work, the roles and responsibilities of difference actors must be established by public authorities	**0.802**		
Public sector leadership is crucial for the development and implementation of MaaS	**0.742**		
Public authorities must lead the process to ensure that MaaS moves towards sustainability	**0.724**		
Integrated mobility services could play a part in achieving a sustainable regional transport system	**0.546**		
There is a high level of incompatibility between public and private goals, such as between public transports' goal of sustainable transport and the commercial goals of a MaaS business		**0.778**	
It is not given that a commercial actor would consider a sustainable society as the goal for the business		**0.734**	
MaaS should be a public task and be run in a non-commercial way		**0.644**	
Overall there is a negative attitude of the private entrepreneurial mindset towards innovation and change, and willingness to participate in pilots or collaborative innovation		**0.615**	
It is not clear who is allowed to sell tickets, who is allowed to give certain discounts and under what conditions			**0.741**	
MaaS implementation is difficult because of State aid and public procurements rule (e.g. PT authority cannot cooperate with specific private firms without procurement and public actors and are not allowed restrict or distort market competition,			**0.731**	
National law is unclear about what is the role of public transport within a MaaS ecosystem that includes both subsidised and commercial services			**0.634**	
There is a clear lack of national vision for MaaS implementation			**0.474**	
There is a public sectors lack of competence in the field so it is not realistic to that a public actor could be able to be the driving force of MaaS				**0.822**
Public transport authorities and their goals are largely designed for their traditional task, i.e. to manage the regional public transport system and not innovate outside the traditional border of public transport				**0.632**

(*continued*)

Table 1. (*continued*)

Loosing own brand image as well as relation to the customers is a big risk that affects the willingness of operators to integrate MaaS Platforms			**0.700**
Entering a MaaS business model will lead to loss of market control for certain participants			**0.642**
Overall, there is an underlying degree of suspicion of even fear of being dominated by other actors of losing control over the development			**0.597**

are the Pearson correlations between the responses to the questionnaire items and the "factors". The numbers shown are sometimes referred to as the "factor loadings". The five factors can be read as five indicative latent variables. The five groupings/factors tell us that the respondents to a degree found these items to more or less represent the same underlying mental representation, i.e., the degree to which the items are a reflection of the same underlying "factor". This is a bottoms-up exploratory data analysis that can point us in the direction of constructs in the area of MaaS and from that further on towards GovTech.

We find that the three items *"For collaborative work, the roles and responsibilities of different actors must be established by public authorities"*, *"Public authorities must lead the process to ensure that MaaS moves towards sustainability"*, *"Public sector leadership is crucial for the development and implementation of MaaS"* are all strongly correlated with factor loadings of 0.724 to 0.802. This indicates the existence of a construct that takes the shape of a strong belief in the public sector. The item *"Integrated mobility services could play a part in achieving a sustainable regional transport"* has with a factor loading of 0.546 a medium strength relation to the central construct, and its topic is less intuitively related to the other three, than these three are to each other. However, the factor loading still indicates that this item has some degree of belonging to this group hence telling us that a belief in "sustainable transport" in the minds of the respondents belong together with a strong belief in the public sector. That is then one potential construct defined, we can call it **Construct 1 - belief in the public sector**. As it indicates a belief that the public sector shall be the normatively leading party to MaaS development and initiatives must be taken by the public sector.

The second factor is the four items *"There is a high level of incompatibility between public and private goals, such as between public transport's goals of sustainable transport and the commercial goals of a MaaS business"*, *"It is not given that a commercial actor would consider a sustainable society as the goal for the business"*, *"MaaS should be a public task and be run in a non-commercial way"*, and *"Overall, there is a negative attitude of the private entrepreneurial mindset towards innovation and change, and willingness to participate in pilots, or collaborative innovation"*. These items group together with factor loadings of 0.615 to 0.778. These all indicate a scepticism towards the private sector as a party to MaaS. While expressing a scepticism of the private sector, this factor does not in any way express a converse positive belief in the public sector in the same way as Construct 1 does. Therefore, we can call this **Construct 2 - scepticism towards the private sector**.

The third factor is the three items *"It is not clear who is allowed to sell tickets, who is allowed to give certain discounts and under which conditions"*, *"National law is unclear about what is the role of public transport within a MaaS ecosystem that includes both subsidised and commercial services"*, *"MaaS implementation is difficult because of state aid and public procurement rules (e.g., PT authority cannot cooperate with specific private firms without procurement, and public actors are not allowed to restrict, or distort market competition)"*, who with factor loadings of 0.634 to 0.741 groups into a factor. This factor expresses a belief in the respondents' minds that the MaaS public-private markets are complex due to the influence of public sector policy making onto the market structures. It can also be noted that the phrasing of the items reads somewhat as if the phrasing speaks from the perspective of a private sector, that puts the blame for the complexity on the public sector. We can call this **Construct 3 - the public-private markets are overly complex, due to public sector policy**.

There is a fourth item who loads onto this factor with the weak factor loading of 0.474, *"There is a clear lack of national vision for MaaS implementation"*. This is a weak loading, still if it falls into any factor it falls into factor three. Topically it can be read as belonging to the topic of factor three. If we interpret it inversely, if there was a clear national vision for MaaS, then the other three items would not be "complain-items" in the way they are. Hence factor three has four items, forming a complaint that public sector norms complicate private-public markets in general and MaaS development in particular.

The fourth factor are the two items *"There is a clear public sector's lack of competence in the field so it is not realistic that a public actor could be able to be the driving force of MaaS"* and *"Public transport authorities and their goals are largely designed for their traditional task, i.e., to manage the regional public transport system and not to innovate outside the traditional border of public transport"* who with factor loadings of 0.632 and 0.822 form one factor. This factor like factor three expresses a general scepticism of the public sector as a market actor in MaaS, still it is not the same kind of scepticism as factor three. While factor three has an aim towards the dominating public sector rules and norms the public sector imposes on the private-public markets, then factor four instead expresses a more direct scepticism of the public sector as a market actor in MaaS development. We can call this **Construct 4 - scepticism towards the public sector**.

The fifth factor is made up of the three items *"Losing own brand image as well as relation to the customers is a big risk that affects the willingness of operators to integrate MaaS platforms"*, *"Entering a MaaS business model will lead to loss of market control for certain participants"*, *"Overall, there is an underlying degree of suspicion or even fear of being dominated by other actors and of losing control over the development"* who with factor loadings of round 0.597 to 0.700 make up one factor. This factor expresses a sense of the insecurities, and downright fears that can come with a public-private partnership. We can call this **Construct 5 – the PPP markets are dangerous**.

The Essence of the EFA. Acknowledging the set of five factors as indicative constructs points in the direction of the following. The respondents show a generic belief that the public sector must be responsible, and an expectation that only given public sector leadership will value from tech utilisation in the public sector be created. However, this is only for as long as there is no interaction with the private sector within a public-private market - then there is a disbelief in the public sector. There is also a generic disbelief in the public sector. That it will not be willing to innovate and change, and that the private sector will not be interested in pursuing sustainability. There is also a distrust towards public-private markets in general, and a projection that neither the public nor the private sector per se would be interested in becoming actors on a market and that any market supposedly to be created, from initiatives taken by the public sector, will be flawed and inefficient, mainly due to the norms and regulations the public sector must follow and impose on those markets, e.g., public procurement rules, and also a risk of general loss of current market positions when the public-private market of MaaS develops.

3.2 Exploring and Testing Constructs with PLS-SEM

We further the exploration of constructs by attempting to put the results of the factor analysis into a partial least square based structural equation model (PLS-SEM). This is a technique for evaluating theoretical relationships between multiple variables, grouped as latent variables, by evaluating the causality of latent variables versus each other [15]. The model is built up out of grouping data items, in our case the survey items, which in this context are called "manifest variables" into groups. The groups are then called "latent variables". The latent variables, like constructs, exist in data sets, but cannot be directly seen. PLS-SEM is a form of casual modelling that can be called "soft modelling" as it is based on a holistic evaluation of outcomes together with theory and where critical exploratory data analysis can be done in parallel with confirmatory data analysis [4].

Connecting latent variables to several manifest variables often allows inferring values of the latent variables based on the measurements of the manifest variables, hence the previous exploratory factor analysis. The five factors do not necessarily equate to five latent variables in a PLS-SEM, but they are in the overall holistic and theoretically inspired process of building a new PLS-SEM, indicator towards latent variables in a PLS-SEM and the basis for the setting up of the PLS-SEM.

It may be worth noting that the dataset was not originally designed for being applied to PLS-SEM, a fact that may in itself impact the PLS-SEM. The implicit structures of a dataset that a PLS-SEM detects may, in this dataset, have another shape than what is optimal for PLS-SEM. We may however apply PLS-SEM to this data set as an instance of a limited exploratory data analysis in the vein of Jebb et al. (2017). We do so because e.g., a multiple regression analysis only takes single item measures, while even a limited PLS-SEM can handle the measurements of plural groupings of data items versus plural groupings of other data items (latent variables) in a way that multiple regression analysis cannot.

Based on our research aim we chose to explore if variance in **Construct 3 - the public-private markets are overly complex, due to public sector policy** can explain variance in **Construct 5 - the markets are dangerous**. In layman's terms if a belief in that the public-private markets are dangerous *can be explained* by a belief in that these markets are so *due* to them being (in the eyes of the respondents) overly influenced by public sector policy. This question was operationalized by putting the constructs into Smart PLS 3^2 for analysis.

PSL-SEM Results. An initial run with all the items from the two constructs showed too much multicollinearity on the item "Losing own brand image as well as relation to the customers is a big risk that affects the willingness of operators to integrate MaaS platforms". It was therefore excluded, and a second and final iteration was done as shown below in Fig. 1. In the second iteration the variance inflation factor (VIF) values, i.e., the measure of the amount of multicollinearity were in the range of 1.425 to 2.146 which is more acceptable.

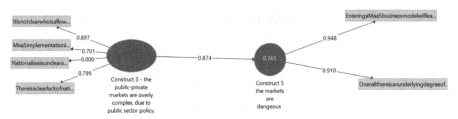

Fig. 1. Relationship between Construct 3 and Construct 5 in PLS-SEM.

Construct Reliability and Validity. Construct Reliability and Validity is an assessment of whether the latent variables measure the concept of what they are intended to measure. Construct validity is assessed by establishing Convergent and Discriminant Validity. Both Convergent and Discriminant validity is established in reflectively measured constructs [14].

Table 2. Measures for assessing construct validity.

	Cronbach's Alpha	rho_A	Composite Reliability	AVE
Construct 3 - the public-private markets are complex	0.569	0.854	0.736	0.484
Construct 5 – the markets are dangerous	0.844	0.886	0.927	0.864

We can note from Table 2 that most of the values are within the acceptable range, with the Cronbach's Alpha and AVE of **Construct 3** on the weak side and the values for **Construct 5** being overall stronger. This can be read as the Construct 5 numerically being a stronger construct than **Construct 3**.

The Fornell-Larcker Criterion. The Fornell-Larcker criterion is a traditional technique used to check the discriminant validity of measurement models. According to

---

² https://www.smartpls.com/ (accessed 2023-03-38).

this criterion, the square root of the average variance extracted by a construct shall be greater than the correlation between the construct and any other construct [14]. In our very simple case, it is only one case we need to observe. As we can see 0.874 is greater than 0.695, which is *not* as it should be and hence discriminant validity between the two constructs is poor. If so, then conclusions made regarding relationships between the two constructs we are investigating may be incorrect. For example, the strength of the relationship could be overestimated, confirming a relationship when in fact there is none. It may also perhaps be so that the two constructs are so strongly related that they are not distinct and should perhaps be more suited as one single construct (Table 3).

Table 3. Discriminant validity.

	Construct 3	Construct 5 -
Construct 3	0.695	
Construct 5	**0.874**	0.929

Heterotrait-Monotrait (HTMT) Ratio of The Model. The HTMT is a measure of similarity between latent variables. If the HTMT is clearly smaller than one, discriminant validity can be regarded as established [17]. In many practical situations, a threshold of 0.85 reliably distinguishes between those pairs of latent variables that have discriminant validity and those that have not. If concepts indeed are theoretically similar, values of up to 0.9 can be accepted but values above that can be seen as indicating a lack of discriminant validity. We have a HTMT-value of 1.003, indicating that the two constructs in the model, in the minds of the respondents, may be overlapping constructs rather than two distinct constructs. That is also what the Fornell-Larcker table indicates.

Cross Loadings. A cross loadings table shows how *all* the manifest variables in a PLS-SEM load onto all the latent variables. Each manifest variable should have *higher* loadings on its own parent latent variable than on the others. If not, then there are issues of discriminant validity between the latent variables, and we by that also see where and how those originate. In our model the cross loadings measure several cases of items loading "wrong", this is in line with what the HTMT-values and what the Fornell-Larcker criterion shows (Table 4).

Table 4. Cross loadings for Construct 5 and Construct 3.

Item	Construct 5	Construct 3
Entering a MaaS business model will lead to loose market control for certain	**0.905**	**0.948**
Overall, there is an underlying degree of suspicion of even fear of being dominated by other actors of losing control over the development	**0.698**	**0.910**
MaaS implementation is difficult because of state aid and public procurement rules	**0.701**	**0.290**
National law is unclear about what is the role of public transport within a MaaS ecosystem that includes both subsidised and commercial services	0.000	0.000
It is not clear who is allowed to sell tickets, who is allowed to give certain discounts and under what conditions	0.897	0.917
There is a clear lack of national vision for MaaS implementation	0.799	0.655

4   Concluding Remarks

The contributions of this paper are two-fold, first as an exploratory data analysis with the aim to identify phenomena to explain and to lay a groundwork for more deductively aimed quantitative research on GovTech and the GovTech market in particular. The analysis was based on a re-interpretation of secondary data, and we shall perhaps not draw too definitive conclusions from it. Yet, what we can see is that in order to understand prerequisites and mechanisms for a GovTech market, then clearer research constructs are needed. We have demonstrated that such clear constructs are not self-evident, at least not in the MaaS data that we took as an example of GovTech.

Second, we still can infer some conclusions for the GovTech market. If it can be read so that a belief that the public-private markets are dangerous is driven by a belief that they are so, due to the regulations and norms the public sector exists to fulfil, which is one interpretation of the exploratory data analysis given the strong connection found, a bleak picture is painted of the way forward for the GovTech market. If so, then that result indicates that in the eyes of the respondents the negative aspects of a public-private market are the norms and regulations the public sector must uphold. If that is the case, it is not necessarily a desirable outcome for the GovTech research area. While those conclusions paint a bleak picture of what may be assumed to be the private sectors' view of the public sector, there is a balance to that in the construct regarding the scepticism toward the private sector. Further, we could see that while those beliefs may appear to be clearly driven by each other, the impression that it is so, may stem from the beliefs being to some or perhaps a large degree overlapping into one construct that tells a different story, but that has not yet been found and is yet to be defined. There is a missing link restricting our capability to understand the GovTech context, and the prima facie constructs across what can be called the GovTech area are disparate and perhaps even contradictory.

What we can do is to observe that if constructs really are abstractions of thought that researchers use to express ideas, and a way of bringing theory down to a hands-on level and for researchers to be able to build the common constructs that are necessary and underlie well conducted quantitative research, then governance, management and business research needs to find ways to work with both the public and the private sectors and aid the sectors in reaching across the aisle. Based on that we prescribe further research into developing constructs that can cut across the research area, enabling for a build-up of a stronger theoretical base of a tech business in public-private markets.

References

1. Alyavina, E., Nikitas, A., Njoya, E.T.: Mobility as a service (MaaS): a thematic map of challenges and opportunities. Res. Transp. Bus. Manag. **43**, 100783 (2022)
2. Babones, S.: Interpretive quantitative methods for the social sciences. Sociology **50**(3), 453–469 (2016)
3. Badri, M.A., Alshare, K.: A path analytic model and measurement of the business value of e-government: an international perspective. Int. J. Inf. Manage. **28**(6), 524–535 (2008)
4. Benitez, J., Henselser, J., Castillo, A., Schuberth, F.: How to perform and report an impactful analysis using partial least squares: guidelines for confirmatory and explanatory IS research. Inf. Manag. **57**(2), 103168 (2020)
5. Bevir, M., Rhodes, R.A.W., Weller, P.: Traditions of governance: interpreting the changing role of the public sector. Public Adm. **81**(1), 1–17 (2003)
6. Beynon-Davies, P.: Models for e-government. Transf. Gov. People Process Policy **1**(1), (2007)
7. Bharosa, N.: The rise of GovTech: Trojan horse or blessing in disguise? A research agenda. *Government Information Quarterly* 39(3), (2022)
8. Butler, L., Yigitcanltar, T., Paz, A.: Barriers and risks of Mobility-as-a-Service (MaaS) adoption in cities: a systematic review of the literature. Cities **109**, 103036 (2021)
9. Casula, M., Rangarajan, N., Shields, P.: The potential of working hypotheses for deductive exploratory research. Qual. Quant. **55**(5), 1703–1725 (2020). https://doi.org/10.1007/s11135-020-01072-9
10. Dener, C., Nii-Aponsah, H., Ghunney, L.E., Johns, K.D.: GovTech Maturity Index: The State of Public Sector Digital Transformation. The World Bank, Washington DC (2021)
11. Digital Journal: GovTech Market Size with Emerging Trends (2022). https://www.digitaljournal.com/pr/govtech-market-size-with-emerging-trends-2022-topkey-players-updates-business-growing-strategies-competitive-dynamics-industry-segmentation-and-forecast-to-2027. Accessed 27 Mar 2023
12. Fabrigar, L.R., Wegener, D.T., MacCallum, R.C., Strahan, E.J.: Evaluating the use of exploratory factor analysis in psychological research. Psychol. Methods **4**(3), 272–299 (1999)
13. Fitzner, K.: Reliability and validity: a quick review. Diabetes Educ. **33**(5), 775–780 (2007)
14. Given, L.: The SAGE Encyclopedia of Qualitative Research Methods, pp. 465–467. SAGE Publications Inc., Thousand Oaks (2023)
15. Hair, J. F., Hult, T., M., Ringle, C. M., Sarstedt, M.: A Primer on Partial Least Squares Structural Equation Modeling (PLS-SEM). 1st ed. SAGE, California (2013)
16. Heeks, R., Bailur, S.: Analyzing e-government research: perspectives, philosophies, theories, methods, and practice. Gov. Inf. Q. **24**(2), 243–265 (2007)
17. Henseler, J., Ringle, C.M., Sarstedt, M.: A new criterion for assessing discriminant validity in variance-based structural equation modeling. J. Acad. Mark. Sci. **43**(1), 115–135 (2014). https://doi.org/10.1007/s11747-014-0403-8

18. Holden, B.: Face Validity. In: Weiner, I.B., Craighead, W.E. (eds.) The Corsini Encyclopedia of Psychology, pp. 637–638. Wiley, Hoboken (2010)
19. Jebb, A.T., Parrigon, S., Woo, S.E.: Exploratory data analysis as a foundation of inductive research. Hum. Resour. Manag. Rev. **27**(2), 265–276 (2017)
20. Karlsson, I., et al.: Development and implementation of mobility-as-a-service–a qualitative study of barriers and enabling factors. Transp. Res. Part A: Policy Pract. **131**, 283–295 (2020)
21. Kattel, R., Mazzucato, M.: Mission-oriented innovation policy and dynamic capabilities in the public sector. Ind. Corp. Chang. **27**(5), 787–801 (2018)
22. Kuziemski, M., Mergel, I., Ulrich, P., Martinez, A.: GovTech practices in the EU. EUR 30985 EN, Publications Office of the European Union, Luxembourg, 2022, ISBN 978-92-76-47234-6, JRC128247 (2022). https://doi.org/10.2760/74735
23. MaaSAlliance: Mobility as a Service? (2022). https://maas-alliance.eu/homepage/what-is-maas/. Accessed 27 Mar 2023
24. Macedo, E., Cicarelli, G., Bandeira, J.M.: Insights from stakeholder's perspectives on barriers and enablers for sustainable MaaS across heterogeneous European cities. Transp. Res. Part A (2023, forthcoming)
25. Nyhlén, S., Gidlund, K.L.: In conversation with digitalization: Myths, fiction or professional imagining? Information Polity **27**(3), 331–341 (2022)
26. PA Consulting: GovTech in the Nordic-Baltic region Part 1: The GovTech situation, challenges and recommendations. Nord 2021:023, Nordic Council of Ministers (2021)
27. Stebbins, R.A.: Exploratory Research in the Social Sciences. Sage, Thousand Oaks (2001)
28. Sundgren, B.: What is a public information system? Int. J. Public Inf. Syst. **1**(1), 81–99 (2005)
29. Velicer, W.F., Jackson, D.N.: Component analysis versus common factor analysis: some issues in selecting an appropriate procedure. Multivar. Behav. Res. **25**(1), 1–28 (1990)
30. Vutsova, A., Ignatova, O.: The role of public-private partnership for effective technology transfer. Appl. Technol. Innov. **10**(3), 83–90 (2014)
31. Watkins, M.W.: Exploratory factor analysis: a guide to best practice. J. Black Psychol. **44**(3), 219–246 (2018)
32. Wirtz, B.W., Daiser, P.: A meta-analysis of empirical e-government research and its future research implications. Int. Rev. Adm. Sci. **84**(1), 144–163 (2016)

Harmonization in eProcurement: Design of a Holistic Solution Model for Pre-award Procedures

Andreas Schmitz[1]([⊠]) [iD], Maria Siapera[2] [iD], Andriana Prentza[2] [iD],
and Maria A. Wimmer[1] [iD]

[1] Research Group E-Government, University of Koblenz, Koblenz, Germany
{andreasschmitz,wimmer}@uni-koblenz.de
[2] Department of Digital Systems, University of Piraeus, Piraeus, Greece
{mariaspr,aprentza}@unipi.gr

Abstract. The standardization of procurement procedures is a complex process requiring multiple layers of interoperability along the European Interoperability Framework (EIF) to be ensured. The high number of distinct actors and different legal frameworks involved hampers efficiency and interoperability of procedures. This problem situation is even more critical during the pre-award phase of procurement, which has so far received less attention from researchers and solution providers alike. While many individual solution components are available for the pre-award phase, these are not orchestrated towards a holistic procedure model. This paper aims to close this gap by A) elaborating a theoretical overview and mapping between issues and proposed solutions, and B) deriving a holistic model for the harmonization of the pre-award phase centered on the orchestration of all identified solution components. Based on the maturity level of the solution components, specific recommendations for action regarding the implementation of the harmonization model are formulated. Methodically, A) is elaborated by iterating three literature review cycles to i) establish relevant concepts in the research field of eProcurement, ii) identify common key issue areas during the pre-award phase and iii) identify solutions for these issues. B) is derived using Design Science Research (DSR).

Keywords: Interoperability · eProcurement · E-Procurement · pre-award · eGovernment · digital transformation · SME · Data Governance · EIF

1 Introduction

The early adoption of eProcurement along the Directives 2014/24/EU [1] and 2014/25/EU [2] demonstrates the European Union's (EU) capability to recognize the significance of utilizing ICT to digitally transform and reduce inefficiencies and costs in public procurement. Despite eProcurement's prominence on the Digital Single Market [3] vision, public bodies have, however, been slow to deploy technology to enhance their

I. Lindgren et al. (Eds.): EGOV 2023, LNCS 14130, pp. 18–33, 2023.
https://doi.org/10.1007/978-3-031-41138-0_2

procedures [4]. Public procurement procedures are complicated, multifaceted processes requiring the coordination of several involved actors and the consideration of multiple interoperability layers (legal, organizational, technical, and semantic) along the EIF [5] while maintaining accountability and transparency.

The current literature on eProcurement indicates that academics are more focused on the post award phase (e.g., eInvoicing) and less so on the pre award phase, which is the entry point of eProcurement processes and where the main data is generated. This paper aims to identify common concepts and issues that emerge in the pre-award phase, and more specifically in the eSourcing, eNotification, eTendering, and eAward phases [6]. It furthermore aims to map these concepts and issues to existing solutions and provide a holistic model and recommendations for the orchestration of such solutions.

The paper is structured as follows: Sect. 2 describes the methodology used to identify the prevalent concepts, key issue areas and solutions appearing in current literature, which is supported by three distinct cycles of literature reviews. Section 3 presents the identified concepts in respect to frequently occurring key issue areas discovered throughout the first two literature review cycles. Section 4 summarizes the results of the final literature review cycle, which maps solutions to the concepts and key issue areas. Section 5 develops a synthesis of the identified solutions and translates these into a holistic model. Finally, Sect. 6 concludes this paper by discussing the results and indicating future research needs.

2 Methodology and Relevant Concepts of the Research

The theoretical foundation for the paper evolves through three cycles of literature review, based on Webster & Watson and Mueller-Bloch & Kranz [7, 8]. These iterative cycles (each cycle following a different objective) provide the knowledge contributions along a structured artefact for the harmonization of the pre-award phase. The first cycle creates an overview of the most relevant literature concepts regarding eProcurement optimization, with an emphasis on the pre-award phase. As a starting point, several literature review studies [9–12] and important EU documents [5, 13] are analyzed and evaluated. Eight concepts, persisting over all sources, are identified, using the methodology prescribed by Vom Brocke et al. [14]. The result of this first literature review is a concept matrix, which structures and supports the subsequent literature review cycles.

The second cycle of literature review identifies key problem areas during the pre-award phase of eProcurement. Based on the identified concept matrix, multiple key word searches are performed based on the concepts. The literature findings for each concept are analyzed and summarized in the sub-sections of Sect. 3 before being synthesized at the end of the chapter. The resulting artifact is a matrix of key issue areas mapped to relevant sources of literature and their corresponding literature concepts. The final literature review cycle maps potential solutions to the previously identified problem areas. In addition to rigorous sources from the literature, relevant sources from EU reports as well as corresponding projects and public initiatives are considered. The result is an extension of the problem matrix by mapping different solution components to each issue areas. Altogether the three cycles of literature review provide a set of concrete solutions for the pre-award phase, supported by rigorous and relevant literature findings, for the development of a model for the harmonization and optimization of pre-award. Figure 1 visualizes the structure of the described literature review cycles.

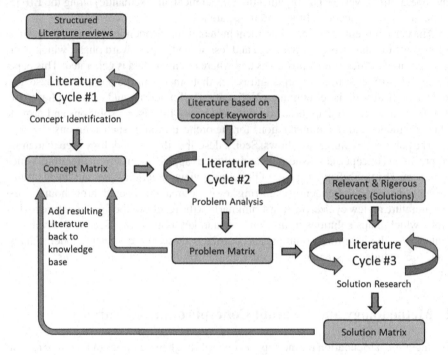

Fig. 1. Overview of literature review cycles

Based on three structured literature reviews from relevant journals and conferences [9–12], a set of eight general literature concepts regarding eProcurement are identified for the problem analysis. Panayiotou and Stavrou focus on electronic G2B services in general, also including procurement services. The authors evaluates 331 publications. Altogether, the study identifies nine dimensions for G2B Services: Interoperability, E-Procurement, E-Customs, SMEs, Personalized Services, Evaluation, Enterprise Architecture, Stakeholder collaboration, Open Data / data sharing, and adoption factors. These dimensions already indicate that interoperability, especially on an organizational layer between different groups of actors, is of high importance [9]. Focusing on implementation issues in eProcurement, Mohungoo et al., provide a different perspective. Based on 165 scientific articles, identified issues are grouped into technical, organizational, and environmental issues. Key technical issues include the introduction of disruptive technologies and digital signatures, while the organizational category mostly covers the coordination between different stakeholders, a lack of personnel, and resistance to change. The environmental category provides insights regarding issues of SMEs and different regulatory frameworks that may be different from country to country, thus yielding interoperability issues [10]. The analysis of critical success-factors for moving from E-Procurement 3.0 to E-Procurement 4.0 is studied by Mavidis und Folinas [11]. A total of 215 sources from literature are evaluated. As in [10], the three categories technical, organizational and technical issues are used to structure the findings. The key findings of [11] and [10] are mostly identical on the categories. However, data quality is added as an important further technological factor in [11]. Finally, Shirzad and Bell evaluate factors for the evolution of e-procurement marketplaces, focusing on establishing flexibility. Based on an initial selection of 493 sources, 22 key studies are evaluated. Four main types of needed flexibility are identified as success factors: Environmental, Technical, Strategic, and Organizational flexibility [12].

Based on the results of the four studies, e-procurement involves the following concepts: Contracting Authorities (CA), Economic Operators (EO), Small- and medium-sized enterprises (SMEs), data governance and the four layers of interoperability of the EIF (Legal organizational, semantic, technical) [5, 15]. The concepts CA, EO, SME can be grouped as an actor related category, while legal, organization, semantic, and technical belong to the concept category of interoperability layers. Since all studies stress the importance of interoperability between different actor groups, dimensions for all relevant stakeholder types are chosen. The layers of the EIF are well suited to represent the different findings regarding interoperability. Finally, Data Governance covers all remaining information related aspects that are not primary considered on the technical and semantic layer. Table 1 provides an overview of the literature concepts and how many relevant literature sources are found for each concept.

Table 1. Concept matrix for public eProcurement

Concept-Category	Concept	High
Actors	CA	**22**: [5, 9–12, 16–32]
	EO	**18:** [5, 9–12, 16–20, 23–28, 33, 34]
	SME	**17:** [9, 18, 20–23, 25, 27–33, 35–37]
Data Governance		**15:** [9–11, 16–18, 20, 23, 24, 26, 33–35, 38]
Interoperability Layers	Legal	**18:** [5, 9–12, 16–18, 20, 22–25, 30, 32, 35, 36]
	Organizational	**20:** [5, 10–12, 16–20, 23–27, 29–31, 36, 37, 39]
	Semantic	**14:** [10–12, 16, 17, 20, 23, 24, 26, 27, 32, 33, 35, 39]
	Technical	**10:** [5, 10–12, 16, 17, 20, 24, 26, 30]

3 Problem Analysis

Based on the literature concepts identified in chapter 2, the second cycle of literature review investigates the main issues along the concepts. The results are presented and synthesized below along the three main concept categories. Key issue areas for each concept are analyzed in the resulting evaluation and presented as an issue matrix.

3.1 Actors: Contracting Authorities, Economic Operators and SMEs

The literature review on the main actors reveals several concerns and challenges that Contracting Authorities face when it comes to efficient use of public procurement. Lack of market knowledge and ambiguity in defining needs impedes the definition of effective and understandable by the Economic Operators, tendering documents and the effective evaluation of vendor suitability [20]. The coordination of heterogenous actors and inter-operability at different levels are essential for ensuring the transparency and account-ability on efficient use of public resources, as well as the fairness of competition among vendors [11, 16]. Organizational, legal, political and social factors exacerbate a diffi-culty of ensuring transparency and interoperability in the public sector [18, 19]. This results in difficulties of translating policies into efficient procurement practices [17] and, at the same time, law-restricted and complex procedures that prevent the participation of Economic Operators and especially SMEs.

SMEs view the public procurement process as excessively convoluted and bureau-cratic [22], which feeds the notion that the public sector market is inaccessible and institutionalized, hence a tradeoff and cost associated with tendering for public sector contracts [40]. The same study and an analysis by the European Commission (EC) [35] also point out that SMEs find the qualification requirements and tender procedures as overly complex and difficult to comprehend. This, combined with the lack of expertise and prior engagement in bidding for public sector contracts, leads to SMEs under-representation, resource constraints [21] and technical barriers, which in turn leads to the inability of SMEs to compete effectively against larger enterprises [40]. In addition, Di Mauro et al. argue that the expenses of bidding, costs of seeking out business opportu-nities and unclear tendering criteria hinder the SME involvement in public procurement [30]. According to Tammi et al., SMEs continue to be under-represented in public sector - supplier relationships despite their significance to national and regional economies [31]. Flynn found out that a restructure of procurement procedures and implementa-tion of SME targeted policies is necessary [36]. Finally Loader, argues that low SME awareness of initiatives and challenges in identifying contract opportunities in the public sector impede SMEs access to public procurement [22].

3.2 eProcurement Interoperability Implementation along EIF Layers

The interoperability layers of the EIF frame the analysis of the implementation of inter-operability in eProcurement procedures [5]. Legal interoperability covers the interop-erability between different legal frameworks and policies. Hardy and Williams have discovered that most issues for eGovernment initiatives and the implementation of pol-icy stem from social and organizational factors rather than technical implementations. The big number of dependencies between different actors during the design and imple-mentation of policies is a key issue [17]. This is further reflected by the Interoperability Maturity model proposed by Concha et al., where legal and institutional affairs are the primary area for the maturity of interoperability and an enabler for technical and semanti-cal interoperability [24]. Kalogirou et al. further exemplify this point by showing several issues for the implementation of European Policies on a practical and national level [26]. Organizational issues can be a main problem factor on all layers of interoperability. This is further exemplified by Palova and Vejacka who show organizational issues faced during the implementation of data standardization on a semantic level [39]. All layers of interoperability are closely connected and the organizational interoperability needs to coordinate between different objectives, policies, actors, and semantical or technical implementations [25]. The creation of networks that can coordinate between all these factors, while ensuring trust and a centralized governance are key for the organizational adoption of interoperability [18]. The definition of suitable tendering criteria and the creation of a clearly structured data flow along the business process are key issues on the semantic layer. The focus on purely monetary tendering is seen as an issue by multiple authors [27, 28, 32]. Instead of focusing on the price, different models are discussed by scholars, such as tendering based on qualification [28], based on the reputation of the bidding EOs and past contracts [27], or partly based on sustainability and environmental concerns [32]. The absence of a clearly structured semantical specification in procedures can disrupt interoperability on other layers, including e.g. the technical exchange of unstructured documents or missing relevant information required for organizational purposes [33]. Finally, the technical layer highly depends on the results of the other layers, since technical failures are mostly caused by insufficient inputs from policy, process organization, or semantic specifications [9, 17].

3.3 Data Governance

Data Governance is concerned with managing and ensuring the quality and value of data along its entire lifecycle [34]. This is an important aspect for the success of eProcurement procedures, especially in the pre-award stage, which needs to supply all information that is used along subsequent steps. Gorgun et al. show that a higher level of quality in notices has significant positive effects on public procurement procedures [23]. Besides poor data quality, the lack of transparency is a key problem for data governance in procurement procedures. Lack of transparency can lead to fraud, corruption, and waste thus leading to financial damage and further hurting the overall integrity and trust of the tendering procedure [38].

3.4 Synthesis of the Second Literature Review Cycle

The combined view on all issues identified during the second cycle of literature review reveals a set of common issues. Generally, most issues of public procurement are at least partly connected to organizational issues. A great number of different stakeholders with different drivers and concerns, combined with numerous dependencies to different layers of interoperability, create an overall complexity on the organizational layer that is hard to handle. Another relevant general observation is the lack of literature focused on the pre-award phase of procurement. While eProcurement in general and the post-award phase in particular are well represented in literature and other relevant sources, the only well researched aspects regarding pre-award are the tendering criteria, the inclusion of SMEs, and other price impacting factors. However, organizational, semantical and technical aspects are scarcely considered by literature. This leads to a literature gap, which this paper tries to close. Table 2 provides an overview of the identified key issue areas and maps them to the relevant literature concepts and findings.

Table 2. Key Issue areas identified in the second literature review cycle

Concepts	Key Issue Areas	Literature References
Organizational (High), Legal (High), CA (High), EO (Medium)	1. Poor Stakeholder coordination on the organizational level	[10, 11, 16–20, 24–27, 29, 30]
SME (High), Legal (Medium), Organizational (Medium)	2. SMEs are not properly included into processes and procurement procedures/policies	[10, 11, 21, 22, 28–31, 35–37]
Semantic (High), EO (High), SME (Medium)	3. Tendering Criteria are not chosen and structured properly	[23, 28, 32, 33, 38, 39]
Semantic (High), Data Governance (High)	4. Tendering Data is poorly structured and not transparent	[10–12, 20, 23, 34, 38]
Organizational (High), Semantic (Medium)	5. Lack of holistically structured and consistent procedures across all layers	[5, 16–18, 24–26, 28]

4 Solution Analysis

The third literature cycle spots potential solutions for problems identified in Sect. 3.

4.1 Introducing Standardized Transactions (PEPPOL)

Ensuring interoperability between buyer's and supplier's systems is a major multi-faceted challenge [41]. Interoperable systems must agree on interfaces that encompass all four layers of interoperability as defined by the EIF [5]. Bilateral agreements on these interfaces are impractical since it would require the implementation of new interfaces and agreements each time a new buyer-supplier connection is established. Hence, standardization is essential for effectively addressing interoperability concerns across all interoperability layers [41]. The objectives of initiatives such as the EU-funded project PEPPOL (Pan-European Public Procurement Online[1]) was to standardize cross-border public procurement processes. It supported the electronic document exchange between buyers and suppliers (both pre-award[2] and post-award[3] eProcurement processes) by first defining a set of specifications (Business Interoperability Specification – BIS), then conducting the exchanges via an open and secure network (eDelivery), and finally by its transport infrastructure agreement[4,5] [42]. In 2012, openPeppol was founded to sustain the project results and to continue the maintenance and further development of the PEPPOL BIS.

[1] https://peppol.org/, last accessed on 26.03.23.
[2] https://docs.peppol.eu/pracc/, last accessed on 26.03.23.
[3] https://docs.peppol.eu/poacc/upgrade-3/, last accessed on 26.03.23.
[4] https://peppol.eu/what-is-peppol/.
[5] https://peppol.eu/what-is-peppol/peppol-profiles-specifications/.

The PEPPOL BIS, which is based on EIF and international open standards, consists of PEPPOL profiles for common eProcurement processes, which can be implemented in existing solutions [43]. Each profile defines the choreography of transactions that can take place between the parties. These also document the underlying eProcurement business process, as well as the technical specifications of each transaction, which are based on worldwide open technological standards [44, 45] (e.g., UBL[6], OASIS ebXML [46]). The PEPPOL BIS in the pre-award supports the following processes: procurement procedure subscription (P001), procurement document access (P002), tender submission (P003), call for tenders questions and answers (P005), tender clarification (P005), search notices (P006), tender withdrawal (P007), publication of notices (P008), award notification (P009) [47].

4.2 Using Enterprise Architecture for Process / Service Design

As identified, the majority of issues in eProcurement and the development of public services in general stem from the incredibly complicated coordination between multiple stakeholders and layers. The usage of Enterprise Architecture (EA) Methods such as The Open Group Architecture Framework (TOGAF) [48] can help to address this complexity by providing a step-by-step approach for different architectural domains and stakeholder views targeting individual problems [49]. Literature has already shown the effectiveness of using EA methods in the public sector, both conceptually [50] and practically [51]. In [44], we propose a framework for designing interoperable public service architectures based on the use-case of eProcurement. Combining the architectural layers of TOGAF ADM with the interoperability layers of EIF enables iterative design of architectures. Following such a holistic approach targets many key issues regarding the implementation of policies into practice, addressing concerns of the relevant stakeholders, and representing each interoperability layer properly. The use of EA Frameworks and methodologies for the design of public services targets the "Poor stakeholder coordination on the organizational level" key issue area by dividing organizational interoperability into multiple architectural views that can assist in translating legal and organizational interoperability concepts to the other layers. Interoperability frameworks such as AgInTef [52] can be utilized during the technical implementation and testing between multiple international stakeholders to provide a tangible solution example.

4.3 Pre-qualification/ESPD

The primary goals of the EC Directives 2014/24/EU [1] and 2014/25/EU [2] is the reduction of administrative burdens for CAs and EOs, including SMEs. The European Single Procurement Document (ESPD) is a crucial part of this endeavor. Its standard form is established by the EC on January 5, 2016 via an implementation regulation. According to the implementation regulation, the ESPD is a *"self-declaration of the business's financial status, abilities, and suitability for a public procurement procedure"* that substitutes the obligation to present all formal evidence and qualification documents as proof of their compliance with legal and specific requirements set by the contracting authorities in

---

[6] https://www.oasis-open.org/committees/tc_home.php?wg_abbrev=ubl#overview.

order to participate in the procurement procedure [53]. Member State CAs are required by law to recognize the qualification criteria established in the ESPD, and EOs can easily qualify for any public procurement in Europe, thereby increasing competition and decreasing transaction costs associated with public procurement participation [53]. The ESPD combined with eCertis[7], a service to check criteria to evidence mapping in other Member States, can enhance tendering criteria selection and structure by standardizing and reusing them when publishing tendering notices.

4.4 Pre-award Catalogues

The usage of electronic catalogues is a well-established practice in post-award procedures. Ordering and delivering goods and the corresponding invoicing can be greatly simplified by using already established and highly structured information from catalogues. This further enables EOs to use their already established product catalogues, reducing effort and making the creation of a tender more profitable and attractive [54]. To enable these benefits during the pre-award phase of procedures, Pre-Award Catalogues are developed, for example the PEPPOL Pre-Award Catalogue[8]. The usage of Pre-Award catalogue follows these steps: First the CA creates a catalogue request with all requirements towards the procured goods and the tender. Second an EO can fill out this catalogue template using its already established product catalogue information. The CA can then easily evaluate all tenders by checking how well the original requirement of the request is adhered to. The usage of Pre-Award Catalogues introduces a full standardization of the procurement contents during pre-award, while also reducing effort for both CAs and EOs. Providing a catalogue request template further enables SMEs to participate, even if they do not have an established catalogue solution. The issues addressed are: First, the public buyer specification can be documented in the form of catalogue requests for future usage and increasing re-usability of tenders for CAs. Secondly, a structured pre-award catalogue can be machine processed and semi-automatically converted into a post-award catalogue.

4.5 Dynamic Purchasing Systems (DPS)

DPS are entirely digital procurement mechanisms that assist CAs in streamlining and enhancing the competitiveness of public procurement procedures [55]. The Directive 2014/24/EU simplifies the DPS regulations, requiring contracting authorities not to limit the number of suppliers that can be admitted to the system, not to impose a time restriction on when an EO can be accepted to the system [1, 56]. EOs can join in at any time if they are qualified and meet the requirements set by the CAs. Moreover, competitiveness is increased since suppliers cannot be awarded contracts directly, but must instead compete for every business opportunity in the DPS, a fact that according to the findings of [29] can influence the participation and success of SMEs [1].

---

[7] https://ec.europa.eu/tools/ecertis/#/about.

[8] https://docs.peppol.eu/pracc/catalogue/1.0/bis/, last accessed 26.03.2023.

4.6 eID

In 2014, the EC published the *"electronic Identification Authentication and Signature Regulation"* (eIDAS) [57] to facilitate seamless interoperable and secure cross-border authentication. Its objective is to make it simpler for European citizens and businesses to utilize electronic identification authentication channels at the European level and establish a common legal framework to increase the trust of individuals, businesses, and public authorities in electronic transactions. The fact that each Member State operates under its own legislative framework and that eIDAS remains technologically neutral and open to different interpretations has resulted in a diversity of digital identification systems and an impediment to interoperability in the European internal market, with just 59% of the population reaping the benefits [58, 59]. Hence, in June 2021, the EC proposed an amendment to this regulation, establishing a "framework for European Digital Identity" to mitigate identified challenges of the previous regulation. The revised regulation includes the adoption of the "European Digital Identity Wallet" and "Self-Sovereign Identity" and a common toolbox to prevent technical fragmentation resulting from divergent standards and interpretations of the regulation [60].

4.7 Core Dataset

The described PEPPOL profiles and extended specifications such as the pre-award catalogue can be combined to cover the entire procurement procedure. While this helps to introduce organizational and semantic interoperability, it does not necessarily introduce sufficient data governance. All relevant PEPPOL specifications during the pre-award phase share a common set of persistent data elements. Based on these data elements, a core dataset artifact can be designed to support partly automatable transformations between process steps and PEPPOL specifications. Furthermore, this enables overarching Schematron[9] validation and even verification of contents across multiple steps, leading to increased data quality. By using core dataset artifacts, different steps of the process can be easily reproduced, thus increasing data transparency and reusability. Altogether, using a core dataset can support data governance along all semantic specifications.

4.8 Matrix to Map Issue Areas with Solutions

Table 3 presents an overview of the previously described solutions, mapped to literature references, maturity level, and the key issue areas where these can be applied.

5 Harmonization of the Pre-award Phase

The different solution components presented in Sect. 4 are selected based on the identified key issue areas in Sect. 3. We now integrate these solution components into a unified holistic model for the pre-award phase's harmonization.

---

[9] HYPERLINK "sps:urlprefix::https" https://www.schematron.com/home/overview.html, last accessed 31.03.2023.

Table 3. Solutions mapped to key issue areas spotted in Table 2

Solutions	Solution Lit. Ref	Maturity	Key Issue Areas
PEPPOL transactions	[41–43, 45]	High	1, 2, 3
EA methodologies	[44, 49–51]	Medium	1, 5
DPS	[21, 55, 56]	Medium	2
Pre award eCatalogues	[54]	Medium	2, 3, 4
Pre-qualification/ESPD	[1, 2, 53]	Medium	2, 3, 4
eID	[58–60]	Low	1, 2, 3, 4, 5
Core Dataset	PEPPOL data mapping	Low	4, 5

Figure 2 depicts the harmonization model, which organizes the solution components across the four interoperability layers vertically and the four main steps of pre-award horizontally. Adoption of EA Methodologies and other structured methods can promote the establishment of legal and organizational interoperability. Especially the challenging implementations of policies and legal frameworks into practical usage can be designed by such methods. This can have further positive effects on the semantical and technical layer since these will result in well-defined and concrete requirements from the top level. When it comes to execution of the processes determined on the legal layer and defined on the organizational layer, structured PEPPOL transaction profiles can provide a cornerstone for semantic coverage of all required business information. However, while the pre-award profiles provide standardized business processes and transaction flows, there are existing gaps. Firstly, the profiles do not entail actual procurement data in a structured format. Secondly, these do not cover the initial phase of eSourcing. Thirdly, these are not optimized towards efficiency for smaller scaled procedures and splitting into lots. These gaps can be filled by introducing pre-award catalogues and DPS processes. The usage of pre-award catalogues both fills the process gap during eSourcing and enables the inclusion of procurement data in a standardized catalogue format. Instead of only providing process control, P002 and P003 can be extended by either providing a pre-award catalogue request (P002) or a filled-out pre-award catalogue as the main content of the tender (P003). This also improves interoperability between pre-award and post-award phases, since the previously structured catalogue data can be easily reused. DPS can be used in conjunction with pre-award catalogues to increase the efficiency of procurement procedures for both EOs and CAs. This can increase the attractiveness of participating for SMEs. However, these are entirely optional and should only be used in smaller-scaled procurement procedures that are suitable for this specialized and restricted approach. Another gap regarding the qualification of bidders can be filled by introducing the ESPD and eCertis. This not only provides clear criteria for qualification that can be easily supplied by EOs, it can also be integrated into the PEPPOL-based choreography of transactions. ESPD artifacts can be attached to the profiles P006 and P008 during the notification to automatically include qualification in a standardized and reusable fashion. To further increase data quality and transparency, a core dataset artifact can be introduced, including all persistent data of an individual procedure. This way procurement data can be easily validated, compared, and reused in each step of the process. Finally on a technical level, eIDs can be introduced to support many parts of the process. The possibility of shareable verifiable credentials and verifiable electronic identifying data of the involved parties can make the attestation of submitted evidences faster and more secure, hence shortening the evaluation time of bidders and improving the entire process chain.

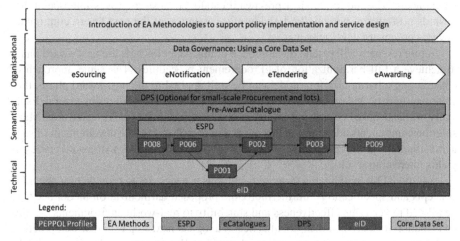

Fig. 2. Pre-Award Harmonization Model

6   Discussion and Further Research Needs

This work provides three main contributions: First, a thorough literature analysis of common issue areas in eProcurement focusing on the pre-award phase. Second, a research and overview of practical solutions that can address the defined issue areas. Third and finally, a harmonization model for the pre-award phase that combines the solution components in a holistic architectural approach. The rigorous foundation is established by conducting three cycles of literature research, resulting in three interconnected concept matrices. These matrices provide a detailed mapping between issue areas, solution components and the scientific sources these maps are based upon. In addition to scientific literature review, the third cycle focuses on researching relevant solution components and introduces several projects and initiatives of the public sector.

Together these findings enable the design of a relevant and rigorous solution model for the pre-award phase as the main contribution of the work. Both the theoretical foundation and the established harmonization model show that solutions to all prevalent issue areas exist but are not aligned to each other.

The proposed solutions have differing levels of maturity, with most of them being still on a piloting level. Therefore, the established harmonization model can target the issues areas in theory but still needs research and development until all needed solutions reach a maturity level that is sufficient for productive usage. This development could be further delayed by the general lack of attention on the pre-award phase. We recommend prioritizing on individual solution components first that are both on a medium to high maturity level and can offer quick wins for the pre-award phase. A focus on establishing a joint usage of pre-award catalogues, ESPD, and DPS procedures along the standardized PEPPOL transactions can help to include a new group of bidders such as SMEs.

Increasing the number of interested participants strengthens the general interest in the pre-award area, feeding more resources into the development of further solution components. The introduction of pre-award catalogues also improves interoperability towards post-award, potentially drawing more attention of the post-award community towards pre-award developments.

Future research will extend the approach of this paper towards the post-award phase to achieve a full harmonization of eProcurement procedures. The same approach of constructing a harmonization model can be well applied to the post-award phase, thus creating a holistic and optimized view towards procurement procedures in general. Especially the handshake between pre-award and post-award is a relevant research area. Many solution components addressed in this paper can be utilized for the development of such a transition. An preliminary analysis how these components affect post-award processes yields interesting results.

Additional research on the proposed solutions is necessary to provide more detailed concepts and specifications. Furthermore, the proposed harmonization model needs to be piloted to verify its effectiveness and suitability to real-world environments. As this contribution focuses on a theoretical concept, a logical next step is to research practical factors that may impact or prevent the real-world implementation of the model. Finally, legal and licensing-based impact factors such as "open specification" rights, patenting and FRAND (fair, reasonable, and nondiscriminatory) terms need to be analyzed.

References

1. Directive 2014/24/EU of the European Parliament and of the Council of 26 February 2014 on public procurement and repealing Directive 2004/18/EC Text with EEA relevance (2014)
2. Directive 2014/25/EU of the European Parliament and of the Council of 26 February 2014 on procurement by entities operating in the water, energy, transport and postal services sectors and repealing Directive 2004/17/EC Text with EEA relevance (2014)
3. Digital procurement. https://single-market-economy.ec.europa.eu/single-market/public-pro curement/digital-procurement_en
4. Kierkegaard, S.: Going, going, gone! e-procurement in the EU (2008)
5. European Commission: New European interoperability framework: promoting seamless services and data flows for European public administrations. DG Informatics, LU (2017)
6. Mondorf, A., Schmidt, D., Wimmer, M.: Ensuring sustainable operation in complex environment: the PEPPOL project and its VCD system. In: MCIS 2010 Proceedings (2010)
7. Mueller-Bloch, C., Kranz, J.: A framework for rigorously identifying research gaps in qualitative literature reviews. Presented at the December 13 (2015)
8. Webster, J., Watson, R.T.: Analyzing the past to prepare for the future: writing a literature review. MIS Q. **26**, xiii–xxiii (2002)
9. Panayiotou, N.A., Stavrou, V.P.: Government to business e-services – a systematic literature review. Gov. Inf. Q. **38**, 101576 (2021). https://doi.org/10.1016/j.giq.2021.101576

10. Mohungoo, I., Brown, I., Kabanda, S.: A systematic review of implementation challenges in public E-Procurement. In: Hattingh, M., Matthee, M., Smuts, H., Pappas, I., Dwivedi, Y.K., Mäntymäki, M. (eds.) I3E 2020. LNCS, vol. 12067, pp. 46–58. Springer, Cham (2020). https://doi.org/10.1007/978-3-030-45002-1_5

11. Mavidis, A., Folinas, D.: From public E-Procurement 3.0 to E-Procurement 4.0; a critical literature review. Sustainability **14**, 11252 (2022). https://doi.org/10.3390/su141811252

12. Shirzad, S.R., Bell, D.: A systematic literature review of flexible E-procurement marketplace. J. Theor. Appl. Electron. Commer. Res. **8**, 49–70 (2013). https://doi.org/10.4067/S0718-187 62013000200005

13. Kouroubali, A., Katehakis, D.G.: The new European interoperability framework as a facilitator of digital transformation for citizen empowerment. J. Biomed. Inform. **94**, 103166 (2019). https://doi.org/10.1016/j.jbi.2019.103166

14. Brocke, J.V., Simons, A., Niehaves, B., Riemer, K., Plattfaut, R., Cleven, A.: Reconstructing the giant: on the importance of rigour in documenting the literature search process. Presented at the http://www.alexandria.unisg.ch/Publikationen/67910 June 10 (2009)

15. European Commission: ANNEX 2 to the communication from the commission to the European parliament, the council, the European economic and social committee and the committee of the regions. DG Informatics, LU (2017)

16. Gottschalk, P.: Maturity levels for interoperability in digital government. Gov. Inf. Q. **26**, 75–81 (2009). https://doi.org/10.1016/j.giq.2008.03.003

17. Hardy, C.A., Williams, S.P.: E-government policy and practice: a theoretical and empirical exploration of public e-procurement. Gov. Inf. Q. **25**, 155–180 (2008). https://doi.org/10.1016/j.giq.2007.02.003

18. Henning, F.: A theoretical framework on the determinants of organisational adoption of interoperability standards in Government information networks. Gov. Inf. Q. **35**, S61–S67 (2018). https://doi.org/10.1016/j.giq.2015.11.008

19. Margariti, V., Stamati, T., Anagnostopoulos, D., Nikolaidou, M., Papastilianou, A.: A holistic model for assessing organizational interoperability in public administration. Gov. Inf. Q. **39**, 101712 (2022). https://doi.org/10.1016/j.giq.2022.101712

20. Riihimäki, E., Pekkola, S.: Public buyer's concerns influencing the early phases of information system acquisition. Gov. Inf. Q. **38**, 101595 (2021). https://doi.org/10.1016/j.giq.2021.101595

21. Akenroye, T.O., Owens, J.D., Elbaz, J., Durowoju, O.A.: Dynamic capabilities for SME participation in public procurement. Bus. Process. Manag. J. **26**, 857–888 (2020). https://doi.org/10.1108/BPMJ-10-2019-0447

22. Loader, K.: Small- and medium-sized enterprises and public procurement: a review of the UK coalition government's policies and their impact. Environ. Plan. C: Polit. Space **36**, 47–66 (2018). https://doi.org/10.1177/2399654417692987

23. Gorgun, M.K., Kutlu, M., Tas, B.K.O.: Information is essential for competitive and cost-effective public procurement. J. Inf. Sci. 01655515221141042 (2022). https://doi.org/10.1177/01655515221141042

24. Concha, G., Astudillo, H., Porrúa, M., Pimenta, C.: E-Government procurement observatory, maturity model and early measurements. Gov. Inf. Q. **29**, S43–S50 (2012). https://doi.org/10.1016/j.giq.2011.08.005

25. Hellberg, A.-S., Grönlund, Å.: Conflicts in implementing interoperability: re-operationalizing basic values. Gov. Inf. Q. **30**, 154–162 (2013). https://doi.org/10.1016/j.giq.2012.10.006

26. Kalogirou, V., Stasis, A., Charalabidis, Y.: Assessing and improving the National Interoperability Frameworks of European Union Member States: the case of Greece. Gov. Inf. Q. **39**, 101716 (2022). https://doi.org/10.1016/j.giq.2022.101716

27. Klabi, H., Mellouli, S., Rekik, M.: A reputation based electronic government procurement model. Gov. Inf. Q. **35**, S43–S53 (2018). https://doi.org/10.1016/j.giq.2016.01.001

28. Qiao, Y., Cummings, G.: The use of qualifications-based selection in public procurement: a survey research. J. Public Procurement **3**, 215–249 (2003). https://doi.org/10.1108/JOPP-03-02-2003-B004
29. Glas, A.H., Eßig, M.: Factors that influence the success of small and medium-sized suppliers in public procurement: evidence from a centralized agency in Germany. Supply Chain Manag. Int. J. **23**, 65–78 (2018). https://doi.org/10.1108/SCM-09-2016-0334
30. Di Mauro, C., Ancarani, A., Hartley, T.: Unravelling SMEs' participation and success in public procurement. J. Public Procurement **20**, 377–401 (2020). https://doi.org/10.1108/JOPP-03-2018-0013
31. Tammi, T., Saastamoinen, J., Reijonen, H.: Market orientation and SMEs' activity in public sector procurement participation. J. Public Procurement **14**, 304–327 (2014). https://doi.org/10.1108/JOPP-14-03-2014-B001
32. Sönnichsen, S.D., Clement, J.: Review of green and sustainable public procurement: towards circular public procurement. J. Clean. Prod. **245**, 118901 (2020). https://doi.org/10.1016/j.jclepro.2019.118901
33. Sciore, E., Siegel, M., Rosenthal, A.: Using semantic values to facilitate interoperability among heterogeneous information systems. ACM Trans. Database Syst. **19**, 254–290 (1994). https://doi.org/10.1145/176567.176570
34. Khatri, V., Brown, C.V.: Designing data governance. Commun. ACM. **53**, 148–152 (2010). https://doi.org/10.1145/1629175.1629210
35. European Commission: SME needs analysis in public procurement: final report. Directorate General for Internal Market, Industry, Entrepreneurship and SMEs, LU (2021)
36. Flynn, A.: Investigating the implementation of SME-friendly policy in public procurement. Policy Stud. **39**, 422–443 (2018). https://doi.org/10.1080/01442872.2018.1478406
37. Harland, C.M., Caldwell, N.D., Powell, P., Zheng, J.: Barriers to supply chain information integration: SMEs adrift of eLands. J. Oper. Manag. **25**, 1234–1254 (2007). https://doi.org/10.1016/j.jom.2007.01.004
38. Soylu, A., et al.: Data quality barriers for transparency in public procurement. Information **13**, 99 (2022). https://doi.org/10.3390/info13020099
39. Paľová, D., Vejačka, M.: Identifying the challenges in e-procurement standardization. IDIMT-2022 (2022)
40. Woldesenbet, K., Worthington, I.: Public procurement and small businesses: estranged or engaged? J. Small Bus. Manage. **57**, 1661–1675 (2019). https://doi.org/10.1111/jsbm.12442
41. Namli, T., Dogac, A.: Testing conformance and interoperability of eHealth applications. Methods Inf. Med. **49**, 281–289 (2010). https://doi.org/10.3414/ME09-02-0022
42. Sonntagbauer, P.: The PEPPOL project – cross border E- Procurement Int public administrations. In: 3rd International Public Procurement Conference Proceedings (2008)
43. Martins, J., Barroso, J., Gonçalves, R., Sousa, A., Bacelar, M., Paredes, H.: Transforming e-Procurement Platforms for PEPPOL and WCAG 2.0 compliance. In: Kim, K.J. (ed.) Information Science and Applications. LNEE, vol. 339, pp. 973–980. Springer, Heidelberg (2015). https://doi.org/10.1007/978-3-662-46578-3_116
44. Schmitz, A., Mondorf, A., Wimmer, M.A.: Framework for designing interoperable public service architectures with exemplification along small-scale procurement and PEPPOL. In: DG.O 2022: The 23rd Annual International Conference on Digital Government Research, pp. 22–34. ACM, Virtual Event Republic of Korea (2022)
45. Sonntagbauer, P.: E-Business, emerging trends in the European Union. In: Gusev, M., Mitrevski, P. (eds.) ICT Innovations 2010. CCIS, vol. 83, pp. 40–50. Springer, Heidelberg (2011). https://doi.org/10.1007/978-3-642-19325-5_5
46. OASIS ebXML RegRep Version 4.0, Part 0: Overview Document. 18 (2012)
47. Works, S.: Pre-award specifications and guidelines. https://peppol.eu/downloads/pre-award/

48. The TOGAF® Standard, Version 9.2. https://pubs.opengroup.org/architecture/togaf9-doc/arch/
49. Guijarro, L.: Interoperability frameworks and enterprise architectures in e-government initiatives in Europe and the United States. Gov. Inf. Q. **24**, 89–101 (2007). https://doi.org/10.1016/j.giq.2006.05.003
50. Mondorf, A., Wimmer, M.: Contextual components of an enterprise architecture framework for pan-European eGovernment services. Presented at the Hawaii International Conference on System Sciences (2017)
51. Ajer, A.K., Olsen, D.: Enterprise architecture challenges: a case study of three Norwegian public sectors. Presented at the Twenty-Sixth European Conference on Information Systems (ECIS2018), June 25, Portsmouth, UK (2018)
52. Siapera, M., Schmitz, A., Wimmer, M.A., Prentza, A.: AgInTeF: Agile interoperability testing framework for orchestrating overarching procedures in verifying digital public services. In: 24th Annual International Conference on Digital Government Research - Together in the unstable world: Digital government and solidarity (DGO 2023). Association for Computing Machinery, New York (2023)
53. Commission Implementing Regulation (EU) 2016/ 7 - of 5 January 2016 - establishing the standard form for the European Single Procurement Document
54. Hudrasyah, H., Nugraha, M.Y.C., Fatima, I., Rahadi, R.A.: E-Catalogue attractiveness study to increase suppliers participation
55. European Commission: Dynamic purchasing systems: use guidelines. DG Internal Market, LU (2021)
56. Eyo, A.: Evidence on use of dynamic purchasing systems in the United Kingdom (UK). Public Procurement Law Rev. **6**, 237–248 (2017)
57. Regulation (EU) No 910/2014 of the European Parliament and of the Council of 23 July 2014 on electronic identification and trust services for electronic transactions in the internal market and repealing Directive 1999/93/EC. (2014)
58. Lips, S., Vinogradova, N., Krimmer, R., Draheim, D.: Re-Shaping the EU digital identity framework. In: DG.O 2022: The 23rd Annual International Conference on Digital Government Research, pp. 13–21. Association for Computing Machinery, New York (2022)
59. A trusted and secure European e-ID - Evaluation of the Regulation | Shaping Europe's digital future. https://digital-strategy.ec.europa.eu/en/library/trusted-and-secure-european-e-id-evaluation-regulation
60. Proposal for a Regulation of the European Parliament and of the COUNCIL AMENDING REGULATION (EU) No 910/2014 as regards establishing a framework for a European Digital Identity (2021)

Government as a Platform in Practice: Commonalities and Differences Across Three European Countries

Peter Kuhn[1,3](✉) ⓘ, Giulia Maragno[2] ⓘ, Dian Balta[1,3] ⓘ, Luca Gastaldi[2] ⓘ, and Florian Matthes[3] ⓘ

[1] Fortiss GmbH, Munich, Germany
{pkuhn,balta}@fortiss.org
[2] Politecnico Di Milano, Milan, Italy
{giulia.maragno,luca.gastaldi}@polimi.it
[3] Technical University of Munich, Munich, Germany
matthes@tum.de

Abstract. Government as a Platform (GaaP) promises better and more efficient public services. More and more countries are applying the approach to eGovernment development. However, there is scant empirical evidence on how to properly implement GaaP in practice. In particular, most of the literature focusses on the adoption in individual countries. We address this gap by investigating and systematically comparing three countries with successful GaaP implementations. By means of expert interviews and analysis of public documents we are able to extract four commonalities and three differences. We discuss our results as lessons learnt. We further contribute to theory and practice by enhancing the knowledge on GaaP approaches, providing a first basis for guidelines toward GaaP.

Keywords: Government as a Platform · Platform-Oriented Infrastructures · Digital Transformation

1 Introduction

Government as a Platform (GaaP) is an approach to the digital transformation of the public sector that promises better and more efficient public services [1]. Coined by O'Reilly [2], GaaP represents the idea of making use of platform structures and principles to improve the public sector. This includes the political level, e.g. in form of platforms for participation [3], as well as the technical level, e.g. in form of platform infrastructures with shared IT components across government entities [4].

In practice, multiple countries have applied the approach. For instance, the UK's Government Digital Service explicitly refers to GaaP as the central approach guiding their activities, but also Italy, Estonia, Singapore, and others follow the GaaP paradigm [5–7]. The individual development paths followed by each one of these countries are

© IFIP International Federation for Information Processing 2023
Published by Springer Nature Switzerland AG 2023
I. Lindgren et al. (Eds.): EGOV 2023, LNCS 14130, pp. 34–47, 2023.
https://doi.org/10.1007/978-3-031-41138-0_3

partially documented in literature – both scientific (e.g. [8, 9]) and governmental (e.g., gds.blog.uk).

However, while information on individual GaaP approaches are available, there is no consolidated knowledge on what the various approaches have in common. Most of the literature provides anecdotal exploration of individual countries' adoption [8, 9]. For countries struggling with GaaP in practice [10], these examples can inspire decision making, but do not provide clear guidance. Consolidated knowledge of commonalities but also differences in the application of GaaP across countries would help to prioritize decisions and, thus, support the application of GaaP by practitioners.

We address this gap by comparing the successful GaaP implementations in Estonia, UK, and Italy. To this end, we conducted two rounds of expert interviews and analyzed public documents. The collected empirical evidence allowed us to extract four common-alities and three differences in the respective GaaP implementations. We discuss our findings and formulate lessons learnt that can be considered by governments that want to implement GaaP.

We contribute to theory by enhancing the knowledge on GaaP approaches in prac-tice. We contribute to practice by providing a first basis for guidelines for GaaP implementations.

2   Theoretical Background

The term "Government as a Platform" was coined by O'Reilly [2], who describes plat-form structures and principles in the private sector and discusses their potential adoption in the public sector. Since then, scholars have investigated various aspects of GaaP. This includes the benefits of GaaP, which can be clustered into efficiency and user-friendliness [10]. The former stems from the concentration on core functionalities of digital public service delivery. For instance, sharing technical components such as elec-tronic IDs across entities allows governments to do "more with less" [1]. The latter is based on the idea that, by concentrating on core functionalities, the resulting freedom outside of those functionalities allows for co-creation and the development of dynamic ecosystems, which foster user-friendly solutions [2, 9, 11].

There is no common definition of GaaP [12, 13], but scholars differentiate vari-ous types of platforms [14], and different perspectives and lenses to understand the phenomenon (e.g. [15] and [16]).

From technical and architectural perspectives, it is a shared IT infrastructure – such as shared components for authentication and payment – that arguably constitutes GaaP [4]. Also, modularity and interoperability models for the automatic exchange of data, e.g. in form of APIs, play a central role [8]. For the scalability and flexibility of GaaP architectures cloud computing is considered an enabler of GaaP [12, 17].

From a governance and managerial perspective, scholars agree that with GaaP comes a new role of government, which is described as platform owner and orchestrator [9, 11]. For the adoption of this role in practice, scholars find that the local stakeholders represent a pivotal element since the new role is associated with changes in responsibilities [10]. The GaaP approach often affects IT systems and responsibilities across different branches of government. Therefore GaaP requires the communication and enforcement of the approach with various actors. The mechanisms for this communication depend on the specific context of the country. For example, federal states require more decentral and cooperative mechanisms [9, 17].

From the perspective of platform principles, scholars describe openness, participation and co-creation as central drivers of GaaP [1, 9, 11]. For instance, [11] describes openness as a means to ensure public value. In an "Open Governance System" the openness of assets, services and engagement leads to participation, co-creation and innovation. In this context, the interpretation of government as an ecosystem has been proposed [16].

Various governments around the world apply GaaP more or less explicitly. These include UK [8], Estonia [6], Italy [9], Russia [18], India [7], Singapore [19], USA, and Australia [20]. The label "Government as a Platform" is used explicitly in the UK, where the Government Digital Service (GDS) has released several blog posts referencing GaaP [21], but also in Italy [22].

In literature, the reporting on GaaP approaches of different countries mostly has country-specific foci, such as federalism [17], orchestration [9], and factors for adoption [12]. While most publications focus on one country, Gil-Garcia considers three countries in a short paper, Australia, the UK and the USA [20]. Also Bender and Heine consider multiple countries, but from a theoretical perspective [4]. To the best of our knowledge, there is no systematic empirical comparison of GaaP implementations across countries.

3 Methodology

This research reports on the investigation and comparison of GaaP approaches in three European countries, which have been chosen for the maturity of their GaaP implementations (cf. Case selection). The investigation is based on publicly available documents and two rounds of expert interviews (cf. Data collection). For the comparison, we use a coding schema based on four dimensions to systematically derive the commonalities and differences among cases (cf. Data analysis).

3.1 Case Selection

To collect data for our analysis, we investigated countries that can be considered advanced in their GaaP approach. Since there is no universal definition of the GaaP approach, we consider it the application of platform structures and principles to IT infrastructure for digital public service delivery. This can happen on purpose, e.g. in form of a deliberate GaaP strategy, or de facto, e.g. without a deliberate GaaP strategy.

Since there are various countries that correspond with that definition, we focused on three countries that are discussed prominently in government and academic literature. We chose Estonia because of its high ranking in eGovernment scores, often being considered the leader in Europe [23]. The country is also considered a role model by other countries [6]. We chose Italy and UK because they explicitly pursue GaaP and reflect on it publicly [21, 22]. Moreover, both countries have been investigated by scholars [8, 9] in major academic outlets as advanced examples of GaaP implementation.

The GaaP approach in Estonia is not officially using the term "Government as a Platform". However, typical steps such as the introduction of an interoperability system can be traced back to 2001, when X-Road was introduced as a distributed data exchange layer for registers and information systems, building the "backbone of e-Estonia" [24]. The e-ID and digital signature followed in 2002.

The GaaP approach in the UK can be traced back to at least 2015, when the founding executive director of the GDS, Mike Bracken, wrote a blog post calling GaaP the next phase of digital transformation [25]. Since then, already existing building blocks GOV.UK and GOV.UK Verify have been complemented by GOV.UK Pay and GOV.UK Notify. Moreover, a set of service standards complete the service toolkit that constitutes the core of the British GaaP approach.

The GaaP approach in Italy can be traced back to 2016, when the founding leader of the Italian Government's Digital Transformation Team laid out a path towards "the new operating system" of the country" [26]. Today, the building blocks of the Italian GaaP approach includes several components, among them a payment (pagoPA), an eID (SPID), and an App (IO) component.

3.2 Data Collection

We collected data from two sources: expert interviews and publicly available documents.

With regard to interviews, we conducted two rounds of expert interviews. The first round of 19 interviews was conducted with experts from UK, Estonia, and Italy from May to July 2021. The interviews were semi-structured and had an exploratory character that aimed at getting an overview over the respective GaaP approaches and understand the relevant areas of decision making.

The second round was conducted with 10 experts from UK, Estonia, and Italy in January and February 2023. The interviews were semi-structured and focused on the specific steps and decisions made when applying GaaP in practice. To recruit for the second round, we contacted the experts from the first round, of whom eight agreed to a second interview and two referred us to colleagues because they didn't have time or changed position. Table 1 gives an overview over the expert interviews in the second round.

The interviewed experts have or had key strategic roles in the application of GaaP in their respective countries. These roles include head of executive bodies, political decision makers as well as consultants. Most of them can be considered IT strategists, with some also identifying as IT architects or IT consultants. In the selection we considered the specific historical circumstances of each country. In Estonia, consultants played an important role, especially at the beginning of the GaaP efforts. In turn, in the UK, digital transformation was and is mostly driven by the GDS. Finally, in Italy, several members of parliament were central in the conceptualization of the Italian GaaP effort. Consequently, we interviewed – among others – consultants from Estonia, heads of GDS from the UK and members of parliament from Italy.

With regard to documents, information was retrieved from publicly available sources based on internet search. The goal of the search was to identify documents summarizing central aspects of the respective GaaP approaches. To validate the selection of documents, the interviewed experts were asked to name relevant documents. In total we selected six

Table 1. Overview over the conducted interviews in the second round.

Interviewee	Organisation	(Former) Role	Country	Duration
I1	Consulting	Expert for Legal Aspects	Estonia	53 min
I2	Consulting	Lead architect of IT infrastructure	Estonia	55 min
I3	Government	Prime minister	Estonia	35 min
I4	Digital Agency	Head of digital agency	UK	45 min
I5	Digital Agency	Head of digital agency	UK	45 min
I6	Digital Agency	CTO of digital agency	Italy	53 min
I7	Parliament	Member of steering committee of digital agency	Italy	48 min
I8	Digital Agency	Lead of core component at digital agency	Italy	57 min
I9	Parliament	Chairman of steering committee of digital agency	Italy	34 min
I10	Government	Minister for digital transformation	Italy	19 min

documents, two from each country. The documents were mostly written by the leaders of the respective digital agencies and lay out a strategy for the coming years or report in retrospective about the lessons learnt in the work of the recent years. Table 2 gives an overview over the analyzed documents.

Table 2. Overview over the analyzed documents.

Title	Type	Outlet	Country
How to build digital public infrastructure: 7 lessons from Estonia [27]	blog article	world economic forum	Estonia
The E-Estonia Story [24]	website post	e-estonia.com	Estonia
Government as a Platform: the next phase of digital transformation [25]	blog article	gds.blog.uk	UK
Government Digital Service: updates on our 2021–2024 strategy [28]	blog article	gds.blog.uk	UK
Toward a new "operating system" for the country [26]	blog article	medium	Italy
Three year plan 2020–2022 [5]	strategic report	-	Italy

3.3 Data Analysis

The first round of interviews was transcribed and coded along the elements of design decisions, i.e. issue, alternative, and justification [29]. The analysis was iterative and had the goal to identify central areas and aspects of decision making in the process of implementing GaaP. These results were the basis for the interview guidelines of the second round.

The second round of interviews and the selected documents were transcribed and coded for design decisions along different dimensions of GaaP, namely architecture, governance, principles and management [4, 8, 11]. The decisions were also distinguished between: (i) descriptive statements that cover GaaP implementation in practice (without judging whether this was or was not a best practice) and (ii) prescriptive statements, in which experts explicitly recommended decisions also to other countries.

To analyze the rich body of data collected, we draw from grounded theory [30]. According to the tips set out for multiple case study theory building, within- and cross-case analyses were performed [31]. The authors first analyzed the interviews of the first round individually and triangulated the data with the documents. Then, adopting an inductive approach [32], we coded the interviews of the second round. The systematic approach suggested by Gioia et al. [33] allowed us to review the transcripts line by line, and develop new concepts while keeping "qualitative rigor" in conducting and presenting our findings.

In the first order analysis, the most promising concepts were extracted and the interviewees' words were left unchanged, to keep a faithful record of the original terms. After that, a second order analysis (cross-case) was carried out by replicating the logic across the cases and grouping sentences with similar meanings. Each group was labelled, and the original terms were retained where possible. At this point, we started making connections between the interviewees' level and the theoretical level, and understanding the theoretical implications of the topics that were emerging from the interviews [33].

Once the cross-case analysis was running, we moved between the case data, the emerging concepts and dimensions, and the academic literature, in order to refine the emerging construct definitions, abstraction levels, construct measures and theoretical relationships.

In the interviews of the first round we asked general questions such as the interviewee's definition of GaaP and the potential of the concepts. This provided the authors with information about the general circumstances of each country. But the coding revealed that the specific steps made towards GaaP were not comprehensively covered, which limited the cross-country comparison. The second round was therefore designed to specifically retrieve the central aspects of the respective GaaP approaches in several dimensions. Consequently, the results are based on both rounds but refers mostly to the second round of interviews.

4   Results

Our research identified commonalities and differences in the GaaP approaches of UK, Italy, and Estonia. Table 3 gives and overview over the results. The commonalities are described in Subsect. 4.1, followed by the differences in Subsect. 4.2.

Table 3. Overview over the GaaP approaches of UK, Italy, and Estonia.

Commonalities	Differences
• Centralization of core functionalities • Strong digital agencies with strong leaders • Carrot and stick management • Openness and Co-creation	• Building blocks vs. data integration layer • Centralization vs. decentralization • Third parties vs. no third parties

4.1 Commonalities

We report on the identified commonalities along four themes. The commonalities are based on the collected data and supported by quotes. The quotes are tagged with the responding country (EE for Estonia, UK for Great Britain, and IT for Italy) and interviewee (01, 02, and so forth) of origin.

Centralization of Core Functionalities. The first set of commonalities concerns the technical architecture of the GaaP approaches in the investigated countries. All three of them centralized certain functionalities in their IT infrastructure. This "platform core" was described as a "set of standards, set of technologies, set of systems, set of services that enable to implement various governmental business processes" (02-EE). The functionalities include but are not limited to the login / authentication functionality, the payment and some form of interoperability functionality. The criteria that decided whether or not to centralize is also similar for the countries. They centralized functionalities that are *"common across all the digital services of the public administration"* (01-IT). Often the functionalities were realized in terms of shared IT components, which are developed and deployed centrally and can be used by all public entities. But the functionalities can also be realized by means of standards and protocols, e.g. X-Road in Estonia. Both, components and standards serve as *"building blocks"* (01-GB) on which the public services of the public entities can be based upon. At the same time all other parts of service provision such as the business logic remains decentral. The reason to centralize functionalities are speed and efficiency: *"If it's decentral, then maybe you don't proceed that fast"* (02-IT). Consequently, centralizing was described as essential for GaaP: *"In my experience, the countries that are consistently in the top 10 governments in the world, have all centralized the key components, and there's really no exceptions to that I've seen"* (01-GB). Despite its advantages, this centralization does not happen automatically when implementing GaaP. The experts described deliberate plans following *"a political choice"* (02-IT). On an operational level, cloud technology is used. *"We defined a national cloud where citizens, where public administrations can [provide] their services."* (05-IT). In summary, our data suggest the centralization of core functionalities as a commonality across countries that implement GaaP.

Strong Digital Agencies with Strong Leaders. The second set of commonalities concerns the governance of the GaaP approach. While the experts emphasized the need to include all ministries and departments, all three countries have a strong entity leading their GaaP approaches. The responsibility of that entity does not include all aspects of GaaP *"but you still need somebody who's in charge of the sort of central issues"* (01-EE).

This "primus inter pares" is necessary because *"it's really difficult to do anything when you have multiple owners and unclear governance. So, the trick is having somebody who can do things despite this situation"* (01-IT). For instance, in Italy the Digital Team – a team within the Presidency of the Council of Ministries focused on eGovernment acceleration – has a strong role. As an example, the Digital Team has the right to take over the ownership of components if it assesses that the progress of development by the current owner is not sufficient. In practice, this possibility was never used, but the existence of this possibility allows the Digital Team to exercise power over other entities. Clear governance in this context was described as the responsibilities being well defined for all actors involved. However, even with well-defined responsibilities and enforcement rights, there is a need for political backing: *"it's quite hard to achieve that without the use of the Prime Minister"* (01-GB). A second aspect, related to this, is the role of single personalities for the success of GaaP. In Estonia it was prime minister Mart Laar, who was significantly advancing e-government in his tenure, and in the UK the heads of the Government Digital Service were credited for their positive role in the advancement of GaaP. The starkest example, however, might be Mr. Diego Piacentini, who for two years acted as special commissioner for digital transformation in the Italian government and served as leader of the Digital Team. He was a former Amazon executive directly reporting to Jeff Bezos. With this past he had the credibility to make changes and use his mandate to its full extent. Beyond strong personalities at the top, multiple experts stressed the importance of skilled personnel in general [27], describing extensive programs and efforts to make sure the according entities in charge of GaaP had employees with skills in IT, design and agile management at their disposal. An example is Piacentini's call for Italians from all over the world to join his Digital Team at the start of his tenure. In summary, our data suggest clear governance with strong leaders and skilled personnel as a commonality across countries that implement GaaP.

Carrot and Stick. The third set of commonalities evolves around the management style of the GaaP approach. All three countries described a management approach that aims at enabling. For instance, central functionalities were designed such that their usage is easy and cheap. One effect of this was the fast adoption of the provided functionalities. *"They were free to choose, but most of them in the end chose to use our tools because they were better in terms of user experience and cheaper as well"* (01-IT). A similar effect was achieved by means of monetary incentives: *"we set aside a pot of money effectively, and said to all our municipalities, if you conform to our standards, we will effectively subsidize your work"* (01-GB). At the same time, all countries complemented their enabling management with standards and regulations. In UK, for instance, the use of GOV.UK as a frontend is mandatory. Also standards regarding accessibility and style guides are part of this regulation. Additionally, the experts pointed out the need for legal adoptions for the implementation of GaaP. *"We don't need different laws because we go further with sort of government as a platform, but maybe the picture of deciding what laws we need changes because the situations are different."* (01-EE). In summary, our data suggests a carrot and stick management approach, complementing incentives with standards and (legal) regulation as a commonality across countries that implement GaaP.

Openness and Co-creation. Beyond certain management decisions, a culture of openness and co-creation was emphasized by the experts as an important ingredient to their

GaaP approach: *"we work with the ministries to make their software open source for example, which was never done before"* (03-IT). Openness includes also the transparency of private data used by public administrations. *"The authorities who have the right to access your data have to be able to explain why."* (01-EE). Besides accountability via transparency, the benefits of this openness were described as innovation and flexibility. For example, during the covid-19 pandemic this openness allowed for faster and better development of new public services: *"if you don't have openness, if you can't access your own code base and change your designs and edit your content very quickly, then you can't service that user need"* (02-GB). Based on openness the countries pushed for participation and co-creation with actors from both within and outside the public sector: *"[...] and then we also created the community, I think we created two. One was called developers, and the other one designers"* (01-IT). These communities constantly contribute to the further development and improvement of services and core functionalities in the respective countries. Finally, open communication of the GaaP approaches and underlying strategies is shared by the three countries. All three countries have been outspoken about their efforts, decisions, and effectiveness, for example, in form of reports or blog posts. *"Celebrate and share wins – and failures"* [27] is one of the lessons Estonia draws from their experience and also recommends to other countries. In summary, our data suggest that embracing platform principles such as openness and co-creation are a commonality across countries that implement GaaP.

4.2 Differences

Despite many commonalities, our investigation revealed also differences in the approaches of the three countries.

Building Blocks vs. Data Integration Layer. Notwithstanding the centralization of core functionalities, the infrastructure architecture differs between countries. Italy's and UK's technical approach to GaaP can be described as an infrastructure of core components, i.e. connected but individual components that provide core functionalities to the public sector. *"Typically within those platforms are things like the notification server. So if you are a municipal or another department, you can link to that notification server"* (01-GB). In contrast, the X-Road in Estonia is described as a decentral data integration layer that connects the IT systems of the public sector entities. A good example for this deliberately decentral approach is the payment functionality which is not realized as a central component in Estonia, but by a private standard, that is used by the data integration layer. *"you can seamlessly pay via the bank's system but it's in the same system."* (01-EE). This suggests that the technical setup providing core functionalities for GaaP can differ between countries.

Centralization vs. Decentralization. Secondly, the degree of centralization of the frontends differs between countries. The UK has the most central approach with GOV.UK being a mandatory frontend for public entities. This follows the idea of a one-stop-shop, which aims at user-friendliness by means of one website for everything *"GOV UK when we built it consolidated 1,780 sites."* (01-GB). Significantly, even the UK's approach has a decentral element. The content of the pages of GOV.UK are provided by the respective entities: *"one content management system, but with federated authority."* (02-GB). The other end of the spectrum is represented by Italy, where the frontend is the responsibility of service providing entities *"we let each administration have its own website."* (01-IT). The reasoning stems from the federal structure of the Italian state. *"If you want to promote the adoption of services you should talk with regions."* (03-IT) Yet, also in Italy, the user-friendliness of the frontend and the idea of a one-stop-shop play a role. To that end, the federal government provides style guides, templates and other standards with the goal to harmonize the frontends within the country. Additionally, the new App IO is aiming at a centralized frontend for mobile phones. Taken together, our investigation suggest that the exact degree of (de)centralization of the frontend can differ between countries that implement GaaP.

Third Parties vs. No Third Parties. Lastly, the openness towards third parties differs between countries. In the UK the login functionality was initially a private sector initiative but subsequently failed for a number of reasons. For instance, the data privacy of the solution was not meeting expectations. *"Access to people's passport details was provided to the private sector and there's been some usage of that"* (01-GB). The consequence was that the public sector built its own solution after all. In contrast, in Estonia, the payment is handled by a private solution of the banking sector *"the banks have been integrated into the system. So the banks were linked to the X-Road"* (01-EE). This system is considered a success and there are no plans to privatize it. In general, the interviewed experts consider the integration of the private sector as challenging *"There are others that have got that facility, Singapore and Iceland, but there's only really about three or four countries that have managed to cross the government and the private sector and use it successfully."* (01-GB). Yet, the two described examples document the openness of governments at the same time. Taken together, our investigation suggest that the inclusion of third parties differs between countries that implement GaaP.

5 Discussion

Based on the presented results we discuss implications for theory and practice.

Firstly, our results suggest that there is **no unique path to GaaP**. Each of the countries has their own history of design decisions and steps toward GaaP. For example, the GaaP efforts of Estonia can be tracked back to 2001, while the Italian journey started only in 2016. The presented differences suggest that a country's context play an important role for this path. This is in line with literature's variety and reported aspects, ranging from managerial themes such as orchestration [9] to specific architectural questions such as constituting elements of GaaP [4]. Further research could investigate how the context of a country such as size and degree of federalism, but also general societal progress in digital transformation affects these paths.

Secondly, our results suggest that – notwithstanding the previous point – GaaP approaches result in **similar structures and principles**. While the implementations follow individual paths, central architectural and managerial patterns can be observed. For example, while the exact set of building blocks differ, the payment and identity functionalities are part of all three investigated GaaP infrastructures. Also, openness in form of co-creation and communication of strategies and lessons learnt are central to all three approaches. This is in line with literature such as [11] and suggests there could be a general blue print or guidelines for GaaP. For practice this means, copying from successful countries can be a valid strategy. With regard to theory, some scholars already attempt to capture these commonalities [4, 8]. However, our results include several aspects that are currently not present in literature - for example, the role of skilled personnel and strong leaders. For theory, this means existing concepts should be extended by important aspects from practice.

Thirdly, our results show that applying GaaP in practice requires the **balancing of trade-offs**. Despite the general commonalities across countries, the approaches differ in the details of their implementation. This can potentially be explained by the different context, with Estonia being smaller and Italy being more federal than the UK. We find that often this adoption can be described as the balancing of two extremes where the equilibrium depends on the context. For example, the ideal degree of centrality might be smaller in a federal than in a more centralized countries. In the UK even the frontend is centralized, while in Italy there are only standards and templates. This is in line with literature from Russia [17] and Germany [10], but has not been explicitly described yet. Similarly, the need for balancing also extends to the governance dimension. In the UK the GDS has the ownership of the main components, whereas in Italy, the ownership remains with the ministries and the Digital Team only orchestrates them. In IS literature, balancing trade-offs in the context of platforms has been described for boundary resources. The so-called "tuning" [34] corresponds with the balancing described in this paper. For practice, this means context matters and it is important to find the right balance for each country individually. For theory, this means the role of trade-offs should be investigated and existing IS literature might contribute to developing theoretical insight into this aspect of GaaP.

6   Conclusion

In this paper we present the findings from an in-depth investigation of three successful GaaP implementations. We find that the countries have several commonalities that can be considered in future conceptualizations of GaaP. Also, we find several differences, which can be interpreted as adherence to individual contexts.

Our research has several limitations. Firstly, we investigated only three countries. This allowed for an in-depth analysis but also limits the generalizability of the results. Many other countries have implemented GaaP and might not have the same commonalities. Our results are therefore only a first basis for further research on commonalities of GaaP implementations. Secondly, the counterfactuals to the decisions of the investigated countries are unknown, i.e. we don't know what would've happened if the governments decided differently. Therefore we cannot know whether the success of the countries is because of or despite their respective GaaP decisions. Future research should also investigate countries that are not successful yet or took different decisions. This could allow for the distinction between critical and non-critical decisions in the application of GaaP. Thirdly, most of our results are descriptive for the current GaaP configuration and less about the steps to get there. While this can be helpful to understand GaaP in these countries, the results are not prescriptive in the sense of a procedure that can be followed. Further research should attempt to provide guidelines in order to further support GaaP in practice.

While limitations exist, we believe this research enhances the structured knowledge on GaaP implementations and can be a suitable starting point towards prescriptive knowledge on the application of GaaP in practice.

Acknowledgments. This research was partially funded by the "Nationales E-Government Kompetenzzentrum e. V.". We thank Vasilisa Poliarus and Dmytro Voitsekhivskyi for their support.

References

1. Janssen, M., Estevez, E.: Lean government and platform-based governance—Doing more with less. Gov. Inf. Q. **30**, S1–S8 (2013). https://doi.org/10.1016/j.giq.2012.11.003
2. O'Reilly, T.: Government as a platform. Innov. Technol. Gov. Global. **6**, 13–40 (2011). https://doi.org/10.1162/INOV_a_00056
3. Al-Ani, A.: Government as a platform: services, participation and policies. In: Friedrichsen, M., Kamalipour, Y. (eds.) Digital Transformation in Journalism and News Media. MBI, pp. 179–196. Springer, Cham (2017). https://doi.org/10.1007/978-3-319-27786-8_14
4. Bender, B., Heine, M.: Government as a Platform? Constitutive elements of public service platforms. In: Kö, A., Francesconi, E., Kotsis, G., Tjoa, A.M., Khalil, I. (eds.) EGOVIS 2021. LNCS, vol. 12926, pp. 3–20. Springer, Cham (2021). https://doi.org/10.1007/978-3-030-866 11-2_1
5. l'Agenzia per l'Italia Digitale, Dipartimento per la Trasformazione Digitale: Piano Triennale per l'informatica nella Pubblica Amministrazione (2020)
6. Margetts, H., Naumann, A.: Government as a platform: what can Estonia show the world? 41 (2017)
7. Mukhopadhyay, S., Bouwman, H., Jaiswal, M.P.: An open platform centric approach for scalable government service delivery to the poor: the Aadhaar case. Gov. Inf. Q. **36**, 437–448 (2019). https://doi.org/10.1016/j.giq.2019.05.001
8. Brown, A., Fishenden, J., Thompson, M., Venters, W.: Appraising the impact and role of platform models and Government as a Platform (GaaP) in UK Government public service reform: towards a Platform Assessment Framework (PAF). Gov. Inf. Q. **34**, 167–182 (2017). https://doi.org/10.1016/j.giq.2017.03.003
9. Cordella, A., Paletti, A.: Government as a platform, orchestration, and public value creation: the Italian case. Gov. Inf. Q. **36**, 101409 (2019). https://doi.org/10.1016/j.giq.2019.101409
10. Kuhn, P., Buchinger, M., Balta, D.: Barriers of government as a platform in practice. In: Ongoing Research, Practitioners, Posters, Workshops, and Projects at EGOV-CeDEM-ePart 2021, Granada (2021)
11. Millard, J.: Open governance systems: doing more with more. Gov. Inf. Q. **35**, S77–S87 (2018). https://doi.org/10.1016/j.giq.2015.08.003
12. Seo, H., Myeong, S.: Determinant factors for adoption of government as a platform in South Korea: mediating effects on the perception of intelligent information technology. Sustainability **13**, 10464 (2021). https://doi.org/10.3390/su131810464
13. Seo, H., Myeong, S.: The priority of factors of building government as a platform with analytic hierarchy process analysis. Sustainability **12**, 5615 (2020). https://doi.org/10.3390/su12145615

14. Thompson, M., Venters, W.: Platform, or technology project? A spectrum of six strategic 'plays' from UK government IT initiatives and their implications for policy. Gov. Inf. Q. **38**, 101628 (2021). https://doi.org/10.1016/j.giq.2021.101628

15. Jamieson, D., Wilson, R., Martin, M.: Is the GaaP wider than we think? Applying a sociotechnical lens to Government-as-a-Platform. In: Proceedings of the 13th International Conference on Theory and Practice of Electronic Governance, pp. 514–517. Association for Computing Machinery, New York (2020). https://doi.org/10.1145/3428502.3428580

16. Rantanen, M.M., Koskinen, J., Hyrynsalmi, S.: E-Government ecosystem: a new view to explain complex phenomenon. In: 2019 42nd International Convention on Information and Communication Technology, Electronics and Microelectronics (MIPRO), pp. 1408–1413 (2019). https://doi.org/10.23919/MIPRO.2019.8756909

17. Styrin, E., Mossberger, K., Zhulin, A.: Government as a platform: intergovernmental participation for public services in the Russian Federation. Gov. Inf. Q. **39**, 101627 (2022). https://doi.org/10.1016/j.giq.2021.101627

18. Smorgunov, L.: Governability and a technocratic approach to government as a platform: critics using the Russian case. Int. J. Electron. Gov. **13**, 4–20 (2021). https://doi.org/10.1504/IJEG.2021.114298

19. Government of Singapure: E-Government Masterplan 2011-2015

20. Gil-Garcia, J.R., Henman, P., Avila-Maravilla, M.A.: Towards "government as a platform"? Preliminary lessons from Australia, the United Kingdom and the United States. In: Proceedings of Ongoing Research, Practitioners, Posters, Workshops, and Projects of the International Conference EGOV-CeDEM-ePart 2019 (2019)

21. Government Digital Service: Government as a Platform: the next phase of digital transformation - Government Digital Service. https://gds.blog.gov.uk/2015/03/29/government-as-a-platform-the-next-phase-of-digital-transformation/. Accessed 19 Jan 2021

22. D.T. Team: Report Digital Transformation Team. https://teamdigitale.governo.it/assets/pdf/Report_DigitalTransformationTeam_09_30_2018.pdf. Accessed 21 Mar 2023

23. European Commission: eGovernment Benchmark 2022 - EXECUTIVE SUMMARY. (2023)

24. The e-Estonia Story. https://e-estonia.com/story/. Accessed 29 Mar 2023

25. Bracken, M.: Government as a Platform: the next phase of digital transformation - Government Digital Service. https://gds.blog.gov.uk/2015/03/29/government-as-a-platform-the-next-phase-of-digital-transformation/. Accessed 29 Mar 2023

26. Piacentini, D.: Towards the new "operating system" of the country. https://medium.com/team-per-la-trasformazione-digitale/new-operating-system-country-technological-competence-plans-11b50a750ea7. Accessed 29 Mar 2023

27. Kaevats, M.: Digital public infrastructure: 7 lessons from Estonia. https://www.weforum.org/agenda/2021/10/how-to-build-digital-public-infrastructure-estonia/. Accessed 29 Mar 2023

28. Read, T.: Government Digital Service: updates on our 2021-2024 strategy - Government Digital Service. https://gds.blog.gov.uk/2022/12/20/government-digital-service-updates-on-our-2021-2024-strategy/. Accessed 29 Mar 2023

29. Potts, C., Bruns, G.: Recording the reasons for design decisions. In: ICSE, pp. 418–427 (1988)

30. Wiesche, M., Jurisch, M.C., City of Munich, Yetton, P.W., Deaken University, Krcmar, H., Technische Universität München: grounded theory methodology in information systems research. MISQ. **41**, 685–701 (2017). https://doi.org/10.25300/MISQ/2017/41.3.02

31. Eisenhardt, K.M., Graebner, M.E.: Theory building from cases: opportunities and challenges. AMJ **50**, 25–32 (2007). https://doi.org/10.5465/amj.2007.24160888

32. Saldaña, J.: The Coding Manual for Qualitative Researchers. SAGE Publ, Los Angeles (2013)

33. Gioia, D.A., Corley, K.G., Hamilton, A.L.: Seeking qualitative rigor in inductive research: notes on the Gioia methodology. Organ. Res. Methods **16**, 15–31 (2013). https://doi.org/10.1177/1094428112452151
34. Eaton, B., Elaluf-Calderwood, S., Sorensen, C., Yoo, Y.: Distributed tuning of boundary resources: the case of Apple's iOS service system. Manag. Inf. Syst. Q. **39**, 217–243 (2015)

The Self-serving Citizen as a Co-producer in the Digital Public Service Delivery

Hanne Höglund Rydén[1]([✉]) [ID], Sara Hofmann[1] [ID], and Guri Verne[2] [ID]

[1] University of Agder, Kristiansand, Norway
{hanne.s.h.ryden,sara.hofmann}@uia.no
[2] University of Oslo, Oslo, Norway
guribv@ifi.uio.no

Abstract. The promotion of digital self-services has generated a shift within digital government, which has implications for citizens that depend on welfare services. From the policy perspective, users can benefit from better service access, process efficiency and opportunities for citizens to co-produce their public services. These opportunities are accompanied by increasing responsibilities for citizens that are expected to serve themselves to a higher extent. This article analyses how vulnerable citizens engage in self-services and their co-production of public services that play out in the digital public service setting. Data were gathered through participatory observations at a service office at the Norwegian welfare administration (NAV) when citizens visited the office to apply for public welfare services. The article provides a novel theoretical framework for conceptualizing dynamic actor-co-production, showing how co-production preconditions can be understood in relation to the actors involved in the service procedure. From a citizen-centric perspective, the article explores the roles of the human state actor – frontline workers, technology state actor – self-service stations, and the private actor – citizens – in the co-production. It sheds light on how participation can be understood at different levels of abstraction and describes the impact of actors' *roles, motives, actions,* and *preconditions* in the co-production of welfare services. The findings show that most citizens that visit the office are vulnerable in relation to financial circumstances and struggle to independently co-produce their services in the public self-service setting.

Keywords: co-production · digital government · digital self-services · vulnerable citizens · actor network theory · participation

1 Introduction

Co-production, which can be described as the involvement of individual citizens and groups in public service delivery [1], has been a central element in the provision of public services for many years. As the old welfare state model with its underlying 'provider centricity' was abandoned, new government reforms such as New Public Management

I. Lindgren et al. (Eds.): EGOV 2023, LNCS 14130, pp. 48–63, 2023.
https://doi.org/10.1007/978-3-031-41138-0_4

and New Public Governance focused on integrating clients, i.e., citizens, into the production of public services [2, 3]. The element of action is essential in co-production [4] since it provides citizens with an active role that can refer to both collective and individual action [5–7]. Co-production can be described as joint activities between a citizen and the public sector that result in value creation and the immediate consumption of a service [8]. Following this understanding, any public service that requires some form of interaction between a citizen and the public sector, is co-produced.

The proliferation of digital self-services in the public sector has led to an even more prominent role of co-production in public service delivery. Compared to traditional public services, digital self-services shift the responsibility of providing relevant and correct information towards the citizens, thus augmenting their role as 'co-producers' [9]. Based on the idea of an active citizenship [10], increasing co-production is seen as promising in the light of an efficient, transparent, and flexible citizen-to-government relationship. For example, the EU has adopted a digital public service agenda that focuses on values such as efficiency and high quality and user-centric services where co-production replaces the old service provision that rests upon a passive consumer logic [11]. Thus, citizens' roles are changing as they are expected to engage in new forms of co-production in digital self-services.

However, the growing emphasis on co-production poses challenges to some citizens as the responsibility for the service procedure moves away from government professionals and closer to the citizen [12, 13]. Digital self-services require citizens to develop capabilities to independently solve problems and serve themselves [14–16]. However, citizens that depend on welfare services, for instance, often face health issues, limited executive functioning, struggle with language barriers, or lack the digital or administrative skills to master digital self-services. Thus, while digitalizing public services can offer new forms to co-produce value, this form of interaction creates new, systematic barriers for some citizens [17].

Despite the increasing interest in co-production, little is known about the practical implications for citizens. There are few empirical studies that consider co-production in action, i.e., that analyze the interaction taking place between citizens and the public sector in the act of co-production empirically [1]. Furthermore, the existing literature does not provide us with an analytical framework that can be used for studying and evaluating co-production from a citizens' point of view. Thus, research is needed to provide us with a conceptual understanding of co-production as well as with empirical data on how co-production unfolds from a citizens' perspective [18].

Therefore, our research goal (RG) is **to design an analytical framework for describing co-production practices in digital self-services**.

Based on this analytical framework, we will answer our research question (RQ) **What are citizens' experiences as they engage in the co-production of digital self-services?**

Our focus is on the individual level of co-production from a citizen's perspective during service delivery, i.e., when a citizen performs activities and contributes to the service procedure to receive welfare service. The focus of this article is self-services co-produced in the NAV office. In this article, we take a two-step approach. First, we develop an analytical framework for understanding co-production in a digital service setting and the implications for the actors involved. Based on actor-network theory, we understand co-production as a network that involves both human and non-human actors. We build on Nabatchi et al.'s understanding of the who, when and what of co-production and extend it by incorporating the actors' motivation (why). Further, we integrate digital self-services as a non-human actor in the framework. Second, we apply this framework empirically to identify implications for citizens that engage in co-production in digital self-services at the stage of co-delivery, also elaborated on from Nabatchi et al.'s. In doing so, we observe citizens' interaction with digital self-service stations and frontline workers at local offices of the Norwegian Labor and Welfare Organization (NAV). These observations are supplemented by frontline workers' perspectives in the observed service setting.

Our article provides conceptual, empirical, and methodological contributions. It provides conceptual clarity by presenting a framework for analyzing co-production in a digital self-service setting. The findings show how digital self-services are co-produced at an office setting, thus challenging the idea of independency that lies in the concept of *self*-service. Empirically, it advances the understanding of implications for citizens engaged in digital self-service co-production and explicitly shows the challenges and obstacles. Finally, we provide methodological contributions for research designs by capturing co-production in action through participant observations.

2   Related Work

2.1   The Concept of Co-production

While there is a broad variety in the definition of co-production, the literature agrees that co-production is about involving citizens in service delivery. According to Brudney and England [19], for example, "coproduction consists of citizen involvement or participation (rather than bureaucratic responsiveness) in the delivery of urban services." while Levine and Fisher [20] describe it more broadly as "the joint provision of public services by public agencies and service consumers". Similarly, Pestoff [21] understands co-production as "a model for the mix of both public service agents and citizens who contribute to the provision of a public service". All these definitions have in common that they mention the involvement of citizens in providing public services.

A further important element in the definition of co-production is the distinction of involved roles. Several definitions explicitly stress that the relationship between actors outside and inside organization is important to optimize the service provision of organizations [22]. Other researchers argue that the essence of co-production is the mutual resource contribution into the service provision [7]. Full co-production is at play when professionals and service users share the responsibility for both service delivery and design [23]. Thus, two central actors in co-production are the public organization that is responsible for delivering the service as well as "individuals who are not 'in' the same organization", i.e., citizens [6].

The literature does not agree as to whether co-production needs to be voluntary from the citizens' perspective or whether also the 'forced' involvement of citizens can be considered as co-production. Some argue that co-production needs to be based on "voluntary cooperation on the part of citizens (rather than compliance with laws or city ordinances)" [18, 23] and citizens can freely decide whether they would like to contribute to a co-production process or not [24]. In contrast to this, others consider all public services where some sort of input is required from a citizen as co-production [2], even when citizens do not want to be involved but have no choice as they are dependent on a public service. This differing view can to a certain extent be explained by noting that the term co-production has previously been used to describe both citizens' involvement in receiving a public service as well as in the (voluntary) development of services, often also referred to as co-design or co-creation [10].

While also creating value for citizens, co-production is strongly motivated by the public sector's financial interests. It is closely linked to the introduction of the public sector reforms New Public Management and New Public Governance [26] and is considered an essential part of social policy in Europe as many governments are forced to balance scarce resources in the public service provision [4]. From an organizational value perspective, co-production can lead to both cost savings and higher service quality as public sector organizations can shift some of the workload towards citizens. Following this argument, co-production ensures both service quality and quantity that will benefit citizens, but to an even higher extent the organizations that create room for the co-production [19].

2.2 Co-production in Digital Self-services

The increased provision of digital self-services has strengthened the importance of co-production in public service delivery. Digital self-services refer to the access to public services through digital technologies without having to deal with government employees. In most cases, this means no direct interaction between citizens and service workers, hence reducing the face-to-face interaction [28]. These technologies alter the roles and expectations of citizens and frontline workers in the service procedure where some scholars consider self-services as a new form of co-production between consumer and the provider [29]. Citizens are sometimes referred to as 'screen level workers', in charge of their own service procedure [31, 32] since digital self-services move the responsibility for the required tasks towards the citizens [14].

In addition to the organizational benefits, co-production in digital self-services offers advantages for citizens as well. Motivated by the arguments of participative politics that foster an active citizenship, the technical development opens for new possibilities of co-production through "self-service politics" [33]. This policy argumentation is in line with the service management literature where the concept of co-production is surrounded with positive connotations of how individuals can benefit from empowerment, ownership, voice, and openness that resonates with the co-production concept [34]. This ideal has been adopted by public policy resulting in more arenas for self-service in the name of co-production [17, 35]. The digital self-service is molded as one arena where the citizen can be an active participant in the public service procedure.

On the other hand, co-production in digital self-services creates severe challenges for both citizens and public sector organizations. One of the greatest obstacles is the exclusion of citizens who struggle to access or lack the ability to benefit from digital services [36]. This exclusion mostly affects vulnerable citizens who need support and personal contact in the service procedure [37]. Disadvantaged or vulnerable people are often racial minorities, those with lower education and in lower socioeconomic situations. They face higher obstacles to participating, which contributes further to existing inequalities [26]. Consequently, co-production can enforce the insider-outsider dynamic as this kind of service provision may only be accessible for some groups [1].

Therefore, this article takes a critical perspective on co-production framed in the context of digital self-services as it argues that co-production will not always benefit the citizen. It also points to the need of understanding the motivation of the different actors in the co-production procedure since co-production is no means in itself [18].

3   Method and Case Description

In this article, we applied a mixed method approach. To answer the research goal of developing a conceptual framework to understand co-production in a digital self-service setting, we developed an analytical framework based on the literature on co-production and digital self-services with a specific focus on Nabatchi et al.'s understanding of the who, when and what of co-production. To evaluate our analytical framework as well as to answer our research question (What are citizens' experiences as they engage in the co-production of digital self-services?), we collected empirical data from citizens co-producing digital self-services in action.

The main method for the data collection was participant observations that positioned the article as a qualitative interpretive case study [38]. The qualitative interpretive methods aim to better understand the lived situations of people from their experiences and realities [39]. Many of the citizens that came to the office where the fieldwork took place were highly depended on the welfare services (see Table 1 for an overview).

The first author carried out participant observations [40] in one office of the Norwegian Labour and Welfare Administration (NAV). NAV is the largest government organization in Norway and administers a third of the national budget by providing both state and municipal services to citizens. The office has a computer area (self-service stations) where citizens can log on to nav.no to apply for services, send information to NAV and collect information and documentation online. Our research focused on the interactions between citizens, frontline workers, and digital self-service stations. From the co-production perspective, the focus is "the moment of truth", when expectations of co-production meet the realization of the same [10]. This is studied in the "single point of interaction", which is the moment of action when services are co-produced [11] that also can be described as the stage of co-delivery [5].

Eleven office visits that lasted four hours each were conducted over a period of four weeks in the spring of 2022. The method has been to observe, interact and ask questions to the citizens during the interactions [41]. Initially, the plan was to conduct passive observation of the citizens' use of the self-service computers, but some citizens approached the researcher with questions when they did not understand how to use the computers or how to interact with the platform of nav.no. The researcher became a volunteer that helped the citizens use the self-service computers turning into an 'involved researcher' [42]. The ability to take on the role as an insider provided insight regarding diverse life situations and get close to participants that otherwise would be hard to connect with due to language and cultural differences. In this way, the observations also enhanced the contextual understanding of the situations that took place in a context that was unknown for the researcher [43]. During most of the observations the frontline workers were present at some point during the interactions and in those cases, questions were also asked to the frontline workers after the interactions took place. These informal talks with the frontline workers served as background information and confirmation of the findings gained from observing the citizens.

We analyzed the data with the help of thematic analysis using our analytical framework. The coding was done in Nvivo and was carried out and refined in three phases. First, the data was coded roughly, and some events were coded according to several nodes. Second, the double-coded nodes were analyzed in relation to the other nodes in the given category and then distributed to the category that they reasoned best with. In a third step, we went through all the nodes to move or remove nodes that where not clearly relating to the category.

4   Results

4.1   Analytical Framework for Co-production in Digital Self-services

Based on related work on co-production, digital self-services and actor-network theory as well as inspired by strategical documents and policies, interviews with frontline workers and observations of citizens at office visits, we developed our analytical framework for understanding citizens' involvement in co-production in a digital self-service setting. We especially build on Nabatchi et al.'s typology of (offline) co-production and extend it to the digital sphere [5].

As co-production can be seen as taking place within a network of actors that are part of the same system framed by a common context, we anchor our framework in the tradition of the actor-network theory. In an actor-network, the different actors perform activities according to their different roles, motives, preconditions, that all together contribute to and make up the design of the co-production process. An actor-network consists of heterogenous actors including both social and technical elements, such as humans, artifacts, or organisations [44]. While we are primarily interested in the citizens' perspective of co-production in digital self-services, we argue that we cannot consider them without account for the other actors involved as the citizens' experiences are linked to them. We consider the other actors as reacting towards the citizens' needs and actions.

Our main point of departure is Nabatchi et al.'s conceptualisation of co-production, which they describe based on the level of co-production (individual, group or collective), the actors involved (who?), the phase within the co-production process (when?) and the activities that the involved actors perform (what?). Nabatchi et al. consider the actors involved as lay and state actors where the lay actor is the user of public services outside the organization and state actors are professionals within the public service organization. The authors outline different steps where co-production occurs in the so-called service cycle, distinguishing between co-commissioning (identifying and prioritizing prospective service elements), co-design (planning and designing services), co-delivery (providing public services), and co-assessment (evaluating services). Our analytical framework will focus on the co-delivery phase representing the performance of co-production in an actual service setting and will consider co-production on the individual level.

Table 1. Overview of data from observations

ID	Gender	Duration	Situation
O1	M	30 min	Came to apply for financial assistance. Struggled with the digital application and tried the digital self-service for a long time without managing to apply before leaving the office
O2	W	5 min	Two women struggled to use the copy machine. Applied on paper for financial assistance and needed to hand in documents on paper because of this
O3	W	10 min	Came for personal assistance regarding her activity plan (for unemployment). Struggled with what and where to type in information in the scheme. Found it difficult to get access to personal assistance at the office as all the frontline workers were busy
O4	M	5 min	Came to access his decision regarding financial assistance. Could not find this at nav.no because he did not have full access due to security level of digital ID
O5	W	10 min	Came because she does not speak Norwegian and needed an appointment regarding financial benefits with a translator. Could not write and the frontline worker needed to copy her personal number from a letter that she brought to the office
O6	W	10 min	Came to print documents to her application on financial assistance. Preferred to hand in documents on paper even if she sent the application digitally
O7	M	10 min	Came to talk to a frontline worker as he got a rejection on his application for financial assistance. Struggled to understand the reason and logics of NAV. Received information about what he needs to do and how to send in his complaint
O8	W	5 min	Two women came to the office to hand in a report to NAV regarding work assessment allowance that was due that day. Because of system failure, they could not send in the report. Came to the office to get help and to get in contact with the counsellor
O9	M	5 min	Came to get help for his friend to register his CV on the digital (unemployment) activity plan. Due to problems with the system, the procedure took long time
O10	W	40 min	Came to get help to apply for financial assistance. Preferred the paper application but did not get access to this at the office. Managed to apply with the help of one of the frontline workers. Much frustration and stress in the interaction
O11	W	45 min	Came to get help to apply for financial assistance. Complex life situation; had contact with NAV for many years. Struggled with the digital application and did not manage to send this in

In our analytical framework for describing co-production in digital self-services, we distinguish three actors: two actors within (state actors) and one actor (lay actor) outside of the organization. We conceptualize the lay actors as the private actor, i.e., the citizen, to emphasize that this actor is outside the organization with private interests in the co-production of services. As our context is a digital self-service setting where citizens interact with both public sector agents and computers, we differentiate between a human state actor, represented by the frontline workers, and a non-human, i.e., technological state actor, represented by the computers, i.e., self-service stations. The idea of the state technological actor as an equal actor in co-production, in our case consisting of technology artefacts and systems, is in line with the actor network theory originally developed by Latour [44].

The actors and their interactions are further described by the four dimensions *role*, *contribution*, *motives*, and *barriers/preconditions*. Roles are the actor's activities in the co-production process, contributions refer to what the actors (co-)produce, motives describe why actors co-produce, and barriers/preconditions are the limitations or pre-requisites for the respective actors to be able to participate in co-production. An example of the role of the human state actor is frontline workers acting as guides that provide consultation regarding services and application procedures. A contribution from the technological state actor is, for instance, to provide access to online information and standardized schemes. The private actor's motives are, for example, to receive personal financial benefits from the NAV's system. Finally, barriers/preconditions for the human state actor can be workload in terms of levels of requests as well as expertise and time.

4.2 Empirical Evidence of Co-production in Self-services

We analyze the empirical data using the presented analytical framework and present how the three actors participate in co-production, centered around the perspectives of citizens. Each actor is described in relation to their role, motive, contribution, and preconditions.

The Private Actor in Self-service Co-production. The private actor is in our case the citizen interacting with the state actors at NAV. The private actor is outside of the organizational structures and does not have the same knowledge as the actor inside the organization. Most of the citizens observed visited the NAV office to receive some interpersonal service in relation to their case.

The citizens often had the role of a passive bystander and informer. Citizens using the digital self-service often requested personal assistance from frontline workers or, when unavailable, from other persons at the office. Some citizens became irritated, anxious, or frustrated when they were encouraged to manage the self-service procedure. Citizens often stepped back and wanted the frontline workers to navigate on the computer on their behalf. Citizens explained their life situations upon frontline workers' request and explained what they wanted to apply for while the frontline workers modified and inserted the information into the system.

The citizens were motivated by familiarity, consultation and to get through the procedure. Many citizens asked for a paper-based application because they were familiar with this procedure. However, they were most often directed to the digital self-service stations instead. They perceived it hard to fill out the digital application, worried about making mistakes, and, thus, wished to get consultation. Some citizens that were directed to the digital application against their will, ended up leaving the office without applying.

Citizens showed little interest in learning about the digital procedures as their primary focus was to get the application right and through the system.

The contribution of citizens was often to download, print, and hand in paper documents rather than following instructions, navigating on platforms, and inserting information. When being directed to the self-service stations, citizens received a note with instructions. However, citizens seldom read this but asked for help instead. When citizens were urged to use the note, many seemed stressed and did not manage to find the application with the help of the instructions. Few citizens succeeded in providing the information themselves. Instead, most citizens resisted to try, or gave up because they struggled to write in Norwegian. Citizens mostly contributed by communicating their needs and providing information verbally. Most citizens also engaged in the activity of downloading, printing and handing in paper documents at the service counter, stating that this was easier for them.

Preconditions of time, language, frequency, digital knowledge, and stress mattered. While some citizens were not in a hurry, others had limited time due to duties such as school or work activities. Most of the citizens were non-native Norwegians and perceived language barriers and, thus, struggled to fill out the digital application without personal assistance. When the office was busy, citizens were often left on their own. Some citizens seemed to lack experience of how to use a computer as they did not have one at home. Others were first time applicants or did not apply frequently and forgot about the procedure between the application periods. Many citizens expressed stress and anxiety when no frontline worker could help them and, finally, they gave up.

The State Human Actor in Self-service Co-production. The state human actor is represented by the frontline worker at the NAV office. During most of the observations citizens were at some point assisted by a frontline-worker.

The human actor had the role as expert, guide, inquirer, and assistant. The frontline workers took on the role of expert and explained the logic of the system and the service procedure. They also informed citizens about the processing time and the next step in the service process. Often, they guided citizens in finding and starting the application. In most of the cases, the frontline workers inserted and retrieved information on the computers on citizens' behalf. Furthermore, the frontline worker often took on the role of an inquirer and asked guiding questions that helped citizens articulate their needs.

The motives were protocol redirection, efficiency, and independence. Most often, the frontline workers redirected citizens to the digital self-service stations according to the protocol of NAV. A frontline worker explained that this made the processes more efficient as less paper handling was needed. When citizens were declined to use paper-based applications, the frontline workers explained that citizens should manage the digital self-service on their own with the support of the instructions to become more independent. However, in the many cases when citizens requested help at the self-service stations, most frontline workers performed the tasks on behalf of the citizen to make the application procedure more efficient.

The contribution was consultation and hands-on assistance in the application procedure. The frontline workers asked questions and translated the answers into the system. This allowed them to check that the information entered was relevant and to reassure that citizens applied for what they needed and were entitled to. Sometimes frontline workers informed citizens about additional support they could be entitled to. During the interaction, the frontline workers informed citizens about rights and responsibilities and the evidence they had to show to support their claims. When misunderstandings occurred, the frontline workers explained again until they noticed that the citizens had understood.

The preconditions were scarce resources and system experiences. The frontline workers had limited time to assist all citizens that required help and sometimes instructed several citizens simultaneously. Some said that they felt stressed when they could not help all citizens that needed it. Sometimes the stressful situation made frontline workers seem tense and irritated during the interactions with citizens. Some frontline workers were experts in specific topic areas, which helped them assist citizens efficiently.

The State Technology Actor in Self-service Co-production. The state technology actor is in our case the digital self-service stations at the NAV office. These stations are composed of hardware tools, computers, printers and copy machines and information system software (platforms). If logged into the system with a digital ID, citizens can use digital services and personal functions depending on each case. All together the office provides eight self-service stations. The identified motives mirror the motives of the designers and managers within NAV, manifested in the state technology actor.

The state technology actor had the role of enabler, visualizer, transmitter, and collector of personal data. The self-service stations provided information and, if logged into nav.no, citizens could see the history of their digital applications as well as messages with information from meetings with NAV. This information confused some citizens who did not understand why the information was presented and what actions were expected from them. Most citizens collected documents at the self-service station by downloading and printing them. The self-service stations also allowed citizens to transmit personal information digitally to NAV. Even though the self-service stations provided functions that enabled independent application, citizens often requested assistance. Some citizens managed to use the digital self-service to a large extent independently, but when digital instructions left room for interpretation, citizens often were insecure in how to proceed.

Motives of the state technology actor were efficiency, standardization, and access. The digital self-service was promoted by frontline workers as a way for citizens to escape the lines to the reception. They also argued that the digital functions saved time for NAV as the steps of receiving, controlling and scanning paper documents into the system disappeared and, thus, would speed up the response time. The digital self-service was motivated by independent access to information and applications. Still, citizens mostly benefited when they were assisted by a frontline worker. According to frontline workers, the self-service provided a standardized application format that should make it easy to apply. However, many citizens perceived this system as more complex.

The contribution to store, print, provide and transmit information was identified. Citizens with a bank ID could in theory use all functions needed to store and send information digitally to NAV. For citizens who struggled to use a bank ID, the self-service stations provided limited functionality. The self-service stations provided general information at nav.no and specific instructions at each step in the digital application process. This information was not always processed by citizens, and some perceived it as vague made them insecure of how to proceed. Especially, when the digital form expected free text entries, many citizens were unsure how and what information to provide. For some citizens, the digital system did not contribute to co-production at all but rather hindered them.

The preconditions of "outside" maintenance, connection, and usability sometimes became a barrier. In several cases, the self-service stations did not allow access to nav.no. Internet connection is a precondition for self-service and according to the frontline workers, the computers needed continuous restarts to work properly. It was often the security guard that solved technical issues. Some citizens became reluctant to use the self-services when they were not working as expected. In some cases when citizens made repeatedly mistakes in the application, technical errors stopped the procedure (Table 2).

Table 2. Findings put in framework (redeveloped from Nabatchi et al. 2017)

	Private actors	State human actor	State technology actor
Roles	Passive informant at the self-service stations, following instructions upon request Informer about own life situation	Guide and expert regarding NAV services, digital self-service, and application procedure Inquirer and assistant	Enabler of self-services by providing functions and applications Visualizer and transmitter of digital information Collector of personal data
Motives	Getting the application done and receiving personal benefits Familiarity by using known paper applications Consultation in the service procedure	Redirecting citizens towards digital self-services according to protocol, efficiency, and empowering citizens' independency	Digital service access and user independency Standardization of application and service efficiency by digital functions and ease of administration
Contributions	Providing application content orally based on life situation and using paper-based applications rather than navigate on the platform to insert information into the digital application Struggling to follow written instructions	Providing interpersonal consultation, control and information and hands on assistance at the self-service stations	Storing, printing, providing, and transmitting information by hardware and online platform Mostly used to convert digital information to analog paper documents
Preconditions/ barriers	Timespan to conduct business within the opening hours of the office, language differences, digital skills, and the level of stress	Time to assist citizens at the self-service stations, depend on the number of visitors, language differences, knowledge, and experience but also the level of stress	Functionality of hardware and system, internet access enable system and platform functionality System failure is a showstopper for actors

5 Discussion and Conclusion

To answer our research goal, we presented an analytical framework for co-production in digital self-services that distinguishes three actors: private actor (citizens), state human actor (frontline workers), and state technological actor (self-service station). In doing so, we have extended Nabatchi et al.'s [5] conceptualization of service co-production to the digital self-service context. The idea of the state technological actor as an equal actor in co-production, in our case consisting of technology artefacts and systems, is in line with the actor network theory originally developed by Latour [44]. Our findings show how co-production takes place within a network of actors that are part of the same system framed by the context of digital self-services. In this network, the three different actors act according to their different roles, motives/protocols, contributions, and preconditions/barriers, which are the four dimensions in our analytical framework that detail the actors' engagement in the co-production process.

All three actors take different roles to jointly co-produce digital self-services. Frontline workers as state human actors provide essential support to citizens. As actors of the organization, they use their organizational knowledge to guide citizens in the system. The self-service stations as state technological actors have the role of the enabler of the service procedure, serving as information vessel and offering digital functionality. However, our findings show that the private actors, represented by the citizens, seldom wish to take part in co-production with the technological actor – at least not without the involvement of frontline workers. This became evident when citizens who were forced to conduct business without human assistance, were faced with system barriers and left the office without accomplishing their errand.

The tensions between actor motives in co-production is based on different underlying logics of the three actors. Organizational motives are transmitted through the practices of the human state actor. They are also inherent in the design of the technological state actor, designed in functions that allow citizens to act. However, if citizens are not equipped or willing to make use of these functions, the technology actor provides little value. Motives of organizational efficiency and empowering user independency showed to be contradictive in practice for many of the citizens that were vulnerable in relation to their life situation and became further vulnerable when they were expected to face the digital system alone. Citizens often resisted the digital self-service and rarely conducted their service independently while frontline workers did not have the resources of time to motivate and guide them to act on their own.

We identified a typical pattern of contributions – or lack thereof – to the co-production process. 1) Frontline workers asked citizens about digital access and their bank ID while citizens tried to negotiate to receive a paper-based application. 2) The frontline workers directed citizens to use the self-service stations and provided citizens a document with written instructions. 3) Citizens often resisted to follow the instructions and asked for interpersonal help. 4) Based on available resources, some citizens received assistance to fill out the steps in the digital application while some left the office without completing the task they came to carry out. These conflicting and interfering contributions indicate that a common understanding of the co-production process is still lacking.

The preconditions for engaging in co-production are similar for the state human actor and the private actor. Citizens had limited time in situations when they had taken time off from other duties whereas frontline workers had limited time in the service interactions as many citizens requested help. The knowledge was also an important precondition as some frontline workers were experts on the digital application but were not always available to citizens. Citizens' prior knowledge from (digitally) interacting with NAV also affected the service co-production. Also, stress created unbeneficial circumstances for the service co-production for both citizens and frontline workers. Furthermore, citizens with language barriers struggled to use the digital self-service stations. Altogether the resources of time, knowledge, the level of stress and language differences that were present in the service interactions between the human actors created barriers for co-production. For the state technological actor, preconditions regarding system functionality, maintenance and design represented potential barriers for all actors involved.

To answer our research goal, we presented a novel analytical framework to analyze co-production from an actor-centered perspective, containing our three actor dimensions: the private actor (the citizen), the state human actor (the frontline worker), and the state technological actor (the self-service station). To answer our research question "What are citizens' experiences as they engage in the co-production of digital self-services?", we demonstrated how the actor-centered framework advances our understanding of how citizens' ability to co-produce in a digital self-service setting is dependent on the support and involvement of the state human actor.

In this sense, our paper makes a theoretical contribution by providing a novel framework for actor co-production that is molded to fit a digital self-service setting. We advance the understanding of co-production and link it to the Information System field by incorporating and framing the IT actor and technology artifacts in co-production, which is often at risk of being hidden in context [45]. In addition, we offer an empirical contribution as we provide insight in how co-production unfolds in practice by framing co-production to the stage of co-delivery understood from the perspectives of vulnerable citizens. In doing so, we answer the call for more empirical studies in co-production of digital self-services. Our finding shows that citizens that visit NAV often are vulnerable in some aspects of life and struggle to co-produce their services in a digital service setting and depend on the support of a state human actor.

Our approach has several limitations and requires future research to understand co-production more comprehensively in digital self-services. First, we only consider co-production in digital self-services that takes place at the NAV office. While this gave us the unique opportunity to observe co-production in action, we acknowledge that citizens often use digital self-services from home and have other experiences with co-production and may only encounter the state digital actor. In these cases, the two state actors will take a different shape. The state technological actor, for example, might only consist of a digital government platform that is accessed via private hardware, which can present a further non-human actor. At the same time, the state human actor might not be visible at all while other human actors such as family might be part of the co-production network. Future research should take these different forms of co-production into consideration. Furthermore, the description of the actors' roles, motives, contributions, and preconditions has been purely based on empirical data. It would be interesting to contrast our empirical findings with assumptions from the literature.

Finally, our data collection took place in a NAV office, which probably entails that those people coming to the office struggle a lot more with digital self-services than others and are (as Table 1 show) dependent on the welfare services of financial assistance to master their daily lives. Thus the empirical findings drawn from the specific context are not representative of the whole population.

References

1. Verschuere, B., Brandsen, T., Pestoff, V.: Co-production: the state of the art in research and the future agenda. Voluntas **23**, 1083–1101 (2012)
2. Alford, J.: Why do public-sector clients coproduce?: Toward a contingency theory. Adm. Soc. **34**, 32–56 (2002)
3. Bovaird, T.: Beyond engagement and participation: user and community coproduction of public services. Public Adm. Rev. **67**, 846–860 (2007)
4. Bovaird, T., Van Ryzin, G.G., Loeffler, E., Parrado, S.: Activating citizens to participate in collective co-production of public services. J. Soc. Pol. **44**, 1–23 (2015)
5. Nabatchi, T., Sancino, A., Sicilia, M.: Varieties of participation in public services: the who, when, and what of coproduction. Public Adm. Rev. **77**, 766–776 (2017)
6. Ostrom, E.: Crossing the great divide: coproduction, synergy, and development. World Dev. **24**, 1073–1087 (1996)
7. Joshi, A., Moore, M.: Institutionalised co-production: unorthodox public service delivery in challenging environments. J. Dev. Stud. **40**, 31–49 (2004)
8. Grönroos, C.: Value co-creation in service logic: a critical analysis. Mark. Theory **11**, 279–301 (2011)
9. Madsen, C.Ø., Lindgren, I., Melin, U.: The accidental caseworker – how digital self-service influences citizens' administrative burden. Gov. Inf. Q. **39**, 101653 (2022)
10. Osborne, S.P., Radnor, Z., Strokosch, K.: Co-production and the co-creation of value in public services: a suitable case for treatment? Public Manag. Rev. **18**, 639–653 (2016)
11. Scupola, A., Mergel, I.: Co-production in digital transformation of public administration and public value creation: the case of Denmark. Gov. Inf. Q. **39**, 101650 (2022)
12. Heggertveit, I., Lindgren, I., Madsen, C.Ø., Hofmann, S.: Administrative burden in digital self-service: an empirical study about citizens in need of financial assistance. In: Krimmer, R., et al. (eds.) Electronic Participation. Lecture Notes in Computer Science, vol. 13392, pp. 173–187. Springer, Cham (2022). https://doi.org/10.1007/978-3-031-23213-8_11
13. Pors, A., Schou, J.: Street-level morality at the digital frontlines: an ethnographic study of moral mediation in welfare work. Adm. Theory Praxis **43**, 154–171 (2021)
14. Breit, E., Salomon, R.: Making the technological transition – citizens' encounters with digital pension services. Soc. Policy Adm. **49**, 299–315 (2015)
15. Rosenthal, P., Peccei, R.: 'The work you want, the help you need': constructing the customer in jobcentre plus. Organization **14**, 201–223 (2007)
16. Forster, R., Gabe, J.: Voice or choice? Patient and public involvement in the national health service in England under new labour. Int. J. Health Serv. **38**, 333–356 (2008)
17. Larsson, K.K., Skjølsvik, T.: Making sense of the digital co-production of welfare services: using digital technology to simplify or tailor the co-production of services. Public Manag. Rev. **25**, 1–18 (2021)
18. Voorberg, W.H., Bekkers, V.J.J.M., Tummers, L.G.: A Systematic review of co-creation and co-production: embarking on the social innovation journey. Public Manag. Rev. **17**, 1333–1357 (2015)

19. Brudney, J.L., England, R.E.: Toward a definition of the coproduction concept. Public Adm. Rev. **43**, 59–65 (1983)
20. Levine, C.H., Fisher, G.: Citizenship and service delivery: the promise of coproduction. Public Adm. Rev. **44**, 178–189 (1984)
21. Pestoff, V.: Towards a paradigm of democratic participation: citizen participation and co-production of personal social services in Sweden. Ann. Public Coop. Econ. **80**, 197–224 (2009)
22. Dunston, R., Lee, A., Boud, D., Brodie, P., Chiarella, M.: Co-production and health system reform – from re-imagining to re-making. Aust. J. Public Adm. **68**, 39–52 (2009)
23. Boyle, D., Harris, M.: The challenge of co-production. London: New Econ. Found. **56** 18
24. Whitaker, G.P.: Coproduction: citizen participation in service delivery. Public Adm. Rev. **40**, 240–246 (1980)
25. Parks, R.B., et al.: Consumers as coproducers of public services: some economic and institutional considerations. Policy Stud. J. **9**, 1001–1011 (1981)
26. Sorrentino, M., Sicilia, M., Howlett, M.: Understanding co-production as a new public governance tool. Policy Soc. **37**, 277–293 (2018)
27. Bovaird, T., Ryzin, G.G.V., Loeffler, E., Parrado, S.: Activating citizens to participate in collective co-production of public services. J. Soc. Policy **44**, 1–23 (2015)
28. Lin, J.C., Chang, H.: The role of technology readiness in self-service technology acceptance. Manag. Serv. Qual. Int. J. **21**, 424–444 (2011)
29. Jeffares, S.: The Virtual Public Servant: Artificial Intelligence and Frontline Work. Springer, Cham (2021). https://doi.org/10.1007/978-3-030-54084-5
30. Hilton, T., Hughes, T.: Co-production and self-service: the application of service-dominant logic. J. Mark. Manag. **29**, 861–881 (2013)
31. Bovens, M., Zouridis, S.: From street-level to system-level bureaucracies: how information and communication technology is transforming administrative discretion and constitutional control. Public Adm. Rev. **62**, 174–184 (2002)
32. Reddick, C.G.: Citizen interaction with e-government: from the streets to servers? Gov. Inf. Q. **22**, 38–57 (2005)
33. Eriksson, K.: Self-service society: participative politics and new forms of governance. Public Adm. **90**, 685–698 (2012)
34. Noveck, B.S.: Smart Citizens, Smarter State: The Technologies of Expertise and the Future of Governing. Harvard University Press, Cambridge (2015). https://doi.org/10.4159/978067 4915435
35. Polzer, T., Goncharenko, G.: The UK COVID-19 app: the failed co-production of a digital public service. Finan. Account. Manag. **38**, 281–298 (2022)
36. Cordelia, A.: E-government: towards the E-Bureaucratic form? J. Inf. Technol. **22**, 265–274 (2007). https://doi.org/10.1057/palgrave.jit.2000105
37. O'Sullivan, S., Walker, C.: From the interpersonal to the internet: social service digitisation and the implications for vulnerable individuals and communities. Aust. J. Polit. Sci. **53**, 490–507 (2018)
38. Myers, M.D.: Investigating information systems with ethnographic research. CAIS. 2 (1999)
39. Klein, H.K., Myers, M.D.: A set of principles for conducting and evaluating interpretive field studies in information systems. MIS Q. **23**, 67–93 (1999)
40. Moeran, B.: From participant observation to observant participation. Organ. Ethnogr. Study. Complexity Everyday Life, 139–155 (2009)
41. Göran, G.: The generation of qualitative data in information systems research: the diversity of empirical research methods. CAIS **44**, 572–599 (2019)
42. Walsham, G.: Doing interpretive research. Eur. J. Inf. Syst. **15**, 320–330 (2006)
43. Nunamaker, J.F., Chen, M., Purdin, T.D.M.: Systems development in information systems research. J. Manag. Inf. Syst. **7**, 89–106 (1990)

44. Latour, B.: Reassembling the Social: An Introduction to Actor-Network-Theory. Oxford University Press, Oxford (2005)
45. Orlikowski, W.J., Iacono, C.S.: Research commentary: desperately seeking the "IT" in IT research—a call to theorizing the IT artifact. Inf. Syst. Res. **12**, 121–134 (2001)

The Digital Cage Dilemma – How Street-Level Bureaucrats at Public Libraries are a Key for Digital Inclusion

Helena Iacobaeus(✉) 🅳

Linköping University, 58183 Linköping, Sweden
helena.iacobaeus@liu.se

Abstract. Ten percent of the Swedish population over the age of sixteen can be counted as digitally excluded. Many of them turn to public libraries for support with e.g. public e-services. As street-level bureaucrats, library staff can support citizens' digital inclusion within the scope of their assignment and institutional framework. However, they face dilemmas when they encounter citizens with needs that fall partly outside this framework.

According to a classic work of Weber, bureaucrats can be seen as locked in an iron cage of rules and norms. It could be argued that digitalization is changing the conditions in bureaucracies even further. As a complement to Weber's iron cage, Peeters and Widlak described the disciplining logic of digital information architecture as a form of digital cage that can exclude citizens and frame the discretion of street-level bureaucrats.

This article elaborates on the concept digital cage, built on the iron cage concept, to analyse how street-level bureaucrats cope with discretionary boundaries in their work for citizens' digital inclusion. Based on an analysis of interviews with library staff at local centres for digital inclusion, policy documents and interviews with local politicians in charge of these centres, the study shows the relevance of the digital cage concept and that the use of new technologies changes and partly limits street-level discretion. However, it also shows that politicians allow library staff a considerable degree of freedom in their work, and that the centres' focus on face-to-face meetings and entrepreneurial solutions is an asset for digital inclusion.

Keywords: Digital Cage · Iron Cage · Digital Inclusion · Street-level Bureaucrats · Discretionary Boundaries

1   Introduction

Ten percent of the Swedish population over sixteen can be counted as digitally excluded [1]. At the same time, the digitalization of public services is increasing in Sweden as in many other countries. As a result, a considerable proportion of the population needs support with understanding and handling public e-services. There are several important actors and institutions involved in lowering the threshold to digital participation among

© IFIP International Federation for Information Processing 2023
Published by Springer Nature Switzerland AG 2023
I. Lindgren et al. (Eds.): EGOV 2023, LNCS 14130, pp. 64–79, 2023.
https://doi.org/10.1007/978-3-031-41138-0_5

citizens: schools, working life, adult education, civil society, and various contact centres, such as civic offices, all play their parts [2, 3]. In a public service context where the use of digital services increases and partly replaces other channels, there is a need for extra support, and it is relevant to explore how increased digitalization changes the discretionary boundaries of street-level bureaucrats (SLBs) in their work to include citizens in a digital society.

Studies of digital government reveal several similarities with what Weber described as far back as 1930 as an 'iron cage' of rational rules and norms that locks bureaucrats in and limits their discretion [4]. Today, it can be added that conditions in bureaucracies are changing, with trends including new technologies that affect the roles of both citizen and bureaucrat. Bureaucrats are more active in several different areas, but their discretion is still constrained by organizational and political decisions and structures. Digitalization can result in new roles for public servants – roles that are characterized by spending less time with citizens and more time with computers [5]. Today's citizens are also more active and use public services more extensively than the citizens of Weber's time, and often do so via digital channels. This article focuses on a complement to Weber's iron cage; Peeters and Widlak [6] described the disciplining logic of digital information architecture as a form of 'digital cage' that can exclude citizens and limit the autonomy and influence of street-level bureaucrats.

To obtain a deeper understanding of street-level discretionary boundaries and the digital cage concept, this article is based on qualitative studies in the public library setting. This setting is an easily accessible node for digital inclusion that many citizens turn to for digital support [7]. While, according to national legislation [8], every municipality in Sweden has to offer library services and work for digital inclusion, these local libraries can be led and managed in very different ways in line with the constitutional local autonomy of municipalities [9]. The chosen public libraries are local centres for digital inclusion, known as Digidel centres. To be able to make a comparison, centres have been selected in ten municipalities spread across the country. These centres are governed and organized in different ways, which might lead to different discretionary boundaries for the SLBs. The article is based on an analysis of interviews with SLBs at the Digidel centres, policy documents and interviews with local politicians who, on a general level, oversee the municipal areas that the centres belong to.

1.1 Aim and Research Questions

The aim of this article is to further the understanding of the concept digital cage in relation to SLB discretionary boundaries. To be able to add to the knowledge on modern-day discretionary boundaries of SLBs, the article analyzes how SLBs, in this case public library staff, cope with their discretionary boundaries in their assignment to support citizens who feel a need to develop their digital skills. The following research questions guide the analysis:

– *How do library staff describe their discretionary boundaries and their coping strategies to adapt to or to bend the bars of the digital cage?*
– *Are there discrepancies between the political expectations and the street-level views of the library staff when it comes to their work for citizens' digital inclusion?*

– *How can the digital cage concept extend knowledge about street-level discretionary boundaries in general, and in relation to digital government in particular?*

1.2   Background – Digital Inclusion and Libraries

The increased digitalization of society is changing our daily lives and, simultaneously, so are the expectations of what a citizen needs to be able to do to play an active part in society. This raises questions about inclusion and exclusion. It is important to note that there is a link between digital inequality and other forms of inequality, and that it can be difficult to bridge the gap with digital means alone [10]. Being digitally excluded is problematic, but it can also reinforce exclusion in other areas. For example, digital exclusion can make it more difficult to make informed decisions on health issues such as selfcare and choice of healthcare providers, something that can have long-lasting effects on an individual's employment and general quality of life.

According to van Dijk [11], the road to digital inclusion can be described as a kind of staircase. The citizen must start with being motivated to use digital services and tools, but he or she also needs to have access to technology, such as broadband, a phone or a computer, and to acquire the necessary knowledge and skills to be able to use digital services. Frequent usage is also an important step towards digital inclusion. Still, even if citizens are motivated and have access and skills, they might use the Internet in different ways, for different reasons, and to a different extent. It is possible to be skilled in certain aspects of the digital society, for example blogging or using video communication tools, without having the necessary skills to use public e-services to apply for education online. This is often referred to as digital diversity.

A lack of access and technology literacy are challenges to digital inclusion [12]. Even users who have sufficient access to the Internet and digital tools can be hampered by a lack of knowledge and skills. Providing citizens with equal access to qualitative and inclusive e-services is pivotal for the successful and legitimate implementation of digital government [13]. However, this cannot be done without considering more than just the individual's access and technology literacy. The usability of the technology, accessibility for all groups and functionality also must be taken into account [12].

On a global scale, the issue of digital exclusion can be described as a digital divide between countries and is closely linked to the level of universalism of a country's welfare state [14]. However, a divide can also exist between different socio-economic groups within a country, and even between groups that are active in the online community but use the Internet in different ways.

Several European digitalization policies, including the Swedish National Digitalization Strategy, describe digital skills as basic prerequisites for full participation in society [15, 16]. However, the European Commission emphasizes that a digital transformation must be inclusive; it *"can only work if it works for all and not only a few"* [17]. This consideration is also emphasized in the Swedish Library Act [8]. The assignment of Swedish public libraries includes several areas related to digitalization, such as making knowledge available and accessible, strengthening the population's digital literacy skills as a democratic value, promoting freedom of opinion, and working for citizens' digital inclusion regardless of their background and economic means [8, 18, 19]. Public libraries have been mentioned in earlier research as institutions with insights into the consequences of digital exclusion among citizens [e.g. 20, 21] and somewhere to turn for support in claiming digital citizenship rights [22].

There are many practical examples of digital support at libraries, notably computer and internet access and IT helpdesks, as well as beginners' courses, mentoring projects, mobile outreach vehicles and makerspaces [21, 23]. The initiatives for digital inclusion include the Digidel centres, nodes for digital inclusion originating from a national, politically independent network for digital inclusion called the Digidel network [24]. The currently 26 Digidel centres are locally run by municipalities, but funding sources can vary and include local, regional and national sources [25]. In many cases, the Swedish Internet Foundation and the Swedish Government have been important contributors. The centres offer digital support free of charge and focus on accessibility and personal meetings. Although a Digidel centre should be recognizable regardless of where it is located, local differences in the activities offered are encouraged in order to meet the needs of each municipality. The focus of a Digidel centre is to provide digital support, but the centre is at the same time embedded in the library organization, which means that it falls under Swedish library law. In many cases, this also results in shared positions where library staff split their time between the centre and regular library services.

2 Theoretical Framing

As a theoretical framing, this article uses Weber's iron cage and the newer concept of a digital cage that can 'trap' citizens but also frame the discretion of SLBs. In the search for a digital cage, SLBs are studied based on theories on digital discretion, especially that proposed by Lipsky [26]. The article focuses on street-level discretionary boundaries and their relationship to the digital cage concept. Thus, it intends to contribute to the understanding of one of the aspects of the development of digital government.

2.1 Street-Level Bureaucrats

The concept of SLBs was proposed by Lipsky to describe the dilemmas of frontline staff in public administration. A wide range of public servants who are in direct contact with citizens can be categorized as SLBs if they have scope for discretion in the execution of their work [26], p. 3. They should achieve certain policy objectives while taking the specific features of each case into consideration, thereby contributing to shaping public policy in their everyday interactions with citizens. While SLBs are supposed to give the best possible support in each case, they are also meant to process cases efficiently to fulfil the high – but possibly vague and conflicting – institutional goals. This, Lipsky argues, could create tension between client-centred and organizational goals, a dilemma that might result in goal displacement and prioritizing methods that produce results that can be measured rather than the kind of results that the process was intended for in the first place. However, SLBs can develop coping strategies like rationing the services they provide citizens with or conserving resources by setting aside more time than necessary for certain tasks [27].

Discretion can be interpreted in different ways, but in SLB literature it means the freedom to make decisions on client cases regarding whether, in what ways and to what extent they should receive rewards or sanctions [28]. Thus, bureaucrats who have strong discretion can exercise power, sometimes referred to as discretionary power, in their daily policy implementation [29].

2.2 From Iron Cage to Digital Cage

The discretion of SLBs is closely linked to Weber's classic bureaucracy model that described bureaucrats as locked in an iron cage. The term was meant as a warning against a formal rationality that causes the ideals and values of organizations to stand back in favour of regulation and calculation of goal fulfilment [4]. In the iron cage of bureaucracy, how things are done and how they can be measured becomes more important than their originally intended meaning [30, 31]. This emphasis on predictability through discipline rather than through expertise can create dehumanizing structures that reduce citizens to *"cogs in a machine"* [6]. Although Weber saw advantages in formal rationality, he also feared that it could end up in a *"disenchanted"* society led by *"specialists without spirit, sensualists without heart"* [4], p. 182.

Bureaucrats can only support individuals within the discretionary boundaries imposed by the institution, and they can therefore face a variety of practical and ethical dilemmas in their daily work when they encounter problems that fall outside these boundaries. Iron cage boundaries often emanate from rules or management based on policies, but they are, in some cases, driven by a collegial point of view and controlled by peer pressure in self-governing teams [32]. Thus, the iron cage can be seen as a socially constructed frame hampering the discretion of the SLBs.

Many researchers have stressed that digitalization is changing the conditions in bureaucracies even further, and partly undermines the foundation of some professions [29, 33, 34]. The roles of SLBs have shifted from providing service to citizens to providing more support than before. As in other sections of society, some of the public tasks that used to be performed by paid personnel have been turned into self-service conducted by citizens [35]. In addition, the digitalization of public services can shift the balance between different professions within an organization. When public servants and case workers are partly replaced by digital services created by other professions, it may become unclear how, and by whom, the core knowledge and values are passed on within the organization [5]. New digital technologies and the extensive data collection that they facilitate can be used for control and hierarchical discipline that might reduce or even end street-level discretionary power [36]. Street-level bureaucrats could be renamed 'screen-level bureaucrats', as they spend less time with individual cases and more time optimizing online information processes in systems overseen by system-level bureaucrats [6].

To develop Weber's iron cage concept, Peeters and Widlak highlighted how information technology can exclude citizens and lead to injustice and inequality in public service provision [6]. In their study of the Dutch population register's data processing system, they argued that the new conditions for SLBs can be seen as a digital cage rather than Weber's iron cage. The disciplining logic of this cage is not only tied to rules and procedures but also to a possibly excluding information infrastructure that rationalizes processes to an extent where citizens and SLBs can be unable to control or influence the outcome. They claimed that a digital cage not only traps the citizen but also reduces the possibilities for SLB discretion and makes the roles of SLBs less important in society: *"The civil servants subjected to a digital cage are no longer the experts of their own rules – as they were in Weber's legal system – but work with a system made by software developers and IT engineers."* [6] Thus, the rapid changes that public administration faces and contributes to with new digital technologies also involves changes at street level; a new and different 'cage' frames the discretionary boundaries of today's street-level – or screen-level – bureaucrats.

3 Method

Sweden is a mature and highly digitalized welfare state where public e-services are common, which makes the country an interesting context for studies of digital inclusion and for reflections on the digital cage. Furthermore, focusing on Digidel centres is one way of giving a direct, frontline view of digital inclusion, or the lack thereof.

3.1 Data Collection

The data collection is qualitative and focuses on daily work for digital inclusion at the Digidel centres, street-level discretionary boundaries in terms of policies, digital systems, etc., and in terms of how the SLBs cope with these boundaries. Here, discretion is both an analytical concept and a concrete way to describe what the SLBs can and cannot do.

A sample of ten Digidel centres was selected from the existing 26. These selected centres are geographically widespread and, with a few exceptions, located in smaller municipalities. The contact person at each centre was approached, and the selected ten SLB respondents were informed about the study design and further use of data before choosing to be interviewed. Two of the centres were visited in person, but all SLB interviews were conducted by video. The ten SLB interviews were semi-structured and followed an interview guide that focused on their work for digital inclusion of citizens and covered the following themes: background, daily work, perceived challenges for digital inclusion and discretionary boundaries related to policy, management expectations, digitalization and competences.

To include other perspectives on the work and boundaries of the SLBs at the Digidel centres, six semi-structured interviews were conducted with local politicians who chair the library-related committees in six of the abovementioned municipalities. This interview guide focused on the politicians' impressions of the daily work at the Digidel centres, the role of libraries in society, challenges for digital inclusion, expectations on the Digidel centres as well as to what extent and how they govern the centres. In addition, policy documents that explain the assignment of the Digidel centres were studied as background data.

All interviews were conducted in Swedish and transcribed verbatim. The quotations used in the article were translated by the author. The SLB interviews (with respondents R1-R10) lasted around 40 min each, while the interviews with politicians (respondents RA-RF) were slightly shorter. Since the focus is on the work and roles of the SLBs, the visitors at the centres were not included in the study and no names or personal data about visitors were included in the interviews. There was no interaction with visitors in the few cases when respondents showed the interviewer around the Digidel centers and, thus, the data collection can be considered to be in line with the ethical guidelines as specified in the Act Concerning the Ethical Review of Research Involving Humans [37]. Apart from quotations, the statements from respondents in the text are used to provide general impressions and are therefore not referenced individually. SLB respondent backgrounds and the political positions of the politician respondents are listed in the table below (Table 1).

Table 1. Respondents.

		Background	Gender	Interview date
SLB respondents	R1	Librarian	M	2022–02-09
	R2	Librarian	M	2022–03-02
	R3	Librarian and educator	F	2022–02-09
	R4	IT, employment services and social care	M	2022–02-16
	R5	Librarian	F	2022–04-25
	R6	Teacher	F	2022–03-01
	R7	Media and information literacy librarian	F	2022–02-18
	R8	Librarian	M	2022–02-19
	R9	Interpreter and social care	F	2022–02-17
	R10	IT educator	M	2022–04-07
		Political position at the time of the interview	**Gender**	**Interview date**
Political respondents	RA	Chairman of the culture- and leisure committee	F	2022–04-05
	RB	Chairman of the culture- and leisure committee	F	2022–04-04
	RC	Chairman of the culture committee	F	2022–04-25
	RD	Chairman of the culture committee	M	2022–04-14
	RE	Chairman of the culture- and leisure committee	M	2023–02-01
	RF	Chairman of the culture- and public health Committee	F	2023–03-02

3.2 Analytical Approach

Using interpretive inquiry, the article focuses on individual experiences of bureaucrats who are directly involved in the work for digital inclusion of citizens. By understanding how they look at their discretionary boundaries and what intentions they give to their own actions, it can add to the knowledge on modern-day SLB discretion in relation to the digital cage concept.

The interview data was read in full to provide an overview. After that, the data was coded in NVivo into the following reoccurring categories: background, daily work, digital exclusion, digital society, discretionary boundaries (with the subthemes competences, digital limitations, management expectations, policies and public expectations), entrepreneurial practices and values. This made is possible to describe and interpret the data as well as to analyse discretionary boundaries and coping strategies.

A possible limitation of this study design is that the respondents are very familiar with digital support because of the nature of their work at the nodes for digital inclusion. Thus, the interview answers could differ slightly from and be more elaborated than they would be in similar studies in libraries without Digidel centres.

4 Results

Digidel centres are generally located in public libraries. However, the staff can be a mix of librarians and other professionals within a wider field of literacy and learning. This is mirrored in the data where some respondents are coming from the educational sector or having experience of working with citizens with special needs. Others come from either the private or public IT sector, or had a traditional library background. Activities vary between the centres, but they all offer digital support through helpdesks and booked appointments. Regular questions concern mobile phones or e-services from agencies such as the Employment Agency, the Tax Agency, regional health care or municipal authorities. Questions related to private actors are also common, e.g. concerning banks and social media use. Apart from this, questions are often asked about cybersecurity or information-seeking skills. The need for support differs between different life situations and age groups. While senior citizens might ask for help with issues such as bank IDs or parking apps, middle-aged citizens may need advice on online job-seeking or e-services, for example. Young citizens may have questions that require other forms of guidance, such as how to react to being subjected to cyberbullying or nude pictures.

Many visitors bring their own devices to the centre when they need support. Ascertaining what the main problem is can involve some 'detective work' since not all visitors will necessarily know the technical terms or the scope of what they are looking for. The SLB role can also be motivating or therapeutic: *"We have many senior visitors, and they like just having someone to talk to... [-] I think it makes a difference just to be able to vent these problems and feelings, that they think it's rather tough. But many realize that they need it to function in society."* (R5).

The centres also offer public computers, printing services, courses, lectures and exhibitions. A Digidel centre is both a physical place and a wider concept that can be moved to branch libraries or other places such as retirement homes. Inspired by book buses, some centres have or plan to obtain digital outreach vehicles (buses, trucks or box bikes) that can raise awareness and support citizens who live far from the centres or have difficulties reaching them.

4.1 Policy-Related Discretionary Boundaries

In terms of policy, the discretionary boundaries of the SLBs are mainly imposed by the Swedish Library Act, GDPR, the National Digitalization Strategy and some local assignments, funding application statements and policies. Of these, the Swedish Library Act has a special position as the most emphasized policy document among the library staff respondents. According to this law, the main stated purpose for all public library services is to act for the development of a democratic society through working for mediation of knowledge and free opinion building [8]. Libraries should be accessible institutions that promote literature, learning, education and research in society. They should also promote knowledge about the use of information technologies. This last part of the mission was further developed by the Digidel network with the goal of strengthening digital inclusion, and thus democratic society. [25] The network defines a Digidel centre as an accessible citizen service node focused on digital inclusion, where citizens can get free digital support face-to-face. The node must have a clear mandate from the municipality and take part in national quality development linked to digitalization.

There are several examples of local policies and assignments linked to the Digidel centres, notably municipal library policies, but also application statements to funding agencies and detailed operational plans for the centres. The boundaries in these local policies are generally drawn both to avoid exposing and handling sensitive information, and to avoid making mistakes that can have serious consequences for the citizen.

Typical limits are avoiding certain banking questions, medical journals or applications for residence permits: *"We have drawn up guidelines for our staff – what kind of service we can offer and what it entails, and where we can draw the line in different subfields [-] For example, that someone wants to apply for residence permit and wants help with applying through the Migration Board website. We don't feel like meddling with the contents, where there is a risk of consequences that can affect the user..."* (R6) This can, however, be interpreted slightly differently at different centres. For example, some SLBs refer all bank ID questions to the bank, while others can help download the ID as long as they avoid looking at the account, and some can go further after informing the citizen and offering a choice: *"... our interpretation is that if they want to show their personal records to get help, then that is a choice that they have made. Obviously, we inform them that 'to be able to help you and explain this, I will see e.g. what you have in your bank account or – if it concerns health care – I will see your medical records – or what you click on here'. And then, they have to choose... if they want this help, they renounce some of their personal privacy to get it. They have to make a choice about what is more pressing."* (R8) Another of the SLBs mentions that he does not deal with hardware questions to avoid unfair public competition with the private sector.

The laws and policies can cause discussions about priority order within the staff groups or with the management. However, the SLBs generally express that the rules are rather clear and that they feel quite free to structure their work as they wish if it fits within the budget.

4.2 Discretionary Boundaries in Political and Management Expectations

The interviewed SLBs rarely give concrete examples of what they perceive as management expectations, but they know or assume that their respective managers want them to provide citizens with digital support, both through their own work and in collaboration with other actors. They also mention expectations of accessibility, like in this quotation: *"[They expect me] to work with digitalization in the whole municipality, based on both the competence at the Digidel centre and the opportunities that we have for citizen contact. Because it is an entirely different thing for a citizen to step into an open and free library or a Digidel centre where they can find staff to talk to, rather than trying to contact someone in a locked city hall..."* (R7) This impression matches the views of the local politicians in charge of the library-related committees in their municipalities. While the politicians highlight the importance of local work for digital inclusion, their governance of the Digidel centres is limited to certain strategic occasions, e.g. making a decision on library policy every fourth year or making budget decisions that concern a centre. Several, although not all, of them also state that they have limited insight into the everyday work of the Digidel centres. However, they all express trust in the SLBs' knowledge and professional assessments. Locating a Digidel centre at the library is seen as a good choice, both because of its accessibility and because of pre-existing trust in the library as an institution. Many of the politicians describe a gradually increasing demand for digital support at libraries, mainly caused by rapid digitalization in general and decreased local presence from the state: *"... from being a physical place for books, it has become more of... you could say that it has been kind of given parts of other societal responsibilities. It has become more like a regular municipal reception."* (RB) This indicates that the politicians see a need for a new and broader role for libraries.

As one of the politicians emphasizes, the work to combat digital exclusion could expand almost indefinitely if it were not for resources (RF). She reflects on the street-level dilemma that higher service levels also affect and heighten the expectations from the public; while she is under the impression that the SLBs at the centre are doing a good and ambitious job, she also has a word of caution that broad assignments like this can cause a strain on public servants.

4.3 Competence-Related Discretionary Boundaries

The SLBs also reflect on their own digital competence and what they can or cannot do for visitors. Here, the answers differ somewhat depending on the background, but several refer to knowledge acquisition via the Digidel network as a strength in their work. They are generally content with their own competence levels, and when they encounter questions that they cannot answer, they often search for a solution together with the visitor. However, it can also be questioned whether library staff, especially librarians, can be expected to handle these issues. Do they generally have the right competencies or do they, as one of the SLBs implies when he talks about a colleague below, have other competencies that are used to a lesser extent than they ought to be because of the demand for digital support? *"... when he got double degrees, he didn't expect to spend his days copying and printing. [...] If we see this as a library mission, I think we should hire different kinds of staff. This is like if a fast-food chain only hired doctors and let them cook."* (R4) The library can, on the other hand, also be seen as the perfect place for digital support: *"No other professional group is so... has a place that is open to all and experience of talking to everyone from different age groups, solving problems without loads of prior knowledge and navigating the societal context needed for handling digital competence."* (R7) Thus, the interviews show a mixed picture, not necessarily of the library´s mission for digital inclusion but of how and by whom it should be carried out.

4.4 Digital Discretionary Boundaries

The support the SLBs can provide is also limited by the visitors' digital skills, their ability to describe the problem, and the kind of technical devices that they bring with them to the support desk. The respondents give examples of the types of systems and e-services that they help with, and highlight what they see as weaknesses in the systems. They see their discretion as being framed by certain digital boundaries that they have no – or limited – influence over, both since they are left *"in the hands of the giant tech corps"* (R10) like Apple and Google, and since they lack ownership of most public e-services. Several public e-services are described as being unnecessarily complicated even for experienced users, and practically inaccessible for vulnerable groups. *"Honestly, some of the public pages and other websites where they are supposed to fill in data are really substandard. They are so counterintuitive that you... I am almost baffled at how bad they are. [...] If you lack the language skills as well, it gets even trickier."* (R8) Their agitation over certain e-services also indicate frustration in their own inability to give support that can make a difference in the long run.

They reflect upon how digital exclusion is context-related and can appear from one day to the next with changing life situations, such as the death of a partner, unemployment or illness. It is also diverse; a citizen can be digitally competent in several areas, e.g. social media, while unskilled in others, e.g. public e-services. Many of their stories of support are focused on the groups that are furthest away from digital inclusion, and they emphasize how stuck, frustrated and lonely some of the visitors seem to be. In combination with their critical stance towards certain public e-services, this can entice SLBs to focus more on the short-term technical solution than on a more general bureaucratic role, as seen in this story of a visitor who needed help to log on to a digital Employment Agency meeting: *"He came by in panic about the risk of having his unemployment benefit stopped. [...] At last, we managed to log him on to a lecture that of course was way... totally pointless, but he needed it to get his benefit. Well, then he thanked me for helping him, put the tablet in a corner and let it lie there while he rattled on with us over a coffee..."* (R4).

Several SLBs see a challenge in the current pace of digitalization of public services and ask for impact analyses to ensure that all citizens have access to the information and services they are entitled to. Other suggestions are for the national coordination of public service digitalization and more inclusive ways to staff system design teams: *"There is this huge gap between those who construct and those who use systems, devices or apps. [...] we live in very different realities, and that can be compared to this urban/rural conflict we have struggled with for a hundred years or so, since we began moving to the cities. In many ways, I think we kind of repeat history. That we create and recreate gaps."* (R7) This indicates that the digital cage rearranges the discretionary boundaries of SLBs and shifts power from the street-level to other professional groups.

4.5   Coping Strategies in the Digital Cage

The SLBs' stories about how they approach questions, support and activities differ between bureaucrats from different backgrounds. The local differences in service are partly due to different perceived needs in the local area, and partly – and to a large extent – to what the individual staff member can do or choose to focus on. Previous networks and experiences, for example from working with certain vulnerable groups or school pupils, come into play. The diversity of digital skills among the SLBs is also relevant; having a background in IT can enable other levels of service than having, for example, a background as a librarian.

The discretionary boundaries highlighted above are handled in different ways by the SLBs, but they largely cope by being entrepreneurial and open, and by getting help from other institutions over which the libraries have no formal influence, such as banks, local companies, associations or national authorities. They have discretionary freedom to choose how they approach the problems and who they work with. Their interests and backgrounds seem to matter in their choices, and are part of the explanation for the *"different help at different times depending on whom you turn to"* (R3), both between the centres and within the same centre.

The SLBs share many positive stories about how visitors are empowered by obtaining new skills. However, there are limits to how digitally inclusive they believe certain groups can become. In some cases, the demands of society are perceived as high or unachievable. They also criticize the tendency to shut down meeting places and offer anonymous, digital services that make it more difficult for already excluded groups. In line with this, clashes between visitor expectations and the aforementioned policy boundaries do occur, especially linked to banking tasks and the content of e-services. This can sometimes cause dilemmas where SLBs see the need for urgent help but are unable to supply it without acting outside their discretionary boundaries. This is exemplified by the following quotation: *"For example, one person came in with a plastic pocket full of bills. Some of them were overdue. She was extremely stressed by not really being able to manage it and the bank office was not in [our city]. She was kind of like, 'Here, just take the bank token, take everything. Just do this because I need help right now.' We felt that we absolutely shouldn't do it, we are not supposed to get involved in this."* (R9) In this specific case, as in many others, the SLBs coped with the dilemma by referring the visitor to another agency. However, some respondents wished that they could contribute more and act as a link for knowledge transfer between cultural and humanistic values on one hand and technological values on the other.

5   Discussion

The scope for discretion among library staff has been changed in several ways by digitalization. While the public inquiry on the national library strategy describes digitalization as a change that increases the power and responsibility of librarians [9], this article shows examples of how digitalization limits their discretion to some extent, for example through indirectly making them the support staff of systems that they cannot influence and, in some cases, have limited knowledge of. However, unlike Peeters and Widlak's argument that the reduction in SLBs' discretion is followed by a more sidelined position in society, the findings in this article do not indicate that library staff become less important. Rather, the fact that they are providing face-to-face support for digital systems and services makes them stand out from the general trends described by Peeters and Widlak, and gives them a key function for citizens who are digitally – and otherwise – excluded. Being able to sort out problems with, for example, public e-services by talking to an SLB in person is important, especially when other doors in society are closing.

The library staff describe several layers of discretionary boundaries related to their work. They are framed by classic aspects such as policy, governance and competence. As seen in the interviews, the client-centred goal of solving citizens' urgent digital problems can come into conflict with the organizational goal of keeping the provided service within policy boundaries. However, they are also formed by digital systems and e-governance, especially since the use of new technologies changes the power relations between professional groups and, in the words of one of the respondents, leaves the SLBs *"in the hands of the giant tech corps"* (R10).

There are no pronounced discrepancies between the local politicians' expectations and the street-level implementation of digital support of citizens. The groups have similar views on the rapid digitalization of society and the need to support citizens. They both emphasize the advantages of digital inclusion, but also the potential problems that can occur when, for example, national authorities switch from office to device. The politicians' governance is limited, which provides the basis for discretionary freedom in policy implementation. These unintrusive attitudes of the politicians, as well as the local differences between approaches and service levels at the various centres, imply that the SLBs are entrepreneurial bureaucrats who are actively involved in shaping policy. In response to the dilemmas that they face, the SLBs form coping strategies; by networking with local community actors, they harness more power than they formally have, which gives them the opportunity to slightly bend the bars of the digital cage.

It is notable that their allegiance is shaped by their close encounters with citizens, in particular the visitors who have identified a need for digital support and chosen to reach out for help. They show care and empathy for the visitors and seem, at times, to identify more with the visitors than with a general image of official Sweden. At the same time, SLBs feel that it can be difficult to help certain groups in society. There is a slight technological pessimism within the group, and some of them picture libraries as a last outpost in a society that contributes to exclusion by demanding too much of certain groups of citizens. Their stories from the street level are, in many cases, stories of citizens who are caught in a digital cage and unable to get out on their own, e.g. because of lack of digital literacy. This is, however, not described as simply a problem of individual motivation and skills. A lack of accessible user design is highlighted, indicating responsibilities for e-service providers and tech companies. The interviews also reveal a street-level frustration with the shifting roles of SLBs. Struggling with the assignment to help citizens with digital services that they have no to limited power over, the SLBs are also framed by a digital cage.

5.1 Conclusions

The classic concept of the iron cage is a relevant way of looking at the discretion of SLBs that remains useful within the field of digital government today. The clear boundaries of

SLB discretion in the data can be explained as a socially constructed frame that creates certain dilemmas between what the citizen needs and what the SLB is allowed to do. There is, however, a difference between the data in this case study and the worst-case scenario that Weber warned us of: the *"disenchanted"* society where formal rationality leads to *"specialists without spirit"* and *"sensualists without heart"*. In this case study, the SLBs express commitment and compassion with their visitors, which leads them to listen, comfort and, in some cases, venture slightly outside the municipal assignment to meet the needs of the citizens.

Although this case study is made in a Swedish context, it illustrates a wider phenomenon within digital government. The concept digital cage does not replace the earlier description of a bureaucracy framed by formal rationality but is an important complement that should not be overlooked. It adds to the understanding of street-level discretionary boundaries today by shining a light on the difficulties of working framed by a more diversified power structure than the classic iron cage bars of legislation and policies. The results indicate that there are ways to facilitate equal and just public service delivery and make the digital cage less limiting. However, that requires a combination of public service knowledge, target group knowledge, user design skills and understanding of how technology can frame bureaucracy and citizens.

While there is a clear ambition from SLBs and local politicians to include citizens in a digital society, the development is swift and governed by a multitude of different actors. The assignment to ensure that as many people as possible are digitally included is demanding and can cause frustration and stress at street level. In relation to digital government, the strive for digital inclusion must, of course, involve more than libraries. However, the valuable competences of the SLBs at Digidel centers provides an opportunity that should be further explored in research and practice. Could the library – a place where the spacing between the bars of the digital cage is somewhat wider – serve as a meeting place between user design and cultural context understanding?

References

1. Swedish Internet Foundation: Svenskarna och internet 2021 (2021)
2. Ranerup, A., Henriksen, H.Z.: Digital discretion: unpacking human and techno-logical agency in automated decision making in Sweden's social services. Soc. Sci. Comput. Rev. **40**(2), 445–461 (2022)
3. Lindgren, I., Toll, D. Melin, U.: Automation as a driver of digital transformation in local government: exploring stakeholder views on an automation initiative in a Swedish municipality. In: DG. O2021: the 22nd Annual International Conference on Digital Government Research, pp. 463–472, (2021)
4. Weber, M.: The Protestant Ethic and the Spirit of Capitalism. Unwin University Books, London (1968)
5. Lindgren, I., Madsen, C.O., Hofmann, S., Melin, U.: Close encounters of the digital kind: a research agenda for the digitalization of public services. Gov. Inf. Q. **36**(3), 427–436 (2019)
6. Peeters, R., Widlak, A.: The digital cage: administrative exclusion through information architecture – the case of the Dutch civil registry's master data management system. Agile Gov. Adapt. Gov. Public Sector Gov. Inf. Q. **35**(2), 175–183 (2018)
7. Bernhard, I., Gustafsson, M., Hedström, K., Sefyrin, J. Wihlborg, E.: A digital society for all? Meanings, practices and policies for digital diversity. In: Proceedings of the 52nd Hawaii International Conference on System Sciences, pp. 3067–3076 (2019)

8. SFS 2013:801. Bibliotekslag [Library Act]
9. Royal Library: Den femte statsmakten. Bibliotekens roll för demokrati, utbildning, tillgänglighet och digitalisering. Linköping: LTAB (2017)
10. Maceviciute, E., Wilson, T.D.: Digital means for reducing digital inequality: literature review. Inf. Sci. Int. J. Emerg. Transdiscipline **21**, 269–287 (2018)
11. van Dijk, J.A.G.M.: Digital divide research, achievements and shortcomings. Poetics **34**, 221–235 (2006)
12. Bertot, J.C., Jaeger, P.T., Grimes, J.M.: Using ICTs to create a culture of transparency: E-government and social media as openness and anti-corruption tools for societies. Gov. Inf. Q. **27**, 264–271 (2010)
13. Bernhard, I., Wihlborg, E.: Bringing all clients into the system – professional digital discretion to enhance inclusion when services are automated. Inf. Polity **27**(3), 373–389 (2022)
14. Alexopoulou, S., Åström, J., Karlsson, M.: The grey digital divide and welfare state regimes: a comparative study of European countries. Inf. Technol. People **35**(8), 273–291 (2022)
15. Helsper, E., van Deursen, A.: Digital skills in Europe: research and policy. In: Andreasson, K. (ed.) Digital Divides, pp. 125–146. CRC Press (2015)
16. Government Offices of Sweden: För ett hållbart digitaliserat Sverige – en digitaliseringsstrategi (2017). https://www.regeringen.se/regeringens-politik/digitaliseringsstrategin/. Accessed 1 Mar 2022
17. European Commission: Digital Economy and Society Index (2020). https://digital-strategy. ec.europa.eu/en/policies/desi
18. Fichtelius et al.: Den femte statsmakten. Linköping: LTAB (2017)
19. Swedish Library Association: Promoting the development of a democratic society: The Swedish Library Act according to the legislator (2015). http://www.biblioteksforeningen. se/wp-content/uploads/2017/01/development-of-of-a-democratic-society.pdf
20. Gustafsson, M., Elvström, R., Skill, K., Wihlborg, E.: DigidelCenter i Motala - Lärdomar för ökad digital kompetens. DINO Rapport, 2019:1. LiU-Tryck, Linköping (2019)
21. Mersand, S., Gasco-Hernandez, M., Udoh, E., Gil-Garcia, J.R.: Public libraries as anchor institutions in smart communities: current practices and future development. In: Proceedings of the 52nd Hawaii International Conference on System Sciences (2019)
22. Gustafsson, M.S., Wihlborg, E., Sefyrin, J.: Technology mediated citizenship: what can we learn from library practices. In: Hofmann, S., et al. (eds.) ePart 2020. LNCS, vol. 12220, pp. 109–120. Springer, Cham (2020). https://doi.org/10.1007/978-3-030-58141-1_9
23. Kolodinsky, J., Cranwell, M., Rowe, E.: Bridging the generation gap across the digital divide: teens teaching internet skills to senior citizens. J. Extension **40**(3) (2002)
24. Digidel: Om Digidelnätverket (2018). https://digidel.se/om-oss/. Accessed 12 Jan 2023
25. Digidel: DigidelCenter (2022). https://digidel.se/digidelcenter/. Accessed 12 Jan 2023
26. Lipsky, M.: Street-Level Bureaucracy: Dilemmas of the Individual in Public Services. Russel Sage Foundation, New York (2010)
27. Gilson, L.: Lipsky's street level bureaucracy. In: Page, E., Lodge, M., Balla, S. (eds.) Oxford Handbook of the Classics of Public Policy. Oxford University Press, Oxford (2015)
28. Busch, P.A.: Digital discretion acceptance and impact in street-level bureaucracy. Ph.D. Thesis, University of Agder, Norway (2019)
29. Busch, P.A., Henriksen, H.Z., Sæbø, Ø.: Opportunities and challenges of digitized discretionary practices: a public service worker perspective. Gov. Inf. Q. **35**(4), 547–556 (2018)
30. Samier, E.A.: Education in a troubled era of disenchantment: the emergence of a new Zeitgeist. J. Educ. Adm. Hist. **50**(1), 41–50 (2018)
31. Kalekin-Fishman, D., Langman, L.: Alienation: the critique that refuses to disappear. Curr. Sociol. Rev. **63**(6), 916–933 (2015)

32. Barker, J.R.: Tightening the iron cage: concertive control in self-managing teams. Adm. Sci. Q. **38**(3), 408–437 (1993)
33. Bovens, M., Zouridis, S.: From street-level to system-level bureaucracies: how information and communication technology is transforming administrative discretion and constitutional control. Public Adm. Rev. **62**(2), 174–184 (2002)
34. Kravchenko, S.A.: From formal rationality to the digital one: side-effects, ambivalences, and vulnerabilities. RUDN J. Sociol. **21**(1), 7–17 (2021)
35. Ritzer, G., Jandric, P., Hayes, S.: The velvet cage of educational con(pro)sumption. Open Rev. Educ. Res. **5**(1), 113–129 (2018)
36. Jorna, F., Wagenaar, P.: The 'iron cage' strengthened? Discretion and digital discipline. Public Adm. **85**(1), 189–214 (2007)
37. Swedish Act Concerning the Ethical Review of Research Involving Humans (2003:460)

Artificial Intelligence, Algorithms, and Automation

Untangling the Relationship Between Public Service Automation and No-Stop Government

Ida Lindgren[1]([✉]) [iD] and Hendrik Scholta[2] [iD]

[1] Department of Management and Engineering, Linköping University, Linköping, Sweden
ida.lindgren@liu.se
[2] ERCIS, University of Münster, Münster, Germany
hendrik.scholta@ercis.uni-muenster.de

Abstract. Public service automation and no-stop government are currently two intensively discussed concepts in digital government literature. Although their definitions point to different meanings, some scholars equate the terms and use them interchangeably. Since a clear shared understanding is crucial for scholars to produce reliable research, this conceptual paper aims to shed light on the two terms and support conceptual clarity. We investigate the meaning and relationship between the concepts of public service automation and no-stop government in digital government research. We review the meaning of each concept and discuss the relationship between the two. Thereby, we show that both terms refer to the substitution of a human in public service delivery, but differences lie in the arrangement of the substitution. In automation, a machine substitutes a public official. In contrast, in no-stop government the public organization substitutes the client. We illustrate the relationship between the two concepts using a three-sided model, showing how the use of digital technologies can create an overlap between the two concepts. This conceptual understanding can be used to guide future research and theorizing in the digital government domain.

Keywords: Digital Government · Conceptual Analysis · Automation · No-Stop Shop · Proactive Public Service

1 Introduction

Two currently discussed terms in digital government literature are *public service automation* and *no-stop government*. Roughly speaking, automation refers to when a machine agent (usually a computer) is used to execute a function that was previously carried out by a human [1], and no-stop government means that a client (citizen or business representative) receives a public service from a public organization without having to do anything to obtain the service [2]. Both terms thus refer to a public service delivery process in which a human is removed from the process by introducing some digital technology; either in the back-office, or on the consumer side.

In the digital government literature, these terms—automation and no-stop government—are sometimes used interchangeably, equating the two. This can be seen in the

© IFIP International Federation for Information Processing 2023
Published by Springer Nature Switzerland AG 2023
I. Lindgren et al. (Eds.): EGOV 2023, LNCS 14130, pp. 83–94, 2023.
https://doi.org/10.1007/978-3-031-41138-0_6

2022 UN e-government survey, stating that *"Invisible government is achieved when services are fully automated, with codified data-oriented processes and AI-driven applications used to complete specific bureaucratic tasks and transactions—often with no human input or interaction"* [3, p. 182]. Here, we equate 'invisible government' with no-stop government. But are the terms automation and no-stop government really referring to the same phenomenon? Although similar, we argue that there are, indeed, important differences between these two concepts and that these differences must be clarified.

In the past, digital government research has been criticized for overlooking previous theories and experiences [4] and for using imprecise and vague definitions of central terms and concepts, e.g., *digital government* [5–7], *e-service* [8], *smart city* [9, 10], and *citizens/government* [11]. We observe a similar problem related to the meaning and relationship of automation and no-stop government. Such conditions are problematic since the foundation of scientific work is a clear understanding of the concepts used. Of course, concepts need to evolve and be adaptable to give scholars the opportunity to account for new insights and developments. Further, a controversial discourse with different viewpoints is essential for fruitful and innovative research. However, to achieve reliable and comparable results, scholars need to have a shared understanding of at least the foundational concepts in their research area.

We see a risk that our collective (mis-)use of the automation and no-stop government concepts obscures important differences between these terms and related phenomena. In this conceptual paper, we therefore investigate the meanings of public service automation and no-stop government and clarify the relationship between these two concepts. Our analysis is guided by the following research question: *What is the meaning and relationship between the concepts of public service automation and no-stop government in digital government research?*

We address our research question by first reviewing definitions and literature on the two concepts. We then proceed to relate the two concepts, discussing similarities, differences, and relationships between the two concepts. By answering the research question in this way, we contribute with conceptual clarifications of two central concepts in digital government literature. This is important to make sure that scholars within the field can engage in fruitful discussion and build cumulative knowledge.

This paper is structured as follows. Section 2 presents related work regarding the terms automation and no-stop government. In Sect. 3, we present the results of our conceptual analysis to provide conceptual clarity regarding these terms. We discuss our results and conclude in Sect. 4.

2   Research Background

Our discussion on automation and no-stop government is positioned in the larger context of *digital government research* and government *digitalization,* where digital government research deals with the ongoing digitalization in public organizations. Digitalization, in turn, refers to processual and organizational changes beyond a mere 1:1 transition from the analog to digital mode [12] and thus brings subsequent effects on, for instance, institutional and organizational design, and stakeholder relationships. We see digitalization as an overarching concept, in relation to which public service automation and no-stop government are different, but partly related, manifestations and applications.

2.1 Public Service Automation

Automation, as a concept and phenomenon, can be traced back to the ancient Greek word for 'self-moving' [13]. In everyday language, the term automation can have several meanings and is associated to terms such as automated and automatic. Today, automation typically refer to *self-operating* equipment/machinery. An important aspect of automation is that the self-operating machinery *replaces human beings* [14]. This is seen also in the research literature, for instance, in the definition by Parasuraman and Riley [1, p. 231], stating that automation refers to *"the execution by a machine agent (usually a computer) of a function that was previously carried out by a human"*. This, in turn, means that automation is both referring to (1) a self-operating machine (a noun) and (2) the process of replacing humans with machines (a verb). The first meaning is also related to the adjective *automatic,* which can both refer to a device that activates, moves, or regulates itself, but also involuntary or reflex actions [15]. The second meaning relates to practices of developing and applying automation/self-operating machines [16]. These differences in meaning may look trivial, but as we will later argue, are important for understanding the relationship between automation and no-stop government.

Automation is easy to spot when it is under development, but harder to observe once it has been successfully implemented, as elegantly put by Parasuraman and Riley [1, p. 231]: *"What is considered automation will therefore change with time. When the reallocation of a function from human to machine is complete and permanent, then the function will tend to be seen simply as a machine operation, not as automation"*. Once in place, the final automation (i.e., the self-operating machine) is thus easily taken for granted.

Automation has been a central theme in digital government literature since the onset of our field, as using digital technologies to automate work is part of the very essence of digital government. In the early 2000's, there was also an ongoing discussion in our field on the need to widen the perspective from government automation to government transformation [17]. As a term, however, 'automation' then turned cold for more than a decade. More recently, automation has re-emerged as a central topic in digital government, triggered by the new spring of artificial intelligence (AI) [18] and the introduction of Robotic Process Automation (RPA) in the public sector [19]. As AI and RPA have become more mature, sophisticated, and affordable, a wider array of processes can now be automated [20], for instance, administrative work and decision-making related to public service [21].

Following on the above, public service automation thus refers to the introduction of software to replace humans in the *internal* machinery of public organizations; predominantly in *administrative* work, as part of the everyday activities of public officials and case workers as they deliver public service [21]. Automation is currently used to replace humans to various degrees in public service processes; from taking over simple data- and information-handling (e.g., cut-and-paste of data between systems, see [22]), to making formal decisions on incoming applications by clients (e.g., parental benefits in Norway, see [23]).

As a final but important note, automation can be achieved without digital technologies. In fact, most automation implemented in the history of mankind has been based on physical machines and apparatuses. The latest trajectory in the history of automation, however, is triggered by digital technology [13]. Public service automation is hence very much a question of *digitally enabled* automation. But, for the sake of our argumentation in this paper, we must remember that automation, as a concept, is not necessarily achieved by digitalization. Automation can be realized by analogue and physical apparatuses, by digital technologies, or a mix thereof.

2.2 No-Stop Government

No-stop government refers to a *proactive* delivery mode of public services, and means that *"the citizen does not have to perform any action or fill in any forms to receive government services"* [2, p. 11]. In the dictionary, proactive is an adjective used to denote an active, rather than passive, role in doing and accomplishing something, and to initiate a change [24]. In the context of public services, the term 'proactive' means that a public organization anticipates a client's potential or actual need for service [25] and acts before the client becomes active [26]. Essentially, proactivity indicates that public organizations' activities in public services are not triggered by the client. Proactivity in public services is intensively discussed in recent digital government literature [e.g., 2, 26–36] and seen as comprising a shift from a "pull" to a "push" paradigm [35]. In the first paradigm, clients pull services and in the second, public organizations push services. Others frame both terms from the client perspective and talk about a shift from "pull" to "pushed" [37], so that clients pull services first and then services are pushed to them.

Proactivity can take various shapes in public services. For example, proactivity can appear in the shape of prefilled form fields or by a public organization suggesting suitable subsequent services to a client. This 'lightest' form of proactivity is also known as *attentive government* [28, 36, 38] and still requires some client activity to complete the delivery process. In its most extreme form, proactivity is realized as *no-stop government* [2, 39] (also discussed as *no-stop shop* in the literature). In no-stop government, a client does not need to do anything to receive a public service and the entire delivery process is completed without any client involvement. A public organization initiates the delivery process itself, collects necessary data, and informs the client about the decision on their eligibility. An intermediate step is the *limited* no-stop government where the client needs to transmit some data to the public organization after the organization has communicated its decision on the client's eligibility [2]. In such a case, the client knows that they will receive a service, but the organization needs more data for the subsequent operational execution of the service, such as the calculation of the exact amount of a regular payment or an address to send regular written information. Thus, in limited no-stop government, data can be captured from a client after the public organization has decided and communicated that the client will receive a service.

A notable example of no-stop government can be found in Austria, where public organizations pay family allowance to parents of a newborn without the parents having to submit an application [40]. After the birth, the hospital informs the central civil registry at the Federal Ministry of the Interior where this data is integrated with further data from the parents. This integrated data is then sent to the Federal Ministry of Finance and forwarded to the responsible local tax office, which makes a decision on the case. When all necessary data is available, the public organization informs the parents that they will receive family allowance from now on (no-stop government). When necessary data is missing, the public organization sends letters to the parents to inform them about the future payment of family allowance and request the bank account number, which the parents need to provide subsequently (limited no-stop government). Similar no-stop government services for family allowance are found in Norway (see [23]) and Sweden (see [41]).

Data standardization and formats for information sharing within and across public organizations are essential to build a solid data foundation and are enablers for the realization of no-stop government [35]. As such, no-stop government is tied closely to digital technologies and digitalization. However, similar to automation, digital technologies are not necessary means for proactivity in a no-stop government, but they sure help. No-stop government can be realized by analogue and manual work, by the use of digital technologies, or a mix thereof.

3 Relating Public Service Automation and No-Stop Government

Why do we need to unpack and relate public service automation and no-stop government? From the accounts above, the concepts look sufficiently different. Still, in the literature, these concepts are often muddled together. Triggered by certain unclarities described below, we want to illustrate how automation can indeed be a means for no-stop government, but automation and no-stop government can also be completely unrelated.

3.1 Different Understandings of Automation and No-Stop Government

For example, we have come across these terms being used interchangeable in public administration literature. To name an example, the public administration scholars Moynihan et al. [42] discuss the possibilities for *automatic enrollment* of clients into public programs, meaning that clients that fit certain criteria for participating in public programs should be 'automatically' assigned to these programs to ensure uptake and realization of citizen rights. However, the meaning of 'automatic' is not clear. It seems as if Moynihan et al. [42] use the adjective 'automatic' to illustrate that the enrollment is made without the client's conscious action (cf. automatic, as meaning self-operating and reflexive). However, in public programs it is not the clients who enroll themselves; the enrollment is done by public officials, i.e., the action that is subject for automation is not performed by the client. Therefore, based on the definitions above, automatic enrollment should then mean that a self-operating machine has replaced public officials to do the enrollment. Looking closer at their arguments, Moynihan et al. [42] use the term 'automatic' to denote that public organizations should use available information about clients to ensure that eligible clients are enrolled to public programs without having to actively apply. Following our argumentation above, this would translate to *no-stop government* and proactive service rather than automation. To be fair, such proactive enrollment can indeed be an *automatic* enrollment, meaning that a software is programmed to enroll citizens into public programs when they fit certain criteria in some system (i.e., digitally enabled automation). However, Moynihan et al. [42] do not discuss automation software in their article and whether or not the 'automatic enrollment' is really based on automation is not clear from their arguments.

Similarly, the sociologists Larasati et al. [43, p. 537] discuss the concept of *digital welfare state* (DWS), defined as a system *"providing welfare services by the state based on the use of technology and data"*. They further define DWS as a system that utilizes digitized data that *"is then processed by algorithms and artificial intelligence to produce effective and efficient policies concerning social services"* [43, p. 538]. The authors' use of DWS thus corresponds with digitally enabled automation, as discussed here, because of the required use of algorithms and AI. The authors also mention that DWS can be used for *"automated system control"* (i.e., prediction, identification, monitoring, detection, targeting and punishment), which is in several ways overlapping with no-stop government.

The two examples used here, automatic enrollment and DWS, are meant to illustrate how the underlying ideas that we call automation and no-stop government are visible under various terms and with various relationships in various streams of literature. In our view, the discussions about no-stop government and automation in public organizations naturally overlap to a large extent. They are similar in the sense that they both relate to removing humans from public organizations' delivery of public service to clients. An important difference, however, is that public service automation deals with reducing human involvement on the public organization side of the interaction, removing humans in the *internal* administrative work. In contrast, no-stop government deals with reducing human involvement on the client side of the interaction, thus removing humans *externally*.

3.2   A Shared Understanding of Automation and No-Stop Government

A reason why automation and no-stop government are treated as similar concepts can be the everyday, common-sense definition of *automatic,* which can both refer to (1) a device that activates, moves, or regulates itself, but also (2) involuntary or reflex actions. If a service is delivered without the client's active engagement, it can be perceived as *automatic* in common everyday language. From the client's perspective, no-stop government's delivery of public services can be perceived as a form of automation, in the sense that they receive something without acting, and we see this understanding of automation mirrored also in the literature [e.g., 21, 23, 27, 44]. This is however not the meaning of automation that we refer to here. Rather, for us, automation concerns whether human employees are doing anything on the *inside* of a public organization to make that service delivery happen. On the supplier side of the interaction, no-stop government services can indeed be delivered using automated computer software, but they are just as likely, or even more likely, to be delivered based on manual work, or a mix of manual and automated work. Automated service delivery is increasingly used by public organizations and the literature on automation of public services in the digital government domain is growing [45–48]. But in these instances, the client still initiates the service interaction, sometimes without being aware of interacting with automated systems. Thus, the conceptual and practical link between automation and no-stop-government are still unclear and needs to be sorted out.

Figure 1 illustrates our proposed link between public service automation and no-stop government. Following the argumentation above, the figure has three axes that represent three interrelated perspectives. The first axis is related to the *internal* organizational perspective. We differentiate between manual and automated work and acknowledge that a mix of both modes of operation can be used. The second axis is related to the *external* organizational perspective. We differentiate between reactive and no-stop services. Again, we acknowledge that a mix of these two modes can be applied. The third axis is related to the *technological* perspective, referring to what artifacts, tools, and equipment are used for communication, administration, and decision-making. We differentiate between digital/virtual and analog/physical modes through which a service is delivered and acknowledge that a mix of both can be used. Put together, these three axes form a three-dimensional cube to which we can relate public services, in relation to internal, external, and technological aspects.

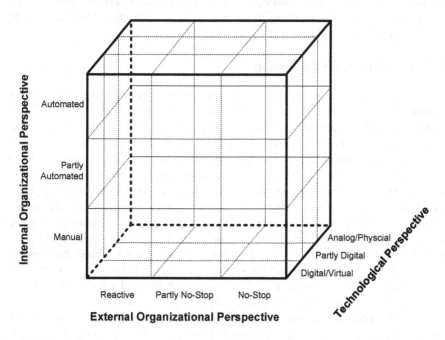

Fig. 1. The relationship between public service automation and no-stop government in digital government research

The cube can be used to classify public services along three perspectives. As a complement to the cube, we furthermore suggest a set of questions to guide the classification of the service delivery process:

- Corresponding to the external organizational perspective: Who is involved in the service delivery process (internal actors and/or the client)?
- Corresponding to the internal organizational perspective: Who or what executes the public organizations' activities (a human and/or machine)?
- Corresponding to the technological perspective: What technology supports the service delivery process (digital and/or analog)?

The most extreme form of public service delivery, when it comes to digitalization and proactivity, is a no-stop government service that is delivered through a digital and fully automated system. In this type of service delivery, the client is not involved in the service delivery process, nor is a public organization employee. Of course, public officials and other human actors are part of the design and set-up of the service delivery process, but once up-and-running, no humans are involved. Another extreme form of public service delivery is the reactive service, delivered through a manual process with only analog/physical tools. Many public services are likely to be automated, digital and proactive to various degrees and located at interior parts of the cube. For example, if a public organization uses a digital IT system to automatically prefill forms or suggest services to potentially eligible clients, but client consent is necessary and finally a public official makes a decision manually and communicates it on paper via mail, then the service is partly automated, partly no-stop and partly digital.

4 Discussion and Conclusion

This conceptual paper aims to clarify the meaning and relationship between the concepts of automation and no-stop government in digital government research. We asked: what is the meaning and relationship between the concepts of public service automation and no-stop government in digital government research? According to our conceptual analysis above, automation and no-stop government are not the same but complementary concepts and phenomena. Both concepts refer to the substitution of humans in public service delivery. All in all, the difference between the two concepts is a matter of perspective and whose actions are replaced or removed from public service delivery. While a machine replaces a public official in public service automation, the client is removed from service delivery in no-stop government. Hence, an important contribution of this paper is that we clarify that automation and no-stop government can go hand in hand, but there can also be automation without no-stop government if clients still perform actions in the process, such as the initiation of the delivery process. Additionally, there can be no-stop government without automation of public officials' work and actions.

Another contribution of this paper is that we highlight that digitalization can facilitate automation and no-stop government, but digitalization is not a necessary means for realizing any of them. Today, however, automation and no-stop government are predominantly achieved using digital technologies and digitalization of work processes. The integral role of digitalization in both automation and no-stop government also contributes to the unclear boundaries between the concepts. Bringing these perspectives together, we distinguish various types of public service delivery as shown in the cube in Fig. 1. By addressing the meaning of automation and no-stop government and possible relationships between the two, we contribute to a deeper understanding and increased conceptual clarity regarding two terms that scholars currently discuss intensively in digital government literature. Some scholars view no-stop government as a form of automation [e.g., 21, 23, 27, 44], but considering that no-stop government can also be achieved through manual work, we argue for a differentiation between automation and no-stop government. The cube in Fig. 1, its explanations, and related questions reflect this viewpoint. Put together, the definitions provided, the cube, and its three questions can guide the classification of different service delivery processes in practice.

We recognize that the conceptual exercise conducted here can seem overly focused on semantic details and that the end-result might be interesting only for a smaller subset of digital government researchers at present. However, as public organizations continue to invest in AI and automation technologies [49–51], the differences between automation and no-stop government will become increasingly visible also in digital government practice. In order to study, document, and explain how digital government applications play out in practice, we need a developed language for differentiating between different types of public service delivery. This is necessary also for theorizing and building cumulative knowledge in the field [11]. An important step towards further theorizing and knowledge development is to clarify theoretical concepts, and thus the labels we put on phenomena in the empirical context. Without clearly defined concepts and labels, comparative studies and mutual learning are made difficult. In this paper, we have detailed the meaning of and relationship between public service automation and no-stop government. From our perspective, this paper thus forms a foundation for a discussion on the meaning of automation and no-stop government, and the interplay between these concepts, that we hope other researchers will find useful.

This paper is purely conceptual and is subject to limitations that can, in turn, spur future work. First, the ideas presented here can be tested empirically by applying them in the analysis of empirical work on automation and no-stop government respectively. Both concepts discussed here need to be investigated and theorized further, separately and in unison. Also, the ideas presented here can be used for further analysis of the interplay between the two concepts. For example, the cube and its three perspectives can guide the investigation of the role played by automation in the realization of no-stop government. Furthermore, the three perspectives in Fig. 1 can be further unpacked theoretically through a deeper conceptual and literature-based analysis. For example, the external organizational perspective can be further explored and extended, e.g., in terms of what happens to our understanding of these concepts and their relationships if clients use RPAs on their own devices to share certain data and complete forms in their interactions with public organizations. Moreover, scholars can incorporate further—especially controversially discussed—terms such as AI and discretion [45, 52] in the conceptual discussion and relate them to automation and no-stop government.

Acknowledgements. Ida Lindgren's participation in this work is supported by AFA Försäkring, as part of the research project "From Form to Robot?" (190200).

References

1. Parasuraman, R., Riley, V.: Humans and automation: use, misuse, disuse, abuse. Hum. Factors **39**, 230–253 (1997)
2. Scholta, H., Mertens, W., Kowalkiewicz, M., Becker, J.: From one-stop shop to no-stop shop: An e-government stage model. Gov. Inf. Q. **36**, 11–26 (2019)
3. United Nations: E-Government Survey 2022: The Future of Digital Government. https://desapublications.un.org/sites/default/files/publications/2022-09/Webversion E-Government 2022.pdf. Accessed 30 Mar 2023
4. Heeks, R., Bailur, S.: Analyzing e-government research: perspectives, philosophies, theories, methods, and practice. Gov. Inf. Q. **24**, 243–265 (2007)

5. Aldrich, D., Bertot, J.C., McClure, C.R.: E-government: Initiatives, developments, and issues. Gov. Inf. Q. **19**, 349–355 (2002)
6. Hwang, S.-D., Choi, Y., Myeong, S.-H.: Electronic government in South Korea: conceptual problems. Gov. Inf. Q. **16**, 277–285 (1999)
7. Yildiz, M.: E-government research: reviewing the literature, limitations, and ways forward. Gov. Inf. Q. **24**, 646–665 (2007)
8. Lindgren, I., Jansson, G.: Electronic services in the public sector: a conceptual framework. Gov. Inf. Q. **30**, 163–172 (2013)
9. Lee, J., Lee, H.: Developing and validating a citizen-centric typology for smart city services. Gov. Inf. Q. **31**, S93–S105 (2014)
10. Nam, T., Pardo, T.A.: Conceptualizing smart city with dimensions of technology, people, and institutions. In: Bertot, J.C., Nahon, K., Chun, S.A., Luna-Reyes, L.F., Atluri, V. (eds.) Proceedings of the 12th Annual International Conference on Digital Government Research (DG.O 2011), College Park, pp. 282–291 (2011)
11. Flak, L.S., Sein, M.K., Sæbø, Ø.: Towards a cumulative tradition in e-government research: going beyond the Gs and Cs. In: Wimmer, M.A., Scholl, J., Grönlund, Å. (eds.) EGOV 2007. LNCS, vol. 4656, pp. 13–22. Springer, Heidelberg (2007). https://doi.org/10.1007/978-3-540-74444-3_2
12. Mergel, I., Edelmann, N., Haug, N.: Defining digital transformation: results from expert interviews. Gov. Inf. Q. **36** (2019)
13. Willcocks, L.P., Lacity, M.: Service Automation: Robots and the Future of Work. SB Publishing, Ashford (2016)
14. HarperCollins Publishers: Automation. https://www.collinsdictionary.com/dictionary/english/automation. Accessed 31 Mar 2023
15. HarperCollins Publishers: Automatic. https://www.collinsdictionary.com/dictionary/english/automatic. Accessed 31 Mar 2023
16. Goldkuhl, G.: The subject matter of process automation practices: through the lenses of research questions. In: Juell-Skielse, G., Lindgren, I., Åkesson, M. (eds.) Service Automation in the Public Sector: Concepts, Empirical Examples and Challenges, pp. 13–33. Springer, Cham (2022)
17. Dixon, B.E.: Towards e-government 2.0: an assessment of where e-government 2.0 is and where it is headed. Public Adm. Manag. **15**, 418–454 (2010)
18. Natale, S., Ballatore, A.: Imagining the thinking machine: technological myths and the rise of artificial intelligence. Convergence **26**, 3–18 (2020)
19. Juell-Skielse, G., Lindgren, I., Åkesson, M.: Towards service automation in public organizations. In: Juell-Skielse, G., Lindgren, I., Åkesson, M. (eds.) Service Automation in the Public Sector. PROIS, pp. 3–10. Springer, Cham (2022). https://doi.org/10.1007/978-3-030-92644-1_1
20. Wajcman, J.: Automation: is it really different this time? Br. J. Sociol. **68**, 119–127 (2017)
21. Roehl, U.B.U.: Understanding automated decision-making in the public sector: a classification of automated, administrative decision-making. In: Juell-Skielse, G., Lindgren, I., Åkesson, M. (eds.) Service Automation in the Public Sector. PROIS, pp. 35–63. Springer, Cham (2022). https://doi.org/10.1007/978-3-030-92644-1_3
22. Lindgren, I., Johansson, B., Söderström, F., Toll, D.: Why is it difficult to implement robotic process automation? In: Janssen, M., et al. (eds.) EGOV 2022. LNCS, vol. 13391, pp. 353–368. Springer, Cham (2022). https://doi.org/10.1007/978-3-031-15086-9_23
23. Larsson, K.K.: Digitization or equality: when government automation covers some, but not all citizens. Gov. Inf. Q. **38**, 1–10 (2021)
24. HarperCollins Publishers: Proactive. https://www.collinsdictionary.com/dictionary/english/proactive. Accessed 31 Mar 2023

25. Bertot, J., Estevez, E., Janowski, T.: Universal and contextualized public services: digital public service innovation framework. Gov. Inf. Q. **33**, 211–222 (2016)
26. Pawlowski, C., Scholta, H.: A taxonomy for proactive public services. Gov. Inf. Q. **40** (2023)
27. Murataj, I., Schulte, M.: No-stop government: expected benefits and concerns of German young adults. In: Janssen, M., et al. (eds.) EGOV 2022. LNCS, vol. 13391, pp. 47–59. Springer, Cham (2022). https://doi.org/10.1007/978-3-031-15086-9_4
28. Scholta, H., Lindgren, I.: Proactivity in digital public services: a conceptual analysis. Gov. Inf. Q. **40** (2023)
29. Scholta, H., Halsbenning, S., Becker, J.: A public value based method to select services for a no-stop shop implementation. In: Proceedings of the 55th Hawaii International Conference on System Sciences HICSS 2022, pp. 2523–2532. Virtual Conference (2022)
30. Erlenheim, R., Draheim, D., Taveter, K.: Identifying design principles for proactive services through systematically understanding the reactivity-proactivity spectrum. In: Charalabidis, Y., Cunha, M.A., Sarantis, D. (eds.) Proceedings of the 13th International Conference on Theory and Practice of Electronic Governance (ICEGOV 2020), Athens, pp. 452–458 (2020)
31. Khasmammadli, G., Erlenheim, R.: Citizens' readiness for proactive public services: a case study from Azerbaijan. In: Amaral, L., Soares, D., Zheng, L., Peixoto, M., Braga, C. (eds.) Proceedings of the 15th International Conference on Theory and Practice of Electronic Governance (ICEGOV 2022), Guimarães, pp. 408–415 (2022)
32. Oude Luttighuis, B., Bharosa, N.N., Spoelstra, F.F., van der Voort, H.H.G., Janssen, M.: Inclusion through proactive public services: findings from the Netherlands: classifying and designing proactivity through understanding service eligibility and delivery processes. In: Proceedings of the 22nd Annual International Conference on Digital Government Research (DG.O 2021), Omaha, pp. 242–251 (2021)
33. Kuhn, P., Buchinger, M., Balta, D.: How to redesign government processes for proactive public services? In: Scholl, H.J., Gil-Garcia, J.R., Janssen, M., Kalampokis, E., Lindgren, I., Rodríguez Bolívar, M.P. (eds.) EGOV 2021. LNCS, vol. 12850, pp. 29–40. Springer, Cham (2021). https://doi.org/10.1007/978-3-030-84789-0_3
34. Kuhn, P., Balta, D.: Service quality through government proactivity: the concept of non-interaction. In: Viale Pereira, G., et al. (eds.) EGOV 2020. LNCS, vol. 12219, pp. 82–95. Springer, Cham (2020). https://doi.org/10.1007/978-3-030-57599-1_7
35. Linders, D., Liao, C.Z.-P., Wang, C.-M.: Proactive e-governance: flipping the service delivery model from pull to push in Taiwan. Gov. Inf. Q. **35**, S68–S76 (2018)
36. Scholta, H., Lindgren, I.: The long and winding road of digital public services—One next step: proactivity. In: Proceedings of the 40th International Conference on Information Systems (ICIS 2019), Munich (2019)
37. Kõrge, H., Erlenheim, R., Draheim, D.: Designing proactive business event services: a case study of the Estonian company registration portal. In: Panagiotopoulos, P., Edelmann, N., Glassey, O., Misuraca, G., Parycek, P., Lampoltshammer, T., Re, B. (eds.) Proceedings of the International Conference on Electronic Participation (ePart 2019), San Benedetto Del Tronto, pp. 73–84 (2019)
38. Brüggemeier, M.: Auf dem Weg zur No-Stop-Verwaltung. Verwaltung Manag. **16**, 93–101 (2010)
39. Kampen, J.K., Snijkers, K.: E-democracy: a critical evaluation of the ultimate e-dream. Soc. Sci. Comput. Rev. **21**, 491–496 (2003)
40. Bosse, J., Burnett, M., Møller Nielsen, S., Rongione, C., Scholtens, H.: European Public Sector Award 2015: The Public Sector as Partner for a Better Society. European Institute of Public Administration, Maastricht (2015)
41. Lindgren, I., van Veenstra, A.F.: Digital government transformation: a case illustrating public e-service development as part of public sector transformation. In: Zuiderwijk, A., Hinnant,

C.C. (eds.) Proceedings of the 19th Annual International Conference on Digital Government Research (DG.O 2018), Delft, pp. 1–6 (2018)

42. Moynihan, D., Herd, P., Harvey, H.: Administrative burden: learning, psychological, and compliance costs in citizen-state interactions. J. Public Adm. Res. Theory. **25**, 43–69 (2015)

43. Larasati, Z.W., Yuda, T.K., Syafa'at, A.R.: Digital welfare state and problem arising: an exploration and future research agenda. Int. J. Sociol. Soc. Policy (2022)

44. Parzer, P., Prorok, T.: Vorschläge zur Entlastung von Bürokratiekosten für Bürgerinnen und Bürger in Österreich. In: Brüggemeier, M., Lenk, K. (eds.) Bürokratieabbau im Verwaltungsvollzug: Better Regulation zwischen Go-Government und No-Government, pp. 83–96. Edition Sigma, Berlin (2011)

45. Busch, P.A., Henriksen, H.Z., Sæbø, Ø.: Opportunities and challenges of digitized discretionary practices: a public service worker perspective. Gov. Inf. Q. **35**, 547–556 (2018)

46. Ranerup, A., Henriksen, H.Z.: Value positions viewed through the lens of automated decision-making: the case of social services. Gov. Inf. Q. **36**, 1–13 (2019)

47. Ranerup, A., Henriksen, H.Z.: Digital discretion: unpacking human and technological agency in automated decision making in Sweden's social services. Soc. Sci. Comput. Rev. (2020)

48. Ranerup, A., Svensson, L.: Value positions in the implementation of automated decision-making in social assistance. Nord. Soc. Work Res. (2022)

49. Zuiderwijk, A., Chen, Y.-C., Salem, F.: Implications of the use of artificial intelligence in public governance: a systematic literature review and a research agenda. Gov. Inf. Q. **38** (2021)

50. van Noordt, C., Misuraca, G.: Artificial intelligence for the public sector: results of landscaping the use of AI in government across the European Union. Gov. Inf. Q. **39** (2022)

51. Ahn, M.J., Chen, Y.-C.: Digital transformation toward AI-augmented public administration: the perception of government employees and the willingness to use AI in government. Gov. Inf. Q. **39** (2022)

52. Busch, P.A., Henriksen, H.Z.: Digital discretion: a systematic literature review of ICT and street-level discretion. Inf. Polity **23**, 3–28 (2018)

ChatGPT Application vis-a-vis Open Government Data (OGD): Capabilities, Public Values, Issues and a Research Agenda

Euripidis Loukis[1] ⓘ, Stuti Saxena[2] ⓘ, Nina Rizun[3] ⓘ, Maria Ioanna Maratsi[4] ⓘ,
Mohsan Ali[4] ⓘ, and Charalampos Alexopoulos[4(✉)] ⓘ

[1] University of the Aegean, 83200 Samos, Greece
eloukis@aegean.gr
[2] Graphic Era University, Uttarakhand 248002, India
[3] Gdansk University of Technology, 80-233 Gdańsk, Poland
nina.rizun@pg.edu.pl
[4] University of the Aegean, 83200 Samos, Greece
{ioanna.m,mohsan,alexop}@aegean.gr

Abstract. As a novel Artificial Intelligence (AI) application, ChatGPT holds pertinence not only for the academic, medicine, law, computing or other sectors, but also for the public sector-case in point being the Open Government Data (OGD) initiative. However, though there has been some limited (as this topic is quite new) research concerning the capabilities ChatGPT in these sectors, there has been no research about the capabilities it can provide to government concerning its wide range of functions and activities. This paper contributes to filling this gap by investigating the capabilities that the ChatGPT can provide concerning one of most recently initiated and novel, and at the same time most promising, activities of government that aims to fuel the emerging data economy and society: the opening of large amounts of government data; furthermore, we investigate the public values that can be promoted through the use of ChatGPT in the area of OGD by both the data publishers as well as their users. At the same time, we investigate the issues that the use of ChatGPT in the area of OGD can pose, which can reduce the capabilities identified as aforesaid as well as the benefits and public values that can be generated from them. For these purposes interviews with 12 experts have been conducted and their responses have been analyzed. Finally, based on our findings we have developed a research agenda concerning the exploitation of ChatGPT application in the OGD domain.

Keywords: Artificial Intelligence · ChatGPT · Open Government Data · Public Values · Research Agenda

1 Introduction

As a major breakthrough in the Artificial Intelligence (AI) landscape, the roll-out of Chat-GPT (Chat Generative Pre-Trained Transformer) in November, 2022 [1], was acknowledged with different reactions across academic circles, social media and electronic media

I. Lindgren et al. (Eds.): EGOV 2023, LNCS 14130, pp. 95–110, 2023.
https://doi.org/10.1007/978-3-031-41138-0_7

[2–7]. In its fundamental form, ChatGPT is "…a variant of the GPT (Generative Pre-trained Transformer) architecture, a neural network trained using a large dataset to generate natural language text suitable for conversational contexts, such as responding to user input in a chatbot or virtual assistant application… (and) it has been trained on a massive text dataset, including various sources, allowing it to generate grammatically correct, contextually appropriate, and coherent text" [8: 1]. Some first limited research (as it is a quite new topic) on the implications of ChatGPT has revealed that it can provide significant and highly beneficial capabilities in diverse sectors like academics, law, medicine, media and computing (software development) to name a few with some concomitant caveats too [9–15].

However, the implications of ChatGPT for the public sector have not been underscored so far. There has been no research about the capabilities it can provide to government concerning its wide range of functions and activities. So, it is necessary to investigate the capabilities that the ChatGPT can provide concerning both the 'traditional' government functions and activities, and also the more recent and novel ones. Our study contributes to filling this gap focusing on one of the most recently initiated and novel, and at the same time one of the most promising, activities of government that aims to fuel the emerging data economy and society: the opening of large amounts of government data to be used by citizens, firms and the society in general [16–19]. Whilst the applications of ChatGPT in the digital government may be a research pointer in itself, the present study seeks to provide an overview regarding the possible research avenues of the ChatGPT applications in the context of Open Government Data (OGD) initiative-the still-evolving digital government innovation across the globe [18]. Given that the success of the OGD initiatives relies on the usability by a range of stakeholders (user side) and the proactiveness of the government agencies (provider side) [20], the present study seeks to provide research pointers across these two broad rubrics; to investigate the implications of ChatGPT for OGD users and providers. Furthermore, we proceed to a deeper investigation of the capabilities that the ChatGPT can provide in the area of OGD from a public values perspective [21].

In particular, this paper contributes to filling this above-mentioned research gap concerning the implications of the ChatGPT for the public sector; our main research questions are:

i) Which capabilities are provided by the ChatGPT in the area of ODG to OGD users and publishers?
ii) What are the public values that can be promoted through the use of ChatGPT by OGD users and publishers exploiting these capabilities?
iii) Which are the issues (e.g., problems, risks) posed the use of ChatGPT in the area of OGD, which can reduce the above capabilities as well as the benefits and public values that can be generated from them?
iv) What should be the future research agenda concerning the exploitation of ChatGPT application in the OGD domain?

For addressing the above research questions interviews with 12 experts have been conducted and their responses have been analyzed; experts' perspectives were synthesized and filtered in alignment with the research objectives.

The theoretical foundation of our study is 'affordances theory', which, though initially developed and used in the ecological psychology domain, is increasingly used in the information systems domain [27]. An affordance is defined as 'the potential for behavior associated with achieving an immediate concrete outcome and arising from the relation between an artifact and a goal-oriented actor or actors' [23]: it constitutes a relationship between an actor and an artefact and concerns the action possibilities provided to the actor, towards achieving his/her goals, by the artefact; however, we might have not only 'positive affordances' but also 'negative affordances' as well [23]. So, in this study we investigate the positive and the negative affordances of ChatGPT concerning the OGD (for both their users and publishers).

Our study makes a contribution to the extant OGD-focused literature across two streams: a) it adds to the OGD-AI linkage literature, which has been limited so far, dealing with the generation of more value from OGD using the 'classical AI' (mainly Machine Learning) [24] it also makes a contribution towards the evolving ChatGPT-related literature.

This paper consists of six sections: In the following Sect. 2 the background of our study is outlined, and then in Sect. 3 our research methodology is described. Next the results are presented in Sects. 4 and 5, while in the final Sect. 6 conclusions are summarized and future research directions are proposed.

2 Background

2.1 Public Values

The 'public value' theory was developed by Moore [21], and elaborated by other researchers [24, 25], in order to provide a new public management paradigm to be used both for activities and resources allocation planning as well as for the evaluation of public sector organizations, which addresses the weaknesses of the two previous dominant public management paradigms: the 'bureaucratic' and the 'new public management' ones. According to the public value theory government has a wide range of objectives, that concern a wide range of collective needs, desires, aspirations and preferences of the citizens, which are associated with values regarded by them as important: efficiency in the use of public sector resources, quality of services, fairness, equal treatment of all citizens, trust, legitimacy, social cohesion, cultural development, transparency, public participation and collaboration, etc. Therefore, public resources should be used by government agencies in order to generate the above types of public value, in a way which is analogous to the generation of private value within private firms.

There has been considerable research concerning the relationship between digital governance and public values [26, 27]. One of its most interesting conclusions was that public value theory constitutes a sound and comprehensive basis for the strategic planning, the evaluation, and in general the analysis, of digital government, as well as specific kinds of information systems and applications for the public sector, which is not limited to the 'traditional' efficiency and cost reduction related objectives, but includes additional political and social objectives concerning the promotion of a wide range of public values, such as the above mentioned ones. An interesting stream of this research concerning the relationship between digital governance and public values is dealing with the identification of specific public values, or categories of public values, that can be substantially promoted through the use of ICT in government. The most representative and widely used of these studies is the one of [27], which identifies four main categories of public values that can be promoted through e-government systems and applications:

- Efficiency-related values: productivity, performance, efficient use of public resources cost reduction, and value for money.
- Service-related values: public services quality, accessibility and utility, as well as citizen centricity.
- Professionalism-related: independent, robust and consistent administration, governed by a rule system based on law (legality), public record, which is the basis for accountability, transparency and equal treatment of citizens (equity).
- Engagement-related: citizens' participation, engagement with the civil society to articulate the public good and facilitate policy development in accordance with liberal democratic principles, deliberation, and 'deeper' democracy.

This framework developed by [27] concerning the public values that can be promoted through e-government has been used for the analysis and evaluation of different kinds of e-government systems and applications, including the application of AI in government [28, 29]. So, in this study we examine the use of ChatGPT in the area of OGD from this public value perspective, by investigating which of the above values (efficiency, services, professionalism and engagement) can be promoted by the use of ChatGPT by OGD users and publishers exploiting the capabilities offered by the former.

2.2 Public Values vis-a-vis OGD

Economic as well as social and political value derivation and innovation via OGD usage is the prime raison d'etre for the implementation of OGD initiatives [16, 17]. As such, public value creation frame encapsulates technical characteristics of OGD initiatives, i.e. system planning and system implementation, as well as people characteristics, i.e. socio-economic status, skills and political development, with the concomitant challenges of citizen familiarity and engagement with the OGD initiatives and the associated legal stipulations [30] as well as the complexity or poor OGD quality, lack of a OGD-supportive management culture or cultural bottlenecks [31].

Given the provisioning of OGD across a range of socio-economic sectors, it is anticipated that the diverse stakeholders, inclusive of the professionals and lay citizens, shall derive value by re-using and harnessing OGD as per their needs and purposes (both social-political and economic) [32]. This is also suggestive of the involvement of a diverse set of stakeholders in the processes of social and economic value co-creation from OGD [33] thereby making this value creation processes more democratic in nature and scope [34]-case in point being the co-engagement of the public and private sector professionals in the OGD value derivation pursuits [35]. Moreover, the lynchpin of such value derivation endeavors lies in the conducive factors pertaining to the linking of granular OGD with congruent as well as non-congruent OGD belonging to the other socio-economic sector, for that matter [36].

2.3 OGD Research Agenda

Since OGD is a relatively recent and novel government activity, and at the same time quite ambitious and promising, aiming to make a strong government contribution to the development of data economy and society, extensive research is required in order to improve its efficiency, effectiveness and in general its maturity, and finally the increase the social and economic value generated from the large amounts of OGD that have been published (which has required a considerable investment). So, there have been several studies aiming to develop a future research agenda for the OGD domain, which are shown in Table 1.

We can see that most of them aim to develop a research agenda concerning OGD in general, while there are some studies aim to develop a more specific research agenda concerning some specific aspects of OGD: its impact on democratic processes [37] and also OGD services quality [19]. Our study aims to contribute to this latter direction: to develop a specific research agenda concerning the exploitation of the ChatGPT application in the OGD domain.

3 Research Methodology

Since our research objective is to investigate a novel research question (for which there is no previous research and knowledge), concerning the positive affordances (capabilities) as well as the negative affordances (issues, e.g. problems, risks, etc.) of ChatGPT in the area of OGD (for both users and publishers of them), we adopted a qualitative app-roach based on structured interviews with experts [41]. Expert opinion is considered as a viable research methodology in cases where the perspectives of experts are warranted for understanding the possibilities of an under-researched or neglected research theme; thus, the experts engage in deliberation and discussion over an issue and their perspec-tives serve as "intellectual bins" for further filtering and analyses. In particular structured interviews were conducted with 12 experts from Universities the authors belonged to or had research collaborations with in the area of OGD (University of the Aegean, Eras-mus University, Gdansk University of Technology) from the domains of management, information systems and business analytics, who had knowledge about OGD on one hand and AI as well as ChatGPT on the other. We believe that such University experts would be a better source of insight concerning the capabilities that the ChatGPT can provide in the area of OGD, as well as relevant problems and risks, than government practitioners in the opening of government data, as the latter might currently have not sufficient knowledge about ChatGPT.

For the present study, the experts were contacted personally via email, which included a brief description of the objectives of our research, explaining that we wanted to elicit their views regarding these research objectives; for the ones who accepted (12 out of 15) to participate in our research an electronic meeting/interview was arranged via skype; all these electronic meetings/interviews were conducted in February 2023. Table 2 sum-marizes the profiles of the interviewees. The following six questions were posed to the experts which concerned the positive affordances (capabilities) of ChatGPT in the area of OGD for their users and publishers (questions A, B, D, E) as well as relevant negative affordances (e.g. possible problems and risks) (questions C and F):

100   E. Loukis et al.

Table 1. Studies for developing OGD-research agenda.

Authors/year	Emphasis	Major pointers for further research
[38]	Development of a taxonomy of OGD research areas and topics	Four main OGD research areas are identified: OGD management and policies, OGD infrastructures, OGD interoperability and OGD usage and value
[37]	Impact of OGD on democratic processes	Systematic literature review with a focus on the impact of OGD initiative across monitorial, deliberative and participatory aspects vis-a-vis government
[39]	Knowledge areas and themes of OGD research are identifies using a co-word analysis and then relevant future research directions are proposed	What opportunities for innovation do open data offer? What business models can be developed through open data? What financial impact do open data have on businesses, and how can this impact be measured? How can open data be applied to improve managerial information systems? How can new educational arenas be developed through open data? How can students develop applications or tools through open data?
[18]	Traces the evolutionary trajectory of OGD research and proposes relevant future research directions	It identities future OGD research directions concerning purpose and benefits of OGD, use of artificial intelligence for creating smartness in OGD, innovation with OGD, theory development - an integral approach of OGD and sustainable OGD initiatives

(continued)

Table 1. (*continued*)

Authors/year	Emphasis	Major pointers for further research
[40]	Systematic literature review of OGD empirical research that identifies six clusters; viz., general/conceptual development (OGD theory); drivers/barriers (OGD antecedents); adoption/usage/implementation (OGD decisions); success/performance/value (OGD outcomes); acceptance/satisfaction/trust in government (OGD impacts), and policies/regulation/law (OGD governance)	Based on the identified research clusters the following future research directions are identified: role of digital intermediaries for closing the OGD demand-supply gap; impact of government activities; status and prospects for economic OGD; specific roles of socio-economic, demographic and cultural characteristics of the economy that spur or hinder OGD implementation; causal linkage between OGD access barriers and the contribution of the digital economy in providing data-based public services; relationship between user-centric OGD initiatives and the customer-centric business models of the intermediaries
[19]	OGD services quality	Dimensions of OGD e-services quality; impact on users' satisfaction, OGD e-services re-use and e-trust; influences of culture; challenges for achieving high OGD e-services quality

A. How do you perceive the efficacy of ChatGPT for Open Government Data (OGD) initiatives?
B. What are the drivers for users' interfacing with ChatGPT with regard to OGD usage?
C. What are the hindrances for users to tap ChatGPT vis-a-vis OGD initiatives?
D. Can ChatGPT help in value creation via OGD? If so, how?
E. How can the government use ChatGPT for OGD publishing?
F. Will ChatGPT be a danger for user privacy while interacting with OGD portals and datasets?

All these electronic meetings/interviews were tape-recorded (with the permission of the interviewees), transcribed and then coded manually by two of the authors separately, using an open coding approach [41]; results were then compared and differences were resolved. Then each of the identified capabilities that ChatGPT can provide in the area of OGD was classified into one of the four categories of public values that can be promoted through the use of ICT in government proposed by the relevant framework of [27] (efficiency-related values, service-related values, professionalism-related and engagement-related). Finally, based on the identified capabilities as well as issues (e.g. problems, risks, etc.) a future research agenda was developed concerning the exploitation of ChatGPT application in the OGD domain.

Table 2. Experts profile/background.

Field of study	Country	Specialty
Information Systems Engineering	Greece	Cybersecurity, Data privacy, Digital forensics, Gamification strategies, Open and linked data ecosystems
Information Systems Engineering	Greece	Data mining, Computer security and reliability, Artificial Intelligence
Business-Society Management	Netherlands	Policy and governance, Planning and decision-making in China, Transport infrastructures, Sustainable urban development
Business Analytics	Poland	Big Data, Computational and Linguistic Analytics, Smart Sustainable Cities

4 Results

Broadly speaking, the experts shared with us their quite interesting perspectives across the capabilities, on the one hand, and the possible downside, on the other hand, vis-a-vis the ChatGPT application in the OGD ecosystem.

4.1 Capabilities

a) The experts pointed out that user engagement with OGD shall be furthered on account of the "open" and easy accessibility of ChatGPT, which can provide to the users substantial assistance in finding the datasets they need (with data about the topic they are interested in), to process them (especially if they are not familiar with data processing tools, as ChatGPT can provide data processing), to draw conclusions from them and in general exploit them either for business purposes (e.g. for developing value added e-services by combining various kinds of open government data and possibly private data as well, for making various business innovations) or for political purposes (for gaining a better and data-based understanding of government actions as well as spending, increasing transparency). Thus, a range of stakeholders, viz., common citizens, private sector entities, journalists, professionals, academia, software developers, and the like, stand to gain from the harnessing of ChatGPT for value derivation and innovation pursuits.

b) Furthermore, the ChatGPT (as it can generate software as well) can provide substantial assistance to programmers for the development of useful applications that are based on OGD, contributing to the generation of more economic and social value from them.

c) Apart from furthering user engagement, OGD awareness may be further bolstered among the potential users-case in point being the essays churned out by the ChatGPT applications with reference to the tutorials, documents, discussion forums, user feedback, data requests, case studies, success stories of value derivation as well as the manner in which OGD might be put to use and even retrieved from the OGD portals. It is anticipated that such essays are more conducive towards developing a more nuanced, comprehensive and enjoyable understanding of the objectives, purposes, applications and utility of OGD per se as well as the technical dimensions related thereto, viz., technical terminology, visualization tools and techniques, searching and discovering OGD, utilizing OGD portal via linkage and/or interoperability, preparation, filtering, analyzing, contributing OGD, for instance.

d) Useful capabilities are provided by the ChatGPT not only to OGD users (or potential users) but also to OGD publishers, the most important of them being the government agencies who open/publish some of their data, in order to acquire valuable insight concerning the OGD needs and preferences of different groups of potential users, to understand better for what kinds and thematic categories of data there is a real demand by citizens and firms, and also to assess the level of awareness about and satisfaction with the data they have already opened. So, ChatGPT can immensely increase the probability of ascertaining the equilibrium between the "demand" and "supply" side of OGD initiatives, which has remained a knotty issue in many contexts. Thus, on the one hand, the ChatGPT application would be helpful in ascertaining the cases where the application has been successful and overwhelming in terms of being responsive to the user queries about OGD, and on the other hand, the negligible or absence of OGD or related information would be an indicator for improvisation of the grey areas by the OGD publishing agencies. Therefore, ChatGPT could assist in the development of better OGD strategies of government agencies, and a better-informed policy making, through a combination of machine and human-derived input.

e) Also, governments can use ChatGPT not only for the design and implementation of their OGD policies and strategies, but also can in their OGD provision portals introduce chatbots backed by the ChatGPT model, which can help with data discovery, recommendations, and better user engagement, as well as with data exploration such as data visualization, insights generation, and suggestions for future potential areas.

Therefore, we can conclude that ChatGPT can provide quite useful capabilities to both OGD users (and potential users) (the above mentioned capabilities a, b and c) and also to OGD publishers (government agencies publishing OGD) (the above mentioned capabilities d and e).

However, some of the experts made interesting remarks, that pertain to the robust technological infrastructures, viz., supervised machine learning and reinforcement learning, on which ChatGPT application rests itself, which are liable to be further improvised with technological breakthroughs in the near future, and, these features are likely to provide glitch-free inferential summaries to the users (as currently definitely there are some mistakes). This is also suggestive of the manner in which customized value-added goods/services might be the resultant of OGD linkage and/or interoperability pursuits. Thus, the stakeholders concerned may get engaged in such value derivation pursuits such that apart from the standalone benefits to be reaped by the ecosystemic entities horizontally and vertically, the collaborative attempts by the public, private and the voluntary sector entities across local, national and international levels are facilitated at the same time. Such inter- and intra- collaborative efforts shall be evidenced across the myriad social, economic, political and legal sectors, for instance.

4.2 Public Values

Wethen analyzed the above identified capabilities that ChatGPT can provide in the area of OGD from a public values perspective, and this led us to the conclusion that they can promote two out of the four types/categories of public values of the framework of [27]: service-related values and professionalism-related.

I) Service-related values: If we view OGD as a service provided by government to the citizens and firms, ChatGPT enables improving the quality of this service, by providing to government insight about the kinds and thematic categories of data that citizens and firms need, which is quite useful for defining their data opening priorities, opening datasets that are really useful, and avoiding wasting valuable financial resources for opening datasets for which there is limited interest and usefulness. One of the experts said: *"The ChatGPT will allow government agencies to identify special needs and preferences of users for data, so that the later can get in a quick and efficient manner the required datasets"*, while another expert mentioned: *"ChatGPT could assist in the prioritization of data categories to be published, as well as the temporal* margin *under which it is optimal (according to customized preferences) to publish certain data"*. Furthermore, ChatGPT enables improving the quality of this OGD provision service with respect to its wider accessibility and use by a much larger numbers of users; indicative for this is the following experts' statement: *"ChatGPT can help with accessibility, efficiency, interactivity, and accuracy of open government data; by leveraging these drivers, ChatGPT can encourage more users to interact with OGD portals or services"*. At the same time ChatGPT will enable users of OGD to visualize and process them easily and rapidly, and draw useful conclusions from them, and finally create more economic value from them; indicative is the following experts' statement: *"New products, services, businesses, jobs, and opportunities can be stimulated by the ChatGPT processing and recommendations concerning the highly valuable dataset"*.

II) Professionalism-related values: The use of ChatGPT in the area of OGD can increase the transparency of government activity and spending, as it enables a much larger number of citizens, journalists, politicians, etc. to find, access and analyze OGD datasets concerning government activity and spending, and draw conclusions from them, easily and rapidly, and this can lead to a higher trust in government; this can also contribute to having political debate of higher quality, with arguments based on real data/evidence (and not on stereotypes and pre-existing biases); indicative of these possible political impacts are the following experts' statements: *"Increasing data understandability and accessibility through the use of ChatGPT can help improve transparency. And in return, trust and confidence in government and other* organizations *by providing greater visibility into their operations and decision-making processes will be increased"* and *"The accessibility of ChatGPT could be one of its most appealing traits to the user. The easy access to the retrieval of knowledge* and *real-time information of any nature, can be an attractive starting point for the user to also use ChatGPT in an OGD context"*.

4.3 Issues

i) With respect to possible privacy violation issues that might be posed by ChatGPT, its developers (OpenAI) claim that it doesn't use any type of private or personal data about individuals until and unless it is publicly available. In the case of OGD, these data usually undergo a strict and careful anonymization before they published. So, it seems that a direct threat is not posed. However, ChatGPT collects data about the sequence of questions and in general the behavior of each registered user, and possibly user's browser data (IP and device information) as well. These personal data, which reflect sensitive attitudes, concerns, interests and sometimes political orientations of future business plans, might be used in inappropriate ways. To mitigate these issues, appropriate measures should be taken to prevent the consent-less transfer, use, or processing of these data.

ii) The ChatGPT has some weaknesses (that might be overcome in the future) in the synthesis of existing information and the development of various kinds of inference, such as summaries and conclusions, so there might be mistakes, which can mislead OGD users (or potential users) with respect to what OGD have been published on topics of user's interest, and/or draw incorrect conclusions from them. This, in combination with the 'black-box' nature of ChatGPT for its users (most of them cannot understand how it works), could scare them away and demotivate them from using it.

iii) In the absence of the requisite regulatory framework for such tools, there are dangers pertaining to cyber-crimes, faulty algorithms, mismatched or biased inferences, misplaced, insufficient, overly generalized, illogical, or culturally-insensitive results.

iv) Linguistic differences across countries might result in algorithmic biases and reinforcement training might be inadequate or inappropriate-for instance, the implications of the etymological differences across languages might be a potential downside of ChatGPT vis-a-vis OGD's understanding and across country comparisons.

v) Semantic issues might pose barriers for ChatGPT to better summarize/analyze OGD.

5 Research Agenda

Based on the above mentioned capabilities and issues described in the previous Sect. 4 we proceeded to the development of a future research agenda concerning the exploitation of ChatGPT in the OGD domain, as this is quite new research topic, so extensive research is required in order to increase its efficiency, effectiveness and maturity in general. The proposed research agenda consists of research areas and specific research topics for each of them that require investigation.

5.1 Research Area I: ChatGPT Application for Furthering OGD Use and Value Generation

– In terms of furthering OGD awareness and use among the potential users, emphasis has been laid on strategic planning and execution by the governments with a personalized and customized target positioning among the target user cohorts [19, 42]. In this vein, harnessing ChatGPT for furthering OGD use and value generation shall serve as a watershed for the users in comprehending the nuances of OGD and the possibilities of value derivation from them, thereby furthering the relevant innovation landscape across numerous socio-economic sectors.

– ChatGPT exploitation by the OGD users hailing from different backgrounds alongside their research and information-seeking behaviors are also important aspects of further research given that the learning-goal orientation is different across the users apart from the personal involvement and perceptions on their occupational performance and social behavior too [14].

– ChatGPT adoption and usage studies vis-a-vis OGD are always a viable line of research across Information Systems theories such that the behavioral intention as well as actual usage and adoption may be gauged across or within cases at individual, group, organizational, regional, country and cultural levels.

– ChatGPT use for processing of data is a very important capability, especially for users who are not familiar with statistics and use of them for data processing as well as drawing conclusions from them; so, it is quite important to investigate to what extent these capabilities are used, and how useful they are for users.

– Also, there are a plethora of research directions springing from the user engagement with ChatGPT vis-a-vis OGD for value creation activities not only with ChatGPT helping out with cues, guidelines, case studies and benchmarked examples for value creation activities by re-using/linking/interoperating OGD [16, 43]. Also, the OGD user would be helping in improvising ChatGPT itself for providing additional features, furthering its user-friendliness or taking into account user privacy while interfacing with ChatGPT functionalities.

5.2 Research Area II: ChatGPT Application for Facilitating/Improving OGD Publishing

– Use of ChatGPT for the development of OGD strategies, for enabling a better understanding about users (or 'potential users') needs and preferences for OGD, as well as about their degree of satisfaction with already opened/published government data (and possibly identify problems and deficiencies of them), and also for enabling the collection of relevant knowledge and experience about opening/publishing government data from other government agencies (of the same country or other countries).

– Use of ChatGPT for developing Tutorials and guides pertaining to the OGD initiatives, in general, and, the country statistics across different indices, data catalogs/sectors or data publishers via ChatGPT may be a potent support mechanism for the government personnel for spearheading the OGD initiatives and this would help in furthering the morale and motivation of the personnel as well.

– Legal and regulatory issues vis-a-vis ChatGPT in terms of OGD applications need to be earmarked with special consideration for individual privacy and security as well as cybercrimes related with impersonation, identity theft, plagiarism, revelation of sensitive content, imprudent behavior, etc.

– Cultural dimensions across local and regional levels cutting across heterogeneous populace are also the potential research areas vis-a-vis ChatGPT invocation for OGD. Furthermore, national comparisons, assessment and evaluation studies, benchmarking, efficacy of ChatGPT for furthering OGD understanding to meet the Society 5.0 and Industry 4.0 as also during the emergency situations like the ones during floods, fires, epidemics, etc. may be considered as viable research pointers.

– Institutionalization mechanisms for furthering user engagement with ChatGPT for better comprehending its utility vis-a-vis OGD need to be analyzed in further research-case in point may be the assessment of the campaign drives, target population, campaign pitch, government incentives, etc.

5.3   Research Area III: The Downside of ChatGPT Application for OGD

Finally, it is necessary to conduct research concerning the downside of the ChatGPT applications vis-a-vis OGD, in order to investigate its possible *dark sides*. This research stream may investigate *possible issues/risks* associated with ethical, privacy and security, technology complexity and technological self-efficacy, addictive behaviors, technology longevity and breakdown on account of systemic failure, etc.; these research pointers may be investigated across individual, group, organizational, national or cultural levels using different research methodologies.

6   Conclusions

The development of the ChatGPT has a great potential to provide quite useful capabilities and benefits for enhancing numerous human activities and economic sectors, and have substantial transformative as well as disruptive effects on them, but the realization of this potential might face significant problems and challenges, and might also pose some threats. These have already started to be researched for some sectors [15], but have not been research for the case of government, despite its high importance for economic and social life.

This study makes a first step towards filling this research gap, focusing on one of the most recently initiated, novel and promising activities of government that aims to contribute to the further development of data economy and society: the opening of large amounts of government data. Using the lenses of 'affordances theory' [22], it investigates the positive affordances (capabilities provided) and the negative affordances (issues posed, such as problems and risks) of ChatGPT in the area of OGD. Furthermore, based on them we proceed to the development of a future research agenda concerning the exploitation of ChatGPT application in the OGD domain. This will allow us to understand the research ramifications of the use of ChatGPT for OGD initiatives from the side of users and publishers. So, our study meets the call for further "multidisciplinary research" with a focus on "enhanced collective cognitive intelligence (human/ICT-enabled) for better governance" [38: 57].

Using a qualitative approach, which is based on a series of interviews with experts, it has been concluded that the use of ChatGPT in the area of OGD can offer significant and highly beneficial capabilities to both OGD users and publishers. From a public value perspective, these capabilities can promote two out of the four main types/categories of public values of the framework of 37: service-related values and professionalism-related values. In particular, with respect to service-related values ChatGPT can improve the

OGD provision service, by enabling government to make it more focused on potential users' needs, and also improve its accessibility and exploitation for the generation of economic and social value. At the same time, the use of ChatGPT in the area of OGD can pose privacy risks, and also can sometime mislead the users, due to its weaknesses in the synthesis of existing information and the development of various kinds of inference, such as summaries and conclusions, which sometimes result in mistakes (though it is expected that these weaknesses will be reduced in future improved versions of the ChatGPT).

Based on the above findings three main future research areas have been identified, which concern the use of ChatGPT for furthering OGD use and value generation, and for facilitating and improving OGD publishing by government, as well as the 'dark sides' of ChatGPT application in the area of OGD. It may be added here that the research areas and topics identified above may be investigated as standalone or integrated too. Besides, the evolution of ChatGPT with time may also lead to different research themes in terms of the efficacious impact and the related challenges vis-a-vis OGD initiatives from the users' and publishers' ends.

Finally, the present study leaves implications on one hand for research and on the other hand for practice and policy-making. With respect to research, it makes a contribution to the limited existing body of knowledge concerning the capabilities and benefits that the ChatGPT can provide to various human activities and economic sectors, which concerns a minimally examined sector with respect to such generative AI applications: the public sector, focusing on one of its most recently emerged and ambitious activity: the opening of government data. With respect to practice, it proposes some useful ways of ChatGPT exploitation by OGD users and publishers, which can improve the economic, social and political value generated by OGD. Our findings indicate that a better strategic blueprint and execution of OGD initiatives may be achieved by government if it takes in account the potential of ChatGPT and the capabilities it can provide. Finally, harnessing ChatGPT evolutionary trajectory would be better witnessed as the users' engagement increases with time thereby prompting the launch of suitable regulatory framework in the near future.

Our study has two main limitations. The first one is that it is dealing with the capabilities provided and the public values that can be promoted, as well as the issues posed, by the use of ChatGPT in one only government activity (that does not belong to the 'core' ones, however it is a very promising one), the opening of government data; so it is necessary to examine the same for the main 'core' government functions and activities (e.g. policy making, welfare, operations, etc. in various thematic domains). The second limitation is that our findings have been based on interviews with experts from Universities (knowledgeable about OGD on one hand and AI as well as ChatGPT on the other); so it is necessary to conduct similar research, based on interviews with government practitioners dealing with opening government data, as well as managers responsible for this (as they gradually gain knowledge about ChatGPT and start thinking about exploiting it in their activities and tasks), or even using Delphi methods.

References

1. Open AI. ChatGPT. https://chat.openai.com/auth/login. Accessed 20 Feb 2023

2. Haque, M.U., Dharmadasa, I., Sworna, Z.T., Rajapakse, R.N., Ahmad, H.: "I think this is most disruptive technology": exploring sentiments of ChatGPT early adopters using Twitter data (2022). https://doi.org/10.48550/arXiv.2212.05856
3. Mashable. ChatGPT. https://mashable.com/category/chatgpt. Accessed 20 Feb 2023
4. Lund, B.D., Wang, T.: Chatting about ChatGPT: how many AI and GPT impact academia and libraries? Library Hi Tech News. https://doi.org/10.1108/LHTN-01-2023-0009 (2023, in press)
5. NBC News. Americans are wary of AI tech like ChatGPT, data shows. https://www.youtube.com/watch?v=rgP6zlP1-OU. Accessed 20 Feb 2023
6. van Dis, E.A.M., Bollen, J., Zuidema, W., van Rooij, R., Bockting, C.L. ChatGPT: five pointers for research. Nature (2023). https://www.nature.com/articles/d41586-023-00288-7
7. CNET. Why we're obsessed with the mind-blowing ChatGPT AI chatbot (2023). https://www.cnet.com/tech/computing/why-were-all-obsessed-with-the-mind-blowing-chatgpt-ai-chatbot/
8. Ventayen, R.J.M.: OpenAI ChatGPT generated results: similarity index of artificial intelligence-based contents. SSRN (2023). https://doi.org/10.2139/ssrn.4332664
9. Aydin, O., Karaarslan, E.: OpenAI ChatGPT generated literature review: digital twin in healthcare. Emerg. Comput. Technol. 2, 22–31 (2022)
10. Choi, J.H., Hickman, K.E., Monahan, A., Scharcz, D.: ChatGPT goes to law school. SSRN. Minnesota Legal Stud. Res. (2023). https://papers.ssrn.com/sol3/papers.cfm?abstract_id=4335905
11. Dowling, M., Lucey, B.: ChatGPT for (finance) research: the Bananarama conjecture. Finance Res. Lett. 103662 (2023)
12. Kirmani, A.R.: Artificial intelligence-enabled science poetry. ACS Energy Lett. 8(1), 574–576 (2023)
13. Pavlik, J.V.: Collaborating with ChatGPT: Considering the implications of generative artificial intelligence for journalism and media education. Journal. Mass Commun. Educ. 78(1), 84–93 (2023)
14. Mhlanga, D.: Open AI In education, the responsible and ethical use of ChatGPT towards lifelong learning. SSRN (2023). https://doi.org/10.2139/ssrn.4354422
15. Dwivedi, Y. K., Kshetri, N., Hughes, L., et al.: So what if ChatGPT wrote it?" Multidisciplinary perspectives on opportunities, challenges and implications of generative conversational AI for research, practice and policy. Int. J. Inf. Manag. 71, 102642 (2023)
16. Jetzek, T., Avital, M., Bjorn-Andersen, N.: Data-driven innovation through open government data. J. Theor. Appl. Electron. Commer. Res. 9(2), 100–120 (2014)
17. Wirtz, B.W., Birkmeyer, S.: Open government: origin, development, and conceptual perspectives. Int. J. Public Adm. 38(5), 381–396 (2015)
18. Gao, Y., Janssen, M., Zhang, C.: Understanding the evolution of open government data research: towards open data sustainability and smartness. Int. Rev. Adm. Sci. (2021, in press). https://doi.org/10.1177/00208523211009955
19. Alexopoulos, C., Saxena, S., Janssen, M., Rizun, N. Whither the need and motivation for open government data (OGD) promotional strategies? Digit. Policy, Regul. Gov. (2023, in press). https://doi.org/10.1108/DPRG-07-2022-0078
20. Gasco-Hernandez, M., Martin, E.G., Reggi, L., Pyo, S., Luna-Reyes, L.F.: Promoting the use of open government data: cases of training and engagement. Gov. Inf. Q. 35(2), 233–242 (2018)
21. Moore, M.: Public value as the focus of strategy. Aust. J. Public Adm. 53(3), 296–303 (1994)
22. Pozzi, G., Pigni, F., Vitari, C.: Affordance theory in the IS discipline: a review and synthesis of the literature. In: Proceedings of Twentieth Americas Conference on Information Systems (AMCIS), Savannah, USA (2014)

23. Gao, Y., Janssen, M.: Generating value from government data using AI: an exploratory study. In: Viale Pereira, G., et al. (eds.) EGOV 2020. LNCS, vol. 12219, pp. 319–331. Springer, Cham (2020). https://doi.org/10.1007/978-3-030-57599-1_24
24. Alford, J., Hughes, O.: Public value pragmatism as the next phase of public management. Am. Rev. Public Adm. **38**(2), 130–148 (2008)
25. Williams, I., Shearer, H.: Appraising public value: past, present and futures. Public Adm. **89**(4), 1367–1384 (2011)
26. Cordella, A., Bonina, C.: A public value perspective for ICT enabled public sector reforms: a theoretical reflection. Gov. Inf. Q. **29**(4), 512–520 (2012)
27. Rose, J., Persson, J.S., Heeager, L.T., Irani, Z.: Managing e-government: value positions and relationships. Inf. Syst. J. **25**(5), 531–571 (2015)
28. Toll, D., Lindgren, I., Melin, U., Madsen, C.: Values, benefits, considerations and risks of AI in government: a study of AI policy documents in Sweden. eJ. eDemocr. Open Gov. **12**(1), 40–60
29. Chen, Y.C., Ahn, M., Wang, Y.-F.: Artificial intelligence and public values: value impacts and governance in the public sector. Sustainability **15**, 4796 (2023)
30. Reyes, L.F.L., Chun, S.A.: Open government and public participation: issues and challenges in creating public value. Inf. Polity **17**(2), 77–81 (2012)
31. Wiedenhoft, G.C., Matheus, R., Saxena, S., Alexopoulos, C.: Barriers towards open government data value co-creation: an empirical investigation. Electron. J. Inf. Syst. Dev. Ctries e12270 (2023, in press)
32. Ubaldi, B.: Open government data: towards empirical analysis of open government data initiatives. OECD Working Papers on Public Governance, 22, OECD Publishing, Paris (2013). https://doi.org/10.1787/5k46bj4f03s7-en
33. Zeleti, F.A., Ojo, A., Curry, E.: Exploring the economic value of open government data. Gov. Inf. Q. **33**(3), 535–551 (2016)
34. Harrison, T.M., et al.: Open government and e-government: democratic challenges from a public value perspective. In: 12th Annual International Digital Government Research Conference: Digital Government Innovation in Challenging Times, pp. 245–253 (2011)
35. McBride, K., Aavik, G., Toots, M., Kalvet, T., Krimmer, R.: How does open government data driven co-creation occur? Six factors and a 'perfect storm'; insights from Chicago's food inspection forecasting model. Gov. Inf. Q. **36**(1), 88–97 (2019)
36. Attard, J., Orlandi, F., Auer, S.: Value creation on open government data. In: 49th Hawaii International Conference on System Sciences (HICSS), Koloa, HI, USA, pp. 2605–2614 (2016)
37. Ruijer, E.H.J.M., Martinius, E.: Researching the democratic impact of open government data: a systematic literature review. Inf. Polity **1**, 1–18 (2017)
38. Charalabidis, Y., Alexopoulos, C., Euripidis, L.: A taxonomy of open government data research areas and topics. J. Organ. Comput. Electron. Commer. **26**(1–2), 41–63 (2016)
39. Corrales-Garay, D., Ortiz-de-Urbina-Criado, M., Mora-Valentín, E.M.: Knowledge areas, themes and future research on open data: a co-word analysis. Gov. Inf. Q. **36**(1), 77–87 (2019)
40. Wirtz, B.W., Weyerer, J.C., Becker, M., Muller, W.M.: Open government data: a systematic literature review of empirical research. Electron. Mark. **32**, 2381–2404 (2022)
41. Maylor, H., Blackmon, K., Huemann, M.: Researching Business and Management, 2nd edn. Palgrave – McMillan Education, UK (2017)
42. Chokki, A.P., Simonofski, A., Frenay, B., Vanderose, B.: Open government data awareness: eliciting citizens' requirements for application design. Transform. Gov.: People Process Policy **16**(4), 377–390 (2022)
43. Shadbolt, N., et al.: Linked open government data: lessons from Data.gov.uk. IEEE Intell. Syst. **27**(3), 16–24 (2012)

The Human Likeness of Government Chatbots – An Empirical Study from Norwegian Municipalities

Asbjørn Følstad[1]([⊠]) [iD], Anna Grøndahl Larsen[1] [iD], and Nina Bjerkreim-Hanssen[2] [iD]

[1] SINTEF, Forskningsveien 1, 0373 Oslo, Norway
{asf,anna.g.larsen}@sintef.no
[2] Prokom, Karl Johans Gate 37B, 0162 Oslo, Norway
nina.bjerkreim@prokom.no

Abstract. While chatbots represent a potentially useful supplement to government information and service provision, transparency requirements imply the need to make sure that this technology is not confused with human support. However, there is a knowledge gap concerning whether and how government chatbots indeed represent a risk of such confusion, in spite of their resemblance with human conversation. To address this gap, we have conducted a study of a Norwegian municipality chatbot including interviews with 16 chatbot users and 18 municipality representatives, as well as analysis of > 2600 citizen dialogues. Interviews with citizen and municipality representatives suggested that citizens typically understood well the chatbot capabilities and limitations, though municipality representatives reported on some examples of humanizing the chatbot in its early phases of deployment. Dialogue analyses indicated that citizens have a markedly utilitarian style in their communication with the chatbot, suggesting limited anthropomorphizing of the chatbot.

Keywords: Chatbot · government · transparency · human-likeness

1 Introduction

Government service provision increasingly make use of chatbots to facilitate service delivery for efficiency gains and improved availability [25]. Chatbots are software agents which provide users with access to information and services through natural language interaction conducted in the form of dialogue [11]. Chatbots are considered an intuitive way of interacting with computer systems, due to the resemblance of the chatbot dialogue with that of a conversation with a fellow human being [17], which potentially lowers barriers to interaction and engagement. Furthermore, the human likeness resulting from a chatbot's use of natural language interaction and resemblance of human conversation, has been suggested as conductive to improved user experience [19] and to reflect positively on users' perceptions of a service provider [4].

I. Lindgren et al. (Eds.): EGOV 2023, LNCS 14130, pp. 111–127, 2023.
https://doi.org/10.1007/978-3-031-41138-0_8

However, humanlike chatbots may also entail negative implications for users and service providers. Human likeness may induce erroneous expectations concerning chatbot capabilities and limitations and lead to unwanted interaction patterns or strategic user behavior [29]. Chatbot human likeness may also lead to uncertainty or deception, where users become uncertain with regard to the chatbot's status as an automated agent or even erroneously believe they are indeed interacting with a human [24]. Curbing such undesirable uncertainty and deception concerning the machine status of a chatbot is important with regards to transparency requirements for trustworthy AI systems [8, 18]. Furthermore, the proposed European Commission AI Act, specifically details such transparency requirements on chatbot providers [10, 33].

In this context, knowledge is needed on how citizens perceive government chatbots. Specifically concerning their perceptions of chatbot human likeness and how this may impact chatbot interaction and, by extension, government service provision. However, while current research has investigated determinants and implications of chatbot human likeness [e.g., 4, 15, 19], there is a lack of knowledge on whether and how such human likeness perceptions impact user interactions with government chatbots.

In response to this gap in knowledge, we have conducted a study to explore whether and how users interact with and perceive government chatbots as humanlike service providers. The study addressed a chatbot for Norwegian municipalities and included three method components. First, we interviewed 16 citizens on their experiences with the chatbot. Second, we interviewed 18 government representatives with a role in maintaining the chatbot. Third, we analyzed > 2600 chatbot dialogues between citizens and a government chatbot.

The study contributes needed knowledge on human likeness and transparency in government chatbots. The interviews with municipality representatives and users contribute knowledge on how the government chatbot is perceived and the implication of such perceptions on behavior and service outcomes. The dialogue analysis contributes insight into users' communication style, indicative of markedly utilitarian goal-orientation.

2 Background

2.1 Government Chatbots

Chatbots are about to become a commonplace channel of government provision of information and services. Already in 2020, a survey identified a substantial appearance of chatbots as part of European government service provision [9]. Currently, chatbots are among the most frequently deployed AI applications in the public sector [36].

Within government service provision, chatbots have been taken up for a broad range of service sectors or areas such as health [31] and social services [37], and by broader service providers such as cities [35] and municipalities [1]. During the pandemic, the uptake of government chatbots saw a marked boost as part of pandemic response [3].

The recent surge in government chatbots seems motivated by beneficial aspects of the technology both for government agencies and for citizens [35]. On the side of the government agencies, chatbots can enable reduced employee workload, and lowered service delivery cost, while improving users' service experiences through providing a more personalized and efficient service delivery [25]. Chatbots have also been explored as a means to strengthen citizen participation and engagement in government [32].

Government chatbots typically are implemented as intent-based solutions, where machine learning is applied to predict user intents from users' free text requests and then provide needed information and services on the basis of predefined content [23]. Most government chatbots are set up as what Makasi et al. [25] refer to as chatbots for service triage, that is, they provide generic information and access to services without adaptation to a user profile.

There is a growing body of knowledge on how users experience government chatbots. Makasi et al. [26], in an interview study with users and designers of government chatbots, found that such chatbots were perceived to enable increased effectiveness and efficiency in service provision, while potentially also strengthening accessibility and ease-of-use for government services. Abbas et al. [1], in an interview study with municipality chatbot users, found users to appreciate the navigation support provided by the chatbot and its potential for simplifying access to government information.

2.2 Chatbot Human Likeness and Its Implications

While users typically have been found to have utilitarian motivations for chatbot use, such as efficiency and convenience [5], chatbots may also potentially improve user experience due to their human-likeness in appearance and communication style [19]. In consequence, there has been substantial industry and research interest in the benefits and limitations of chatbot human likeness [27], and the factors that may determine users' tendencies to *anthropomorphize* chatbots, that is, a tendency to imbue the behavior of an agent with motivations, intention, or emotions reflecting human likeness [7].

While chatbots arguably resemble human communication through their natural language processing capabilities and dialogical interaction [17], chatbot human likeness may be manipulated through the inclusion of humanlike *cues* in the chatbot design [4], that is, design features intended to strengthen users' anthropomorphizing the chatbot. Such design features may concern the visual appearance of the chatbot, such as providing a humanlike avatar, the presentation of the chatbot, such as having it present itself with a human name, the communication style of the chatbot, such as presenting the information in an informal tone of voice, and the communication intelligence of the chatbot, such as its capabilities to mimic a skilled human conversationalist.

Strengthening human likeness in chatbots has been shown to entail a range of potentially beneficial effects for service provision. For example, Go and Sundar [15], in an experimental study of chatbots in the e-commerce domain, found manipulation of human likeness to be associated with changes in user satisfaction and perceived chatbot expertise. Furthermore, Jain et al. [20], in a study of chatbot interaction design, found users to desire chatbot interactions that resemble conversations with humans.

Chatbot human likeness may also hold implications for user behavior and chatbot interaction outcomes. Adam et al. [2], in an experimental study in the e-commerce domain, found increased human likeness in the chatbot to be associated with increased user compliance during interaction. Park et al. [28], in an experimental study, found chatbot human likeness to impact willingness to donate to a fundraising initiative. Hence, chatbot providers may utilize humanlike design cues in chatbots to impact user behavior in a direction considered desirable from the point of view of the provider.

2.3 Chatbot Transparency Requirements

While human likeness may be desired by chatbot users [20], the potential for humanlike design cues in chatbots to unduly impact user perceptions and behavior have caused concern [27], e.g., regarding users' potential confusion of whether they interact with a chatbot or a human [30]. Such confusion could bias user decision-making during chatbot use or induce erroneous user beliefs concerning chatbot capabilities.

For AI-systems, transparency is considered a key requirement in ethics guidelines [18], including that of the EC high level expert group on trustworthy AI [8]. In the latter, transparency is defined so as to concern data, systems, and AI business models, and it is particularly noted that users should "be aware that they are interacting with an AI system, and must be informed of the system's capabilities and limitations".

For chatbots, this requirement implies a requirement on the part of the service provider to ensure that users are properly informed that they are interacting with a chatbot. This requirement has been formalized in the proposed European AI Act [10]. Here, AI service providers are obliged to ensure that users are aware that they are interacting with an AI-system and not a human service person. Chatbots are explicitly mentioned with regards to this transparency obligation.

3   Research Questions

In consequence of the potential implications of chatbot human likeness to user perceptions and behavior, as well as the transparency requirements for chatbots, it is important to know how users perceive and interact with government chatbots and, specifically, whether and how these perceptions and interactions suggest that users anthropomorphize such chatbots. In response to this knowledge need, we explicated the following research question:

RQ1: How do users and service providers consider chatbots as humanlike interfaces to government information and service?

Furthermore, since chatbot human-likeness may impact user behavior, it is also important to explore whether and how users' interactions with government chatbots suggest a tendency to anthropomorphize such chatbots. In response to this, we asked:

RQ2: How do users interact with government chatbots? And does such interaction suggest a tendency to anthropomorphize such chatbots?

4   Method

4.1 Research Design

In response to the research questions, we set up a three-component research design consisting of two qualitative interview series and an analysis of chatbot dialogues. In the first interview series, we interviewed users of the chatbot. In the second series, we interviewed government representatives with responsibilities for chatbot implementations. In the dialogue analysis, we reviewed > 2600 citizen chatbot dialogues.

Through this multi-method approach, we were able to gain rich insight into the research questions, combining the perspectives of users and government representatives with data from actual chatbot interactions.

4.2 The Case: A Municipality Chatbot

The study was conducted in the context of a specific chatbot: the municipality chatbot 'Kommune-Kari'. This chatbot is provided for service triage rather than service negotiation [25], and is available to citizens in about 100 Norwegian municipalities; about one third of the Norwegian population. The chatbot has been operational since 2017 and engaged in several hundred thousand dialogues in 2022.

The chatbot provides access to municipality information and services through a text-based chat user interface. It is provided by Prokom and based on the boost.ai conversational platform. The chatbot is implemented as an intent-based solution [23] leveraging a machine learning model to predict users' intents based on their textual input. Following intent prediction, the chatbot provides a predefined response through a rule-based approach. This response typically includes options for follow-up or refinement of the answer through button or free text interaction. The chatbot is set up for anonymous use. It does not have access to a user profile, but provides the users with general information about the municipality and its services. Information is provided either directly through the chatbot or by links to relevant sources on the municipality website or elsewhere.

Of particular interest to this study, the chatbot is presented through a human-like cartoon avatar resembling a female face (Fig. 1). When activated, the chatbot presents itself in a welcome message greeting the user, states its own name (Kari – a common Norwegian female name), explains that it is a chatbot, encourages the users to phrase their requests in a concise manner, and reminds the user that the service is for anonymous use only. The chatbot avatar, name and presentation was decided by the chatbot provider following an analysis of current practice. The chatbot is arguably a good case for exploring the research questions. First, it has been operational for several years and is a much-used chatbot. Furthermore, it is used for citizen interaction with a relatively large set of government actors and broad range of information seeking. The large number of municipalities in which it is in use allows for variation in how it is implemented and perceived. The broad range of information and services provided through a municipality, spanning, e.g., healthcare, education, renovation, planning and construction, as well as sport and leisure, implies that the chatbot is used for a broad range of citizen requests – which is valuable when exploring user perceptions and interactions.

4.3 Interviews with Citizens and Municipality Representatives

Participants and Recruitment. The study included 16 citizen participants and 18 municipality representatives.

Citizen participants were recruited from four municipalities where the chatbot is implemented, four from each municipality. The municipalities varied in size and regional location to ensure breadth in the data collected. The citizen participants were recruited by a panel provider, Norstat; eight females and eight males in the age range of 21–68 years (median: 47,5). To ensure recent experience with the chatbot, all citizen participants

Fig. 1. Municipality chatbot welcome message. Translated from Norwegian.

were asked to use the chatbot at least twice prior to the interview. Most participants (11) reported also to have used the chatbot prior to this preparatory use.

The municipality representatives were recruited through the network of the chatbot service provider. The municipalities represented 18 different municipalities or municipality constellations of various sizes and regional locations. All participants held roles in the municipality with responsibility for the chatbot. They were mainly organized as part of the communication team (12) or the citizen service centre (5). Most municipalities had been involved in the implementation of the municipality chatbot, hence holding substantial experience on its use in the municipality.

Interview Procedure. The interviews were semi-structured and conducted individually with the participants, in total 34 interview sessions. The interview guide was set up to address ethical and societal aspects of chatbot implementation in government, and focused on perceptions and implications of chatbot human-likeness as one of several topics. In this paper we focus specifically on the participants' reflections on the human-likeness of the chatbot. Analyses and findings focusing on other aspects of the interview datasets, will be presented elsewhere [16]. The interviews were conducted by video link, through Microsoft Teams. The interviews with the citizen participants lasted 20–40 min. The interviews with the municipality representatives each lasted about 1 h.

Analysis Process. The interviews were audio recorded and transcribed. The transcripts were analyzed through thematic analysis following the guidelines of Braun and Clarke [6]. To maintain quality in analysis, the citizen interviews were analyzed separately from the interviews with the municipality representatives. The analysis of the interviews with the citizens was led by the second author, the analysis of the interviews with the municipality representatives was led by the first author.

4.4 Dialogue Analysis

An analysis of citizen dialogues with the chatbot was conducted to understand how users interact with government chatbots. The analysis was conducted as part of a larger research effort to understand user interaction with government chatbots through the lens of an analysis framework for customer service. This larger research effort has been published elsewhere [12]. In the study presented here, we combine the dialogue analysis with findings from interviews data to shed light on whether users' interactions with a government chatbot suggest a tendency to anthropomorphize such chatbots.

Dialogue Sampling. Dialogues between citizens and the chatbot were sampled from six different municipalities. The municipalities varied in size and regional location, as well as how they had chosen to implement the chatbot, so as to enable substantial variation in chatbot users and interactions.

Data were sampled over a two-month period. For sufficient breadth in request topics and communication styles, we sampled between 4–500 dialogues from each municipality, 2663 in total. The sampling was conducted by the chatbot service provider in line with the chatbot terms of use and following confidentiality agreements with the researchers. To ensure dialogue anonymity, all sampled dialogues were checked for person data by personnel at the chatbot service provider prior to analysis.

Analysis Process. The dialogues were first analyzed from perspective of dialogue descriptives, including user request characteristics, e.g., message brevity and predicted user intent, and dialogue characteristics, such as the number of dialogue turns and indications of understandability issues.

Furthermore, and key to this study, the dialogues were analyzed to identify the *users' communication style* in the interactions, that is, their tendency to engage in utilitarian or socially oriented interactions [14]. Dialogues with a socially oriented communication style more closely resemble dialogues to be expected between human conversationalists, with use of politeness markers and first- or second person pronouns. Dialogues with a utilitarian communication style lack one or both of these characteristics.

4.5 Research Ethics

The presented research has been conducted in line with ethical guidelines for research involving human subjects. Interviews were voluntary and only conducted following informed consent, and upon approval of the research organization data protection officer. Chatbot dialogue analyses were conducted in line with terms of use and only following manual checks of user anonymity.

5 Results

In the results section, we first present findings from the interviews with citizens, followed by findings from the interviews with municipality representatives, and the findings from the dialogue analysis.

5.1 Results from the Interviews with Citizens

Chatbot Considered Efficient Complementary Channel. In the citizen interviews, the participants described themselves as highly efficiency-seeking and goal-oriented in their interactions with the chatbot. Such efficiency concerned fast response (16) and navigational support (11). The participants typically also noted that they expect the chatbot to be able to help them with simple, general requests rather than complex and personal questions.

> *I think of it as a more advanced search engine. That can help you to sort out what you need to know. You may ask general questions that everyone would ask [...]. And then you get answers without having to search the website forever* (C1).

In line with this, the participants typically described the chatbot as and additional self-service channel and noted that they appreciated the opportunity for self-service provided by the municipality's digital channels (14). The participants, furthermore, reported on not being worried that digitalization will remove their opportunity to get in touch with humans in the municipality. Rather than a substitute for human communication, the participants considered the chatbot as an additional public service channel, allowing them to get swift responses to general requests around the clock. Participants indeed underlined the importance of available human resources when needed, but they reported to prefer self-service for general requests (14). The following quote illustrates this perspective:

> *Preferably a chat service, because using the phone you have to wait for them to answer the phone, and they don't always respond, [...]. So, I find that the chat service is better. You get a response much faster* (C5).

Humanlike Chatbot Features May Be Pleasant but Not Important. While the chatbot is presented through a humanlike avatar image, a humanlike name, and communicate in an informal style, all participants noted that such humanlike features of the chatbot have little or no implications for their use of it. Some noted that the humanlike features did *not* matter to them whatsoever whereas others said they appreciated such features. The latter participants noted that this made talking to the chatbot more personal and that they found it somewhat "fun" that the chatbot has humanlike features. The following quote illustrates this latter perspective:

> *I wouldn't say it is important to me [...]. But I thought some of the features were fun. That* Kommune-Kari *is a character, and when I did a search on football and sports clubs it said, "football is fun!" with a football emoji. There are some fun features like that [...] it has some personality to it* (C6).

Yet, although some reported to appreciate humanlike features in the chatbot, all participants argued that these had little or no bearing on their assessment or use of the chatbot.

Machine Nature of Chatbot Clear but Interaction May Improve on Experience. All participants expressed that they found it clear that they were interacting with a chatbot and not a human service provider, and they were aware that the chatbot provides general rather than personalised responses to inquiries. The participants further found it relatively easy to understand how to interact with the chatbot. Yet, participants also pointed out that the chatbots' usefulness had increased over time, as they had become more experienced chatbot users, and better understood how to pose questions (*i.e.*, shorter sentences and/or single words). To illustrate, one participant noted that:

> *I tried some longer sentences, and then I realised that it didn't work, and then I started using very short sentences, and sometimes just one word* (C6).

This may suggest that the human likeness and the communication style of the chatbot initially may lead users to ask longer and more complicated questions. Participants did not express this as a drawback, though, noting that they found it easy to figure out how to use the chatbot.

The participants also pointed out that they know someone, or assumed that there may be someone, who may be challenged to use a chatbot (10). One concern among these participants was that other users might fail to understand the chatbot interaction format, where the chatbot input should be presented in a concise manner. That is, they foresaw that some users might use the same interaction strategies that they would when interacting with a human, leading to a suboptimal outcome. Related to this, one participant made specific note that the chatbot did not understand them when asking a difficult question and suggested that this may indicate difficulties for users struggling with reading or writing. Another noted as follows:

> *For chatbots you must be as short and concise as possible [...]. But I helped my mother-in-law, and she had written [a very long sentence]* (C13).

5.2 Results from the Interviews with Municipality Representatives

In the interviews with the municipality representatives, the participants reported on their perceptions of citizen interactions with the municipality chatbot. Their reports were based on their experience from reviewing interaction logs with the chatbot and on feedback from citizens – for example through the citizen service centre.

Chatbot for Efficient Interactions with the Municipality. The participants described the chatbot as a useful navigation support for users (13), that may simplify access to the municipality information and services (11). The participants noted that they considered the chatbot to be particularly useful for general information requests (13), while chatbot responses for precise or personal questions could be insufficient (9).

> *We find the chatbot to answer quite well, with some important limitations. Specific questions and the like do not work that well [...] But very good at general questions. Short, general questions work well.* (M3)

Machine Nature of Chatbot Clear to Most Users. When asked about implications of the chatbot human likeness, the participants considered this to be limited. Several of the participants pointed out that users typically understand what a chatbot is and which opportunities and limitations it entails (7).

Most understand that it is a chatbot. This is actually very clearly explained. That it is not a human. Even though it may appear like one. (M9)

The participants also noted that the chatbot was clearly different from a human service provider also in terms of its relative lack of flexibility (8). While a human service provider may show high levels of flexibility in adapting to the requests and messages of a user, the chatbot does not have such conversational intelligence. Hence, the risk of confusing the chatbot for a human was seen as limited.

I believe it is pretty clear that it is not a person, that is, the dialogue is very structured and it includes new links, new buttons, as you ask new questions. (M15)

Some of the participants also made note of the chatbot being clear on its limitations (4). For example, by asking for questions to be provided in short sentences, or by clarifying to the user in cases of insufficient prediction confidence regarding user intents.

Some may not Understand Chatbot Interaction or Capabilities. While the participants argued that most users understand that the chatbot is a machine and that they should interact with it differently than with a human service person, they also typically noted that some users might misunderstand.

Most participants reported to have observed that some users interact with the chatbot in a manner suggesting that they do not understand how to ask questions to a chatbot in a productive manner (13). This could, for example, be that users were observed to not ask direct questions, but instead presented their inquiries over multiple questions; something that is challenging for the chatbot to interpret correctly.

There are some who ask the chatbot as if they believe they are about to chat with a real human. This can be seen in the way people ask questions and follow up, can be seen sometimes. (M8)

Some participants suggested that chatbot human likeness may lead users to get false expectations regarding chatbot capabilities. For example, they may believe that the chatbot has higher conversational flexibility than it actually does, or they may ask questions at a level of complexity that the chatbot cannot answer.

I find that sometimes they think of her as a human [...] they write long sentences [...] then the chatbot does not work and it becomes a source of irritation (M14)

Signs of Increasing Maturity in Users. While not all users may understand the chatbot interaction or capabilities, some participants noted what they saw as an increased maturity in user interaction with the chatbot over time (4). As an example of this, some noted a reduction in playful or exploratory chatbot interactions and a general tendency to fewer users engaging with the chatbot as if it were a human.

Before we experienced perhaps someone believed it was a real person behind it. This we could see in the questions coming in. But I do not see this much anymore. (M4)

Further Reflections on Implications of Human Likeness. Finally, reflecting further on implications of human likeness in the chatbot, some participants also noted that chatbot human likeness could potentially lead to changes in how citizens engaged with the municipality information and services. Some participants noted that a humanlike chatbot may entail that users see the service interaction as more personal and – thereby – more attractive (4).

The dialogue interaction I believe is beneficial. To feel that you talk to someone, this is a human need basically. (M12)

Others noted that chatbot human likeness may reduce citizens threshold for getting in touch with the municipality, because it is easier to ask questions in an interaction format resembling that of human conversation (3).

I believe that the threshold for getting in touch is a little lower [...] We see that it is used for very much now (M9)

Some participants also noted that the humanlike character of a chatbot may motivate users to ask more personal or specific questions than they would e.g. in a search interface. This may be beneficial as responses may be more relevant to the user, but it may also entail a challenge in cases where the user asks questions at a level of specificity to which the chatbot cannot provide an answer without knowledge of the user context.

We see that there may also be very personal questions in the chatbot, and hard to answer [these] in a general way (M2)

5.3 Results from the Dialogue Analysis

In total, 2663 dialogues were included in the sample from the six municipalities. The dialogues were about equally distributed across the six municipalities involved in the analysis, ranging between 430 and 475 dialogues for each municipality.

The dialogues reflected the breadth of the information and services offered by the municipalities, including general healthcare (18%), COVID-19 (12%), general municipality information (8%), leisure (6%), applications and case processing (4%), contact information (4%), water and sewage (4%), education (3%), and renovation (3).

The dialogues provided insight into the characteristics of the user requests, the length of dialogues, and the users' communication style. We detail these in the following.

User Requests. The user requests to the chatbot were typically brief and concise. In the analyzed dialogues, the initial requests had a median length of 19 characters (25th percentile = 12; 75th percentile = 36). The vast majority of such initial requests (92%) were 60 characters or less, despite the maximum message length in the chatbot was set to 110 characters.

This implies that the user requests to the chatbot typically were highly pointed, with little detail or contextual explanations. Examples of such pointed request formulations include the following: "Where is covid test", "Registration for vaccination", "Dirty water in the tap", "When is the boating license course", and "Summer school".

Dialogue Characteristics. The citizen dialogues with the chatbot were typically brief. Most chatbot dialogues (77%) included only one user message, 15% included two messages, 8% included three or more. Moreover, the dialogue analysis identified that the users typically received useful help (65%), either by information included in the chatbot message or through information or services linked to by the chatbot. Furthermore, only 3% of the dialogues were found to indicate understandability issues such as failure to formulate requests interpretable to the chatbot or failure to make use of interaction mechanisms.

In the following, a typical conversation with only one user message is presented:

- *User:* "Status for vaccination in [municipality name]"
- *Chatbot:* "We provide the latest updates on vaccination status here: [link]"

Users' Communication Style. Dialogues were categorized as having a socially oriented communication style if including social markers such as greetings and use of first- or second person pronouns. Otherwise, the user dialogues were categorized as having a utilitarian communication style. In the analysis, we found an overwhelming proportion of the dialogues to be in a utilitarian style (95%), whereas only a small minority (5%) were in a socially oriented style.

To illustrate the two communication styles of the users, we include below examples of user requests in utilitarian and socially oriented styles respectively:

- *Utilitarian style user request:* "Status for vaccination in [municipality]"
- *Socially oriented style user request:* " Hi. Where in the municipality may I take a rapid test?"

While the low proportion of dialogues with a socially oriented communication style was consistent with the brevity or user requests and short dialogues, it was a surprise as previous research on customer service chatbots has found higher prevalence of socially oriented dialogues [14].

6 Discussion

In the following, we first discuss citizen and municipality perspectives on chatbots with regard to human likeness. Second, we discuss citizen behavior during chatbot interactions and how this may shed light on any anthropomorphizing of the chatbot. Finally, we address implications for theory and practice and reflect on limitations and future research.

6.1 Citizen and Municipality Representative Considerations of Human Likeness

Our findings suggest that citizens typically have an adequate understanding of chatbot capabilities and limitations. Specifically, it is interesting that the citizens were found to hold adequate expectations on chatbot capabilities, since previous research has suggested that chatbot human likeness may induce inflated capability expectations [27]. While the chatbot in this study had marked humanlike characteristics [4, 15] in visual appearance and communication style, with a humanlike avatar, human name, and informal tone of voice, the users did not find this confusing or problematic. Rather, the users argued that the chatbot human likeness was not important for their use of it, and a low rate of understandability issues was found in the chatbot dialogues.

Chatbot human likeness was, however, suggested by some of the citizen participants to have some pleasurable aspects. This is in line with previous findings in the context of customer service, where users have been found to appreciate chatbot human likeness even though humanlike characteristics are not considered key [13]. The relative lack of perceived importance of human likeness in government chatbots may be due to the highly goal-oriented user of such chatbots [1], which is in line also with the participants accentuation of potential efficiency benefits in the chatbot. Hence, while human likeness may be highly important in other chatbots [20], such as for example companion chatbots [34], this characteristic do not seem to be important to government chatbots.

However, the study participants noted that some users may be confused by the chatbot human likeness, shown for example in terms of inadequate strategies for chatbot interaction. Such confusion is reminiscent of what has been found in research on voice-based agents where inexperienced users fail to understand how to interact with a conversational user interface [22]. Possibly, confusion due to chatbot human likeness may be caused by lack of experience. This assumption is supported by our participants noting increased maturity over time for chatbot interactions.

6.2 Reflections of Anthropomorphizing in Citizens' Chatbot Dialogues?

Citizen and municipality representative reports on chatbot human likeness typically not confusing its users, are corroborated by our findings from the dialogue analysis. In these analyses, the concise requests of users and the typically short dialogues suggest that users are highly goal oriented and that their mode of interaction is one of efficiency. This use of chatbots aligns with previous findings, where utilitarian motivation has been identified as users' main motivation to engage with chatbots [5]. Furthermore, efficient interactions are in accordance with the aim of chatbots for service triage [25], where the chatbot is used to identify and access needed information and services.

Furthermore, the utilitarian orientation reflected in the chatbot dialogues are indicative of chatbot human likeness not imposing on users a tendency towards anthropomorphism. On the contrary, the prevalence of socially oriented interactions – found in only 5% of the analyzed dialogues – was lower than in a similar analysis of chatbots for customer service [14]. Also, the social orientation in users' communication style was surprisingly low contrasted with observations in other domains, such as conversational search [21].

In conclusion, the brevity in user requests, efficiency in dialogues, and prevalence of a utilitarian communication style all point in the same direction as the findings from the citizen and municipality representative interviews. In spite of humanlike design cues in the studied chatbot, users perceive and engage with this in a way that suggests a concern for efficiency and effectiveness, rather than one of anthropomorphizing.

6.3 Implications for Theory and Practice

The study findings hold several implications for theory and practice. We note the following implications to be of particular interest for theory:

- **Chatbot objective may determine user perceptions and behavior:** Much previous work has addressed how chatbot design may impact user perceptions and behavior [e.g., 19]. Our findings complement this, by suggesting that also chatbot objective – e.g., to provide government service triage [25] – may potentially determine user perceptions and communication style. This is in particular seen when contrasting our findings on communication style to previous work [e.g. 14, 21].
- **Humanlike chatbot design cues may have limited impact on user behavior:** Previous work has shown that user perceptions and behavior may be determined by humanlike design cues in the chatbot [e.g., 4, 15]. Our findings indicate that while humanlike design cues concerning chatbot presentation and appearance may hold implications for user perceptions, they may have limited impact on user behavior, e.g., in a government chatbot for service triage.

For practice, we see the following implications to be of particular interest:

- **A chatbot for government service triage may comply with transparency requirements:** Chatbots are expected to comply with transparency requirements, as per ethics guidelines [18] and regulatory frameworks [33], that is, it should be evident to users that they are interacting with a chatbot. Our findings suggest that complying with such requirements is indeed feasible for chatbots for service triage.
- **Some users may nevertheless fail to understand the chatbot:** In spite of the machine nature of a chatbot typically being clear to users, the conversational interaction may lead to some confusion, in particular for inexperienced users. Design of government chatbots should take into consideration how to also support users who are inexperienced with chatbots so as to avoid confusion.

6.4 Limitations and Future Research

While the presented study provides needed knowledge on citizen perceptions of human likeness in chatbots, and their limited anthropomorphizing of such chatbots, the study has important limitations. These limitations suggest paths for future research.

First, while the study employs different methods for data collection and analysis, it only involves one chatbot, the municipality chatbot 'Kommune-Kari'. While this chatbot is implemented in a large number of municipalities, it far from covers chatbots at the level of all government services and organizations. Hence, the findings from this study would benefit from being complemented with findings from other chatbots.

Second, the study is limited to a single country, Norway, which may limit findings in terms of the characteristics of citizen population and structure of government. We foresee future studies replicating our approach in other countries or regions.

Third, the study only addresses user perceptions and interactions with a government chatbot for service triage, following the typology of Makasi et al. [25]. While this chatbot type arguably is most commonly deployed in current government service provision, this is likely to change in the future. Both in terms of the increasing availability of chatbots for personalized support, and also the emerging availability of chatbots based on large language models with improved capabilities for humanlike interaction. There will arguably be a need for continued research into the implications of government chatbot human likeness as more advanced technology is taken up in government chatbots and chatbot capabilities for humanlike and personalized interactions change. We hope our study is a useful initial contribution to this important area of research.

Acknowledgement. The study was supported by EC H2020 grant no. 101004594, ETAPAS.

References

1. Abbas, N., Følstad, A., Bjørkli, C.A.: Chatbots as part of digital government service provision– a user perspective. In: Følstad, A., et al. (eds.) CONVERSATIONS 2022. LNCS, vol. 13815, pp. 66–82. Springer, Cham (2022). https://doi.org/10.1007/978-3-031-25581-6_5
2. Adam, M., Wessel, M., Benlian, A.: AI-based chatbots in customer service and their effects on user compliance. Electron. Mark. **31**(2), 427–445 (2020). https://doi.org/10.1007/s12525-020-00414-7
3. Amiri, P., Karahanna, E.: Chatbot use cases in the Covid-19 public health response. J. Am. Med. Inform. Assoc. **29**(5), 1000–1010 (2022)
4. Araujo, T.: Living up to the chatbot hype: the influence of anthropomorphic design cues and communicative agency framing on conversational agent and company perceptions. Comput. Hum. Behav. **85**, 183–189 (2018)
5. Brandtzaeg, P.B., Følstad, A.: Why people use chatbots. In: Kompatsiaris, I., Cave, J., Satsiou, A., Carle, G., Passani, A., Kontopoulos, E., Diplaris, S., McMillan, D. (eds.) INSCI 2017. LNCS, vol. 10673, pp. 377–392. Springer, Cham (2017). https://doi.org/10.1007/978-3-319-70284-1_30
6. Braun, V., Clarke, V.: Using thematic analysis in psychology. Qual. Res. Psychol. **3**(2), 77–101 (2006)
7. Epley, N., Waytz, A., Cacioppo, J.T.: On seeing human: a three-factor theory of anthropomorphism. Psychol. Rev. **114**(4), 864–886 (2007)
8. European Commission: Ethics guidelines for trustworthy AI (2019). https://digital-strategy.ec.europa.eu/en/library/ethics-guidelines-trustworthy-ai
9. European Commission: AI watch - artificial intelligence in public services. Technical report (2020). https://publications.jrc.ec.europa.eu/repository/handle/JRC120399
10. European Commission: Proposal for a regulation on a European approach for artificial intelligence (No. COM(2021) 206 Final) (2021). https://digital-strategy.ec.europa.eu/en/library/proposal-regulation-laying-down-harmonised-rules-artificial-intelligence
11. Følstad, A., et al.: Future directions for chatbot research: an interdisciplinary research agenda. Computing **103**(12), 2915–2942 (2021). https://doi.org/10.1007/s00607-021-01016-7
12. Følstad, A., Bjerkreim-Hanssen, N.: User interactions with a municipality chatbot – lessons learnt from dialogue analysis. Int. J. Hum.-Comput. Interact. (2023). https://doi.org/10.1080/10447318.2023.2238355
13. Følstad, A., Skjuve, M.: Chatbots for customer service: user experience and motivation. In: Proceedings of Conversational User Interfaces - CUI 2019, pp. 1–9. ACM, New York (2019)
14. Følstad, A., Taylor, C.: Investigating the user experience of customer service chatbot interaction: a framework for qualitative analysis of chatbot dialogues. Qual. User Exp. **6**(1), 1–17 (2021). https://doi.org/10.1007/s41233-021-00046-5

15. Go, E., Sundar, S.S.: Humanizing chatbots: the effects of visual, identity and conversational cues on humanness perceptions. Comput. Hum. Behav. **97**, 304–316 (2019)
16. Grøndahl Larsen, A., Følstad, A.: The impact of chatbots on public service provision – a qualitative interview study with citizens and public service providers (2023). Research Paper Submitted for Review
17. Hall, E.: Conversation Design. A Book Apart, New York (2018)
18. Hagendorff, T.: The ethics of AI ethics: an evaluation of guidelines. Mind. Mach. **30**(1), 99–120 (2020)
19. Haugeland, I.K.F., Følstad, A., Taylor, C., Bjørkli, C.A.: Understanding the user experience of customer service chatbots: an experimental study of chatbot interaction design. Int. J. Hum. Comput. Stud. **161**, 102788 (2022)
20. Jain, M., Kumar, P., Kota, R., Patel, S.N.: Evaluating and informing the design of chatbots. In: Proceedings Designing Interactive Systems – DIS 2018, pp. 895–906. ACM, New York (2018)
21. Liao, Q.V., Geyer, W., Muller, M., Khazaen, Y.: Conversational interfaces for information search. In: Fu, W.T., van Oostendorp, H. (eds.) Understanding and Improving Information Search. HIS, pp. 267–287. Springer, Cham (2020). https://doi.org/10.1007/978-3-030-38825-6_13
22. Luger, E., Sellen, A.: "Like having a really bad PA" the gulf between user expectation and experience of conversational agents. In: Proceedings of CHI 2016, pp. 5286–5297. ACM, New York (2016)
23. Luo, B., Lau, R.Y., Li, C., Si, Y.W.: A critical review of state-of-the-art chatbot designs and applications. Wiley Interdiscip. Rev.: Data Min. Knowl. Discov. **12**(1), e1434 (2022)
24. Maedche, A., et al.: AI-based digital assistants: opportunities, threats, and research perspectives. Bus. Inf. Syst. Eng. **61**, 535–544 (2019)
25. Makasi, T., Nili, A., Desouza, K.C., Tate, M.: A typology of chatbots in public service delivery. IEEE Softw. **39**(3), 58–66 (2021)
26. Makasi, T., Nili, A., Desouza, K., Tate, M.: Public service values and chatbots in the public sector: reconciling designer efforts and user expectations. In: Proceedings of the Hawaii International Conference on System Sciences. University of Hawaii, Manoa (2022)
27. Murtarelli, G., Gregory, A., Romenti, S.: A conversation-based perspective for shaping ethical human–machine interactions: the particular challenge of chatbots. J. Bus. Res. **129**, 927–935 (2021)
28. Park, G., Yim, M.C., Chung, J., Lee, S.: Effect of AI chatbot empathy and identity disclosure on willingness to donate: the mediation of humanness and social presence. Behav. Inf. Technol. (2022). https://doi.org/10.1080/0144929X.2022.2105746
29. Rapp, A., Curti, L., Boldi, A.: The human side of human-chatbot interaction: a systematic literature review of ten years of research on text-based chatbots. Int. J. Hum. Comput. Stud. **151**, 102630 (2021)
30. Ruane, E., Birhane, A., Ventresque, A.: Conversational AI: social and ethical considerations. In: Proceedings of AICS 2019, pp. 104–115. DBLP, Dagstuhl (2019)
31. Sagstad, M.H., Morken, N.H., Lund, A., Dingsør, L.J., Nilsen, A.B.V., Sorbye, L.M.: Quantitative user data from a chatbot developed for women with gestational diabetes mellitus: observational study. JMIR Form. Res. **6**(4), e28091 (2022)
32. Segura-Tinoco, A., Holgado-Sánchez, A., Cantador, I., Cortés-Cediel, M.E., Bolívar, M.P.R.: A conversational agent for argument-driven e-participation. In: Proceedings of DG.O 2022, pp. 191–205. ACM, New York (2022)
33. Schaake, M.: The European Commission's Artificial Intelligence Act. Policy Brief, Stanford HAI (2021)
34. Skjuve, M., Følstad, A., Fostervold, K.I., Brandtzaeg, P.B.: A longitudinal study of human–chatbot relationships. Int. J. Hum. Comput. Stud. **168**, 102903 (2022)

35. van Noordt, C., Misuraca, G.: New wine in old bottles: Chatbots in government. In: Panagiotopoulos, P., Edelmann, N., Glassey, O., Misuraca, G., Parycek, P., Lampoltshammer, T., Re, B. (eds.) ePart 2019. LNCS, vol. 11686, pp. 49–59. Springer, Cham (2019). https://doi.org/10.1007/978-3-030-27397-2_5
36. van Noordt, C., Misuraca, G.: Artificial intelligence for the public sector: results of landscaping the use of AI in government across the European Union. Gov. Inf. Q. **39**(3), 101714 (2022)
37. Verne, G.B., Steinstø, T., Simonsen, L., Bratteteig, T.: How can I help you? A chatbot's answers to citizens' information needs. Scand. J. Inf. Syst. **34**(2), 7 (2022)

Automatic Bill Recommendation
for Statehouse Journalists

Michelle Perkonigg[1]([✉])[ID], Foaad Khosmood[2][ID], and Christian Gütl[1][ID]

[1] Graz University of Technology, Rechbauerstraße 12, 8010 Graz, Austria
`michelle.perkonigg@student.tugraz.at, c.guetl@tugraz.at`
[2] Institute for Advanced Technology and Public Policy, California Polytechnic State
University, San Luis Obispo, CA 93407, USA
`foaad@calpoly.edu`
`https://iatpp.calpoly.edu/`

Abstract. AI4Reporters is a project designed to produce automated
electronic tip sheets for news reporters covering the statehouses (state
level legislatures) in the United States. The project aims to capture the
most important information that occurred in a bill discussion to allow
reporters to quickly decide if they want to pursue a story on the subject. In this paper, we present, discuss and evaluate a module for the tip
sheets that is designed to recommend additional bills to investigate for
the reporter that receives the tip sheet. Similar in concept to movie recommendations, this module is designed to find other bills with their own
meetings and discussions, that are most relevant to the discussion captured in the given tip sheet. Specifically we present similarity algorithms
along three dimensions that our investigation suggests are distinct reasons for journalists to be interested in a recommendation. These include
similarity in content, individuals or geographical locations. We validate
the system by fielding a user study of 29 subjects for hour-long surveys
resulting in 870 decisions being captured. We find that between 63.4%
and 82.8% of the human selections are in agreement with our system's
recommendations.

Keywords: digital government · legislatures · bill recommendation ·
artificial intelligence

1 Introduction and Motivation

AI4Reporters [25] is a project aiming to create AI-powered, automated tip sheets
generated for reporters that are otherwise unable to cover the legislature in person. A kind of algorithmic journalism [23], AI4Reporters processes the transcript
and video of a legislative hearing and then generates interesting facts, anomalies
(such as unusual voting patterns), pull quotes, speaker lists, backgrounders and
other useful features in form of a web-accessible interactive tip sheet [25] or a full
news story [27]. Most tip sheets are generated per bill discussion (a subdivision
of a committee hearing focused on discussing and voting on a single bill). The

© IFIP International Federation for Information Processing 2023
Published by Springer Nature Switzerland AG 2023
I. Lindgren et al. (Eds.): EGOV 2023, LNCS 14130, pp. 128–143, 2023.
https://doi.org/10.1007/978-3-031-41138-0_9

idea is this information could provide a tip for a reporter to help them make a decision to pursue a story on the subject.

If the reporter does decide to investigate further, the tip sheet provides many references to useful background information, each linked to verifiable, primary sources for complete transparency and traceability. One of the main elements that is always necessary for such investigations is related or similar bills that are either going through the legislative cycle or have already completed it. In this paper, we present, discuss and evaluate a bill recommendation module for the tip sheets designed to surface a few relevant bills for the reporter to consider. The bulk of our work described here is development and evaluation of an algorithm for this recommendation system. The proposed algorithm is a first suggestion to be adapted by community due to the novelty of the whole system in the application domain.

1.1   Motivation

In this section we present the motivation for the parent project and also for the present work which is a recommendation module for tip sheets.

AI4Reporters. Unlike the US Congress, European Parliament and numerous national legislatures, written proceedings are not officially produced or maintained by US state governments, effectively cutting off meaningful access to vast majority of citizens and researchers [8]. While the governments do publish bill titles, bill texts, committee memberships, and vote outcomes, there is a considerable gap in knowledge in the absence of written, searchable records of spoken language.

Until about the first decade of the twenty first century, the aforementioned gap was mostly addressed in the form of news reporting. While most ordinary citizens in a state like California, could not travel to Sacramento and would not have direct access to legislative information, they would still get the highlights from their hometown newspaper, radio station or TV station. A vibrant cadre of journalists representing many cities, towns and rural areas in the state, used to flood the buildings of the California legislature, be present at hearings, and make sure developments important to their readership would be covered.

A number of factors disrupted the local news economy which in the past twenty years resulted in severe decline in state and local reporting. Among them are competition from internet news sources and media corporate consolidation leading to many traditional regional news media organizations being purchased by large corporations that prioritize national over local coverage. Analysis of the factors leading to the changing media landscape and the reasons for them are beyond the scope of this paper. We only emphasize the present reality of severely diminished news coverage at the statehouse [19,25,39].

The notable absence of media covering the legislature can have some devastating consequences for citizens in a democratic society, even at the state level. Some of the most important legislation with global impact is discussed and debated there. California alone is on the verge of becoming the world's fourth largest economy with \$3.63 Trillion GDP [44]. Not only are citizens deprived of valuable information, but they have decreasing opportunity to hold lawmakers accountable for their actions and statements. Meanwhile, well-resourced and powerful interests who can afford to hire lobbyists have better access and more influence with the legislatures.

Thus the overarching motivation of AI4Reporters is to strengthen local and state media and to help increase accountability and transparency by democratizing access to legislative proceedings [25].

1.2 Recommender Module

When reporters use electronic tip sheets to keep informed on the events of a committee bill discussion, they will at some point decide if there is reason to pursue a news story with a more complete explanation. In order to prepare for that story, or even when trying to decide on writing it, the reporters need to examine other, similar, discussions to be able to get a better context. The recommender module is designed to give them a quick list of one to three references for examination.

Reporters can of course dive deeper and familiarise themselves with a much larger set of bills for their background investigation. They may decide to read every single bill passed in that committee or all the previous bills authored by a certain individual. We aim to provide only the first step, a quick glance on what else could be relevant.

One of the main questions that arises early in this work is "by what criteria should relevance be measured"? Based on discussions with area experts on the project and observations of the state legislative proceedings in California, we identify three main dimensions to this notion of "relevance": people, locations and issues. These are based on typical assignments for a reporter. For example, a local reporter may be primarily interested in their representative or bills mentioning their locale and thus would find recommendations of bills involving the same individuals or geographical entities compelling. Similarly, a reporter may be following an important issue and thus would be open to recommendations of other bills discussing similar issues.

We further present three scoring systems as means to automatically measure each dimension, breaking down each score into components derivable from the given corpus. Our hypothesis is that bills selected based on our system will match user expectations of a good recommendation to a significant degree. We test the system with a user study and generally find that study subjects agree with our algorithms in each of the three areas by majorities of 63.4% (locations), 75.2% (people) and 82.8% (content). See Fig. 4.

2 Background and Related Work

In the domain of legislature and legislative proceedings there is a broad range of different research directions to be considered from prediction of votes on legislators [7], over the prediction of bill survival [45] to supporting the drafting phase of a bill [1], to fully producing articles automatically about a hearing [27].

Due to this kind of support reporters can spent less time crawling through the huge amount of available data and defining relevant facts [25]. Focusing on this data, the documents and the contained language have to be processed which requires the field of Natural Language Processing (NLP) to come into action, along with machine learning and artificial intelligence. The aim is to give computing units the ability to communicate in a human manner, such that natural language can be processed and analyzed correctly and therefore enable a human-like response or behaviour involving semantic appropriateness [4].

NLP pipelines often involve several preliminary or pre-processing stages, such as lemmatization, stemming, tokenization, part-of-speech tagging and entity recognition combined with document clustering [28], semantic analysis [37], supervised machine learning and many more in a broad application area.

2.1 Legislative Analysis

Researchers have explored predicting votes in legislatures. [22] presented a method for that prediction using an ideal point topic model. Therefore historical legislative voting data and bill texts were used to conduct topic modeling on the bill text and determine an ideal point for every legislator to finally calculate the prediction using the model. [24] focused on predicting votes in the U.S. on topic level, also based on using an ideal point estimation for every topic. [9] did it at the state level (California).

Another direction of research is to predict bill survival implying the likelihood of a bill to become a law [7,45].

Another area of interest is the support of individuals in different phases of the legislative proceedings. Those supporting methods can be performed for better understanding of legislation. Within this field, [1] presented a compliance assessment tool for EU legislation that delivers descriptions of legal terms, soft-obligations, exceptions and related legislation to a legislation of interest.

Another supporting system is Quick Check introduced by [43]. Quick Check recommends relevant cases to a legal issue given by a user by applying different methodologies for extracting document structure, determining potentially relevant cases and ranking to present the most relevant cases.

Still in the area of supporting and providing legislative data, [32] shifted their focus on the storage of this information, suggesting, based on the Belgian legislature, approaches for process automaton to improve timeliness and availability of legislative data.

2.2 Digital Democracy and AI4Reporters

Digital Democracy [8], a project launched by The Institute for Advanced Technology and Public Policy at California Polytechnic State University aims at filling the gap of providing valuable and comprehensible information for citizens as mentioned in the citation above.

One of the main challenges in government transparency in the United States is the availability of proceedings at the state legislatures. US state governments are republics with very similar structure to the federal government. But compared to the national legislature, the state legislatures, such as those in California and Texas, are less studied and less transparent. For example there are no official transcripts of discussions in US state legislatures [36].

The AI4Reporters project, as the title of the project already indicates, uses artificial intelligence that processes data from different sources amongst which is the legislative database populated by Digital Democracy, extracts facts and finally shows it in a readable and well structured way, such that reporters can use this information for their report [25].

As part of the quality legislative database are bill texts, which are the formulated ideas that can become law. This type of text follows a simple shape as demonstrated in Fig. 1 [13]. The parts included in the database of the Digital Democracy project are:

- **The bill ID** is a unique identification for the bill in the session year. It is composed by the type (AB - Assembly Bill, SB - Senate Bill, etc.) and a unique number for that session year.
- **The bill title** gives a short statement of what the bill is about.
- **The bill author** lists all authors and co-authors of the bill.
- **The bill status** describes the current status of the bill. This can either be proposed, introduced, amended assembly, amended senate, enrolled or chaptered.
- **The bill digest** presents a short summary of the bill.
- **The bill text** contains detailed information on the bill content.

The length of such bills can vary tremendously, starting with a small bill where only few sentences are necessary for description (see [11]) going up to bills that consists of several pages (see [12]), that outline and explain the bill, its limitations and its influences in detail.

2.3   Recommender Systems

Nowadays recommendation systems are widely used. For example, Amazon recommending books based on shared interest with other users or Netflix recommending movies and series by predicting ratings for a movie or series [38]. The general problem faced by this systems is the pure overload of information that is still increasing with time. Therefore, limited and carefully selected potentially interesting information is presented to the user based on different underlying recommendation techniques [15].

Basically recommender systems are divided into the two most common categories: content-based and collaborative filtering. Those two are often extended by other typical categories, some of them listed and explained below.

Fig. 1. Preview and structure of a bill (Adapted from: [11]).

Collaborative Filtering. Collaborative filtering generates recommendations by matching the users interests and preferences and with information gathered from other users and their preferences. Therefore, this type of recommendation highlights the necessity of available data implying the dependency on the collaboration of users [5]. Collaborative filtering can further be subdivided into user-based and item-based. User based collaborative filtering searches for similarities between users to recommend new items, while item-based is based on similarity between new items and items contained in the users historical data [30]. Context information can also be employed and integrated into a collaborative filtering technique, allowing the system to provide different recommendations in different situations [17].

Content-Based Filtering. Content-based filtering focuses on historical information of the user (e.g. purchases) and the description of items to generate recommendations [33]. The general approach of content-based filtering is to create a user profile by defining the preferences through analyzing behaviour and personal data. This user profile is then matched with information about the items to filter out the best matching one [30].

Other Kinds of Filtering. Demographic filtering considers demographic data of a user and exploits the attributes of demographic categories of users or items to provide suggestions [6]. [3] analyzed different approaches to profile users. The presented approaches are categorized into unified (mixed, categorical and fuzzy) and isolated (cascaded and single attribute) approaches depending on how the attributes are combined, each of them considering age, gender and occupation as demographic attributes.

In contrast to collaborative and content-based filtering, this approach does not rely on collected historical preference data of the user.

Knowledge-based filtering recommends items with the help of a knowledge base that forms information about users and items. Ontologies are often used to represent information in a structured way, capturing concepts and relations of objects in the ontology [41]. [2] proposed a filtering technique using an ontology that is updated dynamically with new information about users and items.

Hybrid filtering is a combination of different techniques to achieve better results and face each others limitations and problems [10]. [46] verified through the conducted study that a combination of collaborative filtering and demographic filtering (gender, nationality and age) can improve results in the application area of music recommendations.

Application Domains. Recommendation system are employed in many different areas [30] to support users by providing a selection of filtered information. Some of the relevant examples include E-Commerce [20, 26], E-Resources focuses on recommending shared content like videos [29], music [16] and documents [43], Digital Libraries [14], E-Government [18, 42].

3   Bill Recommendation System

The bill recommendation system is meant to work as a component of those tip sheets which focus on a single bill discussion in the legislature. It produces a number of other similar bills that may be of interest to the reader. Due to the novelty of the application domain, the general concept of the recommendation system is designed based on the insights given by a domain expert and therefore represents a first approach to be adapted in future. Three types of similarity are considered, and thus up to three different recommendations can be made. These are: geographical entities, participating individuals and bill content. For each type of similarity, the system recommends a bill most similar to the one under review. See system architecture in Fig. 2.

3.1   Recommendation Based on Geographical Entities

Recommendations based on extracted geographical entities focus on delivering results that talk about the same geographical location or places and therefore, draw a connection between discussed bills. For this purpose the state of a bill and geographical locations mentioned in the bill text are considered and weighted, such that bills introduced in the same state are prioritized. As soon as geographical entities are extracted, validation thereof is conducted using a geocoding python library [21] to reduce false positively tagged entities. Equation 1 presents the used formula to determine geographical similarity, in which $locations_{BillX}$ is a set of validated geographical entities extracted from the specific Bill X and $state_{BillX}$ holds the US state where Bill X is presented.

$$score_{geo} = score_{state} * 0.3 + \frac{|locations_{BillA} \cap locations_{BillB}|}{|locations_{BillA} \cup locations_{BillB}|} * 0.7,$$

$$\text{with } score_{state} = \begin{cases} 1, & \text{if } state_{BillA} == state_{BillB} \\ 0, & \text{otherwise} \end{cases} \tag{1}$$

3.2   Recommendation Based on Individuals

The second recommendation type focuses on participating individuals. The basic idea of this recommendation type relies on the assumption of a shared interest between the reader of a certain bill and the participating groups of people and individuals in this bills' life-cycle. We consider the author of a bill, the speakers during all the bill discussions, the affiliations of the speakers and the organizations mentioned in the bill content. Every extracted entity is validated by checking its entry in the legislative database. Moreover, extracting and validating this data allows us to apply a weighted distribution which we derive experimentally. In the final score shown in Eq. 2, $author_{BillX}$ holds if the two bills share the same author, weighted at 20% of overall importance. The next term, $speakers_{BillX}$, is a measure of mutual speakers present in both bill discussions and is also weighted at 20%. $affiliations_{BillX}$ is similarly a measure of mutual speaker affiliations, weighted at 30%. Finally, $organizations_{BillX}$ represents a measure of mutual organizations mentioned in the discussion. also weighted at 30%.

$$score_{individuals} = score_{author} * 0.2 + \frac{|speakers_{BillA} \cap speakers_{BillB}|}{|speakers_{BillA} \cup speakers_{BillB}|} * 0.2$$

$$+ \frac{|affiliations_{BillA} \cap affiliations_{BillB}|}{|affiliations_{BillA} \cup affiliations_{BillB}|} * 0.3$$

$$+ \frac{|organizations_{BillA} \cap organizations_{BillB}|}{|organizations_{BillA} \cup organizations_{BillB}|} * 0.3, \tag{2}$$

$$\text{with } score_{author} = \begin{cases} 1, & \text{if } author_{BillA} == author_{BillB} \\ 0, & \text{otherwise} \end{cases}$$

3.3   Recommendation Based on Bill Content

The last type of recommendation is based on the content, outputting a reference bill that shares some similarity with the bill of interest in their contents. Therefore, the similarity graph introduced by [40] is used, which is basically a bidirectional weighted graph connecting words and sentences to each other relying on their relations retrieved from the lexical database WordNet [31]. To determine similarity a bill has to be linked to the graph appropriately. The graph is then exploited in two ways, contributing to two different scores that are then combined to retrieve the final score for content recommendations. First score exploits the structure of the graph in combination with using the Levenshtein Distance [35] to get a rather fast result for determining bill title similarity. Exploiting the structure, without considering the weight and defining a maximum depth allows us to retrieve only semantically close nodes from the graph. In Eq. 3 $nodes_{TitleX}$ represents this set of extracted nodes for the title of Bill X. The second score ($score_{text}$) uses the similarity calculation as proposed by [40] exploiting the linkages and their weights of the graph, by performing a breadth first search to finally get a similarity score for two bill contents. Hereby $Bill\ A \xleftarrow{all\ paths} Bill\ B$ of Eq. 3 refers to the extraction of all paths in the similarity graph going from Bill A to Bill B having a predefined minimum weight and maximum depth. Final score then is composed by the sum of the equally weighted similarity scores of bill title and bill content as shown in Eq. 3.

$$score_{content} = \frac{1}{2} * (\frac{100 - LevenshteinDistance(Title\ A, Title\ B)}{100}) * 0.5$$

$$+ \frac{|nodes_{TitleA} \cap nodes_{TitleB}|}{|nodes_{TitleA} \cup nodes_{TitleB}|} * 0.5) + \frac{1}{2} * score_{text},$$

$$\text{with } score_{text} = \qquad (3)$$

$$min(\alpha, \frac{\sum Bill\ A \xleftarrow{all\ paths} Bill\ B + \sum Bill\ B \xleftarrow{all\ paths} Bill\ A}{2}),$$

$$\text{where } 0 < \alpha \leq 1$$

3.4 Development

On implementation side, the bill recommendation system is built in a modular way, allowing easy modification but also extension of new recommendation types.

Since journalism is a rapid business that requires the bill recommendation system to be as efficient as possible, a set of well-defined constraints and steps to enhance system performance are incorporated. Potential recommendations are restricted to bills of the same session year and bills having the same main committee, reducing the number of similarity determinations to enhance performance. Further for content recommendations, an additional constraint is given that the title must share some minimal similarity to be considered for computing the full content similarity. We also use domain specific stop word list excluded from similarity consideration.

The system consists of three components (see Fig. 2). For performance reasons, the component 'Similarity Graph' is generating and storing the graph only once and is not to be updated unless the underlying information for graph construction changes. The component 'Content Scores' runs every night calculating

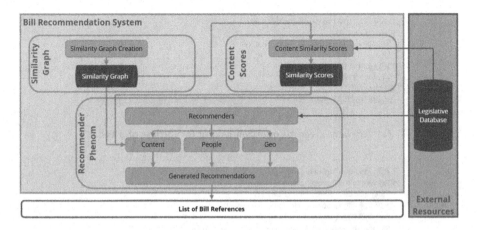

Fig. 2. Conceptual Architecture of the bill recommendation system consisting of three components: Similarity Graph, Content Scores and Recommendation Phenom.

similarity scores for content between bills and lastly the component 'Recommender System' generating scores for a specific bill of interest on demand.

4   User Study

The purpose of the user study is to see if users agree with our systems recommendations and further to see if the underlying recommendation types make intuitive sense to the users.

We use the paid online distributed research participant recruitment service Prolific [34], and choose to restrict participants to those located in California who have completed secondary education. The location restriction is realistic for a target audience for such a tool and increases chances the study subjects have familiarity with bill content, locations and individuals.

After a brief opt-in user study informed consent and explanation, the survey consisted of ten pages of content questions. Each page began by asking the user to follow a hyperlink and read a given bill of interest. After this, they were asked to read three other bills as recommendations for someone who was interested in the first bill. The user was asked to read each of those bills, and then to select between two choices of "this a good recommendation" or "this is a bad recommendation", and provide an explanation as to why they answered the way they did.

Furthermore, two control questions were asked on each page to make sure the users were paying attention: they were asked to type in the author of the bill of interest, and its title in free-form response questions. Those survey returns that did not correctly answer these questions were dismissed. Figure 3 provides an overview of the answers to the control questions.

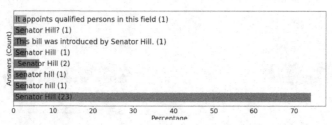

(a) Answers given to question asking for author of a bill.

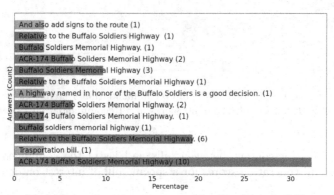

(b) Answers given to question asking for title of a bill.

Fig. 3. Example accepted answers to the two control questions injected into the user study are highlighted in green, the orange answers were subject to rejection. (Color figure online)

The users had no prior information about how the recommendations were selected. In reality, one of the three recommendations was completely random. Another was generated by our system based on one of the similarity measures. The third recommendation was either random or system generated. In this way, either one out of three or two out of three recommendations were random such that the user couldn't intuit that a majority of recommendations are "good" or "bad" per bill of interest. The survey guaranteed exactly half the overall recommendations shown to a user to be random, and the other half system generated, equally distributed among the three different similarity measures.

The data, bills and transcriptions used for this study are from the Digital Democracy project [8] only considering bills from the California legislature 2015–2018 which aligns with the restriction set for distribution. Running the study resulted in valid answers from 29 out of 31 participants each of them having to rate 30 presented recommendations for 10 bills of interest, consequently 870 decisions were collected. The study is estimated to take an hour, highly depending on the speed of reading of the study participants.

5   Results

Overall, we collected 523 (60.1%) 'yes' answers and 347 (39.9%) 'no' answers, thus slightly more than 60% of the recommendations were considered as good ones. Diving into more detail, dividing the ratings into their source of recommendation generation (see Fig. 4), it can be seen that for ratings of random recommendation there are mixed opinions among the participants, as expected.

Moving towards the recommendations produced by the proposed bill recommendation system, a positive trend can be seen. Content based recommendations with 82.8% good ratings are outperforming individual based ones having 75.2% and geographical information based ones with 63.4%. For system generated recommendations there's almost a 2:1 consensus with the user subjects on all three variants.

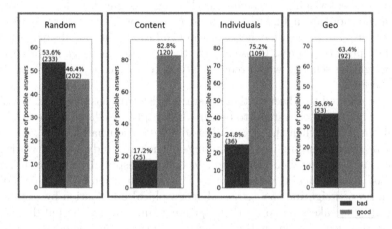

Fig. 4. Breakdown of boolean answers given to the recommendations to be rated in the survey based on their source of generation: random, content based, based on individuals or based on geographical information.

Evaluation of the follow-up short text answers, all of which were coded by the authors, shows that content based recommendations are always recognized as such, due to the answers drawing content-related connections between the two bills. Further investigation into the results conveys the impression that content is the first place to look for similarity of two bills.

With this study we show that the proposed system outputs a relevant but limited set of recommendations with respect to a bill of interest, providing a new source of information to be considered for reporters, with a major advantage that the exact reason for the recommendation can be published alongside it for reader consideration.

6   Conclusion

Proposing a bill recommendation system having a quality legislative database as data source and reporters as target audience is a challenging task, keeping in mind the steady growth of data and the fast business of journalism. With this system a list of related bills for a given bill of interest is presented, that share some sort of similarity, either regarding geographic information, participating individuals or content. Our user study shows the proposed system outperforms randomly presented recommendations significantly. Evaluation of the system-generated recommendations shows that content-based recommendations perform best, followed by recommendations based on involving individuals and those based on extracted geographical information. Further investigation indicates that content is the most important factor when looking for similarity between two bills.

The applied weighting schemes used in our scoring for all three types of recommendation are a first contribution to the community, derived from the provided insights given by experts of the California state legislature active on the AI4Reporters project. Consequently there is the necessity for adaption of those weighting schema, which requires access to a specific group of population to be studied.

An automated tip sheet system for state legislature has never existed before and there are no other systems to benchmark against. We hope to do future field evaluations if and when this proposal is adopted by journalists.

Future work emerging from the findings of the user study point towards more sophisticated and detailed calculation techniques, especially for the individual based and geographical information based recommendation types. This could be in the form of weighting the extracted geographical information by distance, or weighting of speakers based on their speaking time during the bill discussions, but first this needs to be analyzed. However, future work includes analysis for the extension with additional recommendation types, worth to include, while not overpopulating the tip sheet.

References

1. Agarwal, S., Steyskal, S., Antunovic, F., Kirrane, S.: Legislative compliance assessment: framework, model and GDPR instantiation. In: Medina, M., Mitrakas, A., Rannenberg, K., Schweighofer, E., Tsouroulas, N. (eds.) APF 2018. LNCS, vol. 11079, pp. 131–149. Springer, Cham (2018). https://doi.org/10.1007/978-3-030-02547-2_8
2. Alaa El-deen Ahmed, R., Fernández-Veiga, M., Gawich, M.: Neural collaborative filtering with ontologies for integrated recommendation systems. Sensors **22**(2) (2022). https://doi.org/10.3390/s22020700. https://www.mdpi.com/1424-8220/22/2/700
3. Al-Shamri, M.Y.H.: User profiling approaches for demographic recommender systems. Knowl.-Based Syst. **100**, 175–187 (2016). https://doi.org/10.1016/j.knosys.2016.03.006. https://www.sciencedirect.com/science/article/pii/S0950705116001192

4. Allen, J.F.: Natural Language Processing, pp. 1218–1222. Wiley, GBR (2003)
5. Ansari, A., Essegaier, S., Kohli, R.: Internet recommendation systems. J. Mark. Res. **37**(3), 363–375 (2000). https://doi.org/10.1509/jmkr.37.3.363.18779
6. Arce-Cardenas, S., Fajardo-Delgado, D., Álvarez-Carmona, M.Á., Ramírez-Silva, J.P.: A tourist recommendation system: a study case in Mexico. In: Batyrshin, I., Gelbukh, A., Sidorov, G. (eds.) MICAI 2021. LNCS (LNAI), vol. 13068, pp. 184–195. Springer, Cham (2021). https://doi.org/10.1007/978-3-030-89820-5_15
7. Bari, A., Brower, W., Davidson, C.: Using artificial intelligence to predict legislative votes in the united states congress. In: 2021 IEEE 6th International Conference on Big Data Analytics (ICBDA), pp. 56–60 (2021). https://doi.org/10.1109/ICBDA51983.2021.9403106
8. Blakeslee, S., et al.: Digital democracy project: making government more transparent one video at a time. Digit. Hum. (2015)
9. Budhwar, A., Kuboi, T., Dekhtyar, A., Khosmood, F.: Predicting the vote using legislative speech. In: Proceedings of the 19th Annual International Conference on Digital Government Research: Governance in the Data Age, pp. 1–10 (2018)
10. Burke, R.: Hybrid web recommender systems. In: Brusilovsky, P., Kobsa, A., Nejdl, W. (eds.) The Adaptive Web. LNCS, vol. 4321, pp. 377–408. Springer, Heidelberg (2007). https://doi.org/10.1007/978-3-540-72079-9_12
11. California Legislative Information: AB-3235 public employees' retirement (2022). https://leginfo.legislature.ca.gov/faces/billNavClient.xhtml?bill_id=201720180AB3235
12. California Legislative Information: AB-976 electronic filing and service (2022). https://leginfo.legislature.ca.gov/faces/billNavClient.xhtml?bill_id=201720180AB976
13. California Legislative Information: California legislative information (2022). https://leginfo.legislature.ca.gov/
14. Cao, L.: Library personalized recommendation system based on collaborative filtering recommendation algorithm. In: Xu, Z., Alrabaee, S., Loyola-González, O., Zhang, X., Cahyani, N.D.W., Ab Rahman, N.H. (eds.) CSIA 2022. LNDECT, vol. 125, pp. 471–477. Springer, Cham (2022). https://doi.org/10.1007/978-3-030-97874-7_61
15. Carrer-Neto, W., Hernández-Alcaraz, M.L., Valencia-García, R., García-Sánchez, F.: Social knowledge-based recommender system. application to the movies domain. Expert Syst. Appl. **39**(12), 10990–11000 (2012). https://doi.org/10.1016/j.eswa.2012.03.025. https://www.sciencedirect.com/science/article/pii/S0957417412004952
16. Chang, S.H., Abdul, A., Chen, J., Liao, H.Y.: A personalized music recommendation system using convolutional neural networks approach. In: 2018 IEEE International Conference on Applied System Invention (ICASI), pp. 47–49 (2018). https://doi.org/10.1109/ICASI.2018.8394293
17. Chen, A.: Context-aware collaborative filtering system: predicting the user's preference in the ubiquitous computing environment. In: Strang, T., Linnhoff-Popien, C. (eds.) LoCA 2005. LNCS, vol. 3479, pp. 244–253. Springer, Heidelberg (2005). https://doi.org/10.1007/11426646_23
18. De Meo, P., Quattrone, G., Ursino, D.: A decision support system for designing new services tailored to citizen profiles in a complex and distributed e-government scenario. Data Knowl. Eng. **67**(1), 161–184 (2008). https://doi.org/10.1016/j.datak.2008.06.005
19. Enda, J., Matsa, K.E., Boyles, J.L.: America's Shifting Statehouse Press: Can New Players Compensate for Lost Legacy Reporters? Pew Research Center (2014)

20. Esteban, B., Álvaro Tejeda-Lorente, Porcel, C., Arroyo, M., Herrera-Viedma, E.: Tplufib-web: a fuzzy linguistic web system to help in the treatment of low back pain problems. Knowl.-Based Syst. **67**, 429–438 (2014). https://doi.org/10.1016/j.knosys.2014.03.004. https://www.sciencedirect.com/science/article/pii/S0950705114000872

21. GeoPy Contributors: Geopy (2018). https://geopy.readthedocs.io/en/stable/

22. Gerrish, S., Blei, D.M.: The ideal point topic model: predicting legislative roll calls from text (2010)

23. Graefe, A., Bohlken, N.: Automated journalism: a meta-analysis of readers' perceptions of human-written in comparison to automated news. Media Commun. **8**(3), 50 (2020). https://doi.org/10.17645/mac.v8i3.3019

24. Gu, Y., Sun, Y., Jiang, N., Wang, B., Chen, T.: Topic-factorized ideal point estimation model for legislative voting network. In: Proceedings of the 20th ACM SIGKDD International Conference on Knowledge Discovery and Data Mining, KDD 2014, pp. 183–192. Association for Computing Machinery, New York (2014). https://doi.org/10.1145/2623330.2623700

25. Howe, P., Robertson, C., Grace, L., Khosmood, F.: Exploring reporter-desired features for an AI-generated legislative news tip sheet. ISOJ **12**(1), 17–44 (2022)

26. Iftikhar, A., Ghazanfar, M.A., Ayub, M., Mehmood, Z., Maqsood, M.: An improved product recommendation method for collaborative filtering. IEEE Access **8**, 123841–123857 (2020). https://doi.org/10.1109/ACCESS.2020.3005953

27. Klimashevskaia, A., Gadgil, R., Gerrity, T., Khosmood, F., Gütl, C., Howe, P.: Automatic news article generation from legislative proceedings: a phenom-based approach. In: Espinosa-Anke, L., Martín-Vide, C., Spasić, I. (eds.) SLSP 2021. LNCS (LNAI), vol. 13062, pp. 15–26. Springer, Cham (2021). https://doi.org/10.1007/978-3-030-89579-2_2

28. Kumar BP, V., VS, P., et al.: Survey on classification and summarization of documents. In: Proceedings of the Second International Conference on Emerging Trends in Science & Technologies For Engineering Systems (ICETSE-2019), pp. 7–13 (2019)

29. Lee, J., Kothari, N., Natsev, P.: Content-based related video recommendations. In: Advances in Neural Information Processing Systems (NIPS) Demonstration Track (2016). http://www.joonseok.net/papers/video_recs_demo.pdf

30. Lu, J., Wu, D., Mao, M., Wang, W., Zhang, G.: Recommender system application developments: a survey. Decis. Support Syst. **74**, 12–32 (2015)

31. Miller, G.A.: Wordnet: a lexical database for english. Commun. ACM **38**(11), 39–41 (1995). https://doi.org/10.1145/219717.219748

32. Moens, M., Logghe, M., Dumortier, J.: Legislative databases: current problems and possible solutions. Int. J. Law Inf. Technol. **10**(1), 1–22 (2002). https://doi.org/10.1093/ijlit/10.1.1

33. Pazzani, M.J., Billsus, D.: Content-based recommendation systems. In: Brusilovsky, P., Kobsa, A., Nejdl, W. (eds.) The Adaptive Web. LNCS, vol. 4321, pp. 325–341. Springer, Heidelberg (2007). https://doi.org/10.1007/978-3-540-72079-9_10

34. Prolific: Prolific (2022). https://prolific.co

35. Rani, S., Singh, J.: Enhancing Levenshtein's edit distance algorithm for evaluating document similarity. In: Sharma, R., Mantri, A., Dua, S. (eds.) ICAN 2017. CCIS, vol. 805, pp. 72–80. Springer, Singapore (2018). https://doi.org/10.1007/978-981-13-0755-3_6

36. Ruprechter, T., Khosmood, F., Guetl, C.: Deconstructing human-assisted video transcription and annotation for legislative proceedings. Digit. Gov. Res. Pract. **1**(3) (2020). https://doi.org/10.1145/3395316

37. Salloum, S.A., Khan, R., Shaalan, K.: A survey of semantic analysis approaches. In: Hassanien, A.-E., Azar, A.T., Gaber, T., Oliva, D., Tolba, F.M. (eds.) AICV 2020. AISC, vol. 1153, pp. 61–70. Springer, Cham (2020). https://doi.org/10.1007/978-3-030-44289-7_6

38. Shani, G., Gunawardana, A.: Evaluating recommendation systems. In: Ricci, F., Rokach, L., Shapira, B., Kantor, P.B. (eds.) Recommender Systems Handbook, pp. 257–297. Springer, Boston, MA (2011). https://doi.org/10.1007/978-0-387-85820-3_8

39. Shaw, A.: As statehouse press corps dwindles, other reliable news sources needed. Better Government Association (2017)

40. Stanchev, L.: Creating a similarity graph from wordnet. In: Proceedings of the 4th International Conference on Web Intelligence, Mining and Semantics (WIMS14), WIMS 2014. Association for Computing Machinery, New York (2014). https://doi.org/10.1145/2611040.2611055

41. Tarus, J.K., Niu, Z., Mustafa, G.: Knowledge-based recommendation: a review of ontology-based recommender systems for e-learning. Artif. Intell. Rev. **50**(1), 21–48 (2018)

42. Terán, L., Meier, A.: A fuzzy recommender system for eelections. In: Andersen, K.N., Francesconi, E., Grönlund, Å., van Engers, T.M. (eds.) EGOVIS 2010. LNCS, vol. 6267, pp. 62–76. Springer, Heidelberg (2010). https://doi.org/10.1007/978-3-642-15172-9_6

43. Thomas, M., et al.: Quick check: a legal research recommendation system. In: NLLP@ KDD, pp. 57–60 (2020)

44. Winkler, M.A.: California poised to overtake Germany as world's no. 4 economy. Bloomberg (2022)

45. Yano, T., Smith, N.A., Wilkerson, J.D.: Textual predictors of bill survival in congressional committees. In: Proceedings of the 2012 Conference of the North American Chapter of the Association for Computational Linguistics: Human Language Technologies, Montréal, Canada, pp. 793–802. Association for Computational Linguistics (2012). https://aclanthology.org/N12-1097

46. Yapriady, B., Uitdenbogerd, A.L.: Combining demographic data with collaborative filtering for automatic music recommendation. In: Khosla, R., Howlett, R.J., Jain, L.C. (eds.) KES 2005. LNCS (LNAI), vol. 3684, pp. 201–207. Springer, Heidelberg (2005). https://doi.org/10.1007/11554028_29

Assessing Forgetfulness in Data Stream Learning – The Case of Hoeffding AnyTime Tree Algorithm

João Pedro Costa(ID), Régis Albuquerque(✉)(ID), and Flavia Bernardini(ID)

Institute of Computing (IC), Fluminense Federal University (UFF),
Niterói, RJ, Brazil
{almeidajoao,ralbuquerque}@id.uff.br, fcbernardini@ic.uff.br

Abstract. Many efforts around the world have emerged on regulations concerning personal management data guarantee, being one of them related to the 'Right to Be Forgotten'. There are many divergences on what type of data must be considered in this matter. If some governmental policy interprets that some data collected in a given domain is property of an individual, and this individual has the right to request forgetfulness of this data portion, this data must be erased from third-party tools and services, including e-government services. One important challenge in this scenario is when these data portions have been used for constructing machine learning-based models, as the knowledge composing these models were partially obtained by the data to be forgotten. Moreover, there can be of special interest when it is demanded to a company to forget huge parts of their source data, which can lead to lower quality estimators. So, it is fundamental to present machine learning tools to support these types of policies as well as investigating the impact of data forgetting to machine learning-based estimators. In this paper, we investigate the impact of these learning and forgetting policies in Data Stream Learning (DSL) using an algorithm called Hoeffding AnyTime Tree (HATT). This is an interesting algorithm as it incorporates the ability to negatively weighting instances, which can be seen as a property of data forgetting. We subject the HATT algorithm to 4 levels of forgetting and investigate the impact of data forgetting in the obtained predictive performance. They are compared against control instances (upper and lower bound) of the HATT algorithm using four non-stationary stream datasets. Our results showed that as the forgetting rate increases, the model approaches the lower bound behavior in terms of accuracy for 2 out of 4 datasets, indicating that this is a promising approach.

Keywords: Right to Be Forgotten · Machine Learning · Data Stream Mining · Decision Tree

We are thankfull to Saulo M. Mastelini, Leandro Miranda and Prof. José Viterbo for discussions to conduct this work and the anonymous referees for their important suggestions for improve work.

I. Lindgren et al. (Eds.): EGOV 2023, LNCS 14130, pp. 144–159, 2023.
https://doi.org/10.1007/978-3-031-41138-0_10

1   Introduction

In the last years, many laws around the world have been proposed to tackle data privacy issues, such as the General Data Protection Rules (GDPR) [7]. Among other characteristics, these laws state that users have the Right to Be Forgotten (RtBF), whom can require their data to be deleted. This leaded the companies to establish mechanisms for forgetting data, which is simpler when the target information was not processed yet. However, many companies and public organizations may have used these data to infer their models for decision making processes, recommending products or user profiles, predicting user behaviors, among other applications. Although these applications are not directly discussed in GDPR and related rules, multiple researchers are already discussing ethics in Artificial Intelligence (AI). The High-Level Expert Group on AI from the European Comission presented a document, called Ethics guidelines for trustworthy AI [6]. This document dictates that trustworthy AI should be lawful, respecting all applicable laws and regulations; ethical, respecting ethical principles and values; and robust, both from a technical perspective while taking into account its social environment. In our point of view, ethical principles and values include the discussion about not using data that should be forgotten in models constructed by learning algorithms. In this way, our premise for conducting this work is that, when users require to forget their data, they must be excluded from the models constructed by Machine Learning (ML) algorithms.

In literature, we could observe many authors discussing the impacts of the RtBF in the AI and specially in ML domains, as discussed in Sect. 2. One important issue, according to them, is analyzing the impact of forgetting data for future predictions. However, one main concern regards to the performance of the predictors when reconstructing them or excluding data from them. In this work, we present in Sect. 3 some hypothetical scenarios in which we face the issue of having to remove data from the knowledge base to comply with the new regulations. Questions such as "how much prediction performance do the estimators lose in this forgetfulness scenario?" are yet to be answered. One issue related to this aspect is that there is not a widespread approach for evaluating the impact of forgetting data in ML.

In the last decades, many works in literature have focused on dealing with incremental learning for facing the catastrophic forgetting problem in ML [24] i.e., the inability to forget data of many classical ML algorithms for constructing neural networks, decision trees and so on. These works evolved to new algorithms that evolves the models on data streams, in order to tackle recurrent issues in incremental learning, such as concept drift detection [12,17]. Data to be forgotten may change the data distribution over time, which may lead to concept drift. So, concept drift is an important aspect of the forgetting scenario.

More recently, there are frameworks bringing together different data stream mining algorithms for some specific purposes, such as data stream clustering, classification and regression. The last ones belongs to the Data Stream Learning (DSL) approach in the context of data stream mining. Examples of these kind of frameworks are MOA, implemented in Java [2], and River, implemented in

Python [21]. One desirable software requirement in these frameworks is to provide services to also allow forgetting data, which is not yet available. In order to do so, it is important to evolve methodologies for assessing the capability of these algorithms to forget.

In ML, decision trees are considered a classic and natural way of learning. Because they are usually constructed recursively, they are related to the fundamental scientific notion of computing: divide and conquer. They can be visualized through graphs that represent the choice conditions and their possibilities in a tree format [18]. *Hoeffding Anytime Tree (HATT) or Extremely Fast Decision Tree* is an algorithmic version of decision trees that is more resilient to concept drift (*concept drift*) [19].

In this work, we present a methodology for experimentally analyzing how to assess the forgetting ability of the DSL algorithm HATT when forgetting data from the data stream. As a contribution, we subject the HATT algorithm to 4 levels of forgetting (10%, 25%, 50%, 75%) and compare with control instances of the HATT algorithm. In our experimental analysis, we used different types of datasets, which present different patterns of concept drift, also used by Losing, Hammer and Wersing [17]. Our results showed that as the forgetting rate increases, the model approaches the lower bound behavior in terms of accuracy for 2 out of 4 datasets.

This work is organized as follows: Sect. 2 presents a brief discussion regarding the RtBF and the problems this scenario may bring to AI. Section 3 describes fictitious scenarios of forgetting data in estimators constructed by ML algorithms. Section 4 presents the background in ML required for better understanding our proposal and results. Section 5 presents our methodology for conducting our experimental analysis. Section 6 presents the results of our experimental analysis. Finally, Sect. 7 describes our conclusions, limitations of this work, our next steps and future work.

2   RtBF and AI

RtBF is essentially the concept that individuals have the right to request that their data (collected by others) must be deleted. European Union regulated, in 2016, "the protection of natural persons with regard to the processing of personal data and on the free movement of such data" through the General Data Protection Regulation (GDPR) [7]. Also, they state that "a data subject should have the right to have personal data concerning him or her rectified and a 'Right to Be Forgotten' ". According to Politou, Aleksis and Patsakis [25], there are many challenges related to forgetting personal data and revoking consent under GDPR, and they state that "privacy and big data are in many cases contradictory. Big data require massive amount of information to be collected with not a predefined and clear purpose at the time of collection. Users do not have any control on their personal information stored and analysed by the involved data controllers and the parties that participate in data dissemination may be numerous".

In this forgetting scenario, while data deletion may seem like a straightforward topic from the point of view of many regulators, this seemingly simple issue poses many practical problems in real ML environments. Dang [4] review the definitions of RtBF in several major legal documents and the application of this right in practice, as well as they discuss this differential privacy requirement as a framework to support the RtbF. Sengelwald and Lackes [26] states that "Privacy laws grant users to determine that their data should not be used any longer by the data holder (i.e., a data record must be removed)". Even not having yet a consensus whether the estimators must reflect this forgetting scenario, if the estimators need to forget the data, there is a need for strategies to forget the data that must be excluded. The problem associated to the RtBF in AI may be due to our imprecise understanding of privacy in relation to AI [27]. Often, people see privacy as hiding their information from others. This is especially apparent when examining the RtBF principle, under which individuals can request that information made public be deleted (and therefore made private). In the case of public information made private, the metaphor of the human mind forgetting some pieces of information applies well or, at least, no more humans in the future will be aware about the data turned private. However, this idea is not necessarily straightly translated into the era of AI and ML. Our current laws seem to treat human and machine memory in the same way, supporting a fictitious understanding of memory and forgetting that does not fit into reality.

It is worth noticing that the range of RtBF tools or techniques available in this context is still under development. In the RtBF scenario, there are mainly two possible approaches for machine learning: (i) retrain the estimator using batch learning; or (ii) deleting data from the memory, in case of lazy learning or incremental learning when it is possible. In the first approach, even presenting the issue of needing to store all records for the generation of new estimators and being too expensive, it is considered a naive solution [15]. In the second approach, Villaronga, Kieseberg and Tiffany [27] use k-anonymity techniques in databases, for the protection and exclusion of information. However, the authors state that "it may be impossible to fulfill the legal aims of the RtBF in artificial intelligence environments". For the domain of stream learning, Mirzasoleiman, Karbasi and Krause [20] proposed a framework that offers instantaneous data summarization while preserving the right of an individual to be forgotten. They cast the problem as an instance of robust streaming submodular maximization, where the goal is to produce a concise real-time summary. They state that their framework outputs a robust solution against deletions from the summary at any given time, while preserving the same approximation guarantee. The authors tested their work on different scenarios. On the one hand, none of the found studies presents ML algorithms that incorporate such forgetting techniques, facilitating the use of ML algorithms in this context. On the other hand, the framework proposed by Mirzasoleiman, Karbasi and Krause [20] is an interesting approach, discussing the use of memories in the stream mining process.

Particularly in the field of data stream learning, Libera, Miranda, Bernardini, Mastelini and Viterbo [16] investigate the impact of learning and forgetting policies in data stream mining for learning classifier predictors. They modify an incremental K-NN classifier to enable it to erase its past data and investigate the impact of data forgetting in the obtained predictive performance. Their results show that the forgetting-enabled algorithm can achieve similar prediction patterns compared to the vanilla one, although it yields lower predictive performance at the beginning of the learning process. Such a scenario is a typical cold-start behavior often observed in data stream mining and learning applications, and not necessarily related to the employed forgetting mechanisms.

3 Forgetting Data in ML—Motivating Scenarios

Figure 1 shows an schematic diagram that shows the relations between a Data Subject and a Data Processor from the GDPR perspective [7], considering the context of constructing ML-based models. Given an application domain, such as the ones we briefly describe in what follows, a Data Subject is a person who provides both Personal Data and Data Collections to a process, executed by a Data Processor. A Data Processor is a private or public organization, responsible for collecting, processing, managing and constructing ML-based models using data from the Data Subject. Also in the figure, $t_1, ..., t_N$ refers to time instants or slots the Data Subject provides data to the Data Processor (or to the processes of the Data Processor) and t_{N+1} is the time instant that a Data Subject requires to the Data Processor to delete his or her entire data.

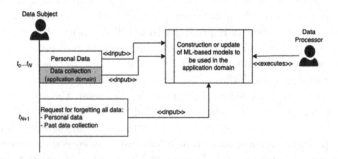

Fig. 1. Process involving (i) a Data Subject – a person who generates both personal data and data collections in a given application domain; and (ii) a Data Processor – an organization responsible for collecting, processing, managing and constructing ML-based models using data from the Data Subject.

From the public government perspective, these ML-based models may help the government managers to make important decisions on policy making and regulations construction. There is not an agreement whether the Data Subject is the Data Owner of the data collections that she or he produces. From one perspective, GDPR states that "The data subject shall have the right to obtain from the controller confirmation as to whether or not personal data concerning him or her are being processed, and, where that is the case, access to the personal data and the following information: [...] the existence of the right to request from the controller rectification or erasure of personal data or restriction of processing of personal data concerning the data subject or to object to such processing" (Art. 15 [7]).

From another perspective, GDPR also states that there are some situations where the Data Subject does not have the right to request to the Data Processor erasure of personal data, which are related to when the Data Processor (i) is exercising the right of freedom of expression and information; (ii) is in compliance with a legal obligation which requires processing by Union or Member State law to which the controller is subject or for the performance of a task carried out in the public interest or in the exercise of official authority vested in the controller; (iii) for reasons of public interest in the area of public health; and (iv) for archiving purposes in the public interest, scientific or historical research purposes or statistical purposes; or (v) for the establishment, exercise or defence of legal claims (Art. 17 [7]). Independently of the case, the Machine Learning and Artificial Intelligence community shall work to develop methodologies and tools for guarantee forgetfulness of data collections, being or not personal or sensitive data of the Data Subject. Besides that, better understanding the behavior of the models in the presence or absence of forgetting is an important research question.

In this way, we present three hypothetical scenarios in order to try to clarify the challenges involved in forgetting data in estimators and models constructed by ML algorithms:

Scenario 1: An electricity supply company collects hourly energy consumption data to forecast the energy consumption of each customer in their home. The company uses this data to forecast energy consumption for the next hour, the next day and the next month. In this scenario, the company aggregates the forecast results to forecast the demand for energy consumption in a city. Also, the local and other levels of government use this data to predict energy consumption in the next days, weeks or months. If someone interpret that the user has the right to ask for the company to delete their historical consumption data, the company (Data Processor) shall remove these data collections or portions from their prediction models, and can be the same in the public organization;

Scenario 2: A social media organization uses data from diverse users to predict consumption behavior. The usage of data was previously consented by users. However, many of them ask the company to forget their data; and

Scenario 3: A local government organization uses opinions and requests from citizens for decision making. The usage of data was previously consented by users, but citizens claim to exclude their data for future analysis.

In our scenarios, if data are used for constructing predictors (classifiers or regressors), we think that could be ethically necessary to chain the data deletion into the forecast estimators, as they are part of the acquired knowledge that composes the estimators. We believe that scenarios like these hypothetical ones will be more and more common in future applications. We also consider that the estimators were constructed using supervised ML algorithms. In this work, we are particularly interested in *eager algorithms* for constructing estimators through diverse approaches (such as symbolic learning, probabilistic learning, statistical learning and so on). Also, they can be constructed either by batch or data stream learning algorithms. In batch learning, the learning algorithm creates an estimator (a model or a set of memories) in only one step and, afterward, the estimator is used to predict the label for unlabeled instances that the estimator builder never saw [2,11]. In DSL (an approach of Data Stream Mining), an estimator is ready to do either one of the following at any time [5]: (i) Receive an unlabeled instance and make a prediction for it on the basis of its current estimator; or (ii) Receive the label for an instance seen in the past, and use it for adjusting the estimator. In the RtBF scenario, there are two possible approaches: (i) reconstructing the estimator if using batch learning; or (ii) deleting data from the memory [20,27].

It is worth noticing that if the dataset to be forgotten is too large, it can change the data distribution over time. Such changes require the use of learning algorithms that tackle concept drift. DSL is one of the approaches largely investigated in ML for constructing adaptive estimators when data stream is available and concept drift is present [2,13]. These DSL algorithms are applied mainly in scenarios where the data distribution happens in a non-stationary way. Consequently, in most cases, there is concept drift arising from the change in the data distribution over time [14]. DSL has been applied and has shown good results in many different domains, such as monitoring and detection of solar energy consumption [10,28], intrusion detection in networks [1], taxi demand prediction [8], anomaly detection [9], vehicle time prediction [23], among others.

4   ML Background

Considering a set of N labeled instances $S = \{(\mathbf{x}_1 \, y_1), ..., (\mathbf{x}_N \, y_N)\}$ in supervised ML, each vector $\mathbf{x}_i$ is of the form $(x_{i1}, ..., x_{iM})$. Each value x_{ij} is a value of the instance $(\mathbf{x}_i, y_i)$ in feature X_j. All $X_j \in X$, where X is the set of input features. All $y_i \in L$, where L is a set of labels and it has a discrete number of labels if we have a classification problem. In *batch learning*, the learning algorithm creates an estimator $\mathbf{h}$ using the entire set S. After, $\mathbf{h}$ is then used to predict the label for unlabeled instances that $\mathbf{h}$ builder never saw. Two common used techniques for constructing or training $\mathbf{h}$ is splitting S into two parts, forming a training and a testing dataset, or constructing $\mathbf{h}$ with the entire S and estimate $\mathbf{h}$ error rate using cross-validation. In any case, there is a first training phase, clearly separated in time from the prediction phase. On the other hand, in *data stream learning*, this separation between training, evaluating, and testing is far less clear-cut, and is usually interleaved. We need to start making predictions before we have all the data, because the data may never end. We need to use the data whose label we predict to keep training the estimator, if possible. Also, we probably need to continuously evaluate the estimator in some way to decide if the estimator needs more or less aggressive retraining [2].

DSL for Classification Problems: Classification needs a set of properly labeled instances to learn an estimator, so that we can use this estimator to predict the labels of unseen instances. In this way, suppose we have a stream of continuously arriving instances. We need to assign a label from a set of nominal labels to each item, as a function of the other features of the item. A estimator can be trained as long as the correct label for (many of) the instances is available at a later time. The most significant requirements for a stream learning algorithm are [2,5]: (i) Process an instance at a time, and inspect it (at most) once; (ii) Use a limited amount of time to process each instance; (iii) Use a limited amount of memory; (iv) Be ready to give a prediction at any time; and (v) Adapt to temporal changes. Typically, *a general DSL algorithm for constructing an estimator* follows these steps: (i) get an unlabeled instance $\mathbf{x}$; (ii) make a prediction $\hat{y} = \hat{f}(\mathbf{x})$, where $\hat{f}$ is the current estimator, under construction by the stream learner; (iii) get the true label y for $\mathbf{x}$; (iv) use the pair (x, y) to update (train) $\hat{f}$, and the pair $(\hat{y}, y)$ to update statistics about $\hat{f}$—the estimator performance. Although this estimator is too simple, it is useful for comparing DSL algorithms.

For evaluating the estimator in DSL, we used a technique called prequential [2]: Each individual instance is used to test the estimator before it is used for training, and from this, metrics such as accuracy can be incrementally updated. When the evaluation is intentionally performed in this order, the estimator is always being tested on instances that has not seen yet. This scheme ensures a smooth plot of accuracy over time, as each individual instance will become less and less significant to the overall average. In this way, only those instances in a sliding window of the most recent ones are used for computing accuracy.

Concept Drift: Formally, concept drift is defined considering two time points t_0 and t_1, and is given by $\exists X : p_{t_0}(X, y) \neq p_{t_1}(X, y)$, where p_{t_0} denotes the joint distribution at time t_0 between the set of input features X and the target variable y [12]. Changes in data can be characterized as changes in the components of this relation. In other terms, the prior probabilities of classes $p(y)$ may change; the class conditional probabilities $p(X|y)$ may change; and, as a result, the posterior probabilities of classes $p(y|X)$ may change, affecting the prediction. In this way, Gama *et al* [12] presents two different types of concept drift: (i) Real concept drift(R), which refers to changes in $p(y|X)$, and such changes can happen either with or without change in $p(X)$; and (ii) Virtual drift(V) happens if the distribution of the incoming data changes (i.e., $p(X)$ changes) without affecting $p(y|X)$. In this way, only the real concept drift changes the class boundary and the previous decision estimator becomes obsolete. In practice, virtual drift changing prior probabilities or novelties may appear in combination with the real drift. In these cases, the class boundary is also affected. Also, changes in data distribution over time may manifest in different forms. A drift may happen suddenly/abruptly(A), by switching from one concept to another, or incrementally(I), consisting of many intermediate concepts in between. Drift may happen suddenly or gradually. Changes can be further characterized by severity, predictability and frequency. Most of the adaptive learning techniques implicitly or explicitly assume and specialize in some subset of concept drifts. Many of them assume sudden non-reoccurring drifts. However, typically, mixtures of many types of concept drift can be observed in real data. In forgetting scenario, depending on the amount of data to be deleted, it also may lead to a concept drift scenario. In this way, it is important to consider this feature in our analysis.

HATT for Data Stream: A classification system needs to rely on learning algorithms for inferring models and consequently future predictions/classifications of test instances. One of the most famous algorithms is *Hoeffding Naive Bayes Tree (HT)*. It uses a decision tree system that performs its predictions by choosing the majority class on each leaf. Its predictive accuracy can be increased by adding *Naive Bayes* models to the leaves of the tree structure. When performing a prediction on a test instance, the leaf will only return a *Naive Bayesina* prediction if it was more accurate than the majority class on the training instances, otherwise it will fall back on a majority class prediction [3]. An interesting modification of *Hoeffding Tree* for the forgetting scenario is the *Hoeffding Anytime Tree (HATT)*, also called *Extremely Fast Decision Tree*. HATT is a version of HT more resilient to concept drift (*concept drift*). For dealing with concept drift, the algorithm may receive a weight associated to an instance in order to indicate the importance of the instance to the model. In case of forgetting data, this weight can be set as -1, indicating that the instance must be not represented anymore in the Hoeffding Tree. HATT can be used as a more accurate substitute for the HT classifier in most scenarios, with a small additional computational cost [19].

5   Our Experimental Methodology

We select four datasets from the ones used by Losing, Hammer and Wersing [17]. The datasets are: **Interchanging RBF** – Fifteen Gaussians are replacing each other every 3000 samples. Abrupt drifts occur in this dataset. **Transient Chessboard** – Virtual drift is present in this dataset. They are generated by revealing successively parts of a chessboard. **Moving Squares** – Four equidistantly separated, squared uniform distributions are moving with constant speed in horizontal direction. When the leading square reaches the limit the direction is reversed. This dataset contains incremental drift. **Poker Hand** – Randomly drawn poker hands are represented by five cards. Each hand is coded with its suit and value. Virtual drift is introduced sorting the instances by rank and value.

Our selection was based on different patterns of concept drift, in order to evaluate the behavior of the models on both possibilities of concept drift: (i) inherent from the dataset domain; and (ii) inherent to the process getting data. Table 1 shows the characteristics of the datasets used in our experiments. In this table, Name refers to the name of the dataset; N, the number of instances in the dataset; $|L|$, the number of labels in the dataset; M, the number of features in X; Drift, the concept drift properties of the dataset, which can be V (virtual), R (real), R+V (various, both real and virtual); AR (abrupt real), IR (incremental real) or ARV (abrupt recurring virtual); and Type, the type of the dataset, which can be Artif., meaning that the dataset was artificially generated, or Real, meaning that the dataset was collected from real world scenarios.

Table 1. Datasets used for our experimental analysis

Name	N	$|L|$	M	Drift	Type
Interchanging RBF	200,000	15	2	AR	Artif.
Transient Chessboard	200,000	8	2	ARV	Artif.
Moving Squares	200,000	4	2	IR	Artif.
Poker Hand	200,000	10	10	V	Real

In order to study the impact of forgetting to the classifiers behavior, we had two premises. The first premise was related to deleting data from a specific window. In this way, we are evaluating the forgetting aspect in relatively recent data seen by the DSL algorithm HATT. We firstly truncated all our datasets in our experimental analysis to have only 200,000 instances (the size of the smaller dataset). In the experiments, we used the Test-Then-Train (TTT) technique to evaluate and evolve the models (HTs) constructed by HATT. This technique, widely used for testing DSL classifiers, is also commonly called Progressive Validation, where the instance is first tested and then the classifier is trained with the labeled instance. Considering that the entire dataset is in fact presented as a data stream to the HATT algorithm, we divided the entire data stream (or dataset) into 1,000 windows, each of them containing 200 instances, i.e., $W_1 = \{(\mathbf{x}_{1-1}\, y_{1-1}), ..., (\mathbf{x}_{1-200}\, y_{1-200})\}$; $W_2 = \{(\mathbf{x}_{2-1}\, y_{2-1}), ..., (\mathbf{x}_{2-200}\, y_{2-200})\}$; ... up to $W_{1,000}$. Each W_k, $k = 1, ..., 1,000$ is then also manipulated for assessing the behavior of the classifiers constructed by the HATT algorithm, better explained next.

Our second premise was related to having an upper bound and a lower bound model in order to test the forgetting impact on the models behavior. The upper bound model $\mathbf{h}_{Upper}$ is the one constructed with the entire dataset, considering the scenario when the dataset to be forgotten is empty – in this case, $\mathbf{h}_{Upper}$ *is the model that never forgets*. The lower bond model $\mathbf{h}_{Lower}$ is the one constructed with only the remaining dataset, the one that was not ever used to be forgotten in any of our intermediate forgetting scenarios – in this case, $\mathbf{h}_{Lower}$ *is the model that never saw the data that would have to be forgotten in the future*.

Considering both premises, we constructed our assessment methodology. Figure 2 presents a schematic diagram for understanding this complex assessment process. In the first window W_1, we construct, using the TTT technique, a first $\mathbf{h}_{Upper,1}$ upper bound model considering the entire window and a first $\mathbf{h}_{Lower,1}$ lower bound model considering only 25% of the entire window that won't be never forgotten ($W_{1,25\%}^*$). Then, we copy the $\mathbf{h}_{Upper,1}$ model to form the models

$h_{10,1}$, $h_{25,1}$, $h_{50,1}$ and $h_{75,1}$ to be the models to be evaluated regarding forgetting rate $r = \{10\%, 25\%, 50\%, 75\%\}$, respectively. So, a function to delete the forgetting percentage rate of each model is applied. In other words, the function Forget(W_1,h_r,r) is applied to the model h_r for each $r = \{10\%, 25\%, 50\%, 75\%\}$, generating the models $h'_{10,1}$, $h'_{25,1}$, $h'_{50,1}$ and $h'_{75,1}$ with the respective data forgotten. These models are then used to TTT again considering the second window W_2. The models $h_{10,2}$, $h_{25,2}$, $h_{50,2}$ and $h_{75,2}$ with their respective accuracies are constructed considering the entire second window $W_{2,100\%}$, as well as the $h_{Upper,1}$ is evolved to $h_{Upper,2}$. $W^*_{2,25\%}$ is also used to evolve $h_{Lower,1}$ to $h_{Lower,2}$. This process continues up to the last window, i.e., $K = 1,000$.

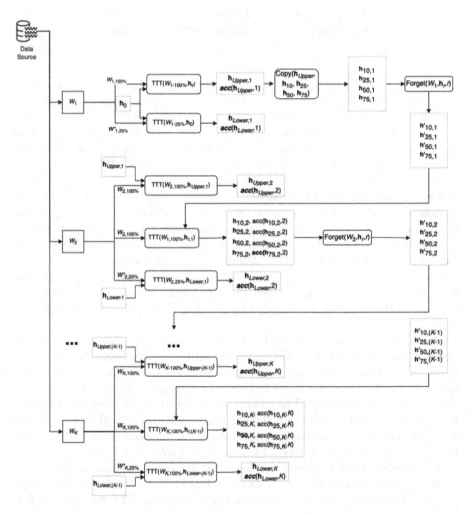

Fig. 2. Our Methodology Diagram for Assessing Forgetfulness in DSL Scenario

For each W_N data window, we divide the window into 5 groups: One set with 25% of the data ($W^*_{N,25\%}$), which will never be forgotten, and the remaining 75% window ($W_{N,75\%}$)is divided in cascade. $W_{N,25\%}$ and $W_{N,75\%}$ sets are mutually exclusive. From the $W_{N,75\%}$ set, we create the $W_{N,50\%}$ subset, with 50% of the original W_N data and $W_{N,50\%} \in W_{N,25\%}$. After, we create the $W_{N,25\%}$ set, with 25% of the original W_N data and $W_{N,25\%} \in W_{N,50\%}$. Lastly, we create the $W_{N,10\%}$ set, with 10% of the original W_N data and $W_{N,10\%} \in W_{N,25\%}$. The instances composing each of these sets are randomly selected. Figure 3 illustrates this division scheme.

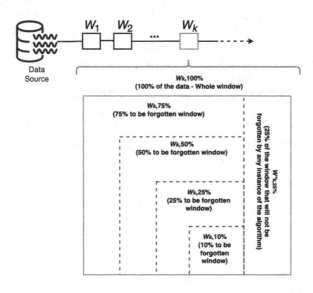

Fig. 3. Windows originated from a data source and a representation of the window W_N division

For each W data window, the accuracies of each tested model are calculated. In Fig. 2 we have a schematic representation of the methodology used. In the first data window (W1), the H_UP model is tested and trained and the Acc metric is calculated, after which 4 copies are generated, setting the forgetting rate for each one (H_75, H_50, H_25 and H_10) and forgetting the window according to the window and the percentage of forgetting each model. In the first window, the accuracy of the H_UP is inherited for the copies, from the following windows it will be calculated according to the prediction of each model. The H_LB model is tested and trained in the X_NonForgettable window (25% of data) and the corresponding Acc metric calculated. The Acc metric (average accuracy) is calculated by the number of correct answers divided by the number of tests.

As the creation of forgetting datasets is random, we reproduced each test 3 times. To perform the computational tests, Scikit-learn was used, a Python module that integrates a wide range of state-of-the-art machine learning algorithms for medium-scale supervised and unsupervised problems. It is distributed under the simplified BSD license, encouraging its use in academic and commercial environments. Source code, binaries and documentation can be downloaded from http://scikit-learn.sourceforge.net [22].

6   Experimental Results

Figures 4a to 5b shows the results obtained for each dataset using HATT without forgetting data (H_UP and H_LB in the subtitles of each figure) and using HATT forgetting data considering $|Forget_{rate}| = \{10, 25, 50, 75\}$, respectively represented by H_10, H_25, H_50 and H_75 in the subtitles. In these figures, we can see that as the forgetting rate increases, the model approaches the lowerbound behavior. This is clearly evidenced in Figs. 4b and 5a. For the base Poker Hand (Fig. 5b) only the H_75 model (with a forgetting rate of 75%) had mostly lower accuracies than the lower bound. We observed a completely unexpected behavior for the Moving Squares base (Fig. 4a). The model with the highest rate of forgetting (H_75) showed better rates of accuracy and the one with the lowest rate of forgetting (H_10) the worst rates of accuracy. Another unexpected behavior was the evolution of the Upper bound rates, which were lower than the rates of the forgetting models.

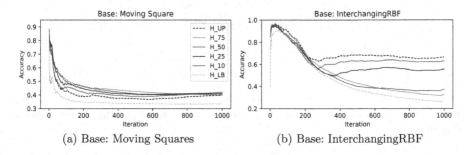

(a) Base: Moving Squares   (b) Base: InterchangingRBF

Fig. 4. Results using Moving Squares and InterchangingRBF dataset

Table 2 shows the average of 3 runs for each model and database. We can observe that with the exception of the Poker Hand base, the models that forget showed better average accuracy in relation to Lowerbound. For the Poker Hand base, only the H_75 classifier (with a 75% forgetting rate) had a lower accuracy rate than the lower bound. For the Moving Squares base, we observed a different behavior than expected: both the Upper Bound and the Lower bound presented lower accuracies than the classifiers subjected to forgetting.

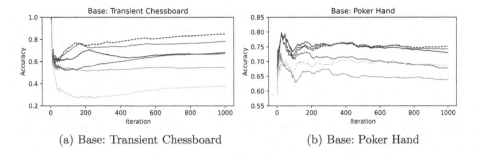

(a) Base: Transient Chessboard   (b) Base: Poker Hand

Fig. 5. Results using Transient Chessboard and Poker Hand dataset

Table 2. Mean value of accuracy obtained on 3 replications of HATT.

Dataset	H_UP	H_LB	H_10	H_25	H_50	H_75
Interchanging RBF	0.7076	0.4598	0.6648	0.6092	0.5089	0.5128
Transient Chessboard	0.7886	0.3383	0.7435	0.6601	0.6174	0.5398
Moving Squares	0.3993	0.3484	0.4187	0.4335	0.4423	0.4457
Poker Hand	0.7510	0.6925	0.7515	0.7498	0.7066	0.6535

7   Conclusions and Future Work

In this paper, we present a methodology for evaluating the behavior of stream learning algorithms in the scenario of RtBF. We specifically used in our methodology the decision tree learning algorithm HATT (Hoeffding AnyTime Tree). We extended this algorithm for forgetting recent data from the stream. As a contribution, we subject the HATT algorithm to 4 levels of forgetting and compare with control instances of the HATT algorithm. We evaluated HATT using prequential technique, typically used for evaluating the performance of DSL algorithms. We also used 4 datasets, previously used in literature, with different patterns of concept drift. We could observe that, as the forgetting rate increases, the model approaches the behavior of the lower bound in terms of accuracy for 2 out of 4 datasets. For the Poker Hand base, only the model with the highest rate of forgetting had mostly lower accuracies than the lower bound. However, we had a totally unexpected behavior for the Moving Squares base: the model with the highest rate of forgetting (75%) showed better rates of accuracy and the one with the lowest rate of forgetting (H_10) worse rates of accuracy. Another unexpected behavior was the evolution of the Upper bound rates, which were lower than the rates of the forgetting models. No conclusion was reached as to what happened to these anomalous behaviors. In order to verify if the behavior of HATT maintain in more datasets, we need yet to conduct more experiments. However, as we achieved these results in 2 out of 4 datasets, we believe our approach is promising.

One important limitation of this work is that we are only evaluating forgetfulness in more recently data. We also only tested one machine learning algorithm (HATT) with only 4 datasets. Future work include exploring forgetfulness in more datasets, as well as in older data. Also, we intend to extend the existing data stream mining frameworks and tools to ensure forgetting data or, at least, assess the algorithms ability to forget, turning it easiser to compare the behavior of different algorithms and related works. We believe this is an important contribution to many public and private organizations that deal with data for constructing predictors based on machine learning algorithms.

References

1. Alves, C., Bernardini, F., Meza, E.B.M., Sousa, L.: Evaluating the behaviour of stream learning algorithms for detecting invasion on wireless networks. Int. J. Secur. Netw. **15**(3), 133–140 (2020)
2. Bifet, A., Gavaldá, R., Holmes, G., Pfahringer, B.: Machine Learning for Data Streams: with Practical Examples in MOA. MIT Press, Cambridge (2018)
3. Bifet, A., Holmes, G., Pfahringer, B.: Leveraging bagging for evolving data streams. In: Balcázar, J.L., Bonchi, F., Gionis, A., Sebag, M. (eds.) ECML PKDD 2010. LNCS (LNAI), vol. 6321, pp. 135–150. Springer, Heidelberg (2010). https://doi. org/10.1007/978-3-642-15880-3_15
4. Dang, Q.-V.: Right to be forgotten in the age of machine learning. In: Antipova, T. (ed.) ICADS 2021. AISC, vol. 1352, pp. 403–411. Springer, Cham (2021). https:// doi.org/10.1007/978-3-030-71782-7_35
5. Domingos, P., Hulten, G.: Mining high-speed data streams. In: Proceedings 6th ACM SIGKDD International Conference on Knowledge Discovery & Data Mining, pp. 71–80. ACM (2000)
6. European Comission: Ethics guidelines for trustworthy AI (2019). https:// ec.europa.eu/digital-single-market/en/news/ethics-guidelines-trustworthy-ai. Accessed 17 July 2020
7. European Parliament: General Data Protection Regulation (2016). https://gdpr-info.eu/. Accessed 31 Mar 2023
8. Faial, D., Bernardini, F., Meza, E.M., Miranda, L., Viterbo, J.: A methodology for taxi demand prediction using stream learning. In: International Conference on Systems, Signals and Image Processing (IWSSIP), pp. 417–422 (2020). https:// doi.org/10.1109/IWSSIP48289.2020.9145097
9. Faial, D., Bernardini, F., Miranda, L., Viterbo, J.: Anomaly detection in vehicle traffic data using batch and stream supervised learning. In: Moura Oliveira, P., Novais, P., Reis, L.P. (eds.) EPIA 2019. LNCS (LNAI), vol. 11804, pp. 675–684. Springer, Cham (2019). https://doi.org/10.1007/978-3-030-30241-2_56
10. Fernandes, L.F.O., Bernardini, F., Meza, E.M., Miranda, L., Viterbo, J.: Energy consumption prediction using data stream learning for commercial buildings. In: International Conference on Systems, Signals and Image Processing (IWSSIP), pp. 441–446 (2020)
11. Frank, E., Hall, M.A., Witten, I.H.: Data Mining: Practical Machine Learning Tools and Techniques, 4th edn. Morgan Kaufmann, Burlington (2016)
12. Gama, J.A., Žliobaitundefined, I., Bifet, A., Pechenizkiy, M., Bouchachia, A.: A survey on concept drift adaptation. ACM Comput. Surv. **46**(4) (2014). https:// doi.org/10.1145/2523813

13. Gama, J.: Knowledge Discovery from Data Streams. CRC Press, Boca Raton (2010)
14. Holzinger, A., et al.: Machine learning and knowledge extraction in digital pathology needs an integrative approach. In: Holzinger, A., Goebel, R., Ferri, M., Palade, V. (eds.) Towards Integrative Machine Learning and Knowledge Extraction. LNCS (LNAI), vol. 10344, pp. 13–50. Springer, Cham (2017). https://doi.org/10.1007/978-3-319-69775-8_2
15. Izzo, Z., Smart, M.A., Chaudhuri, K., Zou, J.: Approximate data deletion from machine learning models. In: Proceedings of 24th International Conference on Artificial Intelligence and Statistics, PMLR, vol. 130, pp. 2008–2016 (2021)
16. Libera, C., Miranda, L., Bernardini, F., Mastelini, S., Viterbo, J.: 'right to be forgotten': analyzing the impact of forgetting data using k-NN algorithm in data stream learning. In: Janssen, M., et al. (eds.) EGOV 2022. LNCS, vol. 13391, pp. 530–542. Springer, Cham (2022). https://doi.org/10.1007/978-3-031-15086-9_34
17. Losing, V., Hammer, B., Wersing, H.: KNN classifier with self adjusting memory for heterogeneous concept drift. In: Proceedings of 2016 IEEE International Conference on Data Mining (ICDM), pp. 291–300 (2016)
18. Mahesh, B.: Machine learning algorithms-a review. Int. J. Sci. Res. (IJSR) **9**, 381–386 (2020)
19. Manapragada, C., Webb, G., Salehi, M.: Extremely fast decision tree. In: Proceedings of 24th ACM SIGKDD International Conference on Knowledge Discovery & Data Mining - KDD 2018, pp. 1953–1962 (2018). https://doi.org/10.1145/3219819.3220005
20. Mirzasoleiman, B., Karbasi, A., Krause, A.: Deletion-robust submodular maximization: data summarization with the "right to be forgotten". In: Proceedings of 34th International Conference on Machine Learning, vol. 70, pp. 2449–2458 (2017)
21. Montiel, J., Read, J., Bifet, A., Abdessalem, T.: Scikit-multiflow: a multi-output streaming framework. J. Mach. Learn. Res. **19**(1), 2915-2914 (2018)
22. Pedregosa, F., et al.: Scikit-learn: machine learning in python. J. Mach. Learn. Res. **12**, 2825–2830 (2011)
23. Pinto, A.S., Bernardini, F., Miranda, L., Viterbo, J., Meza, E.M.: An exploratory study using stream learning algorithms to predict duration time of vehicle routes. In: 2020 International Conference on Systems, Signals and Image Processing (IWSSIP), pp. 299–304 (2020)
24. Polikar, R., Udpa, L., Udpa, S.S., Honavar, V.: LEARN++: an incremental learning algorithm for multilayer perceptron networks. In: Proceedings of 2000 IEEE International Conference on Acoustics, Speech, and Signal Processing (2000)
25. Politou, E., Alepis, E., Patsakis, C.: Forgetting personal data and revoking consent under the GDPR: challenges and proposed solutions. J. Cybersecurity **4**(1) (2018)
26. Sengewald, J., Lackes, R.: The impact of the 'right to be forgotten' on algorithmic fairness. In: Buchmann, R.A., Polini, A., Johansson, B., Karagiannis, D. (eds.) BIR 2021. LNBIP, vol. 430, pp. 204–218. Springer, Cham (2021). https://doi.org/10.1007/978-3-030-87205-2_14
27. Villaronga, E.F., Kieseberg, P.T.L.: Humans forget, machines remember: artificial intelligence and the right to be forgotten. Comput. Law Secur. Rev. **34**(2), 304–313 (2018)
28. Zamora-Martínez, F., Romeu, P., Botella-Rocamora, P., Pardo, J.: On-line learning of indoor temperature forecasting models towards energy efficiency. Energy Build. **83**, 162–172 (2014)

Robot Colleagues in Swedish Municipalities: How RPA Affects the Work Situation of Employees

Daniel Toll$^{(\boxtimes)}$ ⓘ, Maria Booth ⓘ, and Ida Lindgren ⓘ

Linköping University, 581 83 Linköping, Sweden
{daniel.toll,maria.booth,ida.lindgren}@liu.se

Abstract. Robotic Process Automation (RPA) is a popular software used for process automation in order to automate administrative tasks, traditionally performed by knowledge workers. The existing research on RPA is lacking in terms of what is known about how this type of technology affects the work situations of employees and their experiences with it. In this study, we seek to contribute to this knowledge gap by conducting an inductive analysis of employee experiences in three Swedish municipalities to explore the effects of RPA on their work situation. We find that RPA creates different effects during implementation compared to post-implementation, and that these effects can be positive or negative in both cases. Furthermore, we show that RPA may alleviate stress in one area of the organization, but that new stress emerges in another. We also conclude that the experiences on the individual level are interconnected with the organizational and managerial aspects of RPA, showing the need to further interconnect knowledge in these areas. Finally, we present some recommendations for future research, with an emphasis on studying employees' work situations from a work environment perspective.

Keywords: RPA · automation · local government · employees · effects

1 Introduction

Robotic Process Automation (RPA) has become a popular type of software to pursue automation of administrative tasks, i.e., tasks typically performed by knowledge workers. This entails the creation of "robot colleagues" that can take over and perform certain tasks (processes) from people, such as transferring data between systems. RPA is often marketed as simple, fast, cheap, and easily scalable, leading both to high amounts of optimism and highly set expectations [1]. In the Swedish public sector, the setting for this study, the use of RPA has rapidly spread throughout local governments. Most Swedish municipalities already have RPA or plan to implement it [2]. The aim of RPA implementation is to increase efficiency and meet the challenges municipalities are facing with regard to the recruitment of highly skilled personnel [3–4].

The introduction of RPA into local government not only affects how the organization performs its duties, but also has implications for the employees in the organization, as the

I. Lindgren et al. (Eds.): EGOV 2023, LNCS 14130, pp. 160–173, 2023.
https://doi.org/10.1007/978-3-031-41138-0_11

introduction of process automation alters their work situation. From a digital government perspective, there is therefore a need to understand the role and effects of RPA on these types of organizations, as well as what it does to their employees. Additionally, there are also indications that the optimistic portrayals of RPA do not necessarily hold true. For example, RPA suppliers claim that no programming skills or technical expertise are required for successful RPA implementation and use, but empirical findings contradict such claims [5]. As such, there are grounds to approach espoused claims and benefits of RPA with caution and scrutiny, calling for research that follows this development in practice. The need for more research in this area is also supported by recent literature reviews and reports by the Swedish Agency for Work Environment Expertise (SAWEE) that show that research on the work life experiences of people in relation to automation software and AI is almost nonexistent [6, 7]. Relatedly, there have been several calls for research for more empirically grounded studies on the use of artificial intelligence and automation in the public sector context from the academic community (e.g., [8–13]). In sum, while the use of RPA in the public sector is increasing [2], research on how RPA affects employees' work situation, and ultimately the organization itself, is scarce. In this paper, we seek to contribute to this research gap.

The aim of this paper is to explore the effects of RPA on employee work situation by conducting an inductive study of employee experiences of RPA implementation and use in three Swedish municipalities. This study contributes to the growing amount of research on RPA in particular, and process automation and artificial intelligence in general. Its contribution lies in its descriptions of how RPA plays out in practice, as well as recommendations for future research. It also contributes by providing a summarized picture of RPA implementations, which can be used to reflect upon current and future implementations.

The paper is organized as follows. Following the introduction, we provide a background discussing existing research on the topic, followed by a description of our method, introducing our case (three Swedish municipalities) and how we conducted the data generation (interviews). We then describe and motivate our analysis approach (grounded theory), followed by a presentation of our results and subsequent discussion. Finally, we provide our conclusions, discuss limitations and make recommendations for future research.

2 Background

The research on RPA is rapidly increasing. So far, however, the bulk of research on RPA has either focused on exploring the benefits of RPA [5, 14–16], or provided recommendations on how such benefits can be realized (e.g. [14, 17–21]). These studies consider the managerial and/or the organizational perspective of RPA implementation and use, while the experiences of employees who are affected by RPA are rarely explored. On a societal level, some studies discuss social challenges related to RPA, for example the resistance or lack of acceptance of RPA based on a fear of job loss [5]. Simultaneously, there are also contradictory findings related to whether RPA actually leads to job-loss or not. While there are studies showing that RPA will not lead to layoffs for knowledge workers [22], other studies show that the opposite holds [13]. Whether RPA leads to job loss or not, the fear of losing one's job is in itself affecting employees' work situation and may also be a source of resistance amongst employees towards the adoption and implementation of RPA [5, 21, 23]. As such, social issues or challenges discussed in relation to RPA tend to frame resisting employees as the challenge, rather than focusing on how employees are affected by and experience its introduction. The study by Eike-brokk and Olsen [13] argues that one of the reasons 30–50% RPA implementations fail is lack of stakeholder buy-in, thus showing the importance of understanding the employee perspective.

While the importance of understanding the employee perspective on RPA imple-mentation has thus been established, few studies to date have done so. A few notable exceptions have however been found. One study of employee experiences of work mean-ingfulness finds that RPA may lead to increased work meaningfulness, but also that it can lead to more routine work, thus showing that the effects of RPA are nuanced [11]. These authors also note that *"In the literature, the employee perspective appear to be under-appreciated and under-researched."* (p. 165), making a call for further research on this topic. A second study focuses on how workers conceptualize RPA, ranging from burdens and threats to tools, team-mates and innovative enablers [12]. This study also notes that *"we still know particularly little about the implications of RPA implementa-tions on the human workforce."* (p. 22). Following this, these authors too make a call for more research on the effects of RPA and employee's responses to its implementa-tion and use. Additionally, they also make the argument that understanding employee experiences is crucial to realizing the benefits of RPA, corroborating the claims made by [13]. A third study focuses on knowledge embodiment and seeks to understand how knowledge embodiment occurs with the introduction of RPA as an aspect of knowledge management [24]. While this study takes an organizational perspective on RPA, it never-theless sheds some light on how employees are affected as it describes how RPA changes the nature of work in the studied organization. It shows that the work for employees has become more analytical following the introduction of RPA. These authors too make rec-ommendations for more research concerning the interaction between automated systems and humans.

3 Method

This study is part of an ongoing research project [25]. The aim of the project is to map current implementations of automated case handling in local governments and develop an analytical tool that can be used by researchers and practitioners alike to decide if and to what degree a case handling process can and should be automated (ibid.). The research project builds on the principles of engaged scholarship [26] and consists of several case studies. These case studies mainly consist of semi-structured interviews, conducted based on a qualitative and interpretive approach [27, 28]. Data generation is explained in Sect. 3.1. The analysis of the data is based on grounded theory to generate descriptive examples of employee experiences and is further described in Sect. 3.2.

3.1 Case Introduction and Data Generation

This study uses data from three different Swedish municipalities that were chosen based on maximum variation sampling. At the time of data generation, the municipalities were at different stages of implementing RPA. One of the municipalities had developed over twenty automated workflows, while the other two municipalities had recently conducted pilot projects and only had a few RPA- "robots" up and running. In all of these municipalities, the processes automated by RPA were case handling processes. Case handling as such normally requires good knowledge of rules, requirements, and procedures, as well as expertise within the topic area (e.g., social benefits, building permits, or school placements). However, this type of process also typically includes tasks such as double-checking information in different systems, moving and entering data between different software interfaces and sending emails. These tasks are at the moment rule-based and unambiguous, not requiring the element of human judgement. While the processes in which the RPA operates can thus be complicated, the tasks performed by the robots are considered simple from a technical point of view.

When conducting our case studies, we used snowball sampling [29] to identify informants, with the aim of identifying and interviewing different roles in relation to the automation initiatives. Thus, we have interviewed employees from different parts of the organizations, ranging from the strategical to the operational level, including directors, strategists, business process developers, IT personnel, administrators, and case workers. Table 1 presents an overview of the three municipalities, their size, and the amount of data we have generated from each. To distinguish and simultaneously anonymize the municipalities in this paper, we have named them Municipality North, East, and West, respectively. The disparity between the number of interviews and informants in the case of Municipality East is due to repeated interviews with some informants. The opposite type of disparity in the case of Municipality West is due to two interviews being conducted with two people simultaneously.

Table 1. Overview of cases used for data generation.

Municipality	Org. size	Data generation
Municipality North (MN)	40 000 citizens 3 000 employees	10 interviews (10 informants)
Municipality East (ME)	165 000 citizens 8 000 employees	22 interviews (18 informants)
Municipality West (MW)	150 000 citizens 11 000 employees	6 interviews (8 informants)

The interviews were semi-structured, and the interview questionnaire was designed with the larger research project in mind (described above). The interviews lasted approximately 90 min in length, and all but one of them were conducted via video calls. Prior to analysis, all interviews were transcribed. The case studies have been conducted in adherence with the ethical guidelines by the Swedish Research Council [30, 31] and the European Code of Conduct for Research Integrity [32].

The interview questions covered digitalization in general, automation in particular, the informants' roles in their respective parts of the organization, as well as their views and experiences related to the recent push for RPA and its perceived purpose and usefulness in relation to their respective areas of work. We have analyzed this data previously, as part of our larger research project. These analyses have shown that these municipalities have experienced challenges with the introduction of RPA, and that there are different attitudes towards it (e.g. [33]). For this study, we focus on employees' experiences related to the implementation and use of RPA, in particular the employees' own thoughts on how RPA affects their work situation. All of the interviews were conducted in Swedish; quotes from the interviews presented later in this paper have been translated.

3.2 Analysis Approach

The inductive analysis conducted in this study is based on grounded theory [34, 35]. However, we have not used grounded theory with the end goal of developing a new theory that includes mechanisms and explanations. Rather, the end goal has been to apply the principles of grounded theory in order to make sense of and organize our data. As this analysis was conducted with a research objective in mind, its inductive nature occurs within the frames set by the research objective, i.e., including anything in the data that can be interpreted as being an effect of RPA on the work situation of employees. Our analysis was conducted through the following steps:

Step 1 – Open coding: The open coding step consisted of going through the transcripts and looking for any statements relating to experiences of RPA. This typically included statements of how RPA has changed the work situation or work content of the interviewee.

Step 2 – Conceptual refinement: During the second step of analysis, the coded parts of the transcripts from the first step were revisited and underwent conceptual refinement, i.e., interpreting what concept could be used as a label to denote the coded statement. For example, the following quote was labeled as "a challenge concerning process mapping":

> *"I would say that in Municipality West, only a few of our processes have been documented. This means that in a group of, let's say, ten people, in the worst-case scenario there could be ten different ways of performing the process. And in order to get a robot to perform the process we have to first agree on 'how do we want the robot to work?'."* (MW)

Step 3 – Categorization: The labeled concepts from the second step of the analysis were combined to form categories, where a category was defined by combining statements that shared similar conceptual nature. Continuing with the example in Step 2, the challenge concerning process mapping was categorized with other challenges to form a category called "Process-mapping challenges".

4 Findings

In this section we present the findings from our inductive analysis. The analysis resulted in themes of how RPA effects on employees' work situations. Additionally, the chapter has been structured into two main parts: the first concerning effects of implementation phase, while the second is focused on RPA in use. When quotes from the interviewees are provided, each quote denotes which municipality the interviewee belongs to by an abbreviation of the municipality in question, e.g., "MW" for "Municipality West". The following figure provides an overview of the themes (Fig. 1).

Experiences during RPA implementation   Experiences of RPA in use

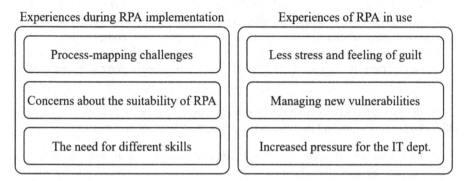

Fig. 1. Overview of themes.

4.1 Effects of RPA During Implementation

We have defined three themes related to the implementation of RPA: "Process-mapping challenges", "Concerns about the suitability of RPA" and "The need for different skills". These are described below.

Process-Mapping Challenges
An important step in RPA implementation is that of mapping the processes that could potentially be considered candidates for RPA. This stage ensures that processes are suitable for RPA in the first place, and also that the RPA is given the correct instructions once it is made active. The first theme, Process-mapping challenges, relates to employee experiences during this crucial stage of RPA implementation. Employees typically involved in process-mapping are those who have been performing the process manually, often with several years of experience. Several of our respondents reported that they found this step difficult for several reasons. One challenge mentioned was that of getting a group of people to agree on how a process is, and should be, conducted, as shown by the following quote:

> "I would say that in Municipality West, only a few of our processes have been documented. This means that in a group of, let's say, ten people, in the worst-case scenario there could be ten different ways of performing the process. And in order to get a robot to perform the process we have to first agree on 'how do we want the robot to work?'." (MW)

Also mentioned is that the employee's knowledge of and familiarity with a process can in itself cause difficulties. Knowledge of how the process works is imperative to the process-mapping, but when that very knowledge leads to employees struggling to see how the process could be performed in new ways, problems arise. As the creation of RPA solutions includes redesigns of the process, the ability to think outside the box becomes of outmost importance:

> "But all processes, if you actually sit down and go through all the processes you have, many of them look quite similar. So, if you focus on those and break them down one more level... Are we talking about a program on a computer, or do we need a piece of paper that we can't get around electronically? (...) But you have to find that person who can see that 'well, this is how we have done it, but why did we do it that way?'."

Some respondents report that the process-mapping stage itself is valuable, due to its effect to spur reflection and discussion regarding the "why" of processes:

> "I think, and we can see this already, that these discussions that are driven by automation and digitalization initiatives lead to us cleaning up our processes. Sometimes we solve things without having to involve technology simply by eliminating them." (ME)

Other employees view process-mapping as less positive, perceiving it as a threat. One respondent in Municipality West mention that some colleagues had found it quite uncomfortable to have their work-processes scrutinized, while another respondent in Municipality North mentions that for some it has felt as if their professional identity is questioned when their processes become the target for automation. One respondent in Municipality East draws on organizational history to explain:

> "Historically, I think that process-mapping has been used in organizational change quite frequently and that [that experience] means that it has quite negative connotations for many of us." (ME)

Process mapping as a stage of RPA implementation is thus a theme of challenging, positive, and negative experiences, as illustrated by the quotes above.

Concerns About the Suitability of RPA
This theme contains experiences that indicate that despite implementing RPA, there are certain apprehensions about its suitability. For example, not everyone agrees that RPA is the way to go to achieve automation, instead preferring other solutions, as indicated by the following quote:

> "So, well, I am positive about automation, but robotization feels a bit, well, like a hobbyhorse. Instead of doing it the right way, we are doing it the wrong way. The right way would have been e.g., APIs along with getting proper info on the actual state of things." (MN)

Related to this are experiences where RPA did not turn out to fulfil expectations, thus making employees working with its implementation question its continued use and future implementations. Several respondents reported that RPA was more complicated than expected, as illustrated by the following quote:

"The first process, then we didn't really know that much about robotic processes in general and we thought that 'that is probably a simple process', but it turned out it had loads of steps with many exceptions and stuff." (MW)

Hence, issues and doubts regarding the implementation of RPA are also experienced.

The Need for Different Skills

The implementation of RPA requires different skills. Getting the right team together and making sure that people have time to work with the automation initiative is mentioned by several respondents as crucial. One respondent in Municipality East mentions the need for employees who understand both the technology (RPA) and the operations (e.g., the processes of a certain department). The same respondent says that when the digitalization department comes in and "speak their own language" it can be perceived as an unwelcome display of power, whereas involving staff who "speak both languages" facilitates the transformation. Another respondent, also in Municipality East, wants to involve even more skills:

"I would say 'it takes three to tango'. Me [project leader for the automation initiative], IT and operations in this case. My role is therefore quite often to translate between the other two. That way we can all understand each other and work together." (ME)

Hence, the implementation of RPA has effects on both those actively working with the implementation process as well as those involved in the processes that have been singled out as RPA-candidates. The combination and interaction between different roles and skills thus becomes a point of consideration when implementing RPA.

4.2 Effects of RPA in Use

We have defined three themes related to experienced effects of finished RPA solutions: "Less stress and feeling of guilt", "Managing new vulnerabilities" and "Increased pressure for the IT department". We describe these below.

Less Stress and Feeling of Guilt

As mentioned earlier, one of the main reasons stated for implementing RPAs in the municipalities is the hope for more efficiently performed processes, thereby freeing up time from employees that can be spent on more value creating tasks. Our data shows that, sometimes, this is also achieved. Municipality West has, for example, introduced an RPA that takes care of invoices that have been sent to the wrong entity within the municipal organization, registering and rerouting them to the correct recipient. According to several of our respondents in Municipality West, the introduction of the RPA has significantly decreased the workload for the employee who normally manages this process. This has resulted in positive experiences, illustrated by the following quote:

"When you arrive at work and realize that you don't have 40 invoices waiting for you, but only 10. Of course... That's pretty sweet!" (MW)

Some respondents also testify that, as was the intention in the first place, the introduction of RPA means that they spend less time on repetitive, "boring" tasks, allowing them to focus on the more value adding aspects of their work. In Municipality West, the introduction of RPA in the salary department means that the salary specialists can focus on more complicated tasks, and also on the more complicated cases that the RPA cannot handle. This sentiment is supported also by a respondent in Municipality North who states that:

"This makes a difference also for the professional identity. Nobody pursues a degree in social work to work as some sort of assistant in accounts. So of course, it's valuable for us to be able to spend time on proper legal assessments, to be able to work closer with clients and to spend time with them. And while I think the value the RPA brings to the citizens is the most important benefit, this comes at a good second." (MN)

However, many of our respondents also talk about how the RPA have improved their work indirectly rather than by the direct removal of tasks. One respondent in Municipality North, for example, says that the introduction of the RPA means that they can access information much earlier in the process, thereby making the process easier to carry out.

A very telling example of how the RPA has improved the work situation without necessarily performing a process more efficiently also comes from Municipality West, where RPA was introduced to handle a rather complicated process. After RPA was introduced, employees testify that the RPA did not necessarily perform the process more efficiently. Previously, however, this process was always put at the bottom of the pile as employees were forced to prioritize more urgent cases. The lead-time for the process could pre-RPA be up to two years, but after implementing RPA most cases are handled within a month. In this case, the introduction of the RPA meant that a process that had previously been systematically de-prioritized, serving as a constant source of stress and source of a guilty conscience among the employees, could now be handled swiftly.

Managing New Vulnerabilities

While the goal of RPA, or automation in general, is the removed need for humans, the technology does need a certain degree of up-keep. Several employees in our study report that the implementation of RPA has resulted in new tasks they have to handle. As RPA solutions are integrated with other systems, it is vulnerable to changes in those systems. This results in an increased need for careful planning. The following respondent from Municipality West sheds some light on this:

"We have changed from a bit more just "well just add this to the system and then we'll up-date" to having to think about all the parts at once. When we do change something, we have to make sure that we inform all involved parties... It is harder to continuously implement smaller improvements." (MW)

While some mentioned the risk of skills being lost when the RPA takes over a process, others mention that that has, so far, not been the case. A respondent in Municipality West, for example, argues that as the RPA cannot yet deal with all cases (some applications are still handled manually), case-managers still need to know what they are doing. However, as repetitive tasks are removed and work becomes more complex, employees also become more specialized. This, according to one respondent in Municipality East, could cause problems in the long run:

"When we become more specialized, we also become more vulnerable. There are no back-up solutions, it's just me and my job, and I have to take care of it and carry it out etc. I very rarely have a colleague at my side who I can discuss things with or feel that 'it's ok if I stay home sick today, somebody else will take care of it'." (ME)

The above examples show how RPA creates new vulnerabilities for the organization; one is associated with the technology itself and the other emerges as a consequence of its implementation.

Increased Pressure for the IT Department
In our data, the IT departments of the municipalities stand out as parts of the organizations that receive new responsibilities due to RPA implementation, in turn creating needs for more resources in this area. For example, one of the main reasons mentioned for introducing RPAs in municipalities is the reduced need for humans, thereby cutting costs and freeing up resources overall. Paradoxically, in Municipality West a RPA solution has replaced two case managers, but created the need for two IT-technicians to be hired to make sure it runs smoothly. In Municipality North another respondent says that:

"They saved loads of time for the case-managers, IT got loads more work. They wanted us to solve all their problems. And we haven't been allocated any extra resources for this work. So, they have automated a process, but they haven't automated the up-keep of the RPA so to speak." (MN)

The belief that RPAs necessarily lead to lower costs is questioned also by other respondents who express a worry that the costs of running an RPA have not necessarily been included in the pre-implementation analysis. One respondent in Municipality North says that:

"We tell our citizens that the RPA will serve them 24/7, but we don't support the RPA 24/7. If the RPA goes down at 17.00 on a Friday, it will remain down until 8.00 on Monday morning when we get back to the office." (MN)

Along the same lines, a respondent in Municipality West says that:

"I am a bit worried about that... Now we're working on these small processes, but if we move to larger processes and systems, an awful lot of maintenance will be needed. And we don't really know how much time and money is needed there. We don't really know how much the maintenance of a robot actually costs." (MW)

In Municipality West, respondents also raise concerns that the RPAs are too dependent on their creators for their up-keep and maintenance and that no-one really knows
what happens if that person, for example, is sick for a longer period of time. In Municipality North, similar concerns are expressed related to the, at times, patchy handover of
a RPA from creators to maintenance. Hence, even though the implementation of RPAs
can improve the work situation for some employees, it cannot be assumed that that
improvement holds for all.

5   Discussion

As our analysis indicates, there are effects of RPA on the work situation of employees
both during and after its implementation. We argue that this is a noteworthy find, as
previous research mostly has focused on the latter, i.e., what happens after RPA has
been implemented. However, the implementation process can be lengthy and include
several different stakeholders [4]. Also, a large portion of RPA implementation projects
tend to fail, where the lack of stakeholder buy-in might be a factor [13]. As such, the
implementation of RPA is not something that goes by quickly and without issues; instead,
the implementation process itself affects employees, and needs to be considered and
managed. The theme "Concerns about the suitability of RPA" indicates that there is some
hesitation amongst employees, which suggests the idea of lacking stakeholder buy-in
(ibid) also in our study. Relatedly, the theme "The need for different skills" also shows the
need for different kinds of stakeholders to be involved during implementation, something
that posed a challenge. Taken together with the theme "Process-mapping challenges",
our analysis indicates that there are several challenges, and ultimately potential barriers,
for implementation. Thus, the employee experiences provide a more nuanced picture
than seen in previous research that generalize the employee perspective to a sense of
fear that causes resistance and affects RPA acceptance (e.g. [23]).

The employee experiences of finished RPA solutions indicate several things. For
one, RPA is associated with both positive and negative experiences. The first theme,
"Less stress and feeling of guilt", being a positive one. There is a lot of hype associated
with RPA, a common claim being that it frees up time, thus allowing employees to
focus on other tasks [5]. Our results show that this is something that RPA is indeed able
to achieve. Notably, our respondents talk about this both in terms of saving time, but
also that it leads to less stress and feeling of guilt and inadequacy, indicating that their
work environment has been changed for the better. However, as our results show, the
situation is also more nuanced, as the remaining themes are of a less positive nature. This
corroborates previous research showing that employees conceptualize robots differently,
ranging from burdens and threats to teammates [12].

The theme "Managing new vulnerabilities" shows how the introduction of RPA
causes organizational changes that affect the work situations of employees. While RPA
may solve certain vulnerabilities, e.g., increasing quality assurance [33], new vulnerabilities are created. Thus, while RPA is sometimes framed as a problem-solver, in practice it
reconfigures the situation, solving one issue and another pops up elsewhere. For example,
the employee who speaks about becoming more specialized is an example of how RPA
can cause the remaining tasks to be more analytical and demanding [24]. Another such

type of reconfiguration is how RPA in Municipality West replaced two case managers, but, paradoxically, two IT technicians had to be hired. Another vulnerability mentioned is how the technological aspects of RPA are unstable and have to be handled, relating to the final theme of "Increased pressure on the IT department".

The increased pressure on the IT department seemingly indicates that in the implementation and management of RPA initiatives, the IT department is an afterthought. Challenges for the IT department have been discussed in previous research [22] and our results show how these challenges affect the employees. While some employees experience less stress (as mentioned in one of the earlier themes), the opposite is true for the IT department. As such, their work environment is negatively affected. This shows the influential connection between managerial aspects and work environment, showing the importance for change management to consider the interplay between these. Thus, we show the importance of connecting knowledge on social aspects of RPA with those of an organizational and managerial nature.

6   Conclusions, Limitations, and Future Research

The objective of this paper was to explore the effects of RPA on the work situation of employees by considering their experiences of the implementation and use of RPA. We have done this by conducting an inductive analysis which resulted in six themes of RPA effects, three of which are associated with the implementation of RPA and three associated with finished RPA solutions in use. Our result contributes to the knowledge gap concerning the lack of empirical studies of RPA in practice. We make the following conclusions:

- The effects during implementation are different than those post-implementation. There are positive and negative effects associated with both.
- RPA leads to reconfigurations of vulnerabilities and work environment effects. While RPA leads to positive outcomes in one place, negative outcomes can occur elsewhere. Relatedly, different stakeholder groups are affected differently. Our results show that the IT department in particular can be negatively affected.
- The effects of RPA experienced by employees on an individual level are interconnected with organizational and managerial aspects of how RPA is managed.

In sum, we find that RPA implementation affects employee work situation directly on an individual level, by e.g., removing repetitive tasks, but also indirectly through changes on an organizational and/or process level, e.g., through changing roles and new vulnerabilities. We also see that the employee work situation is affected both during the implementation phase as well as when the RPA is in use. We recognize several limitations with this study. Our inductive approach, while suitable for our explorative aim, has resulted in mainly descriptive accounts of experiences. We believe that the addition of a theoretical framework would have allowed for a deeper analysis. A recommendation for future research is therefore to consider employee experiences in relation to e.g., work environment legislation and literature. Such research could also benefit from relating the analysis to organizational and managerial factors. Furthermore, we mention that RPA affects different stakeholders differently (e.g., the IT department), but our analysis makes no further distinctions between different groups of employees. As our findings indicate that this is a relevant perspective, we acknowledge the lack of it as a limitation and recommend future studies to consider different employee experiences related to their role and position within the organization. The difference between organizational, individual, and process level effects and the relationship between them also needs further exploration to fully understand how employee work situation is affected by the introduction of RPA. Finally, we recognize that while this study is focused on the public sector context, our analysis is unable at this time to discern which part of the findings is specific to this context, compared to RPA in e.g., the private sector. While this is a consequence of the limited research on this topic, we recommend future studies to compare different contexts to identify differences and commonalities, where this study can be used as an example of RPA in the public sector.

Acknowledgements. This work is supported by AFA Försäkring, as part of the research project "From Form to Robot?" (190200).

References

1. Kregel, I., Koch, J., Plattfaut, R.: Beyond the hype: robotic process automation's public perception over time. J. Organ. Comput. Electron. Commer. **31**(2), 130–150 (2021)
2. Juell-Skielse, G., Güner, E.O., Han, S.: Adoption of robotic process automation in the public sector: a survey study in Sweden. In: Janssen, M., et al. (eds.) EGOV 2022. LNCS, vol. 13391, pp. 336–352. Springer, Cham (2022). https://doi.org/10.1007/978-3-031-15086-9_22
3. SALAR: Automatisering Av Arbete. SALAR, Stockholm (2018)
4. Svensson, L.: Tekniken är den enkla biten. Om att implementera digital automatisering i handläggningen av försörjningsstöd, Lund (2019)
5. Hindel, J., Cabrera, L.M., Stierle, M.: Robotic process automation: hype or hope? In: Wirtschaftsinformatik (Zentrale Tracks), pp. 1750–1762, March 2020
6. SAWEE (Swedish Agency for Work Environment Expertise): Artificiell intelligens, robotisering och arbetsmiljö (2022)
7. SAWEE (Swedish Agency for Work Environment Expertise): Identifierade Kunskapsluckor 2022 – Myndigheten För Arbetsmiljökunskap (2022). https://mynak.se/identifierade-kunska psluckor-2022/. Accessed 26 Mar 2023
8. Germundsson, N.: Promoting the digital future: the construction of digital automation in Swedish policy discourse on social assistance. Crit. Policy Stud. **16**(4), 478–496 (2022)
9. Veale, M., Brass, I.: Administration by Algorithm? Public Management meets Public Sector Machine Learning. Oxford University Press (2019)
10. Wihlborg, E., Larsson, H., Hedström, K.: The computer says no!"–a case study on automated decision-making in public authorities. In: 2016 49th Hawaii International Conference on System Sciences (HICSS), pp. 2903–2912. IEEE, 2016 January
11. Staaby, A., Hansen, K.S., Grønli, T.M.: Automation of routine work: a case study of employees' experiences of work meaningfulness. In: 54th Annual Hawaii International Conference on System Sciences, HICSS 2021, pp. 156–165. Hawaii International Conference on System Sciences (HICSS) (2021)
12. Waizenegger, L., Techatassanasoontorn, A.A.: When robots join our team: a configuration theory of employees' perceptions of and reactions to robotic process automation. Australas. J. Inf. Syst. **26** (2022)

13. Eikebrokk, T.R., Olsen, D.H.: Robotic process automation for knowledge workers – will it lead to empowerment or lay-offs? Bibsys Open Journal Syst. **27**(1) (2019). ISSN 1894-7719. Paper Presented at NOKOBIT 2019, Narvik, 25–26 November 2019
14. Lamberton, C., Brigo, D., Hoy, D.: Impact of robotics, RPA and AI on the insurance industry: challenges and opportunities. J. Financ. Perspect. **4**(1) (2017)
15. Pramod, D.: Robotic process automation for industry: adoption status, benefits, challenges and research agenda. Benchmarking: Int. J. **29**(5), 1562–1586 (2021)
16. Denagama Vitharanage, I.M., Bandara, W., Syed, R., Toman, D.: An empirically supported conceptualisation of robotic process automation (RPA) benefits. In: Proceedings of the 28th European Conference on Information Systems (ECIS 2020). Association for Information Systems, June 2020
17. Kaniadakis, A., Linturn, L.: Organisational adoption of a hyped technology: the case of robotic process automation. In: ECIS 2021 Research Papers, p. 46 (2021)
18. Osman, C.C.: Robotic process automation: lessons learned from case studies. Informatica Economica **23**(4) (2019)
19. Penttinen, E., Kasslin, H., Asatiani, A.: How to choose between robotic process automation and back-end system automation? In: European Conference on Information Systems 2018, June 2018
20. Plattfaut, R., Borghoff, V., Godefroid, M., Koch, J., Trampler, M., Coners, A.: The critical success factors for robotic process automation. Comput. Ind. **138**, 103646 (2022)
21. Stamoulis, D.: Management considerations for robotic process automation implementations in digital industries. J. Inf. Syst. Technol. Manag. **7**(25), 35–53 (2022)
22. Lacity, M., Willcocks, L.: What knowledge workers stand to gain from automation. Harv. Bus. Rev. **19**(6) (2015)
23. Syed, R., Wynn, M.T.: How to trust a bot: an RPA user perspective. In: Asatiani, A., et al. (eds.) BPM 2020. LNBIP, vol. 393, pp. 147–160. Springer, Cham (2020). https://doi.org/10. 1007/978-3-030-58779-6_10
24. Dias, M., Pan, S., Tim, Y.: Knowledge embodiment of human and machine interactions: robotic-process-automation at the Finland government. In: Proceedings of the 27th European Conference on Information Systems (ECIS), Uppsala, Sweden (2019)
25. Lindgren, I.: Exploring the use of robotic process automation in local government. In: EGOV-CeDEM-ePart 2020, p. 249 (2020)
26. Van de Ven, A.H.: Engaged Scholarship: A Guide for Organizational and Social Research. Oxford University Press (2007). on Demand
27. Myers, M.D.: Qualitative research in information systems. MIS Q. **21**(2), 241–242 (1997). https://doi.org/10.2307/249422
28. Walsham, G.: Interpretive case studies in IS research: nature and method. Eur. J. Inf. Syst. **4**(2), 74–81 (1995)
29. Patton, M.Q.: Qualitative Evaluation Methods. Sage, Beverly Hills (1980)
30. Vetenskapsrådet: Forskningsetiska principer inom humanistisk-samhällsvetenskaplig forskning. Vetenskapsrådet, Stockholm (2002)
31. Vetenskapsrådet: God forskningssed. Vetenskapsrådet, Stockholm (2017)
32. All European Academies: The European Code of Conduct for Research Integrity (2017). https://allea.org/code-of-conduct/. Accessed 10 June 2023
33. Toll, D., Lindgren, I., Melin, U.: Stakeholder views of process automation as an enabler of prioritized value ideals in a Swedish municipality. JeDEM-eJ. eDemocr. Open Gov. **14**(2), 32–56 (2022)
34. Corbin, J.M., Strauss, A.: Grounded theory research: procedures, canons, and evaluative criteria. Qual. Sociol. **13**(1), 3–21 (1990)
35. Glaser, B.G., Strauss, A.L.: Discovery of Grounded Theory: Strategies for Qualitative Research. Routledge (2017)

Using Artificial Intelligence in Parliament - The Hellenic Case

Jörn von Lucke[1](✉) ⓘ and Fotios Fitsilis[2] ⓘ

[1] The Open Government Institute, Zeppelin University, 88045 Friedrichshafen, Germany
joern.vonlucke@zu.de
[2] Scientific Service, Hellenic Parliament, Athens, Greece
fitsilisf@parliament.gr

Abstract. Parliaments are looking into using artificial intelligence (AI) technology to do certain tasks. Reflecting on conceivable tools, fields of application, usage scenarios and needs, it is reasonable to expect AI-induced changes in parliaments. However, not much research has been done on how to use AI in the parliamentary workspace. This article contributes to the bridging of this gap by presenting empirical evidence for the future use of AI-based tools and services as well as open questions in a national parliament. The data were collected during a brainstorming exercise in 2020 and a virtual workshop in the Hellenic Parliament in 2021. The analysis sheds light in the prioritization of AI-based technologies within the parliamentary environment. In the course of the study, the relevance and the priority of 210 applications and topics of AI technologies in parliament have been investigated.

Keywords: Artificial Intelligence · Parliament · Hellenic Parliament · Greece

1 Introduction

Parliaments have the opportunity to decide whether or not they want to rely on artificial intelligence (AI) and AI-based applications for performing parliamentary tasks. AI-based applications have the potential to automate several tasks of the parliamentary routine, such as identifying patterns and events, notifying relevant parties, making predictions, recommending actions, making prognoses, initiate precautionary measures, and even making decisions without human intervention. All of this could also happen nearly in real time [7]. Behind this, however, is neither a single technology nor a collection of niche applications. Rather, numerous technologies are assigned to AI today [4, 8–12, 23]. All these applications might provide invaluable support for parliamentarians, enabling them to make informed decisions quickly and efficiently. Despite the benefits, the decision to adopt AI technology in parliamentary tasks ultimately lies with the parliaments themselves, as they must balance the potential advantages against the ethical and legal considerations of AI implementation.

Reflecting potential tools, fields of application, usage scenarios and requirements, AI-induced changes in parliaments are to be expected. To deal with these changes at an

© IFIP International Federation for Information Processing 2023
Published by Springer Nature Switzerland AG 2023
I. Lindgren et al. (Eds.): EGOV 2023, LNCS 14130, pp. 174–191, 2023.
https://doi.org/10.1007/978-3-031-41138-0_12

early stage, thus gaining a broad overall view, the corresponding approaches, potentials and visions for parliaments should be examined. Brainstorming workshops are a good way to gain an initial overview of the areas and fields of AI application in parliaments. The brainstorming results should be locally assessed by national parliaments for their relevance and priority. An efficient way to do so is via interactive workshops. The analysis of such assessment sheds light in the prioritization of AI-based technologies within the parliamentary environment and lays the fundament for the creation of an implementation roadmap for a user-generated development of AI-based solutions.

2 Literature Review

The Hellenic Parliament is the national parliament of the Hellenic Republic. As an important institution of the Greek political system, it has one chamber with 300 parliamentarians elected for four years, who among others perform the role of legislator. It is organized in general directorates and utilizes Information and Communication Technologies (ICT) that facilitate and support its parliamentary functions as prescribed by the Constitution.

In order to evolve in a gradual, non-disruptive manner, the Hellenic Parliament has been setting strategic goals usually expressed in the programmatic statements of its newly elected Speakers. In the digital sphere, some of the goals are materialized through (volunteering) action plans within the framework of the Open Government Partnership. In 2018, the goals were formalized as a four-year long Strategic Plan 2018–2021 [11] (also called "strategy") using a structured development procedure. A combined bottom-up (for the organizational part) and top-down (for the vision, mission and values) approach was used to capture the necessary strategic elements. The draft strategy underwent a concluding consultation step, during which its structure and the distinct strategic options were refined. The development of the strategic plan was guided and supported by the previously formed Strategic Planning and Management Reengineering Unit, which was established in 2017 for this purpose. The strategy contains significant statements pointing at the digitalization of every aspect of parliamentary life and foresees the use of information technology to achieve certain institutional goals.

AI was so far no topic with strategic value for the parliamentary processes. However, this can be explained due to the fact that the strategy was meant to be technology-agnostic. Hence, it contains goals and objectives, and not the (technological) means to achieve them. For instance, specific emphasis was placed in the adoption of interoperability tools (Strategic Goal 2), the use of open data modes and the digital production of "legislative work" (Strategic Goal 6). The latter can be substantially advanced using artificial intelligence.

The use of AI in parliaments is becoming increasingly important and cannot be ignored. Lessons learned from preliminary studies [12] and the use of AI in representative institutions can be transferred and applied economically. In response to societal pressure, parliaments are beginning to analyze the opportunities and challenges presented by AI. The Parliamentary Assembly of the Council of Europe [18] and the Global Parliamentary Network of the OECD [17] have both established groups focused on AI. However, despite broad recognition of the need to introduce AI, there are limited examples of actual implementation in parliaments. The European Parliament has been probably the most thoroughly informed representative institution on AI-related issues to date. As such, it has adopted several relevant resolutions [5] and actively utilizes AI solutions in its Archives Unit [6]. The Brazilian Chamber of Deputies has launched Ulysses, a set of AI tools to improve the legislative process and interact with citizens [21, 22].

In late 2022, the introduction of ChatGPT [2] by OpenAI, caused a sharp rise of interest for AI-based solutions with a direct or indirect impact on legislation [15]. Whether a game changer or not, such AI-tools and the related services need to be taken seriously by legislatures. In fact, parliaments can become leading institutions in the application of AI-based tools and services in both the application and the regulation of AI [8, 9]. In this regard, it is worth mentioning that the European Commission investigated the potential of AI and innovative ICT tools in order to advance legal drafting, a core parliamentary business [19].

3 Research Approach

The design of the study was primarily concerned with finding a suitable research approach that would allow the assessment of a broad, detailed and practical as well as diverse and without one-sided perspective range of possible application areas for AI in parliaments. It should be noted that AI tools can be technically divided into several branches of operation such as summarization, classification, sentiment analysis, semantic analysis, and recommendation. Specific technologies and algorithms, such as NLP, BERT, and GPT-X, can be applied differently depending on the case. However, as technologies and algorithms evolve rapidly, a technology-agnostic study was recommended. Moreover, the study should not only be about the collection of existing solutions but also about the capturing of ideas for the future of parliament, even if they appear to be not yet technically feasible. A lot of these ideas are suitable as guiding pictures that can be further developed into long-term visions and design-oriented approaches, while laying the foundation for impact assessments [13, 14].

The brainstorming method was chosen for the open collection of ideas [3]. The method was applied in two rounds on a group of three experts from academia and parliamentary practice who met the following baseline requirements: sufficient expertise through studies, own research on the topic, practical experience, and professional capacity. XLeap was used as a cloud-based brainstorming platform [24]. In the first round, ideas for the use of AI technologies in parliaments were collected and sorted. In the second round, the contributions were reviewed, complemented, and reflected upon [13, 14].

The preliminary results of the brainstorming can be presented to a parliamentary community for more in-depth assessment. Rather than having a mixed participation from different parliaments (see [12]), administrators and Members of Parliament (MPs) from a single parliament are thought to offer more homogeneous responses. For this audience, a follow-up utility analysis [20] appears to be suitable to determine the benefit, relevance, and necessity of the generated proposals. For this purpose, a utility analysis and an XLeap-based utility survey on relevance and priority of AI proposal was performed through two different questions. First, for each entry, the relevance of the proposal was requested on a scale from 0 (irrelevant) to 5 (relevant) to 10 (must-have). Second, the priority of the proposal was requested with the year of implementation as parameter. In this case, the scale ranged from 0 (2020) to 5 (2025) to 10 (2030). Each of these values can be converted into a concrete date (0: 31.12.2020; 5: 31.12.2025; 10: 31.12.2030). Proposals that should not even be implemented may be rated with the maximum value of 10 [13, 14].

4 Brainstorming Results

Based on the original research concept, on 14th July 2020 a four-hour online brainstorming session was organized with the participation of three designated experts. Overall, 196 contributions were collected by answering the open question: "Which are the fields of application for AI in the work and environment of parliaments?" After eliminating overlaps, the number of proposals was reduced to 181 and the ideas were clustered according to thematic areas. In the course of a further revision, additional ideas were added and all contributions were reviewed, discussed and partly revised. The final clustering included 210 entries that belong to nine thematic areas (clusters): #1: Parliamentarians (13); #2: Legislation (36); #3: Parliamentary Control and Parliamentary Diplomacy (14); #4: Civic Education and National Culture (17); #5: Parliamentary Administration, Parliament Buildings, Driving Service and Police (37); #6: Parliamentary Bureau & Parliamentary Directorates & Elections (19); #7: Scientific Services (13); #8: Framework (47) and #9: Open Questions (14) [14].

5 National Parliament Assessment Results: The Hellenic Case

Eight months after the brainstorming workshop, a virtual workshop was held on 18th March 2021 in the Hellenic Parliament, in order to evaluate the proposals from the brainstorming exercise. The 14 participants, nine men and five women, came from seven different parliamentary sectors. MPs and their staff were also invited to represent the demand side of parliament. The preparation phase lasted two weeks during which several discussions were held to clarify various aspects of the study and specific organizational questions. In order to save workshop time, the participants were sent in advance the Greek translation of the questionnaire.

Initiating the workshop, the procedure and the aim of the rating were presented. All participants were also informed that they would receive the results in the form of an electronic PDF document directly with the end of the workshop. The participants then individually and anonymously evaluated all 210 AI-related proposals, each divided into blocks covering the nine thematic areas. The relevance and priority values for each one of the proposals were captured and documented using the moderation software XLeap in the setup explained in Sect. 3.

Regarding the results from the Hellenic Parliament of the workshop, the relevance scores for all proposals ranged from 4.31 to 9.38, on a scale ranging from 0 to 10. The five highest rated proposals (top 5) received a score of 9.08 or better. Eleven out of 210 proposals (5.2%) had a score of 9.0 or better, while 69 proposals (32.8%) were rated 8.0 points or better. The cut-off point of 7.5 and better, which is crucial for the relevance scale, contained 118 of 210 proposals (56,2%). Surprisingly, 209 out of 210 proposals (99.5%) scored above 5.0 (relevant) and 210 (100%) scored above 2.5. Only the well-known typology of Misuraca and van Noordt [16] has been rated with a relevance of 4.31. These results and the evaluation of the participants' opinions underline a remarkably high interest in AI for the future work operations of the Hellenic Parliament. Overall, there was valuable feedback for the proposals and, by extension, for the research and development agenda of the research team. The recommendations for the implementation of these proposals suggest implementation interval between December 2021 and November 2026 [14].

6 Discussion: Findings and Comments

For further analysis of the findings, four different types of evaluations were drawn from the full data set. Firstly, the top 10 proposals rated as most relevant (Sect. 6.1, Table 1) are compiled, that is which questions must be answered and which projects should definitely be implemented. Secondly, the top 10 proposals rated with the highest priority (Sect. 6.2, Table 2) are put together, i.e. which ones should be implemented most quickly. Thirdly, the respective top 3 options (sorted by relevance, Sect. 6.3, Tables 3, 4, 5 and 6) are discussed for eight topic clusters. This provides an overview across all thematic areas of which priorities are set in each cluster. Fourthly, the top 5 open questions (sorted by relevance, Sect. 6.4, Table 7) are analyzed to determine which topics needs to be addressed and which discussions need to be initiated first.

6.1 Top 10 Relevance of All Proposals

The results of the brainstorming and the evaluation of the participants' choices from the Hellenic Parliament underline a remarkably high interest in AI. The Top 10 of all 210 proposals have received a relevance score of 9,00 or better on a scale from 0 to 10.

Among the ten most important proposals for the Hellenic Parliament, which should definitely be implemented due to their high relevance, there are five open questions (9,01–9,05), four requirements (5,02; 8,01; 8,02; 8,03) and only one concrete proposal (5,01). The design of training courses and a recruitment campaign, ethical aspects and the limits of the use of AI in parliaments, an AI-based restructuring of electoral constituencies and the concretization of the concept of a smart parliament are rated as open questions that urgently need to be clarified. The integration into the European Interoperability Framework and the associated system interoperability as well as specific security requirements for the use of algorithmic systems in the context of human decisions also need to be clarified. There is also a call for a pragmatic approach to the incalculable consequences from the use of AI, for example by presenting lists of permissions and prohibitions to preserve the integrity and working capacity of the parliament. Furthermore, AI-based applications for automatic text entry of manuscripts and speeches are requested. The latter is the highest graded technical proposal regarding its relevance and should be assessed closely for advanced implementation. This is because the Hellenic Parliament is not foreign to such solutions. In the late 2000's a speech-to-text application was unsuccessfully tested. More than a decade later, speech recognition for

Table 1. Multi-Criteria Table for the Hellenic Parliament. Sorted by Relevance.

Nr	Item	Relevance 0..10		Priority 31.12.20–31.12.30	
		↓Ø	SD	Ø	SD
9,01	[131.-] Prerequisites: Training and hiring of new staff in the IT department?	9,38	0,08	02.12.2021	0,06
8,01	[211.-] Link parliamentary AI systems with European Interoperability Framework (EIF, further developed with AI portfolio)	9,38	0,08	19.05.2022	0,12
9,02	[136.-] Ethical aspects of the operation of AI-based systems	9,31	0,08	29.01.2022	0,09
9,03	[97.-] Reflection on the limits of the use of AI in parliament	9,15	0,13	29.01.2022	0,10
9,04	[214.-] Election engineering: Restructuring constituencies by AI to improve the representative function of parliament (sounds like gerrymandering, but it is exactly the opposite)	9,08	0,13	23.04.2022	0,07
8,03	[159.-] Special safeguards when using algorithmic systems in the context of human decisions,	9,08	0,11	19.05.2023	0,25
8,02	[114.-] EU/Mercosur-supported system interoperability	9,08	0,10	06.11.2023	0,24
5,01	[71.-] AI-based automatic text and speech capture	9,00	0,10	15.10.2022	0,23
5,02	[216.-] Limits of parliamentarianism in times of AI usage: consequences unmanageable - Which AI services will be allowed and which must be banned in order not to jeopardise the functionality and integrity of parliament?	9,00	0,11	11.05.2023	0,28
9,05	[139.-] Defining the smart parliament concept, what is involved?	9,00	0,14	16.07.2022	0,26

semi-automatic minute generation was introduced [10], though its development started earlier.

6.2 Top 10 Priority of All Proposals

With regard to priority, also to be related with implementation expectations, it can be observed that the participants in March 2021 set target dates in the years between December 2021 and November 2026 that corresponds to a period of five years and, thus, within a manageable planning horizon. The date of the next parliamentary elections in spring 2023 might have played a role. The maximum value of 10 years (2030) was rarely selected as a target. Although all standard deviations range from 0,06 to 0,35, with 19 values at 0,30 or above (9.0%) indicating a divergent assessment, the deviation within the cohort is kept within manageable limits. The lower the value, the closer together are the experts' assessments over time.

Among the top 10 proposals for the Hellenic Parliament to be implemented as a matter of time priority (until July 2022), there are five open questions (9,01; 9,02; 9,03; 9,04; 9,09), three requirements (8,01; 8,14; 8,19) and only two concrete proposals (4,01 & 7,01). Training and recruitment of new staff, ethical aspects and limits of the use of AI in the parliament are urgently to be clarified. An AI-based document search for the parliamentary library, the digital reading room of the library and the Scientific Services should make it much easier for users to search for and access relevant documents. An AI-based search function on the homepage of the parliamentary website is also expected to relieve burden if it provides a high-quality and rapid response to queries. It also needs to be clarified soon if AI can be used to redraw electoral districts and to carry out security analyses, or if this will create new problems. In addition, a framework is needed for embedding AI in the European Interoperability Framework, for legal protection against discrimination and for minimum data quality requirements for the use of AI in Parliament. Two years later, in March 2023, none of these issues have been addressed by the Greek Parliament. Hence, until recently, this grading seems to have been over-realistic. However, in the ChatGPT era, the timeline for the introduction of these proposals appears feasible yet challenging.

6.3 Top 3 Relevance of Each Cluster

Regarding both top 10 rankings, it is noticeable that there are many questions and framework requirements among them, but relatively few proposals. Perhaps there might be too many unanswered questions that suggest reflecting first on opportunities and risks. For this reason, this section looks at the top 3 for each of the eight clusters and then reflects the distribution of the proposals visually. It is important to add that the top 3 were selected according to relevance and, if applicable, according to the lowest standard deviation. This way, three proposals could clearly be selected for each cluster, suitable for an in-depth analysis, also from a parliamentary perspective.

The first cluster (Parliamentarians) includes 13 proposals. Particularly high scores (Table 3) were given to a voting system for the plenary chamber and the committees that is reliable thanks to AI services (9,00), the use of AI-based text analysis services (8,43) and AI-supported services (8,07) that considerably simplify MPs' work in parliament and in their constituencies. The people in parliament are looking for substantial reliefs for their work, without wanting to question everything in principle. Reliable voting systems,

Table 2. Multi-Criteria Table for the Hellenic Parliament. Sorted by Priority.

Nr	Item	Relevance 0..10		Priority 31.12.20–31.12.30	
		↓∅	SD	∅	SD
9,01	[131.-] Prerequisites: Training and hiring of new staff in the IT department?	9,38	0,08	02.12.2021	0,06
9,02	[136.-] Ethical aspects of the operation of AI-based systems	9,31	0,08	29.01.2022	0,09
9,03	[97.-] Reflection on the limits of the use of AI in parliament	9,15	0,13	29.01.2022	0,10
7,01	[15.-] AI-based intelligent document search in the parliamentary library and in e-publication room of library/scientific services	8,69	0,26	03.03.2022	0,13
4,01	[27.-] Intelligent, AI-based search functions in the front end of the parliament's website	8,57	0,19	17.03.2022	0,20
9,04	[215.-] Election engineering: Restructuring constituencies by AI to improve the representative function of parliament (sounds like gerrymandering, but it is exactly the opposite)	9,08	0,13	23.04.2022	0,07
8,01	[211.-] Link parliamentary AI systems with European Interoperability Framework (EIF, further developed with AI portfolio)	9,38	0,08	19.05.2022	0,12
9,09	[127.-] Potential problem areas: Security analysis and cooperation of these systems	8,08	0,22	17.06.2022	0,11
8,14	[161.-] Legal protection against discrimination	8,69	0,19	17.06.2022	0,16
8,19	[103.-] Ensuring that data quality is fit for purpose	8,46	0,14	16.07.2022	0,13

text analytics and other AI-based services can potentially take a lot of pressure off the MPs and the staff.

The second cluster contains fields of application in the legislation and includes 36 proposals [13]. High ratings (Table 3) were given to the intelligent examination of legislative proposals for possible impacts with other regulations (8,57), the Transformation of legislation (code) into machine understandable e-code (8,57) and a collection of all coded laws (smart law) with the possibility for AI interpretation of the legislation (8,50).

Table 3. Multi-Criteria Table for Top 3 per Cluster - Hellenic Parliament. Sorted by Relevance.

Cluster #1: Parliamentarians Cluster #2: Legislation		Relevance 0..10		Priority 31.12.20–31.12.30	
Nr	Item	↓Ø	SD	Ø	SD
1,01	[137.-] Reliable voting systems (through AI technologies) in plenary and committees	9,00	0,16	17.03.2024	0,29
1,02	[74.-] Use of text analytics	8,43	0,15	15.04.2024	0,25
1,03	[138.-] Smarter MP - AI-based services to support MPs in parliament and in their constituency	8,07	0,12	31.12.2025	0,23
2,01	[20.-] Intelligent examination of legislative proposals for interactions with further regulations	8,57	0,12	02.07.2023	0,19
2,02	[26.-] Transformation of legislation (code) into machine-understandable e-code	8,57	0,20	16.10.2023	0,24
2,03	[125.-] Smart Law - collection of all coded laws with the possibility of AI interpretation of the legislation	8,50	0,13	31.12.2023	0,25

The reason for the high level of enthusiasm for these three proposals is that such complex projects are nowadays only possible, if at all, via complex legal information systems and the use of modern document standards such as Akoma Ntoso [1] and semantic web standards. The complexity and the previous time- and labour-intensive burden of the relevant investigations make "intelligent audits" particularly attractive to parliamentary legal experts.

The third cluster around parliamentary control and parliamentary diplomacy contains 14 proposals. The top 3 of this cluster (Table 4) includes AI-based measures to reduce any bias or discrimination with AI-based proposals for elimination (7,64), algorithmic reviews of legislative evaluation reports (7,21) and the development of AI-based counter-fake news technologies (7,07). The rates for this top 3 group are significant lower and also the lowest comparing all clusters. The reason for this might lie in the complexity of such solutions, that do not allow an easy implementation.

The fourth cluster around civic education and national culture consists of 17 proposals. The top 3 proposals of this cluster (Table 4) are user orientated and easy to implement. The first proposal demands intelligent, AI-based search functions for the front end of the parliament's website (8,57), which might improve the accessibility and brings people to the data and documents they were looking for. An AI-based coach for youth and citizens could explain parliaments works, processes and MP activity in an easy understandable way (8,00). Also important seems to be the capacity building measures for the use of AI in parliament for the parliamentary staff and for MPs (8,00).

Table 4. Multi-Criteria Table for Top 3 per Cluster - Hellenic Parliament. Sorted by Relevance.

Cluster #3: Parliamentary Control & Co Cluster #4: Civic Education and National Culture		Relevance 0..10		Priority 31.12.20–31.12.30	
Nr	Item	↓Ø	SD	Ø	SD
3,01	[165.-] AI-based measures to reduce bias/discrimination with AI-based proposals for elimination (bias reduction and counter-balancing by AI)	7,64	0,20	22.08.2023	0,20
3,02	[143.-] Algorithmic reviews of legislative evaluation reports	7,21	0,26	17.03.2024	0,22
3,03	[188.-] Development of AI-based counter-fake news technologies	7,07	0,26	27.07.2023	0,22
4,01	[27.-] Intelligent, AI-based search functions in the front end of the parliament's website	8,57	0,19	17.03.2022	0,20
4,02	[191.-] AI-based coach for youth and citizens	8,00	0,17	26.07.2024	0,29
4,03	[201.-] Capacity building regarding AI among parliamentary staff as well as MPs	8,00	0,20	11.05.2023	0,21

The fifth cluster around parliamentary administration, parliament buildings, driving service and police contains 37 proposals. Among the three highest rated proposals (Table 5) are an AI-based automatic text and voice capturing solution (9,00), a regulation on permission and prohibition of AI services in parliament (9,00) and AI-based virtual assistants for disabled people on parliamentary websites (8,86). AI can accelerate the digitalization of documents and thoughts by learning to capture and process speech, text and images. AI-based assistants simplify access to complex topics with reading and navigation tools as well as summaries. Through the integration of corresponding services in word processing systems, administrators already get to know and learn to appreciate these features. At the same time, however, there is concern that the use of internet accessible AI may lead to unintended damage, espionage or sabotage, thus jeopardizing the functioning and integrity of parliament. Permission and prohibition lists at least give staff some assurance as to what would be permissible and what would be prohibited, even if this cannot provide complete protection.

The sixth cluster around parliamentary bureaus, parliamentary directorates and elections comprises 19 proposals. The top 3 (Table 5) include remote access to parliament and voting for MPs (8,71), AI-based process automation in parliament (8,29) and a politician earnings index (8,14). To prevent identity hijacking, AI-based security measures can help MPs to engage and vote securely from a distance. AI-based process automation opens up numerous optimizations for parliament, as soon as process management is practiced and electronic processes are fully stored. Because the recording of politicians' income and supplementary income is complex, volatile and lengthy, AI applications can ensure continuous monitoring, comparison and a functioning reporting system.

Table 5. Multi-Criteria Table for Top 3 per Cluster– Hellenic Parliament. Sorted by Relevance.

Cluster #5: Parliamentary Administration & Co Cluster #6: Parliamentary Bureau & Co		Relevance 0..10		Priority 31.12.20–31.12.30	
Nr	Item	↓Ø	SD	Ø	SD
5,01	[71.-] AI-based automatic text and speech capture	9,00	0,10	15.10.2022	0,23
5,02	[216.-] Limits of parliamentarianism in times of AI usage: consequences unmanageable - Which AI services will be allowed and which must be banned in order not to jeopardise the functionality and integrity of parliament?	9,00	0,11	11.05.2023	0,28
5,03	[226.-] Virtual AI assistants for the disabled (e.g., reading and navigation aids) on the websites of the Parliament	8,86	0,11	10.11.2022	0,24
6,01	[223.-] Should MPs generally be allowed remote access (from a distance) to parliament and votes? (possible through 5G networks)	8,71	0,22	16.09.2022	0,19
6,02	[33.-] AI-based process automation in parliament, based on existing process management and electronic processes	8,29	0,17	18.03.2023	0,21
6,03	[205.-] Politicians' merit index - inappropriate disproportionate enrichment of politicians becomes transparent, can be continuously monitored by AI applications	8,14	0,24	31.12.2023	0,24

The seventh cluster around scientific services and the parliamentary library contains 13 proposals. The top 3 of this cluster (Table 6) contains an AI-based document search in the parliamentary library and the e-publication room of the academic services (8,69) that simplifies access to relevant documents, an AI-based library services (8,23) that can generate recommendation lists with reading tips based on recommendations, demand and work profile, and technology development and ethically correct guidelines for the design of AI use in parliamentary work (8,08).

In the eighth cluster, there are 47 proposals relevant for the design of a framework for the use of AI in parliaments. Among them, there are guiding images, fields of application, areas of usage, and relevant boundaries. The top 3 of the framework (Table 6) includes the integration into the European Interoperability Framework (9,38), an EU-wide system interoperability (9,08) and special safety precautions when using algorithmic decision making systems (9,08). The reasons for this rating lie in the chronic lack of interoperability of ICT systems and the intensive discussions in Europe about the European AI law.

Table 6. Multi-Criteria Table for Top 3 per Cluster– Hellenic Parliament. Sorted by Relevance.

Cluster #7: Scientific Services Cluster #8: Framework		Relevance 0..10		Priority 31.12.20–31.12.30	
Nr	Item	↓Ø	SD	Ø	SD
7,01	[15.-] AI-based intelligent document search in the parliamentary library and in e-publication room of library/scientific services	8,69	0,26	03.03.2022	0,13
7,02	[207.-] AI services in parliamentary libraries: reader profile generates AI-based a new recommendation reading list, AI-based reading tips (based on recommendations: Readers who like this book also have,,,,), AI-based literature and study profile (metadata, summary, graphics)	8,23	0,25	30.10.2022	0,17
7,03	[98.-] Research: technology development and ethics-based design for parliamentary work	8,08	0,18	31.12.2022	0,17
8,01	[211.-] Link parliamentary AI systems with European Interoperability Framework (EIF, further developed with AI portfolio)	9,38	0,08	19.05.2022	0,12
8,02	[114.-] EU/Mercosur-supported system interoperability	9,08	0,10	06.11.2023	0,24
8,03	[159.-] Special safeguards when using algorithmic systems in the context of human decisions,	9,08	0,11	19.05.2023	0,25

The visual cluster analysis shows a clumping of the proposals in all clusters, even if each cluster has a different number of proposals. In concrete terms, a certain correlation between relevance and priority can be seen in the Figs. 1, 2, 3, 4, 5, 6, 7 and 8. According to the repeated pattern, higher priority proposals should be implemented more quickly. Projects with lower priority are given more time for implementation. Overall, a tight cluster for values between 6–9 (relevance) and 2–6 (priority: 2022–2026) has formed. Nevertheless, it is important to bear in mind that these are only the impressions from a single workshop and that the results of prioritization might be different in other national parliaments.

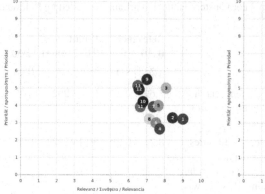

Fig. 1. Cluster #1 – Parliamentarians

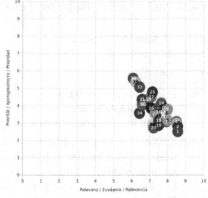

Fig. 2. Cluster #2 – Legislation

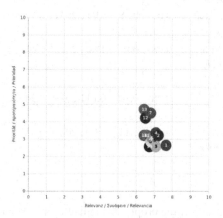

Fig. 3. Parliamentary Control & Co

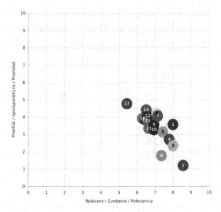

Fig. 4. Civic Education and National Culture

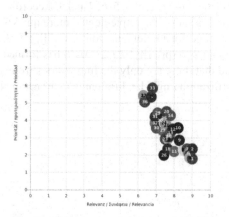

Fig. 5. Parliamentary Administration& Co

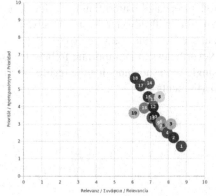

Fig. 6. Parliamentary Bureau & Co

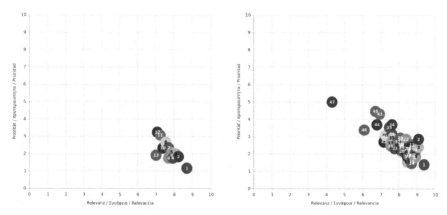

Fig. 7. Scientific Services   **Fig. 8.** Framework

6.4   Top 5 Relevance of Open Questions

Finally, the Top 5 questions on the use of AI in parliaments (Table 7, Fig. 9), considered as open, are examined in more detail. Looking at the following order, it is noticeable that practical, user related questions appear to be more important than general questions and that there are no easy answers: How does the parliament reposition itself in terms of personnel, training and hiring? (9,38) This question is relevant because the use of AI in parliament requires a workforce that is capable of working with AI technologies. Parliament has to reposition itself to attract and train personnel with the necessary skills. Which ethical aspects become relevant? (9,31) The use of AI in parliament raises ethical concerns that must be addressed, especially how the use of AI could impact privacy, security, and other ethical issues. What are the limits of the use of AI in parliament? (9,15) The use of AI in parliament may have limitations in terms of its effectiveness, accuracy, and potential biases. It is important to consider these limitations when implementing AI in parliament. What are the potential advantages and challenges of using AI to restructure constituencies in order to improve the representativeness of parliament? (9,08) This could happen, but it also presents challenges and potential ethical issues that must be considered. What actually constitutes a smart parliament? (9,00) By examining what makes a smart parliament, it is possible to better understand how parliaments can be improved to better serve the needs and interests of citizens. This can ultimately lead to more effective governance and better outcomes for society as a whole.

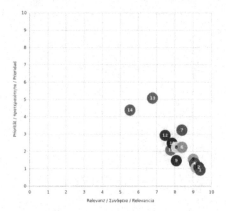

Fig. 9. Open Questions

Table 7. Multi-Criteria Table for Open Questions – Hellenic Parliament. Sorted by Relevance.

Nr	Item	Relevance 0..10		Priority 31.12.20–31.12.30	
		↓Ø	SD	Ø	SD
9,01	[131.-] Prerequisites: Training and hiring of new staff in the IT department?	9,38	0,08	02.12.2021	0,06
9,02	[136.-] Ethical aspects of the operation of AI-based systems	9,31	0,08	29.01.2022	0,09
9,03	[97.-] Reflection on the limits of the use of AI in parliament	9,15	0,13	29.01.2022	0,10
9,04	[214.-] Election engineering: Restructuring constituencies by AI to improve the representative function of parliament (sounds like gerrymandering, but it is exactly the opposite)	9,08	0,13	23.04.2022	0,07
9,05	[139.-] Defining the smart parliament concept, what is involved?	9,00	0,14	16.07.2022	0,26

7   Conclusion and Outlook

A series of constructive proposals for the use of AI in parliaments were gathered and evaluated with a view to their relevance and priority for the Hellenic Parliament by using a creative research approach, engaging an expert brainstorming team and interacting with administrators within an innovative parliamentary environment. The collection of proposals together with the ratings can help to determine in which areas to focus research, where AI-based innovations urgently need to be initiated with a view to a more efficient parliamentary institution.

This approach also provides a good foundation for establishing a research agenda on AI in parliaments. The workshop has shown that the 210 proposals cover a broad range of relevant topics. In view of the chosen procedure, it must be critically questioned whether three experts for a brainstorming are sufficient or other experts would not come to other proposals and alternative ratings at different times. Surprisingly, looking at the results, there are no low rated proposals, even though there was no sorting out of contributions. Ratings will surely change over time and from institution to institution, also taking the technological progress of generative pretrained transformers (GPT-X & Co) into consideration. Further rounds of workshops with other national parliaments are planned and some have already been held (Argentina 2022) in order to prove this assumption. A broad dialogue about the potentially divergent results and working agendas also needs to be initiated using an intra- and transdisciplinary approach.

There is interest in the use of AI in legislatures and it is important that science and parliamentary practice have set out on the path. This study has helped to frame the general understanding in view of the disruptive and perhaps overwhelming changes that the recent success of GPT-X & Co might bring closer. Several proposals are now on the table, in a wide variety, partly in line with expectations, partly surprising. There are many trade-offs to be made between desire and realizability, utility and feasibility, resources and constraints. These results from the Hellenic Parliament might not be widely transferable. Using similar workshops, parliaments can work out for themselves whether, where and which AI-based applications are relevant and derive recommendations for politics and the parliamentary practice.

The proposals prioritized by workshop participants constitute the "tip of the iceberg" of AI-based apps and services linked to a variety of sectors. The relative differences in the relevance factor among these options are small. For the Hellenic Parliament this selection can potentially cause significant implications. When updating the parliament's strategic plan, AI-based tools and services need to be considered to be part of the parliament's strategic goals and choices. Furthermore, when planning for the organization's next generation ICT systems, new AI-based systems and procedures have to be designed.

The workshop in the Hellenic Parliament was conducted in March 2021, right in the middle on the pandemic that caused the disruption of certain parliamentary processes and the acceleration of the digital transformation of others [10]. Inevitably, the implementation of the parliament's strategy, as well as any actions for the creation of a follow-up plan were put into hold. Nonetheless, though just one of the specified AI-based solutions was directly introduced into the parliamentary workspace (see Sect. 6.1 on the speech to text application for semi-automatic minute generation), there were substantial developments regarding the composition of the ICT sector and the study of the relevant framework, which are referred on the top open questions in the examined proposals (see Sect. 6.4). Regarding the former, an extensive administrative reshuffling brought about a new leadership structure in the IT department and the relevant general directorate. Interestingly, two of the new administrative leaders participated at the said workshop, thus gaining important insights that can flow into the development of novel AI-based solutions. When talking about the latter, that is the AI framework, parliamentary researchers from the Hellenic Parliament are currently participating in international networks and working groups for the development of ethical and operational guidelines.

In the coming years, practice will show which of these approaches will gain real relevance and how quickly the Hellenic Parliament will deal with them. As soon as solutions are available and prove themselves in practice, many other parliaments could benefit from them. However, it must be politically clarified whether this would be desirable and technically feasible in terms of national digital sovereignty. In times of tight budgets, a collaborative approach to the introduction of AI in parliaments could be more convincing in that the burden will be shared among several shoulders. However, this option requires trustworthy partners who would support a cloud-based approaches with numerous AI solutions and do not demonize it because of the risk of manipulation.

The new parliament that will emerge out of the 2023 elections will have the unique opportunity to set the rules of the human-machine interaction for the first time in Greek history. It remains to be seen if it will stand up to the expectations of society.

In the future, legislatures and external stakeholders, with academia up front, must talk intensively about the use of AI in the parliamentary environment, discuss controversially about its limits, regulate where necessary and design the solutions by themselves. With a first roadmap available in the Hellenic case, all those involved may suit up for lot of work ahead.

References

1. Akoma Ntoso. http://www.akomantoso.org. Accessed 27 Mar 2023
2. Chat-GPT. https://chat.openai.com. Accessed 27 Mar 2023
3. Clark, C.: Brainstorming - How to Create Successful Ideas, Wilshire Book Company, Chatsworth (1989)
4. Council of Europe: Artificial Intelligence, Human Rights, Democracy, and The Rule of Law – A Primer, Council of Europe and The Alan Turing Institute, Strasbourg (2021)
5. European Parliament: Proposal for a Regulation on a European Approach for Artificial Intelligence, after 2021–04, legislative train 02.2022 (2022). https://www.europarl.europa.eu/legislative-train/api/stages/report/current/theme/a-europe-fit-for-the-digital-age/file/regulation-on-artificial-intelligence. Accessed 27 Mar 2023
6. European Parliament: Historical Archives (2023). https://historicalarchives.europarl.europa.eu/home.html. Accessed 27 Mar 2023
7. Etscheid, J, von Lucke, J., Stroh, F.: Künstliche Intelligenz in der öffentlichen Verwaltung, Digitalakademie@BW & Fraunhofer IAO, Stuttgart, pp. 11–12 (2020)
8. Fitsilis, F.: Artificial Intelligence (AI) in parliaments - preliminary analysis of the Eduskunta experiment. J. Legis. Stud. 27(4), 621–633 (2021)
9. Fitsilis, F.: Imposing Regulation on Advanced Algorithms. Springer, Cham (2019). https://doi.org/10.1007/978-3-030-27979-0
10. Fitsilis, F., Pliakogianni, A.: The Hellenic parliament's response to the COVID-19 pandemic: a balancing act between necessity and realism. IALS Stud. Law Rev. 8, 19–27 (2021)
11. Hellenic Parliament: Stratigikó Schédio (Strategic Plan) 2018–2021, Athens (2018)
12. Koryzis, D., Dalas, A., Spiliotopoulos, D., Fitsilis, F.: ParlTech: transformation framework for the digital parliament. Big Data Cogn. Comput. 5(1), 15, 1–16 (2021)
13. von Lucke, J., Fitsilis, F.: Using artificial intelligence for legislation - thinking about and selecting realistic topics. In: Janssen, M., et al. (Hrsg.) EGOV-CeDEM-ePart 2022 - Proceedings of Ongoing Research, Practitioners, Workshops, Posters, and Projects of the International Conference EGOV-CeDEM-ePart 2022, pp. 32–42 (2022)

14. von Lucke, J., Fitsilis, F.: Research and Development Agenda for the Use of AI in Parliaments (2023, under review)
15. Maruri, K.: Lawmakers Experiment With ChatGPT to Write Bills, Governing, Folsum (2023). https://www.governing.com/next/lawmakers-experiment-with-chatgpt-to-write-bills. Accessed 27 Mar 2023
16. Misuraca, G., van Noordt, C.: Overview of the use and impact of AI in public services in the EU. Publications Office of the European Union (2020)
17. Organisation for Economic Co-operation and Development: The OECD Global Parliamentary group on AI. https://oecd.ai/en/parliamentary-group-on-ai. Accessed 27 Mar 2023
18. Parliamentary Assembly of the Council of Europe [PACE]: Artificial Intelligence: Ensuring respect for democracy, human rights and the rule of law, Strasbourg (2020)
19. Palmirani, M., Vitali, F., Van Puymbroeck, W., Nubla Durango, F.: Legal Drafting in the Era of Artificial Intelligence and Digitisation. European Commission, Brussels (2022)
20. Röthig, P.: Handbuch für Organisationsuntersuchungen in der Bundesverwaltung, 5th edn., p. 31. Bundesministerium des Innern, Bonn (1998)
21. Silva, N., et al.: Evaluating topic models in Portuguese political comments about bills from Brazil's chamber of deputies. In: Britto, A., Valdivia Delgado, K. (eds.) BRACIS 2021. LNCS (LNAI), vol. 13074, pp. 104–120. Springer, Cham (2021). https://doi.org/10.1007/978-3-030-91699-2_8
22. Souza, E., et al.: An information retrieval pipeline for legislative documents from the Brazilian chamber of deputies. In: Legal Knowledge and Information Systems, vol. 346, pp. 119–126. IOS Press, Clifton (2021)
23. Stanford University: Artificial Intelligence Index Report 2021, Stanford (2021)
24. Xleap. https://www.xleap.net

An Ecosystem for Deploying Artificial Intelligence in Public Administration

Areti Karamanou[1]([✉])[iD], Evdokia Mangou[2][iD], and Konstantinos Tarabanis[1][iD]

[1] Information Systems Lab, Department of Business Administration,
University of Macedonia, Egnatia 156, 54636 Thessaloniki, Greece
{akarm,kat}@uom.edu.gr
[2] Region of Central Macedonia, Vasilissis Olgas Avenue 198,
54110 Thessaloniki, Greece
e.magou@pkm.gov.gr

Abstract. The public sector is an immensely valuable resource of data, which has the potential to be harnessed for a wide range of applications. However, there are several challenges that impede the collection and dissemination of this data, including high variability and rapid obsolescence. Despite these challenges, emerging technologies such as Artificial Intelligence (AI) offer the potential to create intelligent applications that can unlock the full potential of public sector data. In this work, we propose a holistic ecosystem that can be utilized for the implementation and evaluation of AI technologies in public administration. To illustrate this, we present a case study focusing on dynamic government data, specifically transport data, in order to extract the various components of the ecosystem and their interdependencies. This case study was chosen due to the fact that real-time dynamic data remains an underexplored form of public sector data.

Keywords: Artificial Intelligence · Public Administration · Ecosystem

1 Introduction

Public sector data represent a vast and diverse resource that holds immense value for society [32]. Within this resource, dynamic data, which are real-time data generated by sensors, are particularly important. Recently, the European Commission recognized dynamic government data as highly valuable, with enormous potential for the economy, the environment, and society. However, collecting and disseminating these data present a range of challenges, including high variability and rapid obsolescence [19].

Fortunately, recent advances in technologies such as Artificial Intelligence (AI) offer the possibility of creating value-added intelligent applications that can unlock the potential of government data. AI has tremendous potential for public administration, offering the possibility of saving up to 1.2 billion hours and $41.1 billion annually [10]. By automating routine tasks, public servants can focus

I. Lindgren et al. (Eds.): EGOV 2023, LNCS 14130, pp. 192–207, 2023.
https://doi.org/10.1007/978-3-031-41138-0_13

on high-value work and make better decisions, detect fraud, plan infrastructure projects, answer citizen queries, adjudicate bail hearings, triage healthcare cases, and provide innovative, personalized public services to citizens [10,42].

This work proposes a holistic ecosystem for the implementation and evaluation of AI technologies, such as machine learning, deep learning, and natural language processing, in public administration. We present a case study focused on dynamic government data, specifically transport data, to explore the ecosystem components and their dependencies. The case was selected because real-time dynamic data is an underexplored form of government data.

2   Method

This study aims to identify the components of an ecosystem for deploying Artificial Intelligence (AI) in public administration and explore their interdependencies through a single exploratory case study. Such a study is useful for gaining insights into a poorly understood phenomenon and generating new theory or propositions about it [45].

For the case study, we examined three open traffic data sets: one from the city of Thessaloniki in Greece, another from the Attica region in Greece, and a third from Switzerland. To identify the ecosystem components, we used "snowballing" to identify AI algorithms, technologies, methods, and cases from technical and policy reports, government documents, and research articles. We also conducted semi-structured interviews with employees of the region of Central Macedonia, the second-largest region in Greece, to create user stories describing potential AI applications based on the traffic data.

3   The Case of Dynamic Traffic Data

3.1   Data Collection

In order to create an ecosystem for deploying Artificial Intelligence (AI) in public administration, we present a case study that focuses on the usage of dynamic government data and, specifically, traffic data to create AI applications for the public sector. The case study uses three open traffic datasets from (i) the city of Thessaloniki in Greece, (ii) the region of Attica in Greece, and (iii) Switzerland. An overview of the three OGD datasets is presented in Table 1.

Traffic Data from the City of Thessaloniki in Greece. The Smart Mobility Living Lab, one of the largest European mobility labs located in Thessaloniki, Greece is the data analysis and modelling laboratory of the Hellenic Institute of Transport (HIT). The lab hosts transportation and mobility related datasets generated by various both conventional and innovative data sources. Among them are the datasets with open data from taxis and Bluetooth detectors in the urban area of Thessaloniki [3]. Specifically, two types of measurements are

Table 1. An overview of the three datasets with traffic data.

	Dataset 1[a]	Dataset 2[b]	Dataset 3[c]
Location	Thessaloniki, GR	Attica region, GR	Switzerland
Access	open	open	open
Accessibility medium	files	files/API	files/API
Historical data	Yes	Yes	No
Aggregation level	minute	hour	minute
Anonymization	Not required	Not required	Not required
Data format	JSON, XML, CSV, KML, MAP	JSON	XML

[a]https://opendata.imet.gr/
[b]https://www.data.gov.gr/datasets/road_traffic_attica/
[c]https://opentransportdata.swiss/

provided. The first one refers to floating car data including the speed measured by the GPS of over one thousand vehicles that operate in the city of Thessaloniki. This dataset is being updated almost real-time providing about 2,000 new records per minute. The second one includes aggregated vehicle detections of over 43 Bluetooth devices located in main road junctions of the city of Thessaloniki at a specific timeframe. Additional data included in the same dataset are trip trajectories with the sequence of locations or the origin and destination. The latest datasets are updated every 15 min. All data can be acquired via proprietary APIs. Historical data are also available as text files.

Traffic Data from the Attica Region in Greece. Data.gov.gr serves as Greece's official data portal for OGD. The portal comprises 49 datasets that span ten thematic areas, including the environment, economy, and transportation. Notably, the new version of the portal incorporates a free Application Programming Interface (API), enabling users to retrieve and access data via a graphical interface or code. Acquiring a token is needed to use the API through completing a registration process. The traffic data for the Attica region in Greece is sourced from traffic sensors that periodically transmit information regarding the number of vehicles and their speed on specific roads in Attica. To mitigate privacy concerns, the data is aggregated hourly and is updated every hour with a one-hour delay. Provided data measurements include the absolute number of the vehicles detected by the sensor during the hour of measurement along with their average speed in km per hour.

Traffic Data from Switzerland. The Open Transport Data Portal of Switzerland (ODPCH)[1] provides access to more than 40 datasets. Among them are datasets with real-time traffic data generated and collected by traffic sensors positioned in road segments throughout Switzerland. Historical data are not available. Data include the number of vehicles passing from specific locations,

---

[1] https://opentransportdata.swiss/en/.

along with their average speed. The data are minutely aggregated and updated every minute and specifically, 20 s after the minute in Coordinated Universal Time (UTC) 0. Data are described using the DATEX II² standard for exchanging road traffic data. An access token is required to get limited access to these data through the corresponding API for six months. The API allows for submitting in total 260,000 requests in the six-month period, which actually, corresponds to the update interval of the data (one update per min).

3.2 Construction

Traffic data has the potential to aid policy-makers and public authorities in designing and managing transportation systems that are efficient, safe, environmentally friendly, and cost-effective. One way to achieve this is through predicting future traffic conditions. There are several methods commonly used for forecasting future traffic conditions, including traditional parametric methods such as Autoregressive Integrated Moving Average (ARIMA) [24], machine learning techniques such as Support Vector Machine (SVM) [2], and deep learning [6,52].

The three datasets analyzed in this study contain sensor-generated traffic data, which often exhibit quality issues [41]. For example, the Attica dataset initially suffered from a high number of missing observations and anomalous values, although most of these issues have been resolved [6,19,20]. Various methods, such as time series analysis (e.g., Seasonal - Trend decomposition using Loess - STL), machine learning (e.g., Isolation Forest), and deep learning (e.g., Generative Adversarial Networks - GANs), can be used to identify anomalous values in the datasets [19]. However, handling missing and anomalous values requires making decisions on a case-by-case basis, depending on factors such as the level of aggregation for the temporal dimension. For example, missing values in the Thessaloniki and Switzerland datasets, which are minute-level aggregated, can be imputed using the average of the previous and next observations, while synthetic data can be used for the Attica dataset, which is hourly aggregated.

Integrating traffic data with other datasets, such as weather data, car accident data, can provide valuable insights and enhance the accuracy of AI models [25]. Using explainable AI techniques can also help understand the reasons behind anomalous values or model decisions [15].

Real-time data access is critical for applications that rely on dynamic data such as traffic intelligent systems. All three datasets are available in Open Government Data (OGD) portals and two of them can be accessed programmatically using an API. The Thessaloniki and Attica datasets are hourly updated, while the Zurich dataset is minutely updated.

Finally, selecting the appropriate AI algorithm for each dataset is crucial. In literature, machine learning approaches such as K-nearest Neighbour [30], and Bayesian models [39], and XGBoost (eXtreme Gradient Boosting) [44] have been used to predict traffic. Recently, the emerging development of deep learning and Graph Neural Networks have achieved state-of-the-art performance in traffic

---

² https://www.datex2.eu/.

forecasting tasks [1,6]. Data may also play a significant role for the selection of the AI algorithm. For instance, the level of granularity and other dataset-specific factors directly affect the quality of the AI model. For instance, the minute-level granularity of the Zurich dataset allows for more accurate traffic flow predictions in the near future, while the hourly-level granularity of the Attica dataset is better suited for predicting traffic flow at the hourly level.

3.3 Evaluation

To assess the performance of the AI model, it is crucial to conduct a performance-based evaluation. Depending on the selected algorithm, various metrics can be employed. For instance, previous studies have utilized metrics such as RMSE, MAPE, and MAE to evaluate the performance of Graph Neural Network models in traffic flow prediction tasks [6]. For the traffic datasets and Graph Neural Networks, the accuracy of the AI model can be affected by the density of traffic sensor locations. Specifically, the Thessaloniki and Attica datasets contain sensor measurements from urban areas, which can lead to the creation of denser graphs when analyzed using Graph Neural Networks. This, in turn, can result in more accurate deep learning algorithms. On the other hand, the Zurich dataset comprises sensor measurements primarily from highways, resulting in sparser graphs [6].

Moreover, explainability can be employed to interpret the decisions made by the AI model. For instance, SHAP has been used to explain the decisions of a neural network that predicts traffic for traffic light control [37,44]. In this case, integrating external data such as weather and vehicle accident data can facilitate better understanding of the decisions made by the model.

3.4 Translation

Traffic forecasts can be used to anticipate future needs and allocate resources accordingly, such as managing traffic lights [28], opening or closing lanes, estimating travel time [33], and mitigating traffic congestion [2]. In order to understand the potential of creating AI applications for the public sector using traffic data, we interviewed a public servant of the Region of Central Macedonia, the second largest region in Greece. The primary objective of the interview was to generate user stories that effectively describe potential AI applications based on the traffic data. These applications should have the potential to streamline the region's operations and enhance the efficiency of its employees.

The interviews resulted in the three user stories, namely (i) Management of vehicle traffic in the wider urban area of Thessaloniki through traffic lights, (ii) Optimal route for scheduled checkpoints, and (iii) Optimal use of GPS Data.

Management of Vehicle Traffic in the Wider Urban Area of Thessaloniki Through Traffic Lights. The Department of Maintenance of Transport Projects, which belongs to the Technical Works Directorate of the region of Central Macedonia in Greece, is responsible for the operation and planning of traffic regulation in the urban web through traffic lights. An application useful for the region of Central Macedonia would be the utilization of traffic/mobility data, traffic load/free flow of vehicles, and real-time reprogramming of traffic regulation and vehicle emptying times in the central vehicle flows, with the aim of immediately relieving traffic congestion and relieving overloaded areas within 10 min by selecting and opening the appropriate vehicle flows with the goal of optimal traffic management, quality of life, more rational resource management, and reduction of vehicle emissions/pollution.

Optimal Route for Scheduled Checkpoints. Many services of the Region of Central Macedonia/Greece (e.g., Technical Works Department, Health Department, Veterinary Department, etc.), whose headquarters are located at the city of Thessaloniki carry out scheduled inspections/checks with teams of competent employees. In these scheduled inspections/checks, the teams of employees visit from 5 to 15 different points (depending on available time). The inspections/checks are carried out within the urban fabric of Thessaloniki and its surroundings, but often also within the wider region of Thessaloniki (as well as in neighboring regions, within the Municipality). An AI application useful for the traffic office and responsible drivers would be to provide them with a proposed route in order to visit the predetermined points. The proposed AI route will be the best possible suggestion in terms of distance/traffic loads/avoidance of bottlenecks, in relation to the evolution of traffic data over time, as theoretically some traffic flows are more congested at specific times. The aim of this application is to save human resources, reduce vehicle emissions/pollution, and provide better working conditions for employees.

Optimal Use of GPS Data. A GPS system has been installed in all vehicles in all regions (Pieria, Pella, Imathia, Serres, Kilkis, Halkidiki, and Thessaloniki) of Central Macedonia. A useful AI application for the supervisors and responsible parties of these vehicles would be to create a notification/report system utilizing the GPS data of each vehicle, indicating, for example, if one of the vehicles is moving at a speed greater than the permitted speed limits, if it goes beyond the allowed routes and movement limits, if it is stationary for a long time so that it can be allocated to another service that needs a vehicle, etc. The goal is the rational management of the resources of the region of Central Macedonia.

4   The Ecosystem

In the previous section, a case study was presented, and its generalization has helped in the development of an ecosystem for deploying Artificial Intelligence (AI) in public administration. The ecosystem, as shown in Fig. 1, provides a comprehensive framework for collecting data from the public sector, using it to develop AI models with various AI technologies, and integrating different techniques for data pre-processing, federated learning, transfer learning, data augmentation, evaluation, explanation, and translation, and, evaluating and explaining the models and, finally, incorporating them in AI applications. The ecosystem is built upon four pillars, namely collection, construction, evaluation, and translation. Additionally, it comprises four key components, namely Data, AI Algorithms, AI Models, and AI Applications.

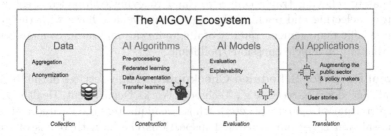

Fig. 1. An Ecosystem for deploying Artificial Intelligence in Public Administration

4.1 Stakeholders

The main stakeholders that have an interest or are impacted by the ecosystem and its functioning include IT stakeholders including agency's AI experts and developers, public service designers, public authorities and public organizations, public servants, regulators, policy makers, citizens and residents, academic and scientific community, businesses and organizations, and practitioners. All of them can undertake both the data and AI applications' producer and consumer roles.

4.2 Data

Utilizing data is crucial for governments to improve public sector intelligence, enabling them to create long-lasting, inclusive, and trustworthy policies and services [29]. Various classifications of government data exist [4,8,38].

Government data can be categorized as open or closed. Open Government Data (OGD) can be freely used and reused by the public, accessible through official OGD portals (e.g., the European OGD portal)[3]. These data are typically provided as downloadable files, but some portals also offer OGD as linked data [21] for integration with other datasets. Additionally, some portals provide an Application Programming Interface (API) for programmatic and real-time access to OGD. In contrast, closed government data includes restricted access data such as employee service records, performance assessments, and confidential or classified government data, which are accessible only to the data owners and authorized groups based on security protocols and public policies.

Government data may also be structured, unstructured, or semi-structured. Structured data have a well-defined format, usually stored in a database, such as public health records organized and stored in columns and rows. Semi-structured data do not have rigid formal structures but contain tags to facilitate separation of data records or fields, such as those found in XML and JSON. In contrast,

---

[3] data.europa.eu.

unstructured data lack any discernible structure, such as text messages, photos, videos, and audio files, transactions, and raw data from scientific research [8].

Government data can also be categorized as real-time or batch data. Real-time data are often produced by sensors (e.g., traffic data), and their provision has only recently begun. These data are high variability and rapidly obsolescent, requiring prompt availability and regular updates. Conversely, batch data are historical data that are not immediately provided but provided some time after their collection.

Finally, government data can be internal or external. Internal data are those produced by a public administration prior to the development of an AI system, existing within the organization's structure (e.g., master or transactional data). In contrast, external government data exists outside an organization's structure or is incorporated specifically for the development of AI systems.

4.3 Collection

Data Aggregation. Government data may be individual or record -level or aggregated. The level and type of aggregation varies. For example, apart from being aggregated (e.g., averaged) geographically (e.g., in the country level), data can also be aggregated based on time (e.g., in the hour level), demographic factors (e.g., gender). In the realm of OGD and especially when it pertains to individual-level data, it is crucial to ensure that data is properly aggregated before publication. The initial level of aggregation may change depending on the requirements of problem.

Data Anonymization. Government data often contains personal information that is protected by regulations, such as the European Data Protection Regulation (GDPR) [31]. As a result, this data cannot be used in its original form without risking privacy violations. To protect privacy while still utilizing the data for analysis with AI, it is important to first anonymize it. There are two main methods for doing so: anonymization and pseudonymization. Anonymization involves removing or encrypting personally identifiable information from datasets so that an individual's identity cannot be directly or indirectly determined. Pseudonymization involves replacing personal information with a pseudonym or unique identifier that can be re-identified when combined with other separately maintained supplementary information [25].

Traditional methods for data anonymization include generalization, suppression, permutation, perturbation, and anatomization [27]. Open-source software for data anonymization, such as AMNESIA[4] and ARX Data Anonymization[5], use various anonymization techniques such as k-Anonimity, k-Map, t-Closeness, and δ-Presence [43]. However, these methods do not guarantee that re-identification is not possible [11]. Therefore, advanced synthetic data generation services have been proposed as an alternative, such as creating synthetic

---

[4] https://amnesia.openaire.eu/index.html.

[5] https://arx.deidentifier.org/.

data using Generative Adversarial Nets (GAN) [46]. AI-generated synthetic data are artificial data that mimic real-world observations and are an accurate representation of the original data.

4.4 Construction

Once data has been collected, it is essential to handle it appropriately to ensure that it can be effectively utilized in creating an AI model.

Artificial Intelligence Algorithms. Some of the most widely recognized and frequently utilized types of algorithms include [5]:

- Computer vision focuses on recognizing, tracking, and interpreting patterns and objects in visual data (e.g., images, videos). Applications include image and video analysis, object detection, and autonomous vehicles.
- Natural Language Processing (NLP) that enables understanding, interpreting, and generating human language. It is used in a wide range of operations, including text classification, sentiment analysis, language translation, chatbot development, and speech recognition.
- Speech Recognition converts spoken language into text or other machine-readable formats. Applications include virtual assistants, voice-enabled devices, and speech-to-text transcription.
- Knowledge-based systems are able to make decisions based on expert knowledge and domain-specific rules. They typically consist of a knowledge base with domain-specific knowledge and rules, and an inference engine, which uses this knowledge to make decisions and solve problems.
- Automated Planning allows generating plans or sequences of actions to achieve particular goals. It enables reasoning about the problem domain, generating plans, and executing them in a dynamic environment. Applications include robotics, manufacturing, logistics, and scheduling.

The selection of the proper AI algorithm from each sub-field of depends on the available data as well as on the requirements of the application.

Pre-processing. Data pre-processing plays a crucial role in converting raw data into a format that is compatible with Artificial Intelligence (AI) algorithms. This essential step involves various techniques and procedures that help to clean, transform, and organize data, making it easier for the AI system to extract meaningful insights and patterns. Data pre-processing methods include:

Data Cleaning. Data cleaning is an essential process in data pre-processing that ensures the accuracy, consistency, and reliability of data, thereby making it suitable for use in AI models. It involves several tasks, such as identifying missing values, which are cells or fields in the dataset that are empty or null, and removing duplicates. Missing values can be imputed using advanced AI techniques like

Generative Adversarial Nets (GAN) [22,47] or simply removed. Data cleaning also ensures that data is in a standard format or structure that is appropriate for use in AI models. This involves identifying and correcting errors or inconsistencies in the data, such as misspelled values and handling anomalous values that are significantly different from the rest of the dataset. Statistical analysis, machine learning, including synthetic data [50], is used for anomaly detection. Effective data cleaning is particularly critical for real-time data like traffic data generated by sensors, which must be promptly accessible without extensive preprocessing before publication.

Data Integration. Government datasets can be leveraged by integrating them with other datasets, internal or external, to increase the value and effectiveness of AI applications [25]. Data integration involves combining data from multiple sources, formats, and structures into a single, consistent, accurate, and comprehensive view. Some previous research has explored the integration and utilization of government data [18,49]. However, the heterogeneity of the original data from different sources presents various challenges, including legal, structural, or other issues [25]. Even if government data are available in formats that facilitate integration (such as linked data), addressing structural challenges is still necessary [18].

Data Augmentation. Data augmentation is a technique used in machine learning to increase the size of a dataset by generating new, synthetic data from the existing data. Data augmentation, hence, is particularly useful in scenarios where the dataset is small, or when the model is prone to overfitting. The aim of data augmentation is to improve the performance and robustness of the machine learning model by exposing it to a larger and more diverse set of training examples [48]. Data augmentation can be used in various types of data, such as text, audio, image, or video. It uses various techniques including GAN.

Federated Learning. Federated learning is a relatively new technique in the field of AI, which has been developed by Google and widely adopted across various research fields and industries [23]. It enables the training of models on decentralized data sources without requiring centralized data storage. In this method, data remains on user devices or edge servers, and the model is trained locally on each device. Federated learning is particularly useful in scenarios where data privacy is paramount, such as healthcare or financial applications, and where data is too large or too sensitive to be stored in a central location. In the public sector, federated learning has been employed to facilitate the development of smart city services [17], develop predictive models in healthcare using sensitive patient data [36], improve traffic management by combining data from multiple sources such as traffic sensors, cameras, and GPS data in transportation [12], and analyze students' behavioral data to understand how students learn in education [13].

Transfer Learning is a machine learning technique for leveraging knowledge gained from one task to improve the performance of another related task. In transfer learning, instead of building a model from scratch, a model pretrained on a dataset is used to train a new model on a different, related dataset saving time and computational resources. The features learned from the first dataset can be used as a starting point for learning new features on the second dataset. Examples of already existing pre-trained models include You Only Look Once (YOLO) [34], a pre-trained model for object detection, and Bidirectional Encoder Representations from Transformers (BERT) [9], a family of pre-trained NLP models. The "Hugging Face"[6] provides a library of a wide range of pre-trained NLP models including BERT.

4.5   Evaluation of Artificial Intelligence Models

Once the AI algorithm is selected and data have been successfully pre-processed, the AI model will be created by training the algorithm on the data. This process involves feeding the model with input data and adjusting its parameters (hyperparameter tuning) to minimize the error between its predictions and the actual outcomes. Hyperparameter tuning can be done with methods such as include grid search, Random search, bayesian optimization, gradient-based optimization, and Ensemble-based methods as well as with cross-validation. Cross-validation partitions the data into training and validation sets and iteratively evaluates the model's performance on different subsets of the data and with different values for the hyperparameters. Cross-validation can be also employed in training to detect and avoid overfitting of the model.

The model needs to be evaluated on a separate validation dataset to ensure its generalizability and performance and ensure that they are effective and reliable in their intended application. Towards this end, several evaluation metrics can be used depending on the type of algorithm. The performance of the model, for example, can be assessed through various metrics such as precision, recall, F1-score, logarithmic loss, the Area Under Curve (AUC), Mean Absolute Error (MAE), Mean Squared Error (MSE), and Mean Absolute Percentage Error (MAPE). These metrics can help assess the model's performance in detecting true positives and minimizing false positives and false negatives.

The efficiency of the AI model is also important and involves measuring its speed and computational requirements. This is important for real-time applications where the model needs to make quick predictions (e.g., in cases where dynamic data generated by sensors are used to create the model). The robustness of the model could also be evaluated in order to assess its ability to perform well under various conditions, such as changes in input data or noisy environments.

In recent years, the importance of explainability in AI models has grown significantly since it helps to improve the understanding of the model's decisions, promoting transparency and trust in the results. This is crucial for the public sector where transparency is a requirement. To achieve this goal, various methods

---

[6] https://huggingface.co/.

have been developed to explain the decisions of both supervised and unsupervised AI models. There are various methods that can be used for explaining AI models. For example, LIME [35] and SHAP [26], which stands for SHapley Additive exPlanation, can be used to explain machine learning predictions. In addition, Class Activation Maps (CAMs) [51] can be utilized to explain Convolutional Neural Network decisions. For neural networks, Global Attribution Mappings (GAMs) [14] can be also employed. These techniques can provide insight into the factors that the AI model is considering when making decisions, allowing users to better understand and interpret the results.

4.6   Translation

Artificial Intelligence (AI) models can be deployed in real-world, intelligent applications for the public sector. AI applications, for example, have the potential to streamline decision-making processes in the public sector. This can be achieved through either fully autonomous decision-making or by providing decision-makers with AI-driven insights and recommendations to aid in the decision-making process. In this sense, humans and machines, rather than competing, could benefit from mutual collaboration and potentially solve problems and achieve better outcomes than each could on their own [7]. AI applications that are built based on government data are able to enhance the efficacy of public services [16], such as the implementation of Integrated Public Services (IPS) [40] that are co-created and continuously evaluated through feedback loops by the public sector.

User stories are essential in designing AI applications, as they ensure that end-users, such as public servants and policymakers, have their needs and preferences fully understood and incorporated into the development process. They serve as a link between data and applications, allowing for the identification of new AI-based applications that can benefit the public sector. User stories can be pulled by the end user who discovers the need for an AI application that could potentially improve their work, or they can be pushed by available public sector data. However, public sector data may not always be of high quality, making them unreliable and inconsistent sources of information. They may contain inaccuracies, errors, and missing values, rendering them unsuitable for developing trustworthy AI applications. Additionally, some public services may not store their data or store them in hardcopies or formats that are not machine-readable. In this case, data themselves can be used as a starting point, and high-quality data can drive the inspiration for the need for an AI application in the public sector. Regardless of whether the user story is pulled or pushed, the ultimate goal is to ensure that the AI application meets the needs of the end-user while utilizing reliable and accurate data.

5   Conclusion

This paper proposes an ecosystem for deploying Artificial Intelligence (AI) in public administration that comprises four main artefacts: Data, AI algorithms,

AI models, and AI applications, built upon three pillars: collection, construction, evaluation, and translation. The data collection process should consider the nature of the source data and the requirements of the AI algorithm, and the collected data should be properly pre-processed and augmented to mitigate the detrimental effects of small sample sizes. Federated learning methods can be employed to overcome data privacy issues. The created AI model should be evaluated for its performance, efficiency, and robustness, and its explainability should be ensured by employing various explainability methods. Finally, the AI model should be integrated into an AI application co-created with the public sector employees, where user stories can be used to describe public sector scenarios that use AI applications.

This ecosystem is a result of an exploratory case study that uses three traffic measurement datasets. The artefacts are complementary, and the selection of the AI algorithm depends not only on the available data but also on the needs of the AI application. The purpose of the AI model will define the AI application that will be used. The requirements for an AI application can be either pulled by the public sector employees or pushed by the available data, where data may create new needs for applications.

We anticipate that the ecosystem for deploying AI in public administration can serve as high-level guidelines for adopting AI in the public sector.

Acknowledgements. This work was supported by the Hellenic Foundation for Research and Innovation (H.F.R.I.) under the "2nd Call for H.F.R.I. Research Projects to support Faculty Members & Researchers" (Project Number: 2412).

References

1. Agafonov, A.: Traffic flow prediction using graph convolution neural networks. In: 2020 10th International Conference on Information Science and Technology (ICIST), pp. 91–95 (2020). https://doi.org/10.1109/ICIST49303.2020.9201971
2. Ata, A., Khan, M.A., Abbas, S., Khan, M.S., Ahmad, G.: Adaptive IoT empowered smart road traffic congestion control system using supervised machine learning algorithm. Comput. J. **64**(11), 1672–1679 (2021)
3. Ayfantopoulou, G., Salanova Grau, J.M., Tzenos, P., Tolikas, A.: Open data from taxis and bluetooth detectors to extract congestion and mobility patterns in thessaloniki. Data Brief **47**, 108899 (2023). https://doi.org/10.1016/j.dib.2023.108899
4. Ballester, O.: An artificial intelligence definition and classification framework for public sector applications. In: DG.O2021: The 22nd Annual International Conference on Digital Government Research, DG.O 2021, pp. 67–75. Association for Computing Machinery, New York (2021). https://doi.org/10.1145/3463677.3463709
5. Berryhill, J., Heang, K.K., Clogher, R., McBride, K.: Hello, world (2019). https://doi.org/10.1787/726fd39d-en
6. Brimos, P., Karamanou, A., Kalampokis, E., Tarabanis, K.: Graph neural networks and open government data to forecast traffic flow. Information (2023, accepted for publication)
7. Carter, S., Nielsen, M.: Using artificial intelligence to augment human intelligence. Distill **2**(12), e9 (2017)

8. Desouza, K.C., Jacob, B.: Big data in the public sector: lessons for practitioners and scholars. Adm. Soc. **49**(7), 1043–1064 (2017). https://doi.org/10.1177/0095399714555751
9. Devlin, J., Chang, M.W., Lee, K., Toutanova, K.: Bert: pre-training of deep bidirectional transformers for language understanding. arXiv abs/1810.04805 (2019)
10. Eggers, W.D., Schatsky, D., Viechnicki, P.: AI-augmented government. Using cognitive technologies to redesign public sector work. Deloitte Insights (2017)
11. El Emam, K., Buckeridge, D., Tamblyn, R., Neisa, A., Jonker, E., Verma, A.: The re-identification risk of Canadians from longitudinal demographics. BMC Med. Inform. Decis. Mak. **11**(1), 46 (2011). https://doi.org/10.1186/1472-6947-11-46
12. Balbin, P.P.F., Barker, J.C., Leung, C.K., Tran, M., Wall, R.P., Cuzzocrea, A.: Predictive analytics on open big data for supporting smart transportation services. Procedia Comput. Sci. **176**, 3009–3018 (2020). https://doi.org/10.1016/j.procs.2020.09.202. Knowledge-Based and Intelligent Information and Engineering Systems: Proceedings of the 24th International Conference KES2020
13. Guo, S., Zeng, D.: Pedagogical data federation toward education 4.0. In: Proceedings of the 6th International Conference on Frontiers of Educational Technologies, ICFET 2020, pp. 51–55. Association for Computing Machinery, New York (2020). https://doi.org/10.1145/3404709.3404751
14. Ibrahim, M., Louie, M., Modarres, C., Paisley, J.: Global explanations of neural networks: mapping the landscape of predictions. In: Proceedings of the 2019 AAAI/ACM Conference on AI, Ethics, and Society, pp. 279–287 (2019)
15. Jacob, V., Song, F., Stiegler, A., Rad, B., Diao, Y., Tatbul, N.: Exathlon: a benchmark for explainable anomaly detection over time series. Proc. VLDB Endow. (PVLDB) (2021)
16. Janssen, M., Charalabidis, Y., Zuiderwijk, A.: Benefits, adoption barriers and myths of open data and open government. Inf. Syst. Manag. **29**(4), 258–268 (2012)
17. Jiang, J.C., Kantarci, B., Oktug, S., Soyata, T.: Federated learning in smart city sensing: challenges and opportunities. Sensors **20**(21), 6230 (2020)
18. Kalampokis, E., Karamanou, A., Tarabanis, K.: Interoperability conflicts in linked open statistical data. Information **10**(8), 249 (2019). https://doi.org/10.3390/info10080249
19. Karamanou, A., Brimos, P., Kalampokis, E., Tarabanis, K.: Exploring the quality of dynamic open government data using statistical and machine learning methods. Sensors **22**(24), 9684 (2022). https://doi.org/10.3390/s22249684
20. Karamanou, A., Brimos, P., Kalampokis, E., Tarabanis, K.: Exploring the quality of dynamic open government data for developing data intelligence applications: the case of attica traffic data. In: Proceedings of the 26th Pan-Hellenic Conference on Informatics, PCI 2022, pp. 102–109. Association for Computing Machinery, New York (2023). https://doi.org/10.1145/3575879.3575974
21. Karamanou, A., Kalampokis, E., Tarabanis, K.: Linked open government data to predict and explain house prices: the case of scottish statistics portal. Big Data Res. **30**, 100355 (2022)
22. Kim, J., Tae, D., Seok, J.: A survey of missing data imputation using generative adversarial networks. In: 2020 International Conference on Artificial Intelligence in Information and Communication (ICAIIC), pp. 454–456. IEEE (2020)
23. Konečný, J., McMahan, H.B., Yu, F.X., Richtarik, P., Suresh, A.T., Bacon, D.: Federated learning: strategies for improving communication efficiency. In: NIPS Workshop on Private Multi-Party Machine Learning (2016)

24. Kumar, P.B., Hariharan, K., et al.: Time series traffic flow prediction with hyper-parameter optimized arima models for intelligent transportation system. J. Sci. Ind. Res. **81**(04), 408–415 (2022)

25. Lee, J.S., Jun, S.P.: Privacy-preserving data mining for open government data from heterogeneous sources. Gov. Inf. Q. **38**(1), 101544 (2021)

26. Lundberg, S.M., Lee, S.I.: A unified approach to interpreting model predictions. In: Guyon, I., et al. (eds.) Advances in Neural Information Processing Systems, vol. 30. Curran Associates, Inc. (2017)

27. Majeed, A., Lee, S.: Anonymization techniques for privacy preserving data publishing: a comprehensive survey. IEEE Access **9**, 8512–8545 (2021). https://doi.org/10.1109/ACCESS.2020.3045700

28. Navarro-Espinoza, A., et al.: Traffic flow prediction for smart traffic lights using machine learning algorithms. Technologies **10**(1), 5 (2022). https://doi.org/10.3390/technologies10010005

29. van Ooijen, C., Ubaldi, B., Welby, B.: A data-driven public sector. OECD Library (33) (2019). https://doi.org/10.1787/09ab162c-en

30. Pang, X., Wang, C., Huang, G.: A short-term traffic flow forecasting method based on a three-layer k-nearest neighbor non-parametric regression algorithm. J. Transp. Technol. **6**, 200–206 (2016). https://doi.org/10.4236/jtts.2016.64020

31. European Parliament: Regulation (EU) 2016/679 of the European parliament and of the council of 27 April 2016 on the protection of natural persons with regard to the processing of personal data and on the free movement of such data, and repealing directive 95/46/EC (general data protection regulation) (text with EEA relevance) (2016)

32. European Parliament: Directive (EU) 2019/1024 of the European parliament and of the council of 20 June 2019 on open data and the re-use of public sector information (recast). Off. J. Eur. Union **172**, 56–83 (2019)

33. Ran, X., Shan, Z., Fang, Y., Lin, C.: An LSTM-based method with attention mechanism for travel time prediction. Sensors **19**(4), 861 (2019)

34. Redmon, J., Divvala, S., Girshick, R., Farhadi, A.: You only look once: unified, real-time object detection. In: 2016 IEEE Conference on Computer Vision and Pattern Recognition (CVPR), Los Alamitos, CA, USA, pp. 779–788. IEEE Computer Society (2016). https://doi.org/10.1109/CVPR.2016.91

35. Ribeiro, M., Singh, S., Guestrin, C.: "why should I trust you?": explaining the predictions of any classifier. In: Proceedings of the 2016 Conference of the North American Chapter of the Association for Computational Linguistics: Demonstrations, San Diego, California, pp. 97–101. Association for Computational Linguistics (2016). https://doi.org/10.18653/v1/N16-3020

36. Rieke, N., et al.: The future of digital health with federated learning. NPJ Digit. Med. **3**(1), 119 (2020)

37. Rizzo, S.G., Vantini, G., Chawla, S.: Reinforcement learning with explainability for traffic signal control. In: 2019 IEEE Intelligent Transportation Systems Conference (ITSC), pp. 3567–3572 (2019). https://doi.org/10.1109/ITSC.2019.8917519

38. Shah, S.I.H., Peristeras, V., Magnisalis, I.: Government big data ecosystem: definitions, types of data, actors, and roles and the impact in public administrations. ACM J. Data Inf. Qual. **13**, 1–25 (2021)

39. Sun, S., Zhang, C., Yu, G.: A Bayesian network approach to traffic flow forecasting. IEEE Trans. Intell. Transp. Syst. **7**(1), 124–132 (2006). https://doi.org/10.1109/TITS.2006.869623

40. Tambouris, E., Tarabanis, K.: Towards inclusive integrated public service (IPS) co-creation and provision. In: DG.O2021: The 22nd Annual International Conference on Digital Government Research, DG.O 2021, pp. 458–462. Association for Computing Machinery, New York (2021). https://doi.org/10.1145/3463677.3463726
41. Teh, H.Y., Kempa-Liehr, A.W., Wang, K.I.-K.: Sensor data quality: a systematic review. J. Big Data **7**(1), 1–49 (2020). https://doi.org/10.1186/s40537-020-0285-1
42. Tinholt, D., Carrara, W., Linden, N.: Unleashing the potential of artificial intelligence in the public sector. Capgemini Consulting (2017)
43. Tomás, J., Rasteiro, D., Bernardino, J.: Data anonymization: an experimental evaluation using open-source tools. Future Internet **14**(6), 167 (2022). https://doi.org/10.3390/fi14060167
44. Wei, Z., Das, S., Zhang, Y.: Short duration crash prediction for rural two-lane roadways: applying explainable artificial intelligence. Transp. Res. Rec. **2676**(12), 535–549 (2022). https://doi.org/10.1177/03611981221096113
45. Yin, R.K.: Case Study Research: Design and Methods, vol. 5. Sage, Thousand Oaks (2009)
46. Yoon, J., Drumright, L.N., van der Schaar, M.: Anonymization through data synthesis using generative adversarial networks (ADS-GAN). IEEE J. Biomed. Health Inform. **24**(8), 2378–2388 (2020)
47. Yoon, J., Jordon, J., Schaar, M.: Gain: missing data imputation using generative adversarial nets. In: International Conference on Machine Learning, pp. 5689–5698. PMLR (2018)
48. Young, M.M., Himmelreich, J., Honcharov, D., Soundarajan, S.: Using artificial intelligence to identify administrative errors in unemployment insurance. Gov. Inf. Q. **39**(4), 101758 (2022)
49. Zeginis, D., Kalampokis, E., Palma, R., Atkinson, R., Tarabanis, K.: A semantic meta-model for data integration and exploitation in precision agriculture and livestock farming. Semant. Web Interoperability Usability Applicability (in press)
50. Zhang, M., Alvarez, R.M., Levin, I.: Election forensics: using machine learning and synthetic data for possible election anomaly detection. PLoS ONE **14**(10), 1–14 (2019)
51. Zhou, B., Khosla, A., Lapedriza, A., Oliva, A., Torralba, A.: Learning deep features for discriminative localization. In: Proceedings of the IEEE Conference on Computer Vision and Pattern Recognition, pp. 2921–2929 (2016)
52. Zhou, Q., Chen, N., Lin, S.: FASTNN: a deep learning approach for traffic flow prediction considering spatiotemporal features. Sensors **22**(18), 6921 (2022)

Open Government and Open Data

Towards High-Value Datasets Determination for Data-Driven Development: A Systematic Literature Review

Anastasija Nikiforova[1]([✉]) [iD], Nina Rizun[2] [iD], Magdalena Ciesielska[2] [iD], Charalampos Alexopoulos[3] [iD], and Andrea Miletić[4] [iD]

[1] University of Tartu, Narva Mnt 18, 51009 Tartu, Estonia
anastasija.nikiforova@ut.ee
[2] Gdańsk University of Technology, Gabriela Narutowicza 11/12, 80-233 Gdańsk, Poland
{nina.rizun,magciesi}@pg.edu.pl
[3] University of the Aegean, 83200 Karlovassi, Samos, Greece
alexop@aegean.gr
[4] University of Zagreb, Savska Cesta 144A, 10000 Zagreb, Croatia
andrea.miletic@geof.unizg.hr

Abstract. Open government data (OGD) is seen as a political and socio-economic phenomenon that promises to promote civic engagement and stimulate public sector innovations in various areas of public life. To bring the expected benefits, data must be reused and transformed into value-added products or services. This, in turn, sets another precondition for data that are expected to not only be available and comply with open data principles, but also be of value, i.e., of interest for reuse by the end-user. This refers to the notion of "high-value dataset" (HVD), recognized by the European Data Portal as a key trend in the OGD area in 2022. While there is a progress in this direction, e.g., the Open Data Directive, incl. identifying 6 key categories, a list of HVDs and arrangements for their publication and re-use, they can be seen as "core"/"base" datasets aimed at increasing interoperability of public sector data with a high priority, contributing to the development of a more mature OGD initiative. Depending on the specifics of a region and country - geographical location, social, environmental, economic issues, cultural characteristics, (under)developed sectors and market specificities, more datasets can be recognized as of high value for a particular country. However, there is no standardized approach to assist chief data officers in this, and there is a clear lack of conceptualizations for the determination of HVD and systematic oversight. In this paper, we present a systematic review of existing literature on the HVD determination, which is expected to form an initial knowledge base for this process, including used approaches and indicators to determine them, data, stakeholders.

Keywords: Open Government Data · High-value Data · Open Data · Public Value · Public Administration · Stakeholder · Open Data Ecosystem

© IFIP International Federation for Information Processing 2023
Published by Springer Nature Switzerland AG 2023
I. Lindgren et al. (Eds.): EGOV 2023, LNCS 14130, pp. 211–229, 2023.
https://doi.org/10.1007/978-3-031-41138-0_14

1 Introduction

Open Government Data (OGD) is seen as an emerging political and socio-economic phenomenon that promises to benefit the economy, improve the transparency, efficiency, and quality of public services, including the transformation of government data-driven actions, stimulate public sector innovations in various areas of public life and promote civic engagement [1, 2]. OGD is considered to have a positive impact on the lives of individuals/citizens, and society, and contributes to tackling environmental problems, contributing to efficient, data-driven, sustainability-oriented development. In other words, OGD is considered to have economic, social, and environmental value. OGD is also one of the pillars of Open Government, which in turn is seen to be supported not only by OGD availability, but by the availability of high-value OGD.

However, the value of data, and open government data in particular, is a complex topic. In other words, although "value" itself is seen as a multifaceted concept, if the user of the data is clearly known, it can be determined from that user's viewpoint/perspective, i.e., needs, expectations and understanding of "value" - what this concept means for this particular user. However, OGD, by definition, does not have a predetermined user – OGD are freely available, accessible and provided without restrictions for their further reuse, which means that they can be used by everyone, regardless of age, gender, education, specialization, and for the purpose they will find necessary for themselves, which, as practice shows, in many cases differs significantly from the original purpose of collecting and using data internally by data producers/owners. The latter, in turn, is seen as a key determinant of the success of OGD as a movement, philosophy and policy, where data are provided for their further re-use and transformation into value (incl. services, products, new business models) when various forms of intelligence, incl. data intelligence, artificial intelligence, embodied intelligence, and collaborative intelligence [3], are used as a method for their transformation.

This makes the determination of OGD value a difficult task, and while several attempts have been made to date, there is considerable room for research and improvement for both academia and public administration. This is all the more so with the reference to the determining *"high-value datasets"* (HVD), particularly being interested in facilitating data provision, i.e., identifying potentially valuable datasets that are not yet available/open, i.e., when *ex-post* assessment of how valuable, interesting and/or useful was the dataset in question is not possible.

In terms of current progress in this area, this refers to a list of initiatives and studies carried out by several organizations and communities, where at the European level, probably most notable progress has been made by the European Commission in the Open Data Directive (originally Public Sector Information Directive (PSI Directive) in relation to the notion of HVD, referring to datasets whose re-use is expected to create the most value for society, the economy, and the environment, contributing to the creation of *"value-added services, applications and new, high-quality and decent jobs, and of the number of potential beneficiaries of the value-added services and applications based on those datasets"* [4]. To date, an agreement on six HVD thematic categories was reached as part of *Directive (EU) 2019/1024 of the European Parliament and of the Council of 20 June 2019 on open data and the re-use of public sector information,* according to which there are thematic data categories of HVD - (1) geospatial, (2) earth observation and environment, (3) meteorological, (4) statistics, (5) companies and company ownership, (6) mobility data that are considered as of high value [4].

Further, a list of specific HVDs and the arrangements for their publication was developed and made available as *"Commission Implementing Regulation (EU) 2023/138 of 21 December 2022 laying down a list of specific high-value datasets and the arrangements for their publication and re-use"* [5] that, however, can be seen as seeking for greater harmonization and interoperability of public sector data and data sharing across EU countries with reference to specific datasets, their granularity, key attributes, geographic coverage, requirements for their re-use, including licence (Creative Commons BY 4.0, any equivalent, or less restrictive open licence), specific format where appropriate, frequency of updates and timeliness, availability in machine-readable format, accessibility via API and bulk download, supported with metadata describing the data within the scope of the INSPIRE data themes that shall contain specific minimum set of the required metadata elements, description of the data structure and semantics, the use of controlled vocabularies and taxonomies (if relevant) etc. In addition, the Semantic Interoperability Community (SEMIC) is constantly hosting webinars on DCAT-AP (Data Catalogue Vocabulary Application Profile) for HVD to discuss with OGD portal owners, OGD publishers and enthusiasts the best approaches to use DCAT-AP to describe HVD and ensure their further findability, accessibility, and reusability. In other words, while it can be seen that progress has been made in this area, an examination of the above documents reveals that these datasets rather form a list of "mandatory" or "open by default" datasets, sometimes also referred to as "base" or "core" datasets, aiming at open data interoperability with a high level of priority and a relatively equal level of value for most countries, which contributed to the development and promotion of a more mature open data ecosystem (ODE) and OGD initiative. Thus, our study can be seen as a response to this call seeking to help countries take these steps.

However, the value of data is known to depend on a perspective such as the user's point of view [6], where [7], for instance, highlights the need to consider both the perspective of the data publisher and the perspective of data re-user when evaluating the value of data and defining HVD. In addition, the value of data depends on country-specific aspects, such as geographic location and its specificities, current environment, social, economic issues, culture, ethnicity, likelihood of crises and/or catastrophes, (under)developed industries/sectors and market specificities, and development trajectories, i.e., priorities. Depending on the above, more datasets can be recognized as having high value within a particular country or region [8–10]. For example, meteorological data describing sea level rise can be of great value in the Netherlands as it has a strong impact on citizens and businesses as more than 1/3 of the country is below sea level, however, the same data will be less valuable for less affected to countries, such as Italy and France [8]. We believe that additional factors such as ongoing smart cities initiatives, and the Sustainable Development Goals (SDG), the current state of countries and cities in relation to their implementation and established priorities affect this list as well.

Therefore, it is important to support the identification of country specific HVD that will increase user interest by transforming data into innovative solution and services. Although this fact is recognized by countries and some local and regional efforts, mostly undertaken by governments with little support from the scientific and academia community, they are mainly faced with problems in the form of delays in their development or complete failure, or ending up with some set of HVD, but little information about how this was actually done. These ad-hoc attempts remain closed and not reusable, which is contrary to both the general OGD philosophy and the HVD-centric philosophy that is expected to be standardized. Most of them are *ex-post* or a combination of the *ex-ante* and *ex-post*, making the process of identifying them more resource-intensive, with an effect only visible after potentially valuable datasets have been discovered, published, and kept maintained, with the need for further evaluation of their impact, which is a resource-consuming task. It is also in line with [11], according to which there is no standardized approach to assisting chief data officers in identifying HVDs, resulting in a failure in consistent identification and maintenance of HVDs.

Considering the importance of this topic, as well as the very fragmented understanding of the topic in the scientific literature and lack of connection between public administration and academia on this issue, it makes sense to turn to the literature and summarize what has been conducted so far in this regard. Thus, the objective is to examine how HVD determination has been reflected in the literature over the years and what has been found by these studies to date, including the indicators used in them, involved stakeholders, data-related aspects, and frameworks. This is done by conducting a Systematic Literature Review (SLR). To achieve the research objective, the following research questions (RQ) were established:

- **(RQ1)** *how is the value of the open government data perceived/defined? how the HVD are defined, if this definition differs from the definition introduced in the PSI/OD Directive? In which contexts has the topic of high-value dataset been investigated by previous research (e.g., research disciplines, countries)? Are local efforts being made at the country levels to identify the datasets that provide the most value to stakeholders of the local open data ecosystem?*
- **(RQ2)** *What datasets are considered to be of higher value in terms of data nature, data type, data format, data dynamism?*
- **(RQ3)** *What indicators are used to determine HVD? How can these indicators be classified and measured? Whether this can be done (semi-)automatically?*
- **(RQ4)** *Whether there is a framework for determining country specific HVD? In other words, is it possible to determine what datasets are of particular value and interest for their further reuse and value creation, taking into account the specificities of the country under consideration, e.g., culture, geography, ethnicity, likelihood of crises and/or catastrophes?*

While the results are expected to be of greater interest to public administration and public agencies to understand which datasets are most in demand with their subsequent opening (or academia to set the research agenda), the current state of affairs and current trends in a broader open data ecosystem perspective suggests that these findings can be of interest to a wider audience, with respect to B2G, C2G and other data governance models. The results are also expected to form the knowledge base for the framework for determining HVD, while the validation of indicators identified as part of this study and derived from government reports will takes place during the workshops with open (government) data and e-government experts (three editions have already taken place).

The paper is structured as follows: Sect. 2 provides an overview of the topic, empha-sizing the importance of HVD, Sect. 3 presents the methodology of this study, Sect. 4 provides the findings/results, Sect. 5 establishes a discussion around the findings, and provides key conclusions and directions for further research.

2 Background

The practice shows that there is often a mismatch between users' needs and the oppor-tunities offered by available datasets [12], where OGD are not relevant to the problems that users want to solve [13]. In other words, open data is often found to be either super-ficial or irrelevant to potential users [2]. However, while the use and value of OGD are often discussed, encouraging data agencies to open their data, governments to support the opening and maintenance of data, citizens, businesses and other data user groups to use these data, there are relatively few studies that analyse the actual use and value of data (and specific dataset), particularly without limiting the scope for a subset of data. This is due to the complexity of the topic and the underlying general paradigm of the OGD – freely accessible and freely reusable, i.e., the license allows to reuse data with-out declaring it in the resulting product or service does, there are a limited number of indicators and approaches to measure the use and the value of data, especially the value of an individual dataset, as well as the success of data opening policies.

Those studies that make such an attempt, typically address the use and value of government data from one of two perspectives - (1) qualitative, (2) quantitative [2]. For the qualitative perspective, motivations for using data, practices, and experiences of users to reuse data and create or co-create value are typically the subject of research [2, 12, 14, 15]. For quantitative approach, the reference to quantitative parameters such as the of views and downloads provided by the OGD portals is related to the use of datasets, although it is clear that these parameters may indicate some interest in the dataset and can be used rather as assumptions to draw onto usage trends [2, 16, 17], i.e., the fact that a dataset has been viewed does not guarantee that it will be actually used, where even the fact of downloading it is not a guarantee, where its actual reuse transforming it into the value is the expected end-result. For the latter, in turn, the "value" into which a dataset has been transformed is also unclear, i.e., *whether this transformation will have either social, economic, or environmental value itself?* This makes it very challenging to estimate the value of existing datasets, not to say about those not yet published.

In 2020, the European Commission attempted to address this issue, by publishing an *"Impact Assessment study on the list of High Value Datasets to be made available by the Member States under the Open Data Directive"* [18]. Based on a literature review of six thematic categories of HVD, six macro characteristics of potential value derived from open data were found, which include economic benefits, environmental benefits, generation of innovative services and innovation (innovation and artificial intelligence), reuse, improving, strengthening, and supporting public authorities in carrying out their mission. Multiple categories of value were found for each macro characteristic, resulting in a total of 32 categories of value and 126 possible indicators (both quantitative and qualitative) to measure this value. However, although it seems to be the longest list of indicators today, three workshops conducted by the authors with e-government and OGD experts found that only a few indicators are sufficiently clear, reasonable, and feasible, i.e., do not require the collection of supporting data, whose amount and complexity is higher than of original dataset.

It should also be noted that as a follow-up to the Directive (EU) 2019/1024 and Commission Implementing Regulation (EU) 2023/138, the Open Data Maturity Report 2022 (ODMR2022) [6] has updated their methodology with a focus on countries' readiness for HVD and the upcoming European Commission Implementing Act, adding relevant indicators to all four dimensions it covers (policy, impact, portal, and quality). These are measured using a questionnaire answered by a representative of the open data initiative in question, asking about the preparatory measures that countries might have initiated before the Implementing Act and the actions taken to date. The recent ODMR2022 [6] also reported that most countries are taking at least some steps to identify HVD and take related activities, and some of them perform well, but HVD list identification is based on categories prioritised at EU level, not the actual needs and interests of countries that can be different.

3   Methodology

To understand how HVD determination has been reflected in the literature over the years and what has been found by these studies to date, we studied all relevant literature covering this topic. In order to identify relevant peer-reviewed literature, the SLR was carried out to form the knowledge base by searching digital libraries covered by Scopus and Web of Science (WoS). Given the specificity of the topic, we covered Digital Government Research library (DGRL) that covers studies related to domains of digital government, digital governance, and digital democracy.

Keyword-based search was carried out using *("open data" OR "open government data") AND ("high-value data*" OR "high value data*")* query, which was applied to the article title, keywords, and abstract to limit the number of papers to those, where these objects were primary research objects rather than mentioned in the body, e.g., as a future work. Only articles in English were considered, while in terms of scope, both journal articles, conference papers, and chapters were studied. The query resulted in 11 articles in Scopus and 5 in WoS (Fig. 1). After deduplication, 11 articles were found unique and were further checked for relevance, all of which were found to be relevant after the first round of evaluation, and one (1) article was excluded from further analysis as non-eligible. One more study was excluded because we were not able to access the full text (neither from Digital Libraries, nor from journal or conference proceedings, nor from ResearchGate). As a result, a total of 9 articles were further examined. Each study was independently examined by at least two authors.

To attain the objective of our study, the protocol was developed based on [19], where the information on each study was collected in four (4) categories: (1) descriptive information, (2) approach- and research design- related information, (3) quality-related information, (4) HVD determination-related information (Table 1). The data underlying the study are publicly available on Zenodo - https://zenodo.org/record/8075918 [20].

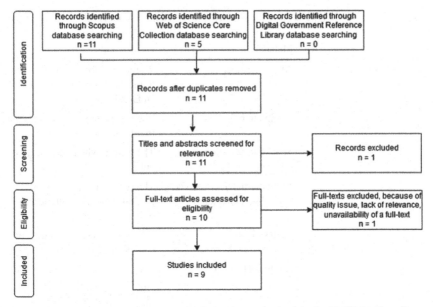

Fig. 1. Study selection, assessment, and inclusion (presented using the PRISMA flow diagram).

4 Results from the Systematic Literature Review

4.1 Descriptive and Quality Analysis

As part of the descriptive analysis, we studied the selected studies' objectives (see Table 2), the journals and conferences where these studies were published, the years of publication, the databases through which we found them, how well they were cited in these digital libraries. Most studies are exploratory and were published between 2012 and 2023. Although neither OGD, nor the importance of the value of data are new topics, scholarly publications dedicated to the topic of HVD are still limited, in contrast to OGD research in general, particularly considering that we did not apply strict exclusion criteria and did not limit the period under investigation – only two studies covered the topic in question in the last three years – [10, 20].

The low number of relevant studies points out the limited body of knowledge on this topic, thereby making this study unique and constituting a call for action. Papers mostly come from Europe with contributions from Belgium, Bulgaria, Germany, Greece, Latvia, the Netherlands, Sweden, Switzerland, although there are several contributions coming from the United Kingdom, the United States of America, Thailand, India, and China.

For most studies HVD is a secondary research object (seven (7) out of nine (9) studies), where their role differs either from an application domain, i.e., a list of already determined HVD categories and the analysis of the correspondence of datasets provided by the national OGD portal to this list [9, 26], or assessing the impact of available datasets focusing on a subset of data represented by datasets belonging to HVD [24]. In some studies, the concept of HVD is referred to more as a buzzword [22, 23, 27], but it is not

Table 1. The structure of the protocol [adapted from [19]].

Category	Metadata	Description
Descriptive information	Article number	A study number, corresponding to the study number assigned in an Excel worksheet
	Complete reference	The complete source information to refer to the study
	Year of publication	The year in which the study was published
	Journal article/conference paper/book chapter	The type of the paper, i.e., journal article, conference paper, or book chapter
	DOI/Website	A link to the website where the study can be found
	Number of citations	The number of citations of the article in Google Scholar, Scopus, Web of Science
	Availability in OA	Availability of an article in the Open Access
	Keywords	Keywords of the paper as indicated by the authors
	Relevance for this study	What is the relevance level of the article for this study? (high/medium/low)
Approach- & research design-related information	Objective/RQ	The research objective/aim, established research questions
	Research method (including unit of analysis)	The methods used to collect data, including the unit of analysis (country, organisation, specific unit that has been analysed, e.g., the number of use-cases, scope of the SLR etc.)
	Contributions	The contributions of the study
	Method	Whether the study uses a qualitative, quantitative, or mixed methods approach?

(*continued*)

Table 1. (*continued*)

Category	Metadata	Description
	Availability of the underlying research data	Whether there is a reference to the publicly available underlying research data e.g., transcriptions of interviews, collected data, or explanation why these data are not shared?
	Period under investigation	Period (or moment) in which the study was conducted
	Use of theory/theoretical concepts/approaches	Does the study mention any theory/theoretical concepts/approaches? If any theory is mentioned, how is theory used in the study?
Quality- & relevance- related information	Quality concerns	Whether there are any quality concerns (e.g., limited information about the research methods used)?
	Primary research object	Is the HVD a primary research object in the study? (primary - the paper is focused on the HVD determination, secondary - mentioned but not studied (e.g., part of discussion, future work etc.))
HVD determination-related information	HVD definition and type of value	How is the HVD defined in the article and/or any other equivalent term?
	HVD indicators	What are the indicators to identify HVD? How were they identified? (components & relationships, "input - > output")
	A framework for HVD determination	Is there a framework presented for HVD identification? What components does it consist of and what are the relationships between these components? (detailed description)
	Stakeholders and their roles	What stakeholders or actors does HVD determination involve? What are their roles?

(*continued*)

Table 1. (*continued*)

Category	Metadata	Description
	Data	What data do HVD cover?
	Level (if relevant)	What is the level of the HVD determination covered in the article? (e.g., city, regional, national, international)

given enough attention, only emphasizing their importance, including their key role for the sustainability of OGD initiative.

Only two (2) studies openly shared the underlying research data – [10, 20], despite not only a growing trend towards open sharing of research data as a good open science practice, but also compliance with the general OGD philosophy and the postulated importance of their re-usability and re-use with another study that provided the reference to the data but whose maintenance was stopped and the data are no longer available. As for those studies that provided an underlying data, it should be mentioned that respective studies were published between 2021 and 2023, which can be argued as related to the growing popularity of open science and OGD as more than data, i.e., rather a philosophy and the mindset that needs to be changed as part of this movement.

For the quality analysis of the articles covered, the research design was mostly appropriate, while several studies were lacking information on approach.

4.2   Content Analysis

The Definition of HVD. Four (4) of nine (9) articles provide a clear definition of what is meant by HVD in each study, and two (2) more studies, where the definition is indirect, but at least a rough definition of such can be extracted. Nikiforova [10] uses the definition proposed in the *Open Data Directive (EU) 2019/1024*. Utamachant and Anutariya [9] uses the "local" definition of HVD given by the Electronic Government Agency of Thailand (EGA). Wang et al. [25] suggests a high-level definition, according to which HVD are "*data that meet the actual needs*". This is somewhat similar to two (2) other studies that limit the definition of HVD to the domain they belong to, i.e., [26] limits HVD to *business data* only, while Zsarnóczay et al. [20] define them as *critical datasets for their work, especially those with greater granularity and spatial extent, with the potential for re-use limited to disaster recovery planning*. Stuermer and Dapp [24], while not defining HVD, refer to specific data categories as defined in the G8 Open Data Charter. Alternatively, Shadbolt et al. [22] does not provide a definition of HVD, but instead postulates that understanding of HVD will be missing until existing data is available in a linked data web (LDW), which will help understand the demand side and collect relevant feedback for local, regional, and national levels.

Since some studies have focused more on data-related aspects, let us refer to them. Five (5) studies reflected on HVD as data categories or specific datasets (Table 3). Two (2) of them refer to classifications such as the 14 categories of the G8 Open Data Charter

Table 2. Overview of studies included in our systematic literature review.

Reference	Study Objective	Primary research?
[22]	To develop an EnAKTing-based integrated account of how to bring OGD into the linked-data Web (LDW)	secondary
[23]	To develop an understanding of the various kinds of technical, administrative & regulatory challenges faced by government agencies in India while trying to release their datasets in open domain	secondary
[9]	To comprehensively analyse the currently available HVDs (in Thailand) in various aspects, including their domain coverage, data attributes and categorization, and intrinsic data qualities	**primary**
[24]	To develop a framework to assess the impact of releasing open data by applying the Social Return on Investment (SROI) approach	secondary
[25]	To summarize the data value evaluation methods of scientific and technological information in the open-source environment	secondary
[26]	To build a bridge between linked data research and new potential adopters of the technology by providing a stepwise introduction on how to move from basic business data described in various formats housed in government registries towards linked OGD	secondary
[27]	To develop a comprehensive understanding of the challenges faced by government agencies with specific focus on India while trying to release their datasets in open domain	secondary
[20]	To prioritize research questions and identify community needs for data and computational simulation capabilities to foster the development of robust tools to simulate the impact of natural hazards on structures, lifelines, and communities	n/a (**domain-specific HVD**)
[10]	To identify the current value of the OGD and their compliance with the term of HVD in users' view, identifying the most valuable areas and datasets for Latvian citizens and businesses (SME)	**primary**

[24], the nine (9) HVD categories defined by the EGA [9], while [20] uses a list of six (6) HVD data categories defined by the OD Directive to design a questionnaire for citizens and SMEs to identify HVD from their point of view, coming up with nine (9) categories that were named as HVDs by respondents in addition to the OD Directive (some of which are rather subsets of these categories). Following a similar survey and

consultation approach, [20] does not use any predefined classification, identified four (4) HVD categories with 12 subcategories for the area of disaster recovery planning.

Table 3. Overview of data categories and datasets recognized as HVD

Ref.	Data categories or datasets
[9]	**9 HVD data categories defined by EGA** (1) Politics and government, (2) government budget and spendings, (3) economic, financial and industry, (4) public healthcare, (5) law, justice and crime, (6) social and welfare, (7) agriculture and irrigation, (8) art, culture and religion, (9) ICT and communication; 22 datasets out of more than 1000
[22]	**14 HVD categories defined by the G8 Open Data Charter** (1) Companies, (2) Crime and Justice, (3) earth observations, (4) education, (5) energy and environment, (6) finance and contracts, (7) geospatial, (8) global development, (9) Government Accountability and Democracy, (10) Health, (11) Science and Research, (12) Statistics, (13) Social mobility and welfare, (14) Transport and Infrastructure
[26]	**1 pre-defined category** - business data, e.g., basic data about a company (e.g., legal name, address, representative, establishment date and company type), company identifiers and annual balance sheets. Authoritative data, LOGD
[20]	**4 categories (12 subcategories) defined by respondents** (1) Buildings; (2) Households, Businesses, and Services; (3) Recovery; (4) Hazard
[10]	**6 HVD categories defined by the OD Directive** (1) geospatial data, (2) earth observation and environment, (3) meteorological, (4) statistics, (5) companies and company ownership, (6) mobility; **9 categories defined by the respondents** (1) medical and health data, (2) detailed tourism data on regions, (3) transport data, (4) data on the suitability of transport and places for people with disabilities, (5) data on streets and traffic lights, (6) data on radiation and noise levels, (7) data on physical and mental health of people, (8) data on social media (e.g., hash tags, fake news, data leaks), (9) sensor data

An analysis of the literature as well as prior work in this area allows us to group these data-related aspects into (1) *data categories*, (2) *specific datasets*, (3) *data type*, (4) *data dynamism*. For the latter groups, they can be seen in part as prerequisites for being considered truly valuable and potentially reusable, mentioning the need for increased interoperability, including providing these data **in LOGD (Linked Open Government Data)** form (the importance of RDF and LOGD is emphasized in [22, 26]). In other cases, it refers to certain features that today make data more prospective for transforming into value-adding products and services, with **geospatial data**, **real-time data** and **sensor-generated data** being predominantly mentioned. Otherwise, some studies, especially more recent ones, are increasingly mentioning datasets that are related to or share the same values as Sustainable Development Goals, the concept of Smart Cities, where both data generated as part of their operation and data that can potentially contribute to the development and maintenance of a smart city are seen as HVD. And yet another category that, though not so often mentioned now, certainly deserves attention, is the emphasis placed by several studies on data that can be seen as **citizen-generated**.

It should be emphasized that although most studies we have reviewed are of national level conducted in Latvia, Greece, Thailand, India, UK, USA, only two of them actually focus on country-specific HVD, namely Latvia [10] and Thailand [9], where the second rather evaluates the list of datasets denoted as HVD on the OGD portal, while [21] focuses on the determination of HVD in a specific domain. This means that determination of country specific HVDs in the scientific literature is very underrepresented.

Otherwise, the vast majority of research perceive HVD as data that will be of interest to be re-used, where the type of value created by this re-use may differ, as well as the beneficiary (business, citizen, government, or both). Thus, let us now discuss what stakeholders and actors these studies cover or consider important.

Which Stakeholders Does HVD Determination Involve? Most studies mention general ODE stakeholders, with only a few focused on those related to the definition of HVD. More precisely, Nikiforova [10] conducts a survey of Latvian (a) citizens/society (individuals) and (b) businesses, in particular small and medium-sized enterprises (SME) since the definition of HVD should take into account the experience of industry reusers, who are characterized by a deeper understanding of this "value", knowing what kind of data may be needed for a particular application. Zsarnóczay et al. [20], conduct the workshops with researchers, developers, and practitioners with expertise in the domain they study, i.e., earthquake, coastal, and wind hazards from engineering, planning, data sciences, and social science, some of whom are also data providers. Their rationale is similar to the above, i.e., the input should be obtained from real users, considering their needs and, as a result having a demand to be reused (corresponds to [7, 28]).

Utamachant and Anutariya [9], who, however, assess the compliance of already published HVD to their perception of HVD, while mentioning that the European data portal recommends that two different points of view be considered when identifying HVD – the data provider and the data re-user, does not follow this recommendation. They argue that OGD public participation in Thailand is still at an immature stage and determining a community data demands is almost impossible, leading to the need to use an alternative approach to identify HVD by referring to the world standards, such as those defined by Government Open Data Index (GODI) and Open Data Barometer (ODB), with further examination of the list by the domain experts, who evaluate the impact of these datasets and readiness for their opening. This, i.e., immaturity of community engagement, should be highlighted as a barrier not only to the HVD determination, but to the overall success of a healthy and sustainable OGD ecosystem. Similarly, Shadbolt et al. [22] argue that OGD is not a rigid government IT specification – it requires a productive dialogue between data providers, users, and developers, where a *"perpetual beta"* should be expected, in which best practice, technical development, innovative use of data, and citizen-centric policies come together to drive data release programs.

As regards the general ODE stakeholders these studies mention, which is not surprising considering that they are all ultimately part of the HVD publishing process, while those listed above are seen the ones who should identify them as potential reusers. [10] also pointed out that the literature suggests that determining the value of a particular dataset is a very complex and multi-perspective task, when the data provider, who tends to have data usage statistics such as views, downloads and number of showcases/use-cases/re-uses seen as one of the popular and most widely used HVD indicators [7, 8, 16], plays a critical role, which is also because there are different views on who should benefit from HVD and an impact they create, i.e., HVD value beneficiary.

Otherwise, two general categories of OGD stakeholders are (1) **data producers**, also called **data publishers, data providers, data suppliers,** who in the traditional OGD ecosystem are government and public agencies, and (2) **data consumers**, also called **data users, reusers,** who can be then broken down into smaller groups such as **citizens, society, NGO, developers/innovators, entrepreneurs, business** and **SME** in particular, **start-ups, media, data journalists, researchers/scientists/academic community, domain experts, private** and **public sector** etc. Government and public agencies should also be considered policy makers, and, more importantly, OGD users, while the rapid changes of the OGD ecosystem suggest that all those listed as data users may also act as data providers, thereby more frequently viewing the OGD ecosystem as a combination of various data governance models that are no longer limited to G2C or G2B, with B2G, C2G becoming increasingly popular as an integral part of the OGD ecosystem rather than an independent, or at least the need for these changes is postulated.

HVD Determination: Indicators and a Framework. As mentioned before only two (2) (and partly [20]) studies address HVD as a primary topic, and even fewer studies focusing on the process of determining HVD. However, we should mention that while the above represents the so-called *"ex ante"* approach, some studies, on the contrary, refer to what is called *"ex post"*, i.e., proposing methods along with indicators for measuring actual impact and value of data. Although they make little contribution to the determination of HVD, they can be seen as an asset in the process of opening and maintaining HVD. In other words, the data are expected not only become publicly available in an open data format, but their actual impact and value must also be measured. These outputs, in turn, may provide some insight into the determination of the next set of HVD, based on public interest in a given category of data or, in contrast to very low reuse rates, although there is evidence that a particular topic of data is in a great demand.

In more detail, given the impossibility of reaching the wider community in Thailand, [9] takes an alternative approach that we would rather define as verification of the HVD datasets determined by their OGD portal. The study proposes an approach to identify HVDs among already published datasets. To this end, they map the datasets denoted as HVD to the Government Open Data Index (GODI) and Open Data Barometer (ODB) data categories, which are then filtered using the UK National Information Infrastructure (NII) datasets, which are then processed by domain experts. Initially, Corruption Perception Index (CPI) was also used along GODI and ODB.

Shadbolt et al. [22], however, consider that such a proposal would only be possible when LDW is ensured, which would help to identify HVD. However, there is no clear idea of how exactly this is supposed to be then done. Stuermer and Dapp [24] proposes a SROI-based (Social return on investment) framework to evaluate the impact of already published datasets. It consists of four (4) values adapted to the given context, namely: (1) *input* - resources such as native data, money, people, infrastructure, equipment, (2) *output* - tangible deliverables/directly controllable results, i.e., setup and operation of an open data portal with metadata, updated content, open format etc., (3) *outcome* -

all direct and indirect consequences of certain output actions of open data users, incl. Hackathons, apps, new firms, data linking, research etc., and (4) *impact* – the outcome adjusted for the effects that would have occurred without the intervention, i.e., actually caused by releasing the data-value-creating consequences. These four values are linked to 14 HVD categories of the G8 Open Data Charter to create a matrix of open data examples, activities, and impacts in each data category. This can be seen as a possible asset in determining the potential of the HVD under consideration.

Wang et al. [25] do not provide a framework, but summarize the knowledge found in literature, according to which two (2) methods are used to evaluate the OGD value, where one is based on a *top-down macroeconomic method* and the other is based on a *bottom-up microeconomic method*. A top-down macro-economic approach evaluates the total value of various industries that use OGD as an investment and shows the total value of OGD to the economy. The bottom-up microeconomic approach is concerned with analysing the productivity of OGD, taking into account the inputs and outputs of individuals and companies when using government data.

Varytimou et al. [26] suggests that the indicator to be used is a high potential for reuse in national and cross-border settings. However, they do not suggest how this high reuse potential can be determined. [20], however, considers that the most appropriate approach is to survey or interview actual real users and data providers, which, however, given the fact that the study is carried out in predefined settings (domain), where the stakeholders are more likely known being also less in nature, is easier than for the whole OGD, where the data users are generally difficult to identify.

Similarly, [10] also does not come up with a framework but believes that consultation with different stakeholder groups should be a mandatory component, where the perspectives of different stakeholder groups should be considered separately, since the value that the OGD brings to them may also differ, i.e., more economic, and entrepreneurial for SMEs and rather social and environmental for citizens. Also, for user groups such as citizens, the author suggests grouping them based on their level of familiarity with OGD and behaviour patterns to reduce the level of noise in the collected data, although considering those who have only used OGD a few times or even never, and those, who are experienced users. The results, however, are subject to interpretation, where it is important to understand what exactly refers to the data and their value, and what – to other ODE components. To structure the survey the author used the six (6) key HVD thematic categories defined in the OD Directive (the list of datasets was not developed at that point), along with the data categories on the national OGD portal, which are evaluated for relevance, after which, when some knowledge base is created, respondents are invited to suggest their own categories, and, more importantly, specify the datasets they consider to be HVD, with further re-evaluation of their interest in OGD, if these datasets are made available. This was considered as the first step towards developing a framework, and the next phase of the analysis was expected to take place with the OGD data re-users, i.e., those who indicated themselves as re-users in the first phase and agreed to be contacted – no other approach is possible in Latvia, where OGD reuse is not monitored. This was expected to be then combined with other approaches found in the literature, incl. Downloads statistics (if the holders of the Latvia Open Data Portal have these data since the portal user interface does not have this data), to ensure more complete analysis of possible indicators to be then.

The findings of the SLR and components associated with HVD determination are summarized in Fig. 2, covering those HVD determination-related features we identified in the literature. Identified approaches and determinants in particular can also be divided into those of more **qualitative** nature and **quantitative**. In other words, some indicators/determinants can be used to quantify the value/potential interest in the dataset in question, while some of them are very qualitative in nature (e.g., citizens awareness of an environmental issue, which, although can be somehow quantified, is still rather qualitative).

Depending on the source of these determinants, i.e., the input data that will be used to determine them, they can also be divided into **internal** – those that imply from the data the data publisher have, the owner of national open government data portal owner (e.g., Google Analytics, log files of the portal etc.), and **external** – where the involvement of external actors or stakeholders (both people and systems) becomes necessary to obtain the input that subsequently transforms into an understanding of potential HVDs or serves as part of the basis for such decision-making.

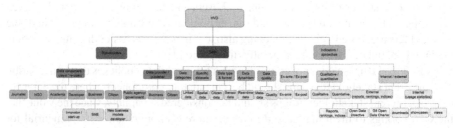

Fig. 2. Conceptualization of the reviewed literature around the HVD concept (for better resolution see - https://zenodo.org/record/8075918 [21]).

We also believe that regardless of the above category, indicators can be divided into those that can be measured by quantifying this "value", and those that cannot. However, most indicators found in the literature and Deloitte report [18], are neither **measurable**, nor **SMART** (Specific, Measurable, Achievable, Relevant, Time-bound), which is contrary to our expectation for the identification of such indicators. What is also important to keep in mind is that the determination of HVD is not a one-time event, but a continuous process in which not only the opening/publishing and subsequent ongoing maintenance of not only the open dataset, but the entire HVD determination process as whole is expected. Thus, we can think of the HVD determination process as a lifecycle similar to the Deming, also PDCA cycle (plan-do-check-act) or define-measure-analyse-improve-control also known as phases of Lean Six Sigma, [29] which consists of at least: identification of a list of potential HVDs, considering the current data supply and stakeholders' needs, including an analysis of the possibilities of opening HVD, opening/publishing HVD, evaluation of an impact of a HVD in comparison with the expected, possibly considering price-to-value ratio, take a decision on the need for adjustments.

5 Conclusions and Future Work

The objective of this study was to examine how the HVD determination has been reflected in the literature over the years and what has been found by these studies to date. After we looked at *how the high-value datasets are defined and whether there are local efforts at the country levels to identify datasets that provide the most value to stakeholders in the local open data ecosystem* (**RQ1**), we explored *which datasets are considered more valuable in terms of the nature, the type and format, and the dynamism of the data* that we identified as the dominant characteristics of HVD (**RQ2**), we examined *what indicators are used to determine HVD and how they can be classified and measured* (**RQ3**), and also analysed *whether there are frameworks for identifying country-specific HVD* to determine which datasets are of particular value and interest for further reuse and value creation, taking into account the specificities of the country in questions, such as culture, geography, ethnicity, likelihood of crises and/or disasters, (under)developed sectors and market specificities (**RQ4**).

Our SLR leads us to conclude that this topic is very underrepresented in the literature, making this study unique. The claim that there is no standardized approach to assisting chief data officers in identifying HVDs has been supported, and a clear lack of conceptualizations for identifying HVD and systematic oversight, where the worlds of "practice" and "academia/research" are highly disconnected, has been identified. The findings of this study are expected to help public administration and government agencies understand which datasets are most in demand with their subsequent opening, as well as the academic community to set the research agenda, where our study and its findings constitute a call for action. The future work will cover examination of publicly available approaches taken by governments, extracting the indicators they use, and assessing their reliability, as well as SMARTness, which would be preferable option that will reduce the overall complexity of the HVD management (determination and maintenance) process. At the same time, it is clear that it is not always the case that non-SMART indicators are not suitable for determining HVDs. Thus, while having as a long-term objective HVD determination framework that would be based solely on SMART indicators, it is clear that they may predominate, but cannot be the only set of indicators used. This, along with the input we received from a series of international workshops with open (government) data experts, covering more indicators and approaches found to be used in practice [30], could enrich the common understanding of the goal, thereby contributing to the next open data wave [31].

Acknowledgement. This research has been funded by the European Social Fund via IT Academy programme (Anastasija Nikiforova). The work of Andrea Miletić was supported by the Young Researchers' Career Development Project - Training of Doctoral Students (DOK-01–2020), established by the Croatian Science Foundation.

References

1. Kassen, M.: Open data and its peers: understanding promising harbingers from Nordic Europe. Aslib J. Inf. Manag. **72**(5), 765–785 (2020)

2. Santos-Hermosa, G., Quarati, A., Loría-Soriano, E., Raffaghelli, J.E.: Why does open data get underused? A focus on the role of (open) data literacy. In: Raffaghelli, J.E., Sangrà, A. (eds.) Data Cultures in Higher Education. Higher Education Dynamics, vol. 59, pp. 145–177. Springer, Cham (2023). https://doi.org/10.1007/978-3-031-24193-2_6

3. Verhulst, S., Addo, P.M., Young, A., Zahuranec, A.J., Baumann, D., McMurren, J.: Emerging uses of technology for development: a new intelligence paradigm (2021). Available at SSRN 3937649

4. Directive (EU) 2019/1024 of the European Parliament and of the Council of 20 June 2019 on open data and the re-use of public sector information (recast)

5. Commission Implementing Regulation (EU) 2023/138 of 21 December 2022 laying down a list of specific high-value datasets and the arrangements for their publication and re-use

6. Carsaniga, G., Lincklaen Arriëns, E.N., Dogger J., van Assen, M., Ceccon, G.: Open Data Maturity Report 2022. Luxembourg: Publications Office of the European Union (2022). https://doi.org/10.2830/70973

7. Bargiotti, L., De Keyzer, M., Goedertier, S., Loutas, N.: Value based prioritisation of open government data investments. European Public Sector Information Platform (2014)

8. Huyer, E., Blank, M.: Analytical Report 15: high-value datasets: understanding the perspective of data providers. Publications Office of the European Union 2020. https://doi.org/10.2830/363773

9. Utamachant, P., Anutariya, C.: An analysis of high-value datasets: a case study of Thailand's open government data. In: 2018 15th International Joint Conference on Computer Science and Software Engineering (JCSSE), pp. 1–6. IEEE (2018)

10. Nikiforova, A.: Towards enrichment of the open government data: a stakeholder-centered determination of High-Value Data sets for Latvia. In: Proceedings of the 14th International Conference on Theory and Practice of Electronic Governance, pp. 367–372 (2021)

11. Ministry of Electronics and Information Technology, 2022, Summary: Draft India Data Accessibility and Use Policy (2022). medianama.com

12. Ruijer, E., Grimmelikhuijsen, S., Van Den Berg, J., Meijer, A.: Open data work: understanding open data usage from a practice lens. Int. Rev. Adm. Sci. 86(1), 3–19 (2020)

13. Bonina, C., Eaton, B.: Cultivating open government data platform ecosystems through governance: lessons from Buenos Aires, Mexico City and Montevideo. Gov. Inf. Q. 37(3), 101479 (2020)

14. Safarov, I., Meijer, A., Grimmelikhuijsen, S.: Utilization of open government data: a systematic literature review of types, conditions, effects and users. Inf. Polity 22(1), 1–24 (2017)

15. Lassinantti, J.: Re-use of public sector open data-Characterising the phenomena. Int. J. Public Inf. Syst. 13(1), 1–29 (2019)

16. Quarati, A., De Martino, M.: Open government data usage: a brief overview. In: Proceedings of the 23rd International Database Applications & Engineering Symposium, pp. 1–8 (2019)

17. Barbosa, L., Pham, K., Silva, C., Vieira, M.R., Freire, J.: Structured open urban data: understanding the landscape. Big data 2(3), 144–154 (2014)

18. Deloitte: Impact Assessment study on the list of High Value Datasets to be made available by the Member States under the Open Data Directive (2020). Deloitte-Study-2020.pdf

19. Zuiderwijk, A., Chen, Y.C., Salem, F.: Implications of the use of artificial intelligence in public governance: a systematic literature review and a research agenda. Gov. Inf. Q. 38(3), 101577 (2021)

20. Zsarnóczay, A., et al.: Community perspectives on simulation and data needs for the study of natural hazard impacts and recovery. Nat. Hazard. Rev. 24(1), 04022042 (2023)

21. Nikiforova, A., Rizun, N., Ciesielska, M., Alexopoulos, C., Miletič, A.: Dataset: A Systematic Literature Review on the topic of High-value datasets [Data set]. Zenodo (2023). https://doi.org/10.5281/zenodo.8075918

22. Shadbolt, N., O'Hara, K., Berners-Lee, T., Gibbins, N., Glaser, H., Hall, W.: Linked open government data: lessons from data.gov.uk. IEEE Intell. Syst. **27**(3), 16–24 (2012)
23. Verma, N., Gupta, M. P.: Open government data: beyond policy & portal, a study in Indian context. In: Proceedings of the 7th International Conference on Theory and Practice of Electronic Governance, pp. 338–341 (2013)
24. Stuermer, M., Dapp, M.M.: Measuring the promise of open data: development of the impact monitoring framework. In: 2016 Conference for E-Democracy and Open Government (CeDEM), pp. 197–203. IEEE (2016
25. Wang, X., Dong, C., Zeng, W., Xu, Z., Zhang, J.: Survey of data value evaluation methods based on open source scientific and technological information. In: Cheng, X., Jing, W., Song, X., Lu, Z. (eds.) Data Science. ICPCSEE 2019. Communications in Computer and Information Science, vol. 1058, pp. 172–185. Springer, Singapore (2019). https://doi.org/10.1007/978-981-15-0118-0_14
26. Varytimou, A., Loutas, N., Peristeras, V.: Towards linked open business registers: the application of the registered organization vocabulary in Greece. Int. J. Semant. Web Inf. Syst. (IJSWIS) **11**(2), 66–92 (2015)
27. Verma, N., Gupta, M.P.: Challenges in publishing open government data: a study in Indian context. In: Proceedings of the 2015 2nd International Conference on Electronic Governance and Open Society: Challenges in Eurasia, pp. 1–9 (2015)
28. Purwanto, A., Zuiderwijk, A., Janssen, M.: Group development stages in open government data engagement initiatives: a comparative case studies analysis. In: Parycek, P., et al. (eds.) EGOV 2018. LNCS, vol. 11020, pp. 48–59. Springer, Cham (2018). https://doi.org/10.1007/978-3-319-98690-6_5
29. López Reyes, M.E., Magnussen, R.: The use of open government data to create social value. In: Janssen, M., et al. (eds.) EGOV 2022. LNCS, vol. 13391, pp. 244–257. Springer, Cham (2022). https://doi.org/10.1007/978-3-031-15086-9_16
30. Nikiforova, A., Alexopoulos, C., Rizun, N., Ciesielska, M.: Identification of high-value dataset determinants: is there a silver bullet for efficient sustainability-oriented data-driven development?. In: 24th Annual International Conference on Digital Government Research - Together in the unstable world: Digital government and solidarity (DGO 2023), 11–14 July 2023, Gdańsk, Poland, 3 p. ACM, New York (2023) https://doi.org/10.1145/3598469.3598556
31. van Loenen, B., Šalamon, D.: Trends and prospects of opening data in problem driven societies. interdisciplinary description of complex systems. INDECS **20**(2), II–IV (2022)

Classification of Open Government Data Solutions' Help: A Novel Taxonomy and Cluster Analysis

Jonathan Crusoe[1,2]([envelope]) [iD] and Antoine Clarinval[3] [iD]

[1] Swedish Center for Digital Innovation, Department of Applied IT, University of Gothenburg, Gothenburg, Sweden
jonathan.crusoe@ait.gu.se
[2] Swedish School of Library and Information Science, University of Borås, Borås, Sweden
jonathan.crusoe@hb.se
[3] Namur Digital Institute, University of Namur, Namur, Belgium
antoine.clarinval@unamur.be

Abstract. Open Government Data (OGD) pose that public organisations should freely share data for anyone to reuse without restrictions. However, the rawness of this data proves to be a challenge for data or information seekers. OGD-based solutions, such as interactive maps and dashboards, could help seekers overcome this difficulty and use OGD to satisfy needs, helping them to work effectively, solve problems, or pursue hobbies. However, there are several challenges that need to be considered when designing solutions, such as seekers wanting to solve problems rather than consuming information and aiming for quick wins over quality. Previous research has classified OGD solutions, focusing on general concepts. The next step is to reveal helpful patterns in OGD solutions, helping seekers. This paper presents a taxonomy with 24 criteria to classify these patterns. It was tested on 40 OGD solutions, and the resulting classifications were grouped in a cluster analysis, identifying 16 key criteria and 6 clusters. The clusters are (1) simple-personalised, (2) proactive multi-visual, (3) lightly-facilitated exploration, (4) facilitated data-management, (5) facilitated information exploration, and (6) horizon solutions. One unexpected finding is that helpful patterns do not cluster following themes, types, or purposes of solutions. Another finding is that the importance of key criteria varies between the clusters.

Keywords: Open Government Data · solution · taxonomy · classification · cluster analysis · information behaviour

1 Introduction

Open Government Data (OGD) pose that data from public organisations should be made freely available for anyone to reuse. These data need to be used to unlock benefits [19] or risk being a costly burden [14]. The potential benefits of OGD include improvements in accountability, value creation, and service development [29]. People who could gain from these benefits are **seekers** who utilise data or information (content) in their everyday life [30] to satisfy various needs [5]. OGD is most often made available through online portals in raw formats such as CSV. The rawness of OGD can make them difficult to use for any meaningful purpose [35]. Therefore, OGD solutions (e.g., interactive maps and dashboards) have a key part in helping seekers understand and act on OGD [16]. **Help** means to make it possible or easier for someone by doing part of the work or by providing, for example, advice or support [33]. OGD solutions could help seekers work effectively, solve problems, or pursue hobbies [25]. However, a challenge is to design solutions to help seekers who tend to prioritise ease of access and use over quality, aim for quick wins, and can find it difficult to express their needs, asking for the wrong content [3, 8, 25]. Consequently, it is important to consider seekers when designing OGD solutions [25, 27].

Previous OGD research has attempted to classify OGD solutions to understand reuse. For example, by their ability to transform data into information [6], as services along criteria like data, themes, and topics [9], and by domain and features [20]. Janssen and Zuiderwijk [17] analysed solutions from a business model perspective with a focus on the source of value and Crusoe [5] identified 23 ways OGD solutions may help seekers. These classifications provide general ideas about the possibilities of solutions being helpful for seekers but open questions about how this helpfulness has been achieved in the design of OGD solutions. As a result, it is time to take the next step to reveal possibly helpful patterns in the design of OGD solutions. We define a **helpful pattern** as the combination of help provided by a solution for a seeker. A helpful pattern could be that a solution acquires, filters, and visualises data for a seeker [see 10].

The paper's objective is to construct a taxonomy (a classification of empirical entities [2]) for helpful patterns in the design of OGD solutions. Hunke et al. [15] explain that a taxonomy can be used to design new solutions by revealing their "anatomy" and key features or properties. Rizk et al. [28] add that a taxonomy can bring understanding to key aspects of utilising data in the design and delivery of solutions. As criteria, our taxonomy must cover the seekers' needing, seeking, using, and distributing of content [5] and be able to classify a broad range of OGD solutions [e.g., 6, 17]. We started the research by synthesising a tentative taxonomy from previous research, which was then refined through iterations of classifying 40 OGD solutions. The research ended with a cluster analysis of these solutions, helping to test the taxonomy and identify clusters of helpful patterns and key criteria. This paper contributes towards explaining how OGD solutions can be designed to be helpful for seekers, and as such realise benefits through the satisfaction of needs.

2   Related Works

In their daily non-professional life, seekers frequently encounter problems that they solve by seeking information related to, e.g., healthcare or hobbies.

According to Savolainen [30], the behaviour undertaken to solve these problems comprises three steps.

First, the evaluation of the importance of the problem. Second, the selection of content sources, such as people, libraries, and digital solutions [32]. Recently, the potential of OGD as a content source has been studied in the context of seekers' everyday life [18]. However, the rawness of OGD makes it hard to directly use to solve a problem, which is a challenge for seekers. As a result, solutions based on OGD are being developed to help seekers. Third, the seekers seek orienting and practical content, which can, for example, be done through active seeking, active scanning, non-directed monitoring, and by proxy [23]. This paper focuses on OGD solutions as a content source, emphasising the third step of [30], namely how OGD solutions help seekers seek information. As a result, we want to understand the design of OGD solutions in relation to seekers. Previous research has classified OGD solutions from three broad perspectives: (1) provision, (2) solution, and (3) usage.

The provision perspective focuses on actors as providers of solutions in some contexts. Gebka and Castiaux [11] have identified roles taken by public organisations, projecting expected roles onto the seekers. The classification of Davies [6] grouped solutions as the ability to transform data into facts, data, information, interfaces, and services. Janssen and Zuiderwijk [17] viewed solutions from a business model perspective, classifying them as single-purpose, interactive, information aggregators, comparison models, repositories, and service platforms. Azkan et al. [1] covered several criteria, such as main value, data types, and payment mode. Similarly, Paukstadt et al. [26] provided criteria like payment mode, pricing model, and value proposition.

The solution perspective has its focus on describing solutions. Foulonneau et al. [9] arranged solutions following criteria like data, themes, and topics. Mainka et al. [20] covered, for example, features and type. Hunke et al. [15] included criteria, such as data generator, data target, and analytic type. On the other hand, Rizk et al. [28] used criteria like data acquisition mechanisms, data exploitation, and insights utilisation. They identified three solution groups: distributed analytic intermediaries, visual data-driven services, and analytic-embedded services. Shneiderman [31] understands criteria as tasks solutions can help seekers with, such as giving an overview of, zooming in on, and filtering content.

The usage perspective approaches solutions from the view of seekers. Virkar et al. [34] classified seekers' usage of legal information solutions, which can be to compare laws and follow legal developments. Crusoe [5] conceptualised solutions following four behaviours of seekers: needing, seeking, using, and distributing content. A solution can help seekers encounter needed content, but also formulate their needs (*needing*). It can also help them find or discover content (*seeking*) while making it easier to understand by representing data, supporting interpretations or adapting its help (*using*). The solution can enable seekers to share or spread content (*distributing*). However, previous classifications of OGD solutions do not explain how functions and properties can be combined into helpful patterns to help seekers satisfy their needs for content. It can, as such, be difficult to construct complete designs for OGD solutions and explain how these designs can satisfy seekers' needs.

3 Research Approach

This research constructed a taxonomy for helpful patterns in the design of OGD solutions. It followed a qualitative artefact study using a qualitative approach [12]. An artefact study generates empirical material about solutions' functions and properties but provides limited information about whether they produce desired results for seekers [12]. However, a qualitative approach gives a deeper understanding of the solutions [24], helping to refine the taxonomy, which is our motivation for following this approach. The taxonomy is made for constructed types, a set of criteria with empirical reference that serve as the basis for comparison of empirical cases [2]. These criteria were the reasons for grouping solutions [21], referring to their functions and properties. We decided to use binary criteria for whether a pattern had a certain help or not. It made the taxonomy possess more criteria but allowed for freer identification of patterns and a reduction in interactive complexity among criteria. This choice also enabled the calculation of objective similarity levels between the helpful patterns [2]. This research followed four steps, iterating between the second and the third: (1) construct an initial taxonomy, (2) select OGD solutions, (3) classify solutions and refine the taxonomy, and (4) test the taxonomy with cluster analysis. The iterations aimed for saturation in the construction of the taxonomy, meaning further data collection no longer sparked new insights nor revealed new criteria [4].

First, we discussed previous research that could help to construct a taxonomy based on previous knowledge. We decided to start by synthesising previous work from multiple fields (e.g., Human-Computer Interaction, Information Behavior, Open Government Data), using [23,30,31], and [5]. Individually, researchers created a conceptual map of how concepts and previous research could be related, which was discussed among them afterwards. The discussion resulted in a tentative list of 25 criteria. Each criterion was named and provided with inclusion criteria and examples. If necessary, exclusion criteria were formulated. Furthermore, a conceptual tree diagram was created to support the classification process. At the centre was a general question (i.e., How is the pattern helping the seeker?), which was then divided into more specific questions with the leaves as the criteria. A researcher could follow and answer these questions to identify applicable criteria. When classifying a solution, colouring the leaves gave an overview of the solution's helpful pattern.

Second, we retrieved a list of 74 solutions identified in [5], enabling us to test the conceptualisation of [5] and provide new insights into previously studied solutions. We chose this list since it was easily accessible and known to contain relevant solutions. Following purposive sampling [7], we started with the solutions presented as good examples, believing them to be easy to classify and have clear helpful patterns. Then, we selected solutions based on the perceived ability to be a negative case or verification, helping to refine the taxonomy. However, some solutions were no longer active, as such we attempted to access them through the Wayback Machine, bringing back six solutions.

Third, the classification started with a small set of agreed solutions. Individually, we classified these solutions using the criteria list and the conceptual tree diagram. We tested each solution, classifying a helpful pattern. We discussed our classifications and underlying reasons, refining the taxonomy and correcting any errors. This step started with classifying a few solutions in quick iterations, allowing for rapid refinement of the taxonomy. When the taxonomy became stable, we increased the number of solutions to classify within one iteration. We reached saturation once 40 solutions had been classified. The taxonomy reduced analytical drift and the sharing of classifications allowed for cross-checking, contributing to research reliability [4]. The discussions of the taxonomy and classifications allowed reflexivity for the researchers, contributing to research validity [22]. At the end of this step, 40 helpful patterns had been classified with a taxonomy of 24 criteria. 11 criteria differed from the tentative taxonomy from the first step.

Fourth, we used cluster analysis to test the taxonomy, aiming to cluster solutions into homogeneous groups based on similarities in their helpful patterns [2]. It is important that criteria help us to group and differentiate between solutions [2,21]. The intent is to minimise differences between solutions within a group while maximising differences between groups [2]. Following this reasoning, we started this step by removing any criteria that we considered too common or uncommon amongst the helpful patterns, as they do not help us differentiate between solutions. We used subjective thresholds of 0.2 and 0.8 (i.e., corresponding to 20% and 80% of classified solutions having a given help), identifying 16 of 24 criteria as key. We applied Gower and Legendres' S9 method to calculate a distance matrix for the criteria, as it is made for binary data and provides high resolution [13]. We then applied divisive cluster analysis [2], which results were visualised as a dendrogram, helping us to determine a cluster number of 6. A **cluster** represents a group of solutions with similar helpful patterns. In order to interpret the clusters, we created a heatmap to represent the proportion of criteria amongst these clusters. Each tile in the heatmap presents the proportion of help for a given cluster. We removed any tile with a value between 0.2 and 0.8 to highlight similarities and differences of the clusters, clarifying any particularities. We then studied the helpful patterns and clusters. If any group contained an odd or puzzling combination of solutions, we revisited the classifications and verified them, helping to reduce errors further. This approach to taxonomy construction has helped to validate the final taxonomy, as it has been tested on a heterogeneous sample of OGD solutions by two researchers.

4   Results

4.1   A Taxonomy for OGD Solutions

The taxonomy comprises 24 criteria and is presented in Table 1 and 2. For each criterion, the definition, examples, the proportion of the 40 classified solutions checking the criteria, and whether it is selected as key or not are indicated. The key criteria are those with a proportion between 0.2 and 0.8. There are 16 key criteria, representing meaningful similarities and differences.

Table 1. Criteria for the taxonomy of helpful patterns. For each criterion, the definition, examples, proportion of the 40 classified solutions checking the criteria, and whether it is selected as key or not are indicated (Part 1, continued in Table 2).

		Criteria and examples	Proport.	Key
NEEDING	ENCOUNTER	**Setup** – Proactive encounters where data or its presentation has an initial structure upon arrival. *For example: start by presenting data for a given year or how data is grouped before the user*	0.550	■
		Suggest – The solution suggests content to the seeker. *For example: Top rankings, alternatives, recent content, and "read more here"-links*	0.525	■
		Reveal – Proactive encounters as highlights or conclusions of data. The solution conveys to the seeker an interpretation of the data. *For example: articles, blog posts, or content panels*	0.375	■
	FORMULATE	**Nudge** – The seeker is nudged towards certain actions. Not instructions nor manuals. *For example: "Click on a country" or search field with example keywords. It can also be more subtle like a label to explain what type of content to input*	0.375	■
		Answer – Presents a question that the pattern aims to answer. It can be intertwined with navigational structures. *For example: "What energy do we produce in the EU?" answered with text, statistics, and diagrams*	0.175	
SEEKING		**Border** – The seeker can draw borders between all content and some content through simple keywords, categories, or parameters. Go beyond predefined divisions. *For example: dashboards and filters*	0.950	
		Sift – The seeker has access to all or most of the data. *For example: a list of data that can be scrolled or various categories with data*	0.775	■
		Detail – The seeker can request more information about some content amongst other content. It is not clicking on items in a search result list. *For example: interactive map where locations can be selected to show some of its information*	0.750	■
		Herd – Data are stored in several datasets, which can be connected to the navigational structure. The seeker manages content as buckets or groups, which can come in categorical hierarchies. The seeker can make clear distinctions and selections between datasets. *For example: open data portals or interactive maps with data inventories*	0.750	■
		Pull – Data are pulled out from a "black box" using various functions. It is not a filter functionality, rather the seeker does not know the large dataset behind the presented data. *For example: search bar, showing results*	0.500	■
		Traverse – The seeker traverses the relationships within the content. Content is similar to a web, network, or layers of aggregation. Data within dataset(s) can follow a hierarchical structure. It is possible that several datasets are combined to produce this effect. It is not tagged data. *For example: animal taxonomies/typologies, some aggregated statistics, politicians and their parties within a governing body*	0.400	■

Table 2. Criteria for the taxonomy of helpful patterns. For each criterion, the definition, examples, proportion of the 40 classified solutions checking the criteria, and whether it is selected as key or not are indicated (part 2).

		Criteria and examples	Proport.	Key
USING	REPRESENT	**Facts** – The content presents facts and information to the user. *For example: tables and summary numbers*	1.000	
		Comparative – The content makes similarities or differences clearly visible. *For example: bar charts and map charts*	0.825	
		Relative – Content reveals relations, occurrences, densities, relativities, or concentrations. *For example: interactive maps, word clouds, or heat maps*	0.625	■
		Movement – The content highlights the transfers of data between nodes or changes in data over time. *For example: Sankey diagrams, line charts, or animations*	0.525	■
	SUPPORT	**Clarify** – Explanations and descriptions of content, easing the understandability. *For example: change language, colours to highlight weight or importance, explanations of terminology or patterns, or about pages*	0.950	
		Facilitate – Make social communication or community building possible or easier. Clear socio-technical purpose. It can be donations, but not pure contact information to developers without a clear purpose. *For example: forums or contact information to politicians*	0.750	■
		Elucidate – Makes the content clearer, enabling the drawing of different conclusions from the same content. *For example: side-by-side visualisations of the same data and map layers*	0.350	■
	ADAPT	**Personalise** – Personalise the offered help by changing content or providing personalised content. Add customisation to the offered help. *For example: drawing tools, measuring tools, or asking for notification on changes in content, put items in a basket*	0.400	■
		Acquire – The seeker can upload or request content. *For example: upload map layers or request evaluation of products*	0.175	
		Record – The actions of the seeker can be undone, replayed, or viewed. A history is kept of the seeker's actions. A seeker could save states. *For example: button to undo the last action*	0.125	
DISTRIB.		**Extract** – The content can be extracted from the solutions. *For example: download a visualisation or underlying data; or print a map*	0.825	
		Refer – The seeker can refer to specific content, which is still part of the solution. *For example: share a link to it or over social media*	0.675	■
		Embed – Other solutions can embed the solution's content. *For example: iframes or API*	0.300	■

4.2   Divisive Cluster Analysis

Only the 16 key criteria were used in the divisive cluster analysis. In total, the
analysis returned 6 clusters represented as a dendogram in Fig. 1. It visualises
the distances between helpful patterns based on their similarities and differences.
Solutions belonging to the same cluster present similarities in their helpful patterns and are coloured alike. Cluster 1 (colored in red) groups 6 solutions. Cluster
2 (chartreuse) has 7 solutions, Cluster 3 (salmon) has 4, Cluster 4 (blue) is the
most populated cluster with 12 solutions, Cluster 5 (purple) has 4, and Cluster
6 (orange) has 7. Table 3 lists the 40 classified solutions sorted by cluster and
the checked criteria for each.

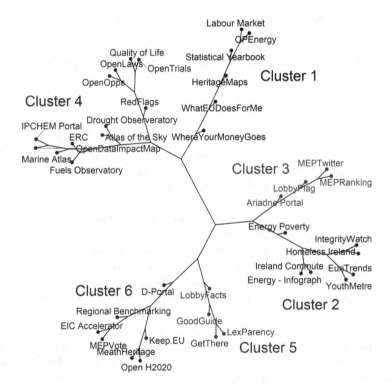

Fig. 1. Dendrogram resulting from the divisive cluster analysis. (Color figure online)

In order to interpret these clusters, it is necessary to analyse the proportion
of each criterion, at the level of each cluster. Figure 2 presents the key criteria
proportions amongst the six clusters. It shows, for example, that solutions in
Cluster 1 always have "Herd" and never "Facilitate" and have a high (resp. low)
likelihood to possess, for example, "Detail" (resp. "Embed"). The most demanding
cluster in terms of criteria to check is Cluster 3. Its solutions must possess 9
criteria. On the contrary, no criterion is a must-have in Cluster 6, but several
criteria have a high likelihood.

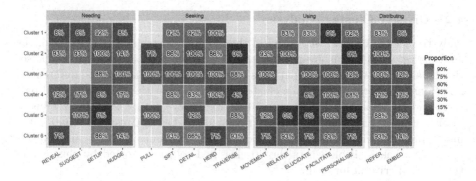

Fig. 2. *Key criteria proportions amongst clusters.*

Given the proportions of the key criteria, the following interpretations can be given for the six clusters.

Cluster 1 – Simple-personalised help. Solutions in this cluster follow a simple pattern compared to other clusters, as they seldom allow seekers to embed content and give limited help to formulate needs or encounter content. They focus on providing personalised information and visualisations, becoming a base or frame for interpretation [5]. They can help seekers see data from various perspectives, as such draw different conclusions.

Cluster 2 – Proactive multi-visual help. These patterns use various ways to visualise data as part of one or more datasets. The patterns are proactive or at least active, seeking to satisfy the seeker's need for data or information [5], meaning they can provide conclusions or guide a seeker's attention towards meaningful insights. This cluster matches visual data-driven services from [28], which visualise data and use storytelling to communicate insights to seekers. However, storytelling is less emphasised in our taxonomy.

Cluster 3 – Lightly-facilitated exploration help. The third cluster patterns aim to help the seeker explore its datasets from multiple perspectives. Some of these patterns allow the seeker to explore relationships within a dataset or details about data. They have some degree of facilitation where the seeker can provide feedback or ask questions.

Cluster 4 – Facilitated data-management help. Solutions in this cluster help seekers manage some larger dataset(s) while facilitating social interactions. While the patterns tend to allow for personalisation, the visualisations are often simple with limited ability to distribute. They seldom reveal any highlights or conclusions in the data.

Cluster 5 – Facilitated information exploration help. These helpful patterns have a limited ability to visualise data. Instead, they focus on information and any related internal connections. This information is often socially complex, such as health information about products, lobbying in the EU, and coordination of lift sharing. Social facilitation can range from community building to feedback or Q&A. While some level of dialogue [17] is possible, the patterns may

Table 3. List of classified solutions and checked criteria (* denotes key criteria).

Name	Reveal*	Suggest*	Setup*	Answer	Nudge*	Pull*	Sift*	Detail*	Border	Herd*	Traverse*	Facts	Comparative	Movement*	Relative*	Elucidate*	Clarify	Facilitate*	Acquire	Record	Personalise*	Refer*	Embed*	Extract
Cluster 1																								
WhereYourMoneyGoes		■				■		■	■	■	■	■	■	■		■	■						■	
HeritageMaps			■	■	■	■	■	■	■	■		■	■		■	■	■		■	■	■	■	■	■
WhatEUDoesForMe	■	■	■			■		■		■	■	■						■			■	■	■	
Labour Market		■				■		■	■	■		■	■	■	■	■		■				■	■	
OPEnergy	■	■				■	■	■	■	■	■	■	■	■	■	■	■				■	■	■	
Cluster 2																								
YouthMetre	■	■	■			■	■	■	■		■	■	■	■	■	■					■	■	■	
Energy - Infograph	■		■	■	■		■	■	■		■	■	■	■	■	■	■				■	■	■	
Ireland Commute	■	■	■				■	■			■	■	■	■	■	■		■			■	■	■	
EnergyPoverty	■	■	■	■	■		■	■	■		■	■	■	■	■	■					■		■	
EuriTrends	■	■	■	■	■		■	■	■	■	■	■	■	■	■	■	■				■	■	■	
Homeless Ireland	■	■	■				■	■	■	■		■	■			■	■				■		■	
IntegrityWatch	■	■	■				■	■	■	■		■	■		■		■	■			■			
Cluster 3																								
Ariadne Portal	■	■			■	■	■	■	■	■	■	■	■	■	■	■	■	■			■	■	■	■
MEPRanking		■			■	■	■	■	■	■	■	■	■	■		■		■				■	■	
MEPTwitter	■	■			■	■	■	■	■	■	■	■	■			■	■	■			■			
LobbyPlag	■			■		■	■	■	■	■		■	■	■	■	■	■	■			■		■	
Cluster 4																								
Atlas of the Sky		■		■	■	■	■		■			■	■	■	■		■	■			■			■
OpenOpps			■	■	■			■	■			■					■	■			■	■	■	
Marine Atlas		■			■	■	■	■	■	■		■	■		■		■	■	■		■			■
IPCHEM Portal	■	■				■	■	■	■			■	■	■	■		■	■	■		■			■
OpenTrials			■	■	■			■	■			■					■	■	■			■	■	
Fuels Observatory	■					■	■	■	■	■		■	■	■	■	■	■	■			■			■
ERC						■	■	■				■	■	■		■	■	■	■		■			■
OpenLaws		■	■	■				■				■					■	■			■			■
RedFlags	■					■	■	■	■	■	■	■	■	■			■	■			■	■	■	■
OpenDataImpactMap	■	■				■	■	■	■			■	■		■		■	■	■					■
Drought Observatory			■			■	■	■	■	■		■	■	■	■		■	■		■	■			■
Quality of Life						■	■		■		■	■	■				■	■				■	■	■
Cluster 5																								
GetThere		■			■	■		■	■			■	■	■			■	■	■					
LexParency		■				■			■	■	■	■	■				■	■				■	■	■
GoodGuide	■	■			■	■	■		■	■		■	■				■	■	■		■			
LobbyFacts	■	■		■		■	■		■			■	■	■	■		■	■						■
Cluster 6																								
Keep.EU	■	■			■	■	■	■		■		■	■		■		■	■			■		■	
MEPVote		■				■	■	■	■	■	■	■		■	■		■					■	■	■
EIC Accelerator		■				■	■	■				■	■		■		■	■				■	■	■
Open H2020	■				■	■	■	■		■	■	■	■		■		■	■				■		■
MeathHeritage	■	■			■			■	■			■	■			■		■	■		■			
D-Portal	■	■	■	■		■	■		■			■	■	■	■	■		■	■		■	■	■	■
Regional Benchmarking		■				■		■		■		■						■				■		■

encourage it to be outside the solutions, for example by providing contact information or sharing content on social media.

Cluster 6 – Horizon solutions. These solutions share most key criteria, but there is little agreement. They are complex to some degree and specialised. This cluster indicates that there are more clusters to be identified. It could also signal innovative designs, as help is combined in new or unique ways. Similar to [28], our taxonomy does not address the structure of helpful patterns. This cluster could be a result of this limitation, and as such, opens new avenues for future research.

5 Discussion

5.1 Novelty of the Contributions

Previous research had classified solutions, following a provision [e.g., 1,6,11], solution [e.g., 9,28,31], or usage [e.g., 5,34] perspective. Our research bridges the latter two, meaning we attempt to classify features and properties from the perspective of seekers. This approach makes our research original within the context of previous OGD research. While it is similar to [34], which focus on classifying seekers, our work is oriented towards solutions. Our research is a step towards designing OGD solutions that can be helpful for seekers but also to evaluate how OGD solutions have attempted to help seekers. It opens questions about possible matches and mismatches between seekers and solutions. Moreover, we constructed a novel taxonomy comprising 24 criteria able to classify helpful patterns in the design of OGD solutions. It enabled the identification of 6 clusters among 40 helpful patterns. 16 of the taxonomy's 24 criteria were key in differentiating and understanding these clusters. The successful identification and interpretation of helpful pattern clusters serve as a test of the taxonomy.

Most of the initial criteria provided in [5,23,30,31] were identified to some degree amongst the helpful patterns. Analysing the proportion of each gives interesting insights into how OGD solutions currently help seekers. First, the rarity of the criteria varies (e.g., 17.5% of solutions have "Acquire" and 82.5% have "Comparative"). Nonetheless, the proportions are mostly included within the 0.2–0.8 range, meaning that most of the criteria are neither too common nor too uncommon. Such criteria can be found in all four categories (i.e., needing, seeking, using, and distributing). This shows the diversity among OGD solutions and reinforces the need for a detailed taxonomy to characterise how they help data and information seekers. Second, the proportion of the criteria within the "Needing" category varies between 0.175 and 0.55. At the same time, the proportions of the criteria in the "Seeking" category and of those related to visualisations in the "Using" category are overall higher. This difference indicates that while OGD solutions help seekers look for and use information, few of them help seekers encounter information or formulate needs for information. Third, few solutions allow for personalising (40%) help and content, and even fewer (12.5%) satisfy the "Record" criteria, which has long been recommended in the literature [31]. Fourth, only 30% of OGD solutions allow seekers to embed the solution's content into other solutions. This lack indicates that it is difficult to build OGD solutions based on other OGD solutions, which would be another approach to increasing the value of OGD instead of working with the raw data directly.

An unexpected finding is that solutions perceived to have similar themes, types, or purposes can be designed following different helpful patterns. We expected similar solutions (e.g., OGD portals and interactive maps) to form clusters or at least follow the classes identified in [17]. It adds to our understanding of taxonomies specialised towards certain fields [e.g., 1,26,28] by explaining why digital solutions, like OGD solutions, can be difficult to classify. For example,

Janssen and Zuiderwijk [17] classified solutions as single-purpose, interactive, information aggregators, comparison models, repositories, and service platforms, while [6] grouped them as facts, data, information, interfaces, and services. It is possible to identify some of these classes among our classified OGD solutions, but none of the identified clusters represents them. There is, as such, a possible disconnect between the combinations of functions and properties that can help seekers and the themes, types, or purposes of solutions. Therefore, the application of helpful patterns could be a new fruitful approach to studying and designing solutions for seekers.

We identified 16 key criteria with proportions ranging between 0.2 and 0.8. It led us to another finding, as the key criteria do not play an equally important role in each cluster (see Fig. 2). For example, Cluster 1 has criteria regarding visualisations with varied expressions, while "Herd" is required. In contrast, Cluster 5 has "Herd" with varied expressions, while criteria regarding visualisations are mostly non-existent. It means that to understand and study some solutions, certain criteria come into the foreground, while others are in the background. The focus may be difficult to make based on the perceived similar themes, types, or purposes among solutions, as the helpful patterns may be different. Consequently, taxonomies with few criteria [e.g., 6, 17, 28] may attribute importance to properties and functions that can be relevant for some solutions, but not others. This finding gives us a new insight into the complexity of solutions, but also possible limitations in classifying them.

5.2 Implications of the Contributions

The two contributions of this research, that is, the taxonomy and the six clusters identified from the 16 key criteria, have utility for researchers and for practitioners. In general, they can be used to describe and analyse helpful patterns in existing solutions. They can also be used to design them. **Researchers** can use the taxonomy to guide data collection or support the analysis of solutions. The 6 clusters can act as the basis for empirical comparisons, providing a stepping stone towards theory development. The 16 key criteria can guide the researcher's attention towards functions and properties that are important to differentiate between solutions but also help to identify functions and properties important to consider when studying specific solutions. **Public organisations** providing OGD can apply the taxonomy as well, on their OGD portal. This would help them to understand how the solution can help seekers, revealing potential areas of improvement. The identified clusters can give them an idea of what solutions could be built from the provided OGD, which can inform relevant help features to include in the OGD portal. **OGD reusers** can use the taxonomy as a basis to brainstorm about innovative designs, helping them to consider important areas. The reusers can also use the taxonomy to evaluate solutions, as it opens to identifying any possible deficiencies or impediments.

However, it must be noted that the utility of the taxonomy depends on the complexity of the solutions being classified. Solutions with tightly related properties and functionalities produce better classifications, while solutions with varied dynamic content (e.g., blogs or descriptions in metadata; allowing for unpredictable variations in help) or specialised parts (e.g., a solution that has a forum, a dashboard, and a news section) can lead to unbalances or gaps in the classification. On the other hand, some of the classified OGD solutions had properties or functionalities difficult to detect for the authors (e.g., hidden within multiple layers of menus or small icon buttons at unexpected locations), which led to classification errors needing to be discussed among researchers. Therefore, we recommend that classification is done independently by at least two individuals and discussed afterwards to lower analytical drift and support reflection. Some errors in our classification also emerged from conceptual unclarity arising from misinterpretable functions or properties (e.g., a text field is presented as a search bar, indicating "Pull', but was used to filter a list of items, as such being "Sift"). It is, therefore, important to understand functions and properties by how they attempt to help the seeker rather than how they describe themselves. Moreover, in our cluster analysis, we could not find any cluster that matches one pattern mentioned by [5]: contextualisation of help to the life of a seeker. Rather, it is spread out over several clusters, meaning the taxonomy may need further refinement towards capturing properties and functionalities that work to contextualise data or information.

5.3 Limitations and Future Research

The research presented in this article has several limitations. We used subjective thresholds for the key criteria and heatmap tiles in Fig. 2, meaning that other clusters may be identifiable among our classified solutions. However, after inspection, the identified clusters contained similar helpful patterns, giving important insights into the helpfulness of OGD solutions. Moreover, a delimitation is that solutions with dynamic content can introduce criteria while being difficult to detect and classify. It relates to a limitation of the taxonomy, as it is not constructed to handle the structure of patterns. If a solution offers different help at various locations, its classification presents these as equally important and related, which is a future research avenue. While the taxonomy construction reached saturation, the taxonomy was only tested with 40 classified solutions. Future research could apply the taxonomy to a larger sample of solutions, going beyond those previously identified by [5], giving insight into how OGD public organisations and reusers have tried to help seekers, but also identify missed opportunities and innovative designs. Another avenue could be to evaluate helpful patterns involving seekers.

6   Conclusion

Our main contribution is the theoretically grounded and empirically tested taxonomy for helpful patterns in the design of OGD solutions. The taxonomy consists of 24 criteria where 16 were identified as key by classifying 40 OGD solutions for their helpful patterns. The helpful patterns were grouped into 6 clusters following the 16 key criteria, which are (1) simple-personalised help, (2) proactive multi-visual help, (3) lightly-facilitated exploration help, (4) facilitated data-management help, (5) facilitated information exploration help, and (6) horizon solutions. Another finding is that the importance of key criteria varies between the clusters. We expected helpful patterns to cluster following themes, types, or purposes of solutions, which was not the case, as different solutions provide similar helpful patterns.

References

1. Azkan, C., Iggena, L., Gür, I., Möller, F., Otto, B.: A taxonomy for data-driven services in manufacturing industries. In: Proceedings of the 26th Pacific Asia Conference on Information Systems, p. 184. Association for Information Systems (2020)
2. Bailey, K.D.: Typologies and Taxonomies: An Introduction to Classification Techniques. Sage, Thousand Oaks (1994)
3. Bates, M.J.: Information behavior. In: Encyclopedia of Library and Information Sciences, vol. 3, pp. 2381–2391 (2010)
4. Creswell, J.W., Creswell, J.D.: Research Design: Qualitative, Quantitative, and Mixed Methods Approaches. Sage Publications, Thousand Oaks (2017)
5. Crusoe, J.: How may an OGD solution help you?-an information behaviour perspective. In: Janssen, M., et al. (eds.) EGOV 2022. LNCS, vol. 13391, pp. 181–195. Springer, Cham (2022). https://doi.org/10.1007/978-3-031-15086-9_12
6. Davies, T.: Open data, democracy and public sector reform - a look at open government data use from data.gov.uk (2010)
7. Denscombe, M.: The Good Research Guide: For Small-Scale Social Research. McGraw Hill, New York (2010)
8. Erdelez, S.: Information encountering: it's more than just bumping into information. Bull. Am. Soc. Inf. Sci. Technol. **25**(3), 26–29 (1999)
9. Foulonneau, M., Martin, S., Turki, S.: How open data are turned into services? In: Snene, M., Leonard, M. (eds.) IESS 2014. LNBIP, vol. 169, pp. 31–39. Springer, Cham (2014). https://doi.org/10.1007/978-3-319-04810-9_3
10. Fry, B.J.: Computational information design. Ph.D. thesis, Massachusetts Institute of Technology (2004)
11. Gebka, E., Castiaux, A.: A typology of municipalities' roles and expected user's roles in open government data release and reuse. In: Scholl, H.J., Gil-Garcia, J.R., Janssen, M., Kalampokis, E., Lindgren, I., Rodríguez Bolívar, M.P. (eds.) EGOV 2021. LNCS, vol. 12850, pp. 137–152. Springer, Cham (2021). https://doi.org/10.1007/978-3-030-84789-0_10
12. Goldkuhl, G.: The generation of qualitative data in information systems research: the diversity of empirical research methods. Commun. Assoc. Inf. Syst. **44**, 572–599 (2019)
13. Gower, J.C., Legendre, P.: Metric and euclidean properties of dissimilarity coefficients. J. Classif. **3**, 5–48 (1986)
14. Hossain, M.A., Dwivedi, Y.K., Rana, N.P.: State-of-the-art in open data research: insights from existing literature and a research agenda. J. Organ. Comput. Electron. Commer. **26**(1–2), 14–40 (2016)
15. Hunke, F., Engel, C.T., Schüritz, R., Ebel, P.: Understanding the anatomy of analytics-based services-a taxonomy to conceptualize the use of data and analytics in services. In: Proceedings of the 27th European Conference on Information Systems, pp. 1–14. Association for Information Systems (2019)

16. Hunnius, S., Krieger, B.: The social shaping of open data through administrative processes. In: Riehle, D., et al. (eds.) Proceedings of the International Symposium on Open Collaboration, pp. 1–5. Association for Computing Machinery (2014)

17. Janssen, M., Zuiderwijk, A.: Infomediary business models for connecting open data providers and users. Soc. Sci. Comput. Rev. **32**(5), 694–711 (2014)

18. Koesten, L.M., Kacprzak, E., Tennison, J.F., Simperl, E.: The trials and tribulations of working with structured data: -a study on information seeking behaviour. In: Proceedings of the 2017 CHI Conference on Human Factors in Computing Systems, pp. 1277–1289. Association for Computing Machinery (2017)

19. Lee, D.: Building an open data ecosystem: an irish experience. In: Estevez, E., Janssen, M., Soares Barbosa, L. (eds.) Proceedings of the 8th International Conference on Theory and Practice of Electronic Governance, pp. 351–360. Association for Computing Machinery (2014)

20. Mainka, A., Hartmann, S., Meschede, C., Stock, W.G.: Mobile application services based upon open urban government data. In: Proceedings of the 2015 iConference, pp. 1–15. iSchools (2015)

21. Marradi, A., et al.: Classification, typology, taxonomy. Qual. Quant. **24**(2), 129–157 (1990)

22. Mays, N., Pope, C.: Assessing quality in qualitative research. BMJ **320**(7226), 50–52 (2000)

23. McKenzie, P.J.: A model of information practices in accounts of everyday-life information seeking. J. Doc. **59**(1), 19–40 (2003)

24. Myers, M.D.: Qualitative Research in Business and Management. Sage Publications Limited, Thousand Oaks (2013)

25. Nicholas, D., Herman, E.: Assessing Information Needs in the Age of the Digital Consumer. Routledge, Milton Park (2010)

26. Paukstadt, U., Strobel, G., Eicker, S.: Understanding services in the era of the internet of things: a smart service taxonomy. In: Proceedings of the 27th European Conference on Information Systems, pp. 1–18. Association for Information Systems (2019)

27. Pettigrew, K.E., Fidel, R., Bruce, H.: Conceptual frameworks in information behavior. Ann. Rev. Inf. Sci. Technol. **35**(43–78) (2001)

28. Rizk, A., Bergvall-Kåreborn, B., Elragal, A.: Towards a taxonomy for data-driven digital services. In: Proceedings of the 51st Hawaii International Conference on System Sciences, pp. 1076–1085. Association for Information Systems (2018)

29. Safarov, I., Meijer, A., Grimmelikhuijsen, S.: Utilization of open government data: a systematic literature review of types, conditions, effects and users. Inf. Polity **22**(1), 1–24 (2017)

30. Savolainen, R.: Everyday life information seeking: approaching information seeking in the context of "way of life". Libr. Inf. Sci. Res. **17**(3), 259–294 (1995)

31. Shneiderman, B.: The eyes have it: a task by data type taxonomy for information visualizations. In: Proceedings of the 1996 IEEE Symposium on Visual Languages, pp. 336–343. Institute of Electrical and Electronics Engineers (1996)

32. Sonnenwald, D.H., Wildemuth, B., Harmon, G.L.: A research method to investigate information seeking using the concept of information horizons: an example from a study of lower socio-economic students' information seeking behavior. New Rev. Inf. Behav. Res. **2**, 65–86 (2001)

33. The Cambridge Dictionary: Help. Cambridge University Press (2019). https://dictionary.cambridge.org/dictionary/english/help. Accessed 1 Oct 2019

34. Virkar, S., Alexopoulos, C., Stavropoulou, S., Tsekeridou, S., Novak, A.S.: User-centric decision support system design in legal informatics: a typology of users. In: Proceedings of the 13th International Conference on Theory and Practice of Electronic Governance, pp. 711–722. Association for Computing Machinery (2020)
35. Weerakkody, V., Irani, Z., Kapoor, K., Sivarajah, U., Dwivedi, Y.K.: Open data and its usability: an empirical view from the citizen's perspective. Inf. Syst. Front. **19**(2), 285–300 (2017)

Verifying Open Data Portals Completeness in Compliance to a Grounding Framework

Flavia Bernardini[1]([✉]) [iD], Catherine Fortes Thedim Costa[1] [iD],
Shaiana Pereira[1] [iD], Victor Antunes Vieira[1,2] [iD], Daniela Trevisan[1] [iD],
and José Viterbo[1] [iD]

[1] Institute of Computing (IC), Fluminense Federal University (UFF),
Niterói, RJ, Brazil
{fcbernardini,daniela,viterbo}@ic.uff.br,
{catherinecosta,shaianazan}@id.uff.br
[2] Acre Federal Institute (IFAC), Rio Branco, AC, Brazil
victor.vieira@ifac.edu.br

Abstract. Open Government Data Portals (OGDPs) are a way of keeping up the information about government's actions, including how the collected taxes are used in favor of its citizens. However, one difficult in some of these portals is guaranteeing accountability on OGDP completeness according to different instruments specifying legal requirements and good practices, especially when they may reinforce some requirements or may be even contradictory. This problem leads to the need for a comprehensive methodology to assess completeness of OGDPs related to data and information availability. This work presents a process for constructing a reference guide, aiming to help analyzing completeness of an OGDP content, in compliance to legal requirements and good practices, presented by textual instruments. We conducted an experimental analysis for evaluating the completeness of Transparency OGDPs (TOGDPs) requirements using our process. We evaluated, as (T)OGDP experts, the constructed reference guide on three different TOGDPs. We also used the output guide to interview managers and users of the Niterói TOGDP, in order to both evaluate the quality of the guide and the Niterói TOGDP completeness. We could observe which items of our guide were well understood and which need to be improved. These results are of interest to the OGD research community as they provide a tool for constructing a reference guide that facilitates the systematic assessment of OGDPs completeness, in compliance to a given legal framework. Future research includes testing our approach on different contexts for various OGDP types and exploring automation possibilities.

Keywords: Open Government Data · Completeness Evaluation · Compliance Assessment · Open Data Reference Framework

This work was partially funded by Niterói City Hall PMN through the Applied Projects Development Program (PDPA). PMN team also collaborated through their productive and constructive participation for conducting this work.

I. Lindgren et al. (Eds.): EGOV 2023, LNCS 14130, pp. 246–261, 2023.
https://doi.org/10.1007/978-3-031-41138-0_16

1   Introduction

In the last two decades, there has been a significant effort from open government and open data community to the government institutions open their data and information and turn more transparent their processes, services, technologies, people and all data manipulated within. In this way, we have seen the fast growth of data volume in Open Government Data Portals (OGDPs) as governmental websites in many countries, considering all administrative levels (federal, state, city and others). The main purpose of the OGDPs is to promote social participation through the empowerment of citizens, giving them access to public data that are of public relevance [1]. In literature, we can find diverse instruments to assess OGDPs quality, in order to enhance their structure and efficiency, thereby increasing their utility [13]. Also, OGDPs may be of different types and may present specific issues to be evaluated depending on the type of the OGDP, such as COVID or Transparency OGDPs [6,10].

On the other hand, the act of turning public data open means more than publishing it in an organized way. There may exist diverse laws, regulations and instruments indicating good practices for constructing OGDPs in many different countries, considering their own realities. However, may not be an easy task to verify if an OGDP fits a legal (reference or grounding) framework, as we discuss in Sect. 2. For instance, in Brazil, there is a specific federal law for legislating governmental transparency – the Transparency Law (TrL)[1] –, stating that all information on bidding, contracts, procurement and others must be available at all government levels in Transparency OGDPs (TOGDPs). TOGDPs also must attend many good practices, pointed out by the Brazilian Federal General Controller, as well as must attend the Brazilian Access to Information Law (AIL),[2] which states that some standards an OGDP must follow, some data types are obligatory, and citizens has the right to request information not present on the portal, either through a computational system or through a request form.

It is also worth noticing that the more than 5,000 municipalities across Brazil are increasingly putting efforts to improve their TOGDPs, as these portals need to fit to mandatory items by law as well as the indicated good practices for constructing these portals. This complex scenario may turn difficult to assess TOGDPs completeness as they be complementary or contradictory. The Brazilian Federal General Controller also applies a huge effort to guarantee the completeness and compliance of these TOGDPs. So, we can observe a lack of a practical and objective instrument to help TOGDP managers, users and controllers to conduct the compliance and completeness verification process.

In this way, this work presents a process for supporting OGDPs evaluators or managers to verify the compliance and completeness of an OGDP based on a grounding reference framework. From our perspective, this grounding framework (GF) is composed by documents or instruments of the following types:

---

[1] In Portuguese. Available at http://www.planalto.gov.br/ccivil_03/leis/lcp/lcp131.htm.

[2] In Portuguese. Available at http://www.planalto.gov.br/ccivil_03/_ato2011-2014/2011/lei/l12527.htm.

(i) laws; (ii) reference models; and (iii) good practices instruments. In our process, these documents must be divided into items to be verified if they exist in the OGDP under scrutiny regarding content completeness evaluation. Other types of documents may be inserted into this GF since they can be divided into items to be verified. From a computing perspective, these items to be verified can also be considered as Non-Functional Requirements (NFRs)[3] of an OGDP. For evaluating our process, we conducted an experimental analysis on Brazilian TODGPs of local governments. We considered in our GF diverse Brazilian laws and good practices instruments, which indicates best practices and "must have" items in TOGDPs. Using our process, we firstly constructed a unified instrument, also called by us a reference guide, containing all items and an indication of the original document from the GF. We firstly manually applied this unified instrument into 3 TOGDPs of 3 Brazilian cities, chosen according to a Brazilian transparency scale and one specific TOGDP, from the city of Niterói, with whom we have an going research project. After, we also assessed the understanding of these users of the instrument we constructed. We could observe that the instrument was very large, which reinforced that a computational tool to assist users could help. A computational tool also turn easier to verify the completeness of an OGDP not only according to the entire GF but also according to each document that composes the framework. We concluded that this completeness assessment process as well as the tool we constructed are helpful for the users to evaluate the completeness of an OGDP.

This work is organized as follows: Sect. 2 describes general concepts and background concepts of OGD, OGDPs and their completeness. Section 3 presents a literature review we conducted, in order to show the state-of-the-art of works tackling the problem of measuring OGDPs completeness. Section 4 presents our proposed process. Section 5 presents an experimental analysis using our proposed process in a real scenario. Finally, Sect. 6 presents our conclusions and future work.

2   OGD, OGDPs and Their Completeness Evaluation

Open data initiatives aim to open all non-personal and noncommercial data, or sufficiently anonymized data, especially all data collected and processed by government organizations—called Open Government Data (OGD). An OGDP, in this context, is a collection of datasets, which can be owned by governments, universities, and other institutions. OGDPs are administrated by authorized users, who are in charge of uploading resources and filling metadata fields. The portal also aims to promote the communication between society and government actors to think about the most appropriate use of data for a better society.

In our initial stage of research, we conducted a literature review to understand the current state of the art in the academic literature to comprehensively explore

---

[3] NFRs are specifications of a system not directly related to the specific functions that the system performs, but to general characteristics such as performance, security, usability, reliability, compatibility, and others.

how different studies are addressing the challenge of assessing the completeness of various instruments available on OGDPs. From our perspective, completeness refers to the degree to which a computational artifact, such as a dataset, a web portal or a tool includes all the necessary or appropriate elements. In the OGDP context, it refers to the extent to which these portals provide all the information, tools, and features necessary for comprehensive data access and analysis.

Initially, we wanted to comprehend the approaches adopted by various studies addressing the issue of evaluating the completeness of different tools employed by OGDPs. We considered that evaluating completeness was according to Non-Functional Requirements (NFRs) of an OGDP, leading to only two relevant references that facilitated our understanding of how existing literature engages with our research question. Additionally, we executed on Scopus a string search, using the terms "open government data" and "legal framework". We selected 5 out of 14 papers, based on their availability at our institution and their unique discussions regarding the legal frameworks that OGDPs are required to comply with. The subsequent text briefly explains and outlines the insights we obtained from these 7 works.

Prieto, Rodríguez and Pimiento [8] present the Open Data (OD) approach tailored for Colombia, mirroring the nation's online government strategy. They propose a model facilitating the regulation of public data accessibility, inclusive of a deployment perspective identifying potential distribution of technical infrastructure components and quality attributes termed as NFRs. They engage in a discussion on their proposal's legal scaffolding, laying out associated definitions and actions relevant to the open data strategy in the national regulations, which were then nascent and evolving. The authors, however, do not furnish verification means to assess if a particular portal aligns with a specified legal framework.

Zubcoff et al [14] detail their methodology for releasing the University of Alicante's data, interpreting their data sources and OGDP as an Open Data ecosystem. They opted to construct their own Data Management System rather than employing existing solutions like CKAN or Socrata. Their justification lies in the failure of these available systems to satisfy certain NFRs, including the utilization of a particular content management system. This highlights the potential complexities of developing OGDPs in light of specific organizational guidelines, which may also encompass external laws and regulations.

Fitzgerald, Hooper and Cook [5] recognized an escalating demand for governmental data access and understanding of appropriate policy, technical, and legal structures to meet economic and societal goals. They emphasized that OGD policies dictate that legal rights over government data should uphold and advance open data accessibility and reusability. In a survey examining Australian Government agencies' information management, they discovered a growing acceptance of open access and proactive disclosure. However, the open access licensing policy isn't distinctly or strongly stated, nor effectively enacted in these agencies. Their study predates the global emergence of the General Data Protection Rules (GDPR). Nonetheless, it underlines the critical need to establish legal boundaries for OGDPs, despite the lack of tools for evaluating OGDP alignment with specific legal frameworks.

Runeson, Olsson and Linaker [9] discuss a legal framework that basis OGDPs. However, they focused their analysis on the legal aspects discussed by the focus groups they used in their experiments. These focus groups focused on GDPR and uncertainties about how this regulation must be implemented, including the need that government information and data must be protected by copyright, as access should be provided under licensing terms that clearly permit its reuse and dissemination.

Osorio-Sanabria, Amaya-Fernández and González-Zabala [7] discuss that, while OGDPs can enhance transparency in public administration, substantial social and technical obstacles may curtail their efficacy. After systematically mapping the OD ecosystem research, they narrowed down from 223 papers to 6, summarizing the elements that empower OD ecosystems to facilitate OGD access and utilization. They argue that considering political and legal frameworks is a key for surmounting these barriers. However, they don't delve into handling complex legal frameworks comprising numerous laws and tools.

Corrêa, Corrêa and Silva [2] observe that Brazil's federal government set out a legal framework to facilitate data opening from all government tiers, with a specific emphasis on internet and transparency portals as essential to solidifying open government. However, they noted that local governments often established transparency websites without adhering to legislative requirements and OGD principles. They conducted an exhaustive evaluation of these websites across 20 Brazilian municipalities, discussing the key parts of the applicable law and assessing portal compliance with OGD principles. Their qualitative analysis found that 95% of the surveyed websites regularly updated, primarily focusing on technological features. However, they didn't provide a straightforward method or process to verify these aspects, nor did they discuss the comprehensiveness of the information provided by these portals.

Egala and Afful-Dadzie [4] performed a qualitative study by interviewing stakeholders within an OGD ecosystem, such as OGD implementers, data suppliers, and users, to assess how well Open Government Data Platforms OGDPs align with national and international legal frameworks. They propose that these frameworks could impact OGD usage at national and subnational levels. They leverage the fit-viability theory, asserting that the legal aspect must be present in the technology's fit part, incorporating Open Data License, Right to Information Law, Data Protection Law, and Open Data Policy. However, they did not provide a methodical approach for OGDP managers to verify these legal aspects. Despite this, their findings could alert governments to potential consequences of excluding key stakeholders when opening government data, and our proposed process could benefit OGDP managers and stakeholders.

While each of these 7 studies has contributed significantly to our understanding of Open Data and NFR completeness theme, none of them provide a systematic and effective approach to assessing an OGDP's compliance with a specific legal framework. In this way, we propose in this work a process for assessing

OGDPs completeness given a legal frameworks, which can be seen as a collection of NFRs. This process, which addresses the noted gap in available tools, involves decomposing each law of the legal framework into NFRs for verification within an OGDP portal. Our approach facilitates a systematic, repeatable, and verifiable alignment of OGDPs with legal requirements, thereby streamlining the compliance process and enhancing data protection measures.

Specifically considering the Brazilian scenario, the Brazilian federal government define its own legal framework to establish what type of information TOGDPs must present. This legal framework can be composed by diverse instruments, either laws (e.g. TrL and AIL) or good practices documents. Verifying the completeness of a TOGDP may be a complex task, as many items should be verified on it. Soares and Rosa [12] analyzed the main transparency portals in municipalities of Rio Grande do Sul, a Brazilian state, with more than 100,000 inhabitants. Their aim was to verify whether they are complying with the requirements based on the Brazilian TrL and the Brazilian AIL, among other items. The research was qualitative, using an observational protocol for collecting and analyzing the TOGDPs information. Their findings show not always the portals attend the laws, which may be directly related to the difficult to analyze their completeness. Machado et al [6] propose an instrument to assess the quality of OGDPs considering 5 groups, being one of them the compliance with the requirements of an AIL. They analyzed TOGDPs of 29 cities in Rio de Janeiro, another state in Brazil, also all of them with more than 100,000 inhabitants, taking into account their evaluation instrument to assess their quality. They observed that some of the portals do not meet some important requirements they defined, in addition to accessibility being neglected. However, they did not consider the TrL in their study and instrument.

These two studies reinforced our perception of the need for tools to verify OGDP completeness in compliance to a GF. Our premise is that not always the stakeholders and managers of an OGDP is necessarily a computing expert, which implies that may be difficult either for them to clearly specify the NFRs of an OGDP or to assess its completeness. This is a particular reality in Brazil, when considering TOGDPs of all government levels. As in Brazil there are more than 5,000 municipalities spread over 26 states, tools for helping these TOGDP managers and other stakeholders to asses their completeness in compliance to a GF are quite important. However, formally defining this process is the first step to achieve these tools.

3   Our Proposed Process

Figure 1 shows our proposed process using BPMN notation. Although we understand that all the information we show in the figure could be represented by BPMN symbols, we chose to enrich the visualization process by adding elements in the figure (in blue) for better explaining the process functioning. Given a Grounding Framework (GF) (Fig. 1 – left), composed by M documents of the following types: (i) laws; (ii) reference models; and (iii) good practices instruments, the aim of our proposed process is to verify the content completeness of a given OGDP under scrutiny (Fig. 1 – OGDP Analysis Object). Our process starts with task 1. Constructing Items Lists from each document of GF. We show in the process that an OGDP evaluator (whom may be the OGDP manager) conduct this task[4]. GF is composed by a set of documents $GF = \{D_1, ..., D_M\}$, and each document is decomposed by a set of items by the OGDP evaluator, i.e., $D_1 = \{Item_{1-1}, ..., Item_{1-N1}\}$ up to $D_M = \{Item_{M-1}, ..., Item_{1-NM}\}$. The output of the task 1. is a list of triples of the form $((Group_k, Item_l), \{SI_{i-l}\}, \{D_{j-l}\})$, where k is the index of all groups of items identified in GF, l is an index of all the items extracted from the documents, each one associated to a group $Group_k$ ((Group,Item) in Fig. 1), $\{SI_{i-l}\}$ (Subitems Set in Fig. 1) is a set of sub-items, obtained by breaking down in a lower granularity of pieces of information from each $Item_l$ and the set $\{D_{j-l}\}$ (Docs Set in Fig. 1) contains an ID of all the documents where $Item_l$ is present. The OGDP evaluator is responsible to identify semantically similar items among the set of documents in $GF = \{D_1, ..., D_M\}$.

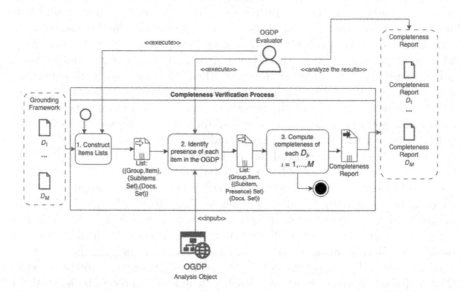

Fig. 1. A diagrammatic schema of our proposed process for evaluating an OGDP completeness based on a grounding framework

Task 2. Identify presence of each item in the OGDP is also executed by an OGDP evaluator or manager. The output of this task is a list of triples of the form $(Item_l, \{(SI_{i-l}, PV_{i-l})\}, \{D_{j-l}\})$ (List: (Item, (Subitem, Presence) Set, Docs Set) in Fig. 1), being the result of adding the presence value PV_{i-l} associated

---

[4] It is worth mentioning that not necessarily the same person must conduct all the 3. tasks of our proposed process.

to each sub-item $SI_{i-l} \in Item_l$. The simplest way of defining the domain of presence value feature is assuming only three values: `true` (meaning the item was found in the OGDP), `false` (meaning the item was not found in the OGDP) or `I don't understand the meaning of the item` (meaning that the OGDP evaluator could not understand what he or she is looking for). Task 3. Compute completeness of each $D_i, i = 1, ..., M$ aims to calculate the completeness of the OGDP regarding each document $D_i \in GF, i = 1, ..., M$. Finally, the OGDP evaluator may analyze the Completeness Report (the final output of our process). This report may allow the OGDP managers to evaluate the portal in order to attend the GF. One interesting aspect of our process is that the OGDP evaluator is able to increment the GF according to his or her needs or specificities.

Our process (Fig. 1) was designed with a dual intention: firstly, to establish a comprehensive and systematic method for examining the completeness of any given OGDP) in compliance to a GF; and secondly, to offer a means of identifying potential areas for enhancement or adjustment within the OGDP under review. The designed process serves as a tool for assessing OGDPs, enabling detailed examination of their alignment with a GF. It allows OGDP managers to identify rectify gaps or discrepancies, ensuring ongoing refinement and improved adherence to legal requirements, reference models, and best practices.

4   Experimental Analysis

We executed Task 1. in order to construct the items lists to be verified in a TOGDP – which we call a reference guide. After, the items lists was used to verify completeness on 3 TOGDPs of three different cities by an OGDP evaluator. The chosen TOGDPs were: TP_1 – Niterói (RJ state)[5], TP_2 – Serra (ES state)[6] and TP_3 – Santana de Parnaíba (SP state)[7]. These choices were due to (i) we had access Niterói TOGDP managers; (ii) Niterói TOGDP managers pointed out that Serra TOGDP is a good example of a TOGDP in Brazil; and (iii) Santana de Parnaíba city hall received a very low grade in a Brazilian transparency evaluation instrument, called Brazil Transparency Map[8]. Finally, in order to better understanding the difficulty level of executing our process, we counted on the participation of 6 coworkers of the Niterói city hall to execute our process using the Niterói TOGDP as the OGDP Analysis Object.

4.1   Constructing Items Lists (Task 1)

In order to construct the items lists, we used the following 4 documents $(D_1, ..., D_4)$: D_1: The Implementation Guide for the Transparency Portal[9]

---

[5] Available at https://transparencia.niteroi.rj.gov.br.

[6] Available at http://transparencia.serra.es.gov.br/.

[7] Available at https://servicos.santanadeparnaiba.sp.gov.br//cecam_transparencia/.

[8] Available in Portuguese at https://mbt.cgu.gov.br/publico/home.

[9] In Portuguese. Available at https://www.gov.br/cgu/pt-br/centrais-de-conteudo/pu blicacoes/transparencia-publica/brasil-transparente/arquivos/guia_portaltranspare ncia.pdf. Last accessed on 2023-03-23.

presents guidelines for the creation of a transparency portal, prepared by the Comptroller General of the Union (CGU), based on the implementation of the Brazilian TrL. Among these guidelines, there are items regarding expenses and revenue, in addition to providing a table with recommendations on the site and content. D_2: The Guide to Requirements and Good Practices for Building Municipal Transparency Portals[10], prepared by the Government of the Espírito Santo State, in Brazil, indicating necessary standards for creating a TOGDP. It separates these standard items into categories: Institutional, Revenues, Expenses, Servers, Agreements, Tenders and Budget. This instrument inspired us as it divides each group into its respective sub-items. D_3: The Access to Public Information booklet, an introduction to the Brazilian AIL[11] for knowledge dissemination of this legislation, which highlights the positive points of an administrative culture pro-access to information. D_4: The Transparent Brazil Map[12] instrument is used to measure public transparency in cities and states in Brazil. Its methodology analyzes whether city halls are complying with the provisions of the Brazilian TrL. Such a scale has several requirements to achieve the ideal scenario of transparency, which are grouped into two topics: regulation (including questions on whether laws items are located on the website of the entity, among others) and passive transparency (including if there is a precise indication on the site of a physical Citizen Information Service, if there is a possibility of post-request follow-up, among others).

Based on $D_1, ..., D_4$, we extracted 12 groups with 82 items, being divided into 256 sub-items. We turned all these items and groups available in a spreadsheet on the Internet[13]. The 12 groups are (with its number of items): **G1. Revenues data (39); G2. Expenses data (76); G3. Financial Information data (9); G4. Bids and Contracts data (37); G5. Public Servants data (20); G6. Agreements data (25); G7. Daily Rates data (7); G8. Follow-up (15); G9. Help and General Information (15); G10. Information Accuracy (2); G11. Interoperability (3); and G12. Regulation (8).**

4.2 Evaluating Completeness of 3 TOGDPs

We performed a manual check on the three portals previously presented. This check consisted of verifying if the items were (Y – Yes) or not (N – No) found, if they were Not Understood (NU) or if they must be verified in anOther System (OS). From this check, we constructed 2 graphs with the percentages of items found in each of the 12 categories – Figs. 2 and 3. Our observations for each group were: **G1:** Most of the information was not located in the 3 TOGDPs.

---

[10] In Portuguese. Available at https://secont.es.gov.br/Media/Secont/DOWNLOA DS/Conselho%20de%20Transparência/guia_requisitos_e_boas_prticas_portal_transpa rencia_municipios%20(2).pdf.

[11] In Portuguese. Available at https://www2.senado.leg.br/bdsf/item/id/496325.

[12] In Portuguese. Available at https://mbt.cgu.gov.br/publico/home.

[13] Available at https://docs.google.com/spreadsheets/d/1X5A8-6QHz3e7vyOLiBtE7 H4_HFsaqpYsqoYZbeFAUyM/ – tab "Version in English".

The search in the recipe group on each site is done in a generic way, encompassing all items. However, four items are specifications of query types, namely: revenues by management unit, global revenues, budgetary and financial execution of revenues by **organ** and budgetary and financial execution of revenues by **revenue**, each one with its respective subcategories, which increases the negative index if that specific type of search is not found. **G2:** despite being the group with the most items to be checked, it has a better found data rate than G1. None of the sites analyzed have a search filtered by document or by area, nor the differentiation between a quick and an advanced search. **G3:** this was the group with mostly positive results in all analyzed samples, which deals with budget guidelines, financial reports, annual balance sheets and accountability. **G4:** this group, which also includes Contracts in our guide, found a higher amount of content on TP_1 compared to TP_2 and TP_3. The item not understood was the "summary of the contract instruments or their amendments and the communications ratified by the higher authority". This instruction is present in one of the references, but without including further details of its meaning. **G5:** We observed that TP_2 has a good result among them. On the other hand, the TP_1 and TP_3 do not have a search on civil servants' remuneration, which indicates almost a third of the information in this group. **G6:** We observed divergences on the level of references of agreements in the three sites. TP_2 handles the most items and, in common with TP_3, has a clear indication of which agreements have been received and which ones have been granted, which does not occur with TP_1. **G7:** TP_1 entirely presented the items of this group but TP_2 and TP_3 portals did not. **G8:** A large part of the follow-up function depends on another system (OS) – the Electronic Citizen Information System, the e-SIC –, and therefore was not analyzed if the information exists in the portal. On the city halls' website, the present data are related to: follow-up of public works, programs, projects and actions; and also results of inspections, audits, provision and accountability carried out by control bodies. **G9:** Most results on help and general information are found on the portals, excepting the possibility of electronically information request, which must be done through another system. **G10:** The three sites indicate the source of their information, in addition to having some relationship indicating the open databases of the municipality. It is noteworthy that this group has only two items to be observed by the evaluators in the respective sites, and they were found in all of them. **G11:** The sites have free access, without having to register to be able to view the pages, and also allow automated access by external systems, but it was not possible to verify whether the portals follow the e-PING (Brazilian Interoperability Standards of Electronic Government). **G12:** This group presents statistics regarding the explicit compliance with laws and the indication that they are being practiced, in addition to checking whether the portals are registered on government sites, and with a standardized URL.

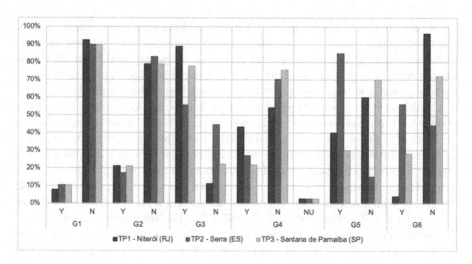

Fig. 2. Percentage of items per group – found (Y), not found (N), not understood (NU) and obtained by other systems (OS) –, by group (G1 to G6) and by TP (TP$_1$, TP$_2$ e TP$_3$).

4.3   Evaluating Completeness of TP_1

The average time to apply the instrument on TP_1 by City Hall professionals (4 participants) was 3 h and by IT professionals (2 participants) was 2 h. Figure 4 shows the percentages of items found, not found and not understood by each of the participants who used the instrument. City hall professionals with an average frequency of using the transparency site are represented by P1, P2 and P3. Participant P4, on the other hand, has daily use experience and we observed that he was the participant who was able to find more items in the guide on the portal, but he was also the one who most evaluated items as not understood. Participants P5 and P6 are IT professionals with no experience using the portal and we see that they were the ones who were able to find fewer guide items on the portal. With this, we see that the understanding of the guide is still well linked to the frequency of use of the portal.

We also analyzed only the results of the evaluation carried out by city hall professionals (P1, P2, P3 to P4 in Fig. 4), in order to observe the rate of items indicated as found by at least one observer, is of 87.25% (226 items out of 259), not found by at least one observer is 57.14% (148 items out of 259) and not understood is 21.6% (56 items out of 259). The high rate of misunderstood items demonstrates how the lack of a clear definition of what to look for can confuse the researcher. P1 and P5 did not respond to 8 different items and it was not possible to identify the difficulty in completing them.

In order to better understand this scenario ,considering only the city hall professionals, we also constructed the graph shown in Fig. 5. The bar on top (first bar) of the figure (Bar 4) is related of the agreement findings of all 4 evaluators; the second bar (Bar 3), the agreement findings of 3 out of 4 evaluators; the

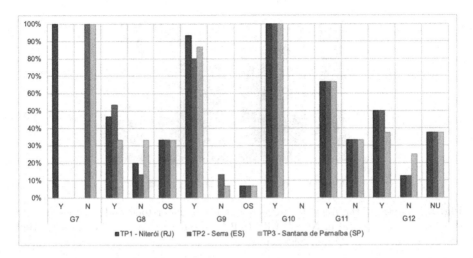

Fig. 3. Percentage of items per group – found (Y), not found (N), not understood (NU) and obtained by other systems (OS) –, by group (G7 to G12) and by TP (TP$_1$, TP$_2$ e TP$_3$).

third bar (Bar 2), the agreement findings of 2 out of 4 evaluators; and the last bar (Bar 1), the findings of at least 1 out of 4 evaluators. We can observe that the total number of items on which the 4 evaluators (Bar 4) were unanimous is 42.8% (111 items out of 259), being 95 items marked as found and 16 marked as not found. We have 32.4% (84 items out of 259) of items agreements for 3 evaluators (Bar 3) and 31.6% (82 items out of 259) items agreement for 2 raters. Considering Bar 1, we can see that 40 items were found by only one of the evaluators, thus indicating that such items are difficult to locate on the portal while the items found by all evaluators (Bar 4) can be considered easily accessible. On the other hand, the 16 items not found by all of the 4 evaluators (Bar 1) can also be considered difficult for users to access or do not exist on the portal. Most of these agreed items marked as not found refer to missing graphs and tables on the viewed page. On the other hand, the items with the greatest divergence being marked as not found by some and not understood by others are related to the use of an specific method where a list of the municipality's open databases is published on the page. In the group of unanimous items not understood by 3 of the evaluators (Bar 3 in Fig. 5), we highlight items from the group G1. Consultation on Revenue, related to the type of document and value of the operation. Another problematic point that was unanimously identified was the item related to the query on expenses by area, where there was confusion over the difference between this and the search for expenses by body. This result makes it clear that these items deserve attention and better clarification.

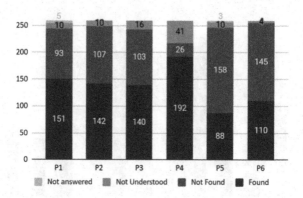

Fig. 4. Analysis of the items found, not found, not understood and not answered in the transparency portal in Niterói City Hall by the participants (P1 to P4 City Hall professionals, P5 and P6 IT professionals)

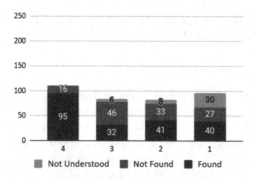

Fig. 5. Number of items found, not found and not understood in the Niterói TP by at least 1 of the evaluators (Bar 1), by 2 out of 4 evaluators (Bar 2), by 3 out of 4 evaluators (Bar 3) and by all 4 evaluators (Bar 4).

5   A Discussion on Our Findings

This study shows the relevance of detailed guides and checklists for the analysis of (T)OGDPs. The lists of items, derived from documents, is a fundamental task when evaluating the completeness of different TOGDPs, due to the semantics the analyst need to identify in each item. The achieved results demonstrated variances in the completeness of TP_1, TP_2 and TP_3. For example, the group G2. Expenses Data showcased more accessible data in all three TOGDPs compared to G1. Revenues data. However, none of the sites offered a search tool filtered by document or area, which indicates a potential area for improvement. Moreover, TP_2 was superior in G5. Public Servants data and G6. Agreement data, while TP_1 excelled in G4. Bids and Contracts data. These variations not only highlight the diverse approaches each city employs for transparency but also underscore the areas where each city could potentially learn from the others to enhance their transparency measures.

The study also examined the ease of use and understanding of the reference guide. We could observe that frequent users, like the city hall professionals, were able to locate more items on the portal compared to those with less familiarity, like the IT professionals. However, even the city hall professionals found about 21.6% of the items difficult to understand. This suggests that, while our guide serves as a useful tool for evaluating TOGDPs, its effectiveness relies significantly on the user's familiarity with the portal and the clarity of item descriptions.

In this context, a more granular analysis was carried out on the TOGDP of Niterói. We discovered that the agreement between four evaluators was limited to about 42.8% of items, indicating the subjective nature of item identification and the potential ambiguity in the items' descriptions. The unanimous not understood items mainly belonged to the group G1. Revenue data, pointing towards a need for better clarification within this category. Such findings illustrate the necessity of improving our instrument's comprehensibility to facilitate a more accurate evaluation.

Despite the thoroughness of the evaluation process, a striking aspect that emerged from the analysis was the limited agreement among evaluators regarding the found items. A mere 42.8% of the items were unanimously recognized by all evaluators as being either present or absent on the TOGDP. This variability suggests multiple potential causes. One hypothesis points towards the evaluators' differential familiarity with the transparency portal. Some of the evaluators had daily interactions with the portal, while others, such as the IT professionals, had less experience navigating it. A second plausible explanation lies in the complexity and diversity of the items, which may not have clear or universal interpretations, leading to discrepancies in evaluations. Lastly, it could also be a reflection of the inherent ambiguity in some transparency guidelines, which may need further clarification or standardization to ensure consistent interpretation and evaluation across different evaluators.

In conclusion, this study underlines the importance of comprehensive guidelines for evaluating TOGDPs, as well as the need to improve the clarity of these guidelines to ensure accurate assessments. The disparities found across different TOGDPs offer a valuable opportunity for shared learning and enhancement of transparency measures. Moving forward, refining the item descriptions in the guidelines, particularly in areas such as "Consultation on Revenue" (G1), would be beneficial for all TOGDP evaluators.

6   Conclusions and Future Work

This work presents a process to assess the completeness of an OGPD in compliance to a Grounding Framework, in a structured and comprehensive way. This process allows portal managers to identify (in)completeness points of OGDPs. We are unaware of international works that propose the type of approach used in this article. We used a diagrammatic scheme in BPMN to propose our process, based on a set of documents composing a reference grounding framework, such as laws, reference models and instruments of good practice. As a result, a Completeness Report is generated, which allows OGPD managers to assess the portal and make necessary improvements. The evaluator is responsible for leading the tasks and can enhance the reference framework as needed. In order to validate our methodology, we applied it in a practical case involving a TOGDP of three Brazilian local governments. Our evaluation showed that the most complete portal has a completeness level of 52%, which indicates that there is still room for improvement in relation to the availability of open information and data. The results also highlighted the importance of having a clear reference framework to guide the completeness assessment of the OGPD and allow comparison with other similar portals. In addition, the results obtained in our case study show the relevance of having a well-defined reference framework and the possibility of comparing the completeness of the OGPD with other similar portals.

Based on our results, some possibilities for future work include: i) testing our approach in OGDPs from different countries and regions to assess its applicability in different contexts and identify possible adjustments and improvements; ii) carrying out case studies to understand how the methodology can be adapted to different types of OGDPs, considering their particularities and specific characteristics; iii) exploring the possibility of automating the OGDP completeness assessment process, using data analysis and machine learning tools; and iv) investigating the relationship between the completeness of the OGDP and the use of available data, assessing how the lack of information can impact its use and generate barriers to transparency and citizen participation. Future research could also explore the Criteria-Based Evaluation [3] method in order to evolve our approach. Another interesting future research may also consider capturing disagreement among participants in different case studies. While this study provided a glimpse of the various users perspectives, more accurate metrics would be beneficial to illustrate these differences. One of the possibilities would be to replicate the use of Krippendorff's alpha (α) [11]. These efforts to quantify and address disagreements could lead to more effective assessment of transparency portals and, ultimately, more refined and user-friendly transparency portals.

References

1. Colpaert, P., Joye, S., Mechant, P., Mannens, E., Van de Walle, R.: The 5 stars of open data portals. In: Proceedings of the 7th International Conference on Methodologies, Technologies and Tools Enabling E-Government (MeTTeG 2013), pp. 61–67 (2013)
2. Corrêa, A.S., Corrêa, P.L.P., da Silva, F.S.C.: Transparency portals versus open government data: an assessment of openness in Brazilian municipalities. In: Proceedings of the 15th annual international conference on Digital Government Research, dg.o 2014, pp. 178–185 (2014). https://doi.org/10.1145/2612733.2612760
3. Cronholm, S., Goldkuhl, G.: Strategies for information systems evaluation-six generic types. Electron. J. Inf. Syst. Eval. **6**(2), 65–74 (2003)
4. Egala, S.B., Afful-Dadzie, E.: Performance of open government data in a developing economy: a multi-stakeholder case analysis of Ghana. Transform. Gov. People Process Policy **16**(3), 318–333 (2022)

5. Fitzgerald, A., Hooper, N., Cook, J.S.: Implementing open licensing in government open data initiatives: a review of Australian government practice. In: Proceedings of 9th International Symposium on Open Collaboration. ACM (2013)
6. Machado, V., Mantini, G., Viterbo, J., Bernardini, F., Barcellos, R.: An instrument for evaluating open data portals: a case study in Brazilian cities. In: Proceedings of the 19th Annual International Conference on Digital Government Research, dg.o 2018. ACM (2018). https://doi.org/10.1145/3209281.3209370
7. Osorio-Sanabria, M.A., Amaya-Fernández, F., González-Zabala, M.: Exploring the components of open data ecosystems: a systematic mapping study. In: Proceedings of 10th Euro-American Conference on Telematics & Information Systems, EATIS 2020. ACM (2021)
8. Prieto, L.M., Rodríguez, A.C., Pimiento, J.: Implementation framework for open data in Colombia. In: Proceedings of 6th International Conference on Theory and Practice of Electronic Governance, ICEGOV 2012, pp. 14–17. ACM (2012)
9. Runeson, P., Olsson, T., Linaker, J.: Open data ecosystems - an empirical investigation into an emerging industry collaboration concept. J. Syst. Softw. **182**, 111088 (2021)
10. Sampaio, I.G.B., Andrade, E.D.O., Bernardini, F., Viterbo, J.: Assessing the quality of Covid-19 open data portals. In: Janssen, M., et al. (eds.) EGOV 2022. LNCS, vol. 13391, pp. 212–227. Springer, Cham (2022). https://doi.org/10.1007/978-3-031-15086-9_14
11. Santos, J.S., Bernardini, F., Paes, A.: Measuring the degree of divergence when labeling tweets in the electoral scenario. In: Proceedings of X Brazilian Workshop on Social Network Analysis and Mining, pp. 127–138. SBC (2021)
12. Soares, C.S., da Rosa, F.S.: What should be published on the transparency portal? Analysis of the electronic portal of the largest municipalities in Rio Grande do Sul. In: XXV Brazilian Congress on Costs (2018). (in Portuguese)
13. Tygel, A., Auer, S., Debattista, J., Orlandi, F., Campos, M.: Towards cleaning-up open data portals: a metadata reconciliation approach. In: Proceedings of IEEE 10th International Conference on Semantic Computing, pp. 71–78 (2016)
14. Zubcoff, J., et al.: The university as an open data ecosystem. Int. J. Des. Nat. Ecodynamics **11**(3), 250–257 (2016)

An Extensive Methodology and Framework for Quality Assessment of DCAT-AP Datasets

Bianca Wentzel[1]([✉])[ID], Fabian Kirstein[1,2][ID], Torben Jastrow[1][ID],
Raphael Sturm[1][ID], Michael Peters[1][ID], and Sonja Schimmler[1,2][ID]

[1] Fraunhofer FOKUS, Berlin, Germany
{bianca.wentzel,fabian.kirstein,torben.jastrow,raphael.sturm,
michael.peters,sonja.schimmler}@fokus.fraunhofer.de
[2] Weizenbaum Institute for the Networked Society, Berlin, Germany

Abstract. The DCAT Application Profile for Data Portals is a crucial cornerstone for publishing and reusing Open Data in Europe. It supports the harmonization and interoperability of Open Data by providing an expressive set of properties, guidelines, and reusable vocabularies. However, a qualitative and accurate implementation by Open Data providers remains challenging. To improve the informative value and the compliance with RDF-based specifications, we propose a methodology to measure and assess the quality of DCAT-AP datasets. Our approach is based on the FAIR and the 5-star principles for Linked Open Data. We define a set of metrics, where each one covers a specific quality aspect. For example, if a certain property has a compliant value, if mandatory vocabularies are applied or if the actual data is available. The values for the metrics are stored as a custom data model based on the Data Quality Vocabulary and is used to calculate an overall quality score for each dataset. We implemented our approach as a scalable and reusable Open Source solution to demonstrate its feasibility. It is applied in a large-scale production environment (data.europa.eu) and constantly checks more than 1.6 million DCAT-AP datasets and delivers quality reports.

Keywords: Open Data · DCAT-AP · Data Quality

1 Introduction

Open Data constitutes a global movement to make data of public interest openly available without any restrictions. Popular providers of Open Data are public administrations, governments, and nonprofit and research organizations. Typically Open Data is published and managed through Web portals and aggregated into central portals. A well-known example for an aggregator is the official portal for European data[1], that provides access to more than 170 individual data catalogs, containing more than 1.6 million datasets.

---

[1] https://data.europa.eu/.

I. Lindgren et al. (Eds.): EGOV 2023, LNCS 14130, pp. 262–278, 2023.
https://doi.org/10.1007/978-3-031-41138-0_17

In order to efficiently disseminate, aggregate, and reuse Open Data a harmonized, standardized, and machine-readable metadata model is paramount. A widely adopted and powerful standard is the DCAT Application Profile for Data Portals (DCAT-AP). It is based on the W3C (World Wide Web Consortium) Resource Description Framework (RDF) Data Catalogue Vocabulary (DCAT)[2] and therefore follows Linked Data and Semantic Web principles. DCAT-AP provides a plethora of properties, vocabularies and guidelines to extensively express information about Open Data. However, currently many published DCAT-AP datasets are affected with quality issues, such as sparse use of properties, wrong or no use of vocabularies, application of incorrect data types or unavailable data. This is caused by several aspects: (1) The DCAT-AP is fuzzy to a certain extent and precise requirements for some properties are missing. (2) Only a few properties are declared as mandatory, allowing datasets with little expressiveness. (3) DCAT-AP only represents the metadata, the actual data is linked and its availability depends on external resources. (4) There does not exist an extensive quality baseline for DCAT-AP, making it difficult for providers to ensure the quality of their DCAT-AP datasets.

In this paper, we present a methodology, framework and software implementation to address these issues and support the iterative improvement of the quality and expressiveness of DCAT-AP datasets. We mainly address two research questions in our work. Firstly, how can we measure and represent the quality, completeness, and validity of DCAT-AP datasets? Secondly, how can we present and communicate these quality assessments to data providers? The main contributions of our work are:

- We designed concrete metrics and a data model to describe and store quality measurements about DCAT-AP datasets based on the Data Quality Vocabulary (DQV) and the FAIR and 5-star principles for Linked Open Data (LOD).
- We implemented a highly scalable processing pipeline to determine the indicators for sets of DCAT-AP catalogs and a reporting tool to browse and download the current and past results.
- We tested and evaluated our approach with a corpus of more than 1.6 million datasets to demonstrate its feasibility and added value.

In Sect. 2 we introduce related work and related projects that deal with quality assessment of Open Data and that act as a foundation for our work. Our qualitative quality metrics and our data model are described in Sect. 3. Our implementation is illustrated in Sect. 4. Our approach is evaluated in Sect. 5 with a feature comparison and a practical use case. Section 6 summarizes our work and gives an outlook for future developments.

2   Related Work

Our work is based on several related standards, specifications, and technologies from the domains Open Data, research data, Linked Data and Semantic Web, as

---

[2] https://www.w3.org/TR/vocab-dcat-2/.

well as data quality. In the following, we present a brief overview of the relevant foundations.

According to the DIN, *quality* is defined as the "totality of characteristics (and characteristic values) of a unit with regard to its suitability to fulfill specified and presupposed requirements"[3]. When referred to data, and more specifically to data and datasets in a scientific context, it can be assumed that there are general requirements for *data quality*, such as verifiability, reusability, relevance or completeness. To ensure high quality standards, improving data quality has been enforced by various public authorities in the past years, e.g. by the Information Quality Act[4]. Such efforts help mitigate the problem that insufficient data quality leads to higher costs and time loss in science projects[5].

DCAT is a mature and popular standard for expressing metadata about data catalogs and foster interoperability between them. The standard consists of multiple classes, where the most relevant ones are dataset and distribution. The first one represents a collection of data, and the second one represents the actual access to the data, e.g. a downloadable file. [12] *DCAT-AP* is a practical extension of *DCAT* which introduces additional metadata fields and mandatory ranges for certain properties. These ranges are provided as a Simple Knowledge Organization System (SKOS)[6] controlled vocabulary, published by the Publications Office of the European Union. For example, properties like language, spatial information or MIME type can be harmonized by applying the provided vocabularies [1].

The *FAIR principles* describe guidelines for data, broken down into "Findability", "Accessibility", "Interoperability" and "Reusability". The principles are intended to ensure a uniform presentation of collected data. Within the four principles, there are 15 sub-principles, as shortly described in the following. *Findability* summarizes that records are tagged with globally unique and persistent identifiers (F1) as well as rich metadata (F2). The data should also be present inside of a searchable resource (F4). In addition, the metadata must specify the data identifier (F3). *Accessibility* describes the need for a simplified access of datasets through standardized communication protocols (A1). Those protocols should be open, free, universally implementable (A1.1) and should allow an authentication/ authorization procedure (A1.2). Furthermore the metadata should be accessible even when the data is no longer available (A2). *Interoperability* ensures that datasets have rich metadata and provide a formal, accessible, shared and broadly applicable language to represent the information (I1). Also metadata (and data as well) should use vocabularies that follow the FAIR principles (I2) and include qualified references to other data (I3). *Reusability* requires datasets to be provided with a variety of descriptive attributes (R1) and a clear and accessible data usage license (R1.1). In addition, datasets should have a traceable provenance (R1.2) and comply with community standards (R1.3) [14].

---

[3] DIN EN ISO 8402 (1995), p. 212.

[4] https://sgp.fas.org/crs/RL32532.pdf.

[5] https://hbr.org/2016/09/bad-data-costs-the-u-s-3-trillion-per-year.

[6] https://www.w3.org/TR/skos-reference/.

The FAIR principles overlap with the *5-star principles for LOD* defined by Tim Berners Lee[7]. While this model also aims at improving FAIRness, it is more focused on interlinking the data to enable the use of Semantic Web technologies. Furthermore, this model refers to Open Data which means that data can be used, modified and shared freely by users[8] while the FAIR principles do not primarily target openness. Based on this model, a dataset is evaluated according to five criteria resulting in a star rating indicating its openness. If the dataset does not comply with any criteria of the model it receives a zero star rating. One star is earned by using an open license, receiving a second star requires the provision of data using a structured format. A dataset has three stars if its format is open and non-proprietary. The fourth star honors the use of URIs to describe properties, and the fifth star evaluates the interlinking of data to provide context.

The *Data Quality Vocabulary (DQV)* is an extension of the DCAT vocabulary, forming the basis for defining and interpreting dataset quality. When interpreting quality, the *DQV* takes into account factors such as the constant updating of data, the possibility of corrections by the user, and persistence obligations[9].

The *Shapes Constraint Language (SHACL)* is used to validate RDF graphs against predefined rules, which are described as RDF graphs as well. These rules specify, for example, specific formats, cardinalities, or relations for properties of an RDF graph. The results are also rendered as an RDF graph and contain detailed information about any errors or violations for the affected properties[10].

2.1 Related Projects

Based on research that is primarily centered around developing standards and metrics to evaluate the quality of Open Data, various solutions have been created to automatically measure the quality of Open Data. A well-known example is the work by Vetrò et al. [11] which resulted in the creation of the Open Data Quality Measurement Framework.

Langer et al. [6] describe the quality assessment tool *SemQuire*, which enables the assessment of Linked Open Data sources based on DQV. Building on a semantic literature review by Zaveri et al. [16] they developed a list of metrics segmented into four dimensions: Accessibility, Contextual, Intrinsic, and Representational. The implementation consists of a user interface, a RESTful API, a set of implemented metrics and the graph database Stardog. The input data can be specified via a direct upload or by fetching a URL or a SPARQL endpoint. Afterwards, the desired metrics can be selected by the user, and the analysis is executed. The measurement results are then shown in the user interface and can be exported into DQV with an overall score.

Another implementation developed by Neumaier et al. [8] is the *Open Data Portal Watch* framework. The metrics used are based on previous work by Reiche

---

[7] https://www.w3.org/2011/gld/wiki/5_Star_Linked_Data.

[8] https://opendefinition.org/.

[9] https://www.w3.org/TR/vocab-dqv/.

[10] https://www.w3.org/TR/shacl/.

et al. [9] and refer to the existing metadata keys of DCAT. They are divided into five dimensions: Existence, Conformance, Retrievability, Accuracy, and Open Data. In contrast to SemQuire, the Open Data Portal Watch framework contains an additional harvesting component that enables the aggregation of data from different Open Data Portals based on various technologies (CKAN, Socrata, OpenDataSoft). The measurement results are shown in a user interface and can be downloaded as a CSV or PDF report. The work of Neumaier et al. [8] serves as the basis for further implementations such as the ODPQ Dashboard [5] and the ADEQUATe platform [7] which enhance the feature set of the Open Data Portal Watch framework, mainly by providing a more advanced dashboard.

In addition to the solutions mentioned above, current research offers implementations with a dedicated focus on evaluating the FAIR principles. These include the *FAIR Evaluator* by Wilkinson et al. [15], which analyzes open datasets using 15 metrics based on the FAIR principles and presents the results in a user interface, as well as the *FAIR Checker* by Rosnet et al. [10] and the FAIR data assessment tool *F-UJI* by Devaraju and Huber [2,3].

3   DCAT-AP Quality Metrics

To determine metadata quality we defined a set of quality metrics called DCATAP Quality Metrics (DCAT-AP-QM) for metadata sets of catalogs, datasets and distributions using DCAT-AP. These metrics are based on the FAIR and 5-star principles and their application results in measurements with qualitative values as well as (aggregated) scores.

3.1   Designing the DCAT-AP Quality Metrics

Inspired by Wang and Strong [13], so-called dimensions are used to categorize different aspects of metadata quality within our DCAT-AP-QM. For each of these abstract classes, metrics are defined that test certain criteria (e.g. timeliness). For each of these metrics, a qualitative or quantitative value describes the metadata quality by directly measuring it (e.g. "yes" in case of timeliness).

For our quality metrics, we define four dimensions, which are in line with the FAIR principles: Findability, Accessibility, Interoperability and Reusability. Additionally, a fifth dimension that emphasizes contextual usability is added: Contextuality. For each of these dimensions metrics are defined adapting the FAIR and the 5-star principles. In the following, for each dimension, the defined metrics are described and the corresponding FAIR (sub-)principles and 5-star principles are detailed. Some metrics are not checked by Piveau Metrics, as they are either out of scope or are always fulfilled due to the way Piveau is implemented. A detailed overview of unchecked principles is provided at the end of this section giving details on why this is the case.

For each metric defined, the name of the tested metadata property is assigned (e.g. Keyword Availability). The semantic representation of this metadata property is added in brackets (e.g. dcat:keyword) consisting of the short version of the respective namespace[11] and the property name. Among the metrics defined, most test either the presence of a certain property ("Availability Metrics", e.g. Keyword Availability) or the matching of certain metadata with values of controlled vocabularies ("Vocabulary Alignment Metrics", e.g. License Vocabulary Alignment). In case of multidimensional properties for Availability Metrics the number of instances is not taken into account, only the sheer presence is measured. Both metric types store their results as boolean values. Additionally, there are some special metrics whose functionality and values will be described in more detail in the following.

Findability. [*Keyword Availability* (dcat: keyword), *Category Availability* (dcat: theme, dct: subject), *Spatial Availability* (dct: spatial) and *Temporal Availability* (dct: temporal)] The metrics cover F2 and R1 of the FAIR principles stating that data should be described with rich metadata.

Accessibility. [*Access URL Status Code* (dcat: accessURL), *Download URL Availability* (dcat: downloadURL) and *Download URL Status Code* (dcat: downloadURL)] The first and third metric describe whether the two specified endpoints can be reached via an HTTP request. The status code returned is used as the value of the measurement. Unlike the download URL, the existence of the access URL is not checked, since it is a mandatory property of DCAT-AP and therefore must be available. The metrics fulfill A1 and A1.1 of the FAIR principles, which state that metadata should be retrievable by their identifier using a standardized, open, free and universal protocol.

Interoperability. [*Format and Media Type Availability* (dct: format, dct: mediaType), *Format and Media Type Vocabulary Alignment* (dct: format, dct: mediaType), *Format and Media Type Non Proprietary* (dct: format, dct: mediaType), *Format Machine Interpretable* (dct: format) and *DCAT-AP Compliance*] The first two metrics check the presence of media type and format information and its vocabulary alignment according to the controlled vocabularies of DCAT-AP. The metrics that deal with the non-proprietary nature and the machine-readability of the format also check against controlled vocabularies but these vocabularies have been defined especially for this purpose[12]. The fifth metric, DCAT-AP compliance, is tested by validating the metadata against the DCAT-AP SHACL shapes[13]. As soon as at least one issue occurs, the metadata is not compliant. This check covers I1 of the FAIR principles demanding the use of a formal, accessible, shared and broadly applicable language for knowledge representation. All vocabulary checks cover I2 of the FAIR principles and the four star level of the 5-star principles requiring the representation of resources using a vocabulary (URIs). Checking the given format for non-proprietary and machine-readability applies to the two star level as well as the three star level of the 5-star principles.

---

[11] dct: http://purl.org/dc/terms/, dcat: http://www.w3.org/ns/dcat#.

[12] https://gitlab.com/dataeuropa/vocabularies/.

[13] https://github.com/SEMICeu/DCAT-AP/tree/master/releases/2.1.1.

Reusability. [*License Availability* (dct: license), *Known License (License Vocabulary Alignment)* (dct: license), *Access Rights Availability* (dct: accessRights), *Access Rights Vocabulary Alignment* (dct: accessRights), *Contact Point Availability* (dct: contactPoint) and *Publisher Availability* (dct: publisher)] Testing the presence of a license covers R1.1 of the FAIR principles demanding the declaration of one. R1 of the FAIR principles, namely a rich description of data using a plurality of accurate and relevant attributes is tested by checking the presence of an access rights description. The usage of controlled vocabularies aligns to I2 of the FAIR principles and the four star level of the 5-star principles which demand the linking of resources using URIs. Additionally, the metrics that look at the contact point and the publisher meet the requirement of R1.2 of the FAIR principles demanding a detailed provenance description.

Contextuality. [*Rights Availability* (dct: rights), *Bytesize Availability* (dcat: byteSize), *Date Issued Availability* (dct: issued) and *Date Modified Availability* dct: modified)] These metrics cover I2 and R1 of the FAIR principles which state that data should be described by rich and relevant metadata.

While the metrics described above cover large parts of the FAIR and the 5-star principles, some (sub-)principles were not considered. F1 and F3 of the FAIR principles demand the usage and integration of a global identifier within the metadata. In order to even be accessible by our tool each DCAT-AP dataset has to have a URL which serves as global identifier, and hence, is a prerequisite. F4 of the FAIR principles, requiring that data should be indexed in a searchable resource, is also not tested, as our tool is designed for an environment that already offers such an index. A2 of the FAIR principles cannot be tested, since (meta)data that is examined is necessarily available. I3 of the FAIR principles as well as the five star level of the 5-star principles are not tested because checking the interlinking of data is out of scope for our tool. R1.3 of the FAIR principles demanding tests against domain-specific standards is also not covered. Our tool is intended for Open Data portals that store data of any discipline, and therefore testing against specific standards is not reasonable.

3.2 Applying the DCAT-AP Quality Metrics

The previously defined metrics serve as a basis to make measurements for each specific metadata set. Statements about the quality of the respective metadata record can then be derived from the totality of the values obtained in this way.

The results are purely qualitative and in most cases only describe the presence of properties in the metadata or the use of controlled vocabularies. While it is necessary to know these details to evaluate and improve the metadata set, they do not provide a quickly ascertainable indication of its overall quality. For this reason, a quantification of each metric in the form of a score is derived to describe the fulfillment of this metric in a quick and easy way.

Aspects that are considered particularly important are given a higher score than less important aspects. An essential criterion for assigning individual maximal achievable scores is the classification of metadata properties into relevance classes according to DCAT-AP (mandatory, recommended, optional). In addition, the importance of the metric in the context of the FAIR and the 5-star principles influences the individual maximal achievable scores.

Each score is computed based on the test results of each metric. Most metric values are boolean, so a value of true receives the maximum score and false a score of zero. There are three metrics that test aspects different to the presence of a property or the use of a controlled vocabulary: In case of DCAT-AP Compliance, the agreement of the metadata with DCAT-AP is tested. As soon as at least one issue is found, the test is considered negative and the score of the metric is zero. In case of the access URL (Access URL Status Code) and the download URL (Download URL Status Code), the returned status must be a HTTP success code 2xx to indicate a successful request, and to receive the maximum score.

Aggregated quality scores enable the comparison of the metadata quality of different catalogs, datasets and distributions. Overall quality scores are computed by summarizing the individual scores. These are provided for each catalog, each dataset and each distribution. Aggregated quality scores are available for each of the five dimensions as well as overall. The higher the ratings, the higher the quality of the metadata set.

3.3 DCAT-AP Quality Metrics Data Model

Table 1. Quality Measurement

DQV Quality Measurement
rdfs:type dqv:QualityMeasurement
dqv:isMeasurementOf
dqv:value
dqv:computedOn
prov:generatedAtTime

Table 2. Quality Annotation

DQV Quality Annotation
rdfs:type dqv:QualityAnnotation
oa:hasBody
dqv:inDimension
oa:motivatedBy
dc:isVersionOf
oa:hasTarget
prov:generatedAtTime

Both the measurements of the metrics as well as the calculated scores are stored using our custom DQV data model. All measurements are stored as *DQV Quality Measurements* except for the DCAT-AP Compliance metric, i.e. the SHACL validation report, which is persisted as *DQV Quality Annotation*. The resulting quality metrics graph contains a set of those classes, one for each metric defined, including additional properties providing detailed information.

The Quality Measurement (see Table 1) describes the metric tested (dqv: isMeasurementOf), the test result (dqv: value), which resource was tested (dqv: computedOn) and when the result was measured (prov: generatedAtTime). The Quality Annotation (see Table 2) includes the SHACL validation (oa: hasBody) property, the dimension this metric is part of (dqv: inDimension) as well as the description of the motivation for the creation of the annotation (oa: motivatedBy). The DCAT-AP version (dc: isVersionOf), the resource the test was performed on (oa: hasTarget) and the point in time those results were generated (prov: generatedAtTime) are also described.

4   A Scalable Metrics Pipeline

This section presents our practical implementation of the DCAT-AP-QM, that we call Piveau Metrics. It consists of four major layers: A persistence layer where the quality data is stored, a pipeline layer, that periodically creates the quality measurements and assessments for a given corpus of DCAT-AP datasets, a service layer that processes the generated data and provides an API for further usage and a UI layer that presents the results to the end user. Each layer consists of several sub-components, where each one is implemented as an individual Web service. Piveau Metrics follows a microservice architecture making the solution highly scalable and extendable. All services were developed in Java and Kotlin and support a container-based cloud deployment. Figure 1 illustrates the layers and their respective services.

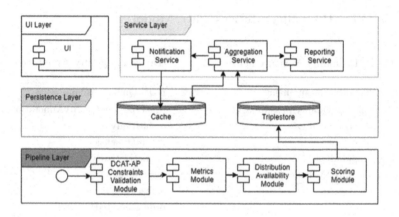

Fig. 1. Overview of Piveau Metrics Layers

4.1   Persistence Layer

The Persistence Layer comprises two different storage solutions: a triplestore graph database and a document database serving as cache. The triplestore is used to store the metric measurements and scores as RDF encoded with DQV. For each DCAT-AP dataset a dedicated named graph is generated. An important feature is that existing graphs are not overwritten, but new ones are created each time the pipeline is triggered providing a history of all previous measurements. The cache is used to store (aggregated) scores that are derived from the metrics graphs - for instance catalog quality scores. This allows for much faster access to this information compared to retrieving them on-the-fly from the DQV data.

4.2   Pipeline Layer

The Pipeline Layer consists of four modules determining the actual scores for each dataset. Ideally, the pipeline is triggered when a dataset is created or an existing one gets updated. Each DCAT-AP dataset passes the services of this layer in a predefined order, where the measurements for each metric and the (aggregated) quality scores are determined. The resulting DQV graph is sent to the triplestore. This pipeline is flexible and easily extendable, so that there is a straightforward path to adding new validation services.

- The *DCAT-AP Constraints Validation Module* constitutes the entry point of the pipeline. It validates the dataset against the official SHACL rules of DCAT-AP. It can manage multiple versions of SHACL shapes to evolve with the standard and support domains beyond DCAT-AP.
- The *Metrics Module* applies the main part of our DCAT-AP-QM to the dataset and returns the result as a DQV encoded payload. It iterates over all properties and applies the defined validations as described in Sect. 3.1.
- The *Distribution Availability Module* checks the availability of each distribution by validating if the access and download URLs are reachable and downloadable. To save resources an HTTP head request is used for the check. If this check fails, an HTTP GET request can also be utilized.
- The *Scoring Module*, as final service of the pipeline, takes all results from previous services and builds the metrics graph incorporating all measurements. In addition, it calculates quality scores for each dataset, each dimension and one overall quality score and adds them to the metrics graph. The complete metrics graph is then stored in the triplestore.

4.3   Service Layer and UI Layer

The Service Layer consists of a set of services that uses the metrics results and shows certain result items in specific formats to the end user. Each service has a scheduling component that can be configured individually.

- The *Aggregation Service* retrieves the current quality scores of datasets and aggregates them into catalog scores and an overall score. These aggregated metrics are stored, ordered by type and aggregation date, in the cache. The Aggregation Service provides an API to return the most recent aggregates as well as averages for specific time frames. Apart from that, an API is offered to retrieve other results from the triplestore that were generated by the Pipeline Layer, e.g. specific measurements for datasets and distributions. These APIs are used by other services in the Service Layer and by the UI Layer.
- The *Reporting Service* provides human-readable and processed reports of the measurements in PDF, ODS or XLSX format. It uses the Aggregation Service API to retrieve the current measurements and generates these reports on a predefined schedule.

– The *Notification Service* requests the measurements and scores for a catalog from the Aggregation Service and sends a notification to the data provider in case of a score deterioration for that specific catalog. The schedule for this service can be activated individually for each catalog.

The *UI Layer* provides an easy-to-use access to the measurements and scores for end users. It is a Web frontend providing diagrams and detailed information about each metric and their evolution in terms of quality. Next to the Notification Service it serves as an access point for data providers.

5   Evaluation

We evaluated our approach on two levels. Firstly, we compared the features of Piveau Metrics with existing and similar approaches to validate the novelty and relevance for the domain of open DCAT-AP datasets. Secondly, we performed a long-term test in a production environment to validate the practical feasibility and impact of the software.

5.1   Feature Comparison

The feature evaluation is based on a set of indicators that cover the theoretical concept and the practical applicability of each solution. The main focus is to evaluate the benefit for the domain of Open Data.

The *Data Check* feature allows to check the accessibility and validity of resources. The *FAIR*, *5-star*, and *DCAT-AP Support* features indicate the consideration of these principles in the different solutions. The *User Interface (UI)* and the *Application Programming Interface (API)* feature ensure that both is available to the user. The *Export* feature allows users to export the measurements as a report (e.g. PDF, JSON) and the *Notification* feature allows users to receive notifications in case a score decreases. The *Score Comparison* feature enables the ranking and comparison of catalogs, datasets and/or distributions (Table 3).

Table 3. Feature Comparison of Open Data Quality Tools

Feature	Piveau Metrics	Sem-Quire	Open Data Portal Watch	FAIR Evaluator	FAIR Checker	F-UJI
Data Check	x	x	x	x	x	x
FAIR Support	x	-	-	x	x	x
5-star Support	x	-	-	-	-	-
DCAT-AP Support	x	-	x	-	-	x
UI/API	x/x	x/x	x/x	x/x	x/x	x/x
Export	x	x	x	x	x	x
Notification	x	-	-	-	-	-
Score Comparison	x	-	-	-	-	-

The evaluation reveals that the related projects utilize distinct standards and principles as a basis for their quality assessment. Similar to our approach, SemQuire utilizes the DQV, and the Open Data Portal Watch framework suggests a set of metrics within the scope of the DCAT specification. The authors of the FAIR Evaluator, the FAIR Checker, and the F-UJI solutions focus on representing the FAIR principles in their implementations. In contrast to our approach, most other solutions restrict the analysis to a single resource at a time. Also, none of the related projects provides a dashboard that presents the quality measurements and quality scores in a comparative view.

5.2   Use Case: data.europa.eu

We applied our solution in a large-scale real-world production system to evaluate its feasibility, scalability, and possible impact on the data quality. Therefore, Piveau Metrics was tightly integrated into the metadata registry and acquisition components of data.europa.eu[14]. The portal is provided by the European Commission and constitutes the central aggregation point for European Open Data. As of March 2023 it lists more than 1.6 million datasets, gathered from more than 170 regional, national, and pan-national data catalogs. It applies DCAT-AP as core data model and storage format. A detailed overview of the underlying software architecture of data.europa.eu can be found in [4]. The Pipeline Layer to create the actual quality information is integrated in the harvesting process, where the metadata is retrieved from the various data sources regularly. Each DCAT-AP dataset is forwarded to the Pipeline Layer, processed and the resulting DCAT-AP-QM is stored alongside the actual dataset in the triplestore of data.europa.eu. The Service Layer is retrieving the quality information from the triplestore to feed the Aggregation Service, the Notification Service and the Reporting Service. (cf. Fig. 1) A dedicated user interface (UI Layer), the Metadata Quality Dashboard (MQD)[15] acts as comprehensive interface providing multiple aggregations (provided by the Aggregation Service) of the scores for the different dimensions and metrics (e.g. the scores for a specific point in time and/or catalog). Figure 2 shows a selection of views. For each catalog users can access a dedicated view and download the reports (provided by the Reporting Service) in multiple formats. Furthermore, for readability the score is transformed into a simple rating with four ranges: excellent, good, sufficient, and bad.

The system is in place since September 2021, when it monitored 74 catalogs. Since then the portal has grown and Piveau Metrics is constantly monitoring the plethora of datasets and catalogs. As of March 2023 the triplestore holds more than 64 million discrete quality values for the current corpus of datasets. The historic data sums up to more than 1.4 billion quality values. Hence, from a technical point of view, including feasibility and scalability, our solution can be successfully applied in a production use case.

---

[14] https://data.europa.eu.
[15] https://data.europa.eu/mqa.

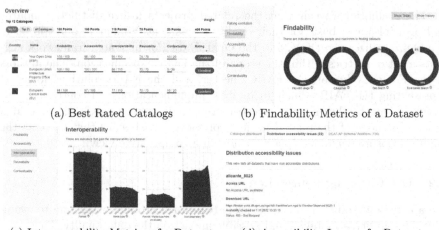

(a) Best Rated Catalogs   (b) Findability Metrics of a Dataset

(c) Interoperability Metrics of a Dataset   (d) Accessibility Issues of a Dataset

Fig. 2. Overview of MQD in data.europa.eu

One objective of our work is the lasting quality improvement of Open Data. Therefore we examined, how the quality evolved over time. The Aggregation Service allows to retrieve scores for specific points in time[16]. We retrieved the overall scores and scores for each of the five dimensions for each catalog and calculated the average across all catalogs. In order to include as many catalogs as possible we chose January 2022 as baseline and the current month March 2023 as comparison. Within this period complete measurements for 164 catalogs are available[17]. Table 4 shows the results and indicates a slight tendency towards better data quality. The overall score has improved and the average rating moved from sufficient to good. Accordingly, the values for the five dimensions improved, with the exception of findability, that dropped minimally. The table also shows the percentage of catalogs that have good/excellent ratings and bad ratings. The increase in the first category and the decrease in the latter reveals a positive progress. In general, we do not claim a correlation between the application of our tool and the improved quality, since many aspects can contribute to this and datasets are constantly added and removed. However, our solution supports a transparent and fine-grained evaluation of the metadata quality. Successive quality improvements can be more evidence-based by both, portal operators and data providers.

---

[16] https://data.europa.eu/api/mqa/cache/.
[17] The raw data can be found here: https://doi.org/10.5281/zenodo.8016840.

Table 4. Average Scores, Values and Ratings between 2022 and 2023

	2022-01	2023-03
Overall Score	218	225
Overall Rating	Sufficient	Good
Findability Value	72	71
Accessibility Value	53	54
Interoperability Value	38	42
Reusability Value	51	52
Contextuality Value	4	7
Good and Excellent Ratings	54%	56%
Bad Ratings	17%	13%

6 Conclusions and Future Work

In this paper we have presented our methodology, data model and practical implementation for assessing and reporting the quality of DCAT-AP datasets. DCAT-AP is a widely adopted RDF-based specification for describing metadata of Open Data. Although DCAT-AP defines many expressive properties and vocabularies to be used, a qualitative and accurate implementation by Open Data providers is challenging. Therefore, we designed quality metrics for DCAT-AP datasets based on a practical view on the FAIR and 5-star principles. We propose a set of specific metrics within the five dimensions findability, accessibility, interoperability, reusability and contextuality. In essence, these metrics cover the valid assignment of critical properties, the compliance with the DCAT-AP specification based on SHACL, and the availability of the actual data. Based on the values of these metrics, we determine overall scores allowing to assess and compare the quality of datasets. The results of the quality evaluations are stored in a custom RDF model based on the Data Quality Vocabulary (DQV), called DCAT-AP-QM data model. We implemented our approach as a scalable and reusable solution to demonstrate its feasibility and implications. Our software is called Piveau Metrics and mainly divided into two processing layers: a pipeline layer to constantly calculate the metrics over a corpus of DCAT-AP datasets and a service layer to provide the results and aggregation reports to applications and users. We compared our approach with existing work in the field of Open Data quality assessment and showed that Piveau Metrics offers the broadest set of features for our application scenario. In addition, with data.europa.eu, we applied our solution in a large-scale production environment. It constantly checks more than 1.6 million DCAT-AP datasets and provides quality reports to the data providers. The DCAT-AP-QM data model and Piveau Metrics is available as Open Source[18].

---

[18] https://gitlab.com/piveau/metrics.

With our work we have shown, that the FAIR principles, the 5-star principles and established RDF standards, such as SHACL and DQV constitute an appropriate foundation to measure and report the quality, completeness and validity of DCAT-AP datasets. This effectively can close the gap between the formal specification and the practical difficulties in applying DCAT-AP.

With data.europa.eu we have built a showcase to demonstrate how quality reports, scoring and rating can be communicated to data providers and interested users. We believe that such an open communication is crucial to increase the quality of Open Data in the future. It introduces a certain degree of gamification and can nudge data providers to improve their data. However, the evolution of the scores illustrated in Sect. 5.2 are only showing a slight improvement. This indicates that data providers need to engage more with the reports and incorporate the insights into their publication processes. Therefore, we aim to improve the feedback loop of our approach and introduce more notification and alert features towards the data providers.

The service-based architecture allows to integrate Piveau Metrics into a variety of management solutions for DCAT-AP. Piveau Metrics is under active development and constantly adapted to changes around the DCAT-AP specification, such as the introduction of Data Services. We want to refine and broaden our quality metrics and include additional aspects, such as the CARE principles[19] and other best practices for Open Data publication. We also intend to extend our quality metrics to data itself, supporting file-type-specific metrics to evaluate the quality of the actual data.

Acknowledgements. This work has been funded by the European Commission under framework contract 10801 (European Data Portal Managed Services - data.europa.eu), by the Federal Ministry of Education and Research of Germany (BMBF) under grant number 16DII138 (Weizenbaum-Institut) and by the German Research Foundation (DFG) under project numbers 441926934 (NFDI4Cat) and 460234259 (NFDI4DataScience).

The authors would like to thank our colleagues Benjamin Dittwald, Fritz Franzke, and Simon Dutkowski for contributing to the development and architecture of Piveau Metrics.

References

1. European Commission: About DCAT application profile for data portals in Europe | Joinup (2021). https://joinup.ec.europa.eu/solution/dcat-application-profile-data-portals-europe/about
2. Devaraju, A., Huber, R.: F-UJI - an automated FAIR data assessment tool (2020). https://doi.org/10.5281/zenodo.4063720
3. Devaraju, A., Huber, R.: F-UJI : An Automated Assessment Tool for Improving the FAIRness of Research Data (2020). https://doi.org/10.5281/zenodo.4068347
4. Kirstein, F., Stefanidis, K., Dittwald, B., Dutkowski, S., Urbanek, S., Hauswirth, M.: Piveau: a large-scale open data management platform based on semantic web

---

[19] https://www.gida-global.org/care.

technologies. In: Harth, A., et al. (eds.) ESWC 2020. LNCS, vol. 12123, pp. 648–664. Springer, Cham (2020). https://doi.org/10.1007/978-3-030-49461-2_38
5. Kubler, S., Robert, J., Neumaier, S., Umbrich, J., Le Traon, Y.: Comparison of metadata quality in open data portals using the analytic hierarchy process. Gov. Inf. Q. **35**(1), 13–29 (2018). https://doi.org/10.1016/j.giq.2017.11.003. https://hal.science/hal-01672652
6. Langer, A., Siegert, V., Göpfert, C., Gaedke, M.: SemQuire - assessing the data quality of linked open data sources based on DQV. In: Pautasso, C., Sánchez-Figueroa, F., Systä, K., Murillo Rodríguez, J.M. (eds.) ICWE 2018. LNCS, vol. 11153, pp. 163–175. Springer, Cham (2018). https://doi.org/10.1007/978-3-030-03056-8_14
7. Neumaier, S., Thurnay, L., Lampoltshammer, T.J., Knap, T.: Search, filter, fork, and link open data: the adequate platform: data- and community-driven quality improvements. In: Companion Proceedings of the The Web Conference 2018, WWW 2018, pp. 1523–1526. International World Wide Web Conferences Steering Committee, Republic and Canton of Geneva, CHE (2018). https://doi.org/10.1145/3184558.3191602
8. Neumaier, S., Umbrich, J., Polleres, A.: Automated quality assessment of metadata across open data portals. J. Data Inf. Q. **8**(1), 1–29 (2016). https://doi.org/10.1145/2964909
9. Reiche, K.J., Höfig, E., Schieferdecker, I.: Assessment and visualization of metadata quality for open government data. In: Proceedings of the International Conference for E-Democrazy and Open Government, CeDEM 2014 (2014)
10. Rosnet, T., Lefort, V., Devignes, M.D., Gaignard, A.: FAIR-Checker, a web tool to support the findability and reusability of digital life science resources (2021). https://doi.org/10.5281/zenodo.5914307
11. Vetro, A., Canova, L., Torchiano, M., Minotas, C., Iemma, R., Morando, F.: Open data quality measurement framework: definition and application to open government data. Gov. Inf. Q. **33**, 325–337 (2016). https://doi.org/10.1016/j.giq.2016.02.001
12. W3C: Data Catalog Vocabulary (DCAT). https://www.w3.org/TR/vocab-dcat/
13. Wang, R.Y., Strong, D.M.: Beyond accuracy: what data quality means to data consumers. J. Manag. Inf. Syst. **12**(4), 5–33 (1996). https://doi.org/10.1080/07421222.1996.11518099
14. Wilkinson, M.D., et al.: The FAIR guiding principles for scientific data management and stewardship. Sci. Data **3**(1), 1–9 (2016)
15. Wilkinson, M.D., et al.: Evaluating FAIR maturity through a scalable, automated, community-governed framework. Sci. Data **6**, 174 (2019). https://www.nature.com/articles/s41597-019-0184-5
16. Zaveri, A., Rula, A., Maurino, A., Pietrobon, R., Lehmann, J., Auer, S.: Quality assessment for linked data: a survey. Semantic Web **7**, 63–93 (2015). https://doi.org/10.3233/SW-150175

Drivers of Dissatisfaction with an Open Government Data Portal: A Critical Incident Technique Approach

Alizée Francey[✉] [iD]

Swiss Graduate School of Public Administration, University of Lausanne, Lausanne, Switzerland
alizee.francey@unil.ch

Abstract. Open government data (OGD) has emerged as a crucial aspect of digital transformation strategies, prompting many governments to establish national OGD portals to facilitate access to large amounts of public sector datasets. However, despite the OGD portals' goal of serving as intermediaries between OGD producers and OGD users, they have faced numerous criticisms for their low use and failure to adequately meet users' needs. The lack of consensus within the OGD community on the sources of dissatisfaction with the OGD portals and their negative impact on their use warrants a detailed examination of users' dissatisfying experiences. Taking a user-centred perspective, I adopt a critical incident technique (CIT) approach to identify the drivers and sources of dissatisfaction with a national OGD portal. Based on my analysis, a descriptive model is proposed to help to comprehend the interrelations between three sources of dissatisfaction with the OGD portal and ten respective drivers: OGD production (i.e., development of high-quality datasets, completeness of the metadata), OGD distribution (i.e., accessibility of the datasets, organisation of the datasets, centralisation of the datasets, search engine, interface, visualisation), and OGD use (i.e., skills and knowledge, and added value).

Keywords: Open Government Data · Dissatisfaction · CIT

1 Introduction

Over the past years, governments have been keen data producers [1]. While government-produced data were initially made accessible through statistical reports or after long and official request processes [2], the emergence of policy debates demanding more transparency gave rise to Open Government Data (OGD). OGD are data produced by state bodies made freely accessible, modifiable, sharable, and usable by anyone with minimal control mechanisms like copyright, price, or repurposing restrictions [3]. As a strong hypothesis in the OGD community is that the value from OGD can best be generated when datasets are being used, previous research pointed out that opening datasets needs to be accompanied by OGD portals to facilitate the distribution of datasets [2, 4–6]. Typically implemented as web-based catalogue systems, OGD portals allow producers

© IFIP International Federation for Information Processing 2023
Published by Springer Nature Switzerland AG 2023
I. Lindgren et al. (Eds.): EGOV 2023, LNCS 14130, pp. 279–294, 2023.
https://doi.org/10.1007/978-3-031-41138-0_18

to upload their datasets while affording users to download the datasets judged to be useful through the portal' search engine or directly via Application Programming Interfaces (API) [4, 6]. Altogether, the OGD portals aim to afford further use by playing the intermediary role between the OGD producers (i.e., public administrations or organisations with a state mandate) and the OGD users (by definition, anyone with interest in the datasets) [2]. These OGD portals received many criticisms fuelled by the fact that datasets are being shared on OGD portals, assuming that they are meant to be further used while their use remains low in practice [7–10].

It is necessary to investigate users' needs to address the low use of OGD portals. Previous research has shown that any information system (IS) not meeting users' needs may not be used [11]. It is thus time to investigate the users' needs [12, 13] especially given that users have reported that OGD portals do not cater to their needs [14]. Given that OGD users can be anyone interested in the datasets, there is a great diversity of user types with respective capacities and interests [15, 16]. However, like for any IS, it can be assumed that there are power and minimalist users. Power users operate the OGD portal with accomplished experience and knowledge, enabling the use of advanced features of the OGD portal. In contrast, minimalist users lack some experience and knowledge to use all the portal's features. Since most users fall into the minimalist category operating the OGD portal with less experience and knowledge [14], investigating their needs enables to identify the lowest common minimum standards of all users' needs. Minimalist users are comprehended as users who are aware of the OGD portal and perceive its usefulness but experience issues when using the OGD portal. As with any IS, when users perceive the IS' usefulness, their overall satisfaction with the IS will make them return [17]. Accordingly, user satisfaction is understood as a successful interaction between the OGD portal and its users, whilst dissatisfaction occurs when the OGD portal does not meet users' needs.

Due to the lack of consensus within the OGD community on the sources of dissatisfaction with the OGD portal and the consequent negative impact on its use, my research seeks to identify the drivers that generate users' dissatisfaction with the OGD portal. Identifying the drivers of dissatisfaction with the OGD portal is needed because the pressure on governments has augmented, given, on the one side, the high investments made by governments and, on the other side, the fact that OGD use remains low in practice [13]. Hence, to ensure minimal use of the OGD portal, researchers and policymakers need to identify the drivers of users' dissatisfaction with the OGD portal. Based on the findings, concrete actions can be taken to improve users' experiences and achieve the desired outcomes of the OGD portal, thereby alleviating the existing political pressure associated with low OGD use. To accomplish this, I adopt a critical incident technique (CIT) approach to identify drivers of dissatisfaction with the OGD portal. Thus, my study's research question is: What are the drivers of dissatisfaction with the OGD portal? Since my approach intends to conduct an in-depth analysis of a national OGD portal, the best outcomes could be achieved by covering the portal to which the author belongs. Therefore, this paper focuses on the national OGD portal of Switzerland. My study is structured as follows: I first outline the background of the paper, then present the research methodology before exposing the results leading to the discussion and conclusion.

2   Background

2.1   Expectation Disconfirmation Theory

Previous research demonstrated the importance of understanding and managing expectations in various contexts through the Expectation Disconfirmation Theory (EDT). Not surprisingly, EDT has also been applied to study IS adoption, use, and satisfaction [18–21]. EDT is often used to explain the level of satisfaction based on users' expectations. According to EDT, outperforming expectations is seen as positive disconfirmation leading to satisfaction [22]. On the other hand, falling short of expectations is seen as a negative disconfirmation leading to dissatisfaction [22]. Disconfirmation is thus a subjective comparison resulting from thinking that performance was better (i.e., positive disconfirmation) or worse (i.e., negative disconfirmation) than expected [22, 23]. While expectations are one's pre-use beliefs about how the IS will perform based on its features, performance is one's post-use beliefs about how the IS performs [23]. EDT posits that users typically compare their perceived performance with their expectations leading to positive or negative disconfirmation affecting satisfaction or dissatisfaction [24]. In the context of my paper, if the OGD portal surpasses expectations, users are likely to be satisfied with the OGD portal (i.e., positive disconfirmation). Conversely, if the OGD portal falls below expectations, it will be perceived as negative disconfirmation by users, leading to dissatisfaction.

2.2   About Users' Dissatisfaction

Understanding users' needs is a critical aspect of developing successful systems. For that purpose, prior research has studied user adoption and intentions to use OGD [5, 25, 26]. However, simply adopting and intending to use OGD is not enough, as a common assumption regarding OGD use is that opening government data is meaningful only so far as they are used [27]. Minimal use of the OGD portal is thus required to ensure that OGD are used, not just published [2, 5]. Accordingly, the OGD portal cannot be considered successful if not used by its users [28]. Combining this with EDT means that if the system performs better than expected, it leads to users' satisfaction and reinforces the users' attitude towards the system. If the system performs worse than expected, it produces adverse effects and complaints, bringing its share of dissatisfaction. In sum, if there have been satisfying past experiences with OGD, users are more likely to interact again with the OGD portal [2, 29], while dissatisfied users tend to stop using it [28].

Studying users' dissatisfaction with the OGD portal is needed to improve users' experience. Studying users' dissatisfaction is all the more relevant given that users' experience is a function of what users remember, and users are better at remembering bad experiences in the government context [30]. One negative incident – such as a poor-quality dataset downloaded from the OGD portal, the search engine, which does not find the desired datasets or the help functionalities not addressing the asked questions – can bring its share of dissatisfaction and discredit the users' overall impression of the OGD portal. By studying users' dissatisfaction with the OGD portal, the aim is to make negative incidents with the OGD portal as rare as possible, especially because negative incidents, in the government context, affect average user (dis)satisfaction four times more than positive incidents [30]. Accordingly, identifying where and when such dissatisfying experiences occur enables targeted interventions to make these negative incidents as rare as possible. Hence, knowing what drivers make users dissatisfied creates opportunities for improving the OGD portal to avoid or limit the recurrence of such negative incidents. To do so, I focus on user experience using the critical incident technique (CIT) because users can only develop dissatisfaction after having hands-on experience with the OGD portal.

3   Critical Incident Technique

I used the CIT to address my research question. Introduced in the social sciences by Flanagan [31], the CIT is a well-established qualitative research tool which consists of "a set of procedures for collecting direct observations of human behaviour" [31]. The choice of the CIT was motivated by three of its features. Firstly, it provides a relatively fast diagnosis of the problematic aspects of users' needs. Secondly, I believe it is the suitable method to identify the drivers of dissatisfaction with the OGD portal because the technique emphasises incidents (i.e., things which happened and were directly observed) that are critical (i.e., things which significantly affected the outcome). Thirdly, CIT brings valuable practical implications [32].

CIT relies on a set of procedures for collecting observations of human behaviour, analysing, and classifying them to be useful in addressing practical problems [33]. By retrieving critical incidents, CIT requires answers based neither on intuitions nor opinions but on facts, which allows for turning factual anecdotes into data [34]. As the data are collected from the respondents' perspective, CIT allows respondents a free range of responses as they can use their terms and languages to recall their experiences [33]. By being sufficiently complete, the critical incident leaves little doubt concerning its effects, allowing inferences and predictions to be made [31]. In that sense, an incident is deemed critical when it contributes to or detracts from the general aim of the activity in a significant way [32, 33]. Applied to my study, I understand by critical incident any story containing a clear and detailed example of a user's experience while using the OGD portal. I focus on the negative critical incident, which is any dissatisfying experience with the OGD portal, that is, all users' encounters with the OGD portal, resulting in frustration and dissatisfaction.

3.1   Data Collection

To investigate the drivers of dissatisfaction with the OGD portal, I employed CIT to collect critical incidents from users of the national OGD portal of Switzerland. This national OGD portal serves as a typical case for other countries due to its adherence to the Comprehensive Knowledge Archive Network (CKAN) [35], which is recognised as the international and de-facto standard for OGD portals [2]. Although minor variations may exist in the front-end implementation of the portals, the CKAN standard ensures a high level of technical interoperability across portals by establishing metadata standards and tools to facilitate the interaction between the portals and their users [2].

To collect my data, I employed the focus-group interview technique due to its ability to reduce the cost in time and personnel while retaining the advantages of individual interviews, such as the interviewer's ability to establish contact, provide explanations, and answer questions [31]. The effectiveness of this technique has been excellent [31]. My sample consisted of 23 public managers from diverse branches (and levels) of the Swiss government, including IT, Education and Research, Health, Finances, Foreign Affairs, and Information Services. Since most users of OGD fall into the minimalist category operating the OGD portal with less experience and knowledge [14], this study aims to investigate their needs. Thus, I followed a purposive sampling strategy to recruit participants following a certificate of advanced studies in Digital Government, a certified on-the-job training program for managers in public organisations from federal, cantonal, and communal levels responsible for or engaged in public digitalisation projects. In consideration of the participants' engagement in public digitalisation projects, participants displayed a level of awareness regarding the OGD portal and acknowledged its usefulness. However, they lacked some experience and knowledge to use all the portal's features, leading to issues when using the OGD portal.

I conducted three focus-group interviews in November 2021, all structured around open-ended questions that encouraged participants to brainstorm and describe their dissatisfying experiences when using the OGD portal. The open-ended questions were designed to focus on the specific features of the OGD portal and the characteristics of the datasets, considering participants' resources and capabilities during their interactions with the OGD portal. Each participant was free to share dissatisfying experiences spontaneously when using the OGD portal, which allowed other participants to bounce back by commenting on the shared experiences, adding new elements, or developing other experiences. The interviewer played the role of facilitator, encouraging the discussion to generate data based on participants' interactions. It was fluent for the interviewer to manage the existing relationships and create an environment where participants were relaxed and encouraged to exchange their experiences. Indeed, participants were well informed about the purpose of the study, knew each other from following the same certificate of advanced studies, and previously agreed to engage in the discussions fully. Participants were asked to provide specific details of their dissatisfying experiences and explain why each experience was particularly dissatisfying. Before starting the focus-group interviews, participants provided informed consent to be recorded. The focus-group interviews lasted approximately one hour and concluded when participants could not report additional incidents. I transcribed the interviews verbatim using the recordings.

3.2 Data Analysis

To analyse the data collected from the focus-group interviews, I used content analysis, a systematic approach to identify and categorise patterns and themes in the data [36]. I used an inductive approach to analyse the data and identify critical incidents that were used as the primary unit of analysis. Only incidents that occurred while users were using the OGD portal contained a clear example of dissatisfying experience and were described in sufficient detail for research analysis were considered. A total of 140 incidents were identified, which I grouped into drivers of dissatisfaction based on similarities in the reported experiences using an analytical induction process [32, 37]. Following the initial content analysis of the critical incidents identified, I elaborated ten drivers of dissatisfaction by grouping the critical incidents according to their meanings. The drivers and their names were not preconceived but flowed from the data [37]. Moreover, to get a higher level of abstraction, I repeated the process and regrouped the ten drivers into three sources of dissatisfaction by identifying where and when the drivers and their respective incidents occurred. This higher level of abstraction enables the identification of the responsible stakeholders and the development of targeted interventions.

Regarding sizes, most studies examined 50 to 100 incidents [38]. My 140 critical incidents provide sufficient theoretical saturation, especially as the last group interviewed did not report any critical incident that required the development of a new driver. My approach captured the essential sources of dissatisfaction while retaining the granularity through the drivers and specific details through the identified incidents.

4   Results

The drivers and sources become essential for understanding dissatisfaction with the OGD portal. The higher level of abstraction allows to identify where and when such dissatisfying experiences occurred and the responsible stakeholders. I present my results through the drivers and sources of dissatisfaction, not by detailing each identified critical incident. However, statements from the critical incidents are cited for illustrative purposes. The results indicate that dissatisfaction with the OGD portal arises from three sources: OGD production, OGD distribution, and OGD use. Hence, dissatisfying experiences with the OGD portal are not limited to issues exclusively related to the OGD portal but also encompass negative incidents related to OGD production and OGD use. From Fig. 1, one can see that when analysing dissatisfaction with the OGD portal, from the 140 critical incidents identified during the focus-group interviews, the most prominent source is OGD distribution (83 incidents), followed by OGD use (29 incidents), and finally, OGD production (28 incidents). Research on critical incidents suggests that what is important is how many times incidents occurred [39]. Given that the frequency of critical incidents is relevant in CIT because it is their frequency which stands these incidents out [40], Fig. 1 relates the number of critical incidents per driver and source. The results show how users fall short of expectations and how dissatisfying experiences and drivers of dissatisfaction lead to negative disconfirmation and dissatisfaction.

4.1   OGD Production

Before being published on the OGD portal, datasets are generated by OGD producers (e.g., public administrations and organisations with a state mandate...). The first source of dissatisfaction stems from OGD production, as it determines if the datasets may (or not) be exploited to their full potential. My results demonstrate that OGD production can lead to dissatisfaction with the OGD portal if the datasets provided do not align with users' expectations. This first source of dissatisfaction with the OGD portal does not pertain to the information produced by the OGD portal itself but is instead the result of the work of OGD producers. This means that the work performed by OGD producers

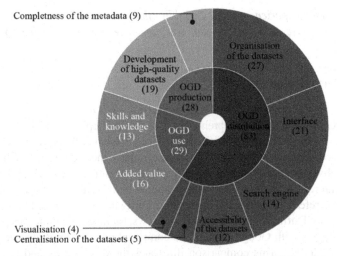

Fig. 1. Drivers and sources of dissatisfaction with the OGD portal

directly affects users' dissatisfaction with the OGD portal. In summary, users' expectations regarding OGD production can result in disconfirmation with the produced OGD, ultimately leading to dissatisfaction with the OGD portal. Two drivers of dissatisfaction related to OGD production are the development of high-quality datasets and the completeness of the metadata.

The first driver contains 19 incidents, including incomplete or outdated datasets, dead links, or empty tables. The lack of high-quality datasets' development impedes the use of the OGD portal, given that users cannot take the best advantage of the datasets, which leads to frustration and dissatisfaction. This is especially true given that the users have a snapshot of several datasets, which inspires ideas for use but is directly hindered by poor data quality. An illustrative example of such incidents is mentioned below:

> *"Typically, some data could be used for marketing purposes to do customer targeting, but the problem is that I don't have a guarantee of having the latest data. I wouldn't have been able to use the found dataset for marketing purposes as it was from 2016 to 2018 and then stopped. […] I cannot set up a customer targeting with a dataset outdated by three years."*

The second driver, containing nine incidents, pertains to the absence of contextual information or incomplete datasets descriptions that are essential for datasets' subsequent use. The fact that the metadata is incomplete produces a feeling of dissatisfaction, as illustrated below:

> *"And even the datasets, when you find them, you think "Ah great, this one looks interesting". But when you export the dataset, you don't have the information on the metadata. I opened one dataset about private use of the internet and internet security. There are some concepts which are not explained. So, when they mention fishing, you think, well, fishing from the person? Fishing from his email?*

Has the person experienced this? I couldn't find out if it were actual experiences or something else... So, in the end, you can't use that data, at least from my experience."

4.2 OGD Distribution

By cataloguing the datasets from OGD producers, the OGD portal facilitates users' access to OGD. Acting as a comprehensive "one-stop-shop", the OGD portal enables users to search and retrieve the desired datasets. Consequently, both the OGD portal and individual perceptions of its performance impact the extent to which the OGD portal can deliver expected benefits. Specifically, the design of the OGD portal interface plays a crucial role in shaping users' expectations. Individuals tend to rely on previous experiences as reference points and expect uniformity in the design and functionality of online interfaces. During the focus-group interviews, for instance, numerous participants drew on analogies with Google search and compared the OGD portal's search engine to the one of Google. This comparison illustrates the discrepancy and misalignment between the users' expectations and what is provided through the OGD portal. As a result, when users' expectations are not aligned with the features offered by the OGD portal, disconfirmation with its features occurs, leading to dissatisfaction. Six drivers related to OGD distribution were identified as drivers of dissatisfaction with the OGD portal. These drivers include the accessibility, organisation, and centralisation of the datasets as well as features of the portal itself, such as interface design, poor search capabilities, or inadequate visualisation tools.

The first driver is the accessibility of the datasets, which contains 12 incidents. The challenges associated with accessing datasets raise fundamental questions about the portal's purpose, as illustrated below:

"The portal doesn't make data access much easier; it puts data in one place but doesn't make accessibility much easier [...]. If I entered the keywords I put on the portal directly into Google, I could reach the data source almost as fast."

The second driver, concerning the organisation of the datasets, includes 27 incidents and relates to issues such as the lack of standardisation, aggregation, and hierarchy of the datasets. In addition, users also expressed dissatisfaction with the absence of a minimal data model, which contributed to their frustration. This sentiment is exemplified in the following statements:

"I have the impression that they did their thing, they said to themselves that's good and then pushed all the information they had, and then if there are cantons that are over-represented and others that don't play the game, that's fine. [...] Okay, we have a lot of stuff... But at the end, it's like when I tell my son to clean up his room, and he puts everything under the bed... The categories are poorly organised. I have the impression they gave a mandate to an intern over the summer."

The third driver pertains to the centralisation of the datasets and includes five incidents. While most incidents are prone to dissatisfaction, incidents relating to the centralisation of the datasets are more nuanced. The nuance arises from the fact that while users acknowledge the advantage of centralising datasets, they are not entirely convinced of how this has been accomplished, as illustrated in the following statement:

"[The portal] main use is to search only in one place... Yeah, it's not bad; it's a kind of reference. [...]"

The fourth driver includes 21 incidents and pertains to the interface design of the OGD portal, particularly concerning the lack of state endorsement, ease of use, and language disparities. While some aspects of the interface design are mentioned positively, users expressed dissatisfaction with practical aspects that hinder their use of OGD, as exemplified in the following statement:

"In terms of features, there are a lot of things; there are nice logos, lots of inputs etc... But in the end, it's a bit like having an aeroplane cockpit full of buttons and possibilities, but the cockpit is put on the handlebars of a bicycle."

"I always come across pages that are not in my language. The page, including the text of the law, is in English. It's not even a national language! And, indeed, the portal is not translated into the national languages, at least not all of them."

The fifth driver contains 14 incidents and pertains to the lack of performance of the search engine and the fact that one needs to be very precise to find relevant datasets, leading to frustration. The poor search engine capabilities lead to frustration and dissatisfaction, as illustrated in the following statements:

"As soon as you know exactly what you are looking for, that's when it's over. If you don't know, you explore the portal, and it's okay."

"I found that it only reasoned at one level, so I don't know if the keywords will also search in the database or if it will only search in the description, in the title or whatever. But as a result, I looked, for example, for things related to mobility, and there were relatively few documents that came up, whereas when you go to the mobility section, there are many things that come up."

The sixth driver pertains to the lack of visualisation options and includes four incidents. According to participants' statements, having more visualisation options would facilitate the use and exploitation of datasets as visualisations are seen as means of supporting the use by inspiring possibilities. The following illustration provides an overview:

"The problem is that the portal also lacks a minimum of visualisation... Let's imagine that the description doesn't provide everything needed for a complete visualisation... We should at least have a minimum of visualisation for some data so that we can tell ourselves: I'm interested in this data because it can be cool to be used as shown. So, at least have an overview of some visualisations' possibilities."

4.3 OGD Use

The third source of dissatisfaction relates to OGD use, which relies on the users and is subject to their capacities. Two drivers of dissatisfaction related to OGD use pertain to the lack of skills and knowledge and the perceived lack of added value. Unaligned expectations related to OGD use can lead to disconfirmation of the OGD use and dissatisfaction with the OGD portal. The critical incidents retrieved indicate that dissatisfaction can arise when users find themselves limited in using the OGD portal, either due to their lack of skills and knowledge or the lack of tutorial and help functionalities available on the OGD portal. However, the 13 incidents identified have been grouped into skills and knowledge, as the quality of support users need depends on their capabilities. An example is illustrated through the following statement:

> "I came across something; now I don't remember exactly what it's called, a kind of format or whatever, that I should have had a program to read [...] I had a pop-up message saying I had to transform the data but couldn't. I couldn't process the datasets in the format I got."

The last driver pertains to the perceived lack of added value of the OGD portal. This driver comprises 16 incidents where users expressed dissatisfaction due to the portal's incapacity to provide good automation and additional guarantees on datasets' quality. This driver highlights how users' dissatisfaction stems from their perceptions that the OGD portal does not offer enough added value compared to alternative data sources. This sentiment is encapsulated in the following statement provided by a user during the focus-group interviews:

> "The portal is a data graveyard, but we don't do anything with the datasets... Whereas if there was an added value... But there is no added value, it's a data graveyard."

5   Discussion

In this discussion section, I synthesise the results into a descriptive model of the drivers and sources of dissatisfaction with the OGD portal, as depicted in Fig. 2. By outlining the interrelations between the sources and respective drivers, the descriptive model provides a framework which helps to comprehend the interrelations between the sources of dissatisfaction with the OGD portal. By showing that the drivers and sources are interrelated and can have a cascading effect on one another, the model also illustrates the necessity to address them as part of a holistic approach. Although my descriptive model also shows the interrelations between the drivers within each source of dissatisfaction, I do not expound on the interrelations as they are inherent to their common source. My focus is thus on the interrelations across the sources and their respective drivers.

By rereading the critical incidents identified, the following interrelations between the sources and their respective drivers could be recognised: 1) Interrelations between OGD production and OGD distribution; 2) Interrelations between OGD production and OGD use; 3) Interrelations between OGD distribution and OGD use.

The descriptive model aids in understanding the process of how dissatisfaction with the OGD portal develops and which stakeholders could be held accountable. The model can help OGD stakeholders become aware of their role in the dissatisfaction with the OGD portal, including how each driver interrelates with one another. The model shows

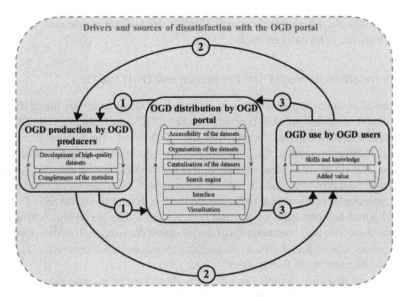

Fig. 2. Descriptive model of drivers and sources of dissatisfaction

that to avoid dissatisfying experiences with the OGD portal, a holistic approach is needed, implying concrete actions from OGD producers, the OGD portal, and OGD users. The descriptive model is developed as a recursive loop that keeps repeating indefinitely if no measure is undertaken. While the interrelations in the model are indicated using arrows, these arrows do not imply a simplistic, unilateral, or causal relationship.

5.1 Interrelations Between OGD Production and OGD Distribution (1)

My empirical evidence suggests that addressing user dissatisfaction with the OGD portal requires considering OGD production and OGD distribution as potential sources of dissatisfaction with the OGD portal. Moreover, my findings indicate that OGD production drivers are interrelated with OGD distribution drivers. For instance, a dissatisfying search engine experience may be related to the lack of structural information about the datasets, hindering their discovery. Although the search engine is a driver of OGD distribution and the responsibility of the OGD portal, its efficiency is contingent on complete metadata provided by OGD producers. This example illustrates how a driver controlled by OGD producers, such as metadata completeness, may be interrelated to another driver controlled by the OGD portal, such as the search engine. Therefore, it is essential to consider the interrelations between these drivers and address them as part of a holistic approach.

The OGD community should thus address the drivers of OGD production and OGD distribution through a holistic approach, as dissatisfaction with the OGD portal is more likely to occur if the interrelations between these sources and respective drivers are neglected. The OGD community should thus foster collaboration by facilitating communication between the OGD producers and the OGD portal to ensure a shared understanding. As an illustrative example, the OGD providers and the OGD portal could set metadata standards, which capture essential information about the datasets needed for the search engine to be more efficient.

5.2   Interrelations Between OGD Production and OGD Use (2)

My empirical evidence suggests that addressing user dissatisfaction with the OGD portal requires considering not only OGD production and OGD distribution but also OGD use as potential sources of dissatisfaction with the OGD portal. The results of my study suggest that drivers related to OGD production are interrelated with drivers related to OGD use. The empirical evidence indicates that dissatisfaction with the OGD portal is more likely if the produced datasets are not aligned with users' needs and preferences. This is particularly relevant since OGD production can determine the perceived value of the OGD portal and prevent it from being perceived as a data graveyard. Additionally, the results show how the characteristics of the produced datasets, such as their formats or timely updates, can impact their use. As an illustration, one participant said, *"I couldn't process the datasets in the format I got"*.

I may posit that understanding users' needs should not be regarded in isolation but rather in the context of what can be produced by the OGD producers. My empirical evidence indicates that dissatisfaction with the OGD portal may arise due to a misalignment between produced datasets and the users' needs. This is especially relevant since drivers related to OGD production are interrelated with those related to OGD use, creating a vicious circle. If produced datasets are not used, motivation to produce and publish datasets diminishes, and if data production is limited, motivation to use the data is also reduced. Consequently, it is crucial to consider the interrelations between these sources and respective drivers and address them as part of a holistic approach. The OGD community should thus foster a feedback loop for OGD producers and users. Engaging the dialogue should enable identifying areas where the produced datasets are not aligned with users' needs. The OGD community could help OGD producers to prioritise the production of datasets aligned with users' needs in terms of interest, format, or update, to mention a few examples. Accordingly, addressing the drivers of OGD production and OGD use through a holistic approach could foster a shared understanding of users' needs and promote a collective effort to improve the OGD ecosystem.

5.3   Interrelations Between OGD Distribution and OGD Use (3)

I may posit that drivers related to OGD distribution are interrelated with drivers related to OGD use. The results suggest an interrelation between drivers that influence the distribution of OGD and those that affect its use. Specifically, drivers related to OGD distribution play a fundamental role in OGD further use by creating a compelling reason for OGD users to visit the OGD portal. As illustrative examples, the accessibility of the datasets or visualisation options can influence users' perceptions of the added value of the OGD portal and their dissatisfaction with the OGD portal. For instance, participants would have required more visualisation options to assess whether the datasets were relevant to their needs quickly. Another key example is how users' perceptions of the added value of the OGD portal are interrelated to the centralisation of datasets.

My empirical evidence emphasises the need to consider the interrelated drivers that influence the distribution and use of OGD, as dissatisfaction with the OGD portal is more likely to occur if the interrelations between those sources and respective drivers are neglected. The OGD community should thus foster collaboration by facilitating exchanges between the OGD users and the OGD portal. For example, the OGD community could establish a users' advisory group to provide ongoing feedback, insights, and recommendations for improving the OGD portal or establish simple feedback mechanisms directly on the OGD portal. Moreover, the OGD portal could also organise workshops, webinars, tutorials, or any other educational programmes to enhance users' data skills and knowledge, which could help them navigate and use the OGD portal. Finally, the OGD community could foster communities of practice and discussion forums where users can share experiences and provide mutual support in using the OGD portal. This could help create a vibrant OGD ecosystem where the distributed OGD can be effectively used, and leverage added value.

6 Conclusion

While CIT has rarely been used in IS research, using CIT can inform practice by gaining valuable practical implications. It enables researchers to maintain scientific rigour while still meeting the interests of practitioners in applied settings [32]. In this sense, CIT provides relevant and concrete information for managers and can suggest practical improvement areas [33]. Accordingly, my study contributes to OGD research in two main ways.

First, this study proposes a descriptive model providing a framework that helps comprehend the interrelations between the sources and respective drivers of dissatisfaction with the OGD portal. Regrouping the critical incidents into drivers and again regrouping the drivers into higher levels of abstraction allows for identifying distinctive sources of dissatisfaction with the OGD portal. Identifying these sources and drivers is crucial as they may individually or jointly affect user dissatisfaction and the subsequent use of the OGD portal. Addressing each source and driver allows to target of the responsible stakeholders, which is needed for prompt and tangible actions. For example, given that drivers related to OGD production and drivers related to OGD distribution are interrelated, close collaboration between the OGD portal and OGD producers is necessary to address drivers such as developing high-quality datasets or the organisation of the datasets. To do so, OGD producers could be forced to endorse a minimal data model, including regular updates for publishing datasets. At the same time, the OGD portal could ensure that the provided datasets comply with the specific requirements of the minimal model.

Second, this study provides some evidence of the importance of studying dissatisfaction. While previous studies have focused primarily on users' satisfaction, neglecting users' dissatisfaction limits the understanding of the users' experiences. Studying dissatisfaction provides valuable insights into users' experiences, particularly since individuals tend to remember dissatisfying experiences more vividly than satisfying ones [30]. Moreover, studying dissatisfaction provides new insights as drivers of (dis)satisfaction are not necessarily two extremes of a continuum. This means that even if certain features generate satisfaction, their absence may not necessarily affect dissatisfaction [41, 42]. While evaluating the OGD portal is not new, research on users' dissatisfaction is in its infancy. The empirical evidence presented in this study serves as a starting point for future research.

Finally, my research has some limitations that could be addressed in future research. Firstly, the results are limited as the focus is on a single national OGD portal. Therefore, future research should consider multiple OGD portals to understand users' experiences comprehensively. Additionally, the sample used in this study was limited to minimalist users, which does not represent the entire population of the OGD portal. While doing so allowed to identify the lowest common minimal standards of users' needs, future research should also include power users to obtain a broader understanding of users' experiences. Finally, while this study identified drivers of dissatisfaction, I call on future research to use quantitative methods to empirically measure the significance of the relationships among the drivers.

References

1. Jetzek, T., Avital, M., Bjorn-Andersen, N.: The sustainable value of open government data. J. Assoc. Inf. Syst. **20**(6), 702–734 (2019)
2. Nikiforova, A., McBride, K.: Open government data portal usability: a user-centred usability analysis of 41 open government data portals. Telematics Inform. **58**(101539), 1–13 (2021)
3. Zhao, Y.P., Fan, B.: Exploring open government data capacity of government agency: based on the resource-based theory. Gov. Inf. Q. **35**(1), 1–12 (2018)
4. Máchová, R., Hub, M., Lněnička, M.: Usability evaluation of open data portals: evaluating data discoverability, accessibility, and reusability from a stakeholders' perspective. Aslib J. Inf. Manag. **70**(3), 252–268 (2018)
5. Janssen, M., Charalabidis, Y., Zuiderwijk, A.: Benefits, adoption barriers and myths of open data and open government. Inf. Syst. Manag. **29**(4), 258–268 (2012)
6. Nikiforova, A., Lněnička, M.: A multi-perspective knowledge-driven approach for analysis of the demand side of the open government data portal. Gov. Inf. Q. **38**(4), 1–19 (2021)
7. Martin, C.: Barriers to the open government data agenda: taking a multi-level perspective. Policy Internet **6**(3), 217–239 (2014)
8. Gascó-Hernández, M., Martin, E.G., Reggi, L., Pyo, S., Luna-Reyes, L.F.: Promoting the use of open government data: cases of training and engagement. Gov. Inf. Q. **35**(2), 233–242 (2018)
9. Ruijer, E., Grimmelikhuijsen, S., Meijer, A.: Open data for democracy: developing a theoretical framework for open data use. Gov. Inf. Q. **34**(1), 45–52 (2017)
10. Quarati, A.: Open government data: usage trends and metadata quality. J. Inf. Sci. **49**, 1–24 (2021)
11. Hughes, D.L., Rana, N.P., Simintiras, A.C.: The changing landscape of IS project failure: an examination of the key factors. J. Enterp. Inf. Manag. **30**(1), 142–165 (2017)
12. Osagie, E., Waqar, M., Adebayo, S., Stasiewicz, A., Porwol, L., Ojo, A.: Usability evaluation of an open data platform. In: International Conference on Digital Government Research, pp. 495–504. ACM (2017)
13. OECD, GovLab: Open Data in Action - Initiatives During the Initial Stage of the COVID-19 Pandemic (2021)
14. Office fédéral de la statistique: Besoins et Attentes dans l'Utilisation et la Mise à Disposition de Données Publiques Ouvertes en Suisse - Résultats de l'Enquête Open Government Data 2022. In: Département fédéral de l'intérieur (ed.), pp. 1–25, Neuchâtel (2022)

15. Lassinantti, J., Ståhlbröst, A., Runardotter, M.: Relevant social groups for open data use and engagement. Gov. Inf. Q. **36**(1), 98–111 (2019)
16. Susha, I., Grönlund, Å., Janssen, M.: Driving factors of service innovation using open government data: an exploratory study of entrepreneurs in two countries. Inf. Polity **20**(1), 19–34 (2015)
17. Bhattacherjee, A.: Understanding information systems continuance: an expectation-confirmation model. MIS Q. **25**(3), 351–370 (2001)
18. Schwarz, C.: Understanding the Role of Expectation Disconfirmation Theory on IT Outsourcing Success, Louisiana (2011)
19. Schwarz, C., Schwarz, A., Black, W.C.: Examining the impact of multicollinearity in discovering higher-order factor models. Commun. Assoc. Inf. Syst. **34**(1), 1191–1208 (2014)
20. Brown, S.A., Venkatesh, V., Goyal, S.: Expectation confirmation in information systems research: a test of six competing models. MIS Q. **38**(3), 729–756 (2014)
21. Premkumar, G., Bhattacherjee, A.: Explaining information technology usage: a test of competing models. Omega **36**(1), 64–75 (2008)
22. Oliver, R.L.: A cognitive model of the antecedents and consequences of satisfaction decisions. J. Mark. Res. **17**(4), 460–469 (1980)
23. Lankton, N.K., McKnight, H.D.: Examining two expectation disconfirmation theory models: assimilation and asymmetry effects. J. Assoc. Inf. Syst. **13**(2), 88–115 (2012)
24. Oliver, R.L.: Satisfaction: A Behavioral Perspective on the Consumer (2014)
25. Wang, H.-J., Jin, L.: Adoption of open government data among government agencies. Gov. Inf. Q. **33**(1), 80–88 (2016)
26. Kaasenbrood, M., Zuiderwijk, A., Janssen, M., de Jong, M., Bharosa, N.: Exploring the factors influencing the adoption of open government data by private organisations. Int. J. Public Adm. Digit. Age **2**(2), 75–92 (2015)
27. Jetzek, T., Avital, M., Bjorn-Andersen, N.: Data-driven innovation through open government data. J. Theor. Appl. Electron. Commer. Res. **9**(2), 100–120 (2014)
28. Bhattacherjee, A., Lin, C.-P.: A unified model of it continuance: three complementary perspectives and crossover effects. Eur. J. Inf. Syst. **24**(4), 364–373 (2015)
29. McBride, K., Aavik, G., Toots, M., Kalvet, T., Krimmer, R.: How does open government data driven co-creation occur? six factors and a 'perfect storm'; insights from Chicagos' food inspection forecasting model. Gov. Inf. Q. **36**(1), 88–97 (2019)
30. D'Emidio, T., Wagner, J.: Understanding the Customer Experience with Government. McKinsey & Company (2018)
31. Flanagan, J.: The critical incident technique. Psychol. Bull. **51**(4), 327–358 (1954)
32. Holloway, B.-B., Beatty, S.E.: Satisfiers and dissatisfiers in the online environment: a critical incident assessment. J. Serv. Res. **10**(4), 347–364 (2008)
33. Gremler, D.D.: The critical incident technique in service research. J. Serv. Res. **7**(1), 65–89 (2004)
34. FitzGerlad, K., Seale, N.S., Kerins, C.A., McElvaney, R.: The critical incident technique: a useful tool for conducting qualitative research. J. Dent. Educ. **72**(3), 299–304 (2008)
35. CKAN Homepage. https://ckan.org/. Accessed 16 Mar 2023
36. Creswell, J.W., Poth, C.N.: Qualitative Inquiry and Research Design: Choosing Among Five Approaches. Sage Publications Inc., Thousand Oaks (2016)
37. Hsieh, H.F., Shannon, S.E.: Three approaches to qualitative content analysis. Qual. Health Res. **15**(9), 1277–1288 (2005)
38. Urquhart, C., et al.: Critical incident technique and explicitation interviewing in studies of information behavior. Libr. Inf. Sci. Res. **25**(1), 63–88 (2003)
39. Hock, S.H., Malcus, L., Hasher, L.: Frequency discrimination: assessing global-level and element-level units in memory. J. Exp. Psychol. **12**(2), 232–240 (1986)

40. Woodley-Zanthos, P., Ellis, N.R.: Memory of frequency of occurrence: intelligence level and retrieval cues. Intelligence **13**(1), 53–61 (1989)
41. Islam, A.K.M.N.: Sources of satisfaction and dissatisfaction with a learning management system in post adoption stage: a critical incident technique approach. Comput. Hum. Behav. **30**, 249–261 (2014)
42. Chan, J.K., Baum, T.: Determination of satisfiers and dissatisfiers using Herzberg's motivator and hygiene factor theory: an exploratory study. Tour. Cult. Commun. **7**(2), 117–131 (2007)

Smart Cities, Regions, and Societies

Design Principles for Developing Open Source Urbanism

Sergei Zhilin[✉] and Marijn Janssen

Delft University of Technology, Delft, The Netherlands
s.zhilin@tudelft.nl

Abstract. In Open Source Urbanism (OSU) citizens self-organize and create Do-It-Yourself (DIY) urban designs to address societal problems. Self-organized citizens develop these designs, but there is no support for the design process based on the co-creation and involvement of citizens. The latter are mainly non-experts. Three aspects characterize OSU: (1) OSU initiatives are initialized by citizens; (2) OSU initiatives are the new commons, are collectively created and managed by self-organized citizens; (3) to last, DIY should be accepted by or co-produced with the authorities as they can change the urban environment. This research offers a set of design principles to guide the cultivation of OSU infrastructures in the self-organized setting of urban commons. We derived the principles from an ethnographic study of an Amsterdam-based citizen initiative. This paper offers a set of design principles to guide the cultivation of OSU infrastructures in the self-organized setting of the urban commons. We introduce eight design principles: (1) Co-creation, (2) Trust-building, (3) Motivating, (4) Growing, (5) Showcasing, (6) Bridging, (7) Open-sourcing, and (8) Peer Production. By promoting self-organized, community-led development, our design principles offer guidelines for urban commons communities, academics, and decision-makers to work towards a shared vision of the future of inclusive cities. Building trust and gaining access to expertise are key aspects of OSU cultivation.

Keywords: citizen initiatives · design ethnography · design principles · urban commons

1 Introduction

As cities become increasingly complex, citizen-led initiatives are emerging as powerful tools for shaping urban environments. Among these initiatives are the urban commons, which are places citizens co-created to collectively manage and utilize shared resources in their communities [12]. *Open Source Urbanism*(OSU) is a type of citizen-led initiative that builds on the concept of the urban commons by integrating open-source principles and digital tools into the co-creation of designs in the urban environment [4,17]. OSU practices aim for *urban transformation*, that is "a process where the dominant structures, functions and identity of urban systems change fundamentally e leading to new cultural, structural

© IFIP International Federation for Information Processing 2023
Published by Springer Nature Switzerland AG 2023
I. Lindgren et al. (Eds.): EGOV 2023, LNCS 14130, pp. 297–312, 2023.
https://doi.org/10.1007/978-3-031-41138-0_19

and institutional configurations" [23, p. 160]. OSU has similarities, but also differences, with *Information Infrastructures* (II). OSU and IIs exhibit the same characteristics, for instance, both phenomena are claimed to be self-organised, decentralised, and evolving. At the same time, OSU differs from the formal organisational contexts that build IIs, such as the lack of resources, clear hierarchies, and control are differences, to name a few. OSU digital tools and practices comprise an OSU infrastructure, i.e., a commons-based information infrastructure (II) that facilitates the co-production of urban design and open source design manuals. IIs are "the entirety of devices, tools, technologies, standards, conventions, and protocols on which the individual worker or the collective rely to carry out the tasks and achieve the goals assigned to them." [21, p. 455]. IIs differ from other Information Systems (IS): the former have no specific purpose but rather a generic idea of supporting a Community of Practice with information-related services, while the latter, such as decision support systems or accounting systems, clearly state their purpose and supported tasks [15].

The self-organized nature of infrastructures requires different approaches than conventional design processes. Designing OSU has no lead designers, and often the designers are not experts or educated for the task. Instead, co-design with the community is needed. OSU differs from II as no experts involved, and co-creation among layman is the central design approach. The literature provides various design principles, including these for IIs [15], however, specific principles for OSU infrastructures are lacking. This paper fills the knowledge gap in designing OSU infrastructures by offering a set of eight guidelines derived from a design ethnography study of an Amsterdam-based urban commons initiative. Design principles might support guiding co-designers in cultivating OSU infrastructures. Design principles are "prescriptive statements that indicate how to do something to achieve a goal." [13, p. 1622]. They are not offered as 'blueprints for strict adherence' but serve as inputs for case-specific design decisions [7]. The urban commons and OSU are not explored by scholars of Information Systems (IS). Thus, we lack knowledge of the design principles in such an idiosyncratic setting. To achieve the research goal of deriving design principles, we adopt ethnographic methods.

The rest of the paper is organized as follows. The second section draws on the literature on the commons and the Community of Practice (CoP) theory, discussing the importance of understanding the context of Open Source Urbanism and the need for a community-driven approach to OSU infrastructures development. The third section presents the research approach. Thereafter the case of our design ethnography is presented. The fifth section offers a set of eight design principles for OSU infrastructures. The sixth section discusses the conclusions and recommendations for future research.

2   Literature Background

This section discusses the nature of OSU in greater detail. Next, an analysis of the design ethnography requires tools for the analysis of communities that share work practices since information infrastructures function in Communities of Practice (CoP) [26], in which members learn from each other by sharing tacit knowledge, such as anecdotes, impromptu comments and opinion exchange, in addition to explicit knowledge.

2.1 What is Open Source Urbanism?

OSU infrastructures occur when citizens self-organize to tackle the issues of their urban environment by creating Do-It-Yourself (DIY) designs. In urban studies literature, DIY urban designs are defined as small-scale, civic-minded design contributions that are designed and constructed by citizens and represent a desire to make improvements to the local urban environment without formal approval of the authorities; however, essentially in a manner that aligns with official urban designs [8]. DIY designs emerge as a response of active citizens to issues in their local environment; they are designed and financed by self-organized citizens and not by public or private companies [11]. Designs can range from alternative energy microstations or Wi-Fi networks to community urban gardens [17]. Active citizens share design knowledge gained during the construction of these designs with the help of design manuals. Design manuals are a written set of rules to follow to create an artefact for achieving a specific goal. The detailisation of design processes in these manuals can be low since most designs are created ad-hoc for a specific local environment to solve a problem at hand; thus, they are not designed to be generalizable. Design manuals are shared on the internet, allowing others to use and alternate them to produce context-specific versions of DIY designs.

OSU unites bottom-up citizen interventions and the open source movement and can be defined as open source production of urban commons [4]. Urban commons and the open source movement are self-organized Communities of Practice that collectively manage, produce and consume resources that vary from urban land to information on the internet. The urban commons focus on the collective management of resources in the urban context (e.g., community gardens, housing cooperatives), while open source communities create digital commons (e.g., open source software, Wikipedia). OSU infrastructures function as peer-to-peer networks in which distinctions between producers and consumers of resources are blurred [17]. Such networks create physical entities, i.e., urban designs and open source manuals covering the design processes. Thus, the second crucial aspect of OSU is that resources are created and consumed in infrastructures that unite urban and digital commons.

OSU emerges as a grassroots response to traditional urban development since active citizens self-organize to improve their local environment outside the traditional public-private dichotomy [4]. Claims of citizens for self-governance over DIY designs challenge the paradigm of governmental control and maintenance over the urban equipment [17]. Nevertheless, citizens cannot simply appoint themselves to alternate their local environment. To last, DIY designs must be authorized by urban officials, i.e., some mechanisms of collaboration with the municipality should be in place. Thus, the third aspect of OSU is that DIY designs should be co-produced with urban authorities.

2.2 Communities of Practice

As with any other kind of Information Infrastructure, OSU infrastructures emerge in and are used by Communities of Practice (CoPs) [26]. The notion of *Community of Practice* (CoP) [18] is an analytical framework for investigating the process of learning through practice. CoPs can be defined as "small groups of people who regularly engage in similar practices and have frequent occasions to interact with each other" [28, p. 549]. CoPs are different from other forms of organization because they are self-organized entities that establish informal membership and leadership [30].

CoPs are characterized by three elements: 1) shared enterprise, 2) mutual engagement, and 3) shared repertoire [30]. CoPs are informal groups of people bound together by an interest in a joint enterprise, for instance, gardening or cooking. Interest in the same domain does not automatically create a CoP. Membership plays a crucial role in CoPs: collective identity and shared competence in the domain of interest distinguish CoP members from outsiders. Mutual engagement connects these people in a community. Over time a CoP develops a unique shared repertoire of community resources, such as routines, jargon, and artefacts [30]. Contrary to formal organizational settings, CoPs are self-organized, which complicates the creation of formal structures with fixed roles and domains of responsibility. Thus, CoP members have to learn from each other during their practice. In this study, we analyzed urban commons as a CoP. Thus, citizens form a CoP to learn how to share responsibilities, tasks, and resources while co-creating DIY designs to solve perceived issues of their local environment.

3   Research Approach

The literature on OSU infrastructures is lacking. This paper addresses this knowledge gap by offering a set of eight guidelines derived from a design ethnography study of an Amsterdam-based urban commons initiative. The research are part of the completed PhD research [33]. The domain of OSU is new in IS discipline, thus, we lack knowledge of the design principles suitable for dealing with the idiosyncratic setting of urban commons. To overcome these barriers, we adopt ethnography, that is "an anthropological research method that relies on first-hand observations made by a researcher immersed over an extended period of time in a culture, with which he/she is unfamiliar" [24, p. 7]. Ethnography is 'one of the most in-depth research methods possible' because it gives the researcher tools to observe interactions and practices of people directly, not relying only on self-reports of their actions [1, p. 40] which is typical for other quantitative methods, such as case studies. Ethnography is a "well suited to providing information systems researchers with rich insights into the human, social and organizational aspects of information systems development and application"

[16, p. 22]. We perceive immersion in an urban commons initiative as necessary to achieve the objective of this study because other methods cannot provide such in-depth knowledge. Ethnography is criticized because immersion in a community's life hardly leaves the researcher space for neutrality. We mitigated this bias in several ways. Firstly, we used various sources of information, such as participant observations, interviews, and documents. Moreover, the CoP members were interested in co-creating an OSU infrastructure for the community, while they did not participate in elaborating design principles. Notably, after completing the fieldwork, we disengaged from the community and conducted data analysis and design principles synthesis as a 'desk research'. Another criticism questions the validity of a theory generation from a single-case ethnography; nevertheless, theories generalized from a single case study are widespread (e.g., [32]). Grounded in one typical case, the offered design principles can be perceived as a departure point for further research.

In ethnography, participant observation is the cornerstone research method which prescribes the researcher to observe but does not disturb the community life [20]. However, some point out that conducting ethnographically inspired research necessarily involves some level of interference in the field being studied; in this way opening opportunities for intervention by the researcher [22]. Thus, ethnography makes possible interventions in the community under scrutiny, however, it provides no tools or approaches for that. Hence, we adopt a method of *design ethnography* in which the ethnographer "is no longer so tentative but rather actively engages with the people in the field" [1, p. 27] which enables an in-depth understanding of a chosen community and allows design interventions. In traditional ethnography, the researcher 'becomes a student of other people's culture' [20, p. 114]; in design ethnography, the researcher also becomes an adviser of the community they engaged with [1]. We define design interventions as the researcher's activities within organizations that aim at solving their practical problems [6]. Design ethnography suits the objectives of this study well, as we aim at co-creating a technology-based artefact with an urban commons community that holds values and performs practices we are not yet familiar with.

This paper derives generalized knowledge (i.e., a set of design principles for cultivating OSU infrastructures) from developing an OSU infrastructure for a real-life case of the urban commons. For this purpose, we conducted the ethnography and four design interventions. We used lessons learned from the design ethnography as input for synthesizing the design principles. The design ethnography took place from July 2018 to December 2020. In total, we conducted four design interventions, one after the other. Each following intervention was chosen based on the reflection on the previous one.

4   Ethnographic Study

The ethnographic case of this study is a self-organised citizen initiative KasKantine (eng. Greenhouse cantina), established in 2014 in Amsterdam, the Netherlands. It temporarily occupies available land plots moving to a new plot every

several years. After each relocation, the construction materials and technological solutions are reused. The main community activity is a donation-based cafe
utilising food from supermarkets and vegetables grown in the community gar-
den. KasKantine is not connected to city infrastructures and produces energy
and water autonomously, thanks to the DIY design created by the CoP. To give
some examples: rainwater filter provides water for non-cooking purposes; grey-
water filter provides water for plant watering; rocket stoves allow heating and
cooking; donated and repaired solar panels provide electricity. We chose this initiative for design ethnography due to several reasons. First, the initiative was
commons-based and gained sufficient DIY design knowledge that can be shared
in the form of design manuals, thus, meeting the definition of OSU. Moreover,
initiatives of this sort are rather rare and exemplify what [32, p. 27] describes as
"unusually revelatory, extreme exemplars, or opportunities for unusual research
access". Finally, the CoP was open to collaboration with the researcher (in the
roles of a volunteer and a design ethnographer).

4.1 Design Intervention 1: Transformation of the Organizational Structure

The first design intervention aimed to create a new organisational structure that
would better achieve the community vision. The rationale behind the organisational transformation was to carry out activities that bring more value to the city
and neighbourhood. The researcher suggested the following design intervention:
KasKantine transforms into a living lab as a testbed for social innovation that
fulfils the needs of local communities. The living lab could include self-organised
initiatives, private companies, public organisations, and knowledge institutions.
The first design intervention did not work out due to several factors (due to
space limitations, we name only the crucial ones). First, the lack of trust since
the researcher joined the community several months prior to the intervention and
was still considered a newcomer. Additionally, the initial top-down design of the
intervention played a role. The researcher assumed that an intervention based
on the literature should be accepted while the understanding of community life
was still lacking.

4.2 Design Intervention 2: Bridging with External Stakeholders

As per the land contract terms, the initiative was obligated to vacate the land
by September 2019. Fearing the possibility of the initiative failing, community
leaders began exploring the development of an OSU infrastructure to address the
challenge of communicating the public value of KasKantine with the municipality. This was necessary to rent a municipality-owned land, and an OSU infrastructure would transform the CoP's tacit knowledge into explicit design manuals.
According to the CoP theory, boundary objects play a critical role in supporting collaboration among actors from different social worlds, as they maintain
different meanings for heterogeneous groups of actors. During the second design

intervention, the CoP required a boundary object to demonstrate to civil servants that KasKantine aligns with the municipality's goals, such as co-creation with citizens and promoting citizen initiatives. At the same time, for CoP members, it would serve as the foundation of an OSU infrastructure. Due to time constraints, the team quickly designed and developed a simple static website without any interactive features. The content included a brief explanation of KasKantine, its social value for the city, and a brief description of DIY designs, along with accompanying photos and generic models of functioning.

4.3   Design Intervention 3: Creating Design Manuals

In August 2019, the municipality offered a five-year contract that would provide the opportunity to further develop the initiative compared to earlier contracts that lasted one or two years only. Moreover, without the pressure of securing a land plot, CoP members were more driven to cultivate an OSU infrastructure. In this design intervention, the team co-designed two artefacts: a pdf booklet with open-source design manuals and a website providing access to the booklet. The booklet format was preferred, allowing independent collaboration on designs separate from website development. Additionally, the one-file structure of the booklet enabled the updating of design manuals without website modifications. The previous version, developed in a short time frame, was inflexible and not extendable. Therefore, an open-source content management system was preferred for future development and maintenance by the community of volunteers, who might leave the initiative at any time.

4.4   Design Intervention 4: Building the Network of Practice

The fourth design intervention aimed at transforming the built website into a digital platform, i.e., "a specific type of civic technology explicitly built for participatory, engagement and collaboration purposes that allow for user-generated content and include a range of functionalities" [10, p. 3]. The resulting platform featured collaboration functionality, such as channels of communication and collaboration spaces. The platform aimed to connect various like-minded CoPs in Amsterdam and other cities. The design intervention was necessary to allow non-professionals to manage the content. In the earlier version, updating the booklet designs required licensed proprietary software and individuals with specialized skills. Likewise, the previous website version was designed to be modified only by individuals with web-development expertise, such as adding a new page or changing the text on the main page.

4.5   Lessons Learned

This section summarizes lessons learned from design interventions. These lessons lay a foundation for design principles. We discuss five important themes that emerged during the evaluation; these themes will serve as the foundation for five design principles of a design method for OSU.

Trust for Co-designer. Establishing trust is a critical component of the process as the researcher must fully integrate into the CoP to co-design an OSU infrastructure through shared practice and engagement in community life. In the first intervention, trust was lacking between the researcher and the CoP, as the former was viewed as an outsider or newcomer. However, over time, as the researcher spent more time with the CoP and demonstrated a commitment to and understanding of the initiative, trust gradually developed.

Motivation of CoP Members. The degree to which CoP members align with the community vision is crucial for finding the motivation to participate in OSU cultivation. Apart from that, CoP members are more likely to engage in cultivation activities if the objectives of the infrastructure align with their personal motivations for volunteering.

Showcasing Community Vision. The simple artefact from the second design intervention laid a foundation for an OSU infrastructure. This simple website showcased the vision of the CoP to external stakeholders, such as the municipality, and demonstrated how KasKantine produce eco-minded public services with the help of DIY designs.

Use of Open Source. The choice of technologies for infrastructure might create lock-ins if the CoP lacks volunteers skilled in the specific technologies. Open Source Software (OSS) solves this problem. The OSS content management platform allowed the CoP to gradually improve the website from a three-pager providing access for downloading the pdf booklet to a digital platform with a dynamic content system. Applying peer production principles.The pandemic forced KasKantine CoP to cultivate an OSU infrastructure via online collaboration further. This eased the application of CBPP principles: we applied three main principles of CBPP: modularity, granularity, and low-cost integration. The modular design of the OSU infrastructure and fine-grained tasks allowed the CoP to work in an asynchronous and geographically dispersed way.

5   Design Principles

Design principles allow embracing the diversity of commons initiatives while providing flexibility in developing case-specific OSU infrastructures. Design principles are not blueprints to implement but serve as inputs for case-specific design decisions. In this paper, we define design principles as follows: *"generic prescriptions and guidelines that are intended to be manifested or encapsulated in the design and implementation of socio-technical systems"*. The principles were synthesised by confronting empirical case observations and literature.

Design principles are applied by a co-designer, i.e., facilitators of the cultivation of an OSU infrastructure, since every user can contribute to the design process. Co-designers should not steer OSU infrastructures but rather facilitate peer production of the digital infrastructure. Co-designers choose methodologies and tools considering their skills and properties of the specific urban commons. Co-designers are interdisciplinary professionals that can grasp such complex socio-technical systems and facilitate their growth. Although not requiring formal education in urban design or computer software design, this role demands a deep understanding of self-organized urban commons initiatives' ethos and work practices, as they are substantially different from organisations based on a hierarchical chain of command and contractual obligations. Civil servants, urban practitioners, active citizens, researchers, or policy-makers can play this role. In the ethnographic study, the researcher played the role of co-designer, facilitating the cultivation of OSU infrastructure.

To describe the design principles in greater detail, we use The Open Group Standard framework for design principles (TOGAF) [27]. In accordance with TOGAF, we provide a short name, statement, a rationale behind each principle using the insights from the literature review and empirical studies. Contrary to the TOGAF standard, we omit to specify the implications, as they are represented in statements.

1. Immersing: immerse in the community life to understand a community vision and practices

Co-design with urban commons initiatives differs from other design projects since these are self-organised, therefore, lack hierarchies and contractual relationships. During the ethnographic studies, we found that proposing a solution in a top-down fashion might be ineffective or not work and, more importantly, may cause resistance. Thus, prior to starting the design process, co-designers should gain a deep understanding of the urban commons CoP, to identify what knowledge can be shared as digital commons. Apart from that, community members might be unaware of their innovative ideas that can be of use to others because they emerged through practice, not as a design project with explicit objectives and deliverables. A long-term involvement in communal practices provides a live experience and deep understanding of the urban commons while not disrupting community life. Over time, the shared practice of the co-designer with the CoP members, paired with reflections, can lead to the understanding of the community vision and practices. The primary condition for co-designers to understand the functioning of the community is to keep in mind that urban commons are based on a self-organised voluntarily-driven organizational structure. As the ethnographic study showed, CoP newcomers that are used to market relations initially have trouble adjusting to the self-organised setting.

We recommend being reluctant to identify the initiative goals from formal documents and interviewing external stakeholders because goals, habits, norms and culture of the CoP can be hidden from outsiders [30] and are subject to change over time. Moreover, CoP members themselves might not be able to clearly formulate their common goals, as they can be expressed not explicitly but rather as a fluid and ever-changing set of ideas and intentions that depend on the changes in the local environment and community composition. Due to this, understanding the community and its history is crucial to acknowledge the evolving nature of the urban commons. Instead, co-designers should grasp what problems in the urban environment they attempt to tackle and what designs they co-create to support their practices. Crucial to identify the problems from the perspective of community members, as the co-designer's perspective may differ.

2. Trust-building: build trust with the community to secure co-creation

Trust between the co-designer and community members is key to securing the relationship paramount for the co-design process. Trust is a basic organising principle for coordinated activities: "whenever actors are simultaneously dependent on and vulnerable to the actions and decisions of others, trust is a relevant organizing principle that warrants consideration." [19, p. 99]. Co-designer is frequently an outsider or newcomer of the CoP, therefore, might hold work ethos and vocabulary quite different from those of CoP members. In order to build trust, the co-designer should secure long-term peer relations with the community. They must immerse in the community life equipped with an open mind, sympathy for their vision, and empathy for their struggles.

In OSU infrastructures, community members must trust co-designers and acknowledge that their intentions are in the collective interest. Trust building is crucial for securing the overall co-creation process because if trust between co-designers and the community is missing, the design activities will bring little to no effect. Trust plays a paramount role in urban commons because self-organised communities operate outside the command and control relations and might resist such structures. Without contractual obligations, they collaborate as peers that cannot coerce each other to perform tasks. Thus, community members negotiate the performance of projects and tasks. The imposition of corporate culture and a hierarchical goal-driven approach might deteriorate peer relations, block or halt the design process, or result in the superficial design of OSU infrastructure that will not function without external support. The latter is undesired as these might result in the existence of nonviable projects that become abandoned when external actors stop supporting the co-creation. Moreover, sources of legitimacy that are standard for bureaucratic structures, such as expertise or social status, are not necessarily automatically recognised in non-hierarchical communities, therefore, other factors play a paramount role, and trustworthiness is a crucial factor.

3. Motivating: look for opportunities to motivate and involve community members

Digital tools, such as source code repositories and wikis, serve as artefacts for knowledge sharing for geographically spread participants. In the case of the urban commons, such artefacts are not necessary, as participants acquire knowledge through practice [2]. Thus, members of urban commons might be unmotivated to support the development of digital tools, as they do not receive direct benefits in exchange for their time and efforts. Building an infrastructure often would take a too high toll on the community, as they are overwhelmed by the everyday activities necessary for the initiative's functioning. Hence, co-creation requires that community members grasp the future individual and communal benefits to motivate them and secure their involvement in OSU cultivation.

Based on the understanding of the community vision and challenges, co-designers formulate goals of an OSU infrastructure, i.e., how it benefits the initiative development. Essentially, the goals of an OSU infrastructure should mirror issues of the local urban environment. This ensures that the community recognises the developed infrastructure's potential benefits and engages in its co-creation. Apart from that, community members can find individual motivations. Frequently idealism and camaraderie motivate peers to contribute. Alternatively, community leaders can find material incentives, for instance, external funding from public or private organisations. Additionally, material incentives may increase the chance of project completion, as it demands higher accountability than voluntary work. On the other hand, it might bring the 'corporate relations' that erode peer production [29].

4. Growing: grow infrastructure on fertile ground to avoid community resistance

We offer the concept of *the fertile ground* for OSU infrastructures instead of *the installed base* well-known in IIs studies [26]. We claim that this new notion fits better the idiosyncratic nature of OSU. The fertile ground highlights the different mode of production in the urban commons that are self-organised, emerging communities driven by the values and visions of people. The urban commons is the fertile ground where an OSU infrastructure grows if cultivated. Organic growth is a slow, natural evolution. In the self-organised setting with no command and control mechanisms, OSU infrastructure grows only if it organically motivations of the community members. This principle prescribes investigating elements of the fertile ground in detail. For instance, which CoP practices are required for the urban commons management and maintenance. Equipped with these, co-designers can grow an OSU infrastructure by fitting new technologies, tools, and practices in the fertile ground of the urban commons.

5. Showcasing: showcase the community vision for communicating with other city actors

The community vision is a declaration of problems in the local urban environment, as perceived by active citizens, and how the urban commons tackle them by means of the DIY designs and community practice. The vision is the alternative urban futures shaped by the collective imagination of the CoP: this is not necessarily a feasible target but rather an ongoing process and a mission to move forward. Community vision could be fluid and changing due to changes in the 'outer world' (e.g., changes in policies, funding programs, and like-minded communities). Nevertheless, urban commons perform community practice aiming at achieving the vision. The focus of an OSU infrastructure is to materialise DIY knowledge on the co-creation of these in the form of design manuals.

The manuals should be exemplified by practical cases to demonstrate their applicability in the real-life context of a specific urban environment. They show the best practices, inspire other urban commons, and support a dialogue with other city actors. Exemplifying the specific community vision with specific designs and related community practices makes shared design manuals tangible, as real-life examples are easy to grasp, unlike abstract designs. Additionally, manuals with examples shared on the internet help communicate the community vision with other city actors. Finally, it has value as it promotes active citizenship, demonstrating that self-organised citizens can solve arising local challenges outside of the standard public-private dichotomy.

6. Bridging: connect heterogeneous groups of actors to align perspectives

The urban commons must comply with urban environment regulations to be authorized by the urban officials. However, external stakeholders with whom the urban commons collaborate might have different perspectives on the same problems and possible solutions. Therefore, the CoP envisions possible solutions to specific urban environment problems that might differ from external urban stakeholders. The different visions can bring tensions. To avoid that, the community should align their vision with that of external stakeholders; they need to find a narrative acceptable to all involved parties.

The urban commons place can be viewed as a *boundary object*, i.e., an entity that is used by different social groups maintaining different meanings for every group, yet holding a shared identity that allows joint action upon them; Boundary objects facilitate collaboration among parties that have conflicting perceptions of it [25]. Urban stakeholders might collaborate upon the authorisation and development of the urban commons without consensus on its meaning for the CoP and the city. Communicating the community vision with urban stakeholders is challenging: community members shape the vision through the practice and do not necessarily have it in the form of ready-made documentation, while other stakeholders do not participate in the practice. Urban officials cannot easily submerge in the reality of urban commons because their goals and background substantially differ from activism and self-organisation. Live demonstrations of the community practice is not necessarily effective, as they belong to different social bubbles and use various vocabularies and perspectives. Instead, decision-makers can evaluate the vision by assessing reports and presentations.

Bridging is required to align different perceptions and interests of stakeholders. According to the CoP theory, some CoP members act as boundary spanners between the CoP and external stakeholders [31]. Boundary spanners have to learn how to convey their vision to urban authorities, for instance, by learning the jargon and work culture of these. They connect the CoP with the 'outside world' and tweak the vision and even vocabulary of the urban commons. They shape the vision influenced by city regulations and community members. Bridging principle change the CoP, as the 'outside world' provoke changes in the community vision, and this, in turn, leads to changes in the physical environment of the urban commons. An OSU infrastructure facilitate this process, as infrastructure transform tacit DIY knowledge into documents in explicit, codified form that can be used as boundary objects.

7. Open-sourcing: apply open source solutions to ease IT development and secure community ownership

Open Source Software (OSS) is well-suited for developing OSU infrastructures, as it is free for use and modification [3]. Notably, many OSS is well-documented, which eases the evolution of IT components of infrastructure. Self-organised communities often face the ongoing flux of members, which raises challenges of maintenance and scaling up the infrastructure. Application of OSS might increase the potential volunteer base since many well-developed OSS solutions have grown vast communities of users. Furthermore, OSU infrastructures based on open source principles prevent data misuse because the community chooses the way the design manuals are stored, managed, and shared. To share design manuals as open source, the co-designer suggests an open source license, such as the software license GNU General Public License or the family of Creative Commons licenses [14].

8. Peer production: apply peer production principles to create a Network of Practice

CoPs are loosely connected into *Networks of Practice* (NoPs) [5] that do not coordinate practice with each other but allow to exchange knowledge [9]. Members of an NoP may never meet each other in real life, however, as their practices are similar, they may be interested in sharing knowledge across CoPs [5]. IIs might facilitate knowledge exchange in loose groupings in which "people are not necessarily collocated but are engaged in practices that share a certain degree of similarity" [28, p. 549]. This principle suggests applying principles of Commons-Based Peer Production (CBPP) [3] in the physical realm of the urban commons. The three main principles of CBPP are modularity, granularity, and low-cost integration. Modularity means that potential objects of peer production must have a modular structure allowing peers to work asynchronously. Granularity refers to the degree to which objects are broken down into smaller modules. This principle allows peers to work on modules according to their level of competence and motivation. The principle of low-cost integration refers to a mechanism by which modules produced by peers are integrated into the end product [3]. We must admit that this principle is more rooted in the literature than in practice since we could not fully test and evaluate this principle in the fourth design intervention.

6 Conclusions and Discussion

Open Source Urbanism (OSU) is a type of citizen-led initiative that builds on the concept of the urban commons by integrating open-source principles and digital tools into the co-creation of designs in the urban environment [4,17]. The digital tools and practices comprise an OSU infrastructure, i.e., a commons-based information infrastructure (II) that facilitates the co-production of urban design and open source design manuals. The literature lacks design knowledge guiding the cultivation of OSU infrastructures. Due to the novelty of the OSU field, a synthesis of design knowledge requires a deep understanding of urban commons involved in OSU practices. Hence, we conducted a long-term fieldwork study within an Amsterdam-based urban commons initiative applying a design ethnography approach. Principles offered in this paper are part of completed PhD research [33].

This paper offers a set of design principles to guide the cultivation of Open Source Urbanism (OSU) infrastructures in the self-organized setting of the urban commons. We introduce eight design principles: (1) Co-creation, (2) Trust-building, (3) Motivating, (4) Growing, (5) Showcasing, (6) Bridging, (7) Open-sourcing, and (8) Peer Production. The design principles proposed in this paper have significant implications for the future of OSU and the co-creation of sustainable and inclusive urban environments. The design principles presented in this paper guide designers to facilitate the co-creation of OSU infrastructure that aligns with the needs of the community and urban environment. OSU infrastructure development requires a co-creation approach that involves community members. OSU represents one of the new alternative approaches to urban development, one that promotes civic engagement by empowering citizens to take control of their local environment and work together to create solutions that meet their unique needs. By sharing design knowledge gained during the construction of these designs, citizens can collaborate and learn from one another, further strengthening community ties and promoting social cohesion.

We highlight that the scope of this study was OSU infrastructure cultivation in the inception stage, i.e., we focused on the bootstrapping problem [15] of OSU infrastructures only, while challenges related to adaptability problem [15], such as adoption, growing user base, and network effect, are outside the scope of this study. Future research can focus on studies of OSU infrastructures in a multi-actor setting, i.e., engaging private companies, decision-makers, and civil servants in cultivating OSU infrastructures. OSU infrastructures are not designed from the top-down, and every user can be a co-designer. This aspect of OSU infrastructures, coupled with possible tensions between self-organized communities and urban authorities, raises questions about the manner of OSU cultivation in such a setting. Especially interesting to investigate an approach that balances different, often even contradictory, interests of various urban stakeholders and maximizes value for city-wide urban development while further enabling citizen-driven initiatives. The second research suggestion concerns the evolution of OSU. This research was limited to constructing design principles for the inception phase of OSU infrastructures, thus, further evolution and growth of these is a possible subject for future studies.

References

1. Baskerville, R.L., Myers, M.D.: Design ethnography in information systems. Inf. Syst. J. **25**(1), 23–46 (2015). https://doi.org/10.1111/isj.12055
2. Bendt, P., Barthel, S., Colding, J.: Civic greening and environmental learning in public-access community gardens in Berlin. Landsc. Urban Plan. **109**(1), 18–30 (2013). https://doi.org/10.1016/j.landurbplan.2012.10.003
3. Benkler, Y.: Coase's penguin, or, Linux and "the nature of the firm". Yale Law J. **112**(3), 369–446 (2002)
4. Bradley, K.: Open-source urbanism: creating, multiplying and managing urban commons. Footprint **9**(1), 91–107 (2015). https://doi.org/10.7480/FOOTPRINT. 9.1.901
5. Brown, J.S., Duguid, P.: Knowledge and organization: a social-practice perspective. Organ. Sci. **12**(2), 198–213 (2001)
6. Checkland, P., Holwell, S.: Action research: its nature and validity. Syst. Pract. Action Res. **11**(1), 9–21 (1998). https://doi.org/10.1023/A:1022908820784/
7. Clegg, C.W.: Sociotechnical principles for system design. Appl. Ergon. **31**(5), 463–477 (2000). https://doi.org/10.1016/S0003-6870(00)00009-0. https://linkinghub. elsevier.com/retrieve/pii/S0003687000000090
8. Douglas, G.C.C.: Do-it-yourself urban design: the social practice of informal "improvement" through unauthorized alteration. City Community **13**(1), 5–25 (2014). https://doi.org/10.1111/cico.12029. http://doi.wiley.com/10.1111/cico. 12029
9. Duguid, P.: "The art of knowing": social and tacit dimensions of knowledge and the limits of the community of practice. Inf. Soc. **21**(2), 109–118 (2005). https:// doi.org/10.1080/01972240590925311
10. Falco, E., Kleinhans, R.: Digital participatory platforms for co-production in urban development. A systematic review. Int. J. E-Plann. Res. **7**(3) (2019)
11. Finn, D.: DIY urbanism: implications for cities. J. Urbanism Int. Res. Placemaking Urban Sustain. **7**(4), 381–398 (2014). https://doi.org/10.1080/17549175.2014. 891149. http://www.tandfonline.com/doi/abs/10.1080/17549175.2014.891149
12. Foster, S., Iaione, C.: The city as a commons. SSRN Electron. J. 281–349 (2015). https://doi.org/10.2139/ssrn.2653084. http://www.ssrn.com/abstract=2653084
13. Gregor, S., Chandra Kruse, L., Seidel, S.: Research perspectives: the anatomy of a design principle. J. Assoc. Inf. Syst. **21**(6), 1622–1652 (2020). https://doi.org/10. 17705/1jais.00649
14. Hansen, A., Howard, T.J.: The current state of open source hardware: the need for an open source development platform. In: Chakrabarti, A., Prakash, R. (eds.) ICoRD 2013, pp. 977–988. Springer, India (2013). https://doi.org/10.1007/978-81-322-1050-4_77
15. Hanseth, O., Lyytinen, K.: Theorizing about the design of information infrastructures: design kernel theories and principles. Sprouts: Working Papers Inf. Syst. **4**(4), 207–241 (2004)
16. Harvey, L.J., Myers, M.D.: Scholarship and practice: the contribution of ethnographic research methods to bridging the gap. Inf. Technol. People **8**(3), 13–27 (1995). https://doi.org/10.1108/09593849510098244
17. Jiménez, A.C.: The right to infrastructure: a prototype for open source urbanism. Environ. Plann. D Soc. Space **32**(2), 342–362 (2014). https://doi.org/10.1068/ d13077p

18. Lave, J., Wenger, E.: Situated Learning: Legitimate Peripheral Participation. Cambridge University Press, Cambridge (1991)

19. McEvily, B., Perrone, V., Zaheer, A.: Trust as an organizing principle. Organ. Sci. **14**(1), 13 (2003)

20. Myers, M.D.: Investigating information systems with ethnographic research. Commun. Assoc. Inf. Syst. **2**(Dec) (1999). https://doi.org/10.17705/1CAIS.00223. https://aisel.aisnet.org/cais/vol2/iss1/23

21. Pipek, V., Wulf, V.: Infrastructuring: toward an integrated perspective on the design and use of information technology. J. Assoc. Inf. Syst. **10**(5), 447–473 (2009)

22. Pors, J.K., Henriksen, D.L., Winthereik, B.R., Berg, M.: Challenging divisions: exploring the intersections of ethnography and intervention in IS research. Scand. J. Inf. Syst. **14**(2), 2–8 (2002)

23. Radywyl, N., Bigg, C.: Reclaiming the commons for urban transformation. J. Cleaner Prod. **50**, 159–170 (2013). https://doi.org/10.1016/j.jclepro.2012.12.020

24. Schultze, U.: A confessional account of an ethnography about knowledge work. MIS Q. **24**(1), 3 (2000). https://doi.org/10.2307/3250978. https://www.jstor.org/stable/3250978?origin=crossref

25. Star, S.L., Griesemer, J.R.: Institutional ecology, 'translations' and boundary objects: amateurs and professionals in berkeley's museum of vertebrate zoology, 1907–39. Soc. Stud. Sci. **19**(3), 387–420 (1989). https://doi.org/10.1177/030631289019003001. http://journals.sagepub.com/doi/10.1177/030631289019003001

26. Star, S.L., Ruhleder, K.: Steps toward an ecology of infrastructure: design and access for large information spaces. In: Information Technology and Organizational Transformation: History, Rhetoric, and Practice, vol. 7, no. 1, pp. 305–346 (1996). https://doi.org/10.4135/9781452231266.n11

27. TOGAF: The TOGAF® Standard, Version 9.2 (2018). http://pubs.opengroup.org/architecture/togaf9-doc/arch/

28. Vaast, E., Walsham, G.: Trans-situated learning: supporting a network of practice with an information infrastructure. Inf. Syst. Res. **20**(4), 547–564 (2009). https://doi.org/10.1287/isre.1080.0228

29. Veen, E.J., Bock, B.B., Van den Berg, W., Visser, A.J., Wiskerke, J.S.: Community gardening and social cohesion: different designs, different motivations. Local Environ. **21**(10), 1271–1287 (2016). https://doi.org/10.1080/13549839.2015.1101433

30. Wenger, E.: Communities of Practice: Learning, Meaning, and Identity. Cambridge University Press, Cambridge (1998)

31. Wenger, E.: Communities of practice and social learning systems. Organization **7**(2), 225–246 (2000). https://doi.org/10.1177/135050840072002

32. Yin, R.K.: Case Study Research: Design and Methods, vol. 5. Sage, Thousand Oaks (1994)

33. Zhilin, S.: Open Source Urbanism: A design method for cultivating information infrastructures in the urban commons. Ridderprint (2023)

Traffic Flow Prediction with Swiss Open Data: A Deep Learning Approach

Petros Brimos$^{(\boxtimes)}$ (iD), Areti Karamanou (iD), Evangelos Kalampokis (iD),
and Konstantinos Tarabanis (iD)

Information Systems Lab, Department of Business Administration,
University of Macedonia, 54636 Thessaloniki, Greece
{bad21024,akarm,ekal,kat}@uom.edu.gr

Abstract. Open government data (OGD) are provided by the public
sector and governments in an open, freely accessible format. Among various
types of OGD, dynamic data generated by sensors, such as traffic
data, can be utilized to develop innovative artificial intelligence (AI)
algorithms and applications. As AI algorithms, specifically Deep Neural
Networks, necessitate large amounts of data, dynamic OGD datasets
serve as supplemental resources to existing traffic datasets, used for performance
comparison and benchmarking. This work examines the effectiveness
of using open traffic data from the Swiss open data portal to
develop a Graph Neural Network (GNN) model for traffic forecasting.
To this end, the objective of this study is to probe the extent to which
dynamic OGD can enhance the accuracy and efficiency of traffic forecasting
models, and more critically, to investigate the potential of this
data in driving the development of cutting-edge AI models for traffic
flow prediction. We posit that strategic utilization of such data has the
potential to catalyze a transformative shift in the realm of traffic management
and control, by fostering intelligent solutions that effectively
leverage the predictive capabilities of AI models. The results indicate
that the GNN-based algorithm is effective in predicting future traffic
flow, outperforming two traditional baselines for time series forecasting.

Keywords: Dynamic Open Government Data · Traffic forecasting ·
Graph Neural Networks · Open Government Data · deep learning

1 Introduction

The Open Government Data (OGD) movement emerged in the early 21st century
[16], advocating for the release of government and public organization data
for private and commercial use. The potential benefits of OGD have been extensively
documented, including improved transparency [25], decision-making [33],
economic growth [23], innovation [38], and public service development [41]. The
deployment of OGD iniatiatives is an evolving phenomenon, with exponential
growth in the volume of data produced and the types of data generated [17].

© IFIP International Federation for Information Processing 2023
Published by Springer Nature Switzerland AG 2023
I. Lindgren et al. (Eds.): EGOV 2023, LNCS 14130, pp. 313–328, 2023.
https://doi.org/10.1007/978-3-031-41138-0_20

Dynamic data, including environmental, traffic, satellite, meteorological, and sensor-generated data, are now recognized as important components of OGD with significant economic value. The use of Dynamic OGD poses unique challenges due to their rapid obsolescence and variability. Immediate availability and regular updates are essential for these constantly evolving datasets. However, meeting these requirements can be difficult, particularly for real-time updates, which must be timely to ensure the data remains relevant. Additionally, dynamic OGD can contain missing values or extreme outliers due to sensor malfunctions or other factors, which can significantly impact the accuracy and quality of the underlying data. For example, traffic dynamic data collected by sensors may have a large amount of missing values or anomalies, resulting in incomplete or inaccurate information. Therefore, ensuring the accuracy and quality of dynamic OGD requires careful monitoring and maintenance to keep up with the evolving nature of the data [18,19]. Traffic data are dynamic data usually generated by sensors and have been recently recognised by the European Union as a part of Open Government Data that has a huge potential economic value [30], and facilitate the creation of added value data-driven services and applications [30]. For example, Open traffic data could be utilized to create applications that predict traffic flow, traffic speed, and traffic demand [13], and enhance the delivery of information and public services in the smart city context, improving quality of life and stimulating economic growth [31].

The core objective of this study is to explore the potential of dynamic Open Government Data in enhancing the precision and efficiency of artificial intelligence models, particularly focusing on traffic forecasting. In addition, this study seeks to substantiate the proposition that the strategic utilization of such data can significantly contribute to the development of innovative AI technologies and provides insights into the potential applications of such technologies in transportation planning and management. Towards this end, a case is used that collects and analyzes traffic data from the Open Transport Data portal of Switzerland, to predict future traffic flow using a Graph Neural Network model, namely Temporal Graph Convolutional Network [43].

This work is organized as follows. Section 2 describes Open Government Data and highlights the importance of dynamic traffic OGD. Section 3 presents the research approach of this study. Thereafter, Sects. 4, 5, 6 present data collection, pre-processing, and traffic forecasting using a GNN model. Finally, Sect. 7 discusses the results and concludes this work.

2   Traffic Open Government Data

Public sector and government agencies collect vast amounts of data from a variety of sources, including citizens, businesses, and other public or private organizations [21]. In the last few decades, the open government data movement and other open data initiatives, such as the Public Sector Information (PSI) Directive in Europe in 2003 [7], have motivated governments to "open" their data, increasing transparency and accountability to citizens, encouraging innovation by creating new added-value services, and motivating citizens to actively participate in governance processes [3]. To this end, hundred of OGD initiatives are taking place across the world providing OGD portals that publish and disseminate several datasets, including geospatial, environmental, transportation, and financial data. For example, the European Data Portal[1] provides 1,604,133 European public sector datasets from 36 European countries.

In recent years, there has been a notable shift in the approach of governments towards the dissemination of information, particularly in terms of the format and frequency of data publication. Traditionally, governments have relied on a paradigm of publishing data in static, infrequently updated formats, which have limited the ability of stakeholders to access and analyze information in a timely and efficient manner. However, a growing number of governments have recognized the value of providing dynamically updated data through online portals, enabling users to access and interact with the most current and relevant information available. This shift towards dynamic data provision has been driven by a range of factors, including the increasing importance of data-driven decision-making in government, the rise of open data initiatives, and the growing demand for transparency and accountability in public sector operations. As a result, many governments have invested significant resources in developing online platforms and tools that enable users to easily access, analyze, and visualize data in real-time, providing a level of flexibility and responsiveness that was previously unavailable.

Many OGD initiatives have promoted freely-accessible and re-usable dynamic data, by providing well-structured and machine-readable data catalogues, portals and interfaces that support automatic data transfer to all the involved target groups of OGD, including citizens, companies, researchers and other public authorities. The European Parliament has recognized the importance of exploiting public sector information [30], particularly real-time, dynamic data which are defined as frequently updated data, often in real time. The significant value of dynamic OGD depends on the immediate availability of data and the frequency of regular updates, facilitating the development of innovative and added-value services and applications. Therefore, dynamic OGD should be immediately available after collection via an API. Dynamic OGD, including environmental, meteorological, traffic and sensor-generated data are increasingly provided by OGD portals. At the same time they are characterized as high-value datasets because their re-use is related to important benefits to the environment, society and economy as well as to the creation of value-added services and applications.

Most recently, a significant increase in the availability of dynamic, real-time traffic data has been observed [11]. This type of data provide mobility related information, such as the total number of vehicles passed from a spatial point and their average speed or the trajectory of a moving object. Open traffic data are usually minutely or hourly aggregated and are available in various standard formats (e.g., using the JavaScript Object Notation - JSON, or eXtensible Markup Language, XML formats). However, that data are not always provided in real

---

[1] https://data.europa.eu/en.

time and cannot easily be retrieved to an external solution using Application Programming Interface (API) [28]. It is indicative that only few of the OGD portals use an API to enable accessing and retrieving the data. In addition, only a few of the OGD portals provide streaming traffic data. Some examples include the Greek OGD portal[2], which provides hourly aggregated traffic data (traffic flow and speed) in CSV or JSON format, and the Norwegian Public Roads Administrations' Traffic Data API[3], that also provides historical hourly aggregated data from 2019. Another example is The Swedish OGD portal[4] that contains streaming traffic data that can be downloaded in XML or JSON format. Finally, this study examines the potential of exploiting the Swiss OGD portal which returns real-time streaming data that are updated every minute, and can also be accessed via an API.

Freely-accessible traffic Open Government Data has the potential to enhance the delivery of advanced public services within the context of Smart Cities [31]. Furthermore, this data significantly contributes to the evolution of Intelligent Transportation Systems (ITS) [26]. ITS encapsulate a range of intelligent applications and technologies [14] addressing myriad transportation issues including, but not limited to, urban traffic congestion [2], traffic-light control, and road safety [35]. Traffic forecasting serves as a critical component of these technologies [22,32], that involves gathering, processing and analyzing massive amounts of traffic data, generated by sensors, to predict future traffic scenarios (e.g., traffic flow, speed, density). The evolution of traffic prediction has been significant in recent years, pivoting from traditional time-series analysis methods to data-driven models [9,22]. The availability of traffic-related data, collected from several sources such as loop detectors, GPS devices, traffic cameras, social media, and IoT-enabled vehicles, has provided an invaluable resource for these data-driven models. There are many forecasting methods considered in the literature, based on classic time-series statistics, such as the Autoregressive Integrated Moving Average [36], and machine learning approaches such as Support Vector Regression [39], K-nearest Neighbour [29] and Bayesian models [34]. These models, especially those based on deep learning, are capable of processing complex, high-dimensional data and extracting meaningful patterns, which are often beyond the reach of conventional time-series methods. They provide higher accuracy and improved predictive capabilities, focusing on the dynamic nature of traffic systems and their contextual factors, such as weather conditions and special events. This paradigm shift towards data-driven traffic prediction models has marked a promising direction for enhancing the efficiency and reliability of traffic management systems. Recently, the emerging development of deep learning and Graph Neural Networks [5,37] have achieved state-of-the-art performance in traffic forecasting tasks [1,12,40,42]. These models manage to capture the complex spatial-temporal dependencies of the road network [13]. Specifically, by modeling the road network (or sensor network) as a graph, these models extend the

---

[2] https://www.data.gov.gr/datasets/.
[3] https://www.vegvesen.no/trafikkdata/api/.
[4] https://api.trafikinfo.trafikverket.se.

convolution operation of Convolutional Neural Networks (CNNs) into the graph domain, effectively capturing the spatial correlations between sensors [6], while dynamic temporal dependencies are captured with the integration of Recurrent Neural Networks (RNNs) and their variants e.g. Long Short Memory Networks (LSTMs) and Gated Recurrent Units (GRUs) [8,10,43].

3   Approach

The research approach of this work uses three steps, namely (1) data collection, (2) data pre-processing, and (3) traffic flow forecasting.

3.1   Data Collection

Traffic data are provided by the Open Transport Data Portal of Switzerland (ODPCH) as streaming data[5]. This implies that historical data are not available since new data always replace old data. The data are minutely aggregated and updated every minute and specifically, 20 s after the minute in Coordinated Universal Time (UTC) 0. As a result, using the provided API to access traffic streams at a particular time will provide access to the traffic measurements of the last minute. The API provides access to two types of data: (a) static data that are actually master data that describe the sensors and their location, and (b) dynamic data with the measurements of the sensors. Both types of data are described using the DATEX II[6] standard for exchanging road traffic data. DATEX II is based on a specific XML schema that can be adapted according to the needs of the data provider. The Swiss profile for DATEX II is based on DATEX II version 2.3. Data were collected and stored using Google Cloud Platform (GCP)[7] services. In particular, streaming traffic data were acquired using Compute Engine, Pub/Sub and Dataflow GCP services. The data were stored in the cloud for the pre-processing and traffic forecasting steps.

Each sensor station employs multiple detectors to record data from different lanes. Detectors within a specific sensor station may be positioned in lanes with opposing directions and in various types of roads (e.g., main carriageways, entry or exit roads, etc.). Across Switzerland, there are 2,302 detectors generating traffic data. Each observation provides measurements for a single detector at a specific timestamp. In particular, every observation includes an identifier in the format "country:sensor station.detector number" to signify the specific detector. For instance, the ID "CH:0002.01" denotes sensor station 0002 and detector 01 situated in Switzerland, whereas "CH:0002.02" refers to the same sensor station but a different detector (i.e., one that is located in a different lane). For each detector the lane number is also provided. Lanes are numbered from right to left in the direction of travel. Each detector generates two types of measurements: (a) traffic flow, indicating the number of vehicles that traversed the lane within a

---

[5] https://opentransportdata.swiss/en/.

[6] https://www.datex2.eu/.

[7] https://cloud.google.com/.

one-minute period, and (b) traffic speed, denoting the average speed of vehicles that passed through the lane within the same minute. The measurements are provided separately for three vehicle classes; (a) light vehicles (e.g., cars, motorbikes, etc.), (b) heavy goods vehicles (i.e., trucks, with or without trailers), and (c) unclassified vehicles. In this study, all vehicle classes were aggregated in one column that represents the total number of vehicles measured by each sensor station per minute. These aggregated historical traffic observations are then used for traffic flow forecasting.

3.2   Data Pre-processing

In this step, traffic data are explored and pre-processed for the deployment of the GNN algorithm. Since this work focuses only on the traffic of the canton of Zurich, only data that were generated by sensors located within this canton were kept. Furthermore, it is common for data generated by sensors to include erroneous values. Erroneous values should be carefully handled (e.g., eliminated or imputed) to prevent inaccurate outcomes and decisions. In this step, we search in the traffic for erroneous values. We consider as erroneous measurements that (i) are missing from the dataset, or (ii) are not normal measurements based the an analysis called flow-speed correlation. Specifically, the missing observations per sensor were counted and observations reported by the portal as erroneous are also explored. In traffic data, the number of cars counted by a sensor and their average speed are strongly correlated. In particular, considering that each sensor measures data that pass from one or more lanes, the maximum number of vehicles that can pass in all lanes in one hour can be calculated using the following equation [4].

$$counted\_vehicles = \frac{speed * 1000}{vehicle\_length + \dfrac{speed}{3.6}} * lanes \qquad (1)$$

where *speed* is the average speed provided by the sensors measured in km per hour and *vehicle_length* is the average length of the different types of vehicles, the fraction *speed /3.6* represents the "safe driving distance" that should be kept between vehicles and is based on the vehicle speed, and *lanes* is the number of lanes in the road each sensor is positioned. The value of *vehicle_length* is set to 4. When the number of vehicles measured by a sensor in an hour is higher than this value, then the measurement is considered as an anomaly. Based on this equation, we calculated the total number of anomalies in the dataset as well as the anomalies per sensor.

Finally, to prepare the dataset for the GNN forecasting model, sensors with a high proportion of missing values and erroneous measurements were removed. The remaining sensors were then aggregated based on their lane IDs to create an aggregated detector that measures the total number of vehicles passing through all lanes corresponding to that sensor ID. Additionally, to align with the methodology used in related research papers, the original one-minute flow data was further aggregated into 5-min intervals. The final preprocessed dataset for the GNN model contains 7537 measurements per sensor, taken from a total of 521 aggregated detectors.

3.3 Traffic Flow Forecasting

Dynamic OGD traffic data can be effectively re-used for advancing cutting-edge deep learning models, such as Graph Neural Networks for traffic forecasting. In this study, we specifically employ the Temporal Graph Convolutional Network (TGCN) algorithm to illustrate the efficacy of this methodology. The TGCN algorithm exploits graph convolutions to comprehend the topology of the sensor network, thereby determining the spatial embeddings for each node. Moreover, it incorporates a Gated Recurrent Unit (GRU) to encapsulate the intricate temporal dependencies present within the traffic data. The aforementioned application serves to exemplify the promising intersection of dynamic OGD and modern deep learning techniques in the domain of traffic forecasting.

The GNN algorithm is created based on the pre-processed dataset of the previous step. For the deployment of the model the traffic data are normalized to the interval [0,1] using the min-max scaling method. Moreover, any missing values that were not excluded by the previous step were imputed using the linear interpolation method. 70% of the data was used for training, 20% for test and 10% for validation. To model the topology of the sensor graph, the adjacency matrix A is created based on the pairwise distances, d_{ij} that represent the distances between the 521 aggregated detectors. Each element on the adjacency matrix takes the value $A_{ij} = 1$ if $exp(-\frac{d_{ij}^2}{\sigma^2}) >= \epsilon$, otherwise $A_{ij} = 0$. This approach uses the Gaussian thresholded kernel, where σ^2, ϵ are thresholds that determine the distribution and sparsity of the matrix and are set to 10 and 0.5 respectively.

To evaluate the performance of the GNN algorithm, its prediction accuracy is compared with two baseline models, namely Autoregressive Integrated Moving Average (ARIMA) and Historical Average (HA). Three evaluation metrics are used in this study, namely the Root Mean Squared Error (RMSE), Mean Absolute Error (MAE), and Mean Absolute Percentage Error (MAPE). The proposed GNN algorithm employs a multi-step forecasting paradigm, where the model takes 12 past observations (corresponding to a time span of one hour) as input to predict the traffic flow for the next 3 (15 min), 6 (30 min), and 9 (45 min) time steps.

4 Data Collection

In this work, dynamic data were repeatedly retrieved using API calls every minute. Specifically, dynamic data were collected for the time period from 14-11-2022 08:24 to 10-12-2022 12:22 which corresponds to 26 days, 3 h and 59 min. To facilitate data analysis, the collected data were transformed into record level data, where each record represents a single observation, i.e., includes the measurements generated by one detector in one minute. Figure 1 presents a sample of the record level data.

sensor_lane_id	timestamp	vehicleFlowRate	number_of_cars	number_of_lorries	number_of_other	average_speed_cars	average_speed_lorries	average_speed_other
CH:0565.05	2022-11-14T08:24:00.000000Z	1560.0	24.0	2.0	NaN	84.000000	81.000000	NaN
CH:0565.05	2022-11-14T08:25:00.000000Z	1680.0	23.0	5.0	NaN	89.300003	83.800003	NaN
CH:0565.05	2022-11-14T08:26:00.000000Z	1680.0	23.0	5.0	NaN	75.199997	75.199997	NaN
CH:0565.05	2022-11-14T08:27:00.000000Z	1860.0	27.0	4.0	NaN	78.900002	78.300003	NaN
CH:0565.05	2022-11-14T08:28:00.000000Z	720.0	11.0	1.0	NaN	89.300003	80.000000	NaN
...	...	...	...	...	...	...	...	...
CH:0565.05	2022-12-10T12:18:00.000000Z	1380.0	23.0	NaN	NaN	91.000000	NaN	NaN
CH:0565.05	2022-12-10T12:19:00.000000Z	1260.0	20.0	1.0	NaN	89.199997	91.000000	NaN
CH:0565.05	2022-12-10T12:20:00.000000Z	1680.0	27.0	1.0	NaN	85.699997	85.000000	NaN
CH:0565.05	2022-12-10T12:21:00.000000Z	1500.0	25.0	NaN	NaN	91.800003	NaN	NaN
CH:0565.05	2022-12-10T12:22:00.000000Z	1560.0	25.0	1.0	NaN	85.699997	82.000000	NaN

Fig. 1. Record level traffic data.

The majority (88.6% or 754 sensors) of the detectors located in the canton of Zurich are positioned in main carriageways, while the rest of them are positioned in lanes of entry or exit slip roads. Finally, 26 detectors are located in emergency lanes. The dataset used in this work includes 28,822,562 observations from 851 detectors that belong to 312 sensor stations all of them located in the canton of Zurich. The mean number of detectors per sensor station is 2.7. In the selected time period, 114,854,670 vehicles passed from the roads of the canton of Zurich, the majority of them being light vehicles (96.15%), followed by heavy vehicles (3.85%).

In order to better understand traffic data, measurements generated by the detectors were statistically analysed. Towards this end, the observations of the 851 detectors were aggregated in 15 min intervals and, thereafter, the median, mean, standard deviation, and interquartile range (IQR) of the vehicles counted by detector were computed. Figure 2 illustrates the distribution of IQR based on the number of vehicles (light, heavy, or other) counted by each sensor-lane id. The right-skewed distribution reveals that few of the sensors count very large number of vehicles.

5 Data Pre-processing

In this work missing values are identified as the number of missing values per detector. Specifically, considering that the dataset doesn't contain any missed observations, the 851 sensors would have generated 32,064,829 observations during the selected time frame (14/11/2022 08:24am to 10/12/2022 12:22pm). Nevertheless, 3,242,267 observations (or 10.11%) are missing. The median percent of missing observations is 9.82% meaning that half of the detectors have less than or equal percents of missing observations to the median, and half of the detectors have greater than or equal percents of missing observations to it. The 50%

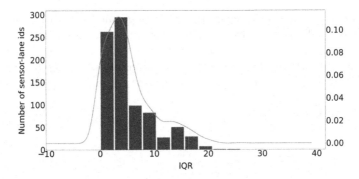

Fig. 2. The IQR distribution of the number of vehicles (of all types) counted by each sensor-lane id.

of the sensors have percent of missing observations in the range 9.75% - 9.83% (interquartile range box). In addition, if we exclude outliers, and based on the bottom 25% and top 25% of the data values, the percent of missing observations of each detector may be as low as 9.75% and as high as 9.83%. Finally, based on our calculations, only 10 detectors have more than 10% missing observations and two above 23%. Specifically, there are two detectors (namely "ZH.CH:0488.01" and "ZH.CH:0488.02") with 99.99% percent of missing observations. For the specific detectors, the available observations include only erroneous measurements. For the flow-speed correlation analysis we calculate the number and percentages of anomalies per (aggregated) detector. Out of the 17,671,322 aggregated observations, only 1478 count more vehicles than the number calculated by the filter (0.0084% of total observations). These anomalies are generated by 41 (aggregated) detectors (7.9% of the aggregated detectors). We also calculated the number of anomalies per (aggregated) detector. This number ranges from 0 to 132 anomalies. In addition, the mean number of detected anomalies per (aggregated) detector is 2.83, while the median is 0 anomalies per (aggregated) detector, meaning that more than half of the (aggregated) detectors have zero anomalies.

In the final preprocessing step of the traffic dataset, we aggregated the sensor lane IDs to create aggregated detectors that measure traffic flow from all lanes at a specific station. As described in Sect. 3, each sensor ID is composed of a sensor station and a detector number. However, in some cases, a station may include multiple traffic detectors, some of which might be in the opposite direction. To address this issue, we extracted additional information from the static dataset, namely the TMC direction, which indicates the direction of the specific road (negative or positive). Sensors from the same station and direction were then aggregated to form a single aggregated detector. For instance, sensors CH:002:01, CH:002:02, and CH:002:03 with a positive TMC direction were aggregated to form CH:002_positive, while sensors CH:002:04, CH:002:05, and CH:002:06 with a negative TMC direction were aggregated to form CH:002_negative. By aggregating sensors based on their station and direction, we ensured that sensors that are not connected on the traffic graph are distinguished and treated as separate nodes. This final step resulted in a total of 521 aggregated detectors, out of the initial 851 sensor lane IDs. These detectors were then used for traffic flow forecasting using the proposed GNN model. Figure 3 shows the 521 aggregated detectors that were used to construct the sensor graph for the GNN model.

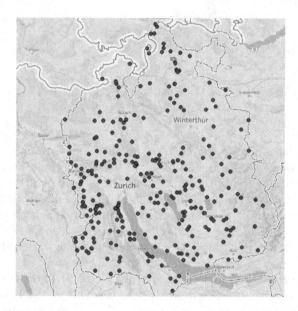

Fig. 3. View of the 521 aggregated detectors in the canton of Zurich. Each point in the map represents aggregated detectors that were created by aggregating the sensor lane IDs during the preprocessing step of the traffic dataset.

6 Traffic Flow Forecasting

In this section, the preprocessed dataset from the previous section is used to perform traffic flow forecasting, including 3,926,777 observations from 521 sensors. TGCN uses 2 graph convolutional layers with 64 and 10 units per layer, and 2 gated recurrent units to capture dynamic temporal dependencies, with 256 units per layer. Among several hyper-parameters of the GNN model, the learning rate is set to 0.001 and the number of training epochs is 100. Table 1 summarizes the results of this study, where we evaluate the forecasting models using three regression error metrics: RMSE, MAE, and MAPE. Our evaluation shows that the TGCN algorithm outperforms the baseline models in terms of prediction accuracy across all forecasting horizons. Specifically, the GNN-based model outperforms the two baselines, with RMSE decreased by 34.4% and 27% compared with HA and ARIMA respectively on the 15-min prediction horizon. As expected the error metrics are increased for the 30 and 60 min prediction, with TGCN achieving the best prediction performance. Figures 4 and 5 show the forecasting visualization regarding sensors CH0286 (positive) and ZH.CH2090 (negative) on the 15 min forecasting horizon. The results show that the TGCN algorithm can effectively predict traffic flow in both morning and evening peak hours. Moreover, both prediction curves indicate that the GNN-based model manage to capture the sudden changes of traffic flow.

Table 1. Performance comparison for GNN and baseline models on the Swiss OGD traffic dataset.

Forecasting Horizon	Metric	HA	ARIMA	TGCN
3 (15 min)	RMSE	27.26	24.42	17.87
	MAE	8.95	10.12	5.67
	MAPE	9.56%	8.98%	4.27%
6 (30 min)	RMSE	27.26	26.78	18.32
	MAE	8.95	11.33	7.32
	MAPE	9.56%	9.02%	6.23%
9 (45 min)	RMSE	27.26	28.39	19.23
	MAE	8.95	9.17	8.22
	MAPE	9.56%	10.13%	8.42%

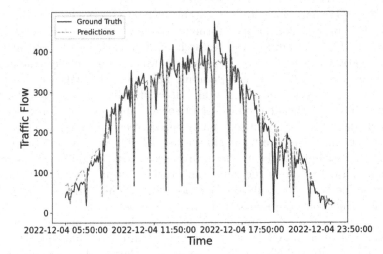

Fig. 4. Comparison of the prediction curve (TGCN) and ground truth for 15 min ahead prediction on snapshot of the test dataset for sensor CH0286_positive.

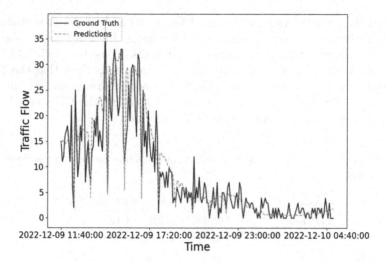

Fig. 5. Comparison of the prediction curve (TGCN) and ground truth for 15 min ahead prediction on snapshot of the test dataset for sensor ZH.CH2090_negative.

7   Discussion and Conclusion

The availability of Open Government Data has created new opportunities for enhancing transparency, accountability, and civic participation in governments [3]. OGD portals have been established by governments worldwide to publish their information in open formats, thereby making them accessible to citizens, other public authorities, researchers, and businesses. Such initiatives aim to create a more inclusive and participatory democracy by enabling the public to engage with government data and hold public officials accountable. In addition to promoting transparency and accountability in governments, OGD initiatives have significant economic and social value. By providing access to high-value datasets, OGD can spur innovation and entrepreneurship, leading to the development of new products and services [15,20]. Dynamic OGD, a subset of OGD that includes real-time data, are particularly valuable in this regard. Real-time data, such as traffic data, can provide insights into traffic patterns, improve traffic flow, and reduce congestion [2,27]. This can result in reduced travel time, fuel consumption, and environmental pollution.

The recent advances in Artificial Intelligence have further highlighted the importance of dynamic OGD. AI algorithms require large amounts of data to function accurately and effectively. However, such data is often available only in closed formats due to privacy concerns and regulations. This creates a challenge for the research community, developers, and both private and public sectors in testing and training various models, as there is a lack of open, freely accessible data. Open government data can help bridge this gap and provide valuable information and datasets for developing efficient algorithms. In particular, dynamic traffic OGD can provide real-time data streams that are necessary for training and testing AI models for traffic forecasting, especially deep learning algorithms [6,8,10,43,44]. Most research papers in traffic forecasting, particularly those that explore state-of-the-art deep learning models such as Graph Neural Networks [6,24,40,42,43] primarily rely on open, benchmarking traffic datasets, such as PEMS[8] and METR-LA [24]. These datasets are limited to specific geographical areas and historical time periods (e.g., 2012). This may limit the generalizability of the AI models trained on these datasets to different traffic environments and periods. To address this limitation and promote the use of AI algorithms such as GNNs in diverse traffic environments, it is necessary to leverage Dynamic Traffic Open Government Data as alternative datasets. Dynamic traffic OGD provide more diverse and up-to-date datasets that are not limited to specific geographical areas or time periods, which is crucial for testing and improving the performance of GNNs and other deep learning models. Therefore, incorporating dynamic traffic OGD in future research studies can enhance the efficiency of GNNs and other AI models for traffic forecasting tasks. This access to OGD can enable the development of more effective AI technologies and applications, leading to significant economic and social benefits. Therefore, governments should continue to invest in dynamic OGD initiatives to promote transparency, accountability, and economic growth in the years to come.

The purpose of this study is to demonstrate the potential use of dynamic OGD for developing state-of-the-art AI models and technologies. In particular, the study focuses on the application of a Graph Neural Network, namely Temporal Graph Convolutional Network, for predicting traffic flow. Traffic forecasting is a crucial area for transportation planning and management. GNNs are considered one of the most effective deep learning algorithms for traffic forecasting, as they can model the road network as a graph and learn the complex spatial and temporal dynamics of traffic flow. The results of this work show that the GNN model trained on Swiss Traffic OGD can accurately predict traffic flow, outperforming two baseline models, namely Historical Average and Autoregressive Integrated Moving Average, and can potentially be used for real-time traffic management and planning.

References

1. Agafonov, A.: Traffic flow prediction using graph convolution neural networks. In: 2020 10th International Conference on Information Science and Technology (ICIST), pp. 91–95 (2020). https://doi.org/10.1109/ICIST49303.2020.9201971
2. Ata, A., Khan, M.A., Abbas, S., Khan, M.S., Ahmad, G.: Adaptive IoT empowered smart road traffic congestion control system using supervised machine learning algorithm. Comput. J. **64**(11), 1672–1679 (2021)
3. Attard, J., Orlandi, F., Scerri, S., Auer, S.: A systematic review of open government data initiatives. Gov. Inf. Q. **32**(4), 399–418 (2015). https://doi.org/10.1016/j.giq.2015.07.006

---

4. Bachechi, C., Rollo, F., Po, L.: Detection and classification of sensor anomalies for simulating urban traffic scenarios. Cluster Comput. **25**(4), 2793–2817 (2022). https://doi.org/10.1007/s10586-021-03445-7

5. Bronstein, M.M., Bruna, J., LeCun, Y., Szlam, A., Vandergheynst, P.: Geometric deep learning: going beyond euclidean data. IEEE Signal Process. Mag. **34**(4), 18–42 (2017). https://doi.org/10.1109/MSP.2017.2693418

6. Bui, K.H.N., Cho, J., Yi, H.: Spatial-temporal graph neural network for traffic forecasting: an overview and open research issues. Appl. Intell. **52**(3), 2763–2774 (2022). https://doi.org/10.1007/s10489-021-02587-w

7. Cox, P., Alemanno, G.: Directive 2003/98/EC of the European parliament and of the council of 17 November 2003 on the re-use of public sector information. Off. J. Eur. Union **46**, 1–156 (2003)

8. Cui, Z., Ke, R., Pu, Z., Wang, Y.: Deep bidirectional and unidirectional LSTM recurrent neural network for network-wide traffic speed prediction (2018). https://doi.org/10.48550/ARXIV.1801.02143

9. Ermagun, A., Levinson, D.: Spatiotemporal traffic forecasting: review and proposed directions. Transp. Rev. **38**(6), 786–814 (2018). https://doi.org/10.1080/01441647.2018.1442887

10. Fu, R., Zhang, Z., Li, L.: Using LSTM and GRU neural network methods for traffic flow prediction. In: 2016 31st Youth Academic Annual Conference of Chinese Association of Automation (YAC), pp. 324–328 (2016). https://doi.org/10.1109/YAC.2016.7804912

11. Gregurić, M., Vujić, M., Alexopoulos, C., Miletić, M.: Application of deep reinforcement learning in traffic signal control: an overview and impact of open traffic data. Appl. Sci. **10**(11), 4011 (2020). https://doi.org/10.3390/app10114011

12. Guo, S., Lin, Y., Feng, N., Song, C., Wan, H.: Attention based spatial-temporal graph convolutional networks for traffic flow forecasting. In: Proceedings of the AAAI Conference on Artificial Intelligence, vol. 33, no. 01, pp. 922–929 (2019). https://doi.org/10.1609/aaai.v33i01.3301922

13. Jiang, W., Luo, J.: Graph neural network for traffic forecasting: a survey. Expert Syst. Appl. **207**, 117921 (2022). https://doi.org/10.1016/j.eswa.2022.117921

14. Kaffash, S., Nguyen, A.T., Zhu, J.: Big data algorithms and applications in intelligent transportation system: a review and bibliometric analysis. Int. J. Prod. Econ. **231**, 107868 (2021). https://doi.org/10.1016/j.ijpe.2020.107868

15. Kalampokis, E., Karacapilidis, N., Tsakalidis, D., Tarabanis, K.: Artificial intelligence and blockchain technologies in the public sector: a research projects perspective. In: Janssen, M., et al. (eds.) EGOV 2022. LNCS, vol. 13391, pp. 323–335. Springer, Cham (2022). https://doi.org/10.1007/978-3-031-15086-9_21

16. Kalampokis, E., Tambouris, E., Tarabanis, K.: A classification scheme for open government data: towards linking decentralised data. Int. J. Web Eng. Technol. **6**(3), 266–285 (2011)

17. Kalampokis, E., Tambouris, E., Tarabanis, K.: Open government data: a stage model. In: Janssen, M., Scholl, H.J., Wimmer, M.A., Tan, Y. (eds.) EGOV 2011. LNCS, vol. 6846, pp. 235–246. Springer, Heidelberg (2011). https://doi.org/10.1007/978-3-642-22878-0_20

18. Karamanou, A., Brimos, P., Kalampokis, E., Tarabanis, K.: Exploring the quality of dynamic open government data using statistical and machine learning methods. Sensors **22**(24), 9684 (2022). https://doi.org/10.3390/s22249684

19. Karamanou, A., Brimos, P., Kalampokis, E., Tarabanis, K.: Exploring the quality of dynamic open government data for developing data intelligence applications: the

case of attica traffic data. In: Proceedings of the 26th Pan-Hellenic Conference on Informatics, PCI 2022, pp. 102–109. Association for Computing Machinery, New York (2023). https://doi.org/10.1145/3575879.3575974

20. Karamanou, A., Kalampokis, E., Tarabanis, K.: Linked open government data to predict and explain house prices: the case of scottish statistics portal. Big Data Res. **30**, 100355 (2022)

21. Karamanou, A., Kalampokis, E., Tarabanis, K.: Integrated statistical indicators from scottish linked open government data. Data Brief **46**, 108779 (2023)

22. Lana, I., Del Ser, J., Velez, M., Vlahogianni, E.I.: Road traffic forecasting: recent advances and new challenges. IEEE Intell. Transp. Syst. Mag. **10**(2), 93–109 (2018). https://doi.org/10.1109/MITS.2018.2806634

23. Leviäkangas, P., Molarius, R.: Open government data policy and value added-evidence on transport safety agency case. Technol. Soc. **63**, 101389 (2020)

24. Li, Y., Yu, R., Shahabi, C., Liu, Y.: Diffusion convolutional recurrent neural network: data-driven traffic forecasting. In: International Conference on Learning Representations (2017)

25. Lourenço, R.P.: An analysis of open government portals: a perspective of transparency for accountability. Gov. Inf. Q. **32**(3), 323–332 (2015)

26. Mahrez, Z., Sabir, E., Badidi, E., Saad, W., Sadik, M.: Smart urban mobility: when mobility systems meet smart data. IEEE Trans. Intell. Transp. Syst. **23**(7), 6222–6239 (2022). https://doi.org/10.1109/TITS.2021.3084907

27. Navarro-Espinoza, A., et al.: Traffic flow prediction for smart traffic lights using machine learning algorithms. Technologies **10**(1), 5 (2022). https://doi.org/10.3390/technologies10010005

28. Nikiforova, A.: Smarter open government data for society 5.0: are your open data smart enough? Sensors **21**(15), 5204 (2021)

29. Pang, X., Wang, C., Huang, G.: A short-term traffic flow forecasting method based on a three-layer k-nearest neighbor non-parametric regression algorithm. J. Transp. Technol. **6**, 200–206 (2016). https://doi.org/10.4236/jtts.2016.64020

30. European Parliament: Directive (EU) 2019/1024 of the European parliament and of the council of 20 June 2019 on open data and the re-use of public sector information (recast). Off. J. Eur. Union **172**, 56–83 (2019)

31. Pereira, G.V., Macadar, M.A., Luciano, E.M., Testa, M.G.: Delivering public value through open government data initiatives in a Smart City context. Inf. Syst. Front. **19**(2), 213–229 (2016). https://doi.org/10.1007/s10796-016-9673-7

32. Qi, Y., Cheng, Z.: Research on traffic congestion forecast based on deep learning. Information **14**(2), 108 (2023). https://doi.org/10.3390/info14020108

33. Ruijer, E., Grimmelikhuijsen, S., Meijer, A.: Open data for democracy: developing a theoretical framework for open data use. Gov. Inf. Q. **34**(1), 45–52 (2017)

34. Sun, S., Zhang, C., Yu, G.: A Bayesian network approach to traffic flow forecasting. IEEE Trans. Intell. Transp. Syst. **7**(1), 124–132 (2006). https://doi.org/10.1109/TITS.2006.869623

35. Varga, N., Bokor, L., Takács, A., Kovács, J., Virág, L.: An architecture proposal for V2X communication-centric traffic light controller systems. In: 2017 15th International Conference on ITS Telecommunications (ITST), pp. 1–7. IEEE (2017)

36. Williams, B.M., Hoel, L.A.: Modeling and forecasting vehicular traffic flow as a seasonal arima process: theoretical basis and empirical results. J. Transp. Eng. **129**(6), 664–672 (2003). https://doi.org/10.1061/(ASCE)0733-947X(2003)129:6(664)

37. Wu, Z., Pan, S., Chen, F., Long, G., Zhang, C., Yu, P.S.: A comprehensive survey on graph neural networks. IEEE Trans. Neural Netw. Learn. Syst. **32**(1), 4–24 (2021). https://doi.org/10.1109/tnnls.2020.2978386

38. Yang, Z., Ha, S., Kankanhalli, A., Um, S.: Understanding the determinants of the intention to innovate with open government data among potential commercial innovators: a risk perspective. Internet Res. (2022, ahead-of-print)

39. Yao, Z., Shao, C., Gao, Y.: Research on methods of short-term traffic forecasting based on support vector regression. J. Beijing Jiaotong Univ. 30(3), 19–22 (2006)

40. Yu, B., Yin, H., Zhu, Z.: Spatio-temporal graph convolutional networks: a deep learning framework for traffic forecasting. In: Proceedings of the Twenty-Seventh International Joint Conference on Artificial Intelligence. International Joint Conferences on Artificial Intelligence Organization (2018). https://doi.org/10.24963/ijcai.2018/505

41. Zhang, J., Puron-Cid, G., Gil-Garcia, J.R.: Creating public value through open government: perspectives, experiences and applications. Inf. Polity 20(2–3), 97–101 (2015)

42. Zhang, Y., Cheng, T., Ren, Y., Xie, K.: A novel residual graph convolution deep learning model for short-term network-based traffic forecasting. Int. J. Geogr. Inf. Sci. 34(5), 969–995 (2020). https://doi.org/10.1080/13658816.2019.1697879

43. Zhao, L., et al.: T-GCN: a temporal graph convolutional network for traffic prediction. IEEE Trans. Intell. Transp. Syst. 21(9), 3848–3858 (2020). https://doi.org/10.1109/tits.2019.2935152

44. Zhou, Q., Chen, N., Lin, S.: FASTNN: a deep learning approach for traffic flow prediction considering spatiotemporal features. Sensors 22(18), 6921 (2022). https://doi.org/10.3390/s22186921

A Systematic Literature Review on the Adoption of Edge Computing for Sustainable Development

May Myat Thwe$^{(\boxtimes)}$ and Kyung Ryul Park

Graduate School of Science and Technology Policy,
Korea Advanced Institute of Science and Technology (KAIST),
Daejeon, Republic of Korea
{maymyatthwe,park.kr}@kaist.ac.kr

Abstract. Digital technologies have been increasingly applied to support the 17 Sustainable Development Goals (SDGs), which address global challenges, including poverty, inequality, and climate change. Edge computing is a rapidly developing digital technology with widespread use, primarily for applications that produce massive amounts of data and require real-time data analysis. This paper examines the potential of edge computing and how it can help achieve the SDGs and advance several development areas. We reviewed the case studies previously published in the literature. A total of 92 primary studies were analyzed, and the cases in those studies were organized based on the various development sectors/industries and use cases and mapped to sustainable development goals. We also identified other emerging technologies that have been cooperatively applied and integrated with edge computing technology. Our findings reveal that transportation is the most prominent development sector adopting edge computing, and we discuss the potential challenges and opportunities associated with edge computing adoption by taking an intelligent transportation system use case as an example. This study aims to guide researchers and policymakers seeking to understand the edge computing paradigm in the context of sustainable development.

Keywords: edge computing · sustainable development · SDG · use case · literature review

1 Introduction

The Sustainable Development Goals (SDGs) adopted by the United Nations in 2015 are 17 goals that aim to address some of the most pressing global challenges, including poverty, inequality, and climate change [3]. Achieving these goals requires innovative solutions [16], and one of the technologies that have

This work was supported by Hyundai Motor Chung Mong-Koo Foundation Scholarship Program.

© IFIP International Federation for Information Processing 2023
Published by Springer Nature Switzerland AG 2023
I. Lindgren et al. (Eds.): EGOV 2023, LNCS 14130, pp. 329–344, 2023.
https://doi.org/10.1007/978-3-031-41138-0_21

been increasingly applied to this effort is edge computing, particularly for applications that generate large amounts of data which require real-time data analysis, such as traffic monitoring, water, and energy management, and disaster response [15, 29]. An increase in data exchange and communication among heterogeneous Internet of Things (IoT) devices has led to massive data generation, which maximizes the demand for data processing. Traditional cloud-computing architecture becomes inefficient due to data mobility constraints and real-time processing delays. Edge computing is a distributed computing paradigm that performs data processing and data storage closer to where it is needed, reducing latency and improving data processing efficiency [7, 8, 35]. Much research in recent years has provided comprehensive surveys of recent advancements in edge computing, highlighting the concepts, technological development, applications, and future research directions [22, 24, 27, 35]. However, no research yet reviews the use cases of edge computing for each SDG, mapping out how it can support sustainable development goals, development sectors/industries and address the challenges of its adoption.

This review paper aims to present a comprehensive review of how edge computing has been adopted to support sustainable development and deployed in areas that are not yet well documented in the literature. and investigate the potential challenges and opportunities of edge computing adoption, which can be helpful for researchers and policymakers to understand the deployment of edge computing to support the SDGs in their specific contexts. The contributions of this paper are as follows:

- To analyze the proportion of edge computing case studies that appeared in existing studies, which are contributing to SDGs and identify which SDG has the significant potential to take advantage of edge computing
- To identify different development sectors/industries, with applications relevant to the SDGs, that have been adopting edge computing
- To present different use cases of edge computing across sectors/industries
- To highlight the emerging technologies that have be integrated and cooperatively applied along with edge computing
- To discuss the challenges and opportunities of edge computing adoption for sustainable development

The remainder of the paper will be organized as follows. Section 2 explains background information on edge computing, SDGs, and their applications for sustainable development. Section 3 provides the related work on the existing edge computing surveys. Section 4 describes a protocol for conducting the review for this paper. Section 5 presents the review results, including the distribution of edge computing case studies for each SDG, use cases in development sectors/industries, and other emerging technologies cooperatively applied with edge computing. Finally, the paper concludes with a discussion of challenges and opportunities associated with using edge computing adoption and future work in Sect. 6 and 7.

2   Background

2.1   Edge Computing

Edge computing has become increasingly popular in recent years as the Internet of Things (IoT) and data volume generated from IoT devices have grown, so streaming the information between IoT devices and cloud data centers becomes inefficient. The horizon of edge computing brings data processing at the network edge near the source of its generation, which improves the speed and efficiency while reducing the cost and complexity of transmitting large amounts of data to a centralized location [35]. IoT devices have limited processing capabilities, and data generated from them have to travel over the network to the cloud for processing, which can be unsuitable for situations where the latency of milliseconds can pose serious threats. Thus, researchers have focused on the edge computing paradigm, which encompasses the data processing and storage to perform at the network edges close to the end-users, fastening the response time and providing better bandwidth availability of IoT systems while enhancing security and reliability. Figure 1 illustrates a sample of the three-layered edge-cloud collaboration architecture of an intelligent transportation system composed of heterogeneous components. The IoT device layer generates data, and edge servers, or nodes, perform the local computations of data produced from IoT devices while the cloud server process and store the data collected from the edge servers.

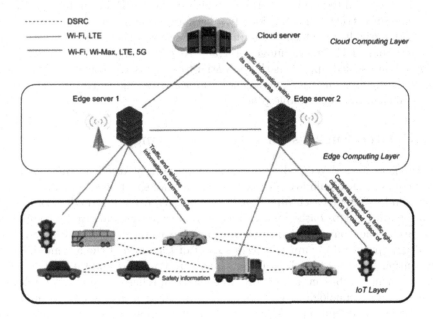

Fig. 1. Overview of Edge-Cloud Architecture for Intelligent Transportation System

2.2   Sustainable Development Goals (SDGs)

"The 2030 Agenda for Sustainable Development" was established by United Nations member states in 2015, acknowledging that ending poverty and deprivations must go together with strategies for improvement in health and education, inequality reduction, and economic growth while addressing climate change and preserving oceans and forests [3]. In this regard, 17 Sustainable Development Goals (SDGs) in a list of 169 SDG targets and 232 unique indicators are defined, a universal call to action to end poverty while protecting the planet and ensuring that all people enjoy prosperity and peace by 2030. Table 1 describes the SDG goal codes and goal names.

2.3   Adoption of Edge Computing for Sustainable Development

Edge computing has been increasingly adopted to transform development sectors/industries and support various Sustainable Development Goals (SDGs). For instance, in the healthcare sector, edge computing has been used to support telemedicine and remote patient monitoring [13,17], which can improve access to healthcare services and support SDG 3 (good health and well-being). Edge computing has also been used to support renewable energy systems and smart grid management, which can help reduce greenhouse gas emissions [10,29] and contribute to SDG 7 (affordable and clean energy). In the manufacturing industry, edge computing has been used to monitor assembly lines, optimize energy consumption and reduce waste [18,36], which supports SDG 9 (industry, innovation, and infrastructure). Additionally, edge computing has been used to support precision agriculture, which can improve food security that can help SDG 1 (no poverty) and SDG 2 (zero hunger) [11,30]. As edge computing continues to be adopted and scaled up, it has the potential to support the achievement of various SDGs by enabling the deployment of innovative technologies and supporting more efficient and sustainable practices.

3   Related Surveys on Edge Computing

Researchers have developed comprehensive surveys of recent advancements in edge computing, highlighting the concepts, technological development, applications, and future research directions. Yu et al. [35] categorized edge computing into separate groups based on architecture and their performance by comparing network latency, bandwidth occupation, energy consumption, and overhead. Mao et al. [27] provided a comprehensive survey of the state-of-the-art mobile edge computing (MEC) research focusing on joint radio-and-computational resource management. Abbas et al. [9] presented a comprehensive survey of relevant research and technological developments in the area of mobile edge computing. It provides the definition of MEC, its advantages, architectures, and application areas. Liu et al. [24] surveyed a comprehensive overview of the existing edge computing systems by introducing representative projects and comparing open-source tools. Khan et al. [22] presented a comprehensive survey of differences in edge and cloud computing concepts, highlighting the characteristics of edge computing and the core applications. Wang et al. [33] organized the application scenarios and the practical implementation methods of deep learning in edge computing frameworks. So far, there has been no survey to analyze edge computing use cases from the perspective of sustainable development goals and sectors/industries, and this is the first survey to provide them.

Table 1. SDG Goals and Names [3]

SDG Goal Codes	SDG Goal Names
1	End poverty in all its forms everywhere
2	End hunger, achieve food security and improved nutrition, and promote sustainable agriculture
3	Ensure healthy lives and promote well-being for all at all ages
4	Ensure inclusive and equitable quality education and promote lifelong learning opportunities for all
5	Achieve gender equality and empower all women and girls
6	Ensure availability and sustainable management of water and sanitation for all
7	Ensure access to affordable, reliable, sustainable, and modern energy for all
8	Promote sustained, inclusive, and sustainable economic growth, full and productive employment, and decent work for all
9	Build resilient infrastructure, promote inclusive and sustainable industrialization, and foster innovation
10	Reduce inequality within and among countries
11	Make cities and human settlements inclusive, safe, resilient, and sustainable
12	Ensure sustainable consumption and production patterns
13	Take urgent action to combat climate change and its impacts
14	Conserve and sustainably use the oceans, seas, and marine resources for sustainable development
15	Protect, restore, and promote sustainable use of terrestrial ecosystems, sustainably manage forests, combat desertification, and halt and reverse land degradation and halt biodiversity loss
16	Promote peaceful and inclusive societies for sustainable development, provide access to justice for all, and build effective, accountable, and inclusive institutions at all levels
17	Strengthen the means of implementation and revitalize the global partnership for sustainable development

Table 2. Research Questions

ID	Research Questions
RQ1	For which sustainable development goals that edge computing have potential to support significantly?
RQ2	Which development sectors/industries, with applications relevant to the SDGs, have been adopting edge computing so far?
RQ3	What are the different use cases of edge computing in those sectors/industries?
RQ4	What are other technologies that have been integrated and cooperatively applied in edge computing environment?

4   Review Protocol

To conduct this literature review, we designed a review protocol that includes the review steps and inputs and outputs for each step, as depicted in Fig. 2. Based on the objective of this review paper, we specified the search strings, automated search engines, and research questions (RQ). The paper articles searched were assessed to determine whether they met the predefined criteria for primary studies. The selected primary studies were examined thoroughly for the data analysis, and review results were reported in Sect. 5. This review paper aims to show the landscape of edge computing use cases for sustainable development. To achieve this goal, we specified research questions, as shown in Table 2. To find the related papers, we used the following search string.

{(**edge computing**) AND (**use case** OR **case study**)} OR (**edge computing**) AND (**SDG**)}

To collect relevant primary studies to answer the RQs, we utilized Google Scholar (https://scholar.google.com) and the Web of Science (https://www.webofknowledge.com) search engines to find related papers. To search for as many related papers as possible, we included articles from different fields as stated in Table 3. The searched papers were organized through the Excel spreadsheet including the titles, abstract, keywords and year of the articles. The searched papers were then evaluated using the predefined selection criteria in Table 3. If a paper satisfied all the inclusion criteria and none of the exclusion criteria, it was selected as a primary study. Following our review protocol, we found 92 primary studies, and conducted data extraction and labelling manually, and collected data were analyzed and categorized to answer the RQs.

In this way, our protocol makes it possible to meet the research questions of the study as follows. RQ1 aims to analyze which SDGs are where edge computing is most applied. Therefore, we examined the case studies described in the primary studies and labeled the goal codes for each paper. We included RQ2 because most primary studies do not explicitly identify specific sustainable development use cases and only present the feasibility of their proposed approaches by providing case studies. Therefore, we clarified the different development sectors/industries where edge computing is being adopted. Additionally, for RQ3, we present the use cases for each sector along with some references. RQ4 examined the challenges and opportunities.

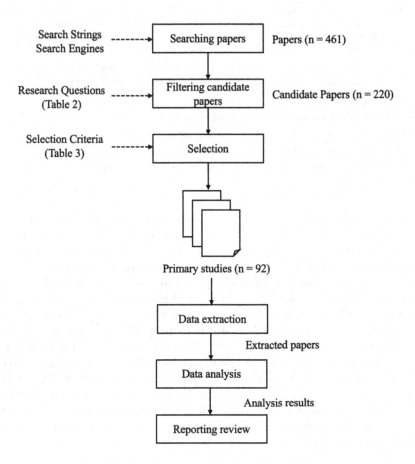

Fig. 2. Overview of Review Protocol

5   Review Results

5.1   RQ1: The Proportion of Edge Computing Case Studies on SDGs

The pie chart in Fig. 3 illustrates the distribution of edge computing applications for Sustainable Development Goals (SDGs) based on an analysis of 92 primary studies. The results show that the majority of the case studies contribute to

Table 3. Selection Criteria

ID	Inclusion Criteria (IC) and Exclusion Criteria (EC)
IC1	Papers written in English
IC2	Research papers peer-reviewed and published in conferences and journals
IC3	Papers in the fields of Computer Science, Engineering, Telecommunications, Transportation, Automation and Control Systems, Instruments and Instrumentation, Energy and Fuels, Science and Technology, Environmental Sciences and Ecology, Government, and Law
IC4	Papers on the topic of edge computing that presented the case study
IC5	Papers that are published between January 2016 to March 2023
EC1	Duplicated Papers
EC2	Papers whose contents are not fully accessible
EC3	Papers not in the form of full research papers (i.e., abstracts or reports)
EC4	Collections of studies (i.e., books, proceedings)
EC5	Papers summarising existing studies or concepts (i.e., surveys)

SDG 11 (Sustainable Cities and Communities) and SDG 9 (Industry, Innovation, and Infrastructure), accounting for 53.4%, followed by 14.2% for SDG 3 (Good Health and Well-being), 8.5% and 6.8% for SDG 12 (Responsible Consumption and Production), and SDG 13 (Climate Action), respectively. The findings also reveal that edge computing has been applied to a lesser extent for 4.5% SDG 2 (Zero Hunger) and 4% SDG 1 (No Poverty). While SDG 7 (Affordable and Clean Energy) and SDG 15 (Life on Land) account for 3.4% and 2.8%, about 2% of the case studies contribute to SDG 10 (Reduced Inequalities), SDG 14 (Life Below Water), and SDG 4 (Quality Education). However, the results highlight that no cases in primary papers describe the application of edge computing for SDG 5 (Gender Equality), SDG 6 (Clean Water and Sanitation), SDG 8 (Decent Work and Economic Growth), SDG 16 (Peace, Justice, and Strong Institutions), and SDG 17 (Partnerships for the Goals). These results suggest the need for further research and exploration to assess the potential of edge computing to support these SDGs.

5.2 RQ2: Proportion of Edge Computing Case Studies for Different Development Sectors/Industries

Edge computing has been widely applied across various sectors/industries to contribute towards achieving Sustainable Development Goals (SDGs). To answer RQ2, we categorized the cases in primary studies into ten development sectors/industries. Among the primary studies, we found that the number of case studies in the transportation sector is 30, followed by 23 cases in healthcare and 15 in manufacturing, which suggests the highest potential to transform the transportation and healthcare sectors/industries. Smart city (with 11 cases), agriculture (7), disaster management (6), and environmental management (4) industries have also adopted edge computing to a significant extent. However,

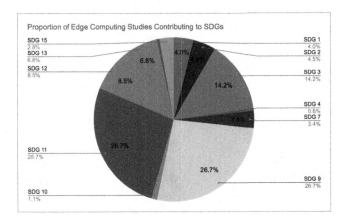

Fig. 3. Proportion of Edge Computing Studies Contributing to SDGs

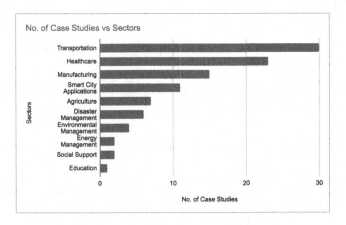

Fig. 4. Number of Edge Computing Case Studies for Different Sectors/Industries

the application of edge computing in the energy, social support, and education sector/industry has been relatively less studied. Figure 4 and Fig. 5 show the number and percentage of edge computing case studies for each sector.

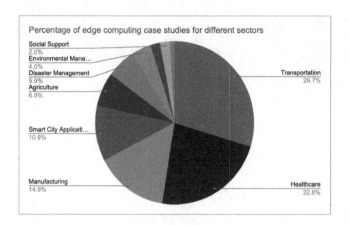

Fig. 5. Percentage of Edge Computing Adoption for Different Development Sectors/Industries

5.3   RQ3: Use Cases of Edge Computing in Development Sectors/Industries

Table 4 describes the different use cases for each sector along with some references.

Table 4. Sectors/Industries and Use Cases where Edge Computing is being deployed

Sector	Use Cases	Ref.
Transportation	Connected vehicles, Vehicle communication (V2V, V2X), Energy efficiency of UAM, Traffic management, Vehicle monitoring, Peer-to-peer (P2P) energy exchange of electric vehicles (EVs)	[12, 25]
Healthcare	Health condition monitoring, Health data analysis, Symptom prediction and diagnosis, Analysis of geo-health big data, Providing mobile health advice	[17, 20]
Manufacturing	Production, Assembly Monitoring, Fault Diagnosis of equipment	[18, 36]
Agriculture	Detection of plant diseases, Water management of plants, Farm management, Smart irrigation, Crop diagnosis	[11, 30]
Disaster management	Earthquake monitoring, Emergency response, Water level prediction, Disaster event detection, Emergency guidance for evacuation	[15, 23]
Environmental management	Managing forests, Air quality monitoring	[13, 31]
Energy	Optimization and automation of energy production from solar energy, State estimation of smart grids	[10, 29]
Smart city	Smart homes, Smart buildings, Smart airports, Smart parking	[21, 26]
Social support	Sign language recognition for disabled people, Voice assistant for elderly	[32, 34]
Education	Q&A with AI agents	[19]

5.4 RQ4: Emerging Technologies Adopted for SDGs

Emerging technologies such as the Internet of Things (IoT), Artificial Intelligence (AI), Big data analytics, Cloud Computing, and 5G have been integrated with edge computing technology. IoT devices are an essential component of edge computing as data sources for edge computing processes and analyses. They have been used to monitor environmental data, track energy usage, and optimize resource usage. Integrating big data analytics and artificial intelligence (AI) with edge computing has enabled real-time analysis of large volumes of data generated by IoT devices and identifying patterns to optimize energy consumption and resource usage. Additionally, the insights generated by AI and big data analytics have been used to predict future environmental conditions, allowing for the implementation of preventative measures. At the same time, cloud computing provides a platform for storing and providing the computing power needed to perform complex analyses of data generated from IoT devices. 5G networks are essential in offering low-latency, high-speed connectivity for edge computing to function timely and effectively. The integration of those technologies with edge computing enables real-time processing and analysis of data, making it possible to implement timely interventions for SDG projects.

6 Discussion

This section discuss the threat to validity of this study and potential challenges and opportunities to be considered when adopting edge computing for the sustainable development by providing a specific case of edge computing-based Intelligent Transportation Systems (ITS) as shown in Fig. 1.

6.1 Challenges and Opportunities of Edge Computing Adoption

Collaborations Between Heterogeneous Edge Computing Systems and Standardization Activities. Edge computing provides decentralized data processing and storage closer to the edge of the network where the data is generated, rather than relying on a centralized cloud infrastructure. ITS plays a significant role in advancing sustainable infrastructure and promoting innovation and creating sustainable cities by improving transportation efficiency, reducing congestion, and promoting multimodal transportation options, contributing to SDGs 9 and 11. As described in the Fig. 1, ITS is composed of heterogeneous and independent constituent system components, including vehicles, people, roadside units, and central control centers, that interact, collaborate, and communicate through vehicle-to-vehicle communication (V2V), vehicle-to-infrastructure (V2X), and so on. However, due to the diversity of the components in edge-cloud environments, which may originate from different vendors, they may have varying protocols, interfaces, and data formats, posing a significant challenge to ensuring interoperability and seamless collaboration among them. It encourages the development of comprehensive standards and guidelines that can ensure the effective integration of heterogeneous components in edge computing systems.

Acknowledging the essence of standardization, academic institutions, industry players, and standard organizations have been actively involved in developing and implementing standards for edge computing, and diverse consortiums, alliances, and working groups have been working to address the standardization needs. For instance, European Telecommunications Standards Institute (ETSI) Mobile Edge Computing (MEC) Industrial Specification Group (ISG) was founded in December 2014 to create a standardized, open environment to allow the efficient and seamless integration of applications from vendors, service providers and third parties across multi-vendor MEC platforms [5]. ITU Telecommunication Standardization Sector (ITU-T) created a group IMT-2020 to study how emerging 5G technologies will interact in future networks, including the requirements and capability framework of the edge-computing-enabled gateway in the Internet-of-Things [8]. Furthermore, ISO/IEC 25010 model [2,4] identified the quality factors applicable in edge computing-based systems. GSM Association also released an edge service description and commercial principles whitepaper [6]. Besides, 3GGPP is also working on Technical Specifications, including standards and architectural principles for enabling edge applications. To sustain IoT momentum, the OpenFog Consortium is defining a new architecture to address infrastructure and connectivity challenges by emphasizing information processing and intelligence at the edge where the data is being produced or used [1].

Although academic, industry, and standard organizations are already functioning to develop standards regarding edge computing adoption, achieving universal standardization remains challenging. The edge computing paradigm is evolving rapidly and requires specific standards for various use cases and application scenarios. Additionally, competing interests among academic and industry players and different technological approaches can further complicate standardization activities. To overcome these challenges, collaboration, and partnership, as emphasized in SDG 17 (Partnerships for the Goals), can create room for opportunities for SDG 17 while promoting multi-stakeholder partnerships to drive standardization efforts forward. By fostering open discussion and sharing best practices, stakeholders can collaborate and cooperate to define common standards to facilitate interoperability and establish guidelines for edge computing to accelerate its successful adoption and benefit various sectors/industries and sustainable development applications.

Potential of Edge Computing Simulation Tools. As described in Table 4, edge computing technologies have been applied for a variety of sectors/industries and use cases including transportation, smart cities applications, healthcare, environmental management, and many more. To consider the ITS example again, developing the ITS infrastructure is complex and requires high financial investment [28]. Besides, when designing edge-cloud collaboration architecture, system architects must consider several aspects, including the entities involved in the hardware infrastructure, application software components, locations to deploy the hardware and software components, and the capabilities of those components. Additionally, they need to ensure that the developed systems can satisfy the stakeholders' needs, how they will use the system, and user-perspective quality requirements. One practical way to address these challenges and design the system in an easy and configurable manner would be the application of simulation tools. There have been many efforts by researchers to use simulation tools to model different edge computing scenarios before the actual development of the systems. Nevertheless, most of the existing simulation tools cannot yet support the metrics to measure various quality attributes such as availability, and security [28] and still lack the implementation constraints which makes them even more challenging to be adopted for some of the scenarios [14], which provide an opportunity for the researchers to initiate the research effort to develop the tools which can provide different quality metrics and implement more complex use cases and scenarios.

6.2   Threats to Validity

Survey papers can have the threat of representativeness of primary studies. Despite the limited search engines and exclusion of relevant studies published before 2016, when the sustainable development goals were first created, we included relevant primary studies from various fields, which can portray the potential application of edge computing in different sectors/industries. The review protocol and comprehensive search strategy we described have minimized the threat of poor representativeness to the extent possible. Another challenge in linking case studies to SDGs is due to the complexity of the goals and the fact that they combine means and ends. ITS can be an example of innovative infrastructure to optimize transportation systems' efficiency, safety, and sustainability, which is associated with SDG 9. At the same time, it can also enhance the livability of cities by reducing traffic congestion, improving air quality, and promoting public transportation, which can contribute to SDG 11. In that case, we categorized ITS as the case relevant to both SDG 9 and 11. SDG classification can be challenging because some goals and targets can contribute to more than one SDG as SDGs are interdependent and interconnected. Different researchers may have different interpretations of which SDGs a case study contributes to. This can lead to inconsistent or biased classifications. The analysis in this study represents the perspective of the authors, which we map the cases in the primary studies to all related SDGs. This study also highlight how emerging technologies have been integrated and applied in edge computing environment, which can suggest future research to explore further their applications and potential in achieving sustainable development. Overall, this survey paper provides a valuable contribution to the landscape of edge computing for sustainable development goals and development sectors/industries while highlighting the need for further research.

7 Conclusion

This paper examines the potential of edge computing in achieving sustainable development goals across various development sectors/industries. We conducted a comprehensive literature review to investigate the use of edge computing for different case studies. A total of 92 primary studies were collected, and cases in those studies were mapped to the relevant sustainable development goals and categorized based on their respective sectors/industries and use cases. Our findings reveal that transportation is the most prominent sector adopting edge computing, and we discuss the challenges and opportunities associated with edge computing adoption by providing the ITS case as an example. This study aims to guide researchers and policymakers seeking to understand the edge computing paradigm, its use cases, and the challenges and opportunities associated with it in the context of sustainable development. In future work, we aim to expand our study by including additional studies collected using other search engines and examine other digital technologies, such as use cases of Artificial Intelligence, to explore further their potential in achieving sustainable development.

References

1. Openfog consortium. https://opcfoundation.org/markets-collaboration/openfog/
2. ISO/IEC systems and software engineering-systems and software quality requirements and evaluation (square)-system and software quality models; ISO/IEC 25010: 2011 (2011)
3. United nations, the 2030 agenda for sustainable development (2015). https://sdgs.un.org
4. ISO/IEC systems and software engineering-systems and software quality requirements and evaluation (square)measurement of system and software product quality; ISO/IEC 25023: 2016 (2016)
5. ETSI, European telecommunications standards institute POC edge video orchestration and video clip replay (2017)
6. GSM association, telco edge cloud: edge service description & commercial principles whitepaper (2020). https://www.gsma.com/futurenetworks/wp-content/uploads/2020/10/gsmatelcoedgeservicedescriptioncommercialprinciplesoct2020.pdf
7. International telecommunication union, digital technologies to achieve the un SDGS (2021). https://www.itu.int/
8. International telecommunication union, requirements and capability framework of the edge-computing-enabled gateway in the internet of things (2021). https://www.itu.int/
9. Abbas, N., Zhang, Y., Taherkordi, A., Skeie, T.: Mobile edge computing: a survey. IEEE Internet Things J. 5(1), 450–465 (2018). https://doi.org/10.1109/JIOT.2017.2750180
10. Agostinelli, S., Cumo, F., Guidi, G., Tomazzoli, C.: Cyber-physical systems improving building energy management: digital twin and artificial intelligence. Energies 14(8), 2338 (2021)
11. Angelopoulos, C.M., Filios, G., Nikoletseas, S., Raptis, T.P.: Keeping data at the edge of smart irrigation networks: a case study in strawberry greenhouses. Comput. Netw. 167, 107039 (2020)

12. Chen, C., Jiang, J., Lv, N., Li, S.: An intelligent path planning scheme of autonomous vehicles platoon using deep reinforcement learning on network edge. IEEE Access **8**, 99059–99069 (2020)
13. Erhan, L., Di Mauro, M., Anjum, A., Bagdasar, O., Song, W., Liotta, A.: Embedded data imputation for environmental intelligent sensing: a case study. Sensors **21**(23), 7774 (2021)
14. Fahimullah, M., Philippe, G., Ahvar, S., Trocan, M.: Simulation tools for fog computing: a comparative analysis. Sensors **23**(7), 3492 (2023). https://doi.org/10.3390/s23073492. https://www.mdpi.com/1424-8220/23/7/3492
15. Gattulli, V., et al.: Design and evaluation of 5G-based architecture supporting data-driven digital twins updating and matching in seismic monitoring. Bull. Earthq. Eng. **20**(9), 4345–4365 (2022)
16. Giovannini, E., Niestroy, I., Nilsson, M., Roure, F., Spanos, M.: The role of science, technology and innovation policies to foster the implementation of the sustainable development goals. Report of the Expert Group "Follow-up to Rio 20 (2015)
17. Goossens, W., Mustefa, D., Scholle, D., Fotouhi, H., Denil, J.: Evaluating edge computing and compression for remote cuff-less blood pressure monitoring. J. Sens. Actuator Netw. **12**(1), 2 (2022)
18. Hästbacka, D., et al.: Dynamic edge and cloud service integration for industrial IoT and production monitoring applications of industrial cyber-physical systems. IEEE Trans. Industr. Inf. **18**(1), 498–508 (2021)
19. Hwang, W.Y., Nurtantyana, R.: X-education: education of all things with AI and edge computing-one case study for EFL learning. Sustainability **14**(19), 12533 (2022)
20. Janbi, N., Mehmood, R., Katib, I., Albeshri, A., Corchado, J.M., Yigitcanlar, T.: Imtidad: a reference architecture and a case study on developing distributed AI services for skin disease diagnosis over cloud, fog and edge. Sensors **22**(5), 1854 (2022)
21. Javed, A., Malhi, A., Kinnunen, T., Främling, K.: Scalable IoT platform for heterogeneous devices in smart environments. IEEE Access **8**, 211973–211985 (2020)
22. Khan, W., Ahmed, E., Hakak, S., Yaqoob, I., Ahmed, A.: Edge computing: a survey, future generation computer systems (2019)
23. Liu, C.H., Yang, T.H., Wijaya, O.T.: Development of an artificial neural network algorithm embedded in an on-site sensor for water level forecasting. Sensors **22**(21), 8532 (2022)
24. Liu, F., Tang, G., Li, Y., Cai, Z., Zhang, X., Zhou, T.: A survey on edge computing systems and tools. Proc. IEEE **107**(8), 1537–1562 (2019)
25. Lu, J., et al.: Analytical offloading design for mobile edge computing-based smart internet of vehicle. EURASIP J. Adv. Signal Process. **2022**(1), 44 (2022)
26. Maltezos, E., et al.: A smart building fire and gas leakage alert system with edge computing and NG112 emergency call capabilities. Information **13**(4), 164 (2022)
27. Mao, Y., You, C., Zhang, J., Huang, K., Letaief, K.B.: A survey on mobile edge computing: the communication perspective. IEEE Commun. Surv. Tutor. **19**(4), 2322–2358 (2017)
28. Thwe, M.M., Hyun, S., Bae, D.H.: Towards the quality assessment of intelligent transportation system of systems using edge computing, pp. 163–165 (2021)
29. Meloni, A., Pegoraro, P.A., Atzori, L., Benigni, A., Sulis, S.: Cloud-based IoT solution for state estimation in smart grids: exploiting virtualization and edge-intelligence technologies. Comput. Netw. **130**, 156–165 (2018)

30. Pérez-Pons, M.E., Plaza-Hernández, M., Alonso, R.S., Parra-Domínguez, J., Prieto, J.: Increasing profitability and monitoring environmental performance: a case study in the agri-food industry through an edge-IoT platform. Sustainability **13**(1), 283 (2020)

31. Silva, M.C., et al.: Wearable edge AI applications for ecological environments. Sensors **21**(15), 5082 (2021)

32. Valera Román, A., Pato Martínez, D., Lozano Murciego, Á., Jiménez-Bravo, D.M., de Paz, J.F.: Voice assistant application for avoiding sedentarism in elderly people based on IoT technologies. Electronics **10**(8), 980 (2021)

33. Wang, X., Han, Y., Leung, V.C., Niyato, D., Yan, X., Chen, X.: Convergence of edge computing and deep learning: a comprehensive survey. IEEE Commun. Surv. Tutor. **22**(2), 869–904 (2020)

34. Xu, D., Zheng, M., Jiang, L., Gu, C., Tan, R., Cheng, P.: Lightweight and unobtrusive data obfuscation at IoT edge for remote inference. IEEE Internet Things J. **7**(10), 9540–9551 (2020)

35. Yu, W., et al.: A survey on the edge computing for the internet of things. IEEE Access **6**, 6900–6919 (2017)

36. Zhang, C., Ji, W.: Edge computing enabled production anomalies detection and energy-efficient production decision approach for discrete manufacturing workshops. IEEE Access **8**, 158197–158207 (2020)

Governance Mechanism of Public-Private Partnerships for Promoting Smart City Performance: A Multi-case Study in China

Jingrui Ju[1]([✉]), Luning Liu[2], and Yuqiang Feng[2]

[1] Huazhong University of Science and Technology, Wuhan, China
jjrrui@sina.cn
[2] Harbin Institute of Technology, Harbin, China

Abstract. Smart city initiatives have evolved into a global movement that is expected to address the severe challenges introduced by urbanization. Most governments adopt a model involving public-private partnerships (PPPs) to advance smart cities because of the lack of associated technical capacity and financial burden. However, with PPPs, it is necessary to choose which governance mechanisms should be adopted to mitigate transaction risks between public and private sectors and promote smart city performance; this is a current knowledge gap. Herein, we conducted a multiple-case study of three smart city projects in China by applying an exploratory case study methodology. Based on an analysis of case interview data, we identified two key aspects of smart city performance and four effective governance mechanisms of PPPs that promote smart city performance. We also discuss theoretical propositions on the relationship between them. The findings presented herein determine scientifically tested aspects for evaluating smart cities and provide guidance for the establishment of PPPs governance mechanisms in smart city projects.

Keywords: Smart city · Public-private partnerships · Governance mechanism · Multi-case study

1 Introduction

Smart cities are expected to mitigate the severe socioeconomic and environmental challenges brought on by unprecedented urbanization by adopting advanced information and communication technologies (Yigitcanlar et al. 2019a; Zhu et al. 2022). This idealized narrative of smart cities has been widely accepted, and smart city initiatives have created a rapidly evolving global movement (Chen et al. 2020; Vu et al. 2020). According to a report released by Deloitte in 2018, more than 1000 cities around the world have launched smart city initiatives. In particular, China has the largest number of smart cities in the world, boasting almost 600 pilot smart cities at the end of 2017.

The degree of investment required to carry out smart city initiatives is enormous in most cases, which puts a burden on government budgets. Most governments consider

© IFIP International Federation for Information Processing 2023
Published by Springer Nature Switzerland AG 2023
I. Lindgren et al. (Eds.): EGOV 2023, LNCS 14130, pp. 345–361, 2023.
https://doi.org/10.1007/978-3-031-41138-0_22

the possibility of engaging the private sector in smart city development, which helps reduce the financial burden and incorporate the innovative capabilities and efficiency of the private sector (especially in terms of ICT) (Lam and Yang 2020; Fishman and Flynn 2018; Lam and Yang 2020). The public-private partnerships (PPPs) model is widely used to advance smart cities. PPPs rely on the cooperation of some sort of durability between governments and the private sector, whereby all members jointly develop products and services and share the risks, costs, and resources associated with these products (Van Ham and Koppenjan 2001; Hodge and Greve 2007).

One of the key goals of PPPs is to improve the performance of smart city projects. As the smart city concept shifts from technology-oriented to governance-oriented, several conceptual evaluation frameworks are proposed on the basis of identifying the key elements of a smart city. For example, Abu-Rayash and Dincer (2021) constructed a framework according to several dimensions (i.e., smart economy, environment, society, governance, energy, infrastructure, transportation, and pandemic resiliency) and listed aspects for each dimension. Meanwhile, Wang et al. (2020) constructed a similar assessment framework. Although these frameworks comprehensively consider the technology- and governance-oriented aspects, there is still a lack of scientific evidence on whether these aspects are applicable to the actual needs of current smart city development projects, which are mostly in the primary stages.

Despite certain benefits to the public and private sectors, challenges and issues remain for PPPs initiatives, as evidenced by various unsuccessful cases (Jamali 2004; Abdul-Aziz and Kassim 2011). One of the crucial challenges is that PPPs are vulnerable to transaction risks, including uncertainty, asset specificity, information asymmetry, and contract incompleteness (Xiong et al. 2019). The lack of appropriate governance arrangements for the majority of cities appears to constitute the most serious obstacle for their effective transformation into being smart (Praharaj et al. 2018). Adopting an appropriate PPPs governance mechanism is crucial for dealing with transaction risks and improving the performance of smart city projects. Xiong et al. (2019) identified eight highly conceptualized governance mechanisms to address transaction risks based on two PPPs power projects. Scholars have also proposed specific governance mechanisms focusing on organizational form and strategy, such as establishing a hybrid organization (Villani et al. 2017), adding a broker (Ruuska and Teigland 2009), and attracting greater investments from private sectors (Tan and Zhao 2019). However, these highly-conceptual governance mechanisms cannot provide sufficient support for systematic mechanism identification in the context of smart cities.

2 Literature Review

2.1 Assessment of Smart Cities

Two categories of smart city assessment frameworks have been identified: technology- and governance-oriented frameworks. The European Smart Cities Ranking initially defined a set of criteria with which to assess the extent of "smartness" in the areas of energy, mobility, community, environment, economy, and buildings (Giffinger et al. 2007; Mattoni et al. 2015; Yigitcanlar et al. 2018). Specific frameworks and indicators used to benchmark the smartness of a given area (e.g., transportation, environment, and energy) were also proposed (Debnath et al. 2014; Garau et al. 2016; Garau et al. 2015; Cook and Schmitter-Edgecombe 2009; Mets et al. 2010; Yigitcanlar et al. 2019a; Yigitcanlar et al. 2019b). These indices were used to benchmark practical projects for the development of smart cities. In contrast to assessment frameworks focusing on the smartness of technological infrastructure, some studies highlight the essential aspects of human and social capital in smart cities; the governance orientation is also a vital component of framework for evaluating smart cities. Scholars have identified the key elements of a smart city under the governance-oriented concept and proposed corresponding conceptual frameworks for evaluating smart cities. For example, Abu-Rayash and Dincer (2021) indicated that a smart city can be characterized according to eight main elements, including a smart economy, environment, society, governance, energy, infrastructure, transportation, and pandemic resiliency. Similarly, Wang et al. (2020) identified a smart city framework that involves smart living, economy, environment, governance, infrastructure, and smart people.

Although the evaluation indicators for these frameworks comprehensively consider the technology- and governance-oriented concepts and various aspects of a smart city, the available literature cannot confirm whether they are applicable in different stages of smart city practice. It has been acknowledged that the project of smart cities is complicated and time-consuming. Most countries are still in the primary exploration stages, and therefore, it is urgent to construct a scientific evaluation framework suitable for current practices.

2.2 Governance Mechanism of Public-Private Partnerships (PPPs)

A PPP project generally involves tasks related to design, construction, operation, financing, and maintenance. These tasks are fully transferred from the public sector to the private sector through long-term contract arrangements in the form of joint-development, build-own-transfer, or build-own-operate-transfer (Bult-Spiering and Dewulf 2006; Savas 2000). Such cooperation can bring intended public benefits, such as enhancing the partnership between the two sectors (Ysa 2007; Erridge and Greer 2002), improving risk management (Shen et al. 2006; Bing et al. 2005), increasing the quality and satisfaction with public facilities and services (Edkins and Smyth 2006), and clarifying government policies (Ball and Maginn 2005; Hart 2003). However, certain problems may also emerge after the failure of a PPP project, e.g., cost overruns, unrealistic price and income projections, and legal disputes. In general, the public sector (but not the private sector) must ultimately shoulder the costs of the failure (Kumaraswamy and Zhang 2001). Therefore, the public sector must attach importance to their cooperative relationship with the private sector and construct an effective governance mechanism to reduce the risk of cooperation failure and promote the performance of PPPs.

A PPP project may involve more risks than conventional public procurement, and therefore, risk sharing is a critical element for the success of PPPs (Wang et al. 2018). PPPs are subject to four common transaction risks at the project level: uncertainty, asset specificity, information asymmetry, and contract incompleteness (Xiong et al. 2019). Uncertainty refers to the fact that it is impossible to accurately describe the current state of PPPs or predict future outcomes (Ball et al. 2003). Cost overruns and demand overestimation are two main sources of uncertainty (Cruz and Marques 2013). Asset specificity measures the extent to which an asset supports transactions and can be redeployed for other uses and users without losing production value (Williamson 1999). The constructed public infrastructure only serves the purpose of public welfare, without adopting alternative uses. Information asymmetry indicates that the government may not be able to identify the true capabilities and actual costs of the private sector at the procurement stage (Hoppe and Schmitz 2013). Contract incompleteness refers to a case where unforeseen contingencies would be so numerous that it would be too costly to describe them all explicitly in a contract. To adequately address the transaction risks, eight governance mechanisms have been identified based on a comparative study of two PPPs power projects: cognition and flexibility for uncertainty, safeguards and credibility for asset specificity, transparency and competition for information asymmetry, and reputation and trust for contract incompleteness (Xiong et al. 2019). These governance mechanisms are highly conceptualized. They provide theoretical support for how PPPs actors construct generalized behavior mechanisms in specific situations (e.g., smart city PPPs in this study).

Studies in the field of organizational management have revealed that some organizational behaviors (e.g., organizational form construction and strategy implementation) can be applied to deal with the transaction risks of PPP projects. These behaviors are actually the manifestation of PPPs governance mechanisms. Specifically, viewing PPPs as a form of hybrid organization can foster value creation for stakeholders in establishing and operating PPPs by combining institutional logics (Villani et al. 2017). Adding a broker in smart city PPPs can help address conflicts and promote mutual communication in large cooperation patterns, wherein the broker is responsible for translating knowledge and facilitating negotiations between the public and private sectors (Ruuska and Teigland 2009). The cooperation form between the actors is of limited importance to the PPPs performance, whereas the use of management strategies can have a significant impact on performance (Kort and Klijn 2011). Attracting greater investments from the private sector rather than state-owned enterprises can help mitigate the financial risks taken by the government (Tan and Zhao 2019). The extent of firm participation can affect the performance and efficiency of smart cities (Wang et al. 2020). These fragmented mechanisms provide necessary support when systematically identifying the general governance mechanism in the context of smart city PPPs.

3   Methods

The present study employed an explorative and inductive research strategy (de Graaf and Huberts 2008; Eisenhardt 1989). We conducted a qualitative case study to explore the impacts of the PPPs governance mechanism on smart city performance (Ospina et al. 2017). We adopted a purposeful sampling strategy (Patton 1990) to determine the case cities. Based on an annual report about smart cities published by the National Development and Reform Commission of China in 2017, our research team considered the top-20 ranked cities that had won national best smart city case awards to solicit participation. Ultimately, three cities agreed to participate, denoted anonymously as SZ, NJ, and YC. In this study design, we interviewed informants of primary stakeholders of the smart city PPPs, e.g., city government officials, general contractors, and private partners. 32 informants from 12 organizations in three cities participated in the interview process.

The interview data analysis began with a case-specific analysis, followed by a cross-case analysis (Miles and Huberman 1994). The coding team (one researcher and two research assistants) familiarized themselves with over 200 pages of transcribed interviews and held multiple meetings after the first round of coding to compare and contrast the three case cities. The interview data analysis started with a case-specific analysis of each case city to understand how and why they had designed such a specific governance mechanism for the PPPs and its impact on the smart city projects. Each coder first read the interview transcripts independently and provided ideas regarding potential aspects for assessment. Subsequent debates among the coders led to either the retention or removal of aspects. The coding team then conducted a cross-case analysis of the three case cities considering the higher and lower levels of smart city performances. City-specific governance mechanisms and common aspects were extracted, collected, and ruled out based on cross-case comparisons, which established the themes of the studied constructs. The aspects were derived from the comments and perspectives of interviewees. Findings from relevant literature sources were incorporated at this stage to conceptually understand the emerging concepts, thereby providing a useful conceptual lens with which to interpret the interview data and an additional source of validation (Eisenhardt 1989). Further, drawing on the relevant literature (e.g., smart cities and governance mechanisms of PPPs), the coding team simplified the themes into constructs.

4 Findings

The theoretical model that was developed based on the interview data analysis is illustrated in Fig. 1.

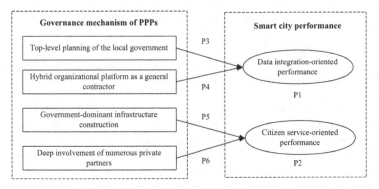

Fig. 1. Theoretical model.

4.1 Aspects of Smart City Performance

During the interviews and the post-hoc review of the transcripts, two key aspects of smart city performance clearly stood out: data integration-oriented and citizen service-oriented performances. These two aspects reflect distinct perspectives related to the outcomes of smart city projects. Some cities may achieve higher-level performance from one perspective, which may not directly transfer into the other perspective. However, some cities may attain high-level performance from both perspectives. In every city we visited, the interviewees largely confirmed these two aspects, although some cities performed well based only on one of the two. The performances of the smart city projects in the case cities are summarized in Table 1.

Table 1. Performances of case cities in smart city projects.

City	Aspects of smart city performance	
	Data integration-oriented performance	Citizen service-oriented performance
NJ	High	High
SZ	Low	High
YC	High	Low

4.1.1 Data Integration-Oriented Performance

A key challenge facing the construction of smart cities is the integration of heterogeneous data sources (Pereira et al. 2022). The vision of a smart city is to integrate a large amount of data from multiple sources; thus, data integration within a smart city is an important challenge to be addressed. In recent years, several technologies have been introduced into smart cities (Pereira et al. 2022), thereby reducing the technical barriers to handling data. An analysis of the interview transcripts indicated that the leaders and directors of smart city projects viewed data integration as a key measurement of the success of smart cities.

The director of the NJ Municipal Commission of Development and Reform placed a strong focus on the importance of data integration in smart city projects. According to him, NJ has achieved a high level of data integration during the project.

> *"As early as the planning process for smart cities, we realized that data integration was the most important task. Compared with other cities in China, our work on government data integration started relatively early. We had collected and integrated all of the data from twenty-eight bureaus in 2012, including data from the Human Resources and Social Security Bureau and the Police Security Bureau, which are the most difficult to collect. Everyone thought data integration was not a good thing at that time, but it is different today, and every bureau realizes the benefits of data integration. All departments need data from other departments."*

NJ ZJSY Information Technology Co., Ltd. Operates a mobile application (APP) to provide public services to more than two million NJ citizen users. The vice president of the company also confirmed that data integration is a key outcome of smart cities.

"A key outcome of smart cities—also a difficult one—is to integrate data. The smart city projects in any city will inevitably encounter this issue."

In summary, all three case cities asserted that a high level of data integration was a key aspect of smart city performance. Based on the statements from different stakeholders of smart city projects in the three case cities, NJ and YC have achieved a high level of data integration, whereas the data integration of SZ was still at a relatively low level. The themes supporting data integration-oriented performance as a key aspect of smart city performance are presented in Table 2. Thus, we propose the following.

Proposition 1: Data integration-oriented performance is a key aspect of smart city performance.

4.1.2 Citizen Service-Oriented Performance

The original intention of smart city projects was to help the local government better govern the city with the support of ICT. Thus, the ultimate objective is to help the government improve their delivery of public services to citizens, thereby facilitating and enhancing human welfare and social flourishing (Marsal-Llacuna 2017; Yigitcanlar et al. 2018). Globally, there are calls for technology to be made more human-centered (Ahmada et al. 2022). The analysis of our interview transcripts suggested that leaders and directors of smart city projects view citizen-centric public service delivery as a key aspect of smart city performance.

For example, the associate director of the NJ Information Klc Holdings Ltd. Stated that citizen service was a critical outcome of smart city projects.

"I think that the most fundamental task [of a smart city] is to help our citizens and make the citizens feel usefulness. In the context of smart city projects, the satisfaction of the citizens is much more important than that of government officials—this is true in NJ city at least. The local government officials of NJ are exceedingly concerned about the evaluations from their service recipients [citizens]."

When asked why one-quarter of the citizens in NJ city have become users of the "my NJ" platform, the vice president of NJ ZJSY Information Technology Co., Ltd. Answered,

"At the initial stages of developing the 'my NJ' platform, we viewed service orientation as a principle that persisted to the present. During the development and operation of the 'my NJ' platform, we just did the things [developed the functions] that citizens required instead of the things [functions] that we needed."

In summary, a high level of citizen service was confirmed as a key aspect of smart city project performance in all three case cities. Compared to the cities achieving a higher level of citizen service (NJ and SZ), citizen service-oriented performance in YC was still at a lower level. The themes supporting citizen service-oriented performance as a key aspect of smart city performance are outlined in Table 2. Thus, we propose the following.

Proposition 2: Citizen service-oriented performance is a key aspect of smart city performance.

Table 2. Explanations and themes of the constructs.

Construct	Explanation	Themes
Data integration-oriented performance	How a large amount of data from multiple sources is integrated in smart city projects	• Data integration is a fundamental but difficult task in smart city projects (N = 15) • Data integration is a basic requirement from the local government and citizens (N = 13)
Citizen service-oriented performance	How much the value of smart city applications can be perceived by the citizens	• The objective of smart cities is to provide better service to citizens (N = 11) • Citizens' satisfaction is a key evaluation criterion of smart city projects (N = 16)
Top-level planning of the local government	Long-term plans for smart city projects should be designed at the top-level by a lead governmental organization	• The local government should be responsible for the clear and long-term plan of smart cities (N = 9) • The long-term plan of smart cities should be designed at the top-level considering how to collect and integrate the requirements from all governmental departments (N = 6) • A specific department in the local government should be assigned to be the lead organization, which carries out the top-level plan of the smart city (N = 8)
Hybrid organizational platform as a general contractor	A hybrid organizational platform should be established and assigned as a general contractor of smart city projects	• A hybrid organizational platform can help the local government implement policies (N = 8) • For continuous operation of smart city projects, the local government should involve private capital and establish a hybrid organizational platform as a general contractor (N = 7)

(continued)

Table 2. (*continued*)

Construct	Explanation	Themes
Government-dominant infrastructure construction	The infrastructures of the smart city should be mainly invested and owned by the local government	• The local government is responsible for investing in infrastructure construction in smart city projects (N = 6) • The local government should fully control the infrastructure of the smart city and then call for private companies to provide citizen services based on the infrastructure (N = 5)
Deep involvement of numerous private partners	The local government should attract numerous private partners to be involved in the smart city projects	• In terms of continuous operation and service delivery, the local government should rely heavily on the private partners (N = 10) • Various private partners should be involved maintain a positive competition environment (N = 7)

4.2 Critical Governance Mechanisms of PPPs and Their Impacts on Smart City Performance

The cross-case analysis of the interview transcripts revealed that there were four critical PPPs governance mechanisms that increased smart city performance: top-level planning of the local government, government-dominant infrastructure construction, hybrid organizational platform as a general contractor, and deep involvement of many private partners. The cross-case comparative evidence regarding how the PPPs governance mechanisms enhance smart city performance is presented in Table 3.

4.2.1 Top-Level Planning of the Local Government

The capacity for top-level planning is critical to the organizations that attempt to implement information systems (Ruuska and Teigland 2009). The logic is similar for the construction of smart cities. The local government should define a long-term plan for the smart cities because it serves a general leadership role in the smart city projects. A top-level long-term plan for the development of smart cities should be designed by considering how to meet and integrate the requirements of all departments in the local government. Furthermore, there should be a specific department in the local government assigned and empowered to be the lead organization, which implements the top-level plan of the smart city.

The director of NJ Municipal Commission of Development and Reform confirmed that they were playing the general leadership role in the Smart NJ project. He also

Table 3. PPPs governance mechanisms and smart city performances for the investigated cases.

City		NJ	SZ	YC
Smart city performance	Data integration-oriented performance	High	Low	High
	Citizen service-oriented performance	High	High	Low
Governance mechanism of PPPs	Top-level planning of the local government	✓	×	✓
	Hybrid organizational platform as a general contractor	✓	×	✓
	Government-dominant infrastructure construction	✓	✓	×
	Deep involvement of numerous private partners	✓	✓	×

expressed the notion that the top-level plan is crucial for promoting the performance of the Smart NJ project.

"At the beginning of the smart city project, we set up two fundamental rules. The first was that the NJ Municipal Commission of Development and Reform should be responsible for top-level planning and coordination. The second was that private capital should play an important role....I think the reason for our success is that we have had a clear strategic plan with a top-level design."

The situation in YC is similar to that in NJ. When explaining why the YC Municipal Big Data Service and Management Bureau was established in 2016, the director began by emphasizing the importance of comprehensive planning.

"The secretary of the Municipal Party Committee of YC is the general leader of the top-level decision team. Mayor Guo is the chief planner and designer. These senior government officials guarantee that our project is carried out in a smooth and orderly fashion. Our bureau, which is the leading governmental organization of the Smart YC project, is responsible for comprehensive planning after a deep review and understanding the requirements of all related governmental departments."

Table 2 presents the themes supporting the top-level planning of the local government as a key driving factor of smart city performance. According to our cross-case analysis based on interview evidence (Table 3), NJ and YC highlighted the importance of the top-level planning of the local government in smart city projects. Both cities have set up an institutional guarantee to facilitate such top-level planning and ensure the leadership position of the local government. The local government of NJ assigned a specific department, i.e., the NJ Municipal Commission of Development and Reform, as the lead organization responsible for planning and managing smart city projects. The local government of YC founded a new department, i.e., the YC Municipal Big Data Service and Management Bureau, to be the lead organization for the Smart YC project. However, SZ failed to select a lead organization, and as a result, there was a lack of top-level planning for the Smart SZ project. Each governmental department in SZ developed its own plan about the smart city according to its own requirements only. This scheme gradually caused considerable difficulties for the local government of SZ to integrate various smart city applications from different fields. As a result, the data integration-oriented performance of the smart city projects was at a relatively higher level in NJ and YC relative to SZ. A clear top-level designed plan can provide an integrative vision and a consistent standard for all governmental departments to develop their smart city applications. This would eventually facilitate data integration, which is a fundamental component of smart city performance. Thus, we propose the following.

Proposition 3: Cities with top-level planning are more likely to achieve high-level data integration-oriented performance in a smart city project.

4.2.2 Hybrid Organizational Platform as a General Contractor

Public-private partnerships require hybrid collaboration to coordinate and align performances across the public and private partners (Caldwell et al. 2017). In the context of smart city projects, such hybrid collaboration is even more important owing to the complexity in governance. Studies have highlighted the central role of hybrid organizations in PPPs (Jay 2013; Skelcher and Smith 2015). According to Williamson (1996), hybrid organizations played an intermediate role by reducing the transaction costs between the public and private sectors. In the present study, the case evidence suggested that a hybrid organizational platform was a critical PPPs governance mechanism, which could enhance smart city performance, especially from the perspective of data integration-oriented performance.

When explaining the organization of his company in the Smart NJ project, the CEO of NJ Information Klc Holdings Ltd. Emphasized the importance of using a hybrid organizational form.

"Our company is defined as a policy-based financing platform, and our capital comes from both government and private [sources]. On one hand, our company is an enterprise that conducts investment businesses focusing on smart cities. On the other hand, it needs policy support from the government."

The director of the NJ Municipal Commission of Development and Reform further explained why the general contractor companies involved in smart city projects should adopt a hybrid organizational platform.

"If the general contractor company of a smart city project is purely state-owned, the relationship between the government and this company is similar to a parent-child relationship—the government can unconditionally issue orders to the company. To avoid this problem, it is critical that private capital is involved in the general contractor company."

However, during our case interview, the director of the SZ Municipal e-Government Resources Center stated that, so far, the SZ municipal government had not set up a particular company to control or oversee the smart city projects.

The themes supporting the hybrid organizational platform as a general contractor as a key driving factor of smart city performance are presented in Table 2. According to the results of our cross-case analysis based on interview evidence (Table 3), the critical role of the hybrid organizational platform as a general contractor in smart city projects has been highlighted in the NJ and YC projects. Specifically, a new company was set up each of these two cities according to the hybrid organizational form to facilitate collaboration between the public and private sectors. Therefore, in NJ and YC, the top-level planning of the local government could be more easily understood and implemented by private companies, with the hybrid organizational platform serving as a broker. As a result, the data integration-oriented performance of smart city projects was relatively higher in NJ and YC relative to SZ, where no such a hybrid organization acting as a general contractor was available. Thus, we propose the following.

Proposition 4: Cities with a hybrid organizational platform as a general contractor are more likely to achieve high-level data integration-oriented performance in a smart city project.

4.2.3   Government-Dominant Infrastructure Construction

Infrastructure construction is the primary task during the initial stages of smart city projects. Public smart city platforms and application systems can often be constructed based on the existing public infrastructure. At a subsequent stage of the smart city projects, the application systems for smart cities should shift to private-dominant, i.e., developed based on the PPPs because private companies use more advanced technologies and customer services than the government. However, there are two major categories to discern how infrastructure construction serves as a foundation of smart cities: government-dominant and private-dominant. The results of the case interviews in this study revealed that NJ and SZ adopted government-dominant infrastructure construction, whereas a private-dominant infrastructure construction was used in YC.

When asked what role the government had played in smart city projects, the director of NJ Municipal Commission of Development and Reform stated that the government was responsible for the investment in smart city infrastructure at the initial stage, and then private companies were involved as the service providers using the infrastructure.

"In fact, our government had played an important role in the initial stage of the smart city projects. In the beginning, most of the investments related to infrastructure construction in the smart city were made by the government, and then [the government] gradually purchased operation services from private companies. For example, the construction of public wireless Internet, which required a significant investment, was funded by the government at first; then, some private companies became involved and helped provide the operational service of public wireless Internet to the NJ citizens."

However, the IT manager of the YC Citizen Center claimed that the infrastructure in the smart city in YC was mostly funded and constructed by a certain famous Chinese

IT company. Therefore, that private company also obtained the operation rights for the smart city infrastructure based on a BOT mode. The manager said,

"ZTE is a world-famous IT company. They are professionals with expertise in both infrastructure construction and IT service delivery. They designed a detailed plan for the Smart YC project according to the requirements of the YC government. Nevertheless, the most important contribution was their idea to build YC as a prototype project of a smart city so they could promote the 'YC model' to other cities in China. Thus, ZTE agreed to invest a large amount of money in the Smart YC project."

The themes supporting government-dominant infrastructure construction as a key driving factor of smart city performance are listed in Table 2. According to our cross-case analysis based on interview evidence (Table 3), NJ and SZ both adopted government-dominant infrastructure construction and had relatively higher citizen service-oriented performance of their smart city projects. In contrast, private-dominant infrastructure construction was adopted in YC, and its citizen service-oriented performance of smart city projects was relatively lower. We speculate that if the local government had invested and owned the infrastructure, then it would have been much easier for the government to select high-quality private companies to provide smart city application services to the citizens. However, if the local government had lost the control over the smart city infrastructure, then the quality of the citizen services could not have been guaranteed without the local government. Thus, we propose the following.

Proposition 5: Cities with government-dominant infrastructure construction are more likely to achieve high-level citizen service-oriented performance in a smart city project.

4.2.4 Deep Involvement of Numerous Private Partners

It is crucial to adopt a network constitution strategy to improve the outcome of PPPs by introducing alternatives to facilitate the search for quality (Klijn and Teisman 2000). The government should involve numerous private partners through new institutional arrangements to provide services for their citizens and to keep alternatives available in PPPs. Therefore, we considered that the involvement of many private partners was another critical governance mechanism of PPPs.

In our case interview, the CEO of NJ Information Klc Holdings Ltd. Confirmed our viewpoint by sharing how they attracted more technology-leading private partners.

"The role of private capital in our platform is two-fold. First, they have very strong research and development capabilities. Second, they have a relatively strong capacity to expand their resources. Therefore, our company's objective is to attract more private capital to be involved in the smart city projects to fill these important roles. First, we look for technology-leading private enterprise in the smart city industry; then, we attract them and establish a platform for them....We set up a fund to sponsor some innovation competitions every year to better seek some outstanding enterprises."

The situation in YC was quite different. In the Smart YC project, only one private partner was involved because this company invested a significant amount of capital in the infrastructure construction of the smart city. The associate director of the YC Municipal Big Data Service and Management Bureau explained the current situation of having a sole private partner and outlined their plans to seek more private partners.

"In fact, this type of cooperation is based on interest swapping. ZTE brought a lot of resources with its arrival in YC and made a great contribution to the local construction. Therefore, although we announced that the market of the smart city is open to all companies, it is not surprising that the local government would support ZTE with a kind of preferential policy. Usually, we sign and assign the sub-projects to ZTE in the first round. Then, ZTE completes the projects by themselves or through outsourcing....Now, we want to seek some more competitors to be involved in our smart city projects. This will help us broaden our insights into the smart city projects."

The themes supporting the deep involvement of numerous private partners as a key driving factor of smart city performance are presented in Table 2. According to the findings of our cross-case analysis based on interview evidence (Table 3), NJ and SZ both attracted numerous private partners to become involved in smart city projects, which led to relatively higher citizen service-oriented performances of their smart city projects. In contrast, only one private partner participated in the Smart YC project, and accordingly, its citizen service-oriented performance was relatively lower. We noted that the involvement of numerous private partners allowed for positive competition, which subsequently guaranteed a high quality of citizen services provided by the private partners. Thus, we propose the following.

Proposition 6: Cities with deep involvement of numerous private partners are more likely to achieve high-level citizen service-oriented performance in a smart city project.

5 Conclusions

The multi-case analysis conducted in this study integrates several literature streams to develop a theoretical framework that helps us better understand PPPs governance mechanisms in the context of smart cities. Our research findings are threefold. First, we determined that data integration- and citizen service-oriented performance are two key aspects for evaluating smart city performance. Second, we discovered that four key PPPs governance mechanisms enhance the performance of smart city projects: top-level planning of the local government, government-dominant infrastructure construction, hybrid organizational platform as a general contractor, and deep involvement of numerous private partners. Third, we proposed that the top-level planning of the local government and the use of a hybrid organizational platform as a general contractor have a positive impact on data integration-oriented performance. Furthermore, the government-dominant infrastructure construction and deep involvement of numerous private partners positively affect citizen service-oriented performance. This research is not without limitations, however. This work is based on a purposeful sample comprising only three cases, with the goal of developing propositions and a theory for future investigations. Additionally, this study only focused on smart city projects in China. Investigations of smart cities in a wide array of countries would increase the generalizability of the results.

References

Abdul-Aziz, A.R., Kassim, P.J.: Objectives, success and failure factors of housing public–private partnerships in Malaysia. Habitat Int. **35**(1), 150–157 (2011)

Abu-Rayash, A., Dincer, I.: Development of integrated sustainability performance indicators for better management of smart cities. Sustain. Cities Soc. **67**, 102704 (2021)

Ahmada, K., Maabrehb, M., Ghaly, M., et al.: Developing future human-centered smart cities: critical analysis of smart city security, data management, and ethical challenges. Comput. Sci. Rev. **43**, 100452 (2022)

Ball, M., Maginn, P.J.: Urban change and conflict: evaluating the role of partnerships in urban regeneration in the UK. Hous. Stud. **20**(1), 9–28 (2005)

Ball, R., Heafey, M., King, D.: Risk transfer and value for money in PFI projects. Public Manag. Rev. **5**(2), 279–290 (2003)

Bing, L., Akintoye, A., Edwards, P.J., Hardcastle, C.: The allocation of risk in PPP/PFI construction projects in the UK. Int. J. Project Manag. **23**(1), 25–35 (2005)

Bult-Spiering, M., Dewulf, G.: Strategic Issues in Public-Private Partnerships: An international perspecitive. Blackwell, Oxford (2006)

Caldwell, N.D., Roehrich, J.K., George, G.: Social value creation and relational coordination in public-private collaborations. J. Manag. Stud. **56**(6), 906–928 (2017)

Chen, B., Liu, T., Wang, Y.: Volatile fragility: new employment forms and disrupted employment protection in the new economy. Int. J. Environ. Res. Public Health **17**(5), 1531 (2020)

Cook, D.J., Schmitter-Edgecombe, M.: Assessing the quality of activities in a smart environment. Methods Inf. Med. **48**(5), 480–485 (2009)

Cruz, C.O., Marques, R.C.: Flexible contracts to cope with uncertainty in public–private partnerships. Int. J. Project Manag. **31**(3), 473–483 (2013)

de Graaf, G., Huberts, L.: Portraying the nature of corruption. using an explorative case-study design. Public Adm. Rev. **68**(4), 640–653 (2008)

Debnath, A.K., Chin, H.C., Haque, M.M., Yuen, B.: A methodological framework for benchmarking smart transport cities. Cities **37**, 47–56 (2014)

Edkins, A.J., Smyth, H.J.: Contractual management in PPP projects: evaluation of legal versus relational contracting for service delivery. J. Prof. Issues Eng. Educ. Pract. **132**(1), 82–93 (2006)

Eisenhardt, K.M.: Building theories from case study research. Acad. Manag. Rev. **14**(4), 532–550 (1989)

Erridge, A., Greer, J.: Partnerships and public procurement: building social capital through supply relations. Public Adm. **80**(3), 503–522 (2002)

Fishman, T.D., Flynn, M.: Using public-private partnerships to advance smart cities. Deloitte Development LLC (2018)

Garau, C., Masala, F., Pinna, F.: Benchmarking smart urban mobility: a study on italian cities. In: Gervasi, O., et al. (eds.) ICCSA 2015. LNCS, vol. 9156, pp. 612–623. Springer, Cham (2015). https://doi.org/10.1007/978-3-319-21407-8_43

Garau, C., Masala, F., Pinna, F.: Cagliari and smart urban mobility: analysis and comparison. Cities **56**, 35–46 (2016)

Giffinger, R., Pichler-Milanović, N., et al.: Smart Cities: Ranking of European Medium-Sized Cities. Vienna University of Technology (2007)

Hart, O.: Incomplete contracts and public ownership: remarks, and an application to public-private partnerships. Econ. J. **113**(486), 69–76 (2003)

Hodge, G.A., Greve, C.: Public–private partnerships: an international performance review. Public Adm. Rev. **67**(3), 545–558 (2007)

Hoppe, E.I., Schmitz, P.W.: Public–private partnerships versus traditional procurement: innovation incentives and information gathering. Rand J. Econ. **44**(1), 56–74 (2013)

Jamali, D.: Success and failure mechanisms of public private partnerships (PPPs) in developing countries: Insights from the Lebanese context. Int. J. Public Sect. Manag. **17**(5), 414–430 (2004)

Jay, J.: Navigating paradox as a mechanism of change and innovation in hybrid organizations. Acad. Manag. J. **56**(1), 137–159 (2013)

Klijn, E.-H., Teisman, G.R.: Governing public-private partnerships: analysing and managing the processes and institutional characteristics of public-private partnerships. In: Osborne, P. (ed.) Public-private partnerships: Theory and practice in international perspective, pp. 165–186. Routledge, London (2000)

Kort, M., Klijn, E.H.: Public–private partnerships in urban regeneration projects: organizational form or managerial capacity? Public Adm. Rev. **71**(4), 618–626 (2011)

Kumaraswamy, M.M., Zhang, X.Q.: Governmental role in BOT-led infrastructure development. Int. J. Project Manag. **19**(4), 195–205 (2001)

Lam, P., Yang, W.: Factors influencing the consideration of public-private partnerships (PPP) for smart city projects: evidence from Hong Kong. Cities **99**, 102606 (2020)

Marsal-Llacuna, M.-L.: Building universal socio-cultural indicators for standardizing the safeguarding of citizens' rights in smart cities. Soc. Indic. Res. **130**(2), 563–579 (2017)

Mattoni, B., Gugliermetti, F., Bisegna, F.: A multilevel method to assess and design the renovation and integration of smart cities. Sustain. Cities Soc. **15**, 105–119 (2015)

Mets, K., Verschueren, T., Haerick, W., Develder, C., De Turck, F.: Optimizing smart energy control strategies for plug-in hybrid electric vehicle charging. In: Network Operations and Management Symposium Workshops (NOMS Workshops), 2010 IEEE/IFIP, pp. 293–299 (2010)

Miles, M.B., Huberman, A.M.: Qualitative Data Analysis: An Expanded Sourcebook. Sage Publications, Thousand Oaks (1994)

Ospina, S.M., Esteve, M., Lee, S.: Assessing qualitative studies in public administration research. Public Adm. Rev. **78**(4), 593–605 (2017)

Patton, M.: Qualitative Evaluation and Research Methods, pp. 169–186. Sage, Beverly Hills (1990)

Pereira, J., Batista, T., Cavalcante, E., Souza, A., et al.: A platform for integrating heterogeneous data and developing smart city applications. Futur. Gener. Comput. Syst. **128**, 552–566 (2022)

Praharaj, S., Han, J.H., Hawken, S.: Towards the right model of smart city governance in India. Sustain. Dev. Stud. **13**(2),171–186 (2018)

Ruuska, I., Teigland, R.: Ensuring project success through collective competence and creative conflict in public–private partnerships–a case study of Bygga Villa, a Swedish triple helix e-government initiative. Int. J. Project Manag. **27**(4), 323–334 (2009)

Savas, E.S.: Privatization and Public-Private Partnerships. Chatham House, New York (2000)

Shen, L.Y., Platten, A., Deng, X.P.: Role of public private partnerships to manage risks in public sector projects in Hong Kong. Int. J. Project Manag. **24**(7), 587–594 (2006)

Skelcher, C., Smith, S.R.: Theorizing hybridity: institutional logics, complex organizations, and actor identities: the case of nonprofits. Public Adm. **93**(2), 433–448 (2015)

Tan, J., Zhao, J.Z.: The rise of public–private partnerships in china: an effective financing approach for infrastructure investment? Public Adm. Rev. **79**(4), 514–518 (2019)

Van Ham, H., Koppenjan, J.: Building public-private partnerships: assessing and managing risks in port development. Public Manag. Rev. **3**(4), 593–616 (2001)

Villani, E., Greco, L., Phillips, N.: Understanding value creation in public-private partnerships: a comparative case study. J. Manag. Stud. **54**(6), 876–905 (2017)

Vu, K., Hanafizadeh, P., Bohlin, E.: ICT as a driver of economic growth: a survey of the literature and directions for future research. Telecommun. Policy **44**(2), 101922 (2020)

Wang, H., Xiong, W., Wu, G., Zhu, D.: Public–private partnership in public administration discipline: a literature review. Public Manag. Rev. **20**(2), 293–316 (2018)

Wang, M., Zhou, T., Wang, D.: Tracking the evolution processes of smart cities in china by assessing performance and efficiency. Technol. Soc. **63**, 101353 (2020)

Williamson, O.E.: The Mechanisms of Governance. Oxford University Press, Oxford (1996)

Williamson, O.E.: Public and private bureaucracies: a transaction cost economics perspectives. J Law Econ. Organ. **15**(1), 306–342 (1999)

Xiong, W., Chen, B., Wang, H., Zhu, D.: Transaction hazards and governance mechanisms in public-private partnerships: a comparative study of two cases. Public Perform. Manag. Rev. **42**(6), 1279–1304 (2019)

Yigitcanlar, T., Foth, M., Kamruzzaman, M.: Towards post-anthropocentric cities: reconceptualizing smart cities to evade urban ecocide. J. Urban Technol. **26**(2), 147–152 (2019b)

Yigitcanlar, T., et al.: Understanding 'smart cities': intertwining development drivers with desired outcomes in a multidimensional framework. Cities **81**(1), 145–160 (2018)

Yigitcanlar, T., Kamruzzaman, M., Foth, M., Sabatini, J., da Costa, E., Ioppolo, G.: Can cities become smart without being sustainable? A systematic review of the literature. Sustain. Cities Soc. **45**, 348–365 (2019a)

Ysa, T.: Governance forms in urban public-private partnerships. Int. Public Manag. J. **10**(1), 35–57 (2007)

Zhu, H., Shen, L., Ren, Y.: How can smart city shape a happier life? The mechanism for developing a happiness driven smart city. Sustain. Cities Soc. **80**, 103791 (2022)

Innovation and Transformation
in Government

Dynamic Capabilities and Digital Transformation in Public Sector: Evidence from Brazilian Case Study

Larissa Galdino de Magalhães Santos[✉] [iD]

United Nations University Operating Unit on Policy-Driven Electronic Governance, 4810225 Guimarães, Portugal
larissamagalhaes@unu.edu

Abstract. The digital transformation of governments addresses a series of challenges to public organizations, especially regarding emerging technologies. There is evidence about the barriers and challenges related to organizational capabilities, resources, skills, and competencies to deal with government strategies. In the continuous digitization process, dynamic capabilities are resources that can allow the improvement and evolution of operations and public services. The article analyzes the mobilization of dynamic capabilities focusing on operationalizing technologies in public sector digital transformation strategies. The Brazilian Digital Transformation Strategy case study provides insights into how organizations can improve their capability to manage change, innovate, and create public value toward digital transformation.

Keywords: Dynamic Capabilities · Public Sector · Digital Transformation

1 Introduction

Capabilities refer to an organization's underlying resources, skills, and competencies. In the public sector, these resources may include human resources, technology infrastructure, and knowledge to carry out policy functions [1]. However, capabilities in the public sector are often identified as constrained and stability-oriented [2]. For capabilities to enable organizations to build and deliver innovations at the service of citizens, they need to be complemented by sources of dynamics.

Dynamic capabilities (DC) [3] refer to an organization's ability to adapt, change, and renew its internal and external competencies in response to the changing environment. For public sector digital transformation, DC can facilitate changes in societal needs, adoption of new technologies, and digital innovations.

Consequently, organizational capabilities provide the foundation for the organization to deliver services, while DC allow for improvements and evolutions in response to changing needs and demands. DC provide a competitive advantage for organizations dealing with new digital realities. Both capabilities are essential to the success of public sector organizations in the digital age. Although first-order capabilities provide the

I. Lindgren et al. (Eds.): EGOV 2023, LNCS 14130, pp. 365–380, 2023.
https://doi.org/10.1007/978-3-031-41138-0_23

resource base, second-order DC are necessary for organizations to effect change, modifying organizational structure and governance through complex resources [4] toward digital transformation.

The literature suggests that dynamic capability is essential to understand the digital transformation capability of organizations [4]. However, more research must be done on DC at the public sector level and their dynamic evolution over time [5]. On the other hand, gaps in skills, coordination, capacities, abilities, and techniques constitute salient structural barriers to the digital transformation of the public sector [6]. Thus, can DC be a critical factor in digital transformation? What DC would be needed to support digital transformation in public sector organizations?

This article aims to deepen the understanding of DC in the public sector, exploring the operationalization of resources for government digital transformation strategies. The study is a case study of the Brazilian Strategy for Digital Transformation, which combines document analysis and interviews with civil servants, and analysis through the DC mobilization framework to detect, apprehend and transform resources, processes, and structures toward the government's digital transformation.

The article is organized as follows. After the initial discussion of this introduction, the theoretical assumptions section discusses the digital transformation of government and the need to review the resource base to deal with emerging technologies, improve performance and serve the citizen. The following section presents the DC development framework and the mobilization of detection, apprehension, and digital transformation capabilities [7]. Case study techniques, semi-structured interviews, and document analysis were attributed to the research. The third section presents the critical description of the case according to DC. Then, the penultimate section presents the analysis of capacity mobilization in the Brazilian strategy. The final section presents the results, contributions, and limitations.

2 Theoretical Assumptions

Capability corresponds to processes and activities learned by an organization that reconfigures the resource base. Dynamics refers to the ability to achieve convergence amid turmoil through integrating, creating, and reconfiguring internal and external resources [8]. Thus, DC[1] Refer to the perception and use of new opportunities for reconfiguring and protecting assets, knowledge resources, and competencies that enable a competitive advantage in changing environments [3].

DC have been used to frame digital transformation analysis in several empirical studies [9]. Digital technologies, which mark the context of digital transformation, reflect a cyber-physical reality based on artificial intelligence, the Internet of Things, Blockchain, etc., whose scalability is marked by different players that generate ever faster innovations, allowing an organization to stay ahead of others.

Concerning public sector organizations, the use of technologies expands technical processes, and consequently, new skills and organizational structures are needed [10] to

---

[1] Dynamic capabilities arise from the theoretical perspective of the resource-based view. Resource-based view discusses how organizations achieve competitiveness in dynamic environments [7, 8].

generate innovation and mediate transformations. Therefore, once the need for transformation is detected, organizations must mobilize resources to achieve the desired strategy. However, with digital transformation, organizations must focus on innovating products and services while optimizing business processes to maintain their operation, influenced by different values and directions [11].

The digital government transformation is an organizational change - second order[2], that results in a new situation, enabled by technologies and processes, cultures, roles, relationships, and all aspects of organizations [12]. Thus, it is a change based on the mobilization of dynamic capacities. Mobilizing DC refers to the process of developing and operationalizing DC. Despite different definitions of DC, such as developing strategies and alliances, restructuring business practices, and optimizing and allocating resources to pursue long-term competitive advantage [13], the most Teece's primitive approach encompasses the convergence in organizational processes that enable organizations to change the resource base.

The structure for developing DC were initially drawn from organizations' processes, positions, and trajectories [3]. Teece reaffirmed the framework by "using the past as a position, the present as a process, and the future as a path through three clusters of high-level capabilities: detect, encompass, and reconfigure [8]". Hence, positions are related to mapping, collecting, analyzing, and learning information and know-how; organizational and managerial processes are related to the ability to apprehend through perceived opportunities, test and create new routines, activities, and products; and paths, refer to transforming assets, modeling, and building partnerships, and redesigning organizational routines [7, 14].

Mobilization of DC corresponds to the ability to detect, apprehend, and transform resources, processes, and structures to adapt and respond to changing environments [7, 14]. Mobilization is achieved through micro foundations [15] that create organizational structures for the perception of opportunities and learning so that knowledge is distributed and apprehended by multiple actors, reconfiguring the organization's capabilities.

Government strategies seeking the digital transformation of the public sector can and should consider the mobilization of DC, which is different from traditional organizational change [16] to achieve change. The literature specializing in DC applied to the public sector has addressed the renewal of operational capabilities [17], capabilities in political and administrative contexts that generate new political practices [5], managerial capabilities related to leaders, and capabilities organizational and process-related capabilities [18], business model to generate public value as a dynamic capability [19], a combination of organizational and DC to create value, and synergistic and external partnerships [20], organizational readiness and the degree of adaptation to changes [21], DC for creating public value [22, 23]; DC and stages of e-government development [24].

Although public sector organizations have historically been identified as slow in adopting changes, the literature highlights the requirement for new organizational capabilities to use technologies that are drivers of digital transformation [11]. Digital transformation is a phenomenon that addresses complex, challenging, and non-routine management tasks for organizations [11], especially the public sector. From the point of view of

---

[2] Second-order capabilities are rare DC that sense, leverage, and reconfigure organizational assets. By default, they are complex and challenging to replicate skills [46].

emerging technologies, it is necessary to reconfigure business operations, management concepts, and structures [25].

The DC is essential to understand the digital transformation capability of organizations [4]. Although the theory of DC applied to public sector organizations is a field on the rise, there still needs to be an in-depth discussion on the operationalization of DC as a responsible driver of the digital transformation of the public sector among companies [26]. It needs a more advanced discussion of how DC evolve in public organizations [27].

The literature covering the interaction between DC and digital transformation is still an open field yet to be explored concerning the composition of digital transformation strategies [26]. This stems from the fact that digital transformation must be understood as a holistic sociotechnical challenge impacting employees, structures, tasks, and organizational procedures [4]. Therefore, digital transformation is a transformational and organizational strategy-related phenomenon [26]. A digital transformation strategy reproduces the effect of various digital innovations, consequently changing the game's rules in organizations [25]. However, there is an imprecision of formal policy documents implemented by governments, which, in most cases, it does not establish precise recommendations regarding organizational aspects Wilson and Mergel [6].

This scenario, of few certainties, results in structural and cultural barriers that include the lack of financial and human resources, outdated privacy and security regulations, gaps in technical and non-technical skills, rigid and isolated institutional arrangements, lack of technological infrastructure, aversion to risk, fear of incentives for change, fear and lack of knowledge of digital tools, and lack of technological awareness, lack of organizational vision, lack of engagement, and lack of strategic thinking Wilson and Mergel [6]. In addition, studies on the technologies and organizational and managerial capabilities underlying the digital transformation of the public sector [28] are incipient. Thus, the digital transformation of public sector organizations is limited to transforming information processes and systems, while culture, routines, and organizational structure are secondary [12].

3   Methodology

This research is based on a case study combined with qualitative methods [29], which have been adopted in the analysis of capabilities, which consist of processes [23]. The conceptual model in Fig. 1 is systematized in Table 1, which presents the expanded definition of the analysis framework: Mobilization of DC. As per Fig. 1 – left to right, document analysis of articles, books, research reports, official documents, and structured interviews aimed to collect data on DC theory applied to the public sector, digital government transformation (DTG), and the Brazilian Strategy (E- Digital).

The collected data were framed in Teece's categories of "positions, processes, and trajectories" [3] in Fig. 1 to identify how the mobilization of detection resources, apprehension, and transformation of the base of knowledge modifies the base of ordinary resources to DC.

The conceptual model is based on the DC' mobilization framework proposed by Teece, Pisano, and Shuen [3] and Teece [7, 14]. The data content analysis protocol and

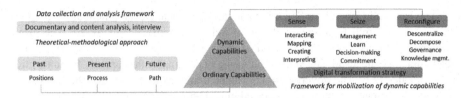

Fig. 1. Conceptual model for mobilizing DC in the public sector.

the interview[3] were based on the categories of "positions, process and path" and "sense, seize and reconfigure". This approach enabled the analysis at the level of processes; that is, it facilitated the interpretation of the mobilization of capabilities at the level of organizational and managerial processes.

As "there are few, if any, empirical studies using hard factual data to confirm the largely anecdotal evidence [30]" on DC mobilization and the digital transformation of the public sector, the conceptual model was synthesized into a Mobilization framework of DC according to Fig. 1 (right). For each dynamic capability and development, we indicate key capabilities that allow a detailed analysis of organizational and managerial processes in the long term.

4 Developing DC for a Digital Transformation Strategy

The public discussion on the Brazilian Strategy for Digital Transformation began in 2017 with the launch of a base document. The following year, a presidential decree instituted the National System for Digital Transformation, with the governance structure of the strategy [31]. Other Federal Government initiatives related to innovation, research incentives, technological development, and digital governance were launched in the same period [32]. However, the detection of environmental knowledge about digital transformation and the interpretation of new opportunities began in mid-2015 with the first activities related to discussions on Industry 4.0 in the Ministry of Science, Technology, and Innovation and the elaboration of the ST&I Plan for Advanced Manufacturing in Brazil [33, 34].

4.1 Sensing and Shaping Opportunities

In mid-2015, civil servants and leaders of the Secretariat for Technological Development and Innovation of the Ministry of Science, Technology, Innovation and Communications (MCTIC) began discussions to learn about the fundamental elements of the Industry 4.0 platform [34, 35]. While the National Confederation of Industry was mapping the potential to take advantage of the opportunities of the new technological cycle, the discussion on the Industry 4.0 ecosystem occupied the saddles of meetings in public sector organizations.

---

[3] The Interview script is incorporated in the analysis Sects. 4 and 4.1. of this article. The transcript of the interview is available at: https://encurtador.com.br/iJVX7.

The National Council for Scientific and Technological Development and more than 40 leaders gathered to discuss policies to induce Industry 4.0 in Brazil. The group interpreted the need for a Triple Helix model between government, companies, and academia to create an advanced manufacturing plan, support the capacity for innovation in companies [34]. The government coordinated actions and proposed guidelines and initiatives to integrate a national advanced manufacturing initiative [33, 35] through the benchmarking on experiences and programs in emerging countries; and opportunities for international cooperation regarding the development of technological and organizational skills for the development of the country's strategy [33, 34]. Furthermore, the Ministry of Industry, Foreign Trade, and Services launched the National Strategy for Science and Technology 2016–2022 to consolidate and integrate the National System of Science, Technology, and Innovation [36]. Then, the strategy also facilitated the constitution of the Science, Technology, and Innovation Plan for Advanced Manufacturing [37].

Within the scope of the MCTIC, the Secretariat for Information Technology Policy articulated the Brazilian Strategy for Digital Transformation with the government, productive sector, universities, and civil society, to define guidelines and goals for digitizing the digitization of the economy [37]. The beginning of 2017 was marked by the recommendations of the Council for Economic and Social Development to the Presidency of the Republic for the implementation of programs to reduce bureaucracy and digital government, digital identity, and a single platform for digital public services, which were incorporated into the "long-term strategy for the digital economy" elaborated by the Ministry of Science, Technology, Innovations, and Communications [38]. Then, the MCTIC officially instituted Interministerial Ordinance n.842, the working group to elaborate the Brazilian digital economy strategy proposal, commonly known as the Brazilian Strategy for Digital Transformation. In mid-August 2017, the government launched a public consultation to discuss the strategy outlined through thematic axes and enablers [39].

Authorities involved in the working group and in managing the strategy participated in a technical mission to Europe to learn about the successful experiences of countries such as Germany, Belgium, Spain, and Portugal [33, 40]. The mission was part of the Technical Cooperation between EU-Brazil Sectoral Dialogues Support Initiative. During the technical mission, some civil servants observed the governance model implemented in the countries. The governance model was "copied" for the Brazilian strategy.

Part of the technical mission and the working group responsible for the strategy, presented the government with a governance model of a multisectoral chamber organized around priority themes [33]. The working group's proposal was submitted for public consultation and after approved the version by the MCTIC, the text was sent as a draft of a Decree to the President in March 2018 as an official strategy.

4.2 Seizing Opportunities

Digital transformation can drive innovations in products or processes as it tweaks the existing business model. The ability to adjust the model is accompanied by incorporating the preferences of customers of public sector organizations, whether suppliers, other governments, and citizens [19]. Seizing the opportunities and transforming products, services, processes, and business models is necessary for reconfiguring. Thus, with the publication of E-Digital, it was necessary to define the governance structure to lead the implementation of the strategy. The mission consisted of technical visits and meetings to deepen dialogue and articulation between the Brazilian delegation and European partners, whose knowledge was destined to implement digital transformation policies [40].

Through the learning and prototyping of European models, E-Digital governance was guided by the triple helix model commonly used in advanced manufacturing plans and combined with the model of multisectoral and thematic chambers [33]. The National System for Digital Transformation (SinDigital), created in 2018, established this governance structure coordinated by the Interministerial Committee for Digital Transformation (CITDigital) and by the Advisory Council for Digital Transformation [31]. The governance structure was inspired by Germany's Industry 4.0 [33], whose private and industrial sector has a decisive role in coordinating discussions on priority topics. It is attributed to the German design, the aggregating vision of existing activities between different ministries and agencies [41]. Although it is noticeable that the emulation of the German model in Brazilian strategies since the first transformation actions of the technological cycle [35], the platform is too ambitious to be reproduced in countries without a base of technological capabilities and accumulated capabilities [41].

The Brazilian structure generated an overcentralized structure based on SinDigital [31], whose decision-making power is divided between specific ministries and controlled by bodies directly linked to the Presidency of the Republic. The management of activities and coordination of E-Digital is the General Coordination of Digital Transformation. Currently, the coordination comprises four employees who provide technical support for elaborating and implementing the strategy articulated with different sectors, accompanying, and monitoring the actions, and rendering accounts to the Federal Court of Accounts. In any case, the E-Digital management methodology was being built as the first version of the strategy was being consolidated, so there were no defined routines [33]. The strategy's governance structure limits the organizational boundaries of CGTD management, so actions are capillaries between different ministries and agencies according to the thematic area. The CGTD and the respective Ministry govern the monitoring of each goal. At the same time, the thematic chambers discuss the agenda with the bodies responsible for the actions, with the participation of CGTD members [33].

Therefore, during the implementation of decision-making and activity management routines, from 2020 onwards, the CGTD began to organize follow-up work with ministries and agencies [33]. First, the CGTD had a moment of knowledge to discuss a specific action of the Ministry. That is, the CGTD mobilizes the ability to detect knowledge about a given action and policy o then mobilizes the ability to learn about the specificities of ministerial execution. For example, to connect a school to the Internet, it was necessary to know the execution of public policies and understand the complexity of actions involving the Ministry of Education and the National Telecommunications Agency.

Although SinDigital and the governance rules were established based on a model detected in the European benchmarking, there needed to be a mobilization of resources to support the management of monitoring actions. After a year of launching E-Digital, CITDigital shows the underutilization of DC. The decision-making routine is attributable to CITDigital, which must propose deliberation routines and decision routines, monitor the progress of activities, issue recommendations, share information, and define the work plan with schedule and priorities for achieving the strategy. The committee can create subcommittees and invite experts to report contributions [31]. However, there needs to be more clarity on the rules for CITDigital's decision-making process [42], and the Advisory Board can only offer recommendations.

Regarding the decision on the allocation of resources, there are no mechanisms related to the budgets of the individual actions in the governance structure or the management of the strategy [42]. Since each ministry or government agency has its budget allocation, the creation of goals depends on the intersectoral nature of the budget allocated to different themes. The CGTD articulates with the institutions the follow-up and monitoring of the targets, whose reports are made available annually on "accomplished actions" or "in progress" [31, 33].

The commitment of employees, whether civil servants or commissioned, is linked to the dedication routine; these resources depend on the means and stimulus the organization supports [7]. There were no training stages for the E-Digital management team after 2018 when the technical mission occurred. In addition, consulting activities are carried out by the Center for Management and Strategic Studies (CGEE), an organization supervised by MCTIC. The CGEE was responsible for public consultations and technical studies, such as the elaboration methodology, and diagnosis. For the strategy review, a legal attribution was instituted by SinDigital. Begovic [43] warns that the tendency to outsource capabilities outside the public sector can mean the failure of commitment capabilities in the public sector.

4.3 Reconfiguring Processes and Opportunities: Transformation Capabilities

Dynamic reconfiguration capabilities generate future resources whose impact must be evaluated after implementation. Structures, routines, and strategic decisions are combined, reconfigured, and aligned to result in transformation. For this reason, capacity must facilitate the decentralization of decision structures, aiming at agility and responsiveness to demands and new technologies, co-specialization of assets that generate value, and the governance and management of internal and external knowledge [7, 14].

E-Digital is an interesting case because, besides being a public sector organization's strategy, it includes transforming the government into a digital government [39]. Furthermore, the strategy review is an opportunity to mobilize capabilities and drive transformation. The evidence already presented indicates that the capacities were detected and apprehended distinctly by the strategy's governance and management. This distinction is evident concerning the mobilization of transformation capabilities.

According to Teece [7, 14], the ability to transform concerns maintaining innovation over time and deviating from unfavorable paths. Even after the OECD assessment [42] on the nebulous governance structure of decision-making and resource allocation, the same aim remained to decentralize the actions of SinDigital and the Interministerial Committee.

Similarly, the review of E-Digital 2018–2022 in the decree creating SinDigital did not result in changes in the governance system. The public consultation and the diagnosis carried out by the CGEE also pointed out inconsistencies in the governance of the strategy [31]. From the point of view of discussions on governance structures for the digital transformation of the public sector, there are relevant criticisms of centralized models and their incompatibility with the generation of public value.

Transformation means redesigning routines, or organizational redesign, involving the structure, processes, and people implementing the strategy. While the management of E-Digital - CGTD - sought to improve organizational performance, knowing the internal processes for the execution of public policies related to the strategy axes and decomposing and following up and monitoring actions, the governance structure remained rudimentary. The management of actions carried out by the CGTD with the Ministries and agencies is still based on dialogue and partnership [33]. The Civil House is responsible for collecting the target, the head of CITDigital.

Through the decomposability of E-Digital actions, CGTD is leading two projects: a project for intelligent monitoring of E-Digital actions and the creation an observatory of digital transformation indicators. For the execution of both projects, CGTD and MCTIC signed a consultancy contract with CGEE to benchmark digital transformation indicators and build a Business Intelligence panel to monitor actions with the bodies of the public sector automatically [33]. The co-specialization of the CGTD took place in two ways. First, given the need to understand the particularities and complexity involved in the execution of public policies related to digital transformation, the coordination was manually involved in meetings between the different ministries and agencies to monitor one hundred actions present in E-Digital 2018–2022 [33].

Then, to subsidize the thematic discussions, the CGTD has participated, since the first edition of E-Digital, in all the thematic chambers and supports and coordinates the involvement of specialists, organizations, and multiple actors in these spaces. CGTD acts established in E-Digital to the chambers and calls the groups involved for discussion, whether governmental or external groups [33]. The CGTD's capacity for co-specialization enabled cooperation with external and internal actors, exposing sources of innovation and reducing the mobilization of resources to promote shared knowledge. Therefore, the CGTD mobilized governance and knowledge management capacity as it developed processes for integrating external actors and specialized learning in the Thematic Chambers. The Chambers function as forums, established through technical cooperation agreements between Ministries, and may have a specific governance system and activity plans [44].

5 Capabilities to Support Digital Transformation in Public Sector Organizations

Mobilizing DC helps understand the organizational capacity of public sector organizations to respond to the demands, challenges, and opportunities of digital transformation. The DC framework [7, 14] explored the determinants of the public sector's digital transformation strategy. Although this article did not intend to stress the debate, the DC mobilization analysis for the digital transformation strategies of public sector organizations is a novelty.

The analysis of the Brazilian Digital Transformation Strategy, based on the detection, apprehension, and reconfiguration capabilities of organizational resources, serves as a call for specialized studies to understand how to expand and deal with organizational and managerial capabilities for strategies of public sector organizations. In the case of E-Digital, dynamic knowledge-sensing capabilities, agenda-setting ability, the combined ability to understand, interact and learn, the capability to foster and manage external partnerships, and the capability to decompose follow-up measures and progress of the strategy play a crucial role in the continuity of the government's strategy for digital transformation in the long term, that is, from the elaboration of E-Digital, implementation, and recent revision.

To a large extent, managerial leaders were the mobilizers of DC. From the detection of opportunities, a combination of multiple capacities to apprehend opportunities and threats is mobilized by managers. Unlike Kattel's [45] analysis, the managers are career civil servants in the public service, are involved in different functions within the MCTIC, and had the political support of decision-makers to propose agendas and strategies.

Decision-makers did not mobilize dynamic apprehension capabilities in the case of E-Digital; the governance of the strategy established rules, decision-making processes, and an organizational structure centralized in the hands of decision-makers, whose decision-making routines are locked within the central committee. In addition, the routine processes of resource allocation and decision-making are unrelated to the organizational and managerial processes of the strategy. However, different dynamic capacities are mobilized by the governance structure and strategy management coordination. The mobilization of different capabilities at different stages of strategy implementation confirms Konopic's perspective [4] that digital transformation is a capacity-building process of continuous strategic renewal.

The CGTD, for example, mobilizes more DC than the governance structure. As it mobilizes knowledge management capabilities, it also mobilizes the ability to detect and learn from external and specialized actors to achieve future projects of evaluation and measures of Strategy progress. Therefore, it results in continual renewal and capabilities. On the other hand, the governance structure needs help in implementing decision-making routines, resource allocation, and governance of external alliances [31, 42].

In particular, mobilizing capacities for detecting agendas and taking advantage of opportunities needs a debate on leadership and agenda. According to Teece [46], the organization's management must be entrepreneurial, as managers need to get involved and learn about trends, emerging markets, and business models through managerial skills. Likewise, the entrepreneurial approach must be disseminated to the entire organization, including the governance structures; this is different from the governance structure of E-Digital.

The inaction related to the capabilities to take advantage of resources is related to the scope of high concentration of decision-making power of government representatives, distant and dissociated from the strategy management [31]. Given this, there are flaws related to the business model for creating public value from the governance of E-Digital; due to the inability to include stakeholders, remaining a traditional and bureaucratic view, there are flaws related to governance performance concerning the digital transformation strategy. The dichotomy between governance and management must be revisited regarding the challenges that public sector organizations face to implement dynamic resources in support of digital transformation.

Table 1 Mobilization of DC identifies the organizational and managerial capabilities desirable for digital transformation strategies, differentiating the capability needed according to the focus during the training process.

Table 1. Mobilization of DC framework for digital transformation in the public sector

Capabilities to detect and shape opportunities for digital transformation	
Focus on positions	Understand approaches related to digital transformation, such as industry 4.0, e-government, data revolution, and SDGs
	Interact with different stakeholders such as technical consultancy, research and citizens involved in the discussion of digital transformation
	Evaluate internal information and resources for valuable models and strategies
	Establish partnerships and launch an ecosystem of actors relevant to digital transformation at the local and national level
	Interpret the challenges of digital transformation from the perspective of different sectors, in addition to the public
	Integrate, engage, and lead innovation agendas among organization members
Capabilities to seize opportunities for process transformation	
Focus on processes	Structure adequate governance and adapt if necessary
	Enjoy and learn best practices related to the public, including business model, value generation, technologies, and products
	Manage processes and define rules, routines, and performance thresholds to ensure the benefit of innovation
	Establish a decentralized decision-making protocol related to the allocation of resources and assets
	Encourage employee commitment to the strategy and in line with the culture of innovation
Transformative capabilities	
Focus on the path	Decentralize the governance of the strategy, aiming to meet the demands of multiple actors
	Decompose follow-up and monitoring measures of actions related to the digital transformation strategy
	Create specialized tools and exchange spaces, such as themed chambers and technical cooperation
	Govern and manage the strategy through knowledge of the processes, the integration of external actors and specialized learning

The DC identified in Table 1 have the potential to contribute to the debate on organizational obstacles and barriers found in the literature [6, 12] and initiate research that unpacks transformation processes in stages, taking advantage of the approach oriented to processes common to capabilities [4]. The focus on mobilizing DC identified in the table above also highlights the prospect of continuous renewal of capabilities being mobilized at different times.

The results of the E-Digital analysis indicate the need to analyze capabilities from the point of view of mobilizing decision makers and managers, that is, the perspective of management and governance of strategies as sources of mobilization of DC. This data is essential because the literature also needs an appropriate discussion about the governance paradigms related to the digital transformation of the public sector [31, 47].

First, because it is evident that a digital transformation governance model has the role of enabling the mobilization – development, and implementation – of DC, however, buying the idea that new approaches to public governance that claim to maximize value and react to fixation of the market, start to mobilize organizational capabilities as a capacity to respond to citizens' demands, technological and economic changes, it may be too outdated. Second, emerging technologies are being institutionalized as part of organizational routines and respond to different paradigms of governance, agile government, regulatory government, government as a platform, and sectoral digital government [48]. Third, a well-designed governance model can emphasize collaboration and partnership between different agencies, the private sector, and stakeholders, and therefore mobilize different capacities at different stages, allocate resources, manage risk, collaborate, and make decisions.

6   DC as a Driver for the Digital Transformation of Public Sector

This article explores the mobilization of DC applied in public sector organizations with a focus on digital transformation strategies. The mobilization of DC framework for digital transformation in the public sector (Table 1) is an empirical framework drawn from the Brazilian case study's analysis and the results of related research (Sect. 2) on DC in the public sector. Public sector and government digital transformation. It is also a conceptual framework based on the microfoundations of DC, as shown in Fig. 1, and on key capabilities unpacked to cover organizations' past, process, and path. Therefore, the framework informs the essential or desirable resources for digital transformation strategies, detecting opportunities, capturing opportunities and threats, and reconfiguring resources to generate competitive advantage, better performance, and innovation.

The DC view is a popular approach in private sector management. Case studies are part of the effort for empirical analysis and still need to be explored on mobilizing DC in public sector organizations. While the constitutive elements – micro-foundations- of DC can often be context-specific [45], as illustrated by the problems of E-Digital governance structure, it is essential to understand capabilities in a broader context of the state and government policies.

DC can serve the public sector's strategic approach to dealing with multiple challenges, including digital transformation. The hypothesis question of this research is informed by the view that dynamic capability works [3, 7, 8, 14] as a driver for digital transformation for public sector organizations. The study was based on the discussion of the literature on organizational capabilities, DC, and digital transformation [4, 11, 13, 25, 26], DC applied to the public sector [2, 5, 18, 20, 21, 23, 27], and digital transformation government and organizational capabilities [6, 11]. Despite studies by innovators by Kattel [45] and Barrutia [20] that discuss digital government strategies and smart cities, the literature has yet to devote much to discussing the mobilization of DC for organizational and managerial barriers and challenges of the digital transformation of the public sector.

The data show that mobilizing DC helps support digital transformation strategies in public sector organizations. It also confirms that the procedural perspective of DC favors the analysis of the different stages of the evolution of digital transformation. At the same time, managers and decision-makers mobilize capabilities in a sequential order different from the procedural order of detection, apprehension, and transformation mechanisms. Therefore, new case studies must be designed to test the combination of DC, or the strategic renewal of DC mobilized by different actors. The governance structure and public management are mechanisms that need an improved debate regarding the mobilization of capabilities and the definition of routines, rules, and partnerships. The evidence from the frontier literature, and the results of this analysis, support the hypothesis that DC are a crucial factor in the digital transformation of the public sector.

6.1 Contributions and Limitations

The study emphasizes the importance of organizational capabilities due to the digital transformation public sector organizations undergo. It offers an empirical framework for applying DC in public sector organizations, which requires more sophisticated versions. Also, it provides a framework for digital transformation "leaders" to assess their internal and essential resources, prioritize capabilities, and mobilize capabilities to support government digital transformation strategies.

Thus, the study also facilitates the operationalization of detection, apprehension, and transformation capabilities, and respective specific capabilities, for other studies to explore the organization's antecedents - past and explain how the mobilization of capabilities influences processes and impacts the trajectory of the future. Furthermore, defining a framework of desirable DC for digital transformation strategies opens up opportunities for further research to test the causality between organizational barriers and obstacles of strategies, applied DC, and long-term performance.

Finally, as a practical result, the DC mobilization framework can be combined with other tools, such as Business Process Management (BPM), to develop and improve strategies continuously. BPM applied to public organizations has been related to transformational government reform and e-government [50] and digital government as a support to the "life cycle of transformation processes, activities and resources [49]".

The sample size of a single case is a limitation, however this study has an exploratory character, although the results indicate paths for future research. Although there is a discussion on the approach of DC, different points of view, and inconsistent division of dimensions [13], we chose not to deepen this debate, given that in the public administration literature, there are studies that use the DC to explore strategic approaches at the organizational and managerial level [21]. Concerning the results, it would be essential to learn to what extent the establishment of DC fails, as decision-making resources and resource allocation relative to the governance structure of the E-Digital strategy are criticized for centralization and inaction.

Funding. This paper is a result of the project "INOV.EGOV-Digital Governance Innovation for Inclusive, Resilient and Sustainable Societies NORTE-01-0145-FEDER-000087", supported by Norte Portugal Regional Operational Program (NORTE 2020), under the PORTUGAL 2020 Partnership Agreement, through the European Regional Development Fund (EFDR).

References

1. Wu, X., Howlett, M., Ramesh, M. (eds.): Policy Capacity and Governance Assessing Governmental Competences and Capabilities in Theory and Practice. SPEPP, Springer, Cham (2018). https://doi.org/10.1007/978-3-319-54675-9
2. Mazzucato, M.; Qobo, M.; Kattel, R. Building state capacities and dynamic capabilities to drive social and economic development: the case of South Africa. UCL Institute for Innovation and Public Purpose, Working Paper Series (2021)
3. Teece, D.J., Pisano, G., Shuen, A.: Dynamic capabilities, and strategic management. Strateg. Manag. J. **18**, 509–533 (1997)
4. Konopik, J., Jahn, C., Schuster, T., Hoßbach, N., Pflaum, A.: Mastering the digital transformation through organizational capabilities: a conceptual framework. Digit. Bus. **2**(2) (2022). https://doi.org/10.1016/j.digbus.2021.100019
5. Mazzucato, M., Kattel, R.: COVID-19 and public-sector capacity. Oxf. Rev. Econ. Policy **36**(1), 256–269 (2020). https://doi.org/10.1093/oxrep/graa031
6. Wilson, C., Mergel, I.: Overcoming barriers to digital government: mapping the strategies of digital champions. Gov. Inf. Q. **39**(2), 101681 (2022). https://doi.org/10.1016/j.giq.2022.101681
7. Teece, D.: Explaining dynamic capabilities: the nature and microfoundations of (sustainable) enterprise performance. Strateg. Manag. J. **28**, 1319–1350 (2007)
8. Teece, D.: The foundations of enterprise performance: dynamic and ordinary capabilities in an (economic) theory of firms. Acad. Manag. Perspect. **28**(4), 328–352 (2014). https://doi.org/10.5465/amp.2013.0116
9. Teece, D.: The evolution of the dynamic capabilities framework. In: Adams, R., Grichnik, D., Pundziene, A., Volkmann, C. (eds.) Artificiality and Sustainability in Entrepreneurship. FGF Studies in Small Business and Entrepreneurship, pp. 113–129. Springer, Cham. (2023). https://doi.org/10.1007/978-3-031-11371-0_6
10. Lanzolla, G., Pesce, D., Tucci, C.L.: The digital transformation of search and recombination in the innovation function: tensions and an integrative framework*. J. Prod. Innov. Manag. **38**, 90–113 (2021). https://doi.org/10.1111/jpim.12546
11. Faro, B., Abedin, B., Cetindamar, D.: Continuous transformation of public-sector organisations in the digital era. In: Americas Conference on Information Systems (2019)
12. Tangi, L., Janssen, M., Benedetti, M., Noci, G.: Digital government transformation: a structural equation modeling analysis of driving and impeding factors. Int. J. Inf. Manag. **60** (2021). https://doi.org/10.1016/j.ijinfomgt.2021.102356
13. Liu, L., Yu, B., Wu, W.: The formation and effects of exploitative dynamic capabilities and explorative dynamic capabilities: an empirical study. Sustainability **11**, 2581 (2019). https://doi.org/10.3390/su11092581
14. Teece, D.: Dynamic Capabilities and Strategic Management: Organizing for Innovation and Growth. Oxford University Press, New York (2009)
15. Helfat, C., Peteraf, M.: Managerial cognitive capabilities and the microfoundations of dynamic capabilities. Strateg. Manag. J. **36**(5), 831–850 (2015). https://doi.org/10.1002/smj.2247

16. Lukito, D., Suharnomo, Perdhana, M.: Transformation management capabilities for digital transformation initiatives: a construct conceptualization in alignment with the dynamic capabilities framework. J. Organ. Manag. Stud. **2022** (2022). https://doi.org/10.5171/2022.845443
17. Piening, E.: Dynamic capabilities in public organizations. Public Manag. Rev. **15**(2), 209–245 (2013). https://doi.org/10.1080/14719037.2012.708358
18. Gullmark, P.: Do all roads lead to innovativeness? A study of public sector organizations' innovation capabilities. Am. Rev. Public Adm. **51**(7), 509–525 (2021). https://doi.org/10.1177/02750740211010464
19. Wirtz, B., Langer, P., Schmidt, F.: Digital government: developing a business model for creating public value - a framework based on dynamic capabilities. Public Adm. Q. **45**, 232–255 (2021). https://doi.org/10.37808/paq.45.3.2
20. Barrutia, J.M., Echebarria, C., Aguado-Moralejo, I., Apaolaza-Ibáñez, V., Hartmann, P. Leading smart city projects: Government dynamic capabilities and public value creation. Technol. Forecast. Soc. Change **179**(C). (2022). Elsevier. https://doi.org/10.1016/j.techfore.2022.121679
21. Guenduez, A., Mergel, I.: The role of dynamic managerial capabilities and organizational readiness in smart city transformation. Cities **129**, 103791 (2022). https://doi.org/10.1016/j.cities.2022.103791
22. Luna-Reyes, L., et al.: Exploring the relationships between dynamic capabilities and IT governance: implications for local governments. Transform. Gov.: People Process Policy **14**(2), 149–169 (2020). https://doi.org/10.1108/TG-09-2019-0092
23. Trivellato, B., Martini, M., Cavenago, D.: How do organizational capabilities support continuous innovation in a public setting? Am. Rev. Public Adm. **51**(1), 57–71 (2021). https://doi.org/10.1177/0275074020939263
24. Klievink, B., Janssen, M.: Realizing integrated government—dynamic capabilities and stage models for transformation. Gov. Inf. Q. **26**(2), 275–284 (2009). https://doi.org/10.1016/j.giq.2008.12.007
25. Frössling, C., Ek, L., Ranerup, A.: Relating integrative capabilities and institutional logics to digital transformation a case study of a public sector organization. Master theses, Institutionen för tillämpad informationsteknologi (2020)
26. Leso, B.: Unlocking the digital organization: a view of the digital transformation capabilities. Doctorate theses. Engenharia de Produção da Universidade Federal do Rio Grande do Sul, Brazil (2022)
27. Kattel, R., Takala, V.: Dynamic capabilities in the public sector: the UK Government Digital Service case. UCL (IIPP WP 2021 p. 01) (2021)
28. Panagiotopoulos, P., Klievink, B., Cordella, A.: Public value creation in digital government. Gov. Inf. Q. **36**(4), 101421 (2019). https://doi.org/10.1016/j.giq.2019.101421
29. Ben Dhaou, S.I.: Towards a repository of e-government capabilities. In: Janssen, M., et al. (eds.) EGOV 2017. LNCS, vol. 10428, pp. 154–165. Springer, Cham (2017). https://doi.org/10.1007/978-3-319-64677-0_13
30. Dubey, R., et al.: Dynamic digital capabilities and supply chain resilience: the role of government effectiveness. Int. J. Prod. Econ. **258** (2023). https://doi.org/10.1016/j.ijpe.2023.108790
31. Magalhães, L.: Brazil's over-centralized governance of digital transformation. Afr. J. Inf. Commun. (AJIC) (30) (2022). https://doi.org/10.23962/ajic.i30.14843
32. Wachowicz, M., Canut, L., (Org.): Análise da estratégia Brasileira para transformação digital: comentários ao decreto n° 9319/18 Curitiba: GEDAI/ UFPR (2018)
33. Coordenação Geral de Transformação Digital. (CGTD). Interview I. Ministry of Science, Technology, and Innovation. Federal Government of Brazil, February 2023, Vitória (2023).

One .mp3 file (46:43 min.), one .pdf file. Pinpoint by Google. https://encurtador.com.br/agBHM

34. Velho, S.K.: Como ocorreu o início da Indústria 4.0 no MCTI. https://pt.linkedin.com/pulse/como-ocorreu-o-in%C3%ADcio-da-ind%C3%BAstria-40-mcti-s%C3%A9rgio-knorr-old-msc-. [Post]. Accessed 16 Mar 2022

35. Arbix, G., et al.: O Brasil e a Nova Onda de Manufatura Avançada: O que aprender com Alemanha, China e Estados Unidos. Novos estud. CEBRAP **36**(3), 29–49 (2017). https://doi.org/10.25091/S0101-3300201700030003

36. Brasil. Estratégia Nacional de Ciência, Tecnologia e Inovação 2016–2022. Ministério da Ciência, Tecnologia, Inovações e Comunicações. Brasília, DF (2017a)

37. Brasil. ProFuturo. Plano de CT&I para Manufatura Avançada no Brasil. Validado pelo Conselho Nacional de Ciência e Tecnologia (2017b)

38. Conselho de Desenvolvimento Econômico e Social. (CDES). ATA DA 46ª REUNIÃO PLENÁRIA. Casa Civil, Presidência da República Federativa do Brasil (2017)

39. Brazil. Estratégia Brasileira de Transformação Digital. E-Digital. Ministry of Science, Technology, Innovations, and Communications. Brasilia, DF (2018)

40. Diálogos. Diálogos União Europeia – Brasil. Técnica em Políticas e Programas de Manufatura Avançada. Ministério da Ciência, Tecnologia, Inovações e Comunicações. Cooperação e Direcção-Geral de Redes, Conteúdos e Tecnologias de Comunicação. Disponível em: Diálogos Setoriais. Cooperação Técnica em Políticas e Programas de Manufatura Avançada (eubrdialogues.com) (2017)

41. UNIDO. What can policymakers learn from Germany's Industry 4.0 development strategy? Inclusive and Sustainable Industrial Development. Department Of Policy, Research, and Statistics Working. Working Paper Series, WP 22 (2018)

42. OECD. On the Way to the Digital Age in Brazil, OECD Publishing, Paris (2020). https://doi.org/10.1787/45a84b29-pt

43. Begovic, M., Kattel, R., Mazzucato, M., Quaggiotto, G.: COVID-19 and the Need for Dynamic State Capabilities: An International Comparison. UCL Institute for Innovation and Public Purpose and United Nations Development Program (2021)

44. Gov.br. (2023). https://www.gov.br/mcti/pt-br/acompanhe-o-mcti/transformacaodigital

45. Kattel, R. Dynamic capabilities of the public sector: Towards a new synthesis. UCL Institute for Innovation and Public Purpose. Working Paper Series 2022/07 (2022)

46. Teece, D.: Business models and dynamic capabilities. Long Range Plann. **51**(1), 40–49 (2018). https://doi.org/10.1016/j.lrp.2017.06.007

47. Chantillon, M.: A governance framework facilitating the digital transformation of the public administration. Ph.D. thesis. Institute Overheid voor, KU Leuven (2021)

48. Janowski, T. Digital government evolution: From transformation to contextualization. Gov. Inf. Q. **32**(3), 221–236 (2015). ISSN 0740-624X. https://doi.org/10.1016/j.giq.2015.07.001

49. Delgado, A., Garcia, F., Astudillo, H.: Introduction to the HICSS'55 mini-track on digital government and Business Process Management (BPM). In: Proceedings of the 55th Hawaii International Conference on Systems Sciences (2022)

50. Niehaves, B., Plattfaut, R., Becker, J.: Business process management capabilities in local governments: a multi-method study. Gov. Inf. Q. **30**, 217–225 (2013)

The Vicious Cycle of Magical Thinking:

How IT Governance Counteracts Digital Transformation

Susanna Hammelev Jörgensen ⓘ, Tomas Lindroth ⓘ, Johan Magnusson ⓘ,
Malin Tinjan ⓘ, Jacob Torell ⓘ, and Robert Åhlén(✉) ⓘ

University of Gothenburg, Forskningsgången 6, 417 56 Göteborg, Sweden
robert.ahlen@ait.gu.se

Abstract. Digital transformation is associated with a fundamental change in the operating models of organizations and industries alike. At the same time, previous research highlights that existing governance practices may act as a deterrent to digital transformation. In this study, we explore how the IT governance of a large university counteracts necessary digital transformation in higher education over time. We show how the adoption of an industry-standard IT governance framework, through a series of generative mechanisms, leads to a vicious cycle that restricts digital transformation into mere computerization, thereby successfully counteracting digital transformation. In other words, the IT governance framework increasingly protects the organization from the organizational change brought on by new digital opportunities. This is discussed in relation to the literature on IT governance and digital transformation with the intent of contributing with a critical perspective on the widespread adoption and use of standard IT governance framework.

Keywords: Digital transformation · IT governance · Vicious cycle · Higher education

1 Introduction

Digital transformation, here understood as organizational change due to the utilization of digital solutions, fundamentally revamps and disrupts existing industries and society [1]. Research identifies two primary dimensions of digital transformation. First, digital transformation has an innate potential to enhance operational efficiency through automation, process redesign, and algorithmic work. Second, digital transformation can create new value streams through innovation, new value offerings, and the dismantling of obsolete and non-value-adding market activities [2–4].

As noted by several researchers [5–7], higher education is one of these industries currently on the cusp of disruption, i.e., under heavy duress for significant change due to changes in its outside environment. On top of this, the aftermath of the COVID-19 pandemic with physical distancing has decimated the social value of college life [8], while simultaneously opening for new, campus-free all digital options from new entrants such

© IFIP International Federation for Information Processing 2023
Published by Springer Nature Switzerland AG 2023
I. Lindgren et al. (Eds.): EGOV 2023, LNCS 14130, pp. 381–396, 2023.
https://doi.org/10.1007/978-3-031-41138-0_24

as Google and Amazon promising full employability at a fraction of the cost, hassle, and risk of enrolling in a university. What we are experiencing here could be referred to as an increased commoditization and de-professionalization of higher education, a development leaving several of the presidents of higher education institutions in a worrisome state [9].

With digital transformation leveraging information technologies, it is positioned in the context of existing IT governance. If we wish to increase the utilization of digital solutions, it will invariably have to pass through the existing loops and hoops of how organizations have set up their decision rights and accountabilities for IT [10]. Previous studies have shown how "pathologies" of IT governance directly counteract innovation capabilities of digital transformation [11], and how shifts in IT governance practice are needed [12]. IT governance is said to be either a constraint or a facilitator of digital transformation [11]. Current configurations of IT governance have an overarching tendency to favor continued operations over new ones, directly counteracting building necessary capabilities for change. If higher education is expected (or more frankly needs) to tap into the benefits of digital transformation, expedient IT governance becomes a critical aspect of what needs to be in place.

Based on this brief rationale, our study aims to answer the following research question: *How does IT governance impact digital transformation in higher education?*

This is answered through a clinical case study of a large, public university in Sweden that revamped its IT governance in 2017. The research team was contracted in 2021 to audit the impact of IT governance on the organization's ability for digital transformation and to suggest necessary changes.

The study contributes by answering previous calls for research from Wiener et al. [13] on an increased emphasis on the enactment rather than the design of governance and control, Rof et al. [5] on the need for more research into business model innovation within higher education, and Magnusson et al. [14] on balancing practices in digital transformation.

The paper is organized accordingly. After this short introduction, we present the previous research on digital transformation and IT governance, particularly within higher education. This is followed by the method of the study where the clinical case study method is described and motivated. After this we present the results in the form of an identified vicious cycle of magical thinking, followed by the discussion where we discuss the findings from the perspective of how IT governance constraints digital transformation in higher education.

2   Previous Research and Theoretical Framing

2.1   Digital Transformation in Higher Education

Higher education institutions are highly affected by surrounding changes because of globalization and digitalization, and the future of higher education is yet to be seen [15]. The universities' reaction to this new digital environment has been sluggish [15, 16] and western universities need to align with external demands [17] to build competitive advantages and to continue to conduct sustainable education [5, 16, 18].

Research about digital transformation in higher education institutions is increasing, implying there is an urge to understand in which ways digital transformation affects higher education and its missions [16, 19]. Yet, the focus is still on the digitization of education and digital systems used for teaching.

Policy making and planning regarding the digital transformation of the organization itself is still in its early stages [6] or has had a very limited impact on the digitalization of higher education institutions [20]. This indicates that the driving force of digitalization of higher education has a bottom-up perspective rather than a top-down one [21]. On the other hand, teachers and students only have a limited set of digital skills [22] and use EdTech primarily to organize classes and share digital documents [6, 19, 21].

Universities need to develop internal strategies and governance models for digital transformation [18, 23] but in most organizations managing digital transformation is not an easy task [24–26].

2.2 The Impact of IT Governance on Digital Transformation

IT governance, here defined as the decision rights and accountability for ensuring the desired behavior in the organization's use of IT [27], requires an understanding of the competing forces in a large organization and needs to create harmony among business objectives, governance archetype, and business performance to be effective [10]. While several IT governance frameworks have been developed over the years to help organizations govern and manage their IT in order to obtain business value, implementation proves to be hard (Dietrich, 2005, referenced in Boonstra et al. [28]). Other findings show that competing institutional logics of key stakeholders influence IT governance practices within the organization [28].

Research shows that IT governance reinforces the existing organizational identity while digital transformation involves introducing a new organizational identity [29]. Digital transformation is dependent on the strategic use of new technologies in organizations [30]. But as noted by Bharadwaj et al. [31], and others [32, 33], IT strategies usually focus on the government of the IT infrastructure and on existing operations while digital transformation origins from the business-centric perspective. Other studies highlight the impact of IT governance on digital transformation through the issue of how IT governance is enacted [2, 28] and the mechanisms of how digital infrastructure constrains ambidexterity in public organizations [34].

2.3 Theoretical Framing: Vicious Cycles

A vicious cycle, as described by Masuch [35] (as "circle" though "cycle" has become the de facto standard) is a generative chain of events without equilibrium, i.e., it is self-enforcing, resulting in ever-increasing detrimental effects for the organization in which it exists [36]. A common version is the "vicious circle of bureaucracy", where a change of sorts is introduced, followed by increased formalization, like new rules. This triggers dysfunctional reactions from the workforce, which are met by more formalization by management. This escalation ends in a blocked system: "Control measures are constantly enacted, as is apathy. The circle has become a normal, yet suboptimal state of affairs" [35 p. 18].

Smith and Lewis [37] drew upon research on tensions and paradoxes in organizations to explain how cycles could become either vicious or virtuous, further elaborated by Cuganesan [38]. Wimelius et al. [39] used it in the context of information systems, to find that virtuous cycles happen when management either tries to integrate two poles of tension or split the tension by choosing one pole. If management is pretending to have decided or is avoiding the tension altogether, vicious cycles can develop. This study uses the vicious cycle theory as an analytical lens to highlight how seemingly isolated events are in fact tightly connected.

3   Method

In the fall of 2020, the research team were approached by executive representatives from a university currently experiencing challenges in its IT governance. The university had implemented a new framework for IT governance in 2017 but was unsure whether the framework produced the effects they originally aspired for. With the research team having a long history of clinical research projects [40], the request was formulated into an assignment for auditing the existing practice and suggestions for the future configuration of IT governance. The research team were given full autonomy in designing the study as well as afforded the possibility of future publications coming out of the project.

After initial workshops and discussions with an executive team from the university with the intent of sensitizing the research team and arriving at a scoping of the assignment of relevance to both the organization and research, the project was formally commenced at the beginning of 2021.

The data collection involved 22 interviews with key stakeholders in the IT governance of the organization (7 from portfolio management, 7 from portfolio support, 4 from IT, and 4 from business support). This involved individuals from different parts of the organization, as well as from both core operations (education and research, departments) and operations support (IT, HR, finance, portfolio management). The interviews spanned 40 to 90 min and were sound recorded and transcribed verbatim. In parallel with the interviews, we collected a large amount of secondary data in the form of project charters, annual reports, steering documents, budgets et cetera.

The interview data were analysed using thematic coding and analysis [41] based in critical realism [36, 42]. After initial inductive coding of first-order constructs, we iteratively worked with finding new first-order and refining them into second-order constructs to function as the basis for our continued analysis. The continued analysis utilized inspiration from previous research on IT governance [10] and institutional theory [43] to theorize on the generative mechanisms [35] underlying the enactment of the IT governance framework.

4   Results

4.1   Case Background

The university is one of Europe's largest with around 50 000 annual students and a faculty of 5 000. The IT governance framework implemented in 2017 is an adaptation of a framework that during the past ten years has become industry standard in the Swedish public sector. The original framework was designed in the late 1990's to counteract the accelerated spend on IT through increasing cost control of primarily maintenance activities and to distribute responsibility for IT across the organization.

The framework as it is applied in the university controls the project pipeline for both maintenance and development. The original rationale for implementing the framework was, according to the initiator and then administrative director: *"We wish to create better conditions to capture demands and viewpoints from business. With the new model the university attains the possibility to do so. The model makes it possible to lead the development and maintenance of systems, processes, and information jointly, toward strategic objectives."*

The project had two direct effect goals, expressed as 1) "increased allocation to development rather than maintenance", 2) "increased business value through an established governance that can prioritize the right development- and maintenance activities" (from the implementation project charter).

4.2 The Vicious Cycle of Magical Thinking in IT Governance

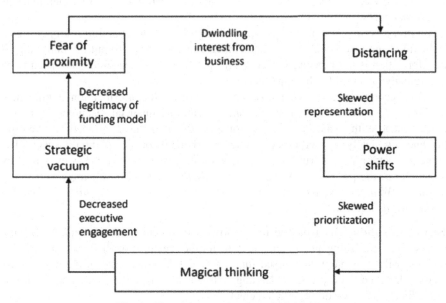

Fig. 1. The vicious cycle of magical thinking.

Our study identifies a vicious cycle of generative mechanisms that we refer to as "magical thinking", i.e., the irrational belief that using the same method repeatedly will result in varied outcomes in the future. We present the different parts of the mechanisms below (Fig. 1).

Strategic Vacuum. The organization lacks a common definition of digital transformation, and within the upper echelons of management it is primarily seen as either a vague extrinsic force or simply market hyperbole. With this as the dominant view, the organization is faced with significant challenges when it comes to setting strategic objectives for digital transformation. *"Who has the right to interpret to create the content of digital transformation? That is something we at [omitted] have not yet landed in: What is digital transformation for us?"*.

The lack of clarity in terms of what digital transformation is and implies, subsequently leads to a retreat of the executives of the organization from any type of discussions or involvement in governance. Digital transformation is seen as something not relevant to the strategic direction for the organization, whereby it is handed over to the lower levels of management to make tactical and operative decisions without any overarching digital transformation strategy or strategic objective. *"But [omitted name of executive in charge of digital transformation] said: 'Now we have digitalized GU, because now we have [Microsoft] Teams'. That is not digital transformation to me, but I think we have very different notions of what digital transformation is."*

A brief overview of the level of integration of digital transformation into the existing vision, strategy, and annual reports of the university corroborates this perception. There are no mentions of anything related to digital transformation in the formal vision and strategy, and within the annual reports digital transformation is primarily mentioned as an external factor.

In other words, the university displays a high level of decoupling of digital transformation from its core operations and strategic management. To put it bluntly: digital transformation is not perceived to be a strategic issue, and hence does not need to be strategically managed by the upper echelons of management.

This becomes apparent when observing meetings in the prioritization board, where decisions are made on how to utilize and allocate the financial resources for digital development. Without any overarching strategic objectives and direction, the discussions become completely focused on cost rather than benefits of the potential projects. The strategic vacuum is rendering the prioritization process pointless. Or as explained by a member of the prioritization board: *"The only thing [portfolio management] thinks about is: 'Well, as long as it is within budget, then we have no opinions.' Then you govern but do not lead."*

Fear of Proximity. Given the lack of executive involvement and the perception of digital transformation as being a non-strategic issue for the organization, there was not enough political will to create a centralized funding model. This was one of the key success factors identified in the pre-study leading up to the new IT governance setup, yet it was immediately scrapped during implementation.

In the absence of a centralized funding model, two things happened. First, there was an increased utilization of investment funding, i.e., capital expenditure. As seen in Fig. 2, this practice has resulted in decreases in the maneuverability of the university, with a mere 20% of the yearly budget now being actionable for new IT initiatives and the rest tied up in the depreciation of previous initiatives.

Second, other types of initiatives that would have to be funded through operating expenses in the core business units became hard to prioritize. Utilizing this type of investment for common solutions inadvertently led to certain parts of the university advocating

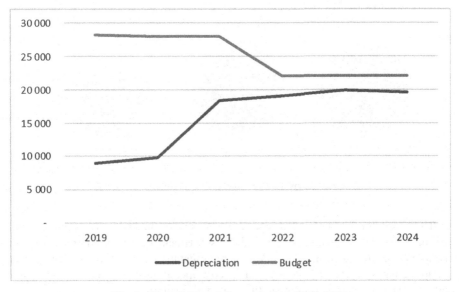

Fig. 2. Cost of depreciation vs budget 2019–2024.

down-prioritization since it would be associated with additional costs allocated without clear benefits. With clear differences in financial resources between the different units, increases in cost that may seem like a minor thing to more financially sturdy departments, were perceived as an almost existential threat by units with less strong finances.

Business units then shy away from lofty transformation projects since the financing is so unclear. They do not want to run the risk of getting the cost but no benefits. The missing central funding model hence has substantial impacts on the pace of digital transformation of the university. *"…but now we are to take these funds from having less guidance counselors at the education unit, so this prioritization happens in operations, so individual managers are then to say: we will take these funds from a different type of operations and allocate it to digital transformation. This is not a feasible option."*

The consequence of this is found in an increased distancing of the core operations from digital transformation. Close involvement is seen as leading to an increased risk of unexpected cost that they can neither justify in the short term or finance without decreasing the quality of their work.

Distancing. Figure 3 displays an overview of the representation in the three boards, councils and forums tasked with governing IT at the university. As seen, portfolio management (prioritization) and the antecedent preparatory council (where the business cases are prepared for portfolio management) are totally devoid of representation from core operations, i.e., departments tasked with teaching and research. Instead, they comprise representatives from supporting functions such as finance, HR, and IT. The only representation from core operations is found in the IT strategic forum, where more general discussions related to core IT systems are handled.

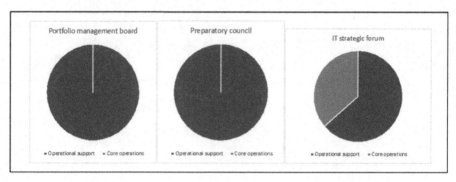

Fig. 3. Overview of representation in three governance fora.

The reason for the low level of representation is associated with the aforementioned lack of a centralized funding model and the subsequent fear of proximity from core operations. At the same time, the skewed representation leads to a shift away from initiatives that would be deemed relevant for core operations (educational- and research development), to issues pertaining to these support functions.

Another aspect directly affecting the involvement of core operations is the underfunding of IT. Over the past three years, the IT cost per user has decreased by 20% (Fig. 4). No funds have been allocated for continuous modernization and the IT governance setup has resulted in an accumulated digital debt in the form of postponed re-investments in digital infrastructure.

The result is a situation where the IT staff and individuals involved in prioritization of new initiatives express feelings of frustration and shame. *"Well, we always do things because we have to, since things are breaking down. So, there is really never any business perspective to prioritize on. It is never like: 'Shucks, does the business want bells and whistles or green pastures?'. Instead, it is just like: 'Does the business want this system crashed or that system crashed?'."*

During this period there has been growing discontent from the business side, and a major incident where the entire email system went down for several months. This inability to deliver services and IT on par with expectations also increases the distancing between core operations and the IT governance.

Powershift. With skewed representation from core operations, the IT governance (contrary to its design) pushes increasing power over prioritization from the business side to IT. With IT being perceived as complex and risky by the other members of the prioritization board (i.e., business support functions such as HR, finance), they increasingly retreat into a passive mode in the meetings. The vacuum is hence filled by the CIO and other representatives from IT that push the initiatives they see as most critical to continued operations, i.e., biasing digital transformation into safeguarding efficient maintenance and the avoidance of down-time.

Figure 5 shows the relative allocation of funds for maintenance vs development in the portfolio. From 20% being spent on development in 2018, this is reduced to 15% by 2020. In other words, the effect goal of the IT governance framework implementation

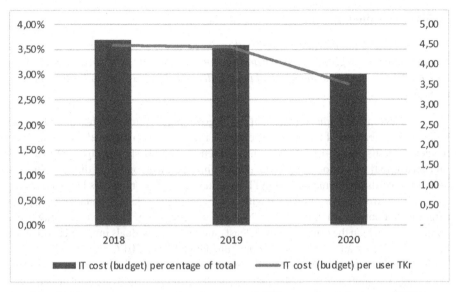

Fig. 4. IT cost as percentage of total revenues and IT cost per user in thousand SEK.

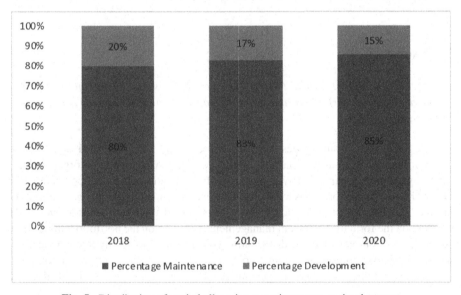

Fig. 5. Distribution of capital allocation to maintenance vs development.

of "increasing spend on development" is directly counteracted and the framework is in essence pushing the organization in the opposite direction. More and more of the resources spent are being allocated to maintenance.

Magical Thinking

... it becomes something of a ritual, rather than real governance. There is a model that is intended to give us direction and all that, but in reality, so to speak, questions and problems and such are handled in operations and in between and within these projects...

As presented, the implementation of the IT governance framework has directly counteracted the objectives of the project itself. Less money is spent on development and less business benefits are accrued due to a shift in focus on merely supporting functions. Digital transformation, i.e., organizational change through the adoption of digital solutions, is in other words counteracted by the IT governance framework as it is being enacted.

The framework is also associated with significant drawbacks. For instance, it displays a significant control cost and high levels of project escalation. Despite these drawbacks being well known in the organization, at least among the individuals involved in portfolio management, the framework has remained unchanged since 2017.

This leads to our conclusion that the organization is engaged in what can be referred to as "magical thinking", i.e., the belief that the continued utilization of a particular method will in some manner create different outputs in the future.

With the increasing emphasis on maintenance issues rather than business development within IT governance, the cycle continues to enforce a continued decrease in executive engagement, perpetuating the strategic vacuum and strengthening the vicious cycle.

5   Discussion

...'Yeah, you should do like this so that everything is correct in [the portfolio management system]'. It is not about method or quality or output, it is about bureaucracy.

The case displays similarities to what has previously been described as a "vicious circle of bureaucracy" as summarized by Masuch [35]. A change in an organization's ways of working, accompanied by an increase in formalization and bureaucratization (the IT governance framework), has led to dysfunctional reactions from the organization (for instance ignoring the prioritization board's decisions). This in turn leads to even more pressure on the formalization from management (focusing on the portfolio management system). This doubling down leads to continued and walled-in apathy (having meetings without business representatives, just going through the motions, etc.) that continues over time in a similar fashion as the generative mechanisms described by Henfridsson & Bygstad [44].

From the perspective of Meyer and Rowan [43], we see the vicious cycle as an instantiation of a focus on the microscopic rationalities rather than the institutional purpose, i.e., "It should not be assumed that the creation of microscopic rationalities in the daily activity of workers effects social ends more efficiently than commitment to larger institutional claims and purposes." [p. 360].

Instead of creating microscopic rationalities (formalization and bureaucratization), the organization should be focused on creating a common understanding of the "what" and "why" of digital transformation. As we find in our study, the absence of executive interest and the inability to create a centralized funding model cannot be ameliorated by a microscopic desire for documents, meetings, and processes. Here, a tendency for over-compliance will only continue to enforce the vicious cycle [45, 46].

When a framework fails to deliver on its promise, it is easy to blame the framework itself. However, recent research on governance and control highlights that research should be focused on enactment rather than the design of the models per se [13, 47–49]. In our study, the enactment of the framework has increasingly been pushing power over prioritization from the business side to IT, as opposed to what was intended in the original framework. In relation to this increased power on the IT side, previous research is divided on whether or not it is a positive force for digital transformation. IT championship is positively associated with successful transformation [50], but it can also bias the organization into avoiding more fundamental change [14].

To succeed with digital transformation, studies [51, 52] have demonstrated that organizations must adapt their governance. The university needs to become more adaptive and use new mechanisms for its governance rather than relying on its established ones [53], and leadership and the people of the organization need to support changes in processes and policies rather than relying on IT [54]. Organizations hence need to focus more on the actual enactment rather than the original design of the IT governance framework. In this light, we see a possibility for frameworks that may seem antiquated to live on through clear changes in their enactment rather than in their design. This does, however, require a sound understanding of the underlying assumptions in the framework(s) and a careful scoping of its use. As seen in the university in question, these two aspects of the framework and its enactment were not addressed, resulting in the vicious cycle of magical thinking. As noted by Wimelius et al. [39 p. 219], "persistent patterns of pretending and avoiding" only reinforce the viciousness of the cycle.

Our study offers three contributions to research. First, we answer calls for research [13] on more studies of the enactment of governance. Our findings, that there is a vicious cycle of magical thinking that persists over time, can be considered a core element of a potential pathology of IT governance, where we design frameworks that are enacted in a counter-productive manner over time. Second, we contribute to the stream of literature [12] on the necessity for IT governance to change as the design and utilization of technology change. Since IT governance is there to afford the organization beneficial behavior in its use of technology, dramatic changes in technology need to be met with similarly dramatic changes in IT governance. Here, we believe and hope that our particular focus on the enactment of frameworks introduces additional nuancing that may prove beneficial to future research. Third and final, this study also contributes more specifically to studies of IT governance in higher education and how a university lags behind in its digital transformation [55–57].

We also offer two contributions to practice. First, our findings identify the need for changes in existing governance if digital transformation is to be relevant to the organization. Managers in organizations aspiring for digital transformation need to assess their current IT governance to make sure that it is not built on counterproductive assumptions.

If the organization's IT governance is designed to delimit IT-related costs, then this needs to be addressed in order to afford digital transformation.

Second, we argue that IT governance frameworks should not be conflated with frameworks for digital transformation strategy execution. Having an IT governance framework based on values such as cost-efficiency and demand management will deliver IT that is low cost and where demands are queued up evenly (that is, a strategy where IT leads, and business follows). Having a model for executing a digitalization strategy, sets the business transformation in the center, where IT will have to follow and respond to an uneven flow of demands [24].

We acknowledge two major limitations in our study. First, our study suffers from data bias where we have excluded broad representation from the universities core operations (i.e., teaching and research). The rationale for this is that core operations exited involvement in portfolio management in the early stages of the introduction of the model. With our focus on exploring how the framework and its enactment counteract digital transformation, we hence acknowledge this delimitation. Second, we see a limitation in the transferability of findings. As noted by Bannister [58], studies of public sector organizations suffer from low transferability between institutional environments due to the institutional arrangements varying significantly between countries.

We propose future research in the form of two concrete projects. First, if IT governance empirically counteracts digital transformation, we would need additional studies for how the enactment of IT governance may be designed to facilitate a shift into a situation where IT governance supports and facilitates digital transformation. This type of study would need to take a longitudinal approach, either retrospectively or prospectively, and focus on the evolution of enactment. Second, we call for research into the underlying assumptions associated with the different frameworks currently employed as "best practice". We believe that the future design of IT governance frameworks needs to be built on assumptions that acknowledge the innate difference of digital logic [59], and here we need additional studies to aid us in this design.

6 Conclusion

This study finds that the enacted IT governance framework counteracts digital transformation in higher education through a vicious cycle of magical thinking. The adoption of a framework designed for reducing IT cost skews the focus through a series of interrelated activities in the organization, resulting in a self-enforcing vicious cycle where less and less emphasis is placed on innovation and business development. Instead of opening for both sides of digital transformation (efficiency and innovation), more and more of the total resources are pushed to maintenance and assurance of going concern under the guise of increased internal efficiency in IT. This directly counteracts digital transformation in the organization.

References

1. Hanelt, A., Bohnsack, R., Marz, D., Marante, C.A.: A systematic review of the literature on digital transformation: insights and implications for strategy and organizational change. J. Manag. Stud. **58**, 1159–1197 (2021). https://doi.org/10.1111/joms.12639

2. Magnusson, J., Khisro, J., Björses, M., Ivarsson, A.: Closeness and distance: configurational practices for digital ambidexterity in the public sector. Transform. Gov. People Process Policy. **15**, 420–441 (2021). https://doi.org/10.1108/tg-02-2020-0030

3. Vial, G.: Understanding digital transformation: a review and a research agenda. J. Strateg. Inf. Syst. **28**, 118–144 (2019). https://doi.org/10.1016/j.jsis.2019.01.003

4. Warner, K.S.R., Wäger, M.: Building dynamic capabilities for digital transformation: an ongoing process of strategic renewal. Long Range Plann. **52**, 326–349 (2019). https://doi.org/10.1016/j.lrp.2018.12.001

5. Rof, A., Bikfalvi, A., Marquès, P.: Digital transformation for business model innovation in higher education: overcoming the tensions. Sustainability-Basel **12**, 4980 (2020). https://doi.org/10.3390/su12124980

6. Bond, M., Marín, V.I., Dolch, C., Bedenlier, S., Zawacki-Richter, O.: Digital transformation in German higher education: student and teacher perceptions and usage of digital media. Int. J. Educ. Technol. High. Educ. **15**(1), 1–20 (2018). https://doi.org/10.1186/s41239-018-0130-1

7. Santos, H., Batista, J., Marques, R.P.: Digital transformation in higher education: the use of communication technologies by students. Procedia Comput. Sci. **164**, 123–130 (2019). https://doi.org/10.1016/j.procs.2019.12.163

8. Shahbaz, S., Ashraf, M.Z., Zakar, R., Fischer, F., Zakar, M.Z.: Psychosocial effects of the COVID-19 pandemic and lockdown on university students: understanding apprehensions through a phenomenographic approach. PLoS ONE **16**, e0251641 (2021). https://doi.org/10.1371/journal.pone.0251641

9. Wingard, J.: The College Devaluation Crisis: Market Disruption, Diminishing ROI, and an Alternative Future of Learning. Stanford Business Books, Stanford (2022)

10. Weill, P., Woodham, R.: Don't just lead, govern: implementing effective it governance. SSRN Electron. J. (2002). https://doi.org/10.2139/ssrn.317319

11. Magnusson, J., Khisro, J., Melin, U.: A pathology of public sector IT governance: how IT governance configuration counteracts ambidexterity. In: Viale Pereira, G., et al. (eds.) EGOV 2020. LNCS, vol. 12219, pp. 29–41. Springer, Cham (2020). https://doi.org/10.1007/978-3-030-57599-1_3

12. Gregory, R.W., Kaganer, E., Henfridsson, O., Ruch, T.J.: IT consumerization and the transformation of IT governance. MIS Q. **42**, 1225–1253 (2018). https://doi.org/10.25300/misq/2018/13703

13. Wiener, M., Mähring, M., Remus, U., Saunders, C., Cram, W.A.: Moving IS project control research into the digital era: the "why" of control and the concept of control purpose. Inf. Syst. Res. **30**, 1387–1401 (2019). https://doi.org/10.1287/isre.2019.0867

14. Magnusson, J., Päivärinta, T., Koutsikouri, D.: Digital ambidexterity in the public sector: empirical evidence of a bias in balancing practices. Transform. Gov. People Process Policy **15**, 59–79 (2020). https://doi.org/10.1108/tg-02-2020-0028

15. Pucciarelli, F., Kaplan, A.: Competition and strategy in higher education: managing complexity and uncertainty. Bus. Horiz. **59**, 311–320 (2016). https://doi.org/10.1016/j.bushor.2016.01.003

16. Posselt, T., Abdelkafi, N., Fischer, L., Tangour, C.: Opportunities and challenges of higher education institutions in Europe: an analysis from a business model perspective. High. Educ. Q. **73**, 100–115 (2019). https://doi.org/10.1111/hequ.12192

17. Jackson, N.C.: Managing for competency with innovation change in higher education: examining the pitfalls and pivots of digital transformation. Bus. Horiz. **62**, 761–772 (2019). https://doi.org/10.1016/j.bushor.2019.08.002

18. Mohamed Hashim, M.A., Tlemsani, I., Matthews, R.: Higher education strategy in digital transformation. Educ. Inf. Technol. **27**, 3171–3195 (2021). https://doi.org/10.1007/s10639-021-10739-1

19. Abad-Segura, E., González-Zamar, M.-D., Infante-Moro, J.C., García, G.R.: Sustainable management of digital transformation in higher education: global research trends. Sustainability-Basel. **12**, 2107 (2020). https://doi.org/10.3390/su12052107
20. Tømte, C.E., Fossland, T., Aamodt, P.O., Degn, L.: Digitalisation in higher education: mapping institutional approaches for teaching and learning. Qual. High. Educ. **25**, 98–114 (2019). https://doi.org/10.1080/13538322.2019.1603611
21. Bygstad, B., Øvrelid, E., Ludvigsen, S., Dæhlen, M.: From dual digitalization to digital learning space: exploring the digital transformation of higher education. Comput Educ. **182**, 104463 (2022). https://doi.org/10.1016/j.compedu.2022.104463
22. Treve, M.: What COVID-19 has introduced into education: challenges facing Higher Education Institutions (HEIs). High. Educ. Pedag. **6**, 212–227 (2021). https://doi.org/10.1080/237 52696.2021.1951616
23. Frick, N.R.J., Mirbabaie, M., Stieglitz, S., Salomon, J.: Maneuvering through the stormy seas of digital transformation: the impact of empowering leadership on the AI readiness of enterprises. J. Decis. Syst. **30**, 1–24 (2021). https://doi.org/10.1080/12460125.2020.1870065
24. Chanias, S., Myers, M.D., Hess, T.: Digital transformation strategy making in pre-digital organizations: the case of a financial services provider. J. Strateg. Inf. Syst. **28**, 17–33 (2019). https://doi.org/10.1016/j.jsis.2018.11.003
25. Hinings, B., Gegenhuber, T., Greenwood, R.: Digital innovation and transformation: an institutional perspective. Inform. Organ.-UK **28**, 52–61 (2018). https://doi.org/10.1016/j.infoan dorg.2018.02.004
26. Smith, P., Beretta, M.: The Gordian knot of practicing digital transformation: coping with emergent paradoxes in ambidextrous organizing structures*. J. Prod. Innov. Manag **38**, 166–191 (2021). https://doi.org/10.1111/jpim.12548
27. Weill, P., Ross, J.W.: It governance on one page. SSRN Electron. J. (2004). https://doi.org/10.2139/ssrn.664612
28. Boonstra, A., Eseryel, U.Y., van Offenbeek, M.A.G.: Stakeholders' enactment of competing logics in IT governance: polarization, compromise or synthesis? Eur. J. Inf. Syst. **27**, 1–20 (2017). https://doi.org/10.1057/s41303-017-0055-0
29. Wessel, L., Baiyere, A., Ologeanu-Taddei, R., Cha, J., Jensen, T.B.: Unpacking the difference between digital transformation and IT-enabled organizational transformation. https://aisel.ais net.org/jais/vol22/iss1/6/. Accessed 04 Nov 2022
30. Matt, C., Hess, T., Benlian, A.: Digital transformation strategies. Bus. Inf. Syst. Eng. **57**(5), 339–343 (2015). https://doi.org/10.1007/s12599-015-0401-5
31. Bharadwaj, A., Sawy, O.A.E., Pavlou, P.A., Venkatraman, N.: Toward a next generation of insights. MIS Q. **37**, 471–482 (2013)
32. Drnevich, P.L., Croson, D.C.: Information technology and business-level strategy: toward an integrated theoretical perspective. MIS Q. **37**, 483–509 (2013). https://doi.org/10.25300/misq/2013/37.2.08
33. Hess, T., Matt, C., Benlian, A., Wiesböck, F.: Options for formulating a digital transformation strategy. MIS Q. Exec. **19** (2016)
34. Khisro, J., Lindroth, T., Magnusson, J.: Mechanisms of constraint: a clinical inquiry of digital infrastructuring in municipalities. Transform. Gov. People Process Policy. **16**, 81–96 (2021). https://doi.org/10.1108/tg-01-2021-0014
35. Masuch, M.: Vicious circles in organizations. Admin. Sci. Q. **30**, 14 (1985). https://doi.org/10.2307/2392809
36. Bygstad, B., Munkvold, B.E., Volkoff, O.: Identifying generative mechanisms through affordances: a framework for critical realist data analysis. J. Inform. Technol. **31**, 83–96 (2016). https://doi.org/10.1057/jit.2015.13
37. Smith, W.K., Lewis, M.W.: Toward a theory of paradox: a dynamic equilibrium model of organizing. Acad. Manag. Rev. **36**, 381–403 (2011). https://doi.org/10.5465/amr.2009.0223

38. Cuganesan, S.: Identity paradoxes: how senior managers and employees negotiate similarity and distinctiveness tensions over time. Organ. Stud. **38**, 489–511 (2017). https://doi.org/10.1177/0170840616655482

39. Wimelius, H., Mathiassen, L., Holmström, J., Keil, M.: A paradoxical perspective on technology renewal in digital transformation. Inform. Syst. J. **31**, 198–225 (2021). https://doi.org/10.1111/isj.12307

40. Schein, E.H.: Clinical inquiry/research. In: Reason, P., Bradbury, H. (eds.) The SAGE Handbook of Action Research. SAGE Publications Ltd. (2008). https://doi.org/10.4135/9781848607934.n26

41. Braun, V., Clarke, V.: Thematic analysis, pp. 57–71 (2012). https://doi.org/10.1037/13620-004

42. Blom, B., Morén, S.: Analysis of generative mechanisms. J. Crit. Realism. **10**, 60–79 (2011). https://doi.org/10.1558/jcr.v10i1.60

43. Meyer, J.W., Rowan, B.: Institutionalized organizations: formal structure as myth and ceremony. Am. J. Sociol. **83**, 340–363 (1977). https://doi.org/10.1086/226550

44. Henfridsson, O., Bygstad, B.: The generative mechanisms of digital infrastructure evolution. MIS Q. **37**, 907–931 (2013)

45. Currie, W.L., Gozman, D.P., Seddon, J.J.M.: Dialectic tensions in the financial markets: a longitudinal study of pre- and post-crisis regulatory technology. J. Inf. Technol. **33**, 304–325 (2018). https://doi.org/10.1057/s41265-017-0047-5

46. Sordi, J.O.D., de Paulo, W.L., Jorge, C.F.B., da Silveira, D.B., Dias, J.A., de Lima, M.S.: Overcompliance and reluctance to make decisions: exploring warning systems in support of public managers. Gov. Inf. Q. **38**, 101592 (2021). https://doi.org/10.1016/j.giq.2021.101592

47. Cram, W.A., Brohman, K., Gallupe, R.B.: Information systems control: a review and framework for emerging information systems processes. J. Assoc. Inf. Syst. **17**, 216–266 (2016). https://doi.org/10.17705/1jais.00427

48. Remus, U., Wiener, M., Saunders, C., Mähring, M.: The impact of control styles and control modes on individual-level outcomes: a first test of the integrated IS project control theory. Eur. J. Inf. Syst. **29**, 1–19 (2020). https://doi.org/10.1080/0960085x.2020.1718008

49. Zimmermann, A., Raisch, S., Cardinal, L.B.: Managing persistent tensions on the frontline: a configurational perspective on ambidexterity. J. Manag. Stud. **55**, 739–769 (2018). https://doi.org/10.1111/joms.12311

50. Gregory, R.W., Keil, M., Muntermann, J., Mähring, M.: Paradoxes and the nature of ambidexterity in IT transformation programs. Inf. Syst. Res. **26**, 57–80 (2015). https://doi.org/10.1287/isre.2014.0554

51. Lacombe, I., Jarboui, A.: Governance and management of digital transformation projects: an exploratory approach in the financial sector. Int. J. Innov. Sci. (2022). https://doi.org/10.1108/ijis-02-2022-0034

52. Janowski, T.: Digital government evolution: from transformation to contextualization. Gov. Inf. Q. **32**, 221–236 (2015). https://doi.org/10.1016/j.giq.2015.07.001

53. Janssen, M., van der Voort, H.: Adaptive governance: towards a stable, accountable and responsive government. Gov. Inf. Q. **33**, 1–5 (2016). https://doi.org/10.1016/j.giq.2016.02.003

54. Mergel, I., Edelmann, N., Haug, N.: Defining digital transformation: results from expert interviews. Gov. Inf. Q. **36**, 101385 (2019). https://doi.org/10.1016/j.giq.2019.06.002

55. Demartini, C.G., Benussi, L., Gatteschi, V., Renga, F.: Education and digital transformation: the "Riconnessioni" project. IEEE Access **8**, 186233–186256 (2020). https://doi.org/10.1109/access.2020.3018189

56. Giang, N.T.H., Hai, P.T.T., Tu, N.T.T., Tan, P.X.: Exploring the readiness for digital transformation in a higher education institution towards industrial revolution 4.0. Int. J. Eng. Pedag. IJEP. **11**, 4–24 (2021). https://doi.org/10.3991/ijep.v11i2.17515

57. Rodríguez-Abitia, G., Bribiesca-Correa, G.: Assessing digital transformation in universities. Futur. Internet **13**, 52 (2021). https://doi.org/10.3390/fi13020052

58. Bannister, F.: The curse of the benchmark: an assessment of the validity and value of e-government comparisons. Int. Rev. Adm. Sci. **73**, 171–188 (2007). https://doi.org/10.1177/0020852307077959
59. Yoo, Y., Henfridsson, O., Lyytinen, K.: Research commentary —the new organizing logic of digital innovation: an agenda for information systems research. Inf. Syst. Res. **21**, 724–735 (2010). https://doi.org/10.1287/isre.1100.0322

The Maturity of Knowledge-Based Management in Finnish Central-Government Organizations: The Need for Managing the Knowledge-Based Management

Emma Partanen[1] , Pasi Raatikainen[2](✉) , Pasi Hellsten[2] ,
and Jussi Myllärniemi[2]

[1] Creatido Oy, Finlaysoninkuja 21 A, 33210 Tampere, Finland
emma.partanen@creatido.fi
[2] Tampere University, Korkeakoulunkatu 8, 33720 Tampere, Finland
pasi.raatikainen94@gmail.com, {pasi.hellsten,
jussi.myllarniemi}@tuni.fi

Abstract. Assessing the maturity of knowledge-based management (KBM) in public sector organizations is crucial for several reasons. Firstly, it helps identifying strengths and weaknesses, which enables organizations to improve their knowledge management practices. Secondly, it serves as a standard for evaluating the effectiveness of knowledge resource management, which can enhance decision-making, problem-solving, and operational efficiency. Thirdly, KBM maturity assessment aids in prioritizing investments, allocating resources, and improving return on investment. Fourthly, evaluating KBM maturity can help identify best practices and lessons learned, leading to better knowledge management practices across organizations. Finally, studying KBM maturity can demonstrate an organization's commitment to effective knowledge management, increasing transparency and accountability. This study assesses the maturity of KBM in Finnish Central-Government Organizations by surveying eight organizations and analyzing the data. The study identifies areas that require more attention, where the need of managing the KBM being highlighted as a significant area for improvement. This research provides insights for researchers and practitioners to address KBM themes that need further attention.

Keywords: Knowledge-based Management · Knowledge Management · Public Sector · Maturity-model

1 Introduction

The existing circumstances within public sector organizations pose a substantial impediment to their operational capacities, as they confront financial limitations alongside mounting expectations from stakeholders and the public [1, 2]. In order to tackle these challenges effectively, the comprehensive harnessing of knowledge assumes paramount

© IFIP International Federation for Information Processing 2023
Published by Springer Nature Switzerland AG 2023
I. Lindgren et al. (Eds.): EGOV 2023, LNCS 14130, pp. 397–413, 2023.
https://doi.org/10.1007/978-3-031-41138-0_25

importance. This criticality has been duly recognized in the governmental strategy of Finland, wherein knowledge-based initiatives have been identified as a principal objective [3]. Specifically, the Finnish government has issued a decision by the Council of State, addressing the utilization and accessibility of knowledge [4]. It is imperative for organizations to continually adapt and progress in response to evolving circumstances [5–7].

In the knowledge economy, post-industrial organizations are increasingly recognizing the importance of KM. KM encompasses various activities such as knowledge creation, acquisition, storage, utilization, sharing, dissemination, and transformation [8]. It is a comprehensive concept that helps organizations address challenges across different areas of their operations. By acknowledging knowledge as a valuable production factor and a key resource for competitive advantage, KM strives to maximize the utilization of diverse knowledge-related resources within organizations. However, the approach to KM can vary depending on the specific circumstances [9, 10].

In the face of rapidly increasing data volumes, organizations are confronted with the challenge of discerning the most relevant information, transforming it into a more meaningful format, and harnessing its potential effectively [11]. To address this issue, knowledge-based approaches have emerged to elucidate how both internal and external knowledge resources of organizations contribute to their competitive advantage [12–15]. In addition to KM [16], the literature has explored this phenomenon through various concepts, including business intelligence [17], data-based value creation [18], knowledge-based value creation [19], and knowledge-based management [20]. These concepts collectively refine data and information, aiming to enhance their significance, thereby sharing a common underlying objective.

This study focuses on KBM, which involves the management of knowledge and knowledge processes within organizations. KBM encompasses the collection, refinement, and utilization of organizational knowledge assets to support decision-making and strategic development [20]. Evaluating the maturity level of KBM within organizations is crucial as it provides insights into the current state of information and knowledge management maturity. Furthermore, it aids in identifying specific areas that require further attention to enhance maturity status and ultimately enhance organizational performance [21]. The evaluation of KBM maturity carries significant implications for both private and public sector organizations. In the public sector, in particular, it has the potential to greatly improve the delivery of public services and contribute to the overall well-being of society. However, there is a notable scarcity of evaluation tools for knowledge management, which should encompass not only technical aspects but also the human elements [22]. This research underscores the importance of knowledge-based development, as well as cultural and strategic considerations.

This study aims to provide propositions for improving KBM in public sector organizations. The recommendations are intended to be applicable across organizations while remaining specific enough for effective implementation. To identify these propositions, the maturity of KBM in public sector organizations needs to be assessed. Therefore, this research focuses on evaluating the maturity of KBM in central-government organizations in Finland. The primary research question is: *"What is the maturity level of KBM in Finnish central-government organizations?"* The study involves conducting a survey and qualitative analysis to examine the collected data. The findings highlight the areas that central-government organizations in Finland should prioritize to enhance the effectiveness of their KBM practices. Based on these areas, propositions are derived to enhance the maturity of KBM in public sector organizations.

This paper is structured into six chapters. In the second section, we discuss our theoretical background, which encompasses the concept of KBM in organizations. In the third chapter, we explain our research approach. The fourth chapter presents our findings, while in the fifth chapter, we discuss the implications of our results. Finally, in the sixth and final chapter, we conclude our study by summarizing our key findings and discussing their broader implications for future research and practice.

2   Theoretical Background

This section delineates the theoretical underpinnings of the present study, which draw on the amalgamation of KBM and public sector organizations. The exposition commences with a portrayal of public sector organizations, followed by an explication of the concept of KBM.

2.1   KBM in Public Organizations

Knowledge is an outcome of human action that takes place, for example, in interaction and decision-making situations. Knowledge is based on information, know-how and experiences. It is refined from information and data and therefore it is valuable for decision-makers. Information, on the other hand, is data in the structured form. Data is unstructured facts that have the least impact for managers [4].

KBM is about turning knowledge into action. Public sector is largely about service provision and managing the operations therein [23, 24]. There are multiple angles to the phenomena under scrutiny. Citizens, taxpayers and other funding sources, various sources within the public and third sector, are some of the stakeholders. Factors, such as citizens' expectations and those of the businesses, public pressure, and reducing resources result in the growing need for effective KBM. The operations need to evolve according to the overall development in societies [25]. In order to meet the challenges and needs presented by stakeholders, e.g., flexibility and easier reachability [25–27] well executed KBM is needed. When utilizing the information and communication technologies (ICT) public sector organizations are not considered to be relatively efficient in it [28–30]. To develop these capabilities, especially to meet the demand, it is beneficial that the knowledge is managed properly and used in the management of the organization. Another step to address this issue is to clarify the maturity of the KBM and how well it is used in managerial activities, i.e. KBM.

KBM would benefit, if not require, overarching and holistic technologies, e.g. info-searching, social networks, and the wide communicating in the services they are to offer [31]. These in turn, are examples of KBM tools by which the knowledge resources are tried to be used in the best possible way to produce the best possible outcome. It is not unheard of that the services and their communications are directed only to a certain target audience and purpose according to the focal responsibilities of the office instead of being wide, multiple operations linking or crossing organizational boundaries. The risk in this approach is that services may be disintegrated and isolated from one another thus presenting the management with difficulties to understand and to formulate the big picture and to make the right decisions therein. It may be claimed that the management should have as transparent process to deal with as possible.

Recognizing and acknowledging the various angles to be included in the public sector decision-making is not always easy [32]. The areas need the approach that suits their operation and the suitable measures for their context, according to the individual objectives set for each branch. There may also be other types of effects, e. g. knowledge needs, caused by the changes in the ever-evolving political settings, expectations of the citizens, or the processual improvements. These developments affect the evaluation of the circumstances and the needed actions, decision making. There is thinking to be done when the measures and their visualization is considered.

A public sector operation as a whole is a multifaceted entity with a huge number of tasks. To make administration run smoothly, there is a need to consider development schemes coming from different areas with different interests and ambitions [33]. The administration needs to consider a number of areas, like the community and the environment, economical viewpoint, education and culture issues, social and healthcare areas, to name but a few. The administrative areas have their own practices, processes, and personnel even though they are parts of the same administration. Furthermore, even though they do have similar features, the management of the operation, the data forming the information, and the processes refining the information into knowledge is different in each area. The prerequisite of the innovating in digitalization is within today's public sector and its management [34, 35]. The knowledge needs need to be well planned and justified.

Digital transformation is often used to mean the renewal of the way of operating, i.e. the business model. This may be seen to entail the different ways of the daily operation. Digital transformation is often also about the resource re-allocation in and for the actual operation [36]. When changing how an operation is executed, it simultaneously affects both individual activities and the overall processes. This is bound to affect also the organizational culture [37]. How far the digitalization initiatives are able to be taken in individual organizations depends also on the overall attitude towards change and how willing and able the organization is to develop itself [38]. Similarly, these effects cover also the probable success in implementing the renewals, like KBM.

Even maintaining the prevailing level of services, let alone developing them, may prove to be a challenge when the resources and their allocation are scrutinized [39]. Many branches and areas need extra attention and development, while the resources are scarce. Simultaneously, however, the services repertoire should be developed, [39]. The personnel and their attitudes, readiness to use new services play a significant role [40]. These may be directed with properly executed KBM. Whilst developing the operations in organizations, the employees are expected to remain active and productive in their everyday routines throughout the development schemes. This underlines the significance of various managerial skills, i.e. the need for understanding of the workplace dynamics, which are indeed skillsets under the knowledge management umbrella [25, 41]. Managing any digitalization initiative is a complex task, a different management approach is required to accomplish organizational transparency and full use of more holistic approach [42]. To develop measures for assessing the effects and the results of such initiatives is equally challenging [43, 44].

KBM is a useful way of public service for increasing productivity and effectiveness [45]. Managing the public sector with knowledge aims to make the operation of public organizations smarter and more efficient. Public sector organizations face requirements concerning efficiency, productivity and effectiveness both from inside and outside the organizations, which is one reason that drives the public sector to focus for KBM and quality decision-making. KBM requires a system accurate, reliable and timely information. If, for example, there is in the planning phase ignored some information, this can weaken the strategic management of public activities to do [46]. Virtanen et al. [46] state that in the public sector strategic management is often replaced by tactical and operational management.

2.2 Maturity of KBM

We assume that public organizations do not take full advantage of the data and information available. In order to do so, the broad understanding about knowledge utilization is necessary. To gain broader understanding of organizations' KBM and to recognize benefits as well as challenges of KBM in organizations, its status, maturity, should be determined [47, 48]. Maturity models can be used as a tool in describing and evaluating the object of the organization, e.g. KBM or performance management. With the help of these models, the maturity of the object under consideration could be determined, i.e. the transition from the initial state towards the desired state [49–51]. The maturity of the organization is typically assessed using the questionnaire based on the selected model, through which it is possible to examine selected object in detail [52].

Most of the maturity models are generic and are not aimed at specific industries [21]. The models are mainly aimed at meeting the needs of the private sector. In Sect. 2.1 we described some typical challenges and characteristics of the Finnish public sector which should be considered when choosing a maturity model. The characteristics of the Finnish public sector and few maturity models [21, 53, 54] form the basis for themes that make it possible to explore comprehensive picture of KBM of the public sector: *The organization's management structures and style, Status of KBM, Systematic development of KBM, Structures of KBM, Structures of information management, Information and knowledge utilization practices and capability and From knowledge to action and effectiveness.* The model we used is seen in Fig. 1.

The model includes the above-mentioned seven themes and also several illustrative topics to make model concrete and to identify areas for improvement. This model contains five maturity levels from insufficient to optimal level. The maturity of KBM is assessed by a questionnaire targeted at entire personnel aiming to identify all knowledge utilizer's experiences regarding KBM, audition of organization's KBM structures, and interviews of key people giving further insight of processes and KBM development focus areas. In this research, the interviews were omitted due to evaluating multiple organizations rather than focusing further on one, which is the way the maturity model is originally intended to be used as.

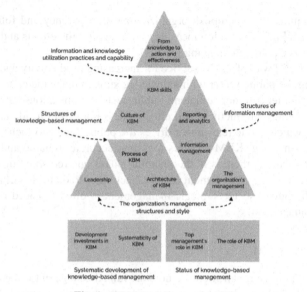

Fig. 1. KBM maturity model [55]

3 Research Approach

The primary objective of this study is to propose actionable recommendations for enhancing Knowledge-Based Management (KBM) within public sector organizations. To accomplish this aim, an evaluation of the KBM maturity levels in Finnish central government organizations is conducted. The research approach adopted for this study is exploratory and deductive in nature. Exploratory research is generally useful when the aim is to identify and define research problems, questions, or propositions. Additionally, deductive reasoning is particularly appropriate when the research aims to utilize theories or theoretical frameworks, present propositions based on established principles, or draw logical conclusions from general principles to specific instances. To elaborate, in our research, we utilized a predetermined theoretical framework for data analysis, facilitating the derivation of meaningful insights. This theoretical framework guides the assessment of specific areas of KBM within the organizations, enabling both an overall evaluation of KBM and the identification of discrepancies across different KBM domains. Given the objective of evaluating maturity levels, quantitative data is employed to provide tangible metrics for assessing the varying degrees of maturity.

The Finnish central government is composed of more than one hundred organiza-tions in 12 administrative branches (see www.valtioneuvosto.fi). Each branch and the organizations within it are led and guided by a ministry. To obtain a sample that is both reasonable and representative of this population, we employed a random sampling tech-nique that targeted four administrative branches. Specifically, we randomly selected one ministry and one bureau from each branch. We took care to avoid hand-picking specific organizations that might offer biased results based on general expectations towards them. This approach ensures that the results can be considered representative of the average state of the studied population. It reduces bias and increases the generalizability of the findings by providing each member of the population with an equal chance of being selected for the study. The resulting sample size for this study consisted of eight organizations: the Ministry of Education and Culture, Finnish Heritage Agency, Ministry of Finance, State Treasury, Ministry of Transport and Communications, Finnish Meteorological Institute, Ministry of Agriculture and Forestry, and Natural Resources Institute Finland.

Our theoretical framework for this study was based on the maturity model, which we presented in Sect. 2.2. This model comprises seven distinct themes: *Organization's management structures and style, Status of KBM, Systematic development of KBM, Structures of KBM, Structures of information management, Information and knowledge utilization practices and capability, and From knowledge to action and effectiveness,* which are clarified by several topics [cf. Fig. 1]. Collectively, these themes and topics offer a comprehensive perspective on an organization's maturity level with respect to KBM.

To obtain a large dataset within reasonable resource and time constraints, we employed a survey methodology to collect data for this study. We designed our survey questionnaire based on the aforementioned maturity model, and it consisted of 57 questions that are relevant for the maturity model's themes. Examples of the questions used are presented in Appendix. The questionnaire was targeted at the entire personnel of each organization to identify their experiences and perceptions regarding KBM. Additionally, as part of the maturity model, we conducted an audit of KBM, which involved two workshops in the present study.

Our present study employs Likert questions in its survey to obtain information regarding the attitudes, opinions, and perceptions of respondents towards a particular topic or issue. Likert questions are widely used in surveys and questionnaires due to their capacity to quantify and evaluate people's viewpoints. The Likert scale provides a standardized and simple format for respondents to express their views, and the resulting numerical data can be analysed using statistical techniques. Thus, Likert questions are considered a reliable and efficient tool for data collection and analysis in social science research. These closed-ended questions prompt respondents to indicate their level of agreement or disagreement on a scale of 1 to 5, with the values at the extremes representing "strongly disagree" or "very unlikely," and "strongly agree" or "very likely," respectively.

The survey was administered through SurveyMonkey, a web-based survey platform. The survey was conducted in the Finnish language. The questionnaire was sent 25.10.2022. We distributed the survey link to representatives of the organizations being studied via email, who in turn disseminated the link to potential respondents within their respective organizations. Data collection was concluded, and data analysis commenced in 15.11.2022.

In our analysis of survey data, we employed a method that involved calculating averages of measures. Specifically, we aggregated the responses of all participants for each question and computed the mean score. Participants were asked to rate their level of agreement with a statement using a five-point scale, and the average score was obtained by summing all individual responses and dividing by the total number of responses. This approach allowed us to succinctly summarize the collective attitudes, perceptions, or opinions of participants pertaining to a particular issue related to KBM. Additionally, it facilitated comparisons of responses across different questions within the survey. By utilizing this method, we were able to discern patterns, trends, and inconsistencies in the data, which enabled us to draw conclusions and make inferences about the target population.

4 Findings

We received a total of 676 responses from the 8 studied organizations. The average response rate inside an organization was found to be 19%. To determine the maturity of KBM among Finnish central government organizations, the average results of each organization were calculated and then averaged to produce an overall index. To maintain anonymity, the organisations are labelled from A to H in Table 1.

Table 1. Survey Results

Theme/Organization	A	B	C	D	E	F	G	H	Total maturity
The organization's management structures and style	3,89	3,73	3,92	3,86	3,67	3,64	4,04	3,82	3,82
Leadership	4,06	3,95	4,09	4,07	3,89	3,72	4,20	4,04	4,00
The organization's management	3,71	3,52	3,75	3,65	3,45	3,56	3,89	3,61	3,64
Status of KBM	2,42	2,94	2,99	2,71	2,60	3,01	3,07	3,03	2,85
Top management's role in KBM	2,56	3,18	3,23	2,90	2,87	3,24	3,33	3,22	3,07
The role of KBM	2,21	2,58	2,63	2,43	2,21	2,67	2,70	2,74	2,52
Systematic development of KBM	2,75	2,71	2,78	2,46	2,42	2,82	2,93	2,70	2,70
Development investments in KBM	3,08	2,85	2,88	2,47	2,54	2,92	3,19	2,73	2,83
Systematicity of KBM	2,42	2,57	2,67	2,46	2,30	2,72	2,67	2,66	2,56
Structures of KBM	2,83	2,81	3,08	3,02	2,81	3,02	3,11	2,86	2,94
Architecture of KBM	2,96	2,92	3,19	3,20	2,95	3,35	3,20	3,09	3,11
Process of KBM	2,71	2,72	3,00	2,85	2,68	2,75	3,03	2,66	2,80
Structures of information management	2,63	2,61	2,73	2,62	2,55	2,90	2,98	2,67	2,71
Reporting and analytics	2,58	2,61	2,79	2,61	2,49	2,94	3,01	2,67	2,71
Information management	2,71	2,61	2,65	2,64	2,65	2,84	2,94	2,68	2,72
Information and knowledge utilization practices and capability	2,93	3,15	3,31	3,11	3,08	3,41	3,46	3,39	3,23
Culture of KBM	2,98	3,19	3,30	3,16	3,07	3,34	3,47	3,43	3,24
KBM skills	2,88	3,09	3,32	3,06	3,09	3,50	3,45	3,34	3,22
From knowledge to action and effectiveness	3,21	3,10	3,37	3,15	2,96	3,16	3,35	3,22	3,19
Impact of KBM	3,15	3,00	3,29	2,89	2,86	3,10	3,36	3,14	3,10
From knowledge to action	3,28	3,20	3,46	3,39	3,06	3,22	3,34	3,30	3,28
Total	2,95	2,98	3,17	3,01	2,88	3,14	3,27	3,08	3,06

The resulting average maturity index was found to be 3.06, indicating a developing level of maturity. The maturity index was calculated as the mean of all organizations' results. The range of possible results varies from 1 to 5. Upon studying the results, it was observed that the maturity level for each topic varied between 2.52 and 4.00. The standard deviation for this measure was 1.10. The levels of maturity in KBM displayed minor variations across the organizations under study, with means ranging from 2.88 to 3.27. Figure 2 illustrates the maturity of KBM based on our findings across the studied organizations.

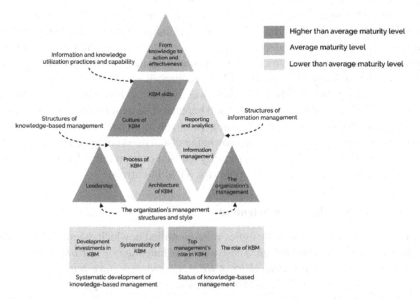

Fig. 2. The established maturity of KBM in Finnish Central-Government Organizations

The primary objective of this study was to gain a comprehensive understanding of KBM practices within the Finnish central government, rather than to compare the performance of individual organizations. However, interestingly, the study does indicate potential differences in the maturity of KBM among administrative branches and between ministries and bureaus. The results indicate that two out of the four administrative branches displayed a slightly higher level of maturity. This difference could be attributed to the inclusion of the Ministry of Finance, which plays a prominent role in enhancing KBM practices in the Finnish public sector. Furthermore, based on our findings, the maturity of KBM was marginally lower in ministries compared to bureaus. Additionally, our analysis revealed that the topics of KBM process and KBM culture exhibited the most significant variation, even within individual organizations.

4.1 Topics with High Level of Maturity

Our analysis indicates that *leadership, organization's management*, and the *culture of KBM* received higher ratings than the average in the Finnish central government organizations.

The participating organizations reported a high level of *leadership*, with an average score ranging from as high as 3.72 to 4.20, while the overall maturity level of KBM was 3.06. Respondents perceived their supervisors as supporters, enablers, and sparring partners in their work, and they had a high level of trust in their colleagues.

Organization's management was viewed as a supporting factor for KBM in the Finnish central government. The structure, practices, operations, aims, and vision were mostly clear, and respondents understood their own goals, responsibilities, and roles in achieving the organization's objectives. However, there was more variation between organizations in terms of management than in leadership.

Information usage was perceived as a natural component of the daily operations in the Finnish central government. It served as a foundation for the *culture* of KBM, with over half of the respondents (51.2%) expressing a shared aim and enthusiasm to utilize information for more effective decision-making and management compared to before. The majority of respondents felt encouraged to actively seek new information to enhance operations. However, there were variations between organizations and differences observed between ministries and bureaus. The willingness to leverage information and knowledge was slightly higher in ministries compared to bureaus. Ministries also provided more opportunities for knowledge discussions compared to bureaus. The development areas for KBM culture primarily focused on promoting discussions around knowledge and ensuring sufficient support for KBM initiatives.

4.2   Topics in Need for More Attention

Based on our analysis, six specific topics were identified in which the maturity of KBM was lower than the overall average. These topics include *the role of KBM in the organization's management, the systematicity of KBM, development investments in KBM, the role of top management in KBM, information management*, and *reporting and analytics in the process of KBM*.

Although knowledge-based decision making and actions are shared goals in the public sector, only a few targeted organizations seem to have recognized KBM as an objective in their strategy, and none have defined a separate strategy or roadmap for its development. Consequently, our results indicate that only 22% of respondents were aware of the KBM objectives pertaining to their own organization. Additionally, in most organizations, roles and responsibilities regarding KBM had not been defined.

It appears that a significant challenge regarding KBM is the differing interpretations of the concept. Our results indicate that only 11.5% of respondents believed that there is a shared understanding within their organization of what KBM entails, and only 22% had knowledge of its components. The absence of a shared understanding and clear definition of the concept can hinder the systematic development of KBM. Moreover, investments in KBM development appear to be primarily focused on technology. In most organizations, there does not seem to be a specific allocation in the budget for KBM, and development projects seem to be isolated in nature.

The role of top management in KBM exhibited variations among organizations. While most respondents believed that top management is willing to incorporate knowledge into decision-making, only 37.1% of respondents believed that top management fully grasps the significance of KBM, and 41.6% perceived a commitment to KBM from top management. Overall, it appears that active involvement and participation of top management in discussions pertaining to knowledge is lacking in many organizations.

In terms of reporting and analytics, the maturity level across all organizations was consistently low. Only 19.4% of respondents considered the available analytical services to be adequate for their information requirements. Additionally, 21.7% had received ready-made reports that facilitated their work, and a mere 23.5% found it easy to obtain the necessary information from the reports. It appears that only a few organizations had manuals and guidelines dedicated to reporting and analytics. Furthermore, a significant portion of respondents (38.7%) expressed dissatisfaction with the quantity of predictive analytics and foresight information available.

The questions pertaining to information management received low ratings across all organizations. In particular, the process of reviewing, utilizing, and making effective use of information from various sources was identified as a challenge, with only 11.8% of respondents finding it easy.

Despite investments in technical and structural improvements in KBM within the Finnish public sector, there seems to be a discrepancy between the knowledge requirements of users in their daily work and the information readily accessible in the systems. Moreover, only 19.1% of respondents believed that the information documented in various systems is valuable and can be utilized to support KBM.

5 Discussion

Our present study has identified a noteworthy finding that merits the attention of organizations under examination. Our assessment of the maturity of KBM in Finnish central-government organizations imply that the management of KBM demands greater attention. According to our findings the maturity of the topics inside this theme were consistently low.

The management of KBM pertains to the organizational structure and understanding of their approach to KBM. This encompasses the active management and development of KBM practices within the organization. As a crucial area of focus, it establishes the foundation for KBM and its continued development, as shortcomings in this area will invariably manifest in other KBM domains.

Our findings indicate the following four propositions for improving the management of KBM. We consider that these propositions include generality in sense that they are relevant for public sector organizations in a large sense. However, these propositions are pragmatic and specific enough so that they include clear actionability for public sector organizations who wish to increase the maturity of their KBM.

5.1 Organizations Should Focus on Defining the Role of KBM in their Organization's Management

First, according to our findings, the role of KBM in organizational management requires more attention. The management and steering of KBM development necessitate defining the scope of KBM and its developmental objectives. A KBM strategy or development plan is an integral part of change management [56]. However, our study revealed that none of the Finnish central government organizations in our sample had a strategy for KBM, despite being mandated to develop one. Only a few personnel were aware of KBM objectives, even though some organizations recognized it as a strategic goal in their strategy. To promote the strategic and comprehensive development of KBM, we recommend defining its objectives and creating a roadmap for its integration into the organizational management development plan. Communicating the KBM objectives and implementing the strategy are crucial for enhancing personnel understanding of KBM and its role in organizational management [56, 57]. Moreover, organizations should assign roles and responsibilities regarding knowledge-based approaches, such as KBM [58].

In practice, this could mean that the organizations' relevant individuals or their representatives participate in discussions, such as workshops, in which they define their organization's view on KBM and specify its objectives. These definitions should encompass the views of personnel at different levels within the organization, while aligning with the organization's overall strategy. Such definitions, including the different roles they indicate, should be made explicit and shared across the organization.

5.2 Organizations Should Focus More on Establishing Systematicity in their KBM

Secondly, our findings suggest that organizations lack systematicity in their approach to KBM. Our study revealed that the scope and content of KBM have not been clearly defined within organizations, leading to a lack of coherent and shared understanding of the concept. To holistically and systematically develop KBM, it is imperative to define its scope and content within the organization. By defining KBM as a whole and comprehending its dependencies on the organization's operations and structures, it becomes easier to understand how the concept relates to everyday operations. The attitude and mindset towards knowledge and KBM should be changed and demystified [11, 58, 59]. Additionally, to promote a shared understanding of the concept, it is necessary to construct terminology specific to KBM.

In practice, this could involve relevant individuals, such as those from different management levels and representatives of the operative level, taking the time to consider what KBM means in practice in their organization. Subsequently, in order to establish systematicity, it would be beneficial to establish processes and generate manuals that represent the defined KBM approach of the organization.

5.3 Organizations Should Have an Active Top-Management in its KBM Efforts

Third, we have identified that the role of top management in KBM requires greater attention in organizations, which is also supported by the literature [32]. According to Kianto et al. [60], knowledge resources are key factors determining an organization's value creation potential, but management plays an equally important role. The development of KBM maturity necessitates the active participation and support of top management [61, 62]. Therefore, it is imperative that top management comprehends the advantages of KBM and commits to its development within the organization. Leading by example and actively participating can be achieved by defining procedures for sharing information and utilizing knowledge in decision-making, as well as enabling further discussions on the available knowledge. Improving transparency in the use of knowledge in decision-making processes and participating in knowledge discussions support the development of KBM culture in the organization, while also providing concrete examples of how KBM can benefit the organization.

In practical terms, this could mean that top management demonstrates KBM by managing with knowledge, making the data and reasoning behind their decisions visible to the personnel, actively participating in discussions and workshops regarding KBM in the organization, and promoting investments for KBM development.

5.4 Organizations Should Invest Specifically to KBM

Fourth and finally, our study indicates that organizations should allocate a budget for KBM investments. Budgeting is a crucial aspect of supporting the systematic development of any managerial area. Investing in KBM development enables holistic and long-term growth rather than isolated development projects. It is important to balance the budget equally between developing KBM know-how and culture, as well as structural and technological advancements. To enhance an organization's KBM capabilities, investments in personnel, processes, and culture are necessary. Given that personnel capabilities and attitudes influence the readiness to adopt new services [40], development efforts should prioritize training to use the necessary technologies and implementing new ways of working. It is widely recognized that decision-making requires human intuition and experience to refine data and information into a more meaningful form, complementing the use of data and technologies [63]. This approach leads to more effective results in decision-making, particularly in strategic decision-making [64].

In practical terms, investments specifically targeted at KBM could be manifested by explicitly allocating funds for KBM investments in the annual budget. In addition to technical infrastructure, these investments could include hiring new professionals, training existing personnel, establishing workshops for discussions and innovation, and developing the enterprise architecture.

6 Conclusion

The purpose of this study was to present propositions for improving maturity KBM in public sector organizations. This purpose was approached by assessing the maturity of KBM in Finnish central-government organizations. To achieve this, a maturity model was employed to evaluate the level of KBM maturity of eight organizations, and a survey was conducted to gather data from nearly 700 respondents across these organizations.

The results of our study highlight the need for greater emphasis on the management of KBM within these organizations. Specifically, we suggest that attention can be directed towards this by: (1.) defining the role of KBM in organizational management; (2.) establishing systematicity in KBM; (3.) investing in KBM specifically; and (4.) having active top management involvement in KBM efforts. Through such efforts, organizations can work towards achieving higher levels of KBM maturity and ultimately use data more effectively.

This study makes valuable contributions to both KBM research and practice. By utilizing a novel maturity model, this study provides an additional perspective to consider when assessing the maturity of an organization's KBM. Additionally, the management of KBM adds a meta-level of interest to KBM researchers, as it highlights the importance of incorporating knowledge of appropriate management styles and practices into KBM discussions. From a practical standpoint, this study offers specific and actionable areas of focus for organizations, which can be particularly useful for management-level decision making.

It is worth noting that the present study also has some limitations that need to be considered. One limitation is that the results are based on self-reported data, which can be influenced by social desirability bias, where participants may provide answers that they think are more socially acceptable. Additionally, response rates are constant issue in surveys, leading to a potential selection bias where respondents may not be representative of the population being studied. Finally, survey studies may also suffer from the limitations of the survey design, such as poorly worded questions or limited response options, which can lead to inaccurate or incomplete data.

This study presents potential avenues for future research. Firstly, this approach may be used for evaluating the maturity of KBM in public sector organizations in the future. This could lead to the development of more refined maturity models that aid in understanding the organizations' current levels of maturity and areas that require improvement. Currently, in ongoing research of Finnish municipalities' KBM maturity is assessed with this model which provides possibilities to comparison and further research. Secondly, future studies may apply our propositions for enhancing KBM maturity in public sector organizations. This would enable further empirical evaluation of the propositions and provide practical guidance on their implementation. Such studies could significantly enhance the maturity of KBM in public sector organizations, leading to improved service delivery to citizens.

Appendix

Examples of the questions form theme "The status of KBM.":

We ask you to evaluate the following knowledge-based management related topics based on your own experiences and conception. (Scale used: 1 = Strongly disagree … 5 = Strongly agree)

7. *"I am familiar with our organisation's knowledge-based management goals"* (topic: The role of knowledge-based management in the organisation's management)

10. *"The management of our organisation is committed to developing knowledge-based management"* (topic: The role of management in knowledge-based management).

References

1. Boselie, P., Van Harten, J., Veld, M.: A human resource management review on public management and public administration research: stop right there…before we go any further. Public Manag. Rev. **23**(4), 483–500 (2021)

2. Rosengart, T., Hirsch, B., Nitzl, C.: The effects of legal versus business education on decision making in public administrations with a Weberian tradition. Bus. Res. **12**(2), 455–478 (2019)
3. Ministry of Finance. Public Service Leadership. https://vm.fi/en/public-service-leadership
4. Thierauf, R.J.: Effective Business Intelligence Systems. Praeger, Westport (2001)
5. Birkinshaw, J.: The critical need to reinvent management. Bus. Strategy Rev. **21**(1), 4–11 (2010)
6. Nunes, P., Breene, T.: Reinvent your business before it's too late. Harv. Bus. Rev. **89**(1/2), 80–87 (2011)
7. Osterwalder, A., Pigneur, Y., Smith, A., Etiemble, F.: The Invincible Company: How to Constantly Reinvent Your Organization with Inspiration from the World's Best Business Models, vol. 4. Wiley, Hoboken (2020)
8. Bolisani, E., Bratianu, C., Bolisani, E., Bratianu, C.: The emergence of knowledge management. In: Bolisani, E., Bratianu, C. (eds.) Emergent Knowledge Strategies. IAKM, vol. 4, pp. 23–47. Springer, Cham (2018). https://doi.org/10.1007/978-3-319-60657-6_2
9. Dalkir, K.: Knowledge Management in Theory and Practice. MIT Press, Cambridge (2017)
10. Hislop, D., Bosua, R., Helms, R.: Knowledge Management in Organizations: A Critical Introduction. Oxford University Press, Oxford (2018)
11. Hellsten, P., Myllärniemi, J.: Business intelligence process model revisited (2019)
12. Grant, R.M.: Toward a knowledge-based theory of the firm. Strateg. Manag. J. **17**(S2), 109–122 (1996)
13. Myllärniemi, J., Laihonen, H., Karppinen, H., Seppänen, K.: Knowledge management practices in healthcare services. Meas. Bus. Excell. **16**(4), 54–65 (2012)
14. Salonius, H., Käpylä, J.: Exploring the requirements of regional knowledge-based management. J. Knowl. Manag. **17**, 583–597 (2013)
15. Siuko, V., Myllärniemi, J., Hellsten, P.: Knowledge-based management challenges in the asset life cycle. In: European Conference on Knowledge Management, pp. 1079–1087 (2022)
16. Wiig, K.M.: Knowledge management: an introduction and perspective. J. Knowl. Manag. **1**(1), 6–14 (1997)
17. Shollo, A., Galliers, R.D.: Towards an understanding of the role of business intelligence systems in organisational knowing. Inf. Syst. J. **26**(4), 339–367 (2016)
18. Xie, K., Wu, Y., Xiao, J., Hu, Q.: Value co-creation between firms and customers: the role of big data-based cooperative assets. Inf. Manag. **53**(8), 1034–1048 (2016)
19. Laihonen, H., Lonnqvist, A.: Knowledge-based value creation: grasping the intangibility of service operations in Finland. Int. J. Knowl.-Based Dev. **1**(4), 331–345 (2010)
20. Siuko, V., Myllärniemi, J., Hellsten, P.: State of knowledge-based management in project networks-case in Finnish infrastructure construction sector (2022)
21. Jääskeläinen, A., et al.: Designing a maturity model for analyzing information and knowledge management in the public sector. VINE J. Inf. Knowl. Manag. Syst. **52**(1), 120–140 (2022)
22. Edwards, J.S., Handzic, M., Carlsson, S., Nissen, M.: Knowledge management research & practice: visions and directions. Knowl. Manag. Res. Pract. **1**, 49–60 (2003)
23. De Vries, H., Bekkers, V., Tummers, L.: Innovation in the public sector: a systematic review and future research agenda. Public Adm. **94**(1), 146–166 (2016)
24. Higgins, B.: Reinventing Human Services: Community-and Family-Centered Practice. Routledge, Abingdon (2017)
25. Hellsten, P., Pekkola, S.: The impact levels of digitalization initiatives. In: IFIP (2019)
26. Bakıcı, T., Almirall, E., Wareham, J.: A smart city initiative: the case of Barcelona. J. Knowl. Econ. **4**, 135–148 (2013)
27. Taylor Buck, N., While, A.: Competitive urbanism and the limits to smart city innovation: the UK Future Cities initiative. Urban Stud. **54**(2), 501–519 (2017)
28. Karagoz, Y., Whiteside, N., Korthaus, A.: Context matters: enablers and barriers to knowledge sharing in Australian public sector ICT projects. J. Knowl. Manag. **24**(8), 1921–1941 (2020)

29. Lecomber, A., Tatnall, A.: Project management for IT professionals: education and training issues. In: Passey, D., Tatnall, A. (eds.) ITEM 2014. IAICT, vol. 444, pp. 12–24. Springer, Heidelberg (2014). https://doi.org/10.1007/978-3-662-45770-2_2

30. Tatnall, A., Davey, B., Dakich, E.: Major eGovernment projects in health, education and transport in Victoria. In: Bled eConference, p. 30 (2013)

31. Lindgren, I., Jansson, G.: Electronic services in the public sector: a conceptual framework. Gov. Inf. Q. 30(2), 163–172 (2013)

32. Ylinen, M., Pekkola, S.: Searching Success in a Successful IS Acquisition (2018)

33. Aichholzer, G., Schmutzer, R.: Organizational challenges to the development of electronic government. In: Proceedings 11th International Workshop on Database and Expert Systems Applications, pp. 379–383. IEEE (2000)

34. Bason, C.: Leading Public Sector Innovation: Co-Creating for a Better Society. Policy Press, Bristol (2018)

35. Demirkan, H., Spohrer, J.C., Welser, J.J.: Digital innovation and strategic transformation. IT Prof. 18(6), 14–18 (2016)

36. Agutter, C., van Hove, S., Steinberg, R., England, R.: VeriSM-A Service Management Approach for the Digital Age. Van Haren, s-Hertogenbosch (2017)

37. Wirtz, B.W.: Business model management. Des Von Geschäftsmodellen, vol. 2, no. 1 (2011)

38. Ding, F., Li, D., George, J.F.: Investigating the effects of IS strategic leadership on orga-nizational benefits from the perspective of CIO strategic roles. Inf. Manag. 51(7), 865–879 (2014)

39. Arnaboldi, M., Lapsley, I., Steccolini, I.: Performance management in the public sector: the ultimate challenge. Financ. Account. Manag. 31(1), 1–22 (2015)

40. Moe, C.E.: Research on public procurement of information systems: the need for a process approach. Commun. Assoc. Inf. Syst. 34(1), 78 (2014)

41. Beck, D.E., Cowan, C.C.: Spiral Dynamics: Mastering Values, Leadership and Change. Wiley, Hoboken (2014)

42. Goldfinch, S.: Pessimism, computer failure, and information systems development in the public sector. Public Adm. Rev. 67(5), 917–929 (2007)

43. Baily, P., Farmer, D., Crocker, B., Jessop, D., Jones, D.: Procurement Principles and Management. Pearson Education, London (2008)

44. Srai, J.S., Lorentz, H.: Developing design principles for the digitalisation of purchasing and supply management. J. Purch. Supply Manag. 25(1), 78–98 (2019)

45. Jalonen, H.: Tiedolla johtamisen näyttämö ja kulissit. Tiedolla Johtaminen Hallinnossa Teor Ja Käytäntöjä 2015, 40–68 (2015)

46. Virtanen, P., Stenvall, J., Rannisto, P.H.: Julkiseen politiikkaan liittyvä oppiminen ja tietoon perustuva päätöksenteko (2015). https://trepo.tuni.fi/handle/10024/101388. Accessed 15 Jun 2023

47. Gabriš, P., Bielik Marettová, M., Pavlenda, P., Ličko, M., Šujanová, J.: Knowledge manage-ment maturity aspects in industrial enterprises (2012)

48. Suwarsi, S., Harahap, D.A., Amanah, D.: Maturity analysis of knowledge management imple-mentation on organizational performance (survey on state-owned enterprises in Indonesia). J. Contemp. Issues Bus. Gov. 27(2), 5672–5682 (2021)

49. Gastaldi, L., et al.: Measuring the maturity of business intelligence in healthcare: supporting the development of a roadmap toward precision medicine within ISMETT hospital. Technol. Forecast. Soc. Change 128, 84–103 (2018)

50. Röglinger, M., Pöppelbuß, J., Becker, J.: Maturity models in business process management. Bus. Process Manag. J. 18, 328–346 (2012)

51. Wendler, R.: The maturity of maturity model research: a systematic mapping study. Inf. Softw. Technol. 54(12), 1317–1339 (2012)

52. Hribar Rajterič, I.: Overview of business intelligence maturity models. Manag. J. Contemp. Manag. Issues **15**(1), 47–67 (2010)
53. Aho, M.: Konstruktio suorituskyvyn johtamisen kypsyyden arviointiin (2011)
54. Davenport, T.H., Harris, J.G., Morison, R.: Analytics at Work: Smarter Decisions, Better Results. Harvard Business Press, Brighton (2010)
55. Creatido 2023. Knowlede-based Management Framework (2023)
56. Juppo, V.: Muutoksen johtaminen suomalaisessa yliopistouudistuksessa rehtoreiden näkökulmasta (2011)
57. Ranki, S.: Strateginen johtaminen suomalaisissa korkeakouluissa (2016)
58. Myllärniemi, J., Helander, N., Pekkola, S.: Challenges in developing data-based value creation. In: International Joint Conference on Knowledge Discovery, Knowledge Engineering and Knowledge Management, pp. 370–376. SCITEPRESS (2019)
59. Bojesson, C., Fundin, A.: Exploring microfoundations of dynamic capabilities–challenges, barriers and enablers of organizational change. J. Organ. Change Manag. **34**(1), 206–222 (2021)
60. Kianto, A., Ritala, P., Spender, J.C., Vanhala, M.: The interaction of intellectual capital assets and knowledge management practices in organizational value creation. J. Intellect. Cap. **15**, 362–375 (2014)
61. Gudfinnsson, K., Strand, M., Berndtsson, M.: Analyzing business intelligence maturity. J. Decis. Syst. **24**(1), 37–54 (2015)
62. Kulkarni, U., Robles-Flores, J.A., Popovič, A.: Business intelligence capability: the effect of top management and the mediating roles of user participation and analytical decision making orientation. J. Assoc. Inf. Syst. **18**(7), 1 (2017)
63. Liebowitz, J., Chan, Y., Jenkin, T., Spicker, D., Paliszkiewicz, J., Babiloni, F.: If numbers could "feel": how well do executives trust their intuition? VINE J. Inf. Knowl. Manag. Syst. **49**, 531–545 (2019)
64. Ransbotham, S., Kiron, D., Prentice, P.K.: Beyond the hype: the hard work behind analytics success. MIT Sloan Manag. Rev. **57**(3), 18 (2016)

Affording and Constraining Digital Transformation:
The Enactment of Structural Change in Three Swedish Government Agencies

Malin Tinjan⁽⊠⁾ ⓘ, Robert Åhlén ⓘ, Susanna Hammelev Jörgensen ⓘ,
and Johan Magnusson ⓘ

University of Gothenburg, Forskningsgången 6, 417 56 Gothenburg, Sweden
{malin.tinjan,robert.ahlen,susanna.hammelev.jorgensen,
johan.magnusson}@ait.gu.se

Abstract. Public sector organizations need to adapt to the ongoing societal changes and new technologies emerging, and as public sector organizations engage in digital transformation, they are confronted with the need to re-arrange and change themselves to be successful. Previous research has identified factors for digital transformation in both public and private sector settings, yet there is still an absence of research into how public sector organizations deal with this transformation. In this study, we explore how government agencies enact structural changes related to digital transformation. We do so through a multi-case study of three government agencies in Sweden, interviewing key actors to explore the organizations' enactments. Our findings show that public sector organizations display a high level of variance in how they enact structural changes to succeed with digital transformation. This is discussed in relation to previous research on management commitment to digital transformation, as well as dialogue and tensions when changing, with the intent to contribute to research and practice in relation to digital transformation.

Keywords: Digital Transformation · Public sector · Structural changes

1 Introduction

The diffusion of new digital technologies puts pressure on organizations to capitalize on these opportunities. Understood as organizational changes brought on by the adoption and utilization of digital technologies [1], digital transformation affects how organizations plan, prioritize, and operate. It challenges how organizations structure the workplace, allocate resources, and build a culture of innovation [2]. Since digital transformation is going on everywhere and affects everything and everyone, it is important that officials in the public sector understand this phenomenon. Magnusson et al. show that digital transformation in incumbent organizations is hindered by their established routines, inertia, and dependencies [3]. There is a need for internal organizational enablers, such as skills development, cultural changes, and different leadership models, to manage this re-organization [4].

© IFIP International Federation for Information Processing 2023
Published by Springer Nature Switzerland AG 2023
I. Lindgren et al. (Eds.): EGOV 2023, LNCS 14130, pp. 414–430, 2023.
https://doi.org/10.1007/978-3-031-41138-0_26

We can, at the same time, see that studies of digital transformation and the organizational changes required in the public sector are in fact uncommon, and multi-case studies are even rarer, although they exist [5, 6]. Most empirical studies on digital transformation in the public sector to date have been conducted in single organizations [7], and on specific projects or initiatives [8]. To better understand digital transformation in the public sector, studies having a more holistic view of organizational changes due to digital transformation are needed [9].

A common assumption in research is that the public sector is uniform and can be standardized. For instance, in a recent study [10], the authors generalize their results to the public sector from a single case study, where they "stud[y] the barriers for digital transformation in a 'typical' public organization" [p. 277]. This is also acknowledged by Mergel et al. who call for more research on digital transformation within the public sector, its different types, and subsectors [11].

This paper aims to contribute to a more nuanced understanding of digital transformation in the public sector by focusing on a single Swedish subsector: national level governmental agencies. Our research question is: *How are structural changes associated with digital transformation enacted among Swedish national level government agencies?*

This question is answered through a multi-case study of three different Swedish government agencies and how they address digital transformation. The three organizations have different settings and configurations, varying from 40 to 1 700 employees, and have different assignments: one in government administration, one in environmental administration, and one in public higher education. Our study contributes by offering empirical insights into organizations within a subsector of the Swedish public sector.

Using Vial's framework for digital transformation [12] as a starting point, we analyze the three organizations' enactments of structural change across four concepts, by developing and using an abductively created conceptual framework.

The remainder of the paper is structured accordingly: This first introduction is followed by a description of the literature on digital transformation in the public sector and on affording and constraining factors in relation to digital transformation. In the third section, we describe our chosen method, our empirical cases, and our conceptual framework used when analyzing and its creation process. The fourth section describes our results, while the fifth section discusses the results in the context of digital transformation. To round off, we discuss the paper's limitations, suggest directions for future research, and make recommendations to practitioners and policymakers.

2 Precursory Findings and Theoretical Framing

2.1 Digital Transformation in Public Sector Organizations

While public sector organizations are under general pressure to be more efficient and increase quality, they are also under specific pressure to become more digital to provide more online services [13] as well as to adapt policies, legislation, and internal structures [14]. Public sector organizations are however governed by complex institutional elements [15], which, combined with a lack of analytical clarity [16], makes the transformation brought on by e-government "still relatively poorly understood" [17]. As Mergel et al. identify [11], the terms *e-government* [16], *digital government* [13], and *transformational government* [18] are often used in similar ways, with similar meanings, ending up in conceptual unclarity.

As noted by Vial [12] as well as Mergel et al. [11], the construct of digital transformation is pluralistic and fragmented. The key aspect in the definition offered by Vial, is that the value creation paths of the organization are altered [12]. The definition put forth by Mergel et al. entails a more "holistic effort", which includes revising core processes [11]. In this study, we focus on the definition of digital transformation offered by Hanelt et al. as *organizational change brought on through the utilization of digital technologies* [1].

Regardless of the exact definition, however, we can see that studies of digital transformation in the public sector are rare, and that there is still much to be learned on how public sector organizations manage digital transformation. Recent studies have shown that digital transformation involves, among other things, creating a new organizational identity, which is a complex and paradoxical endeavor [19] that sometimes includes complicated intra-group power dynamics and introspection [20]. How government officials view themselves and their own organization's ability for digital transformation is therefore of interest. Several years ago, Meijer & Bekkers pointed out that individuals were rarely the object of e-government research [16]. Since then, several studies [21, 22] have heeded their call and shown that officials differ on the reasons, objects, processes, and results of digital transformation [11].

2.2 Factors Affording and Constraining Digital Transformation

In our stated definition of digital transformation, organizational change is emphasized. This change is facilitated by affording factors and hampered by constraining factors, carried out within the organization. There has been some research done on barriers to digital transformation in the public sector. Wilson & Mergel drew upon their analysis of the U.S. public sector and created concepts of barriers in two dimensions: *structural barriers* containing governance, capabilities, and resources; and *cultural barriers* containing a lack of awareness and internal culture [21].

Tangi et al. analyzed the Italian public sector and identified *organizational barriers* (including lack of political will, top management support, and coordination between divisions) and *cultural barriers* (including bureaucratic culture and employee resistance due to fear of losing jobs or control) [22]. In Sweden, Magnusson et al. identified ill-fitting IT governance models as a constraint to digital transformation in the public sector [23].

Some success factors for digital transformation have been stated by Osmundsen et al., such as a supportive organizational culture, well-managed transformative actions, and engaged managers and employees [24]. Escobar et al. instead explored eight concepts of success factors containing *people* (including team awareness and digital skills) as well as *organization* (including multilevel governance and management structures, changes in organizational structures, and changes in organizational culture) [25].

Based on a literature review, Vial proposes a broad conceptual framework designed to understand the phenomenon of digital transformation in its entirety, including the influence of affording and constraining factors [12]. Vial's framework describes digital transformation as a process initiated by ongoing technological development, which causes organizations to react to these changes and adjust their value-creation paths to stay competitive. These reactions and adjustments can be constrained by organizational barriers and afforded by structural changes, generating positive or negative impacts.

Vial's affording factors are grouped under the headline "structural changes" that affect the organization's development and are said to be needed for digital transformation. These changes include *organizational structure*, for instance, cross-functional collaboration, *organizational culture* regarding organizational agility and experimentation [op. cit., p. 127], *leadership* towards fostering a digital mindset, and having *employees* take new *roles* and develop new *skills* [op. cit., p. 129].

3 Method

In this study, we expand on Vial's conceptual framework and use it as a lens to analyze our organizations on whether they lean more towards affording factors, or more towards constraining factors, across the four concepts of structural change. Although Vial's framework is based on studies of the private sector, the framework can be equally useful for studying the public sector [26], as value creation likewise occurs in the public sector [27].

The research design in this paper is a qualitative [28], exploratory [29] multi-case study [30] which allows us to explore the emerging and under-researched phenomenon of digital transformation in the public sector. To answer our research question, we chose three Swedish national level government agencies to study, according to a most different systems design [31] with adequacy sampling [32], see Table 1. The organizations were chosen because of their differences and because of the research team's proximity to them as three of us are Executive Ph.D. students, employed in the organizations.

To gain insight into how the studied organizations enact digital transformation, we chose to conduct expert interviews [33] to understand how the individuals themselves describe the enactment. The research team did a total of 56 semi-structured interviews, between 16 and 23 per organization, of about 60 min each, over a period of three months, between December 2022 and February 2023. Both managers and employees involved in organizational development and digital transformation were interviewed, around themes such as digitalization, business improvement, and the relationship between core operations and the IT department. The interviews were recorded and transcribed.

After 56 interviews, we made a "situated, interpretative judgment" [34] that we did not need further interviews. We sensitized ourselves to our data by reading and watching all the interviews and deep coding 15 of them, five per organization, while iteratively developing our conceptual framework. The selection of interviews to code was made through purposive sampling [35] making sure to get both managers and employees, from both IT and core operations, and selecting at random when we had several interviewees in a category; see Table 2. After coding those 15 interviews, we again decided that we had enough empirical data to understand the organizations and to analyze them through our framework, and that coding more interviews would not yield any different results.

Table 1. Case descriptions

	Case A	Case B	Case C
No. of employees	~40	~1 700	~300
Annual turnover	EUR 3,2 million	EUR 140,1 million	EUR 69,4 million
Established in	Independent authority since 2002, in current configuration since 2016	First formed in 1977, in current configuration since 1999	Formed through the merger of several other (parts of) agencies in 2011
Subject matter	Government administration	University	Environmental administration
Sourcing of IT	In a long-term government mandated collaboration with a much larger host authority, supplying IT and administrative services	In-house IT but decentralized sourcing, where each department are hosting and managing various IT systems on their own	Heavily dependent on external consultants in IT, due to external financing generally not allowed to be used towards salaries

Table 2. Coded interviews sample overview

	Case A	Case B	Case C
Managers	CEO + 2 top-level managers	CIO + 2 top-level managers	CDO + 2 s-level managers
Employees	2 from core	1 from core + 1 from IT	2 from IT

The data from the interviews were primarily triangulated by the fact that three of the research team members were employed by the investigated organizations and therefore embedded in the context as a type of prolonged engagement in the field [36]. The research team thus had useful knowledge about whom to interview and had the organizational knowledge to interpret their statements with contextual nuance. The potential bias in interpretations and selection of respondents was managed by not interviewing within one's own organization, collaborating intensively during coding and analysis [37], and using the snowball method to add to our selection of respondents [38].

As the method of analysis, we followed the five phases of Braun & Clarkes reflexive thematic analysis [39] where analysis starts immediately. Our coding scheme and conceptual framework (see Table 3) developed abductively over time, while we still were interviewing and coding interviews.

We familiarized ourselves with the data (phase 1) by conducting, reading, or watching all 56 interviews. In phase 2, we constructed a deductive code sheet for affording digital transformation, originating from Vial's four structural changes. The idea was originally to code for affording factors for digital transformation, but as we searched for themes (phase 3), we discovered constraining factors as well. So, we expanded the conceptual framework and create new themes to include constraining factors as well.

We contrasted affording and constraining factors side by side as we reviewed our themes (phase 4) meaning that we had identified, defined, and named (phase 5) both affording and constraining factors over each of the type of structural change.

Table 3. Conceptual framework

Vial's concepts	Some examples of quotes	First-order codes	Second-order themes
Organizational structure	"No, we are special, and we want to do this" "IT helps, but we have to, on our own, come up with the ideas of what we want to digitalize" "I would like to say that our relationship is a very strong and intimate collaborative relationship"	*Affording*: Cross-functional networks, Unified planning and prioritizing, Non-hierarchical organization, Few silos, Holistic view of the organization	*Affording*: Cross-functional collaboration [40, 41]
		Constraining: Lack of cooperation or collaboration, Lack of knowledge of other organizations planning/ structure/ strategy, Language that shows uniqueness, IT decides which systems to use in business, Getting "help" from IT function	*Constraining*: Silo-thinking [21, 22]
Organizational culture	"We need to have proper investigations in a number of areas" "My view is that we are very cautious and like to do things that someone else has done before us" "I like continuous business development and not big projects because then you can constantly change a little bit"	*Affording*: Agility/flexibility, Courage, Goals or results of projects are unclear or not defined, Common language/definitions, Multi-media mindset, POC/pilots	*Affording*: Willingness to experiment and take risk [42]
		Constraining: Separation between IT and business functions, Waterfall methods, Focus on solutions instead of customer need, Fear, Preparatory studies instead of action	*Constraining*: Culture of planning and fear [21]

(*continued*)

Table 3. (*continued*)

Vial's concepts	Some examples of quotes	First-order codes	Second-order themes
Leadership	"When we recruit managers outside the organization, it is explicitly stated that you must have experience in, for example, business development, digitization" "To work with digital business development in a structured way, we are not … very good, strategically anyway"	*Affording*: (New) leadership roles, Leader/ roles tasked with closing the gap between business and IT, Aligning technology with strategy and ways of working, Models, methods, and actions supporting integration between IT and business	*Affording*: Leaders act to develop a digital mindset/ digital strategy [43, 44]
		Constraining: No leadership roles tasked with digitalization, Top management lacks digital strategy, Top management silent on digitalization	*Constraining*: Governance and management not targeting digital transformation [5, 45]
Employee roles and skills	"We have a manager level and an employee level that varies a lot in the ability to make use of the possibilities of digitization or to even be able to drive digitization forward" "There is a lack of internal competence in how to work with digitization" "We have also worked hard and put an incredible sum of resources into IT development"	*Affording*: Business leads IT projects, Competence development of employees, Employees want to be involved in digitalization (projects), Digital skills requested from all new personnel when hired, not only IT	*Affording*: Employees take/get new roles, tasks, or titles [41]
		Constraining: Lack of people with relevant/ right competence or skills, Employees lack interest, knowledge, or skills in digitalization, Forced to hire consultants	*Constraining*: Lack of personnel working with digital transformation [46]

4   Results

The results are presented following the four structural concepts as per our conceptual framework. Each sub-section expands on the differences and commonalities between the three cases in relation to their enactment of digital transformation. The second-order themes from Table 3 are written **in bold**. The last sub-section summarizes our findings from each organization.

The quotes have been translated into English by the authors and are being referenced as "Manager 1", "Employee 2", etc., in a sequential order to preserve their anonymity.

4.1 Organizational Structure

Case A have started to change their organizational structure to enable themselves to make the best use of digital technology. This is done by embracing **cross-functional collaboration** in both formal and informal ways: *"So, we continue to work on getting this together with us and them. So that it won't be us and them, but that it will be us, together"* (Manager 1, Case A).

In Case B there is a lack of unified commitment to digitalization, and they used to collaborate more in the past, leaving them with a current state of **silo thinking**: *"Man ... well, no, I'm not ... well, as you can hear, I miss these meetings where we actually had the opportunity to meet and discuss issues that concern everyone, and work together above all, that's really important"* (Employee 1, Case B).

Case C is undergoing a major top-down re-organization affecting roles, titles, responsibilities, assignments, and governance models. The CDO has a clear vision of unified planning and execution, and has disbanded the previous Digitalization Council, leaving the rest of the organization without insight into what is happening and why. Employees are frustrated about how these new ways of working are supposed to be executed: *"We have business developers, but how they work... it's very ad hoc. The role is not super defined, it depends on the department and the head of the department, so they are doing different things"* (Employee 1, Case C).

Both Cases B and C refer to **cross-functional collaboration** as an ideal. In Case B it is described as an ideal state, i.e., how it "ought to be" (without any reference to any codified rules or operating practices). In Case C it is described in terms of how it "will be" (once the new models and ways of working are put in place). Case A displays a unified starting point, having a single vision that everybody seems to rally around, leading to **cross-functional collaboration** being a reality.

4.2 Organizational Culture

Managers in Case A want the organization to expand, be more assertive, and be more future-oriented than its current financing and institutional arrangements allow. One of them says: *"I am quite critical towards the lack of understanding [from the government] that development work needs to be ongoing continuously in order to get the changes that are needed"* (Manager 2, Case A).

The management of Case C has grand plans for the organization, as mentioned in Sect. 4.1. Individual projects can be given free rein to be more agile and iterative, so there is a **willingness to experiment**, but this has not yet become the norm: *"But [being a project manager] has been like walking in a minefield in an organization that constantly refers to control models for project management that do not ... there is no possibility that the project can use them. The project is losing forward momentum, we will not meet the target because we are moving towards a moving target where the development both in the users' maturity to use digital tools, and the functionality and performance of the tools themselves, is going extremely fast"* (Employee, Case C).

Cases A and C display similar patterns and express a desire to be more agile and make use of iterative ways of working. The **culture of planning** in Case B is, however, unparalleled in Cases A and C. It is so strong in Case B that one manager explained how they planned to plan: *"But then it will be more like we have to plan to raise the need for it. If we plan, for example, in the fall of 2022 that in 2023 we will raise the need with the administrative director, then we might talk about a process that will come in 2024 at the earliest or 2025, so there are very long lead times"* (Manager 1, Case B).

In Case B suggestions of organizational need can be submitted by anyone to a prioritization group, but without a designated project manager already designated in the submission, the suggestion is usually rejected. Like cross-functional collaboration, their idea of a **willingness to experiment** is mostly an ideal pushed by managers of how things ought to be, their stance on the matter, is not so much backed up by actual examples.

4.3 Leadership

Leaders in Cases A and C highlight the importance of adopting a team-based and agile approach. Case A does so more formally by creating teams within core operations and implementing a new software development scheme. In Case C **leaders act to develop a digital strategy** by appointing a CDO, an Enterprise Architect, and setting up an entire digital transformation department. They have the ambition to work in a more professional team-based agile manner, but the organization is currently characterized by a lot of individual work. *"…if we want to be an attractive workplace, if we are to retain people, and if people want to start working with us, we need to work in a way that people understand and recognize"* (Manager 1, Case C).

Those interviewed in Case B highlight the need to act quickly and bring new and scalable solutions into the organization, but struggle to gain understanding and attention from the core business, due to an absence of a clear digital transformation strategy: *"I think there is a need for somebody who knows about management, control, keep track, and takes inventory: 'What do we have? What are we doing?' [Digital transformation and IT] is a bit too scattered"* (Employee 1, Case B).

Interviewees from Cases A and C emphasize being a traditional government bureaucracy with a primary obligation to deliver on their democratic assignments, allowing for development and innovation only when time and resources permit. The picture of **unclear governance and management without a focus on digital transformation** emerges in all three cases but more so in Cases B and C. Governance are fragmented in Case B with two different lines of decision-making which are not unified in a joint vision. Or as one employee says: *"I would like to say that no one dares to decide. Within the administration, that is. I think it should be, developed within the departments or within the academy, how can we make it as good as possible for students and teachers, and what kind of support can the administration provide for that?"* (Employee 1, Case B).

All three organizations suffer from a lack of clarity regarding responsibilities and decisions-rights regarding digital transformation.

4.4 Employee Roles and Skills

In both Cases A and C, employees have been given **new roles to drive digital transformation**. In Case A, a new software development scheme is being put in place. This has brought on some tensions and unclarity towards those in other roles: *"We need to find a way of working where we have both people who take these [new] roles, but also those who do not have [software development] roles, how should they work with the [IT] organization?"* (Manager 3, Case A).

In Case B, the IT department perceives itself as a catalyst for digital transformation, as stated by the CIO, and the **business is expected to take the role of project leader**, despite the lack of both skills and sufficient resources: *"When I started, I got push-back from the business units: 'No, I won't send anyone to your reference group'... Well then, how I am supposed to know what is needed without input from users?"* (Employee 1, Case B).

There is also a lack of project managers in Case B, so projects are sometimes halted and delayed: *"That is a question in the prioritization: Do you have a project manager? - No? Then you must wait until someone is available"* (Manager 2, Case B). This is counter-acted by leaders trying to encourage employees and pushing them to step up to take on project leadership. However, as the **lack of personnel working with digital transformation** is a systemic problem, our understanding is that the problem will not be solved merely through encouraging individuals.

In all three cases, there is a lack of skills to run IT projects. Case A has historically relied heavily on external consultants in both management and development and is now more actively working to increase its internal skills, although through a different organization that brings in IT competence as a host authority. Case B makes less use of external consultants and **lacks internal resources**.

In Case C they continue to rely on external consultants despite investment in **new roles** and the creation of a new digital transformation department and the gap between the internal employee and the external consultants is wide. This quote describes the gap in skills between the external project manager and internal project members: *"But they are very novice and ignorant in the field, on a level that I am surprised by, I must say. It feels more like you have to educate, and go back to ABC, to make them understand what we are really doing here. Very... if the level of knowledge had been higher, it would have been a completely different journey"* (Employee 2, Case C).

4.5 Summary of Results

Figure 1 contains a summary of the results of the three case studies, presented across our four concepts.

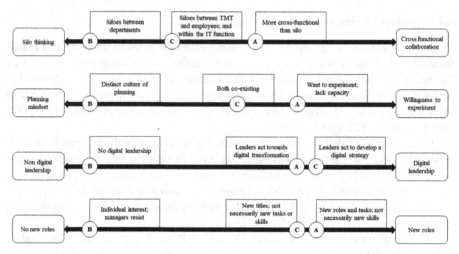

Fig. 1. Summary of results

5 Discussion

In this section, we first discuss our results across the three organizations, where we see that alignment of views and dialogue of digital transformation both within the top management team, and between the top management and the employees is a key factor influencing other factors. This is then discussed in relation to prior studies on the importance of leadership and management's commitment to digital transformation. Finally, we discuss similarities in the organizational changes in the three organizations in terms of duality, tension, and paradoxes.

The three organizations show different ways of enacting digital transformation and even though there are some similarities, they are overall more different than alike. We see that the organizations differ in degrees of alignment and consensus, both between and within the top management team and employees on how the organization faces digital transformation. Meaning making through dialogue is essential for organizational change or "rather, issues are made meaningful (or not) through communicative practices" [47, p. 34]. In Case A, there is alignment in the dialogue between top management and employees regarding the organization's need for digital transformation. They mention the same digital initiatives for the organization and discuss the same re-organization efforts in the same way. Whereas in Case B, there is a lack of conversation across the organization and between management and employees about digital transformation. All levels mention a need for digital transformation, but there is no consensus on how it is supposed to be done and who is supposed to champion it. In Case C, digital transformation is prioritized by some in senior management, but despite a re-organization, the organization does not seem to get clarity on what digital transformation actually means for them. There is no alignment between management and employees, as the employees call for clearer roles, processes, working methods, and priorities across the board.

Research has highlighted that leadership is essential for digital transformation [43], and that a lack of management commitment [48], support [49], and ownership [50] drives inadequate resource allocation and weak decision-making, which drives other barriers. The consequences of a lack of commitment are evident in Case B, where questions about how to adapt to digital transformation are not on the agenda at all, creating frustration among both employees and managers. In Case C, on the other hand, we do find a commitment to digital transformation, but only in a selection of top management and consultants.

The structural changes to enhance digital transformation include more than just altering the organization. Employees' mindsets and participation in the change process, and management explaining why changes are being made [51], are important to employees' commitment and positive attitudes [49]. Here, top management in Case C has not been active in any strategic change management focused on people's contribution to the new ways of working. Like in Case B, this leads to frustration among both managers and employees, creating tension and increased distancing. This means that even if managers in Case C are aware of the need for digital transformation and have started to change the organizational structure, such as a new prioritization board, new governance models, and new roles and titles, the people within the organization are not changing, and the (absent) effects are the same as in an organization where no decisions have been made at all, such as Case B.

In Case A there is also a commitment to digital transformation, but from both managers and employees, although to a low degree, as the organization does not seem to know how to move from "want" to "do". But even if the transformation is slow or small, there is no frustration or lack of commitment to the common vision of Case A's need to digitally transform.

Albeit the direct enactment of organizational changes differs in the three organizations there are some similarities. Research suggests that thinking of structural changes as dualities, rather than either/or-situations that need to be resolved can be beneficial to relieve tensions and to overcome organizational barriers [52]. In all three cases, they mention how they perform a balancing act between old and new ways of working, thinking, and acting. They refer to walking in minefields when choosing how to realize digitalization and that formalized structures, routines, and models counteract development. These dialectics and organizational contradictions were present within all three organizations, creating tensions, but with different contents and expressions [53, 54].

The three agencies also describe tensions from all different levels of the organization, from the top management level to the employee level, and in various manners, such as expressing it in words, through facial expressions, and by showing emotions [55]. They all mention how they want something *more* or something *else*, but not *how to change* or *how to become* more of what they want to be. We, therefore, hypothesize that there are competing demands and existing contextual paradoxes in these three agencies that work interdependently and at multiple levels affecting how they conduct and succeed in their organizational changes [55, 56].

5.1 Contributions, Limitations, and Future Research

Our study has two main contributions to research. First, we have contributed to more multi-case studies of the public sector by offering empirical insight into three different government agencies. Second, we have demonstrated that not all public sector organizations are the same, not even within the same subsector, as they differ greatly in attitude, enactment, and commitment toward digital transformation. Becoming aware of the public sector's similarities and differences in relation to digital transformation might open up new discussions, arguments, and formats for researchers in a variety of fields.

We offer three central implications for practice. First, we underline the contention from Aditya et al. [48] that lack of commitment has the most impact when enacting digital transformation. It may seem obvious, but as our study shows, it is still lacking. Second, we can see that commitment is not enough. There needs to be a dialogue on changes and action behind what top management says, and then change leadership behind the action, to get digital transformation going. Third, organizations may be advised to, instead of focusing on if the organization is following old or new ways of working, accept that these concepts exist simultaneously, which in turn might help them to overcome barriers to organizational changes.

We see some limitations to the presented study. First, we have not actually studied digital transformation as such; we do not know if any value creation paths have been altered. Second, as change is a key aspect of digital transformation, there is a limitation in that we only studied these organizations at one point in time and have not followed them over time [57]. Third, we have not tried to explain why the organizations' enactments are the way they are, which could be a theme for forthcoming research.

More empirical studies into the public sector and its subsectors are needed, both in this subsector and in others. We suggest a longitudinal study, following public sector organizations over time, tracking their change, as Svahn et al. did for a car manufacturer [54]. Second, we suggest evaluating whether public sector organizations really undergo digital transformation and how. Third, studying the public sector through a paradox lens to see how competing demands affect organizations' digital transformation [58].

6 Conclusion

This study offers empirical insight into how structural changes are differently enacted in three Swedish government agencies in relation to their digital transformation. There really is no single "public sector organization" ideal type that easily can be referenced to. While there exists a lot of research on how digital transformation affects and is enacted in the private sector, less is said about the public sector; especially studies comparing different subsectors and organizations within the public sector are lacking. Our study shows how these three organizations in different ways struggle with understanding how to change and their enactment of digital transformation and that there are some factors, for instance, communication and commitment of leadership, that trigger tensions and create barriers.

References

1. Hanelt, A., Bohnsack, R., Marz, D., Marante, C.A.: A systematic review of the literature on digital transformation: insights and implications for strategy and organizational change. J. Manag. Stud. **58**, 1159–1197 (2021). https://doi.org/10.1111/joms.12639

2. Jackson, N.C.: Managing for competency with innovation change in higher education: examining the pitfalls and pivots of digital transformation. Bus. Horizons **62**, 761–772 (2019). https://doi.org/10.1016/j.bushor.2019.08.002

3. Magnusson, J., Elliot, V., Hagberg, J.: Digital transformation: why companies resist what they need for sustained performance. J. Bus. Strategy **43**, 316–322 (2022). https://doi.org/10.1108/jbs-02-2021-0018

4. Brunetti, F., Matt, D.T., Bonfanti, A., Longhi, A.D., Pedrini, G., Orzes, G.: Digital transformation challenges: strategies emerging from a multi-stakeholder approach. TQM J. **32**, 697–724 (2020). https://doi.org/10.1108/tqm-12-2019-0309

5. Pittaway, J.J., Montazemi, A.R.: Know-how to lead digital transformation: the case of local governments. Gov. Inform. Q. **37**, 101474 (2020). https://doi.org/10.1016/j.giq.2020.101474

6. Hafseld, K.H.J., Hussein, B., Rauzy, A.B.: An attempt to understand complexity in a government digital transformation project. Int. J. Inf. Syst. Proj. Manag. **9**, 70–91 (2021). https://doi.org/10.12821/ijispm090304

7. Gong, Y., Yang, J., Shi, X.: Towards a comprehensive understanding of digital transformation in government: analysis of flexibility and enterprise architecture. Gov. Inform. Q. **37**, 101487 (2020). https://doi.org/10.1016/j.giq.2020.101487

8. Gil-Garcia, J.R., Flores-Zúñiga, M.Á.: Towards a comprehensive understanding of digital government success: integrating implementation and adoption factors. Gov. Inform. Q. **37**, 101518 (2020). https://doi.org/10.1016/j.giq.2020.101518

9. Vogelsang, K., Liere-Netheler, K., Packmohr, S., Hoppe, U.: A taxonomy of barriers to digital transformation. In: Presented at the 14th International Conference on Wirtschaftsinformatik, 24 February (2019)

10. Bjerke-Busch, L.S., Aspelund, A.: Identifying barriers for digital transformation in the public sector. In: Schallmo, D.R.A., Tidd, J. (eds.) Digitalization. MP, pp. 277–290. Springer, Cham (2021). https://doi.org/10.1007/978-3-030-69380-0_15

11. Mergel, I., Edelmann, N., Haug, N.: Defining digital transformation: results from expert interviews. Gov. Inform. Q. **36**, 101385 (2019). https://doi.org/10.1016/j.giq.2019.06.002

12. Vial, G.: Understanding digital transformation: a review and a research agenda. J. Strateg. Inf. Syst. **28**, 118–144 (2019). https://doi.org/10.1016/j.jsis.2019.01.003

13. Janowski, T.: Digital government evolution: from transformation to contextualization. Gov. Inform. Q. **32**, 221–236 (2015). https://doi.org/10.1016/j.giq.2015.07.001

14. Janssen, M., van der Voort, H.: Adaptive governance: towards a stable, accountable and responsive government. Gov. Inform. Q. **33**, 1–5 (2016). https://doi.org/10.1016/j.giq.2016.02.003

15. Weerakkody, V., Omar, A., El-Haddadeh, R., Al-Busaidy, M.: Digitally-enabled service transformation in the public sector: the lure of institutional pressure and strategic response towards change. Gov. Inform. Q. **33**, 658–668 (2016). https://doi.org/10.1016/j.giq.2016.06.006

16. Meijer, A., Bekkers, V.: A metatheory of e-government: creating some order in a fragmented research field. Gov. Inform. Q. **32**, 237–245 (2015). https://doi.org/10.1016/j.giq.2015.04.006

17. Nograšek, J., Vintar, M.: E-government and organisational transformation of government: black box revisited? Gov. Inform. Q. **31**, 108–118 (2014). https://doi.org/10.1016/j.giq.2013.07.006

18. Omar, A., Weerakkody, V., Daowd, A.: Studying Transformational Government: a review of the existing methodological approaches and future outlook. Gov. Inform. Q. **37**, 101458 (2020). https://doi.org/10.1016/j.giq.2020.101458

19. Wessel, L.: Unpacking the difference between digital transformation and IT-enabled organizational transformation. J. Assoc. Inf. Syst. **22**, 102–129 (2021). https://doi.org/10.17705/1jais.00655

20. Jarvenpaa, S.L., Selander, L.: Between scale and impact: member prototype ambiguity in digital transformation. Eur. J. Inform. Syst. 1–19 (2023, ahead-of-print). https://doi.org/10.1080/0960085x.2023.2175474
21. Wilson, C., Mergel, I.: Overcoming barriers to digital government: mapping the strategies of digital champions. Gov. Inform. Q. **39**, 101681 (2022). https://doi.org/10.1016/j.giq.2022.101681
22. Tangi, L., Janssen, M., Benedetti, M., Noci, G.: Digital government transformation: a structural equation modelling analysis of driving and impeding factors. Int. J. Inform. Manag. **60**, 102356 (2021). https://doi.org/10.1016/j.ijinfomgt.2021.102356
23. Magnusson, J., Khisro, J., Melin, U.: A pathology of public sector IT governance: how IT governance configuration counteracts ambidexterity. In: Viale Pereira, G., et al. (eds.) EGOV 2020. LNCS, vol. 12219, pp. 29–41. Springer, Cham (2020). https://doi.org/10.1007/978-3-030-57599-1_3
24. Osmundsen, K., Iden, J., Bygstad, B.: Digital transformation: drivers, success factors, and implications. In: Presented at the MCIS 2018 (2018)
25. Escobar, F., Almeida, W.H.C., Varajão, J.: Digital transformation success in the public sector: a systematic literature review of cases, processes, and success factors. Inf. Polity **28**, 1–21 (2022). https://doi.org/10.3233/ip-211518
26. Boyne, G.A.: Public and private management: what's the difference? J. Manag. Stud. **39**, 97–122 (2002). https://doi.org/10.1111/1467-6486.00284
27. Pang, M.-S., Lee, G., DeLone, W.H.: IT resources, organizational capabilities, and value creation in public-sector organizations: a public-value management perspective. J. Inform. Technol. **29**, 187–205 (2014). https://doi.org/10.1057/jit.2014.2
28. Yin, R.K.: Qualitative Research from Start to Finish. The Guilford Press, New York, London (2011)
29. Stebbins, R.A.: Exploratory Research in the Social Sciences. SAGE Publications, Thousand Oaks (2001). https://doi.org/10.4135/9781412984249
30. Eisenhardt, K.M.: Better stories and better constructs: the case for rigor and comparative logic. Acad. Manag. Rev. **16**, 620 (1991). https://doi.org/10.2307/258921
31. Anckar, C.: On the applicability of the most similar systems design and the most different systems design in comparative research. Int. J. Soc. Res. Method **11**, 389–401 (2008). https://doi.org/10.1080/13645570701401552
32. Bowen, G.A.: Naturalistic inquiry and the saturation concept: a research note. Qual. Res. **8**, 137–152 (2008). https://doi.org/10.1177/1468794107085301
33. Bogner, A., Littig, B., Menz, W.: Interviewing Experts, pp. 1–13 (2009). https://doi.org/10.1057/9780230244276_1
34. Braun, V., Clarke, V.: To saturate or not to saturate? Questioning data saturation as a useful concept for thematic analysis and sample-size rationales. Qual. Res. Sport Exerc. Heal. **13**, 201–216 (2021). https://doi.org/10.1080/2159676x.2019.1704846
35. Sandelowski, M.: Sample size in qualitative research. Res. Nurs. Health **18**, 179–183 (1995). https://doi.org/10.1002/nur.4770180211
36. Creswell, J.W., Miller, D.L.: Determining validity in qualitative inquiry. Theor. Pract. **39**, 124–130 (2000). https://doi.org/10.1207/s15430421tip3903_2
37. Vaughn, P., Turner, C.: Decoding via coding: analyzing qualitative text data through thematic coding and survey methodologies. J. Libr. Adm. **56**, 41–51 (2016). https://doi.org/10.1080/01930826.2015.1105035
38. Goodman, L.A.: Snowball sampling. Ann. Math. Stat. **32**, 148–170 (1961)
39. Braun, V., Clarke, V.: Thematic analysis. In: Cooper, H., Camic, P.M., Long, D.L., Panter, A.T., Rindskopf, D., Sher, K.J. (eds.) APA Handbook of Research Methods in Psychology: Research Designs: Quantitative, Qualitative, Neuropsychological, and Biological, vol. 2, pp. 57–71 (2012). https://doi.org/10.1037/13620-004

40. Earley, S.: The digital transformation: staying competitive. IT Prof. **16**, 58–60 (2014). https://doi.org/10.1109/mitp.2014.24
41. Duerr, S., Holotiuk, F., Wagner, H.-T., Beimborn, D., Weitzel, T.: What is digital organizational culture? Insights from exploratory case studies. In: Proceedings of the 51st Hawaii International Conference on System Sciences (2018). https://doi.org/10.24251/hicss.2018.640
42. Hartl, E., Hess, T.: The role of cultural values for digital transformation: insights from a Delphi study. In: Presented at the Twenty-Third Americas Conference on Information Systems, Boston (2017)
43. Li, W., Liu, K., Belitski, M., Ghobadian, A., O'Regan, N.: E-leadership through strategic alignment: an empirical study of small- and medium-sized enterprises in the digital age. J. Inform. Technol. **31**, 185–206 (2016). https://doi.org/10.1057/jit.2016.10
44. Ehlers, U.-D.: Digital leadership in higher education. J. High. Educ. Policy Leadersh. Stud. **1**, 6–14 (2020). https://doi.org/10.29252/johepal.1.3.6
45. Volberda, H.W., Khanagha, S., Baden-Fuller, C., Mihalache, O.R., Birkinshaw, J.: Strategizing in a digital world: overcoming cognitive barriers, reconfiguring routines and introducing new organizational forms. Long Range Plann. **54**, 102110 (2021). https://doi.org/10.1016/j.lrp.2021.102110
46. Caputo, F., Cillo, V., Fiano, F., Pironti, M., Romano, M.: Building T-shaped professionals for mastering digital transformation. J. Bus. Res. **154**, 113309 (2023). https://doi.org/10.1016/j.jbusres.2022.113309
47. Thomas, R., Sargent, L.D., Hardy, C.: Managing organizational change: negotiating meaning and power-resistance relations. Org. Sci. **22**, 22–41 (2011). https://doi.org/10.1287/orsc.1090.0520
48. Aditya, B.R., Ferdiana, R., Kusumawardani, S.S.: A barrier diagnostic framework in process of digital transformation in higher education institutions. J. Appl. Res. High. Educ. **14**, 749–761 (2022). https://doi.org/10.1108/jarhe-12-2020-0454
49. Ashaye, O.R., Irani, Z.: The role of stakeholders in the effective use of e-government resources in public services. Int. J. Inform. Manag. **49**, 253–270 (2019). https://doi.org/10.1016/j.ijinfomgt.2019.05.016
50. Syed, R., Bandara, W., Eden, R.: Public sector digital transformation barriers: a developing country experience. Inf. Polity **28**, 5–27 (2023). https://doi.org/10.3233/ip-220017
51. Pollitt, C.: Structural change and public service performance: international lessons? Public Money Manag. **29**, 285–291 (2009). https://doi.org/10.1080/09540960903205907
52. Sutherland, F., Smith, A.C.: Duality theory and the management of the change–stability paradox. J. Manag. Org. **17**, 534–547 (2011). https://doi.org/10.5172/jmo.2011.17.4.534
53. Clegg, S., Cunha, M.P.E.: Organizational dialectics. In: Smith, W.K., Lewis, M.W., Jarzabkowski, P., Langley, A. (eds.) The Oxford Handbook of Orgaizational Paradox. Oxford University Press (2017)
54. Svahn, F., Mathiassen, L., Lindgren, R.: Embracing digital innovation in incumbent firms: how Volvo cars managed competing concerns. MIS Q. **41**, 239–253 (2017). https://doi.org/10.25300/misq/2017/41.1.12
55. Andriopoulos, C., Gotsi, M.: Methods of paradox. In: Smith, W.K., Lewis, M.W., Jarzabkowski, P., Langley, A. (eds.) The Oxford Handbook of Organizational Paradox, pp. 513–528. Oxford Academic (2017, Online)
56. Smith, W.K., Erez, M., Jarvenpaa, S., Lewis, M.W., Tracey, P.: Adding complexity to theories of paradox, tensions, and dualities of innovation and change: introduction to organization studies special issue on paradox, tensions, and dualities of innovation and change. Org. Stud. **38**, 303–317 (2017). https://doi.org/10.1177/0170840617693560

57. Pettigrew, A.M.: Longitudinal field research on change: theory and practice. Org. Sci. **1**, 267–292 (1990). https://doi.org/10.1287/orsc.1.3.267
58. Soh, C., Yeow, A., Goh, Q., Hansen, R.: Digital transformation: of paradoxical tensions and managerial responses. In: Fortieth International Conference on Information Systems, Munich (2019)

The Evolution of Government Strategies from IT to Digitalization: A Comparative Study of Two Time Periods in Swedish Local Governments

Aya Rizk[1]([⊠]) [ID], Daniel Toll[1] [ID], Leif Sundberg[2] [ID], and Marcus Heidlund[2] [ID]

[1] Linköping University, 581 83 Linköping, Sweden
{aya.rizk,daniel.toll}@liu.se
[2] Mid Sweden University, 851 70 Sundsvall, Sweden
{leif.Sundberg,marcus.heidlund}@miun.se

Abstract. In this paper we explore the evolution of the use of digital technology in the public sector. We do so by analyzing a corpus of IT- and digitalization strategies from Swedish local governments, produced from two time periods, using topic modeling. Our analysis reveals salient topics covered in these two sets of strategies and classifies them into three types: topics that persist across the two periods, topics that are unique to each period, and topics that evolved in content. We suggest that local government strategies became more general and optimistic in terms of the technologies' new opportunities, specific in terms of management practices, and increasingly blurry in terms of organizational and material boundaries. We also provide evidence of digitalization strategies becoming more homogenous in their covered topics than their IT counterparts. By doing so, we contribute to research devoted to analyzing the discursive landscape of digital government by investigating the official content found in these strategies. Thus, we contribute to research devoted to studying policy in order to historically situate contemporary use of digital technologies and its evolution. We conclude the paper with important implications for practice.

Keywords: Digitalization · IT · Public policy · Local government · Topic modeling

1 Introduction

In this paper we examine the evolution of topics related to the use of digital technology in the public sector by studying a corpus of IT- and digitalization strategies from Swedish local government produced over two time periods. By doing so, we contribute to research devoted to analyzing the discursive landscape of digital government by investigating official narratives found in these strategies.

The field of digital government, or e-Government[1], has evolved from a practice-oriented field that emerged in the 1990s, influenced by the success of e-commerce [1], to a

---

[1] In this paper, we use e-government to denote the research area, while digital government to denote the phenomenon of digital technologies transforming government.

© IFIP International Federation for Information Processing 2023
Published by Springer Nature Switzerland AG 2023
I. Lindgren et al. (Eds.): EGOV 2023, LNCS 14130, pp. 431–445, 2023.
https://doi.org/10.1007/978-3-031-41138-0_27

multi-disciplinary research field, influenced by disciplines such as public administration and information systems [2]. In the early years, government activities and scholarly attention focused on the use of information technology (IT), fueled by the possibilities enabled by widespread adoption of the Internet. Since then, the terminology used in both practice and research has shifted: from IT to digitalization, or digital transformation, and from e-Government to digital government. Janowski [3] showed how the focus areas in e-Government research have changed over time in four stages, and Scholl [4] argued that digital government constitutes a second phase as the "d" replaced the "e". These changes are reflected by name changes in research tracks (e.g., the digital government track in the HICSS conference), literature databases (e.g., the digital government reference library, see [5]), thus indicating an evolutionary trajectory. However, it is important to remember that digital government research has also been accused of reproducing techno-optimistic stories about the transformative capabilities of the latest technologies [6]. Thus, there is a need for more empirical-based evidence to outline if the shifts in research focus have been accompanied by actual changes in the way governments perceive and work with digital technologies. In other words, we aim to answer the research question (RQ): *"How have digitalization strategies changed (from IT strategies) over the past two decades?"*.

To answer the RQ, we argue that government policies, investigations, and strategies play a key role in understanding the discursive landscape of digital government. Such documents carry purpose and intention [7], create shared problems, definitions and solutions [8], and stabilize and materialize certain narratives [9, 10]. Therefore, they are important research objects to study the evolution of digital government over time. Our contribution consists of a comparative analysis of IT and digitalization strategies, which are policy documents produced in the Swedish local government context.

This paper is structured as follows: first, we review previous research on digitalization in the public sector and the role of digitalization strategies in the discourse of digital government, concluding with a more elaborate description of why such a comparative analysis is needed. Second, we present the research method, including data collection and analysis using topic modeling. Third, we discuss the findings through an analysis of the topic contents and their distribution over the selected strategies. Finally, we discuss our findings against digital government literature and the wider digitalization literature within information systems.

2 Previous Research

Digitalization strategies have become drivers for the development of digitalization and digital government everywhere. Such strategies exist at the EU level in Europe [11] as well as on the national and regional levels in many countries [e.g., 10, 12]. These types of strategies are typically written as policy documents that set the goals of digital transformation and are designed to instigate the changes that are needed to reap its supposed benefits [7, 13]. Thus, digitalization strategies are reflections of their contemporary settings regarding how digital transformation is, or was, perceived.

Previous research presents conflicting findings regarding how changes in the terminology for digital technology in the public sector have been paralleled with changes in focus, purpose, and narratives associated with the implementation of these technologies.

Ilshammar et al. [14] argued that the shift from "automatic data processing" in the 1960s to "IT" in the 1990s did not entail any shifts in the expected values with the use of these technologies. Most initiatives aimed to increase government efficiency, hence the authors' choice of title, "old wine in new bottles". Melin [15] described the discursive landscape in Swedish action plans of e-Government as rather static, referring to "The emperor's new clothes". Giritli-Nygren [16] identified in the same Swedish action plan that the use of IT is focused on efficiency and increased service. Service and efficiency are common themes in e-government policies where Sundberg [17] highlights a shift towards a more service-dominant logic as the terminology shifted around 2010, from "IT" to "digitalization". Moreover, the two are sometimes expressed together, known as the e-Government paradox [18]. These types of values could be identified in different government policies [e.g., 19, 20]. Heidlund and Sundberg [21] conducted a study of digitalization strategies in Swedish municipalities and found a repository of general and identical optimistic statements, which these authors referred to as the "parrot syndrome." Meanwhile, findings from the Danish context suggest that the values proposed in strategies on the use of digital technology were relatively static between 1994–2016, and the role of e-democracy was minimal during these years [20]. Furthermore, Schou and Hjelholt [22] identified that Danish digitalization strategies were built on the idea of an ideal citizen to whom certain needs have been attached.

The above examples demonstrate previous research on digitalization strategies. However, to the best of our knowledge, research providing insights into the evolution of IT and digitalization strategies over a longer time period is scarce, and the current study aims to fill that research gap. Lately, novel methodologies to study the evolution of digital government have gained popularity [see, e.g., 23]. As outlined in the next section, we contribute to this strand of research by using topic modeling on a corpus of strategies authored in the Swedish public sector.

3 Research Method

In order to identify the respective scopes of IT and digitalization strategies at the local government level, and be able to compare them, we turn to topic modeling. Topic modeling has been increasingly used in IS research in general [24, 25] and in e-government research specifically [7, 26] due to its ability to inductively uncover dominant topics in large text corpora. We apply topic modeling to quantitatively, yet inductively, extract topics from IT strategies published in the early 2000s as well as those from digitalization strategies published in the years around 2020. Extracted topics are used to highlight the main concepts of interest covered by these strategies. By comparing these two sets of strategies, we aim to understand the evolution of digitalization from IT. Hannigan et al. [27] refer to this process as a rendering process in which topic modeling acts as a "means to juxtapose data and theory" (p. 590). As such, this paper also addresses the recent calls for mid-range theorizing within information systems research using topic modeling [28]. Before detailing our data collection and analysis, we first briefly describe the Swedish local government context.

3.1 The Swedish Context

In the Swedish context, the government has emphasized over a long period of time the importance of utilizing the opportunities of digital technology for the benefit of citizens, companies, and organizations in general. In 2004/2005, a proposition made to the government emphasized the need to shift perspective from IT politics for the benefit of society, to politics benefiting an IT-integrated society [29]. In this proposition, the possibilities related to ICTs and their potential consequences in care and education were of particular emphasis. By 2011, Sweden had the vision to "become the best in the world in utilizing digitalization's opportunities" [30, p. 5], which was reiterated in 2017 [31].

Digitalization strategies can exist on several levels of government, as is the case in Sweden. The Swedish local government consists of 290 municipalities, each of which enjoys a high degree of autonomy vis-à-vis the national government. As a result, there are such strategies both on the national and local levels, with the local level strategies being specific versions and interpretations of the goals set by the national level strategy.

3.2 Data Collection

Since the terminology and context describing the documents is shifting, we apply the following demarcations to outline what constitutes an IT/digitalization strategy: The document has a clear focus on IT/digitalization and is authored on a strategic level in the local government. The document must be an overarching strategy for the entire municipality and should not be a general strategy concerning government operations, of which IT/digitalization is a subset. Lastly, the document should be a formal strategic document (i.e., not a PowerPoint presentation or text on a website). After establishing what constitutes an IT/digitalization strategy we collected the two different types of strategies in two phases as follows:

Collection of IT Strategies. All 290 municipalities were contacted by e-mail to request their respective IT strategies for the years 2000–2003 or the closest strategy to that period written by the municipality. The Swedish law requires public authorities to respond to such requests for public documents within a reasonable timeframe, typically within a few weeks. Within two weeks, we received over 90 documents, without the need to send reminders. After this period, our analysis commenced, which meant that any documents received later were not included in this analysis. We excluded plans attached to strategies for the same year (e.g., a plan for IT in education). We also excluded strategies after 2005 to maintain at least a 10-year buffer period between the two sets, since the earliest digitalization strategy in our dataset was published in 2015. This resulted in 71 IT strategies published between 1997 and 2005, with the majority published in the years 2000–2003.

Collection of Digitalization Strategies. The contemporary digitalization strategies were gathered from the official websites of the Swedish municipalities. Opting for a different approach for this dataset stems from our earlier experience where municipalities refer us to their official websites when requesting publicly accessible documents. The search was performed in two steps:

- Using search engines and/or navigation tools on the websites, looking for keywords (in Swedish) such as "digitalization AND policy OR strategy OR plan."
- If no strategic document could be found in step one, we used Google to search for "MunicipalityName AND digitalization," with further refinement as needed.

In case these steps did not lead to any documents, we concluded that the municipality did not have a digitalization strategy. This search also revealed that many municipalities are currently working on formulating this type of strategy, as expressed in, for example, city council protocols. If multiple documents were found (e.g., both a strategy and a policy), the most recent document was used. This process resulted in 85 strategies published between 2015 and 2021. Many of these strategies focused on developing digitalization for several following years (e.g., a strategy published in 2019 for the digital municipality 2020–2023).

3.3 Data Pre-processing

The digitalization strategies were primarily in pdf format (except 3 that were in MS Word formats such as.doc), which were all readily machine-readable; a requirement for the software used for our topic modeling approach. The older IT strategies contained 33 scanned, 31 machine-readable pdf, and 7 MS Word documents. Accordingly, we first applied optical character recognition (OCR) to the scanned documents to make them machine-readable. The following pre-processing steps were applied on both sets of documents using the data science platform RapidMiner:

- Tokenization: transforming the text into a sequence of tokens, or words, and removing special characters and punctuation. However, dashes and slashes were kept, because some of the strategies often contained tokens such as "e-strategy", "IT-strategy" or "IS/IT" which we wanted to keep as single tokens.
- Case transformation: transforming all text to lower case.
- Filter stopwords: removing the most common Swedish stopwords such as "är", "bara", and "inte" (en: "is", "only", "not"). We also removed a list of stopwords customized for this analysis which focused on municipal contexts including all municipality names, the words "stad" and "kommun" (en: "city", "municipality"), along with their variations.
- Stemming: transforming all tokens/words to their stem. E.g., "infrastruktur", "infrastrukturen" and "infrastrukturer" are all stemmed to "infrastruktur" (en: "infrastructure", "the infrastructure", "infrastructures").

The main purpose of these preprocessing activities is to minimize the variations across the corpus and create a more accurate representation of the recurring tokens [25, 28, 32].

3.4 Topic Extraction and Interpretation

In order to choose the best number of topics, we relied on the rate of declining perplexity score (i.e., the trained model's ability to predict words on unseen data). We chose the range of 1 to 20 topics to consider the feasibility of the researchers' interpretation of the output topics [27]. Figure 1 shows the perplexity graph for both corpora. The optimization algorithm showed the lowest decline in perplexity taking place between 11 and 12 topics for the digitalization strategies, and between 9 and 10 for the IT strategies. Accordingly, we chose 11 and 9 topics, respectively. The topics were extracted using the Latent Dirichlet Allocation (LDA) algorithm based on Newman et al. [33].

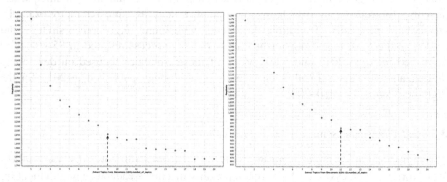

Fig. 1. Relationship between number of topics and perplexity (Left: IT; Right: Digitalization)

For each topic, the top 20 words along with their weights were extracted and interpreted collectively during three workshops by the four co-authors. The first workshop focused on digitalization strategies, where the noise in the topics informed the list of customized stopwords described in the previous section. After adding to that list and rebuilding the model, the second workshop focused on the interpretation of the refined topics and words. The third workshop focused on interpreting topics extracted from the IT strategies. Upon examining the topics and top words, three cases of topic mergers took place under the condition that at least three top words were common across the pair of merged topics. In that case, the weights were summed for the merged topic, and the unique words were added with their original weight. This resulted in 10 and 7 unique topics for digitalization and IT strategies, respectively.

4   Results

Our analysis suggests that while some topics are unique to each period, other topics persist and evolve in their focus. IT strategies are clearly focused on material elements of IT, such as the broadband infrastructure and security of files and programs on PCs. They also focused on the administration and governance in the – then emerging – IT units, with frequent use of words such as *system responsible* and *system owner*. Whereas digitalization strategies included topics dedicated to the economical and budgetary aspects of digitalization, and relating the local level to other levels, such as the national. Figure 2 illustrates the relationship between the topics now and then (for a list of topics and associated words, see the Appendix). It is important to note here that the arrows do not indicate any causal relationship between topics, they represent our interpretation of how the topics evolved over time. Following the figure, these topics are described.

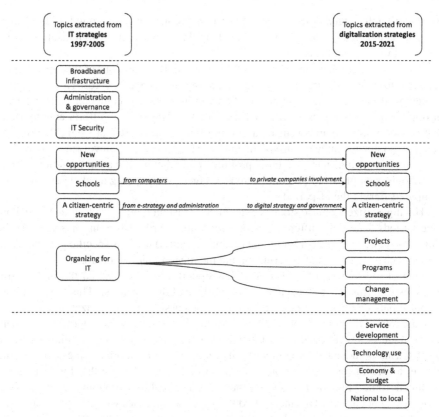

Fig. 2. Topics evolution from IT to digitalization strategies

The first three topics that can be seen on top of Fig. 2 are specific to the IT-strategies, i.e., they are not observed in the later digitalization strategies. The first of these, "Broadband infrastructure" contains words that are focused on internet and the underlying infrastructure, reflecting the fact that broadband development was a focus area in Sweden in the early 2000s. The topic "Administration & governance" includes words such as "system", "responsibility" and "system owner", thus being focused on system management procedures in municipalities. The third topic unique to the IT strategies is "IT Security", that is focused on security and personal responsibility in relation to using IT on an individual user level and password management.

Some of the topics persist over time, from IT strategies to digitalization strategies. One of the these we refer to as "Organizing for IT", which handles the organizational activities needed to accomplish related goals. While this topic is expressed in a single topic in IT strategies, we observed that there are three related topics in the corresponding digitalization strategies, namely: projects, programs, and change management. In projects, "digitalization work" is a frequent term, along with the notions of "responsibility", "follow-up" and "support". In programs, target groups and values associated with such programs are in focus. In change management, application (of technology), current state, activities, and concerns with such activities are frequently mentioned. It is

438   A. Rizk et al.

worth noting that standardization is frequently mentioned in Organizing for IT, whereas no equivalent has appeared in the top words in the corresponding digitalization topics (or any other topic in the corpus).

"Schools" is another topic that persists over time. Both versions of the topic include students, teachers, schools, and pedagogy among the frequent words. However, in IT strategies, these words are complemented by computers and computer halls, whereas in digitalization strategies, terms such as agenda, company and efforts emerge (note that the term "insats" in Swedish can be translated to "efforts" or "stake"). With the potential double meaning of "insats" in mind, we interpret that the involvement of private companies in schools has been more prominent and that having a digitalization agenda for schools is emphasized (in contrast to focus on e.g., equipping local classrooms with computers during the IT period).

Having a citizen-centric strategy is another persistent topic in such strategies in both time periods. The only difference between the top words describing this topic is the shift from general administration (and e-administration) towards specific governmental bodies such as the national government and the local municipal boards.

One of the topics, referred to as "New opportunities" contained the highest frequencies of terms most associated with both IT and digitalization. This topic (in both corpora) puts emphasis on new opportunities or possibilities, organization and development. While the topic may seem very similar in both analyses in terms of frequent terms, there is a difference in its relative weight to the other topics within the same corpus. This is indicated by comparing its relative weight to other topics (Fig. 3) and by the document-topic predictions (Fig. 4) in both corpora. Note that Fig. 4 presents document-topic predictions based on the highest probability (dominance) for a given topic in said document. This means two things: a) some topics will not appear in Fig. 4 if no document is predicted to be primarily discussing that topic, and b) each document will be counted towards only one topic based on this highest probability, even if other topics are present in the document.

Fig. 3. Avg. Weighted topics (Left: IT; Right: Digitalization)

The last four topics are specific to digitalization strategies. The first of these is "Service development", a topic focused on services, and methods, leadership and needs related to developing services. The topic "Technology use" is a topic that generally denotes words pertaining to technology and the use of technology. "Economy & budget" is a topic that contains both financial words and words such as "responsibility",

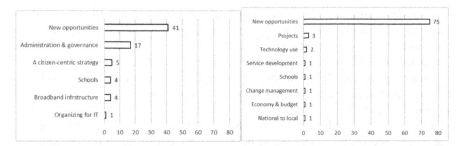

Fig. 4. Number of documents predicted to belong to topics (Left: IT; Right: Digitalization)

"digitalization overview" and "current", seemingly indicating that it is common for digitalization strategies to discuss the costs of digitalization at current and in the future. Finally, the topic "National to local" is a topic that mentions other levels of government (pan-national, national, and regional) as well as other influential institutions that affect policymaking. Thus, the digitalization strategies do not only discuss the respective municipalities in a vacuum, rather, the strategies are related to a wider societal context.

5   Discussion

As our analysis suggests, digitalization is neither old wine in new bottles nor a completely new phenomenon. It can be argued that it is an evolution from IT with both a difference in degree and a difference in kind. The difference in kind can be represented by the topics distinct to each period, while the degree in difference by the topics that persist and change in scope.

At first glance, the results make intuitive sense. For example, it is unsurprising to see that the strategies from twenty years ago were preoccupied with the development of broadband infrastructure. This corroborates well with the history of societal development in Sweden, where there was a push in the late 1990s and early 2000s to rapidly develop Internet infrastructure [34, 35], in combination with initiatives to increase adoption of computers by citizens. Consequently, it is only natural that this topic should have died down since then. Another aspect of this evolution is the visibility of topics focusing on service development and technology use after said infrastructure has been developed as a precondition [36].

On the other hand, the lack of an equivalent security topic in the digitalization strategies seemed surprising at first. There are two potential explanations for this observation. First, the notion of IT security has evolved from focusing on specific users and password protected information to a much broader issue of cybersecurity that is not addressed in digitalization policy anymore. Rather, there are other policy documents that address that very topic in detail. Second, the issue might still be addressed in digitalization strategies, yet, not in the frequency required to be picked up by the topic modeling algorithm. Our insights from the data collection process suggest that the former explanation is more plausible, as IT strategies would normally be accompanied by IT plans, while the later digitalization strategies have various other attachments, including cybersecurity policies.

Meanwhile, there are also differences between the two corpora that suggest that digitalization draws more from regional, national, and pan-national strategies than the IT counterparts. Keywords such as "regional", "national" and "europ*" refer to policies formulated at higher levels of government, such as the digital agendas of the European Commission [37, 38] or the National Swedish digitalization strategy [31]. Such influence from other levels of government can also be observed in another topic "New opportunities", albeit indirectly.

We noted in our results that the topic "New opportunities" persisted between the two datasets and became even more prevalent in the recent one (in digitalization strategies). The focus on "new opportunities" goes back to the official Swedish IT and digitalization strategies, which state that "The overarching goal is that Sweden shall be the best in the world at utilizing the opportunities created by digitalization." [31, p. 6]. As such, the relative increase in the "New opportunities" topic is likely a result of the more visceral top-down push from the Swedish government regarding digitalization, which was established in the years preceding the digitalization strategies [10]. This lends credence to previous research that claims that this type of content exhibits a state of equilibrium, as suggested by Persson et al. [20]; what can be referred to as "old wine in new bottles" [14] or "the emperor's new clothes" [15] highlighting a reoccurring rhetoric but the class of technology changes (e.g., IT to digitalization). However, since the goal of utilizing the new opportunities created by digitalization is an abstract goal, the recreation of this goal on the local level possibly makes these strategies difficult to operationalize on the local level. As the landscape of digital technologies is far from static, and thus the prevalence of this topic can also be seen as a reflection of the fact that municipalities find themselves in a chronic state of catching up with the latest opportunities.

On the other hand, we observe an evolution towards more specific digitalization strategies in terms of working practices. This can be reasoned from the comparison of the IT strategy topic "Organizing for IT", which we consider related to the digitalization strategy topics "Projects", "Programs" and "Change management". Based on the similarity between these topics, we view the latter ones as more specific instances of the broader theme of "Organizing for IT" that has emerged over the last decades. In the early 2000s, the role of IT in organizations was still unclear, and implementation and management of IT was similar (or, usually conducted by an IT-department). In the years since, however, the area of IT, or digitalization, has become more pervasive and prevalent for most, if not all parts of organizations, with more well-established practices. It can also be interpreted that there is a recent focus on the (articulation of) value of digital technology realized through programs, as opposed to earlier strategies [19, 20].

Notably, there also exists a trend towards a "service" ideal associated with digitalization (see, [17]). A few years after the millennium shift, municipalities aimed to become "24h governments", referring to increasing the availability of digital (or, e-) services published via their web sites [36, 39]. Thus, where the IT strategies emphasized physical aspects such as broadband and infrastructure, the digitalization strategies are more concerned with intangibles. Echoing Löwgren and Stolterman's [40] notion of the digital as a material without qualities, digitalization is transcending the physical to a higher degree than IT and is thus associated with less borders and more blurriness. This blurriness does not only apply to the physical vs intangible but also to the boundaries between local and national governments. A potential concern here is that national discourses are incorporated on a local level without any translation, which may hamper the possibilities to locally adapt the content of these strategies.

6 Conclusions, Limitations and Future Research

In this study, we sought to answer the research question: *"How have digitalization strategies changed (from IT strategies) over the past two decades?"* Based on our analysis we observe the following changes. First, digitalization strategies are more homogenous than IT strategies, indicating that local government strategies on digitalization are becoming more similar to one another, reinforcing the national discourse concerning digitalization. Second, the practices of managing digitalization have become more specific over time, with digitalization strategies presenting a more nuanced picture of how digitalization is organized. Third, we note that strategies over time have become blurry regarding organizational and material boundaries. The newer digitalization strategies mentioned other levels of government, the European union and the private sector, thus relating the strategy to organizations other than the local government in question. Similarly, the older IT strategies present a clearer distinction between the material aspects of digitalization (such as infrastructure) and e.g., software. In the digitalization strategies, however, these distinctions are not as present, indicating that digitalization over time has become a more amorphous phenomenon where these different aspects are intermingled.

By performing topic modeling on a corpus of IT- and digitalization strategies, we contribute to research and practice as follows. First, we contribute to a research stream devoted to studying policy to historically situate contemporary use of digital technologies in its evolution. By doing so, this study constitutes an important contribution of both a snapshot of stories about digitalization, and how they relate to previous ideas about the use of technology in the public sector.

Second, we present a novel methodological approach to studying the evolution of narratives associated with the use of digital technology in the public sector. The use of topic modeling enables us to process large numbers of policy documents and retrieve an overview of the topics linking such documents together and their respective representations of terms or words.

Third, our study has important implications for practice. As we noted the trend towards increasingly homogeneous "general" content in the policies, streamlined with national and pan-national ideas, we ponder what value these documents provide to actual operations in the local governments? While digitalization entails more intangible qualities than "IT", we encourage policymakers to aim to be more specific and focus on local challenges; e.g., to find ways to translate general ideas about digitalization to local conditions.

The dataset included in this study has some inherent limitations. For instance, the different municipalities release their strategies in different years, resulting in both sets being published over extended periods, risking that the strategies belonging to the same corpus were handling different narratives. We mitigated this risk by ensuring a 10-year gap between both sets. The datasets also do not represent strategies from the same set of municipalities, even though there is a large overlap. Our assessment is that given the overarching scope of this paper, such lack of 1:1 mapping is not crucial. However, we suggest that future research include a qualitative analysis of a sample of the chosen strategies where the comparison would consider the specific evolution of the same municipality's IT-digital discourse. The selection of these municipalities can be informed by our analysis, for example, by choosing municipalities covering a wide range of topics for maximum variation.

Appendix: Topic Interpretations and Top Words[2]

IT strategies		Digitalization strategies	
Topic	Top words	Topic	Top words
Broadband infrastructure	internet, infrastructure, urban areas, capacity, broadband *nät, infrastruktur, tätort, kapacitet, bredband*	Service Development	Service, fulfill, way of working, method, leadership *tjänst, uppfylla, arbetssätt, metod, ledning*
Administration and governance	System, operation, responsib*, system owner, collective *system, drift, ansvar, systemägare, gemensam*	Technology use	Technology, technical, system, unit, functions, use* *teknik, teknisk, system, enhet, fungerar, använd*
IT security	User, information, responsib*, password, staff *användare, information, ansvar, lösenord, personal*	Economy and budget	responsib*, finance, conducted, estimat*, exist* *ansvar, finansiering, genomfört, beräkna, befint*
New opportunities	opportunit*, organization*, develop*, goal, new *möjlig, verksam, utveckling, mål, nya*	New opportunities	Service, organization*, opportunit*, develop*, condition, new *tjänst, verksamhet, möj, utveckling, förutsättning, nya*
Schools	Student*, school, computer, pedagogical, child* *elev, skolan, dator, pedagogisk, barn*	Schools	Agenda, student, teacher, company, effort, child* *agenda, elev, lärare, företag, insats, barn*

(continued)

[2] A sample of the top words are selected for each topic based primarily on their weight. The words are presented in English (authors' translation) and Swedish (original). Since the words are stemmed, an asterisk * is added to the English word to indicate possible variations (e.g., the responsib* stems from words such as responsible, responsibility and responsibilities.

(*continued*)

IT strategies		Digitalization strategies	
Topic	Top words	Topic	Top words
A citizen-centric strategy	Citizen, administration, e-strategy, proposal[a] *medborgare, förvaltning, e-strategi, förslag, tjänstutlåtande*	A citizen-centric strategy	National government, digitalization strategy, citizen, municipal board, open* *regering, digitaliseringsstrategi, medborgare, kommunstyrelse, öpp*
Organizing for IT	Systematic, before, goal, function, activity *systematisk, inför, målet, funktion, aktivitet*	Projects	Digitalization work, project, responsib*, follow-up, support *digitaliseringsarbet, projekt, ansvar, uppföljning, stöd*
		Programs	Service, program, effect, target group, value *service, program, effekt, målgrupp, värd*
		Change management	Concern*, application, change, proposal, activity, focus area *koncern, tillämpning, förändring, förslag, aktivitet, fokusområde*
		National to local	Region, inhabitant, national, government, SALAR[b], external environment, local, europ* *region, invånare, nationell, regering, skl, omvärld, lokal, europ*

[a]Both Swedish terms "förslag" and "tjänsteutlåtande" can be translated to the English term "proposal". The difference is that "förslag" is a general suggestion while "tjänsteutlåtande" is a specific to proposals by public servants, typically preceding a decision.
[b]The Swedish Association of Local Authorities and Regions, an interest organization for local and regional governments.

References

1. Grönlund, Å., Horan, T.A.: Introducing e-gov: history, definitions, and issues. Commun. Assoc. Inf. Syst. **15**(1), 39 (2005)

2. Heeks, R., Bailur, S.: Analyzing e-government research: perspectives, philosophies, theories, methods, and practice. Gov. Inf. Q. **24**(2), 243–265 (2007)
3. Janowski, T.: Digital government evolution: from transformation to contextualization. Gov. Inf. Q. **32**(3), 221–236 (2015)
4. Scholl, H.J.: Digital government: looking back and ahead on a fascinating domain of research and practice. Digit. Gov.: Res. Pract. **1**(1), 1–12 (2020)
5. Scholl, H.J.: The digital government reference library (DGRL) and its potential formative impact on digital government research (DGR). Gov. Inf. Q. **38**(4), 101613 (2021)
6. Bannister, F., Connolly, R.: Forward to the past: lessons for the future of e-government from the story so far. Inf. Polity **17**(3–4), 211–226 (2012)
7. Guenduez, A.A., Mettler, T.: Strategically constructed narratives on artificial intelligence: what stories are told in governmental artificial intelligence policies? Gov. Inf. Q. **40**, 101719 (2022)
8. Sundberg, L.: If digitalization is the solution, what is the problem?. In: Papers Presented at the 19th European Conference on Digital Government ECDG 2019, pp. 136–143 (2019)
9. Lindberg, J., Kvist, E., Lindgren, S.: The ongoing and collective character of digital care for older people: moving beyond techno-determinism in government policy. J. Technol. Hum. Serv. **40**(4), 357–378 (2022)
10. Nyhlén, S., Gidlund, K.L.: In conversation with digitalization: myths, fiction or professional imagining? Inf. Polity **27**, 1–11 (2022)
11. European Commission: European Commission Digital Strategy. The European Commission (2022). https://ec.europa.eu/info/publications/EC-Digital-Strategy_en
12. Kinnunen, J., Androniceanu, A., Georgescu, I.: Digitalization of EU countries: a clusterwise analysis. In: Proceedings of the 13rd International Management Conference: Management Strategies for High Performance, pp. 1–12 (2019)
13. Dolfsma, W., Seo, D.: Government policy and technological innovation—A suggested typology. Technovation **33**(6–7), 173–179 (2013)
14. Ilshammar, L., Bjurström, A., Grönlund, Å.: Public e-services in Sweden: old wine in new bottles? Scand. J. Inf. Syst. **17**(2), 3 (2005)
15. Melin, U.: The emperor's new clothes? Analysing the Swedish action plan for e-government. Int. J. Public Inf. Syst. **5**(2), 97–122 (2009)
16. Giritli Nygren, K.: The rhetoric of e-government management and the reality of e-government work: the Swedish action plan for e-government considered. Int. J. Public Inf. Syst. **2009**(2), 135–146 (2009)
17. Sundberg, L.: From automatic data processing to digitalization: what is past is prologue. In: Lindgren, I., et al. (eds.) EGOV 2019. LNCS, vol. 11685, pp. 31–42. Springer, Cham (2019). https://doi.org/10.1007/978-3-030-27325-5_3
18. Bertot, J.C., Jaeger, P.T.: The E-Government paradox: better customer service doesn't necessarily cost less. Gov. Inf. Q. **2**(25), 149–154 (2008)
19. Toll, D., Lindgren, I., Melin, U., Madsen, C.Ø.: Values, benefits, considerations and risks of AI in government: a study of AI policy documents in Sweden. eJournal eDemocracy Open Gov. **12**(1), 40–60 (2020)
20. Persson, J.S., Reinwald, A.K., Skorve, E., Nielsen, P.A.: Value positions in e-government strategies: Something is (not) changing in the state of Denmark. In: 25th European Conference on Information Systems, pp. 904–917. The Association for Information Systems (AIS) (2017)
21. Heidlund, M., Sundberg, L.: What is the value of digitalization? Strategic narratives in local government. Inf. Polity 1–17 (2023, preprint)
22. Schou, J., Hjelholt, M.: Digitalizing the welfare state: citizenship discourses in Danish digitalization strategies from 2002 to 2015. Critical Policy Stud. **13**(1), 3–22 (2019)
23. Puron-Cid, G., Villaseñor-García, E.A.: Applying neural networks analysis to assess digital government evolution. Gov. Inf. Q. **40**, 101811 (2023)

24. Jeyaraj, A., Zadeh, A.H.: Evolution of information systems research: insights from topic modeling. Inf. Manag. **57**(4), 103207 (2020)
25. Müller, O., Junglas, I., Brocke, J.V., Debortoli, S.: Utilizing big data analytics for information systems research: challenges, promises and guidelines. Eur. J. Inf. Syst. **25**(4), 289–302 (2016)
26. Isoaho, K., Gritsenko, D., Mäkelä, E.: Topic modeling and text analysis for qualitative policy research. Policy Stud. J. **49**(1), 300–324 (2021)
27. Hannigan, T.R., et al.: Topic modeling in management research: rendering new theory from textual data. Acad. Manag. Ann. **13**(2), 586–632 (2019)
28. Rizk, A., Elragal, A.: Data science: developing theoretical contributions in information systems via text analytics. J. Big Data **7**, 1–26 (2020)
29. The Swedish Government Offices: Från IT-politik för samhället till politik för IT-samhället (2005). https://www.regeringen.se/rattsliga-dokument/proposition/2005/07/prop.-200405175. Accessed 20 Mar 2023
30. The Swedish Government Offices: Med medborgaren i centrum Regeringens strategi för en digitalt samverkande statsförvaltning. Näringsdepartementet (2012)
31. The Swedish Government Offices: För ett hållbart digitaliserat Sverige – en digitaliseringsstrategi. The Swedish Government Offices (2017). https://digitaliseringsradet.se/media/1191/digitaliseringsstrategin_slutlig_170518-2.pdf. Accessed 14 Nov 2022
32. Debortoli, S., Müller, O., Junglas, I., Vom Brocke, J.: Text mining for information systems researchers: an annotated topic modeling tutorial. Commun. Assoc. Inf. Syst. (CAIS) **39**(1), 7 (2016)
33. Newman, D., Asuncion, A., Smyth, P., Welling, M.: Distributed algorithms for topic models. J. Mach. Learn. Res. **10**(8), 1801–1828 (2009)
34. Hansteen, K.: Norwegian and Swedish broadband initiatives (1999–2005). Hoykom report, no. 505 (2005)
35. The Swedish Government Offices: Utredningen Bredband 2013. SOU 2008:40: Bredband till hela landet (2008)
36. The IT Commission: SOU 2003:55: Digitala tjänster - hur då? En IT-politik för resultat och nytta. Näringsdepartementet (2003)
37. European Commission: Digital Europe Program (2018). https://ec.europa.eu/commission/presscorner/detail/en/IP_18_4043
38. European Commission: Digital Europe Program (2021). https://ec.europa.eu/commission/presscorner/detail/en/ip_21_5863
39. The 24-hour Delegation: SOU 2005:119: e-tjänster för ett enklare och öppnare samhälle. Finansdepartementet (2005)
40. Löwgren, J., Stolterman, E.: Thoughtful Interaction Design: A Design Perspective on Information Technology. MIT Press, Cambridge (2004)

Exploring Digital Innovation Paths in Healthcare: The Case of a Large Swedish Healthcare Organization

Johan Magnusson$^{(\boxtimes)}$ [ID], Andrea Gajic [ID], Leman Isik [ID], and Christina Nilsson [ID]

Swedish Center for Digital Innovation, University of Gothenburg, Gothenburg, Sweden
{johan.magnusson,andrea.gajic,christina.nilsson}@ait.gu.se,
leman.isik@gu.se

Abstract. Digital innovation has been advocated as bringing new opportunities to organizations. At the same time, here is still a gap of empirical research on the paths, i.e., choices in directions manifested over time, of digital innovation in public sector healthcare. In this study, we aim to fill this gap through analyzing a complete set of three years of centrally funded innovation projects in a large incumbent healthcare organization. Using a previously proposed framework combining the Resource Based View and Organizational Ambidexterity into a positioning of digital innovation opportunity, we investigate the paths of digital innovation. The findings show that the predominant path of digital innovation lies in exploitative innovation through utilizing internal and shared resources. In contrast with the literature the use of complementary assets in the form of external resources i.e., engaging customers and other external parties in value creation, is only found in one of the projects. We describe this as a case of path dependency, where the organization avoids tapping into some of the core opportunities in digital innovation. This is discussed in relation to the digital innovation literature and the future paths of digital innovation in public sector healthcare.

Keywords: Digital Innovation · Digital Transformation · Digital Opportunities · Path

1 Introduction

Digital transformation, here understood in line with Hanelt et al. [1] as the organizational change brought about through the utilization of digital solutions is opening a plethora of new opportunities. Said opportunities lie both in increased operational excellence and in new value creation and revenue streams [2]. As noted by Chanias et al. [3] and their study of emergent digital transformation strategies, the direction sought in terms of operational excellence or new value offerings constitutes a core aspect of the aspired path of digital transformation [4, 5]. Increased emphasis on digital transformation brings an increased emphasis on digital innovation [6].

© IFIP International Federation for Information Processing 2023
Published by Springer Nature Switzerland AG 2023
I. Lindgren et al. (Eds.): EGOV 2023, LNCS 14130, pp. 446–461, 2023.
https://doi.org/10.1007/978-3-031-41138-0_28

Digital innovation, i.e., "the creation or adoption, and exploitation of an inherently unbounded, value-adding novelty (e.g., product, service, process, or business model) through the incorporation of digital technology" [7] has been advocated as bringing new opportunities to organizations. Digital innovation is innately different from previous forms of innovation, through introducing a new logic [8]. Core to this new logic are the notions of unbounded, open-ended and emergent as characteristics for the new innovation landscape [9]. In other words, digital innovation differs from previous forms of innovation through tapping into the innate characteristics of digital materiality [10].

Oberländer et al. [11] studied organizations that existed before the digital transformation era to investigate how they are adapting to the changes brought about by digital solutions. The study focused on how these organizations are resourcing and directing their innovation projects to take advantage of the new opportunities created by digital innovation. According to Oberländer et al., projects may be either exploitative or explorative, i.e., they could either be focused on exploiting existing opportunities (e.g., increased efficiency of existing operations) or exploring new opportunities (e.g., innovation of new value creation opportunities). This differentiation, stemming from the organizational ambidexterity literature has previously been widely studied within the information systems discipline [12–14]. Oberländer et al. further adds the dimension of resources, where the innovation initiative may use internal (e.g., employees), shared (e.g., employees and customers) or external (e.g., customers) resources. We pose that these two dimensions (activity and resources) constitute a feasible basis for assessing the paths of digital innovation.

Healthcare has experienced a surge in digital innovation during the past decade. From having had a predominant focus on infrastructural information systems such as electronic patient records and hospital management systems [15, 16], the field of e-health has increased its emphasis on more lightweight digital solutions [17], i.e., primarily patient-centric solutions built on top of the existing (or completely stand-alone) digital infrastructure. As noted by Jovanovic et al. [18] this type of digital innovation has significantly supported the handling of recent disruptive events such as the COVID-19 pandemic. Despite the intricate and apparent value of digital innovation in healthcare, little is still known about its changing role in healthcare [19].

Albeit a core aspect of digital transformation strategy the path, i.e., choices in directions manifested over time, of digital innovation has so far received only limited empirical attention within research [4, 5]. As noted by Magnusson et al. [12], further research is needed to understand the development of digital innovation and Chanias et al. [3] highlight the need for more longitudinal studies of the same. Based on this brief rationale, the research question we answer in this study is:

What are the current paths of digital innovation in healthcare?

We answer the question through a retrospective longitudinal, three-year study of a healthcare organization's centralized innovation portfolio, seeing the decision to fund as a starting point of digital innovation. The initiatives are analyzed through Oberländer et al.'s [11] differentiation between the type of activity (exploit/explore) and resourcing (internal/shared/external). We employ Oberländer's methodology to analyze the paths of digital innovation within the organization. We contribute to previous research through answering the calls from Oberländer et al. [11] on future studies of digital opportunity, as well as Chanias et al. [3] balancing the prioritization of efficiency and innovation during the process of digital transformation.

The paper is organized accordingly: After this brief introduction, we present the previous findings in the form of a review of the digital innovation literature and the theoretical framing in a depiction of the analytical framework used. This is followed by the method of the study, where the details on data collection and analysis are presented. After this we present the results of the study, showing the direction of intent and its development over time. This is followed by a discussion, where the findings are contrasted with previous findings, leading up to a conclusion and directions for future research.

2   Previous Research and Theoretical Framing

Since its inception, the concept of digital innovation has been subject to various interpretations and definitions. As found in Hund et al. [7] and their review of 227 papers in eight disciplines, multiple studies refrain from making an explicit definition of the concept. Of these reviewed papers only 29 provide an explicit definition to digital innovation. There is also significant diversity in how digital innovation is defined, primarily in terms of what is emphasized. While Nambisan et al. maintains a focus on the process of innovation, seeing digital innovation as a process of innovation supported by digital technology, Yoo et al. [8] see it as a type of new products infused with digital technology. In this study, we adhere to the definition as offered by Hund et al. [7] in seeing digital innovation as "the creation or adoption, and exploitation of an inherently unbounded, value-adding novelty (e.g., product, service, process, or business model) through the incorporation of digital technology".

Digital innovation has been suggested as one of the ways for organizations to meet the challenges associated with our times [20], and there is a plethora of studies on digital innovation in various disciplines [6, 7, 21, 22]. In relation to digital innovation in healthcare, there have been numerous studies that highlight its emerging importance and potential in solving significant challenges [15, 18, 23].

Following the ideas of Hanelt et al. [1] digital innovation can be utilized in two basic ways: generating new opportunities and improving existing ones. These two trajectories correspond to the organizational ambidexterity notions of activities for exploration or exploitation [24–26]. Through the previous research, we see exploration as being equated with the generation of new opportunities, and exploitation with the improvement of existing opportunities [12].

Several studies have shown the tendency for digital innovation to focus on exploitation rather than exploration [12]. An empirical study in the public sector displayed that 84% of the portfolio's digital projects were attributable to internal efficiency [5]. In relation to the findings from Wu et al. [27], incumbent organizations display a tendency where the path of their utilization of technology is path dependent on the complementary assets of the organization. In other words, previous investments are expected to set an organization on a particular path in terms of digital innovation, decreasing explorative activities related to new technology.

In addition to the dimension of activities from Hanelt et al. [1] and the organizational ambidexterity literature, Oberländer et al. [11] introduces the dimension of resources. Here, we see that digital innovation may utilize resources that are either internal, shared or external. Key to Oberländer's view of resources is that they constitute the core elements of how value is created in the digital innovation.

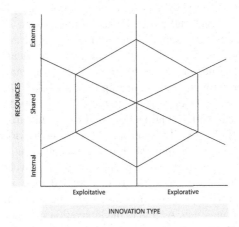

Fig. 1. Conceptual framework employed in the study (from Oberländer et al., [11])

In terms of the internal, these resources refer to resources that are owned by the organization in question, i.e., internal users of the digital innovation. We may think of a digital innovation such as an app for making reservations for meeting-rooms or facilities in the corporate office. In terms of the shared resources, value is created through an interplay of internal and external resources, such as in the case of a digital health solution where the physicians consult the patients, and the patients give feedback that is utilized for quality assurance (both internal and external). External resources refer to value creation that is completely external to the organization in question, such as solutions where value creation is externalized yet captured by the organization in question in the form of social media platforms et cetera. Previous studies in healthcare such as Enticot et al., show the importance of involvement and collaboration with stakeholders and other actors outside the organization to succeed in digital innovation. Likewise, Temiz et al. [28] in a study conducted during the covid-19 pandemic find that gathering interdisciplinary teams both from the public and private sectors to develop solutions, resulted in significant growth in digital healthcare. In line with Oberländer et al. [11], we use these two dimensions, activities, and resources, to assess the paths of digital innovation in a portfolio of digital innovation projects as displayed in Fig. 1. The types of activities and resources are mutually exclusive, and the types of activities are exploitative innovation vs explorative innovation.

3 Method

This study focuses on the digital innovation projects centrally coordinated and funded in one of Sweden's largest healthcare organizations. The organization has a budget of 6,6 billion € and employs 56 000 across various organizational levels. The organization cater to the healthcare needs of over two million citizens (20% of the national population). The healthcare services offered by the organization encompass all aspects of acute care, primary care, specialist care and public health among others. The central innovation fund was created in late 2016, supports innovation in healthcare, is annually financed with €2 million by the political healthcare board in the organization.

The innovation fund has the aim to facilitate "bottom-up innovation". This is done by two calls per year, with co-workers having the possibility of proposing projects in two different categories. Category 1 refers to projects with a budget of under €10 000, and category 2 to projects (often continuations or direct results from category 1 projects) with a budget up to €150 000. These projects may have previously received funding from various sources and may require additional financing, leading to an application to the innovation fund. Alternatively, some projects may exclusively obtain funding from the innovation fund. Thus, we aim to clarify that the budgetary resources available can exceed the amount received from the innovation fund. The innovation fund comprises the empirical selection of our study. Access to the innovation project charters was provided through members of the research team being employed in the organization in parallel with their research engagement. The first call of the innovation fund was given in 2017, and in 2018 a new, digital administrative system was implemented for assessment and approval of innovation projects. It was through this platform that the research team accessed the data for the purposes of this research, i.e., projects funded in 2017 were omitted from the sample.

The research team has examined documents related to the innovation fund, where it is established that the innovation fund aligns with the organization's objectives regarding innovation. Data was collected in the form of all formal documents (business-cases, project charters and budgets) of innovation projects that had been approved for funding during the past three years (Table 1). Hence, in focus for this research is the innovation funds project portfolio. In addition to this, we collected secondary data in the form of policies and strategies for the innovation fund to sensitize ourselves with contextual information.

Table 1. Overview of collected data.

	2019	2020	2021
# Project charters	36	59	54
Total budget	€1,8M	€2,8M	€1,9M

After the data collection, we started the coding process. We organized our coding schema into two main categories—background information and digital opportunity class. Background information included codes such as portfolio, objective, budget, involved parties, and digital technology, among others. Digital opportunity class nested codes such as innovation types and resource types, which were adopted from previous research on this topic. In the framework of this research, we distinguish two innovation types, exploitative and explorative (with three recognized resource types: internal, shared and external [11]. Both innovation types and resource types with more detailed descriptions for the coding are presented in Table 2. The portfolio was also examined by nominal versus monetary value, large versus small projects and solitary versus collaborative projects to identify additional patterns.

Table 2. Overview of coding scheme.

Type of Resources	
Internal	Digital innovation constitutes a basis for internal value creation (solution intended for solely internal use, e.g., sick-leave registration app)
Shared	Digital innovation constitutes an interface between internal and external value creation (solution shared between internal and external parties, e.g., digital consultations with reviews conducted by the patients)
External	Digital innovation constitutes an externalization of value creation by external parties (solution intended for solely external use, e.g. Facebook)
Type of Innovation	
Exploitative	Projects primarily focused on exploiting existing opportunities (i.e., increased efficiency as effect goal)
Explorative	Projects primarily focused on exploring new opportunities (i.e., sensing, experimenting, learning)

Coding was conducted by three researchers of the author team. All the codes were logged into an Excel file, which was shared by the authors. The coding process started with three randomly sampled project charters, resulting in an inter-coder reliability scoring below 70% [29]. Given this result, the coding was continued in parallel for three other projects until reaching inter-coder reliability of 100%. After this, the remaining projects were evenly distributed to the three researchers for individual coding. During the coding process, we had general discussions with the whole author team to check the progress and discuss preliminary results. For example, during our meetings, we realized that an innovation initiative could be a first-time project or a continuation project. As such, we refined our coding schema to include this new category and re-coded the projects to capture this information. After the coding was completed, we explored the data to find meaningful representations of patterns that would help us answer our research question and be of value to future research. As such, we engaged in descriptive analyses of our data. During the data analyses, we looked for patterns and relations that could directly relate to Oberländer's [11] framework and for the background data.

4 Results

The results are presented in two sections. First, we present a general overview of the results, including descriptive statistics of frequencies and patterns. Then, we present the findings related to the path of digital innovation in healthcare.

4.1 Digital Innovation Projects in Healthcare

Table 3 contains an overview of the descriptive characteristics of the results.

Table 3. Descriptive results.

	2019	2020	2021
Number of projects	36	59	54
Number of digital innovation projects	24	43	42
Percentage digital innovation	67%	73%	78%
Portfolio turnover (ratio of projects previously not funded by the platform)	69%	63%	44%
Average budget per projects	€52 000	€44 000	€35 000

The sample is comprised of two types of projects, referred to as single and continuation. The single projects are one-off projects that do not result in continued applications for centralized funding. The reason said projects are not continued may be either that the results were not promising enough or that the results were promising enough to warrant local funding for continuation. With this data not being part of the sample, we are restricted from further analysis. The continuation projects are projects with a tradition of centralized funding, i.e., they have been funded in multiple iterations by the central fund. The innovation fund enables applying for the same project in different phases, which means that the same project can be granted funding for several rounds and years.

The innovation portfolio includes 149 projects. In terms of digital innovation, these comprise 73% of the total projects. In other words, digital innovation is the dominant form of innovation in the centrally funded projects over the period. The portfolio displays an increase in the level of digital innovation over the period 2019–2021, from 67% to 78%. This increase indicates an increasing prevalence of digital innovation, with a 179% increase in the frequency of digital innovation from 2019 to 2020. We attribute this sharp increase to the COVID-19 pandemic, which raised the awareness of the need for digital innovation in the organization. At the same time, we see a decrease in the average size of each project in the portfolio, from €52 000 to €35 000 along with a decrease in portfolio turnover from 69% to 44%, attributable to the increased tendency to focus centralized funding on the continuation of projects that had previously been funded.

To add further nuance and richness to the paper, we include some examples of projects based on classification. With some projects being active and under intellectual property arrangements that refrain from complete transparency, we have aspired to obscure some of the descriptions (Table 4).

Table 4. Selection of examples of digital innovations studied.

Categorization	Brief description
Explorative, External, Small, Solitary	Autonomous drones for CPR machine delivery to remote locations
Exploitative, Internal, Large, Solitary	AI for dictation
Explorative, Internal, Large, Solitary	3D printing of orthopedic aids in the orthopedic departments using specialized software. The project will investigate the obstacles and opportunities of this initiative and will involve writing, testing, and evaluating the add-on
Exploitative, Internal, Small, Solitary	Digitization of decision trees - towards more automated dental care Currently, there is an analog decision tree that guides receptionists on how to book emergency patients. The aim of this preliminary study is to investigate whether this decision tree could be developed into a digital tool to assist receptionists and clinicians. The ultimate goal is to achieve more efficient dental care
Exploratory, Shared, Large, Collaborative	App for medication effect monitoring
Exploratory, Shared, Large, Collaborative	Digital parental support via 1177 for children with speech and/or language impairment Completely new way of working. Develop, complete and implement a digital parental support
Exploitative, Shared, Large, Collaborative	DigiFysASP – a digiphysical AntiStressProgram via 1177 for stress-related mental illness Increase the availability of Antistress Programs (ASP) and replace physical visits with digital ones. The digital solution is combined with physical visits

4.2 The Paths of Digital Innovation

Figure 2 displays an overview of the nominal (i.e., number of projects) and monetary (i.e., budgets of said projects) allocation into resources and types of activities based in Oberländer [11] methodology.

The predominant path of digital innovation is mainly exploitative, utilizing internal and shared resources. Only one project in three years utilized external resources. The project portfolio is primarily focused exploitative innovation. Approximately 57% of the projects are exploitative while 43% are explorative in nominal terms. In terms of monetary allocation, 63% of capital is allocated to exploitation and 36% to exploration. This emphasis aligns with the organization's intent of improving existing ways of working rather than emphasizing the more radical "change". Figure 3 illustrates changes in the

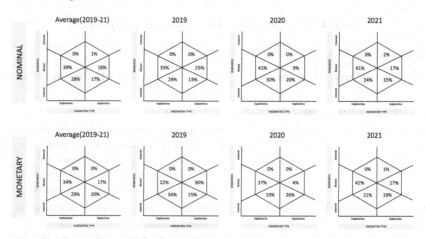

Fig. 2. Overview of path of digital innovation per year and total (monetary vs nominal).

distribution of both number of projects and the budgets of over time 2019–21 in relation to innovation activities.

Fig. 3. Exploitative vs explorative innovation (nominal and monetary).

In relation to the differentiation of resources utilized in the digital innovation, there is an almost complete absence of external resource utilization. Only one of the 109 projects in the portfolio was categorized as utilizing external resources. At an aggregate level, we find that internal resource utilization is employed in 45% (nominal) vs 49% (monetary). Shared resource utilization is employed in 55% (nominal) vs 51% (monetary). In other words, shared resource utilization is more predominantly employed in digital innovation than internal resource utilization. In Fig. 4 we show how the distribution of both number of projects and the budgets of said projects changes over time during 2019–21 in relation to resources.

We also controlled for size in the projects. Categorizing the projects based on budget's (below/above €100 000), we identified differences in terms of trajectories (Fig. 5).

As seen in Fig. 5, 2019 displayed the largest impact of project size on digital innovation path. Large projects were here 7% points less exploitative more focused on shared resources. This impact of size diminishes and shifts into large projects being more exploitative (2% points) in 2020 and less exploitative (2% points) in 2021. Similar developments are seen in shifts to less shared resources (2% points) in 2020 and more (2% points) in 2021. On an aggregate level, there are only minor differences between the

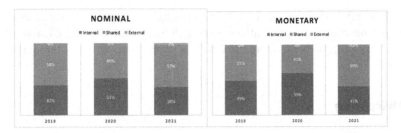

Fig. 4. Internal, Shared and External resources (nominal and monetary).

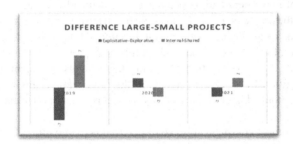

Fig. 5. Differences per year between large and small projects (percentage points).

two types of projects based on size with large projects being 2% points less focused on exploitative innovation in terms of activities, and more (1% point) focused on utilizing internal resources and shared resources (2% points). In other words, size only has a limited (inconclusive in terms of mediation) impact on the digital innovation path of the project. In relation to the collaborative arrangements in the project portfolio, i.e., if the project has one party (solitary) or several parties (collaborative) involved, we do find clear differences in digital innovation trajectories (Fig. 6).

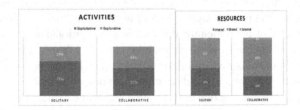

Fig. 6. Comparison of digital innovation path in solitary vs collaborative projects.

71% of the solitary projects are exploitative, compared to 57% of the collaborative projects. Solitary projects are also more prone to utilizing internal resources (48%) when compared to the collaborative (34%). Regarding the single instance of a project that utilizes external resources, this is a collaborative project. In other words, the collaborative arrangement has a substantial impact on the digital innovation path of the project, with solitary projects being more directed into exploitative activities through internal resources.

5 Discussion

This study finds that the predominant digital innovation path in the central innovation fund in the studied healthcare organization is exploitative rather than explorative, using internal and shared resources rather than external. In other words, the innovation projects follow a logic of incumbent path-dependence [30], with a high level of risk averseness and reliance on the previous transactional logic of the hospital and the medical profession as manifestations of healthcare delivery. Digital innovation is used to amalgamate the incumbent logic of the organization, well in line with previous findings from research [9, 31, 32]. With digital innovation becoming increasingly prevalent as a percentage of all centrally funded innovation projects in the organization, this predominant path risks being strengthened over time, resulting in entrenchment rather than new practices emerging.

There is an almost complete absence of external resource utilization, i.e., the innovation projects in the portfolio display an avarice toward relinquishing control over the production of healthcare to its patients. We interpret this as an instantiation of the previously identified inability of incumbents to tap into new opportunities provided through digital transformation [9, 11, 32]. With the digital introducing the possibility for more radical shifts in the logic of value creation, the healthcare organization's digital innovation projects clearly are steered away from this option. Instead, they display a tendency to enforce the previous logic of centralized delivery of healthcare, in direct contrast with the current developments in healthcare-related digital technologies and solutions [33–35].

Healthcare organizations are highly institutionalized organizations [36] and as such associated with significant caveats for change and transformation [37, 38]. In Martin et al. [41] a study of change in healthcare identifies significant differences in identity work between established doctors (prone to reject changes in logic) and consultants (prone to welcome changes in logic). According to these findings, medical reform is directly counteracted by doctor tenure, resulting in a foundational problem for healthcare organizations experiencing in need for transformation. Gollop et al. [42] identify the need for accepting and acknowledging the skepticism and resistance for transformation prevalent among doctors, and to build structures and processes that may counteract said sources of inertia. The finding that collaborative setups, i.e., where more than one e.g., department or clinic where active parties in the project are set on a path that is more explorative and less internal resource centric can be interpreted as an indication of this type of arrangement may afford more chances for tapping into more aspects of digital innovation.

The function of the digital innovation projects can here be seen as a means through which the organization explores the practice of innovation, learning for future transformation rather than instrumentally testing and implementing new solutions for direct realizable benefits [43]. Through this perspective, we can see our findings on the digital innovation paths from a new vantage point. As noted by Ozalp et al. [19], healthcare is under constant pressure from external, major platform vendors such as, e.g., Amazon looking for an opportunity to "colonize" medicine. In this competitive position, the innovation projects we have studied constitute a necessary ingredient for increased resilience in incumbent organizations facing strong external pressures. In other words, the innovation projects fulfil a dual function of both localizing innovation practices to train healthcare staff in transformative action, as well as increasing the resilience of the organization over time. As far as we have seen, this less than directly instrumental perspective to digital innovation is still missing from the core literature [44, 45].

Our study offers two primary contributions to research. First, this is the first study of its kind to assess a complete set of an organization's centralized digital innovation fund projects. Building on Oberländer et al. [11], we have shown the dearth of external resource utilization and the dominance of exploitative innovation in healthcare, and through this we offer a concrete empirical contribution to the digital innovation literature. In line with previous findings, we empirically show the myopia of the incumbent in resisting to "saw off the branch they're sitting on," avoiding to assess and evaluate logics that may contrast with the existing [46]. This can be interpreted along the lines of either path dependent [47, 48] or risk aversion [6, 49], yet in both interpretations the results are detrimental to the sustained relevance of the organization through sub-utilizing the scope of opportunities brought on through digital innovation [11].

Second, in line with Wu et al. [27] the inability to utilize external complementary assets in the innovation initiatives (i.e., limiting the resource utilization to the internal/shared and not the external) can be seen as hampering the new digital innovation path of the organization. With complementary assets offering the possibility of being "prisms" and not only "pipelines" [27] (p. 1257), the use of said resources has the potential to create new trajectories and not merely enforce the existing path of innovation. In other words, increased use of external resources for digital innovation would be expected to develop new options for the organization in question, hereby counteracting the tendency for path dependency and offering the possibility for increased strategic agility [32, 50].

We identify two implications for practice from our study. First, incumbent organizations should be aware of the risk of path-dependency and enforcement of existing logic in their choice of digital innovation trajectories. There is a significant risk that funds spent doubling down on the existing, traditional logic and operating model of the organization will be associated with both increased path dependence for the organization and significant opportunity cost. Here we believe that the conceptual model from Oberländer et al. [11] utilized in our study would offer a valuable contribution to organizations aspiring to make better prioritization decisions in their digital innovation. Using the conceptual model as a basis for a new form of portfolio management can be a fruitful path ahead. Second, organizations experiencing a risk of obsoleteness brought about through increased digital transformation on the societal level should aspire for increased utilization of complementary resources in line with the findings from Wu et al. [27]. This perspective offers strong empirical support for the costs associated with not amply utilizing external resources.

Our study identifies one implication for policy. Policy makers should continuously monitor the direction of opportunity in healthcare innovation. As found by Kizito and Magnusson, current digital healthcare policies display an over-emphasis on exploitation rather than exploration, which will invariably lead to impacts on the organizations' tendencies to actuate digital innovation opportunities. From this perspective, the bias on exploitative innovation found in our study may be the result of national or regional policy decisions. To ensure that policy is designed to afford the right organizational behavior, the method used in our study should be scaled nationally and the results can be used as a basis for future policy design.

Based on our findings, we identify two major avenues for future research. As noted, most of the innovation projects did not include concrete plans for implementation, i.e., they exist in a pre-value creation state for the organizations. Until the projects are implemented and (potentially) scaled, they will stay mere actualized opportunities and not realized. We hence propose two follow-up studies. First, we propose a study of how the results of the projects are implemented and how the identified benefits are realized. Previous research has long highlighted the inadequacy of benefits realization in relation to digital initiatives [51], and here we see the need for additional studies. Second, we propose a study on scaling, i.e., if the results are scaled outside of the involved organizational entity. Given the unique characteristics of digital innovation, we see a need for additional research [52, 53].

Our study has two main limitations. First, our sample consists of solely the centralized digital innovation projects. Previous research has identified the lion share of digital innovation being decentralized and not centralized, whereby our results should not be generalized to the complete set of digital innovation initiatives. Second, with this being a single case study we acknowledge the inability to generalize the empirical findings to other organizations. Despite this, we believe that the application of Oberländer et al.'s [11] framework holds merit and should inspire future cross-case comparisons. Third, we acknowledge the innate problems associated with the transferability of findings across national contexts, as noted by Bannister [54]. With the organization in question being part of the Swedish public sector, it is poised in a very particular institutional environment, and any attempts at transferring the results into other national contexts should be made with great care.

6   Conclusion

Our study finds that the path of digital innovation in the studied healthcare organization is predominantly focused on exploitative innovation activities, utilizing a combination of internal and shared resources. Neither project size nor collaborative configuration is found to be mediating said path, yet the development over time (2019–2021) involves increased emphasis on exploitative innovation with shared resources. We argue that this may be interpreted as indications of path-dependencies and subsequent myopia. With digital innovation increasing in frequency and percentage of total projects over time in the studied organization, we argue that the organizations need to be aware of the potential suboptimization involved in increasingly utilizing digital innovation for continuous improvements to existing operations rather than utilizing the more disruptive affordances of digital innovation.

References

1. Hanelt, A., Bohnsack, R., Marz, D., Marante, C.A.: A systematic review of the literature on digital transformation: insights and implications for strategy and organizational change. J Manag. Stud. **58**, 1159–1197 (2021). https://doi.org/10.1111/joms.12639
2. Vial, G.: Understanding digital transformation: a review and a research agenda. J. Strateg. Inf. Syst. **28**, 118–144 (2019). https://doi.org/10.1016/j.jsis.2019.01.003
3. Chanias, S., Myers, M.D., Hess, T.: Digital transformation strategy making in pre-digital organizations: the case of a financial services provider. J. Strateg. Inf. Syst. **28**, 17–33 (2019). https://doi.org/10.1016/j.jsis.2018.11.003
4. Norling, K., Lindroth, T., Magnusson, J., Torell, J.: Digital decoupling: a population study of digital transformation strategies in Swedish municipalities. In: Dg O 2022 23rd Annual International Conference on Digital Government Research, pp. 356–363 (2022). https://doi.org/10.1145/3543434.3543639
5. Lindroth, T., Magnusson, J., Norling, K., Torell, J.: Balancing the digital portfolio: empirical evidence of an ambidextrous bias in digital government. In: Dg O 2022 23rd Annual International Conference on Digital Government Research, pp. 307–314 (2022). https://doi.org/10.1145/3543434.3543641
6. Drechsler, K., Wagner, H.T., Gregory, R., et al.: At the crossroad between digital innovation and digital transformation.pdf. Communications of the Association for Information Systems (2020). https://doi.org/10.17705/1CAIS.044XX
7. Hund, A., Wagner, H.-T., Beimborn, D., Weitzel, T.: Digital innovation: review and novel perspective. J. Strateg. Inf. Syst. **30**, 101695 (2021). https://doi.org/10.1016/j.jsis.2021.101695
8. Yoo, Y., Henfridsson, O., Lyytinen, K.: Research commentary—The new organizing logic of digital innovation: an agenda for information systems research. Inform. Syst. Res. **21**, 724–735 (2010). https://doi.org/10.1287/isre.1100.0322
9. Svahn, F., Mathiassen, L., University, G.S., Lindgren, R.: Embracing digital innovation in incumbent firms: how Volvo cars managed competing concerns. MIS Q. **41**, 239–253 (2017). https://doi.org/10.25300/misq/2017/41.1.12
10. Faulkner, P., Runde, J.: Theorizing the digital object1. MIS Q. **43**, 1279–1302 (2019). https://doi.org/10.25300/misq/2019/13136
11. Oberländer, A.M., Röglinger, M., Rosemann, M.: Digital opportunities for incumbents – a resource-centric perspective. J. Strateg. Inf. Syst. **30**, 101670 (2021). https://doi.org/10.1016/j.jsis.2021.101670
12. Magnusson, J., Koutsikouri, D., Päivärinta, T.: Efficiency creep and shadow innovation: enacting ambidextrous IT Governance in the public sector. Eur. J. Inform. Syst. **29**, 329–349 (2020). https://doi.org/10.1080/0960085x.2020.1740617
13. Xue, L.: How do industry environments moderate the effects of firms' IT asset portfolios? MIS Q. **36**, 509–528 (2012). https://doi.org/10.2307/41703465
14. Mithas, S., Rust, R.T.: How information technology strategy and investments influence firm performance. MIS Q. **40**, 223–245 (2016). https://doi.org/10.25300/misq/2016/40.1.10
15. Sheikh, A., et al.: Health information technology and digital innovation for national learning health and care systems. Lancet Digit. Heal. **3**, e383–e396 (2021). https://doi.org/10.1016/s2589-7500(21)00005-4
16. Wimelius, H., Mathiassen, L., Holmström, J., Keil, M.: A paradoxical perspective on technology renewal in digital transformation. Inf. Syst. J. **31**, 198–225 (2021). https://doi.org/10.1111/isj.12307
17. Bygstad, B.: Generative innovation: a comparison of lightweight and heavyweight IT. J. Inf. Technol. **32**, 180–193 (2017). https://doi.org/10.1057/jit.2016.15

18. Jovanovic, K., et al.: Digital innovation hubs in health-care robotics fighting COVID-19. IEEE Robot. Autom. Mag. **28**, 40–47 (2021). https://doi.org/10.1109/mra.2020.3044965

19. Ozalp, H., Ozcan, P., Dinckol, D., Zachariadis, M., Gawer, A.: "Digital Colonization" of highly regulated industries: an analysis of big tech platforms' entry into health care and education. Calif. Manag. Rev. **64**, 78–107 (2022). https://doi.org/10.1177/00081256221094307

20. Eom, S.-J., Lee, J.: Digital government transformation in turbulent times: responses, challenges, and future direction. Gov. Inform. Q. **39**, 101690 (2022). https://doi.org/10.1016/j.giq.2022.101690

21. Hinings, B., Gegenhuber, T., Greenwood, R.: Digital innovation and transformation: an institutional perspective. Inf. Org. **28**, 52–61 (2018). https://doi.org/10.1016/j.infoandorg.2018.02.004

22. Lyytinen, K., Yoo, Y.,Boland Jr., R.J.: Digital product innovation within four classes of innovation networks. Inf. Syst. J. **26**, 47–75 (2016). https://doi.org/10.1111/isj.12093

23. Bygstad, B., Øvrelid, E., Ludvigsen, S., Dæhlen, M.: From dual digitalization to digital learning space: exploring the digital transformation of higher education. Comput. Educ. **182**, 104463 (2022). https://doi.org/10.1016/j.compedu.2022.104463

24. March, J.G.: Exploration and exploitation in organizational learning. Stud. Organ. (2009). https://doi.org/10.3280/so2008-002006

25. Birkinshaw, J., Zimmermann, A., Raisch, S.: How do firms adapt to discontinuous change? Bridging the dynamic capabilities and ambidexterity perspectives. Calif. Manag. Rev. **58**, 36–58 (2016). https://doi.org/10.1525/cmr.2016.58.4.36

26. Zimmermann, A., Raisch, S., Cardinal, L.B.: Managing persistent tensions on the frontline: a configurational perspective on ambidexterity. J. Manag. Stud. **55**, 739–769 (2018). https://doi.org/10.1111/joms.12311

27. Wu, B., Wan, Z., Levinthal, D.A.: Complementary assets as pipes and prisms: innovation incentives and trajectory choices. Strat. Manag. J. **35**, 1257–1278 (2014). https://doi.org/10.1002/smj.2159

28. Temiz, S.: Open innovation via crowdsourcing: a digital only hackathon case study from Sweden. J. Open Innov. Technol. Mark. Complex. **7**, 39 (2021). https://doi.org/10.3390/joitmc7010039

29. Lombard, M., Snyder-Duch, J., Bracken, C.C.: Content analysis in mass communication: assessment and reporting of intercoder reliability. Hum. Commun. Res. **28**, 587–604 (2002). https://doi.org/10.1111/j.1468-2958.2002.tb00826.x

30. Priyono, A., Moin, A., Putri, V.N.A.O.: Identifying digital transformation paths in the business model of SMEs during the COVID-19 pandemic. J. Open Innov.: Technol. Mark. Complex. **6**, 104 (2020). https://doi.org/10.3390/joitmc6040104

31. Magnusson, J., Elliot, V., Hagberg, J.: Digital transformation: why companies resist what they need for sustained performance. J. Bus. Strat. **43**, 316–322 (2022). https://doi.org/10.1108/jbs-02-2021-0018

32. Warner, K.S.R., Wäger, M.: Building dynamic capabilities for digital transformation: an ongoing process of strategic renewal. Long Range Plann. **52**, 326–349 (2019). https://doi.org/10.1016/j.lrp.2018.12.001

33. Burau, V., Nissen, N., Terkildsen, M.D., Væggemose, U.: Personalised medicine and the state: a political discourse analysis. Heal. Polic. **125**, 122–129 (2021). https://doi.org/10.1016/j.healthpol.2020.10.005

34. Casino, F., Dasaklis, T.K., Patsakis, C.: A systematic literature review of blockchain-based applications: current status, classification and open issues. Telemat. Inform. **36**, 55–81 (2019). https://doi.org/10.1016/j.tele.2018.11.006

35. Dillard-Wright, J.: A radical imagination for nursing: generative insurrection, creative resistance. Nurs. Philos. **23**, e12371 (2022). https://doi.org/10.1111/nup.12371

36. Meyer, J.W., Rowan, B.: Institutionalized organizations: formal structure as myth and ceremony. Am. J. Sociol. **83**, 340–363 (1977). https://doi.org/10.1086/226550
37. Amarantou, V., Kazakopoulou, S., Chatzoudes, D., Chatzoglou, P.: Resistance to change: an empirical investigation of its antecedents. J. Organ. Chang. Manag. **31**, 426–450 (2018). https://doi.org/10.1108/jocm-05-2017-0196
38. Detert, J.R., Pollock, T.G.: Values, interests, and the capacity to act. J. Appl. Behav. Sci. **44**, 186–214 (2008). https://doi.org/10.1177/0021886308314901

Correction to: Construct Hunting in GovTech Research: An Exploratory Data Analysis

Mattias Svahn⬥, Aron Larsson⬥, Eloísa Macedo⬥,
and Jorge Bandeira⬥

Correction to:
Chapter "Construct Hunting in GovTech Research:
An Exploratory Data Analysis" in: I. Lindgren et al. (Eds.):
Electronic Government, **LNCS 14130,**
https://doi.org/10.1007/978-3-031-41138-0_1

In the originally published version of chapter 1, there was a typing error in the name of the author Eloísa Macedo. This has been corrected.

The updated original version of this chapter can be found at
https://doi.org/10.1007/978-3-031-41138-0_1

Author Index

Printed in the United States
by Baker & Taylor Publisher Services